IT DOESN'T
TAKE A HERO

GENERAL H. NORMAN SCHWARZKOPF

THE AUTOBIOGRAPHY

IT DOESN'T TAKE A HERO

WRITTEN WITH PETER PETRE

BANTAM PRESS

LONDON · NEW YORK · TORONTO · SYDNEY · AUCKLAND

TRANSWORLD PUBLISHERS LTD
61–63 Uxbridge Road, London W5 5SA

TRANSWORLD PUBLISHERS (AUSTRALIA) PTY LTD
15–25 Helles Avenue, Moorebank, NSW 2170

TRANSWORLD PUBLISHERS (NZ) LTD
3 William Pickering Drive, Albany, Auckland

Grateful acknowledgement is made to Ruth Ann Schwarzkopf for permission
to quote from her story "Daddy's Girl" on page 20

Speech quoted on pages 102–103 from *Ben Franklin in Paris*, a musical play
by Sidney Michaels and Mark Sandrich, Jr. © 1965

Published 1992 by Bantam Press
a division of Transworld Publishers Ltd
Copyright © H. Norman Schwarzkopf 1992
Reprinted 1992 (five times)

Art Direction by Maria Carella
Maps Designed by Natasha Perkel

The catalogue record for this book is available from the British Library

ISBN 0593 025938

Printed and bound in Great Britain
by Mackays of Chatham PLC, Chatham, Kent

**To my family
and my troops**

LIST OF MAPS

PREFACE

This book almost didn't get written. On the day of the Gulf War victory parade in Washington, D.C. in 1991, I attended a memorial service at Arlington Cemetery for the men and women who had died in Desert Shield and Desert Storm. I sat on the stage behind the President and looked out at an audience filled with families who had lost loved ones. The grief that marked their faces made me think that writing a memoir that included the Gulf War would only cause them more pain. But over the course of the day, as I talked with some of them, they surprised me by saying they wanted me to write. Two days later the same thing happened at the ticker tape parade in New York City. On the reviewing stand, family members of people who had died also asked, "When are you going to write your book? We need to hear the full story." Without their encouragement, I never would have gone ahead.

My original goal was to model my account on the *Personal Memoirs of U.S. Grant*—the great two-volume work that, to my mind, is still the finest military history of the Civil War. But unlike Grant's, my book was to be a full autobiography, not primarily the story of a war. Writing it turned out to be a more personal process than I'd bargained for, and the following pages contain more emotion than their nineteenth-century model. That was the only way to tell the story, even though I had been taught at West Point that an officer should avoid any public display of feelings. For the entire first part of my career, I prided myself on being unflappable even in the most chaotic of circumstances. That guise lasted until Vietnam, where I realized that I was dealing with human lives and if one were lost, it could never be replaced. I quickly learned that there was nothing wrong with being emotional.

One of the toughest personal decisions I had to make was whether to discuss my mother's drinking in these pages. Her alcoholism had as much to do with shaping me as did the fact that my father was a general. During my boyhood her illness was our family's unspoken secret, and I carried it with me for twenty-five years before I felt I could mention it even to friends. Today there are many organizations and agencies to help alcoholics and their families; I hope that children of alcoholics reading this book will realize that they are not alone.

As Peter Petre and I worked, I found myself telling the story of the U.S. Army along with my own. From the time I was twelve years old until I retired last year at the age of fifty-seven, the Army *was* my life. I loved commanding soldiers and being around people who had made a serious commitment to serve their country. I was lucky to be given exciting assignments in places ranging from southern California to West Berlin. But while I was good at soldiering and was promoted rapidly, I wasn't always happy with the Army: often I hated what I saw going on around me, and came close to resigning not once but several times. When I received my commission as a second lieutenant, the Army was suffering from the aftereffects of the Korean War; in many ways it was ethically and morally bankrupt, which led eventually to the debacle in Vietnam. By the end of my second tour in Vietnam, the Army had not only reached its nadir but also lost the confidence of the American people. I agonized over the question of whether to stay in—and decided I would, in the hope of someday getting a chance to help fix what I thought was wrong. As I rose to senior rank over the years, I saw the Army transform itself into a force that Americans *could* be proud of. The units I commanded during Desert Storm were the product of twenty years of reform, and soldier for soldier, officer for officer, we had the best-trained, best-equipped army in the world.

———

In my account of Desert Storm, I've tried to lay out an enormously complex set of events as clearly, concisely, and completely as possible. I've made it a point not to digress into military or political analyses that were not central to the events as they unfolded. Similarly, I avoided going back to justify or excuse the various choices we made. I've tried to reconstruct the behind-the-scenes decision-making process on the basis of my recollections and the detailed notes I kept throughout the crisis. As my account of conversations with President Bush, Secretary of Defense Cheney, and General Colin Powell will show, the process was tortuous and sometimes filled with emotional strain and debate—we knew our choices would affect the lives of hundreds of thousands of people as well as the prestige of the United States. The discussions and disagreements recorded here are *not* meant as criticism of the leaders. I respect and admire the President, Cheney, and Powell, and we ended up in unanimous agreement on every major issue.

My account of the war omits a handful of operations, some behind Iraqi lines, that remain classified, and I have also been careful to avoid any mention of classified programs or information. Such discussions would have changed none of the conclusions I've presented. Also, many generals and foreign leaders confided in me in the course of events, and I have honored their trust. Finally, throughout the book and in my depiction of Desert Storm, on some occasions when I have criticized a fellow officer in such a way that I felt it might be embarrassing to him or his family, I have chosen to omit his name.

There are other omissions, however, that I regret. I wish I could have mentioned the thousands of people who helped me, taught me, supported me, encouraged me, and served by my side: the secretaries who made it look as if I knew how to spell; the drivers who got me there on time most of the time; the enlisted aides who helped me entertain foreign dignitaries in my home; the aides-de-camp who ran my life better than I myself could have; the chaplains who ministered to me and the doctors who sewed me up; the military game wardens who showed me all the great places to hunt and fish; the civilian personnel who held together installations I commanded and adapted gracefully whenever I came up with one of my bright ideas; the privates, NCOs, and officers who took my orders and delivered results that made me look better than I deserved; my chiefs of staff, assistant commanders, and other deputies whose lives I didn't always make easy but who gave me their loyalty and never let me down; the senior officers who took the time to develop me as a subordinate; and the foreign friends who not only welcomed me into their countries but initiated me into the nuances of their cultures. I wish I could have named more of my West Point classmates and their wives, and dozens of my other friends and peers. Finally, I wish I could have named the hundreds of Central Command staff members who gave such superb support before, during, and after Desert Storm. They kept track of the troops, gathered the intelligence, transmitted the orders, wrote the reports, saw to the supplies, wired up the phones, served the meals—and otherwise made things happen. A little piece of this book belongs to each of them.

Tampa, Florida
August 2, 1992

"It doesn't take a hero to order men into battle. It takes a hero to be one of those men who goes into battle."

—General H. Norman Schwarzkopf,
from a television interview with
Barbara Walters, March 15, 1991

1

When my father went off to war in August 1942, his last act was to make me the man of the house. I was with him and my mother in the backyard, which to me always seemed like a magical place, with tall evergreen shrubs and fragrant lilacs and a mysterious old stone barbecue shaped like a throne. It was dusk and the first few fireflies were out; my older sisters, Ruth Ann and Sally, were busy inside the house. I was seven years old.

Pop stood in front of me and gave a little talk about how he had to leave because he was going off to serve our country. Because he was leaving, he said, I was now going to have a big job. It was up to me to look after the girls, because men are the protectors of women. He said he had great confidence in my ability to do this, and as a demonstration of his confidence, there was something he wanted me to have. Then he went into the house while I waited with Mom. When he came back out, he was carrying his Army saber. "I'm placing this sword in your keeping until I come back," he said, and laid it in my hands. "Now, son, I'm depending on you. The responsibility is yours."

My father's saber was a sacred thing in our family. We called it his West Point sword, because he'd gotten it the year he graduated, in 1917. He was always quick to tell you that West Point had shaped his entire life. "Duty, Honor, Country," the West Point motto, was his creed, and it became mine.

He kept the saber on a table in his study, and when I was a tiny boy he would sometimes pull it from its scabbard and show me where his name was engraved on the blade. (It actually said N. Norman Schwarzkopf, because the engraver had made a mistake, but that didn't matter.) The sword had special meaning for me because it was my name, too, and because from the first day I could remember, my parents had told me I was going to West Point. My sisters didn't like it a bit, because girls were left out. But there was never any question about what my role was going to be.

When he handed me the saber I felt an awesome obligation. To be accountable not only for it, but for Mom and the girls! I was overwhelmed. My mother I thought I could handle. It was my sisters I was more worried about, since I had *no* control over anything my sisters did.

Mom made sure I put the saber back in its place in the study. Then it was time for bed. My mother was a registered nurse and always insisted we get our sleep. Pop kissed me one last good-night, and I lay looking out the window. It was still twilight, and I watched the stars start to come out. I fell asleep thinking, "How am I going to do this?"

The next morning when I woke up, my father was gone. Nothing was ever the same again.

Up to then I'd had a wonderful boyhood, filled with dogs, Christmases, birthdays, tree climbing and sled riding, and all kinds of friends. Despite the Depression, we had plenty of food on the table; the most we ever saw of hard times were the tramps who would show up at the back door. Mom would have our maid give them lunch, but when they'd eaten, they had to leave immediately.

We lived in a great stone fortress known as the Green House, on Main Street in Lawrenceville, New Jersey. The walls were covered with ivy, and a plaque beside the door said "1815." The house had previously been leased by the Lawrenceville School, an exclusive boys' school whose practice fields stretched out behind an iron fence across the street. Princeton was six miles down the road to the left; Trenton, the state capital, was six miles to the right. We had a large front yard with a copper beech tree that reached all the way to the heavens, like Jack's beanstalk. The year Pop left I carved my initials on the trunk. Next to the beech was a big Camperdown elm—a great climbing tree whose branches drooped in such a way that you could go up and be hidden in the leaves. Beyond the barbecue pit in back, my parents owned an acre of land where they'd built a badminton court and where Mom had a flower garden with a little brick path weaving through it.

The house had a feeling of great space inside: high ceilings, a big parlor with antique furniture where we were forbidden to play, Pop's study with its bay window and deep leather chairs, and a large living room centered around the family radio, one of those big curved-top radios with a lighted-up dial. We'd sit by it and listen to *The Shadow* and *The Lone Ranger* and *The Green Hornet* and our own dad. Millions of Americans knew Pop's name because he'd been head of the New Jersey State Police at the time of the Lindbergh kidnapping. After he left the police, he became the voice of *Gang Busters*, a crime series that was one of America's most popular radio shows. It came on at eight o'clock on Saturday evenings, the only night of the week we were allowed to stay up late.

The *Gang Busters* lead-in was a simulated prison break. First you would hear the sound of prisoners marching. Then, all of a sudden, sirens would start to wail and you'd hear running footsteps and whistles blowing. Next, machine guns would open up. Finally an announcer would say, "Philips H. Lord presents *Gang Busters*!"

Philips H. Lord was the producer; Pop was the interviewer. An announcer would describe that week's crime and say: "We will now hear from the principal law enforcement officer who was involved in this heinous crime. He will be interviewed by Colonel H. Norman Schwarzkopf, former superintendent of the New Jersey State Police."

Then Pop would come on. He had a nice, measured, reasonable-sounding voice, not too deep. He'd say: "Well, Sheriff Smith, we're here tonight to talk about the Joe Ludwig murder case. I know that you were the principal law officer involved in this in Morristown, New Jersey. Can you tell us what happened on the night of the twenty-sixth of October, 1933?"

"Why, yes, Colonel Schwarzkopf. As a matter of fact, I will never forget that night. I was sitting in my office and snow was falling outside, and all of a sudden the phone rang . . ."

You'd hear a phone ring, and then the actors would read their parts. When it was time for a commercial the actors' voices would fade and Pop would come on and say, "That's very interesting, Sheriff Smith. We need to talk about that in more detail." Then the announcer would say, "But first a message from Palmolive Brushless Shaving Cream."

After the commercial, Pop would say, "Now, tell me more about what happened to that stolen automobile as it was careening down the road . . ."

It was absolutely fantastic.

The stories enacted in these *Gang Busters* scripts were all true crimes: Murder Inc., Louis Lepke. My mother objected for a while to letting me listen because the show was so violent, and one night her concerns were borne out. The program was about the Blonde Tigress, a gang leader who had escaped from prison after murdering a guard by sticking a knitting needle through his eardrum right into his brain. For months afterward, every time I thought about that I wanted to cover my ears so no one could stab me.

The show always ended with a bulletin about a criminal at large. That was the climax for me. They'd describe some horrible felony and say, "Be on the lookout for a man five feet seven, a hundred and forty pounds, black hair, brown eyes," and I'd be hanging on every word, even though I had no more idea than the man in the moon what "five feet seven" meant. But I'd try to conjure up a face. The criminals I imagined all had black mustaches and looked a lot like Adolf Hitler.

At the back of our house, down a long hall and through the dining room, was the Schwarzkopf family's favorite place: the kitchen. It was big and warm and always smelled good. My mother had a pantry with all sorts of delicious things on the shelves. She did a lot of canning in those days. There was a breakfast nook, a big stove, and a wooden table covered with sheet metal in the middle of the room. When my dad brought home pheasants he'd shot or fish he'd caught, they would be cleaned on that table, and Mom would roll out her pie crusts there, too.

Most days I rode my bike to school, down Main Street, left, up a ways, right, down that road, left, and up a hill. After class I'd link up with my friends Johnny Chivers, Billy Kraus, and Jimmy Wright. We'd spend nickels at the Jigger Shop, which was the town's most popular soda fountain, play cops and robbers, and smash empty Coca-Cola bottles on sewer grates. Near Johnny Chivers's house the trolley that ran from one end of Lawrenceville to the other crossed a little brook on a trestle about four feet high. One afternoon, after we got tired of defying death by walking on the rails, we snuck into Billy Kraus's father's farm and pulled up some carrots and potatoes. Then we found an old tin can, filled it with brook water under the trestle, built a fire, and set the vegetables to cook. We felt very daring because this was just what hoboes did. Though the potatoes were so underdone that biting one was like eating an apple, I've never had a better meal.

My boyhood would have been perfect had it not been for the fact that I had older sisters. I spent most of my young life thinking my middle name was "Stupid," as in "Here's my stupid brother Norman" or "Norman, you're so stupid." Sally and Ruth Ann went to a private girls' school in Princeton called Miss Fine's School. Ruth Ann, who was born four years before me, was Pop's favorite. He called her "Yan." She had blonde hair, loved dresses and braids, and embodied all the feminine virtues expected in a little girl. She'd come home after school, practice her piano, read, and think up interesting questions to discuss with Pop. Sally, who was two and a half years older than I was, was more of a tomboy. Though she played the recorder and read even more books than Ruth Ann, she preferred to play outside. If Ruth Ann wasn't around, she would sometimes pal around with me and my friends, provided she got to be in charge.

When the two of them deigned to include me in their backyard games, Ruth Ann would be a princess, Sally would be a general—and I would be a serf. They constantly made me the butt of their jokes. One day they tricked me into thinking Snow White was on the phone. I had a crush on Snow White—I had seen the Walt Disney movie and I thought she was everything a boy could ever want—so I grabbed the receiver and listened. "What did she say?" Ruth Ann asked.

"She said, 'Number please,'" I answered. My sisters, who had called the operator, thought this was hilarious. They rolled around on the floor, holding their stomachs and laughing uproariously.

Sometimes I got revenge. One afternoon, the year before Pop went overseas, Mom took us to see the movie *Geronimo*. I was big on Indians and thought the movie was great—full of blood and gore. One thing Geronimo did in this movie was scalp lots of women and children. The next day I was in the kitchen, bothering my mother, and she said, "Why don't you go out and play?"

"I don't have anybody to play with."

"Why don't you go upstairs and play Geronimo?" I had just gotten a toy war bonnet and tom-tom, and that encouragement was all I needed. I took a hammer from the kitchen drawer, went into my sisters' room, and tomahawked their dolls, punching a neat round hole in each one's forehead. When Sally and Ruth Ann came home, they screamed bloody murder, and I said to my mother, "But you *told* me to play Geronimo."

It was up to my mother to settle such disputes, because even then Pop was hardly ever around. When President Roosevelt had called up the National Guard in November 1940, Pop had left his job as a vice president of Middlesex Transportation Company, a subsidiary of Johnson & Johnson, and gone on active duty. He only came home on weekends. But he and my mother made sure his presence was felt. When he came home on Friday night, we'd have a great reckoning of how we had behaved while he was gone. If we'd been good children, we got medals. He had a ready supply because over the years he'd won all sorts of awards for marksmanship. Getting a medal was the highlight of my week. The fact that the medal might say "Left-Handed Pistol Champion, New Jersey State Police 1925" was irrelevant to me because I couldn't read anyhow.

Fortunately Mom was very forgiving, and usually did not report transgressions like my tomahawking the dolls. However, she did report my attempt to build a campfire next to the garage in December 1941. She discovered the burnt matches and sticks in the snow and confronted me; I denied knowing anything about it. That Friday, Pop gave me a talking-to. He and my mother had some neighbors over, and after dinner we all went into the formal parlor, where Pop took me aside and sat me down on a loveseat near the door. It was an uncomfortable place to sit, covered in scratchy brown upholstery and with springs so tight that they had no give. My father said he knew about my fire and that he was worried I'd hurt myself or burn down the house. As he spoke he pulled out his cigarette lighter. Pop was a chain-smoker and that Zippo fascinated me. He lit a cigarette, then held out the lighter and said, "If you want to play with fire and burn yourself, you might as well use this lighter and put your hand in the flame right now. Do you want to do that?"

"No," I said.

"Good," he said. "I want you never to play with matches again."

Then he went on to the subject of honor. He told me: "No matter what happens, no matter how bad a situation is, no matter what you think the consequences will be if you tell the truth, an honorable man does not lie. A Schwarzkopf does not lie."

———

When Pop reported back to the military in 1940, he was one of the Army's most unusual colonels. The bulk of his experience involved commanding not soldiers but police. Pop had grown up in Newark, the only child in a German-speaking household, and graduated from West Point in time to serve in World War I. He fought in the battle of the Marne and was gassed with mustard gas, which made him prone to pneumonia all his life. After the armistice, the Army appointed him provost marshal, or military police chief, of an occupied German town, because he spoke the language. A couple of years later, though, Pop had to leave the military because his father, a jeweler, had become crippled with arthritis, and Pop couldn't support his parents on his Army pay.

Then, in 1921, Teddy Edwards, the governor of New Jersey and father of an officer who had served with my dad in the war, chose Pop to organize the state police. Prohibition had just come in, and New Jersey was more like the Wild West than the land of suburbs and traffic jams you see now. If you ventured between towns at night in some parts of the state, you did so at your peril. There were bootleggers and smugglers bringing liquor and cigarettes from down south into New York, and gangs of highwaymen roamed the countryside. Governor Edwards, a political maverick, wanted a police superintendent who had no ties to the northern New Jersey political machine, which was linked to some of the gangs. Even though Pop was only twenty-five years old, he had the right qualifications: on top of his experience as a military police chief he was enterprising, honest, and tough. He'd played Army football and had been captain of the polo team and heavyweight boxing champion of his West Point class.

That first summer, my dad recruited over one hundred men. He housed them in tents and subjected them to weeks of tough physical training based on drills used by the U.S. Cavalry. He turned out to be a natural at the job: he loved every aspect of organizing the force, from setting up training schedules to designing uniforms to inventing exercises that would build morale. There are photographs of his "monkey drills"—competitions in which trainees would do stunts like standing astride a team of four horses galloping abreast. Of one hundred and sixteen recruits, eighty-one made it. My dad assigned about half of them, on horses, to the southern part of the state, where roads were still primitive, and the other half, on motorcycles, to the north.

Pop loved to talk about those days before any of us children had been born. He'd tell how he and his men once borrowed motorboats to nab some pirates who had been raiding coal barges on the Raritan River, and how bootleggers would offer him bribes to keep the troopers off certain roads so they could take contraband through. Pop approached the job like the western sheriff who says to the bad guy, "Get out of town by sundown." A gang would be moving into a town, and he'd take a couple of troopers, big gorillas, and pay the leader a visit. He'd say, "You do not want to move into Red Bank. Let me explain what's going to happen if you do. . . ." Pop served under five governors and ran the force for fifteen years, and gradually the force got New Jersey under control.

Dad kept lots of interesting objects from his police days at our home. On the bar in the basement was a slot machine the troopers had confiscated. It was rigged so it could only take slugs, and Pop kept a stack of them there for anybody who wanted to play. The basement also had a pistol range, consisting of a cast-iron box on a stand. You would hang targets inside. At the back of the box was a slab of armor plate, mounted in such a way that the bullet would go through the target, smash against the plate, and slide down to where the plate curved under. I liked to reach in and touch the crushed bullets—they felt dirty, the way lead does.

In the living room we had photographs from the Lindbergh kidnapping, the most notorious crime of the 1930s. Because it occurred in rural New Jersey, and kidnapping was not yet a federal offense, the state police led the investigation, which resulted in the conviction of Bruno Hauptmann, an immigrant German carpenter, in 1935, and his execution in 1936. The case against Hauptmann was built entirely on circumstantial evidence, which led some people to call it brilliant police work, while others called it a frame-up. As kids, we knew the case was controversial, but Pop told us the outcome was just and we thought this must be correct. But by the time the case ended, Harold Hoffman, a politician Pop despised, had been elected governor. He used the controversy as a pretext to replace my father with a political ally.

The controversy continues even to this day. My father was a great record keeper, and in our attic in Lawrenceville there was a filing cabinet filled with duplicates of every document that ever came across his desk regarding the Lindbergh case. When I grew older I read the files. These left no doubt in my mind that the outcome of the trial was just. When my father died, my mother gave these records to the New Jersey State Police, and when the state of New Jersey reinvestigated the case from 1977 to 1981, they came to the same conclusion I had.

My first memories of Pop are from after the Lindbergh case, when he was doing the *Gang Busters* shows in the late 1930s. He was far from wealthy, but earned enough money to afford the Green House, employ a maid, and send my sisters to private school. While Lawrenceville wasn't as fancy as parts of Princeton—our neighbors included storekeepers and farmers as well as teachers from the Lawrenceville School—we owned one of the town's finest houses and my parents were prominent in the Princeton and Lawrenceville social scene. Their friends were professors, businesspeople, and town leaders; they belonged to the country club set, the contract bridge set, and the badminton set—though not to the social-register and coming-out-party crowd. On some nights, my dad's state trooper friends would show up to play poker. Pop had taught me the rules, and I'd sit with him at the table so I could watch what was going on. My parents liked to hold cookouts in the summer and noisy parties at Christmastime. Theirs was a pretty hard drinking crowd. The morning after a party I'd go around eating olives and maraschino cherries from the cocktail glasses.

When Pop was called back into the Army in 1940, not much changed. He and Mom kept up their social life on weekends, and sometimes he brought me to visit his encampment. The first was Camp Kilmer, midway between Princeton and New York. I remember following him down long rows of tents until we came to the one where he slept, with his cot all neatly made up, its blanket so tightly stretched that you could drop a quarter on the cot and see it bounce. He also showed me a tent with the regimental flag out front, where his office was. After almost a year, he transferred to Fort Hancock, one of the installations that guards the approach to the Port of New York. When I visited there I was in a frenzy of anticipation, because he'd promised to show me the fort's "disappearing guns." The idea of something that disappeared fascinated me. These were the days of Mandrake the Magician, who could make himself vanish and come back. I didn't want to be too pushy when we got to the fort, but I could hardly wait to see the guns. When I finally did, I was horribly disappointed. They were guns mounted on platforms that could be elevated above the embankment when it was time to fire, then quickly brought back down so the enemy couldn't shoot at them directly. But if you were standing behind the embankment, where we were, they didn't disappear at all. I don't think he realized how literal-minded a seven-year-old can be.

He took me to the room where he slept and showed me a book on his bedside table. It was *Mein Kampf.* He told me Hitler was a bad man and that a great deal of what he had written in that book was now happening in the world. The title appeared on the cover in German script. I was learning my alphabet and recognized this was a different kind of writing entirely. That was in November 1941.

A few weeks later came the attack on Pearl Harbor, and it finally dawned on me that something momentous was happening. When the news hit, I was sitting in a tree at Johnny Chivers's house. His mother told me, "This is terrible. It means your father will have to go to war!" I didn't understand what she meant—he was a soldier and away from home already. In the days that followed I listened to the news reports with my mother and sisters, but things didn't get any clearer. Christmas was coming soon, and as I tried to make sense of what was going on, Tojo and Hitler and Mussolini and Santa Claus got all jumbled in my mind.

Soon Lawrenceville was full of commotion. All the families had to put blackout shades on their windows, and the town ran air raid drills. When the air raid siren went off, that was the signal to pull down your shades. Then some obnoxious local official who had been appointed air raid warden would come around and berate people who had failed to do so, or who had lowered their shades but dared allow light to creep around them. Once we had a near panic because a blimp at Lakehurst Naval Air Station detected a

German submarine off the coast. We really thought the Germans were about to invade New Jersey. We kept our blackout shades down continually for about a week.

By then, we boys were all armed to the teeth with toy machine guns and dressed in soldier suits and camouflaged helmets, and we fought the Germans and the Japanese on a daily basis in our backyards. At school, the worst thing you could call somebody was a Nazi or a Jap. *Dummkopf* became a popular insult, and a few times at school I had to explain that "Schwarzkopf" had nothing to do with *Dummkopf*. These incidents rarely led to blows because I was big for my age. But I never liked to fight—I was worried I would hurt my adversary.

About six months passed, and I assumed this was what life would be like for the duration of the war. But in June 1942 my father was summoned to Washington to meet with General George C. Marshall. My parents were astounded: as chief of staff, he was the top-ranking general in the entire Army, the boss of Eisenhower, Bradley, and Patton. Going down the chain of command, there were probably thousands of officers between him and a guy like Pop. But Marshall had a reputation for reaching down and picking West Point men out of the ranks when he had a problem to solve. On the path leading from the locker room to the West Point football stadium, there is a plaque engraved with a remark Marshall supposedly made: "I want an officer for a secret and dangerous mission. I want a West Point football player." In this case, the West Point football player was Pop, and the mission was Iran.

Marshall's problem involved delivering military aid to the Soviets. Stalin's soldiers were in desperate need of weapons and supplies: in the southern part of Russia the Nazis were closing in on Stalingrad; their main thrust was to seize the oil fields near the Caspian Sea and the Caucasus, opening the way to the Middle East. To help thwart them, the United States was pouring in vast quantities of materiel. Much of it went through the so-called Persian corridor: ships would sail to the head of the Persian Gulf, where their cargoes would be unloaded and trucked north through Iran, across the Caucasus, and into the Soviet Union.

But too many shipments weren't making it through. In the wilds of Iran, mountain tribes would ride down, attack convoys, and help themselves to whatever they wanted, or block the roads and charge exorbitant tolls. When the U.S. ambassador complained to the shah and said that he must stop these raids, the shah said, "We can't." Iran had a 22,000-man national police force, called the Imperial Iranian Gendarmerie, that was supposed to maintain order in the countryside, but the name was more imposing than the organization. So General Marshall had to take time out from getting several million GIs ready for combat and worry about policing the back roads of Iran. That was where Pop came in. The general ordered Pop to Tehran to be an advisor to the Imperial Iranian Gendarmerie and come up with a way to make it an effective force.

From my point of view as a seven-year-old, all I knew was that my dad had gone to Washington to meet with a guy named George Marshall. After he'd been gone a couple of days the telephone rang and he told Mom the news. I was in the hammock on the side porch, missing him, while they talked. Then Mom called us together and announced Pop was going to Tehran. We had no idea where that was, so she got out the globe and we started searching. It seemed as if we spun it a great distance. Suddenly Ruth Ann jabbed her finger down and said, "Here." It was halfway around the world! Mom turned to me and explained that Pop was about to travel to an exotic, magical, faraway place, the land of the Thousand-and-One Nights, where people wore long robes and carried knives in their belts and rode camels across the desert. I'm sure she knew all too well what could happen if the Wehrmacht attacked across the Caucasus, but she didn't talk about that. I still hadn't made the connection that this was war and that my father might get killed.

So his leaving was no big tragedy. He was going off for a long time. Well, what was a long time? He was gone all week long anyhow. That was already a long time. Nobody expressed it to me in terms of months and years. Even if they had, I doubt I'd have understood.

2

think Mom would have been glad if she could have gone off to war, too. I can imagine her running a field hospital, coordinating teams of harried doctors and nurses, finding ways around shortages of bandages and supplies, and staying absolutely collected because that was the way to save the most lives.

Instead, she found herself in tedious, completely unheroic circumstances on the home front. Most of my parents' social life had revolved around Pop—he was the one who attracted attention and she was content to be at his side. Now she found herself a single mother with a large house, three kids, and a way of life that was impossible to sustain on Army pay. Worse, there was no one in Lawrenceville who shared our situation—the other fathers were all well beyond draft age. So was Pop, but he was the only one in the National Guard. This was not the kind of war Mom was equipped to fight.

She was a remarkable woman. She was born Ruth Bowman in 1900 in Bluefield, West Virginia, a little town where as a girl she had made pocket money taking tourists up a mountain to look at the sunrise. Her father was county school superintendent and her mother head of the Woman's Christian Temperance Union. Her parents got divorced when she was eighteen, partly because my grandfather liked to drink and my grandmother couldn't make him give it up.

Mom used to say she'd left Bluefield because she loved them both and they kept trying to get her to pick sides. She came north and studied nursing at Trenton's largest hospital, working her way up to assistant superintendent of nurses; then she went into private-duty nursing for wealthy families. She made a successful career at a time when women mostly stayed home.

She and Pop met at a Trenton reception in 1928, when he was still head of the state police. He asked her out and she said yes. She loved to tell the story of how, upon spotting him the following weekend in a parade, decked out in his uniform and riding a white horse, she pointed him out to one of her friends and said, "That's the man I'm going to marry." It was a tempestuous romance. Pop was thirty-three years old and quite the man about town; he courted my mother, but even though she turned down another beau, he wouldn't commit. So Mom said, "The hell with you, buster," moved to New York, got a job at Columbia Presbyterian Hospital, and started dating other men. That drove my father wild, so he went to New York, fetched her back, and married her.

It had been decades since she'd left Bluefield behind, but Mom stayed faithful to her West Virginia roots, and you could see that in the way she sized people up. She hated inherited wealth or privilege. Organizations like the Daughters of the American Revolution and the First Families of Virginia irritated her, even though she was proud that on her father's side of the family she could trace her ancestry to Thomas Jefferson. She'd talk about getting invited to join the DAR and burst out, "I want nothing to do with that bunch of nitwits! I wouldn't waste my *time* doing that." The people she held in respect were those who earned their position through hard work, rather than having it handed to them.

My father taught me honor, but I learned tolerance from her. The year he left she transferred me from Lawrenceville Elementary to the Princeton Elementary School, where she thought I'd get a better education, and I traveled back and forth each day on the Princeton–Lawrenceville bus. While I was on my way home one afternoon, a black lady who had been our maid got on. I had been taught that when a lady gets on a bus, you offer her your seat. So I gave her mine, but some kids started snickering and whispering as though I had done something really dumb. When I got home, I told this to Mom, who was fixing dinner at the long table in the kitchen. She stopped what she was doing, sat me down opposite her in the breakfast nook, and told me what I'd done was right. Then she said: "You have to understand that you're one of the luckiest people in the world. You were born white, you were born Protestant, and you were born American. That means you'll be spared prejudices that a lot of other people have to put up with. But always remember: you had nothing to do with the fact that you were born that way. It gives you no right to look down on anybody who wasn't. No matter what the other children say, you must never look down on anybody."

Putting aside her career and being part of the Princeton and Lawrence-ville social scene had made sense to my mother as long as she shared it with my father. They were a great couple, happy with each other, their lives, and their friends. With my dad around, she felt confident and independent, proud of his accomplishments and also proud of her own. But once he went away, everything she loved about their life disappeared, and she was left with the burdens.

The worst headache was the house—it carried a large mortgage and high taxes, and cost too much to run. Soon after my dad left they tried selling it, but there were no buyers. Next, Mom thought she could find a family to lodge with us, but after she had one all lined up they made another arrangement. Meanwhile, she had to have the oil burner taken out, as all of America's oil was needed for the war effort. So to heat the house that winter of 1942–43 we had a big coal furnace installed, and Mom had to go down to the basement at least twice a day to shovel coal. Household help was hard to find, because all the maids now had jobs in Trenton munitions factories. Gasoline became very scarce as well. We owned a wonderful Pontiac sedan called a "torpedo back," whose roof came down to a point in the rear—a real *Gang Busters* car. But all of a sudden we couldn't go anywhere, which bothered Mom, because she liked to drive. You had to have a ration sticker on your windshield, and ours was a black "A," the lowest status possible. Our allotment dropped to three gallons a week by the end of 1942 and was even lower in 1943. Mom saved most of our ration for visits to Grandma Schwarzkopf in Newark, about fifty miles away. She and Grandma Schwarz-kopf didn't like each other very much—the first thing Grandma Schwarz-kopf said to Mom when Ruth Ann was born was, "A German woman would have had a boy first"—but Mom was a dutiful daughter-in-law.

I always enjoyed our visits to my grandmother's house for the first half hour. She spoiled me rotten because I was my father's *son*. There was always plenty of candy around and some special little present for me, like a toy soldier. After the first half hour, however, I was ready to go home. I felt that old people talked too much, I didn't like them always hugging and kissing me, and besides, they smelled funny!

———

We all tried to do our bit for the war effort in Pop's absence. That first year, Mom trained women in Lawrenceville to be nurse's aides. Ruth Ann and Sally worked at British War Relief in Princeton, unraveling old sweaters so the ladies could knit them into socks. We listened to the war bulletins, and when word came of the Allies winning in North Africa and invading Sicily, we cheered, even though I was too little to grasp the details of what was going on. My school was participating in a War Department fundraising program, and I went around collecting nickels and dimes to help buy a jeep for the war. I think we had to collect seven hundred and fifty dollars. When we reached that goal we had Jeep Day, a miraculous occasion when the Army actually brought your jeep to the school. I'll never forget how fantastic that jeep looked. It was way up in the air, on a platform truck, was painted Army green with white stars on the side, and was draped in red, white, and blue banners. Of course, the same jeep was probably brought to every school in New Jersey, but we didn't know that. This was the jeep *we* had bought. The Princeton Elementary School jeep was going over to fight the Germans and the Japs.

Collecting money for the war effort got me interested in making some money for myself. Mom was great at encouraging this entrepreneurial spark. The spring after Pop left she helped me get a paper route. Each afternoon I had to report to a loading dock in town to pick up my bundle of the *Trenton Times*. You had to fold the papers a certain way, and if you did it right, you could ride your bicycle and chuck a paper all the way up onto a customer's front porch. I was the slowest folder. The other paper boys would come in after me, fold their papers, load their bikes, and be on their way, while I was still standing there folding mine. Once I got on my bike, I was no good at hitting the customer's front porch; my papers usually landed in the shrubbery between the house and the street. Then I had to decide whether to stop, get off my bike, pick up the paper, and lay it on the porch, or let it stay where it had landed. Usually I'd let it stay. Meanwhile, I'd be running late, and the newspaper office would be getting complaints that the paper hadn't been delivered. I lasted about three weeks. Mom and I finally had a little business conference and agreed that my future was not in newspapers.

Next I got interested in selling seeds. Seed companies put fascinating ads in comic books that showed terrific premiums you could earn selling door-to-door. I studied those ads and decided to try for the complete fishing outfit, which included a rod and reel and a box of tackle. Mom helped figure out how much I'd have to sell and we filled out the order form. "Are you sure you want to order this many seeds?" she said. "Maybe you should try for the magnifying glass instead." But I'd made up my mind.

The seeds came in little packets that sold for a dime each. The packets had marvelous pictures of the things you could grow—exotic melons, tropical flowers, pyracantha vines that would climb up and cover your house. I couldn't understand why more people didn't want them. I spent weeks knocking on doors all over Lawrenceville, but I still had hundreds of unsold packets. Meanwhile the seed people started sending letters that said, in effect, "You've got our seeds. We're waiting for the money." Mom helped think of new people to ask and new neighborhoods to try. But as more weeks passed, the seed people's letters turned nasty, and finally she declared that I'd done a good job and sold everything I could. She paid for the rest of the seeds herself. I waited eagerly for my rod and reel to arrive. When the package finally came, it wasn't shaped like a rod and reel—it was rectangular. I thought they must have folded the rod somehow, but when I opened it, it was a Bible. With it came another letter from the seed people, referring to fine print in the contract that said if you took too long to pay, the company could determine your premium. I thought it was unfair, but Mom took no position except to say, "Next year we will not sell seeds, Norman."

Meanwhile, Pop sent mail. His letters and packages came not just in a stream, but in a *torrent*. He'd gotten hold of a typewriter in Tehran, and even though he'd never learned to type, he churned out thousands and thousands and thousands of words every week. Deliveries were uneven, so often there would be nothing for three weeks and then suddenly twelve or fifteen letters would arrive. Mom would sit us down in the living room and read them aloud. Those letters were something to see. Pop had a set of colored pens and he'd illustrate the pages with intricate drawings of things he'd observed and funny cartoons. He wrote about everything. Marble palaces and mosques, bread riots, raids by wild mountain tribes, tedious diplomatic lunches, goings-on in the Big House, which was the villa he shared with other members of the U.S. mission, his houseboy Ali, the politics of the Iranian parliament, and his troubles with his teeth. A lot of this went right over my head, but there was always something to capture my attention, such as the way Tehran rug makers would take a new rug on which they might have slaved for months and age it to increase its value. "They lay them out in the streets," he wrote, "let people walk on them for days at a time, let donkeys and sheep and camels that go along the sidewalks tromp all over them, and the other day I saw one that a man wanted to make real old lying out in the street where cars and horse-carts would ride over it."

Pop also sent packages filled with gifts from the bazaars—silver filigree jewelry, prayer rugs, and lamb's wool hats. Mine were all-boy things I could really relate to: a tribal hunting knife, a camel bell, the cured horn of an ibex he'd shot. The best was a three-hundred-year-old Persian battle-ax he sent for my tenth birthday, a lethal-looking thing about two feet long, inlaid with silver and engraved with Farsi verses and an inscription that said it was intended for a young nobleman. With the ax came a letter in which he called it "a prediction of your worthy success in the 'Battle of Life'" and spoke warmly about his love and ambition for me:

> It really is something to have completed the first decade of your life, and to look back over the years and realize all the joy and pleasure that you have brought to Mommy and me, the grand association with your lovely sisters, your accomplishments and realizations, your friends, your experiences and progress along life's highway. I am proud of you, my boy, and look into the augury of the past and see a glorious future. Deep in Mommy's heart and my heart lie unspoken hopes and ambitions for you, an abiding love and understanding, and the knowledge that the success of our lives will be written in your deeds.

My parents exchanged mail privately as well. Those couldn't have been happy notes, because all through 1943 Mom was struggling to make ends meet and gradually losing heart. That summer, she and Pop decided that we should move out of the Green House and have it broken up into rental apartments, so it would pay for itself until a buyer could be found. One of Pop's friends helped with the plan, but the bank that held the mortgage was reluctant to finance the conversion, and there were other problems. Meanwhile, the burden was on Mom to find us an affordable place to rent, and get us packed and moved by the end of the year.

At the height of all this, in October 1943, Pop came home briefly. He'd flown to Washington to plead for trucks and boots for his gendarmes, and was with us for only a few days. That visit is a blur in my mind except for something that happened to Sally on Halloween. She and Ruth Ann had come in the front door from trick-or-treating. I was already in bed, and Mom and Pop were in the kitchen. Sally walked back and found them at the long wooden table, sitting next to each other, smoking cigarettes, in serious conversation. Mom was crying. My sister worried about it for days: she had no idea why Mom was so sad. Of course, the grown-ups were keeping all their problems from us. When Pop left soon after, Mom found herself facing another winter alone.

A few weeks later I got home from school and found my mother sitting on the front steps, hugging her knees and in tears. She had just come up from the basement and was all smudged with coal dust. I was scared and kept trying to find out what was wrong, but she was jumbling her words. She said we didn't have anything to eat, there was nothing in the house, nothing was ready for dinner. But I knew we had food. Something was happening to my mother and I didn't know what it was.

We moved to Princeton in early December, first to an apartment, then to a rental house on Hibben Road in a prosperous old neighborhood near the Princeton Theological Seminary. The house was smaller and easier to manage than the Green House had been, but my sisters, who were used to living at the best address in Lawrenceville, thought it was a comedown because it was made of wood while most of the nearby houses were grander and made of stone. But it had bay windows and a screened-in front porch, and there was really nothing wrong with it, except that the two years we spent there were so unhappy. After we left Lawrenceville it became apparent that Mom was drinking heavily and that that was what caused her to slur her words and not be herself. Maybe she'd been drinking before we moved and we hadn't known. But in Princeton the problem grew too severe to hide. Within six months it had become the central fact of our lives.

I used to dread coming home at night. I'd go around the side of the house, where there was a window that looked into the kitchen. I'd stand in the dark and look inside and try to judge what kind of night it was going to be. Mom had a Jekyll-and-Hyde personality. When she was sober, she was the sweetest, most sensitive, loving, and intelligent person you could ever meet. But when she was drunk she was a holy terror.

Mom did her drinking before dinner. Sometimes she'd take an eight-ounce glass, fill it three quarters full of bourbon, and swallow it down. Then we'd sit at the table and she would start. When Mom was drunk, a terrible meanness would come out, mostly in the form of personal attacks on my sisters. She might look at Sally and say, "Sit up straight! Why are you always slouching? Why don't you sit up straight at the table?" Then it would be, "Just look at you. You're such a mess. Look at that hair." The small jabs would go on until she sensed she'd hit on something my sister was particularly sensitive about, and then she'd bore in until my sister broke down in tears. Sometimes the vulnerability involved a boyfriend, or school, or weight; whatever it was, Mom found it.

My defense was to isolate myself as much as I could: get in there, have dinner, and disappear upstairs to my room. But after dinner Sally and Ruth Ann had to wash the dishes; they had no escape. They'd stand at the old cast-iron sink with their backs to Mom, who sat at the kitchen table and continued to criticize them. Anybody who hasn't lived with an alcoholic parent would find it hard to imagine how those kitchen scenes unfolded.

Years later Ruth Ann wrote an account of one in a short story. She changed her name to Bethesda and Sally's to Lena, but the rest is fact:

Last night Mother kept them standing against the wall in the kitchen until nine o'clock, all because they had talked French while doing the dishes.

"You think you're so smart, talking about your Mother, well you just stand there," she had said over and over, watching them as she ate from the saucepan, stuffing her mouth with string beans.

"What do you have to do that's so important? You just stand there. And you, Miss Bethesda, you stand with your legs together. Do you hear me? You put those fat thighs together!" String beans fell out of her mouth when she said "fat thighs."

"Miss High-and-Mighty," Mother stuck out her lower lip, "looking down her nose at her mother. You think you're so smart talking French. Why can't you stay on your diet, answer me that!"

"I don't know, Mother," Bethesda answered. Actually, she didn't know. She wished she could! It made her ashamed to think how ugly she was now with her big body and frizzy hair.

"You think you're so special working with Miss Fine's girls," Mother made her voice real high for those three words, "proud as peacocks down at British War Relief with the society ladies. . . . How about some war relief for your mother! How about some of that, Miss Bethesda!" on and on. Lena hadn't said a word. Then Mother started in on Daddy, how he was living-the-life-of-Riley, whatever that was, with his houseboy, Ali Akbar. Bethesda didn't know why Mother hated Ali Akbar so. "Ali Akbar. Ali Akbar. The colonel and his little houseboy, Ali Akbar," Mother had said making little eyes, mouthing the words at them. That's when Bethesda answered back.

"He's doing his part," she told Mother, even though she knew what would happen next. Mother sent Lena upstairs. Then she slumped on the table and began to cry.

"Nobody cares about me. Not one person in the whole wide world cares what happens to me."

Bethesda watched her carefully. "Pull yourself together," she wanted to say. "Roll with the punches! There's a war on!" But she didn't say anything. She watched Mother's dark head rolling back and forth on her arms. She waited for what was coming. She knew that now Mother would make her cry.

When we moved to Princeton, Mom made a new friend whom the three of us hated. Her family had a lot of money but she was just the kind of idle rich person Mom usually did not want anything to do with. This woman was a falling-down drunk. I don't think I ever saw her sober. She was one of those women who wears heavy makeup put on carelessly, so that it looks like it's melting—lipstick smeared around the lips, eyebrows plucked and haphazardly painted back on. We viewed her as *the* cause of Mom's alcoholism because Mom would go out sober with her and come home drunk.

They spent a lot of time with the woman's brother, a great big guy, grossly overweight, who seemed to be in a perpetual sweat, oozing perspiration out of every pore of his body. I think he must have been making a play for my mother. Another guy was always hanging around, too, a big buddy of theirs who looked just like the movie star Sonny Tufts—tall and husky, with slick blond hair, blue eyes, and a million-dollar smile. He tried to chum it up with Sally and me. Once he even took us pheasant hunting, in open country not far from the courthouse where the Lindbergh trial had been held. But I thought he was a total phony and wanted no part of his friendship; if I'd had my way, I would have taken my Persian battle-ax to him. These weren't the kind of friends Mom and Pop had had before Pop left.

Each of us dealt with the turmoil in a different way. Ruth Ann always argued: the older she got, the fiercer her quarrels with Mom became. Sally would tough it out: she became the daughter who tried to hold the family together. I didn't like confrontations, but sometimes I fought back with sabotage: when Mom was out of the house I'd search the kitchen for the bottles of bourbon and gin, pour them out behind the garage, and smash them. At times it was anger that overwhelmed me, at other times fear, but what I felt most often was complete helplessness. I simply retreated, which Mom let me do because I was the youngest and her favorite. Deep inside me was a place where I would withdraw when things were unhappy at home. I discovered I could hide the painful feelings and still make friends and love dogs and help old ladies across the street and be a good guy. I had lots of buddies, but no really close friend. I learned to be self-contained and independent. Maybe that was a gift my mother gave me.

———

I was still pretty happy when I was out of the house. The school offered a detailed course on the Revolutionary War, particularly as it related to our area—the Battle of Princeton and the Battle of Trenton and Washington's crossing of the Delaware. I loved the idea that I was walking the very same ground as George Washington. I was also fascinated by natural history, particularly birds. There wasn't a bird that flew in the state of New Jersey that I couldn't identify. I could tell the males from the females and could look at the color of an egg or the shape of a nest and identify the kind of bird it belonged to.

I imagined myself to be a mighty hunter. We had a garage and some apple trees behind the house, and I was constantly back there setting traps. My earliest trap was a white box propped up by a stick with a string tied to it, like you see in cartoons. I found out very quickly that animals are too smart for that—you couldn't even catch a house cat. Then I discovered a book at the library called *A Boy's Guide to Wilderness Living* and learned to make rock falls and deadfalls and snares, all of which were too clumsy to work. Finally I sent away for a wire mesh trap with a little spring door that could capture chipmunks alive. I was really excited. My plan—once I had caught and trained a large menagerie of chipmunks—was to produce H. Norman Schwarzkopf's Trained Chipmunks of World Renown, an act Barnum & Bailey would covet for their center ring. Then I caught one. I got up one morning and found a little chipmunk in the trap, scared to death and squeaking like crazy. I immediately let him go and felt ashamed that I'd taken away his freedom even for the short time I had. Compassion always got the better of my predatory instinct.

I remember the first thing I ever killed. It was a robin. I was big into my bow and arrow at the time, constantly launching arrows at all sorts of targets, figuring I'd never hit any of them. One day I spotted a robin in the backyard. I lined up, let loose the arrow, and my God, I'd hit it! The arrow was sticking right through the bird, which flapped around on the ground for a few minutes before it died. There was no way for me to bring the robin back to life, and it was my fault.

I went inside, got the fanciest box I could find, lined it with the very softest fabric I could find, and buried the bird, digging a deep hole and saying all the prayers I could remember. I vowed to heaven that I would never, ever, ever again shoot at a bird, or anything else, if I could just be forgiven for having committed this terrible crime. Pop used to preach endlessly that you should never point a weapon at anyone or any living thing unless you intended to use it, and now I saw he was right. After that I wasn't so blithe about shooting my bow and arrow or my BB gun at anything that moved. Sometimes I'd fake it with my buddies. We'd be stalking something with BB guns and when we got close enough I'd shoot, but I always aimed to miss.

Mom seemed to understand my need to get away. She signed me up for all the organized activities we could find. Because of the war, there weren't that many—the Cub Scout troop had disbanded, and there was no Little League or soccer league. But I went to a boys' club every Saturday, where I learned to shoot a twenty-two. I also sang soprano in the boys' choir at Trinity Episcopal Church. One of the reasons I joined the choir was that you got paid: for one long practice and one Sunday service per week, each boy got fifty cents, which seemed like a lot. I even went to dancing school, and though I'd have been mortified if my friends had found out I was learning ballroom dancing, I loved it. Part of the reason was that it was a coed class, with several pretty girls. Even at age eight or nine, I was a very romantic young man.

When Mom reported on my activities to Pop, he started to worry that I was becoming a sissy. Although he'd sung in the West Point choir himself and was an excellent dancer, he wanted to see me more active in sports. In his letters all through 1944 he mounted a get-Norm-on-the-field campaign, assigning me manly tasks such as reporting the Army football score to him each week. He had a point: though I swam and hiked at summer camp and played pickup games of baseball and kick the can with my friends, I really wasn't athletically inclined.

———

My father's wartime adventures began to seem quite unreal to me, compared with the battles in our own house. The longer we lived in Princeton, the more irrelevant his letters seemed. No one told him the family was in trouble, and Mom hid her drinking whenever one of Pop's officers stopped by to visit on his way to Iran. My father had no idea what was happening in our lives. His letters often included messages such as "I know I can depend upon you to be the man in the house," and I had a sense of having failed utterly at the job. But the letters didn't speak to what I cared about or needed. I missed having a father. Many of my friends whose fathers taught at Princeton or Lawrenceville School had their dads around. The men were nice to me, but no one tried to be my surrogate father. If they had, I would have resisted with all my might, because nobody could replace my own.

We prayed he would come home and rescue us, but we didn't know when that would be possible. The first war bulletin that ever made sense to me was in June 1944, when I heard about D-Day on the radio. The announcer quoted Ohio governor John Bricker's now-famous line that this was "the beginning of the end of the forces of evil and destruction." I was excited, astounded, mesmerized—it meant the war was almost over and maybe my dad would come home. But when the defeat of Nazi Germany finally came the following spring, the shah's government was dependent on the United States, and Pop wrote that his mission could go on for years. Then he was unexpectedly called back for consultations in Washington and came up to Princeton for a month's leave. It was June 1945.

I later learned that my father was stunned at the condition in which he found Mom, but he never showed it at the time. When she'd launch into a tirade at dinner he'd change the subject or wait for an opportunity to excuse us children from the table. Eventually he talked to Ruth Ann and Sally about Mom's drinking, but it was only to explain that he couldn't stay with us to solve the problem. To Ruth Ann, who was fifteen, he said: "There's still a war on. There's a job to do for the duration, and you have a part. You have to take care of your mother. I'm counting on you to carry the ball." To Sally, who was thirteen, he said, "You have to roll with the punches."

He and I didn't discuss her drinking at all, but what he did for me was much more effective. I asked him to send me away to military school, and he agreed. Pop had gone to military school, and I had already tried the idea on Mom. I told him, "I'm tired of being in this house with nothing but girls. It's turning me into a sissy." That was all it took. I couldn't tell him I wanted to get away from my mother's drinking and the constant fighting. It would have embarrassed me to say those things.

That September, I entered the sixth grade at Bordentown Military Academy. I was delighted, because I was marching to the program my father had set out for me. I'd seen pictures of him in his military uniforms as a little boy; now I was going to military school, and maybe someday I'd go to West Point. If I had any worry, it was whether I would measure up.

Bordentown was a picture-postcard military academy midway between Princeton and Philadelphia—a big old white stone building with a parade ground out front and dormitories and playing fields behind. For the first time I became a success—scholastically, athletically, and militarily. My grades had always been only average or a little above, and my report cards had consistently said things like "Norman is doing fine, but he's not working up to his potential." Now I was getting straight A's. It was all a matter of structure and focus; the classes at Bordentown were somewhat harder than those at Princeton Elementary School, but Bordentown had mandatory study hall at night, and no pretty girls or radio shows or adventures with my buddies to distract me.

Physically I thrived, too. I grew that winter to nearly six feet tall, and played soccer and learned to throw the javelin and shot put. Militarily, I got promoted to private first class, the highest rank you could achieve in sixth grade. I liked wearing a uniform, sitting formally at the dining table, and marching to class. And I liked the discipline; if you come from a home as chaotic as mine had become, it's very reassuring to know what's expected. We younger boys lived in a dormitory run by a house mother named Mrs. McKay, a warm old lady who took a special liking to me and made me feel totally safe and secure. In the space of a year I changed from a shy chubby boy to a tall bold adolescent. I'm sure my sisters had mixed feelings about this transformation, especially in its crude early phase. When I came home at Christmas I wanted to show them they could no longer push me around, so I'd hold up my fist with one knuckle jutting out, bang them in the arm, and say, "If you scream I'll hit you again."

I didn't spend much time at home after Pop's visit in 1945, and he made sure it stayed that way. The following June, after school let out, he wrote to my mother saying now that the war was over, he wanted me to live with him in Iran. She came into my room one day and said, "How would you like to go to Iran and join your father?" She had to repeat the question before I could believe it was real. All I could say was, "When do I leave?"

Pop had arranged for me to travel with Major Dick Waters, who was to depart in August to join Pop's staff. The plan was for us to start in Washington, D.C., drive to Florida, where Major Waters would say good-bye to his family, and then catch a plane at the Army Air Force base at West Palm Beach. Within a week Mom and I were wandering the halls of the Pentagon, getting my passport and arranging endless shots to immunize me against cholera, the plague, diphtheria, and other diseases you could catch in Iran. The Pentagon was new in those days. I remember being amazed that you could walk and walk and walk inside it and never seem to go anywhere. Everybody was nice to us, not least because Pop had just been promoted to brigadier general as a reflection of the importance of the United States's link to Iran.

It took almost a month and several trips to Washington to get all the inoculations. We stayed with one of Mom's friends from nursing school and also spent a couple of weeks with my sisters at the shore, in the little town of Sea Girt, New Jersey. I met a girl there named Eileen, whom I was convinced I'd love for the rest of my life. I took her to the movies and worked up enough nerve to hold her hand—big stuff for an eleven-year-old. Then we had to say good-bye forever because I was going off to join Beau Geste in the desert.

Finally, on my twelfth birthday, August 22, 1946, Major Waters pulled up at the curb in his white sedan. I stuck my suitcase in the backseat and kissed Mom good-bye, and we drove off. I mark that day as the start of my military career because, from then on, I lived in an Army world.

3

There was no easy way to reach the Middle East. In the last week of August we took off from West Palm Beach in a crowded Air Force passenger plane. We flew back up the Eastern Seaboard, across the North Atlantic via Newfoundland, Labrador, and the Azores, through Europe, and across North Africa, stopping to refuel every six or eight hundred miles. Counting layovers and connections, it took five days to reach Cairo, where a beat-up two-engine cargo plane sent by Pop waited to carry us the final thousand miles to Tehran.

That was my first encounter with desert heat. We sat with a half dozen other passengers strapped to metal seats along the walls of the cargo bay. The cabin had tiny windows and the temperature was over a hundred degrees. We climbed to maybe three thousand feet, and soon the plane began hitting thermal currents rising from the desert floor, and started bouncing up and down, up and down. Everybody got airsick, and I decided I never wanted to set foot in a plane again. We stopped to refuel at Baghdad. Around the airport was sand, yellow sand, in every direction. The afternoon air was hot and utterly dry, and there was a breeze blowing like no breeze I'd ever felt. It wasn't refreshing; it made me feel as though I were inside a giant balloon with someone pumping in hot air. The airport had no terminal and no shade, so we ended up sitting under the wing while the plane was being refueled. When I climbed back in I fell asleep, exhausted from airsickness and heat, and didn't wake up until we landed at Tehran.

My father wasn't there to meet us, but he'd sent a couple of aides in an Army car. We drove along a dusty highway, past shabby men on donkeys and women in veils, into Tehran, around a traffic circle, and then back out, toward some mountains. Finally we pulled up in front of a big metal gate, and I recognized the villa I'd seen in photos. I went up the front steps, and just as I reached the top, Pop burst through the door to greet me and passed me right by. I'd grown so much that year that he didn't even recognize me. I had to chase him down the steps and grab him, and we hugged. For the first time in four years I was under my father's roof.

By then the two most powerful Americans in Iran were my father and Ambassador George Allen, with whom he worked closely. My father had access to the shah, conferred constantly with the Iranian prime minister, was friends with important tribal chiefs, and had even better connections outside Tehran than Ambassador Allen did. He had built the gendarmerie into a well-trained, well-paid, highly organized force of twenty thousand men—not huge, considering it had to police an area as big as the eastern United States. But with fifteen regiments stationed at strategic points across the country, it acted as a powerful and stabilizing force, probably the strongest in Iran.

Long before the war ended, Pop's mission had changed. The United States and the Soviet Union were still allies against the Nazis in Europe, but the Soviets were maneuvering to bring Iran into their sphere, and Pop's job was to keep communism out. Stalin did not like the influence the United States was gaining in Tehran, and did not like the fact that a strong gendarmerie meant a stronger shah, even though the Soviet Union was desperate for those shipments of American aid that the gendarmerie helped protect.

The shah, Mohammad Reza Pahlavi, was still only in his twenties and struggling to consolidate his power. When Soviet and British troops withdrew from Iran's outlying provinces in the spring of 1946, a few months before I arrived, it was Pop's gendarmes who filled the vacuum, keeping order in the countryside, confiscating guns, and backing up local police when antimonarchy demonstrations got out of hand. So my father became a target for Soviet propaganda. Tass published reports denouncing him, and when Iranian communists staged demonstrations, there were always "Down with Schwarzkopf" signs. That was fine with Pop, who made no bones about the fact that he was anticommunist and prided himself on helping to keep Iran out of the Soviet bloc.

Pop shared the Big House with four of his officers, two of whose wives had recently been allowed to join them; there were no kids besides me. It was a beautifully proportioned villa with terraces and balconies and white marble walls. Around it were two acres of manicured gardens that you reached by going out French doors and down sweeping marble steps. There were two swimming pools, which astounded me, since I'd never dreamed of having even one. Downstairs was a huge dining room, huge living room, and giant foyer, all with white marble floors and magnificent Persian carpets. The upstairs was divided into rooms and suites. The offices were in the basement. Pop made a big ceremony of introducing me to the servants—his houseboy, Ali (not a boy at all, I was surprised to learn, but a grown man of thirty-five with a family of his own), the cook, the waiters, the gardener. Then there was the handyman, Bussorgy, an awesome-looking but mentally retarded giant.

To get away from the heat inside the buildings at night, most people in Tehran slept outside. My room had no balcony, so my bed was on the roof, where I could see south across the city and the desert that lay beyond. To the north was the Elburz mountain range, and in the distance Mount Damāvand, more than 18,000 feet high. At dawn that first morning I woke to the sound of muezzins chanting the call to prayer from their minarets. I liked the sound, a beautiful, lilting vocalization. There were mosques all over Tehran, and I learned to pick out voices from three different directions.

During the day, the most astonishing scenes would unfold in front of our gate. The Big House was on a road that led up into the Shemran foothills of the Elburz, and camel caravans on their way into town would pass right by. The camels wore sets of big bronze bells under their necks: usually a bell within a bell, and sometimes a bell within a bell within a bell. As the camels walked, the bells would go ba-*bong*, ba-*bong*, ba-*bong*, and I would hear them passing the wall outside. Rug merchants would bang on our gate, and occasionally one who looked promising would be allowed to present his wares. All the adults would gather as he'd throw his rugs out one at a time on the living room floor, and sometimes the bargaining went on for two or three hours.

Even our water came through the gate, from a big concrete gutter called a "jube" that paralleled the road. Tehran had no underground pipes, so the water system made use of the fact that the city was built on a slope. Twice a day the city engineers would flood the jube, and the water would run down the hill. Each day the gardener and Bussorgy would build a little dam and divert some of the flow to a cistern on the roof, and that was the water we used for washing. Wealthy people lived up above, where we were, and the poor people down below, so for the wealthy the water was clean, but by the time it ran all the way down to the other end of town it would be filthy. Our drinking water came from the American embassy, which had a well. They would deliver it on a donkey cart with a big barrel on the back, and we'd store it in vodka bottles left over from parties. There was always a bottle in the bathroom where we brushed our teeth.

Right away I loved Tehran. The day after I arrived Pop and I got in a car and he had his driver take us downtown. He pointed out the palace square, where three marble palaces faced each other, one rose-colored, one a beautiful green, and one (the shah's) pure white. He pointed out historic mosques and government ministries where he'd fought bureaucratic battles for the gendarmerie. I couldn't take my eyes off the people and animals on the streets. There were camels and donkeys burdened with huge woven saddlebags and driven by fierce-looking tribesmen with daggers in their belts. There were mullahs in black robes and beggars and lepers. There were animals running loose, and jabbering voices. Battered horse-drawn taxis called "doroshkes" were everywhere and the scraggly little horses that pulled them looked very strange, because to identify them their owners would dip a hand in henna and put a bright red handprint on the horse's rear, and paint on other decorations as well. Pop took me down stone steps into the underground bazaar, a maze of tunnels lit with candles and bare electric bulbs. Along the tunnel walls were holes, and in every hole was some kind of shop. He greeted his favorite rug merchant, who was serving a customer a cup of coffee as they haggled over prices, and we stopped to watch an old bronzeworker, working by candlelight and using only a little hammer and a nail, tapping absolutely gorgeous motifs on a huge brass tray.

Each morning I ate an all-American breakfast of eggs, toast, orange juice from powdered concentrate, and Spam—which the Moslem cooks were willing to prepare because they didn't realize it was pork—with the grown-ups in the dining room. Pop sat at the head of the table and I sat to his right. Then I was off to school. My father had signed me up for the Presbyterian mission school, where all the Americans sent their kids. My school bus was an Army truck with a big white star on each side and a canvas cover on the back, and my bus driver was an Army sergeant. On the way we'd pick up the ambassador's sons at the embassy. My classmates were a hodgepodge of Americans, Iranians, and children whose refugee parents had ended up in Tehran—Armenians, White Russians, German Jews, and Jews from Palestine. I made lots of friends and was constantly switching from culture to culture. I'd walk an Armenian girl home after school, trying to sell her on the American custom of holding hands. Or I'd go home with my best friend,

Michael Lieberman, a Palestinian Jew, and we'd listen to his older brother Jacob talk about joining the terrorists fighting the British to establish the Jewish state. Or I'd go into a British home, where people were sipping tea.

Pop's schedule was laid out from morning till night, and it was impossible for him to drop everything to look after me. So he adopted the strategy of including me whenever he could. He brought me to diplomatic receptions and formal dinners; whenever there was a party at the Big House, he expected me to attend. And he didn't stay with me. He'd say, "Get out there and mingle, Norm. Introduce yourself to these people; tell 'em who you are."

He loved to share the adventure of the Middle East. One night in late September he said, "We're going out." We got in the car and Pop explained we'd been invited to have dinner with a chief of a Baluchi tribe, who was visiting Tehran. The Baluchi were nomads from the eastern part of the country who considered themselves autonomous, but this chief was loyal to the shah. When they came to town, Pop explained, the Baluchi didn't check into a hotel. They literally brought their town with them. We drove to the outskirts of the city, and at dusk we came to the edge of a mesa where we could see the dark brown tents of the Baluchi encampment spread out below. There was a large tent for the chief, and dozens of family tents all around it, in no apparent order. Goats, donkeys, camels, and horses seemed to be everywhere, some in rudimentary corrals, some wandering around, tended by children.

We descended into the camp on a narrow dirt road and pulled up in front of the main tent. About twenty tribesmen in long robes and armed with rifles and knives talked to Pop and his interpreter while I waited nearby. After fifteen minutes we were ushered into a central tent, where the floor was covered with tribal rugs in bright geometric patterns of white, blue, and varying shades of red, and there were rough-woven cushions to lean on. I was seated next to Pop. The fierce-looking tribesmen scared me a little and I started to talk to Pop, but he said I should keep quiet and try to mimic what he did. Before us were mounds of rice of every description heaped on three-foot-long platters and laid out on the rugs. There was sweet rice with bits of red and green and yellow flavoring; saffron rice; rice prepared with chicken; even rice with fruit. There were salads of raw vegetables, which Pop had warned me not to eat because of the impurity of the water in which the vegetables had been washed. The servants brought in sheep that had been spit roasted whole, laid them on top of the long platters of rice. I literally had an entire sheep in front of me. There was much talking and laughing and gesturing as servants came around and piled everybody's plates high. But no one touched the sheep.

Once the plates were filled, servants started plucking out the sheeps' eyeballs. The Baluchi considered eyeballs a delicacy and there was a feeling of great ceremony as they were given out. Pop, the honored guest, received the first, and I watched as he scooped it up with some rice in his right hand, popped it in his mouth, and solemnly chewed. The chief got one, and two or three of his top men. Then they started discussing me, saying, "The general's son is here! Shouldn't we give the general's son the sheep's eye?" It seemed half joking and I desperately hoped they weren't serious. "The next person we are going to honor is the general's son!" the chief announced, and everybody laughed and clapped. My father was beaming.

So they gave me a sheep's eyeball. With all the roasting and basting it didn't look like a staring eye—more like a brown fig. But it was still an eyeball as far as I was concerned. I said to my father, "I'm not going to eat that." He said out of the corner of his mouth, "You *will* eat it!" As a stranger to the tribe, I'd been given a spoon to use with my meal. Holding my breath, I spooned the eyeball up and swallowed it whole, and everyone applauded. Afterward Pop said he was glad I'd done as I was told. "They were paying you a great tribute, and if you hadn't eaten the eye, you'd have insulted them," he said. "But instead you ate it, and by doing that you made a contribution to American-Iranian relations. I'm proud of you." Hearing him say these things made up for the fact that I'd just had to swallow a sheep's eye.

That fall, every once in a while, I'd think about my friends back in Princeton, joining the Boy Scouts and raking leaves, and I'd marvel at my good fortune. I was with my dad in the Arabian Nights, having manly experiences, with no women bossing me around. I was living every boy's dream.

It never occurred to me to feel homesick. Even the disease and filth of the Middle East didn't get me down. I swam in the Big House pools despite the fact that they had no filtration system and you sometimes had to peel off leeches afterward. I got used to sleeping under netting to ward off sand flies, which carried a fever similar to malaria. Exotic diseases were an everyday event. We'd all been immunized against cholera, typhoid, typhus, and yellow fever, but you could catch something called "undulant fever" if you ate Iranian ice cream or drank the milk—it caused an officer in Pop's command to waste away over the course of a year and die. And another of Pop's aides was diagnosed as having a thirty-foot tapeworm. Then there were everyday ailments related to impurities in the water, such as diarrhea and jaundice. At the mission school, kids were always turning bright orange-yellow from jaundice. I got it a couple of times—I'd feel a little run-down but I'd take some medicine and continue right on with classes, and in a week or so it would pass.

Turning yellow was something you expected to have happen; it was all part of the adventure.

———

When he couldn't spend time with me, my father would arrange for me to see things he had discovered. Once I drove with an interpreter downtown to the central bank, where an Iranian official and a guard met us and took us to the underground vaults. They opened a door and I walked into a room that was filled from one end to the other with the fabled crown jewels of the shah. I saw the imperial crowns on display, with rubies and emeralds the size of fists. There were diamond-studded sashes and gem-encrusted golden swords. In the corners of the room were piles of emeralds and rubies. Piles! And from the ceiling hung what looked like sausages of pearls—pearls on strands entwined to form thick ropes. The entire ceiling was covered with them. But the thing that really stunned me was a globe that stood in the middle of the room. It was solid gold. All the oceans on this globe were formed in emeralds, and all the countries—except Iran—in rubies. Iran was all diamonds. I gasped and stared and babbled to the man from the bank, "Look at this globe! Look at this!"

"Oh," he said, "that's just something they made with leftover jewels."

Then he asked if I would like to see the gold. It was in an adjacent and much larger vault. Walking in was like entering a library of wealth. The gold was in bricks, piled up to the ceiling in row upon row of iron beams. They seemed to stretch in every direction. There was an Iranian guard by the door, standing with his arms crossed like the genie from Aladdin's lamp. He chuckled and said something in Persian, and the interpreter asked me, "Do you know what he said?"

"No."

"He said to tell you that you can have all the gold you can carry out."

I said, "Really?" I went over and grabbed a gold brick. It was about the size of a loaf of bread and I couldn't even get one end off the iron beam. All the guards had a laugh over this.

Some nights, when Pop didn't have to go out, I'd ask him for help with my homework and we would end up just talking. His room had four overstuffed chairs grouped around a small oil stove, and we'd sit, sometimes for hours. We talked about all sorts of things—people we'd met, things we'd seen on the streets, my volleyball team at school, the Iranian parliament, the latest run-in between the gendarmes and the bandits. We talked about military things, about West Point, about honor. Occasionally he'd discuss the men in his command. There were officers he admired, who were selfless and loyal, and others who were duplicitous and self-serving. He'd say things like, "Be careful of that guy. He's not what he seems to be on the surface." I loved those nights alone with my father, because he was all mine. Sometimes I wasn't that interested in what he was saying, but it didn't matter. What was important was being together.

Unfortunately for me, this arrangement didn't last. In November, after I'd been in Tehran only two months, my father called me into his room and said, "We need to have a serious talk." He showed me a letter from Mom in which she said she wanted to come to Iran with my sisters. By this time the house in Lawrenceville had been leased, so there was nothing holding her in Princeton except my sisters' education at Miss Fine's School—which she had mixed feelings about anyway. The war was over, Army wives were allowed to join their husbands abroad, and she wanted our family reunited. She was determined to come.

"What's going to happen if Mom comes over?" he asked. He knew she was an alcoholic and he was concerned about how it would affect his ability to function with the Iranians, with the diplomatic community, and with his own men. He was also worried about how it would affect his life and mine. Maybe he expected me to lend a sympathetic ear while he weighed his decision. But I had a very definite opinion and blurted out: "I don't want them to come. If you let them come, everything is going to change. It's going to be just like it was in New Jersey. There's going to be fighting and arguing and our house is not going to be a happy house. I don't want to go back to living in an unhappy house!"

This led to the first conversation we'd ever had about what had happened back in Princeton. Pop talked about coming home on leave at the end of the war and discovering Mom's drinking. I was surprised—I thought he'd known about it all along. Then he asked what our lives had been like, and we talked about the fact that when Mom got drunk her personality changed. My father saw this cause-and-effect almost as an excuse for her behavior. "Your mother is a sweet, wonderful nurse, an angel of mercy," he told me. "But she is ill, and when she acts that way, it's not really her, it's this illness coming out." It was as if he were talking about two different people.

By now I'd figured out that he was going to let her come, and that this was his way of preparing me. He said, "She is my wife and your mother. How can I say no? Even though we know this is going to change our lives completely, and it's going to knock things all out of whack, we have no choice." I didn't like being dragged back into the man-of-the-house role, but he was asking for my support, and as the conversation went on, I acquiesced. Finally he said, "We have to stick together and deal with this—protect ourselves, protect the girls, and figure out how to make it work." And I told him, "Okay, Pop. I'm with you. We'll make it work."

I'm sure he went to bed satisfied that he'd talked through this difficult matter with his son, that his son now had a positive attitude, and that things would be fine. I was in turmoil: I tried to believe that, since it was Pop's absence that had caused Mom's drinking to start, having him back as head of the family would make it stop. But I knew in my heart that things probably weren't going to be fine at all.

————

My father went to great pains to prepare for Mom's arrival. There was no space at the villa for all five of us, so he arranged for us to move to a house downtown, right next to the palace square, on a street called Khiaban Khoch. The house was a three-story building made of large pale bricks, not opulent like the Big House but furnished comfortably in the western style. The big front door opened on the street and there was a garden on one side; from the third floor, where I slept, I could see over the garden wall into a maze of houses, courtyards, other gardens, and alleys, all of which were hidden from the street. Ali and a chauffeur came with us, and Pop hired an Iranian gardener, a White Russian maid, a chef named Kachev who had previously cooked at the French embassy, and tutors for the girls, because Tehran had no suitable English-language high school. All of this was provided at no cost by the Iranian government. Meanwhile Mom and my sisters crossed the Atlantic on an Italian ocean liner in great style. It docked in Alexandria, Egypt in early December, and Pop was waiting to escort them to the Cairo airport, where he had flown in the cargo plane.

The instant she set foot in the house, Mom made her presence felt. Kachev served lunch, and for dessert he presented a fantastic sugar confection called a Queen Anne's Bonnet. Mom declared it too rich—and we never saw a dessert like it again. She moved all the family photographs from Pop's office into the living room. He tried to talk her out of that, because he liked the room to be formal, but she told him it didn't look like a home. Then she went into the kitchen and ordered Kachev to disinfect his utensils. There was no question about it: family life had returned.

She very much objected to some of the habits that I had picked up. I'd gotten used to having servants, for example. Every room in the house had a button on the wall. If I pushed the button, Ali would magically appear, and I'd say, "Ali, may I have a Coca-Cola, please?" He would say, "Yes, sir." And he'd be back five minutes later with a Coca-Cola. It was terrific! But from the day Mom arrived, there was no more button pushing. If we wanted Coca-Cola, we went and got our own.

She immediately put curbs on my comings and goings. She didn't like the thought of my staying up for poker parties and hanging out with the men. I was "being matured too quickly," she told my father, and there was no longer any need to take me to dinner parties and receptions, because I wasn't being left at home alone. When my father had to go out at night, she now went with him. I felt that my mother and sisters had ruined my life. They were forcing me to go back to being a normal twelve-year-old boy.

Pop had his hands full with Mom's drinking but she liked being the general's lady, and when it was important she managed to behave. At home, when she got drunk and began to run down one of my sisters or me, Pop would step in. We'd be sitting at the table and he would say, "It's time for you to go do your homework," and we'd be excused. I admired him for that, because then the attack would shift to him. He was much more able to deal with it emotionally than we were. And I think it was much harder for her to hurt him than to hurt us.

Sally and Ruth Ann had made an unbelievable splash in the social circles of Tehran. They were full-fledged teenagers now, aged fourteen and sixteen. General Moshiri, the most senior officer of the gendarmerie, had a daughter who was Sally's age and spoke English perfectly, and she introduced my sisters to all the boys. Both Sally and Ruth Ann ended up with Iranian boyfriends; Sally must have gone through three or four. This surprised me because Sally had always seemed to be a tomboy. One was the shah's half-brother Gholam, whom she had met the year before when he was a student at Princeton. The fact that he was dating a westerner was a scandal among the Iranians. So whenever he took Sally out, they'd ride in a van with curtains drawn across all the windows. Then she threw over Gholam—another scandal. Her next flame was the heavyweight boxing champion of Iran, a guy named Jimmy. When he asked her out, my father said Sally absolutely could not date that sort of man. But Mom went into her egalitarian mode and said, "Nonsense. She can go out with anybody she wants!" So Jimmy would take my sister dancing on the terrace of the Palace Hotel, while the diplomatic community gossiped and Pop tried to convince Mom she should put a stop to it.

Ruth Ann, on the other hand, dated only one man. He was General Moshiri's son Changes. I remember him as a gentle, intelligent, somewhat aloof, quiet man who seemed to have great inner strength. He had a natural quality of leadership that caused the other young Iranians to show him respect. He also seemed to have a stabilizing effect on Ruth Ann, and I recall her days in Tehran as some of her happiest.

I tried not to pay a lot of attention to my sisters and the fuss they caused. Even with my freedom curtailed, I was much more independent than I ever had been in Lawrenceville. I was off doing my own thing, going hunting with Pop's men, playing tennis with the British, and riding bicycles around Tehran with my best friend, Michael. One of our favorite pastimes was to throw our bikes on top of one of the rattletrap Iranian buses that ran from the center of Tehran into the Shemran foothills. Those foothills were green and lush; there were goat and sheep herds and almond plantations and melon fields. The bus would unload in the market square of one of the agricultural villages, and we'd get on our bikes and coast all the way back down into Tehran, sharing the road with donkey carts and camel caravans.

Living near the palace square, we were much less insulated from the life of the city than we had been at the Big House. One day the shah had a triumphal parade right past our door. This was in April, several months after the Iranian army marched into the provinces of Azerbaijan and Kurdistan, where Soviet troops had been stationed during the war and where the communists had tried to establish separatist governments. The shah made a trip to Azerbaijan to formally reclaim it for Iran, and his supporters in Tehran organized a hero's welcome for him on his return. All along the route from the airport to the palace they built lavish wooden arches, some draped with Persian carpets, others spectacularly carved with animal heads and intricate designs. On the morning the shah arrived, thousands of people turned out to cheer. His motorcade moved slowly down our street, and each time it came to an arch, people would sacrifice goats and sheep and let the blood run across the road, so that his car would drive over it. The men at the arch by our house jumped the gun, sacrificing their animals as soon as the police escort zoomed past. The blood spilled into the street, but there was no shah, and it was all clotted by the time he got near. I saw him in his limousine, a slender young guy dressed in an elaborate beribboned khaki uniform. The men were so determined that he not miss their sacrifice that they dragged the carcasses into the road and jumped on them to force more blood out. The shah acknowledged this, and then they dragged the animals aside and on he went.

In our new quarters I became much more aware of my father's work. Beyond his duties with the gendarmerie there was cloak-and-dagger stuff that I never really understood. I'd paid no attention at the Big House, when people would be shown to the offices in the basement. But at the Khiaban

Khoch house, very peculiar people sometimes came to our door. I'd answer the bell and there would be a dirty, disheveled Iranian, not the sort of man I associated with the gendarmerie. But then he'd say in perfect English, "I have an appointment to meet with your father." And Pop would say, "That's right, show him in." They'd go into his study and the doors would close with a loud clunk. Afterward Pop sometimes said, "Forget you ever saw that person." I didn't know who the person was to begin with, but I'd say, "Yes, sir." I assumed the meetings had to do with confronting the Soviets, and that these were agents of some sort, but I figured not asking too many questions was part of being a general's son.

That spring there was much discussion about where my sisters and I would go to school. My parents never saw tutors as more than a stopgap for Sally and Ruth Ann, and I was almost ready for high school, too, because I'd skipped ahead into the mission school's eighth grade. The nearest American schools were ones for U.S. military dependents in occupied Germany, 2,400 miles away; but they were only day schools, and my parents would have had to find people to look after us and a place for us to live. Finally, on the advice of Pop's diplomat friends, they picked the École Internationale, a boarding school in Geneva.

Sally and Ruth Ann were overjoyed. Swiss boarding school fit their self-image and I think secretly they'd been afraid Mom and Pop would send us back to Newark to live with Grandma Schwarzkopf. I had no idea what Switzerland would be like, but I was curious and willing to try. I figured that no matter what happened I would come back to Iran the following June.

As a way of saying good-bye, some of the Americans and Iranians who worked for my dad invited me on a special hunt. Until then all my hunting had consisted of day trips with Pop or one or two other people, in the foothills near Tehran. The day typically consisted of scrambling up and down rocky hills with rifles. I'd never shot anything. This trip was different—we were going out overnight in the desert to hunt the wild ass, an animal that had almost mystical meaning in Iran. The Iranian desert was one of the few places in the world where the wild ass was found. It was very rare, a highly sought-after trophy, treasured for its long, woolly brown-and-gray coat. Hunters lucky enough to spot a herd in the desert almost never got close enough for a shot.

We set out in midafternoon in an open Army truck—ten Iranian gendarmes, three other Americans, and me. There were no high-ranking officers, and there was a feeling of camaraderie. It was very hot—the same blast-furnace heat I'd felt at the Baghdad airport the summer before. But by this time I was totally acclimated. I loved the weather and had long since gotten so suntanned that I didn't burn anymore. We drove away from the city, through a string of villages that dwindled in size. At the last one we bought several dozen green melons, which the Iranians used instead of canteens to ward off thirst. As the sun went down, we drove on into the desert.

After about five miles, somebody spotted a male gazelle grazing in the dusk. The truck stopped and a number of us grabbed rifles and took aim. I didn't know it, but the men had agreed that the shot should be mine, so they all held back and I was the only one who fired. To my amazement, the gazelle dropped. The Iranians jumped out of the truck and ran to the gazelle. As Islamic custom calls for an animal to be bled as soon as it is killed, someone cut its throat. I was appalled. I'd killed the gazelle, but I hadn't figured on seeing so much blood. The Iranians made a tremendous fuss about the fact that I'd shot a gazelle. To them it was a joyous event, a passage into manhood. Right there in the desert, they butchered the animal and built a big fire to cook some of the meat. By now it was night, and the winds were coming up, and with great ceremony they served the cooked heart of the gazelle to me. This time, I didn't need my father to tell me what to do. I ate the meat, and I savored it rather than choking it down. Then we got back in the truck and drove late into the night until eventually we set up camp. By now the desert had turned very cold, and I was lying on rocks, bundled up in every scrap of clothing I could find, but I couldn't get warm. I was too excited to sleep anyway.

The next morning we drove on in search of the wild ass. The track was very rocky, and we were bouncing along, jolting so hard I felt like my teeth were shaking right out of my head. Suddenly someone spotted a herd of asses running in the desert. At that very instant we came to a dry riverbed that led in the direction the animals were headed, and the driver took off at high speed. Everybody grabbed for his gun as we zoomed along. The Americans had carbines and the Iranians long, heavy bolt-action rifles that probably dated back to World War I. We made a dead intercept just as the asses crossed the riverbed. They burst over the bank at a gallop, no more than fifteen yards away, and we saw that the leader was so old he was pure white. Just as we opened fire, the truck veered out of the riverbed to chase the herd and started careening over rocks. Weapons were going off in every direction and people were clinging to the sides of the truck and falling on the floor. The asses must have been running at fifty miles an hour, and at the sound of the guns they went into fifth gear. They put five hundred yards between us and themselves in what seemed like no more than ten seconds.

The entire herd got away and there was nothing for us to do but turn around. We made the long drive back to Tehran, with everybody telling stories to everybody else, making excuses as to why they'd missed. But I knew that even if we hadn't hit the rocks, the herd would have escaped. Every round went at least five feet too high, because we'd all had our sights set for three-hundred-yard shots, figuring the wily ass would never let us get closer than that.

4

Switzerland's Alpine forests and blue lakes were an astonishing change from Iran's rocky deserts. Geneva had escaped World War II totally undamaged, and I was startled to see a city with churches instead of mosques, trolley cars instead of doroshkes, and medieval town houses instead of palaces. It looked like a picture from a chocolate box. The city was built along the Rhône where the river drains from Lake Geneva; on the northern bank was a modern section, and on the southern bank, the Old Town, which extended up a hill crowned by the great cathedral of St. Pierre. Nestled in its narrow streets were wonderful little restaurants that served Swiss fondue and wine and beer—even, we quickly discovered, to high school kids.

The École Internationale was a cluster of red-roofed whitewashed buildings about a kilometer east of the Old Town. On my first day, as I entered the main building, I saw a very attractive girl coming down the steps dragging a trunk. She wore blue slacks and a bright colorful shirt, and had long dark hair with a band around it. I hadn't seen anyone this pretty in quite some time. She noticed me gawking and said, "Are you going to stand there, or are you going to help me with this thing?" I ran over, realizing that I was no longer in Iran, where it was a breach of propriety for a man to offer a woman help.

The school dated back to the founding of the League of Nations and had been set up so the children of delegates would have someplace to study. "Écolint," as everybody called it, was egalitarian, not very fancy, and reasonably inexpensive. This made it fundamentally different from the *other* Swiss boarding schools, where the world's millionaires sent their kids. The war had had a dramatic effect on everyone at Écolint. My schoolmates included children of British aristocrats who had been sheltered there from the time of the Blitz, as well as tough teenagers from Eastern Europe who had been raised in communist partisan groups and were there to catch up on their formal education. One girl, a survivor of Dachau, showed my sisters the tattoo on her arm; another had been at the school when the Nazis rounded up her family in Paris—the only reason she survived. There were French, Germans, Americans, Indians, Swiss, Poles, Czechs, Yugoslavs, and even Ethiopians.

Just being there was an education, and I saw again and again that events have more than one side. When the communists staged a coup in Prague in the middle of the school year, Madame Maurette, our French headmistress, called a student convocation. She made a passionate speech calling the coup the death of liberty. But there were kids in the audience whose fathers were part of the takeover, as well as kids whose parents had been overthrown.

Adjusting to the place was an even greater challenge than I'd faced in Tehran. While my sisters had wisely spent the summer practicing their French, somehow I'd figured that because Écolint was trilingual—people spoke English, French, and German in class—I'd be able to get along in English. But the everyday language was actually French. I realized that my first night, when I sat down to eat in the dining hall. There were ten of us at the table, and even the British were speaking French. I didn't know one word of it, except the minuscule amount I'd learned at the Presbyterian mission school, and now speaking French was a matter of survival: If you didn't know how to say, *"Du pain, s'il vous plaît,"* you couldn't count on getting bread.

My salvation was my size: I dwarfed most of my classmates. I was immediately recruited for the soccer team, which was big at Écolint. I'd never played before, but because I could kick the ball a mile and because I was so big, the coach made me a fullback. My main duty during a game was to lurk in the backfield until an opposing player broke clear and raced toward our goal. I was then to separate that player, who was generally two thirds my size, from the ball. At the start of the season, I usually accomplished this by colliding with the guy; but gradually, with help from my teammates and coach, my footwork improved. We were really good, too.

Not only did we beat the big-deal schools around the lake, but we went on to win the boarding school junior championship for all of western Switzerland. Being a soccer player helped transform me into a somebody on campus. By November I even spoke enough French to get along.

My closest friends were fellow soccer players in the Stump House, the dorm for young teenage boys: Jack, the son of an Italian businessman and an Indian woman; Uri, a French Jew; and Jiro, a Czech. We had lessons nine hours a day and the course-load was more than twice that of a typical American high school. I never really struggled except in Latin, which I kept getting mixed up with French. In Latin I got a D. On weekends Jack, Uri, Jiro, and I explored the town. Even though my weekly allowance was only five francs ($1.25), nothing cost very much. We'd go to a French movie or an outdoor concert along the lake, and afterward treat ourselves to fantastic pastries and hot chocolate. Evenings we weren't allowed to go out unchaperoned, but the school held dances—I learned how to jitterbug and tango—and sometimes the proctors took us to the Swiss symphony, where I decided Tchaikovsky was my favorite composer.

I heard my first opera and smoked my first cigarette on the same night. The opera, *Aïda*, made a big impression on me, with its spectacular Triumphal March and its Egyptian scenery that reminded me of Tehran. During intermission we strolled outside. Some of the seniors had cigarettes and I took one and suavely lit up. I could see the others were doing something with the smoke besides blowing it out, but I had no idea how to inhale. So each time I took a puff, I swallowed the smoke. Presently we went back in. I was seated next to an elderly Swiss gentleman who wore wire-rim glasses, a big cravat, and a stiff collar. Just as the singing started I belched, and a big puff of smoke came out of my mouth. He gave me the most startled look. I belched again, and out came another puff. After that he turned away, and never again looked in my direction.

I was equally urbane the first time I kissed a girl. Claudine was a sexy French sophomore who decided around the time of our winning the soccer championship that she had a crush on me. She invited me for a walk on a wooded path that wound around behind the athletic fields. This was where couples went; there was a tree along the way where everyone was expected to kiss. I'm sure that Claudine, being a sophomore and French, expected a passionate French kiss. But what she got was a mere peck from my puckered lips. That was it for our romance; she dropped me the next day.

My sisters lived in the girls' dorm and each went her own way. Ruth Ann got interested in Marxism and for a while her boyfriend was a Yugoslav communist named Stanko Borchich, who lectured her about the evils of

Dad's work. Dating Stanko was a terribly rebellious thing for a Schwarz-kopf to do, given Dad's opinion of communists. Meanwhile, Sally became an aesthete. She and her friends would read poems by Shelley and Byron late into the night. My crowd didn't take life so seriously. We played ball, went to dances, and dated girls.

The only time I saw much of my sisters was during the holidays. We were too far away to go back to Tehran, so our parents let us sign up for various chaperoned trips around Europe. The most memorable was during the Easter holidays in 1948, when my sisters dragooned me into joining a small group going to Florence, purportedly to look at art. Our chaperon was a Mr. Henderson, a pale, red-haired forty-year-old Englishman who taught political science. To make a little extra money on the trip, he had taken an assignment from an Australian newspaper to write about Italy's upcoming national elections. The elections had attracted worldwide atten-tion because there was a chance the communists might win. So in between visits to churches and Renaissance museums, Mr. Henderson took us along when he did his reporting. In the town of Stresa on the shores of Lake Maggiore, we first went to the Christian Democrat office, which seemed staid and boring, full of people wearing spectacles and typing. Then we went to the Communist Party headquarters in a big, dank underground bar with huge casks of wine along the walls. The party members were fishermen, wearing caps and heavy wool jackets, drinking a lot and having a great time. They welcomed us with big smiles and handshakes and pats on the back and loaded me up with piles of literature—posters of Karl Marx and Garibaldi together, stuff with red stars and hammers and sickles. I loved it and took it all back to Geneva and hung it on the walls of my room. I thought the communists would do very well in that district, because they were more fun than the Christian Democrats. As for the spread of global communism, life was moving too quickly for me to worry. I agreed with Pop that it was bad, but I figured, "We beat the Nazis, we beat the Japs, and we'll beat this, too."

Much as I was enjoying myself at the École, I looked forward to June, when I could go back to Iran. But in the spring Mom and Pop wrote, shattering my hopes. Pop had gotten orders transferring him to the Army's European headquarters, in Frankfurt, to work with the military police. I was sure that I'd never again see Iran and that I'd have to leave Switzerland and live with my parents. I was crushed, but got no sympathy from Ruth Ann and Sally because their lives weren't going to change—they knew they would be allowed to stay at the École because they were so close to graduating. So I was left to brood, and after a couple of days I sat down and wrote a vow that someday I would return to Iran. I fully intended to sign that note in blood. But then I realized cutting myself would hurt, and decided the oath would carry almost as much weight if I signed it in ink.

Frankfurt in the summer of 1948 still bore the scars of its conquest by Patton's Third Army three years before. On the outskirts of the city, displaced persons camps were filled with thousands of Germans and Hungarians and Poles who had fled the Soviet armies in the east. Downtown we saw bombed-out buildings and walls with bullet holes everywhere. Food was very scarce for the Germans, and in the camps men and women lined up to get their family's daily ration of potatoes, vegetables, eggs, and powdered milk. The black market thrived, despite efforts by the military police to stamp it out.

My father's new assignment was as deputy provost marshal of U.S. forces in Germany. This meant that he was the number-two policeman in the American zone of occupied Germany. While he didn't like being number two at anything, especially since he was working for a West Point classmate he despised, he undertook his new duties with his usual organizational zeal. His first task was to establish a highway patrol (organized along the lines of the New Jersey State Police, naturally) to police the high-speed autobahns running the length and width of Germany. This done, he organized a special customs unit to stop the flood of contraband pouring across the inter-German border.

As Americans we lived in relative luxury. Most Army officers and their families had never had it so good. Generals and colonels lived in a green, undamaged neighborhood on the northwest side of town, in houses that had belonged to Nazi officials and wealthy industrialists. Ours had a walnut-paneled foyer and a big, elegant dining room, and looked across the street to a beautiful park. The Central Housing Office provided us with a German maid and gardener, and my parents had a driver and military sedan to take them around. Social life centered on the officers' clubs and on the posh restaurants previously reserved for the rich. One night my father took me to the Carlton Hotel, where the splendid dining room had crystal chandeliers that had somehow survived the bombing. There, by candlelight, he showed me how to eat lobster. He had a special technique for extracting every morsel of meat, which he'd learned from his father and imparted to me as if it were a secret of the ancient world. I'd have loved any food dunked in butter, but the lobster was delicious and the ritual made it special. Even today I can get more out of a lobster than most men can.

You could live in Frankfurt for years and never make a German friend. There were thousands of American soldiers and dependents in the area, and the Army ran its own hospital, dental clinic, and post exchange, and even had a movie theater where admission cost a quarter. And of course there was Frankfurt American High School, complete with football, sock hops, cheer-leaders, and a yearbook, which drew Army brats from miles around.

I had been away from the United States for two years, and the world of the American teenager was totally alien to me. When I showed up in Frankfurt in July, I was wearing Swiss summer clothes while all the other Americans had on blue jeans and white socks and loafers. I had long, stringy European hair; but in Frankfurt crew cuts were in style. I don't think I've ever felt more out of place. I spent hours poring over a Sears, Roebuck catalog, looking at men's clothes. I wanted Levi's and western shirts and western belts but didn't know you could place an order from Germany. In Switzerland a schoolmate whose father worked for a relief organization had given me a used overcoat that some kind soul in the United States had sent as a gift for a displaced person. I wore it everywhere and it became my trademark.

One day I came downstairs for breakfast and found a pair of football shoes under my chair. My dad desperately wanted me to play football, but I didn't know anything about the game. I couldn't block, couldn't tackle, and didn't have a lot of speed. I went out for the team and practiced with them every day, but when the weekend came the coach never had me suit up for the game. Dad knew this bothered me, so at the end of the season he hired a German trainer named Herr Schultz, who had coached field events for the prewar German Olympic teams, to work with me. Herr Schultz and I agreed that part of my problem was that I wasn't strong enough, so he taught me to use dumbbells, with the visual aid of photos that showed German guys built like blacksmiths, in sleeveless undershirts, lifting weights. I'd be ready for football the following year.

It took months before I unlearned Switzerland enough to fit in, but gradually I became Americanized. By springtime my life revolved around Frankfurt's two great centers of Army brat activity: the teen club and the snack bar at the PX. My friends and I would go to one or the other every day after school. At the snack bar we'd sit for hours, drinking milkshakes, eating french fries, flirting with girls, and joking around. The teen club, across the park from my house, had a pool table and a jukebox. Unlike some of the other kids, I always had to be home for dinner or I'd be "put on restriction"—Army talk for getting grounded. On school nights I was forbidden to go out at all, so I would go up to my room. I had my own world up there: I'd play the radio, lift weights, and read, and I liked to write poetry on romantic subjects like young soldiers dying selflessly in combat. I never admitted *that* to any of my friends.

Pop and I increasingly butted heads. On weekends I had the strictest curfew of any of my friends—11:30 P.M.—and when I came home late he was always waiting, mad. He also started getting very tough about school. I never brought books home; what little homework I had, I'd knock off during study hall. For me, passing my courses was a cinch; I was carrying only four a semester now, compared with ten at Écolint. But when I came in the door Pop would say, "How'd you do on that test today?"

"I did great. I got an eighty."

"Do you realize that means you don't know twenty percent of the subject?" That infuriated me.

He measured everything against what he thought I needed to get into West Point. I dreaded getting my report card, because he would accept nothing less than a B. If I brought home one C, *wham*, that was grounds for restriction. If I argued that two A's more than offset one C, he'd say C meant average, and you didn't get into West Point if you were just average.

In retrospect, the pressure he put on me was nothing out of the ordinary, but compared with his lenience in Iran, it seemed arbitrary and harsh. I was almost two years older now and in my own mind more mature, but he required me to operate under strict rules, and our camaraderie had disappeared. I missed the easygoing friendship we'd had.

Mom's drinking was also a barrier between us, and it embarrassed me terribly. I'll never forget the Friday night I was on restriction and my friends Harold Nunn and Gene Heady dropped by to keep me company. Mom was drunk, and before I could get downstairs she let them in. She was stumbling and slurring her speech. When Harold started snickering, she bored in on him the way she did with my sisters. He didn't know how to react and tried to cover up by laughing even more and poking Gene in the ribs. I was dying inside: these were my buddies. I jumped in and said, "Hey, you guys have got to get over to the teen club. Sorry I can't make it."

I literally pushed them out the door, with my mother saying, "Yes, I think they should leave!"

That night I lay in bed with my stomach churning, thinking, "How am I gonna face these guys tomorrow? They're over at the teen club right now telling everybody that Schwarzkopf's mother is a drunk." But the subject never came up. It was something you just didn't talk about.

Pop didn't make the problem any easier. At night he would walk in and have at least two stiff drinks before going upstairs to get out of his uniform. The same routine probably went on in every house up and down the street, because the Army was a hard-drinking world. But of course, when he drank, Mom drank too. He'd even encourage it. "Would you like another drink?" he'd ask her. And I'd look at him and think, "Goddammit, don't you know where this is going to lead?" I loved him and admired him, but when he gave her alcohol, I hated him for it.

When the school year ended, Sally and Ruth Ann came home from the École, and we took a train to Bremerhaven and put them on a boat for New York. They both had scholarships in the United States, Ruth Ann at Barnard College and Sally at Smith. For my parents, shipping them off was a big relief: the girls had gotten too cosmopolitan for their taste and were even making plans to stay in Europe for college until Pop found out and put his foot down. Ruth Ann's flirtation with Marxism drove him wild—the year before, she'd asked if she could spend the summer at a Bulgarian youth camp—but Mom reassured him by saying, "Now, dear, she's just going through a stage. We'll get her back in the United States, and she'll go to a nice American college, and she'll be fine." I think Pop believed that.

Army headquarters was shifting from Frankfurt to Heidelberg, fifty miles to the south in the Neckar Valley, and we got ready to move again. I arrived at Heidelberg American High School wearing Levi's, a denim shirt, a western belt with a big buckle, and GI boots—this time I was ready to do high school right. I went out for football and now had enough strength and coordination to make the team. The coach, Lou Barth, was a military police major who had played for the Philadelphia Eagles. He and I really hit it off, and he made me a tackle, as he had been. Though I wasn't Heidelberg's greatest player, I held my own and got better with each game. That season we beat all six American high school teams in Germany and won the European championship. We were big men on campus and I felt as though I'd really come into my own.

Socially my life revolved around a group of eight guys called the "Hoods." Teenage gangs were big in the United States—we'd seen them in movies. And though there was nothing criminal about us—we were all athletes, lettermen, and good guys, and considered ourselves the junior class elite—we loved the gang trappings. We each had a Hoods nickname: there was Babyface and Chopper and the Chief. I was Cuddles, as a result of having smooched with one of my girlfriends on a city bus. We had a gang uniform: a white dress shirt with the sleeves rolled up and a pack of cigarettes in the pocket, white socks, loafers, letter sweaters, and Levi's. Our hangout was Bohler's bar on Heidelberg's main street. It was in an historic district for drinking—just a few doors from the Red Ox, a student bar that dated back to 1703. Herr Bohler was shrewd. When we started going there, he recognized that having American teenagers around would put off his German customers, but by the same token, he wanted our money. So he gave us a little upstairs room with a three-seat bar and tables and decorated with Bavarian wood carvings. That became the Hoods's clubhouse. On weekend nights we'd start at the teen club at around six-thirty, where we'd shoot pool and dance. By nine o'clock we'd take our girlfriends and go to Bohler's to drink beer and eat thick slabs of brown bread with smoked ham. I was having a wonderful time.

My dad was proud to see me playing football, but not happy to have me running around the streets. He refused to eliminate or extend my curfew, even though I was practically the only Hood who had one. And he was constantly after me about my grades. I liked the school and was so popular that I got elected to the student council, but studies were not high on my list.

It all blew up one night in the spring. The MPs accused the Hoods of brawling with some Germans (which we hadn't done) and arrested us. Even though Pop believed me, he could see my chances of getting into West Point heading down the drain. Since I was still only fifteen, two years short of being eligible to apply, he began to look for a way to keep me out of trouble until then. Coach Barth made the obvious suggestion: send me back to military school. He knew the coach at Valley Forge Military Academy near Philadelphia and offered to get me a two-year football scholarship.

My father's fear that I'd somehow strayed from the path he'd set was unfounded. While I wasn't happy at home, I felt none of the rebelliousness that gets teenagers into gang wars or shotgun marriages or trouble with the police. I was thrilled I'd been able to transform myself into a European kid in Geneva, and into a teenage Army brat in Germany. But while I was proud of those experiences, West Point was still my goal. So when he decided it was time for me to leave my buddies and girlfriends and the pleasures of Europe, and buckle down at Valley Forge, I did it willingly.

But I wasn't the only one causing him headaches. His and Mom's idea of straightening out Ruth Ann by sending her to college in the United States had backfired. At Barnard her grades were so bad she was in danger of losing her scholarship, and the school wrote to Pop complaining about her political activities. She had joined the NAACP and something called the Columbia Labor Youth League. When Pop wrote to ask Ruth Ann what was going on, she replied that she'd found causes she could be proud of, and accused Pop of ruining her life: "I would like to join the Communist Party, but they told me I can't because of *you*!" My father was fit to be tied. Ruth Ann had always been his favorite, and I can remember him pacing up and down our living room in Heidelberg saying: "Your sister is going crazy in New York City! What the hell is happening to my daughter? Where did I go wrong? I've spent my life fighting communism and now she's becoming a communist!"

We spent the summer in Rome, where Pop had been ordered to oversee the delivery of U.S. military aid as chief of an organization called the Military Assistance and Advisory Group. We lived like wealthy Italians in a beautiful penthouse apartment a few doors up from the Villa Borghese. In my Levi's and letter sweater I quickly made friends with young U.S. expatriates, such as the son of the U.S. naval attaché, and we went out looking for fun every single night. We would drink at a little beer joint across the piazza from the Spanish Steps, order ice cream at some sidewalk cafe, and then buy cut-rate tickets to the opera at the Baths of Caracalla, an ancient bath that had been converted into a theater. I saw *Carmen* there for the first time, and in the scene outside the bull ring they brought real horses and carriages on the stage. I also saw *Aïda* again, in a production that featured real elephants.

In July I fell madly in love with a dark-eyed beauty named Rosario, the daughter of the Spanish ambassador. I remember walking her home from a party one night in July, stopping behind every Roman column to kiss. We walked until we got to the Fountain of Trevi and went behind it and kissed some more. The moon was out, the air was sweet, and life was absolutely wonderful. My favorite spot was the Colosseum, which we called Joe's Place. The naval attaché's son had discovered a way to sneak in at night: how much more romantic can life be than when you're fifteen, in Rome, and necking in the Colosseum?

It was all innocent fun, but when my parents saw me going out every night they assumed the worst. My friends and I played nickel-ante poker, which somehow gave my parents the idea that I had a serious gambling problem. Mom told me Pop was afraid that if he ever gave me his West Point ring, I'd lose it in a poker game. I probably could have put their minds at ease by talking to them more, but communication between us was at an all-time low.

They must have been relieved when August finally came and I got on a boat bound for New York. For military dependents, troop transport ships were the primary mode of transportation between Europe and the United

States. Such ships were usually named after presidents or generals, such as the *President Tyler* or the *General Patch*, but Pop booked me on the *Private Johnson*, which was an accurate reflection of its size. To make the voyage interesting for me, he had me assigned to a compartment in the bow, where I bunked with a crew of Turkish sailors who were on their way to New London, Connecticut, to pick up a war surplus submarine. We reached the Atlantic and hit seas so rough that everybody in the compartment was seasick for days. I'll never forget finding myself on deck one afternoon, lying on a hatch cover and wishing I could die, surrounded by seasick Turks who all wished *they* could die. It made me wonder why anyone would ever join the Navy.

I'd been away from America for four years and was looking forward to coming home. Seeing the Statue of Liberty as we entered New York harbor sent a chill down my spine, and I stood at the ship's rail with pride welling up inside me, thinking, "I'm back in my country. I'm back in America. I'm so happy to be back!"

In a way I'd come full circle. Valley Forge was only forty miles from Bordentown Military Academy, where I'd lived five years and five schools before. Like Bordentown it had beautiful colonial brick buildings, a manicured parade ground, and the same strict discipline under which I had thrived. I fell in right away with the routine. Each day we got up, went to mess hall for breakfast, ate in the allotted time, returned to our dorms, and got ready for class. Before leaving our rooms for the day, we made our beds and left everything ready for the daily inspection. We went to class in uniform—a gray shirt with necktie, trousers with a stripe on the side, a short navy blue overcoat, and an overseas cap. At lunchtime we went outside, formed up with our companies, and marched to the mess hall. After school came sports—for me, football and then track and intramural wrestling later in the year. We marched to dinner at night, and after dinner went straight back to the dorm for study hall. This meant sitting in our rooms with our doors open and our books in front of us on our desks. You did not talk. You did not joke. You did not play the radio. Monitors patrolled the halls, and if they caught someone goofing off, they wrote up a disciplinary report. I liked the marching, I liked the discipline, and academically I shot up to the honor roll. Valley Forge was a junior college as well as a high school, and while I had enough credits to have graduated from high school the day I arrived, I found plenty of courses to take—college-level classes with names like "West Point English" and "West Point Math."

Football was different from the game at Heidelberg High: at Valley Forge it was serious business. The coach was an ill-tempered major named

Novak who made it clear that if you had a football scholarship, he owned a piece of you. He'd say things like, "Schwarzkopf! You call that hitting? Can't you remember we're paying you to be here?" We competed in a military academy conference that served as a kind of farm league for big-name universities. For example, if Navy recruited a high school star and decided he needed more schooling to be able to get by in college, they'd stick him in our league for a couple of years. There were ten guys like that on my team, superb athletes, and even though our record was only 2–9 during my first year, I had to play hard just to keep up. The next year we got a new coach, Major L. Maitland Blank, and our record improved to 5–3. My performance improved, too: Coach Blank noticed I played best when mad, so he'd arbitrarily yank me out of the game and bench me for a few minutes to get me riled.

I could handle tough treatment on the football field, but it disturbed me that the student body was divided into two groups, the have-nots and the haves. The have-nots were people like me, on football or band scholarships. We were far outnumbered by the haves, rich kids like those you would expect to find at a military boarding school: boys from Latin America, boys from broken homes, boys who'd been kicked out of other private schools. Some of them liked to flaunt their wealth, and the school did nothing to discourage them from flashing huge wads of money and lording it over the have-nots. As part of our scholarships we had to wait tables in the mess hall, and some of the rich boys would say, rudely, "Get me more bread."

"I'm not your slave," I'd tell them, and I was big enough that no one dared to insist.

Valley Forge prided itself on maintaining an honor system like West Point's. We were taught the fundamental West Point rule of self-discipline—a cadet neither lies, cheats, nor steals, nor tolerates anyone who does—and cadet officers were responsible for the enforcement of the code, just as at West Point. That was well and good, but Valley Forge applied the code so clumsily that the school's discipline sometimes crossed the line into cruelty. One day shortly after I arrived, a fourteen-year-old boy was drummed out of the academy for stealing. We were standing in formation before lunch, and drummers from the band took up positions near the front gate. Then the cadet regimental commander called the boy in front of him and cut all the buttons and insignia off his uniform so there was nothing left that said "Valley Forge." With that, the drums started beating, a grim, hollow sound, and the boy had to walk with his shirt open past the entire corps of cadets, down the drive, and out the gate, never to return. I replayed that scene in my mind many times, wondering whether the boy's parents had agreed to his humiliation, and worrying about where he had gone.

A couple of months later I got my only black mark in discipline. We were eating Christmas dinner in the mess hall on the night before our holiday break. The meal was great until dessert, which turned out to be doughy, undercooked pumpkin pie. Cadets started complaining and all of a sudden *boomp!* in the middle of our table landed a slice of pie that someone had thrown. Instantly the air was filled with flying pieces of pumpkin pie. I contemplated the slice on my plate, then temptation got the better of me and I tossed it.

We went back to our barracks in high spirits, but an hour later the cadet regimental commander called us all to a meeting. It was his responsibility to maintain order in the corps, and he was furious that things had gotten out of hand. He harangued us and finally said, "I hereby put anyone who threw pie *on his honor* to report himself. Anyone who does not report himself will be guilty of an honor breach, and can be thrown out of Valley Forge. Dismissed."

We went back to our rooms and I sat on my bed, remembering the boy who'd been drummed out of the corps. Clearly I had to turn myself in. I went to the head cadet's room, where he was talking to two other cadet officers.

"What do *you* want?" he said.

"I'm here to tell you that I threw a piece of pie tonight in the mess hall." They all jumped on me, threatening, as punishment, to confine me to barracks and cancel my Christmas vacation. The head cadet said, "Get your weapon, go outside, and march until your punishment is determined."

I obeyed. It was snowing that night, and they left me outside for hours—the only cadet marching. I was seething at the unfairness of it: yes, I'd thrown food, which was a minor regulatory breach, and yet because I'd been the only cadet to take the honor system so seriously that I'd turned myself in, they'd made me the scapegoat. Finally, at two in the morning, they ordered me inside, saying I could go on vacation but that I hadn't heard the end of it: during vacation the administration would decide my ultimate fate. Wonderful! Merry Christmas! I got to carry that worry to my grandmother's house in Newark, where I spent the holiday.

The matter ended with only a letter of reprimand in my record, but it taught me a crucial lesson about running an honor system. Honor is fundamentally a code of conscience; any institution that wants to foster it should not use a person's sense of honor against him, as Valley Forge did. We'd been wrong to throw pie, but the cadet regimental commander had shown even poorer judgment by escalating a relatively minor situation into a matter of personal honor.

The main objective of my two years at Valley Forge was to find a way into West Point. That goal had become as important to me as to my father. The U.S. Military Academy had produced the leaders of the armies that had defeated the Axis Powers—Eisenhower, Bradley, MacArthur, Patton, and many more—and its prestige was at an all-time high. This, plus the fact that a West Point education was free, made the academy one of the most sought-after colleges in the United States. You couldn't simply mail in your application; to get one of the 816 slots in the entering class, each man had to win one of a limited number of competitive appointments or be nominated by a senator or congressman and then pass a set of academic, physical, and medical tests.

Pop came to Valley Forge in February 1951 and we strategized. At his urging I made a list of congressmen from New Jersey and sent each a letter introducing myself and saying I'd like to be considered for nomination to the class entering West Point in 1952. In response I got back nothing but form letters that said things like, "Dear Cadet Schwarzkopf: Thank you very much for your inquiry. It has been noted that neither you nor your parents are constituents of Congressman Jones, and his practice is to appoint only candidates from his district. Thank you very much for your interest in the national defense." It was terribly frustrating to me; I was the son of an Army officer serving his country overseas, and because he was out of the country, I couldn't get a nomination.

I sent out more letters, to congressmen in Pennsylvania and New York. When someone told me representatives from South Carolina were having trouble finding candidates, I mailed letters to them, too. But by May 1951, when my father retired from active duty and moved back to the United States with my mother, I still had nothing. One Saturday, Pop and I sat at the kitchen table of their new house in Maplewood, New Jersey, trying to figure out what to do. He'd been able through some old connections to get me an interview with a senator from New Jersey, H. Alexander Smith. We knew that Senator Smith had already chosen his candidate for 1952, as well as a backup, but it turned out he liked my credentials enough to make me his number-three choice. This gave me the right to take West Point's entrance exams the following spring, but it probably wasn't enough to get me in. The candidates ahead of me were just too good to fail.

As much as Pop wanted to see me at West Point, he didn't intercede earlier or really try to pull strings. He had faith in me and faith in the admission system, and figured I'd get in fair and square. I was just as confident: all my life I'd been told I was going to West Point, and it was unimaginable that I wouldn't get in. We didn't dwell on the reality, which was that I might be in for a long wait. The valid ages for admission to West Point were seventeen to twenty-two, so if I didn't make it in 1952, I could enroll in a junior college or enlist in the Army and try again the next year.

Pop urged me to go after something called an "Honor Military Appointment." Each year West Point held open a few slots that candidates from military schools could compete for. Winners were picked on the basis of leadership potential, high school grades, athletics, school activities, and a nationwide exam similar to the college boards. It was a long shot—there were hundreds of candidates and just five positions open that year—but Dad was so sure I could win that I went back to Valley Forge determined to stand out in every way I could. That year I earned varsity letters in football and track. Militarily I became one of the highest-ranking cadets. Academically I was at the top of my class. A friendly English teacher, Lieutenant Esrey, took me under his wing, named me editor of the yearbook, and encouraged me to compete in a debating contest, which I won. I became an ace at taking multiple-choice tests, from the civil service exam to the Stanford-Binet, so that when the honor military exam came along, I scored very high. To top it all off, Valley Forge named me valedictorian. Everything had fallen into place—except that I still had no appointment to West Point. It was the *Navy* that recruited me—they offered a full ROTC scholarship to the college of my choice, with the promise that when I got out I could join the Marines. That did not go over big in the Schwarzkopf household.

When graduation came I gave my speech and said good-bye to my buddies, claiming, "I'm going to West Point next year." Then I went home to Maplewood and whiled away several uneasy weeks. Plebe year at West Point started on July 1, and as the days of June ticked by, I started reconciling myself to my fallback plan, which was to live at home and enroll in the Newark College of Engineering, a little school where I would take a year of technical courses while I tried again to get into West Point.

Then a telegram arrived on June 26. It said:

ENTITLED ADMISSION WEST POINT AS COMPETITOR HONOR MILITARY SCHOOL STOP REPORT SUPERINTENDENT WEST POINT NEW YORK BEFORE ELEVEN OCLOCK AM DAYLIGHT SAVING TIME ONE JULY FOR ADMISSION AS CADET

I read it three times. Pop was at work, but I showed it to my mother and she cried a little. Then I went to the town barbershop and got a crew cut, which seemed like the appropriate thing to do. I didn't know how else to celebrate.

Finally Pop came home. He walked in the door and said, "Hey, I like your haircut."

I said, "Here, you're going to like this a lot more," and showed him the telegram. He gave me a big hug and took me into the kitchen, and we celebrated with a beer.

5

n the morning of July 1, 1952, I kissed Mom good-bye, hugged Pop, and got a lift from one of his friends who sold Chevrolets in a town near West Point. On my lap I clutched an athletic bag containing the few items I'd been instructed to bring—a razor, a toothbrush, a three-hundred-dollar check to cover toiletries and other essentials during the next four years, and not much else. I was excited and scared: I felt the way I had the summer before, when my parents and I had taken a sightseeing cruise up the Hudson. As the boat drew even with West Point, Pop had pointed out the cadets strolling with their girlfriends along a path overlooking the river called "Flirtation Walk." I'd looked at the cadets in their uniforms and thought, "That could be me. But am I good enough? Can I measure up?" Now I was about to find out.

We drove in the granite main gate and followed a series of arrows marked "New Cadets Report Here." They led to a sally port entrance between two imposing stone buildings. I got out, bag in hand, and gave my name to a clerk who said, "Fine. Go in this door." I walked into a gymnasium-sized room full of clerks sitting at tables stretched along the walls and dozens of new cadets. You started at the first table and worked your way around, answering questions, filling out forms, and turning over your three hundred dollars. It was all very well organized, just as I expected of West Point. At the far end came the embarrassing part: you had to strip, step up on a platform, and get photographed wearing nothing but a jockstrap. They took two views, rear and side, and these so-called posture pictures would hang in your locker all year to remind you of where you'd started. After I pulled my clothes back on a clerk instructed, "Go out that door."

The minute I stepped through that door, my world—and everyone else's—changed. Waiting for us on the other side were the "first classmen," or seniors, who had been assigned to whip the new plebes into shape. Whatever status any of us had achieved back home as a valedictorian or star athlete meant nothing. Right away they started bellowing: "You! Come over here! Line up! Stand at attention! Do you call that standing at attention, Mister? Drag in that chin! Get your shoulders back! More yet! More yet! Drop your bag! Pick it up! Not fast enough! When I tell you to drop your bag, you drop your bag right away!" I'd expected this—Pop had warned me—but when someone hollers in your ear it's impossible not to tense up. Within minutes I was sweating like everybody else.

Officially, the first eight weeks of cadet training is called "plebe summer"; unofficially—and more accurately—it is known as "Beast Barracks," and the first classmen are the "Beast Detail." It's an initiation far harder than Army basic training—designed to drive out those plebes who can't handle physical and psychological stress, and teach the survivors the discipline and basic skills they need to get along at West Point.

We were in a football-field-sized courtyard called "Central Area," bordered by four-story-tall granite barracks. The Beast Detail immediately taught us enough rudimentary marching moves—left face, right face, double time—to maneuver us in squads of ten into those buildings. I got lumped into the First New Cadet Company, which occupied a section of barracks near the door where we'd entered. They hustled us into the company office, called the "orderly room," for more paperwork. I filled out some forms and a guy threw them back in my face and said, "Dumb smack! Can't you read? It says put your first name and middle initial!"

"Sir, I do not have a first name. My name is H. Norman Schwarzkopf. I only have an initial."

"Who ever heard of not having a first name! What does your birth certificate say?" While I didn't like being harassed, I was secretly glad because Pop was finally getting his revenge. (His full name was Herbert Norman Schwarzkopf, and though he hated "Herbert" and preferred "H. Norman," he'd experienced this very scene as a cadet, and as a result was called Herbert on all his Army records. To prevent this from happening to me, he'd officially named me "H. Norman.") It took the Beast Detail several minutes to look up the regulation Army solution. They finally instructed me to write "H. (F.I.O.) Norman Schwarzkopf." "F.I.O." meant "first initial only."

They made us run up the stairs to our rooms on the fourth floor, where we put down our bags. Then they ran us back down: to the barber for crew cuts much more severe than the one I already had, to the dispensary for a checkup and shots, and to the quartermaster. There we got measured for uniforms and loaded up with fatigues, shirts, underwear, and socks until we each had two huge laundry bags balanced on our shoulders that had to be double-timed back to the barracks. Everything at Beast Barracks was done eyes forward, on the run, with first classmen shouting at you every step of the way.

At noon, we marched to the mess hall to be "taught our manners" over lunch. You had to eat sitting at attention on the front six inches of your chair. No conversing, no looking around. You had to cut your food, put down your knife, take a bite, and put down your fork while you chewed. As I did this a first classman kept yelling in my ear things like, "Keep your eyes to yourself, dumbjohn!" and "That was too big a bite!" From the surrounding sounds in the mess hall, every other plebe had a first classman hollering in *his* ear. It was pandemonium. If you made a mistake, the first classman would say, "Sit up!" which meant you had to stop eating, pull in your chin, and stay still while he upbraided you some more. Then he'd say, "Okay, eat," and you could take another bite. Hardly any food actually got in our stomachs before they cleared the plates away.

So much abuse rained down on us that the day became a blur. But by five o'clock, the Beast Detail somehow had us all dressed in "plebe skins"—plain gray trousers, gray shirt, a visored cap—and then they marched us out to Trophy Point, a beautiful spot overlooking the Hudson, where we took our oath of allegiance, the one all officers swear when entering military service: to support the Constitution of the United States. Then they fired a cannon and lowered the flag to the sound of "The Star-Spangled Banner." It was a milestone in my life, but I had trouble paying attention because people had been shouting at me all day and I wondered what was waiting for us when we marched back. I still couldn't believe I'd made it to West Point—and now it seemed like it was going to be a challenge to survive the first month.

Our physical training began the next morning—hours of calisthenics and marching. We also took a swim test, which meant lining up alongside the pool, jumping in on command, and paddling back and forth for three hundred yards. One guy in my group, a big muscular fellow, didn't know how to swim. But by now we'd been conditioned to do everything we were told, so when the first classmen said, "Into the pool!" in he jumped. Several minutes elapsed before the Beast Detail realized he was drowning. They dragged him out, pumped the water out of his lungs, and then started screaming, "Dumb smack! Why didn't you tell us you couldn't swim?"

Most of the rules plebes had to follow made no sense—for example, you weren't allowed to look out the window of your room. The penalty for any screw-up was extra abuse, either on the spot or later in the day. The harassment applied to me included a routine called the "Gang Busters Poop," which a first classman had invented after realizing the connection between my name and the radio show. "Schwarzkopf! Do the Gang Busters Poop!" they'd say. I'd have to stomp my feet, simulate the sirens and machine-gun noises from the beginning of Pop's show, and then announce, "Philips H. Lord presents *Gang Busters*!" I knew the best defense in Beast Barracks was to have a sense of humor, so I never let the harassment get to me. In fact, one of my problems was that I often couldn't keep a straight face. A first classman would catch me smiling and say, "You're smirking, dumb smack! Grind your chin in! Stand at attention!" He'd stick his nose right in my face, and if he was a little guy looking up at me, I would burst out laughing—which naturally made things worse.

During the eight weeks of Beast Barracks, physical training got increasingly tough. We progressed into obstacle courses, calisthenics with our rifles, and cross-country hikes—and dozens of cadets quit as they found they couldn't keep up. I felt a little sorry for them, but everybody understood it was the right thing. If a cadet wasn't physically and mentally tough enough to make it through Beast Barracks, he'd never withstand the demands of four years of West Point—not to mention the rigors of leading men in war.

The most important lesson drilled into us during those weeks was the honor code. West Point was still reeling from the first cheating scandal in its history, which had resulted in a mass dismissal of ninety cadets the year before. The scandal had involved nearly the entire football team: a tutoring system for the athletes had deteriorated into the passing of questions that were to appear on upcoming exams. When the scandal broke, it was front-page news because Army was one of the top teams in the nation; to cleanse its reputation, West Point had kicked out most of its best players.

We were the first plebes to come in after the scandal, and West Point went to great lengths to make sure we understood how the honor system worked. Beast Barracks included ten lectures on the subject. The basic rule was simple—a cadet does not lie, cheat, or steal, or tolerate anybody who does—and all of West Point was grounded on the assumption that cadets would abide by it. Both in and out of the classroom, we had lots of opportunity to break the rules. Instructors would typically give the identical test to several sets of cadets over the course of two days. There was nothing to stop those who took it first from leaking the questions to their buddies whose turn came later—except that they were on their honor. In the barracks, if we left during the weekend, we filled out cards saying our absence was legitimate—meaning that we were not at some local tavern swilling beer. As long as the officer in charge of the barracks had those cards, he never checked up on us.

The purpose was to instill a standard of truthfulness that an officer would follow for the rest of his life. I liked living by a code of behavior that applied twenty-four hours a day, and I liked having my word be my bond. One afternoon in my plebe year, there was a parade, called a "bandbox review," going on in Central Area. A plebe who lived on the other side of the building came to my room and said, "Mind if I look out your window?"

"You know we're not supposed to do that."

"Don't worry. I'll stand on this chair way back from the window and no one will ever know."

I should have told him no, but all I said was, "It's your neck. If you want to do it, it's fine with me."

Right after the review a first classman named Nerone burst into my room. This was a guy with whom I'd had run-ins before and who had told me he would drive me out of West Point if he could. I never understood what he had against me, but his hatred seemed intense and personal. He stood me at attention and chewed me up one side and down the other for sneaking a look out the window, saying I was going to pay a terrible price. When he finally paused, I said, "Sir, I did not watch the review."

"I saw you standing on that chair! Who do you think you're trying to fool?"

"Sir, I did not watch the review."

"You didn't?"

"No, sir."

"All right," he said, and walked out the door. That was the end of the matter. Because of the honor code, despite his dislike for me, he accepted my word. And I was not expected to report the guy who had actually watched from my window, because that was a regulatory breach, not an honor violation.

When the academic year began, our Beast Barracks companies dissolved and we were distributed among the twenty-four companies of cadets.

Whereas before we'd had only first classmen bossing us around, we now had hundreds of second and third classmen doing it, too. But I'd made it through Beast Barracks and I was growing confident that I'd succeed.

Even though the most grueling military training was reserved for the summer months, during the academic year everybody had his hands full. West Point was a good, tough engineering school. Our classes put heavy emphasis on physics, engineering, math, history, and social science; in addition we studied tactics, starting with Alexander the Great and working our way through all the important battles up to the end of World War II. Each day also had its measure of marching, inspection, and drill—not to mention athletics, since the intercollegiate and intramural programs involved every cadet. There were evenings when I'd drag into my room from wrestling practice and sleep right through supper, only to have to get up for study hall. Months passed during which I was only vaguely aware of the momentous happenings in the world: the testing of the H-bomb, the end of the Korean War, the defeat of the French at Dien Bien Phu, even the Army's confrontation with Joseph McCarthy in the congressional hearings that led to his downfall.

But when I went home during the Army-McCarthy hearings at Easter in 1954, I sat riveted in front of the TV. I thought McCarthy was a lunatic, right out there with the Ku Klux Klan. He had no concept of the rights of the individual and I hated his methods. But I also thought he was probably right about the communists: they probably did have cells everywhere—for all I knew, my sister Ruth Ann was in one! The Hiss and Rosenberg cases made it clear that America's secrets were being stolen. The Soviets were catching up with us in atomic weaponry, and they really did want to take over the world. I was a dedicated anticommunist and looked forward to working in America's defense.

West Point taught the military ethos in the most effective way imaginable: it gave us war heroes for teachers. In my plebe year I studied tactics with Lieutenant Colonel James Hollingsworth, who'd been a tank commander in World War II. He was a colorful character, profane as could be. He'd digress from the lesson plan and instead of explaining how to place a machine gun in an infantry defensive position, he'd be off in North Africa or charging across Europe in a tank column: "There we were, me and Georgie Patton with our tanks at the Kasserine Pass . . ." He described glorious scenes of victory and we loved every minute. Guys like Hollingsworth made all the pettiness and harassment we went through tolerable.

For a long time Hollingsworth had me convinced I wanted to be a tank commander—tanks had mobility and firepower and shock action, he would tell us, whereas infantry "means walkin' and thinkin' at two and a half miles an hour." He really knew how to inspire me. Once, during plebe year, I was on a target range with a 3.5-inch rocket launcher, a long tube that you put on your shoulder and fired like a World War II bazooka. We were shooting dummy rounds at targets shaped like tank silhouettes 150 yards away. Hollingsworth was walking up and down behind us as I aimed and fired my rocket, and *clunk!* it hit the tank silhouette. He patted me on the back and said, "That's great, Mister! You're just the kind of killer we want to have in our Army!" I felt as if I'd been blessed by God.

Then there was Captain Alton H. Quanbeck, our junior-year engineering mechanics professor, who'd been a Korean War fighter ace. He was always on the tail of a communist MiG, getting ready to shoot it down. Captain Paul F. Gorman, Jr., who taught social science, had fought in the infantry during the retreat from the Yalu River. He didn't talk about the war much, but he was missing the ring finger from his left hand. Rumor had it that the Chinese had overrun his position and a Chinese soldier, taking him for dead, had cut off his finger to get his West Point ring. Every time Captain Gorman waved his hand to make a point, we were reminded of what we had to be prepared to endure.

One of my mentors was Captain Samuel Rucks Martin, my senior-year English teacher, who had commanded a tank company in Korea. Not only was he a hell of an officer, but he understood poetry, which I confess I still liked. His adventure stories were wonderful—tales of rescuing cases of beer off exploding boxcars and the like—but more important he taught us things about leadership that weren't in our books. For example, he told how he'd sparked the morale of his troops in Korea by letting them dispense with salutes. He'd be sitting in his tank, parked at a road junction, and as his men rumbled by in their tanks, they'd give him a jaunty wave. The rule book called for a salute, and to a stickler, what Martin described would have been intolerable. But Captain Martin made us see that, far from a breakdown in discipline, the wave signaled something crucial: a buildup in unit pride and morale.

We hungered for stories that showed what it meant to be an officer. We had no practical experience against which to judge the tales we were told, only our own idealism and what we read in books. The foremost question on everyone's mind, of course, was, "How will I perform the first time I'm in combat?" We also worried how we'd do if we were captured: "Am I tough enough to hold out? What about if I'm subjected to torture?" We listened hard as a couple of Army psychiatrists gave a fascinating lecture about brainwashing in Korea. Their research indicated that one out of every three Americans captured had become a collaborator, and they described shocking case histories of soldiers who had caused the deaths of fellow prisoners by betraying them to the guards. The study attributed the collaborators' behavior to a lack of self-discipline—a failing of which we hoped we'd never be guilty.

One of the most disturbing classes I ever attended was a showing of *The Triumph of the Will*, Leni Riefenstahl's famous propaganda film about Hitler's Nuremberg rally of 1934. As I watched, even knowing about the atrocities the Nazis had committed and hating everything about them, I still felt swept up by the martial music, marching feet, and obvious esprit. We spent days trying to come to terms with the fundamental immorality of war. We never resolved anything in our debates, but by encouraging us to ask questions, West Point tried to prepare us for the ethical and moral ambiguities we might someday face as officers. The academy wanted to ensure that we would never be like those Nazi generals who stood up after World War II at the Nuremberg trials and shrugged off their participation in atrocities by saying, *"Dienst ist Dienst"*—in effect, "I was only doing my duty."

We all liked to think we'd be fierce warriors when the time came, but few of us were really bloodthirsty. During spring training one year we had a class called "Methods of Instruction" in which we learned how to teach troops. Each cadet had to pick a topic and give two lessons: first a lecture and then the hands-on application. I discussed judo. My classmate Charlie Sarkis, who was an expert outdoorsman, decided to talk about survival. For his lecture, he came into class with a tub of water and a rabbit, explaining that the best way to kill a rabbit is to drown it. He then drowned the rabbit and demonstrated how to skin it. After that he brought in twelve more rabbits and invited us to follow his example. We balked, and the instructor called the whole thing off but gave Charlie an A. Nobody was going to drown innocent bunnies!

———

We were quizzed and graded every day, and yet with only a little studying I was able consistently to make the dean's list. I had no wish to do better than that. Each class had what were called "goats" and "hives." Goats were the cadets at the bottom, the nickname being pejorative—the goat is the mascot of the Navy. Hives were people at the very top, the buzzing bees who were gunning for Rhodes scholarships or who were just driven to excel academically for the sake of excelling.

My buddies would say, "Oh, Schwarzie, you're a hive." That bothered me because I wanted to be accepted as a regular guy. My goal was to be good academically, good socially, good athletically, and good militarily—but not get carried away. I ran with cadets who saw the world the same way—not just wanting to be people with high grades, but people who were fun to be with and who didn't take life too seriously.

Leroy Suddath and David Horton were my roommates all four years. Leroy was a big, blond Georgian with a deep drawl and a terrific sense of humor. Both Leroy's father and eldest brother had been at the academy and flunked out: this was a family tradition he was determined to break. When he came to West Point he'd already been in college three years—he'd played basketball for Auburn—but he still had to struggle to get by. And yet Leroy was obviously a leader. Other cadets sensed it right away, but he was so laid back and had such poor grades that it took the administration a couple of years to appreciate him. Finally, after our junior year, they sent him to a summer training program at Fort Dix, New Jersey, where he served as a stand-in for a lieutenant. Leroy came back with rave reviews: the troops had absolutely worshiped the guy.

I was probably a terrible influence because I didn't need to study much. Instead of hitting the books, Leroy and I were constantly telling stories and playing pranks that sometimes drove my other roommate, David, crazy. He was a big, strapping guy from Cove Creek, North Carolina, who was conscientious about homework. One December night we were studying probability, but Leroy and I got bored and decided to liven things up with an experiment. We opened the window, and as an icy wind blasted into the room, we began a solemn discussion of the statistical likelihood of a leaf blowing in. Poor Dave was clutching the papers on his desk, saying, "For cryin' out loud, you guys, I gotta work!" Studiousness earned Dave a spot in the middle of the class, but he too was right at the top when it came to leadership.

We had Saturday afternoons and nights off, but weren't allowed to leave the post, so we relied on girls who would drive up from New Jersey and Long Island hoping to meet a cadet. Most Saturday nights the class would have a formal, heavily chaperoned dance, at which we appeared in dress uniforms and the girls kept dance cards. Public displays of affection were strictly forbidden—no holding hands, no putting your arm around your date, and certainly no kissing while in uniform. Upperclassmen could take their girls to Flirtation Walk, but plebes weren't allowed to do so. The only private spot available to us was Fort Putnam, a Revolutionary War ruin up the hill behind the main campus.

After plebe year things improved. Now, on occasional weekends, our dates could pick *us* up in their cars, and we'd go to New York City for plays and restaurants and parties. There was a ramshackle hotel called the Piccadilly near Times Square that catered to cadets. Six or seven of us would rent a room and pack in there with our dates. The hotel management set aside an entire floor for cadets, so that if we were running up and down the hall whooping and hollering at three in the morning, the only people we disturbed were ourselves. As far as West Point was concerned, what we did in Manhattan was our business, particularly if we were not in uniform. The only regulation was that cadets could not get married—as long as Uncle Sam was paying for our college education, he did not want us distracted by wives or babies. When we checked back into the barracks on Sundays, we had to sign a statement saying, "I am not married, nor have I ever been married."

At Christmas and Easter, I had a regular routine. First I'd visit my parents, who had settled into a surprisingly quiet life in Maplewood, New Jersey, a suburb of New York. Before retiring from the Army Pop had accepted the newly created position of administrative director of the Department of Law and Public Safety for the state of New Jersey. He was running an investigation into waterfront rackets, and every morning he'd make the ninety-minute commute to his office in Trenton. He loved to drive: he had a state-owned Buick with license number 12 and was always on the lookout for state troopers. Whenever he passed one he'd wave. "That's my outfit," he'd say. At the end of the day he'd drive back, have drinks with Mom, eat dinner, and watch TV. Even though Maplewood was a fashionable place to live, not unlike Lawrenceville and Princeton, they weren't that active socially, partly because of Mom's drinking and partly, I think, because they'd been obliged to socialize so much in Tehran, Germany, and Rome that they'd gotten tired of it.

After the holiday I'd borrow the car and take off for Washington, D.C., where a couple of my buddies from the Hoods now lived and where I had a series of girlfriends. While there I'd often link up with other cadets, and we'd all stay with my sister Sally in her small house in Georgetown. By this time, Sally had graduated from Smith and launched herself on a career at the National Security Agency that she could never discuss. I rarely saw Ruth Ann, who had become a social worker and moved to Providence, Rhode Island, where I was sure she was stirring up more trouble.

Pop had had an extraordinary athletic record at West Point, and mine never equaled his. Football was my major disappointment. I went out for the plebe team as a tackle, but right away it was obvious I wasn't effective on the field. West Point used the "one platoon" system: a single squad played both offense and defense. On defense I was fine, but on offense I was so slow I kept getting in the way of our running backs. When the season ended I moved on to other sports and did make the varsity in wrestling, soccer, and track. (Running was not my specialty—my events were shot put and discus.)

Militarily I thrived. I liked wearing the uniform, enjoyed it when a girlfriend or Mom and Pop came to see me on parade, and was proud when I started gaining rank. In my junior year I was made a cadet corporal, an honor reserved for about a third of each class. In my senior year I was made a cadet captain and company commander. Captain was the highest rank you could hold at West Point. Our chain of command consisted of the first captain, who was top dog, two regimental commanders, six battalion commanders, and twenty-four company commanders, each in charge of a hundred men.

It was my first taste of leadership and I found I was good at it. In the West Point system, first classmen ran the corps of cadets, with Army officer faculty members supervising. As a company commander, I was responsible for all that went on in our barracks from reveille until lights-out: everything from conducting daily formations to manning the orderly room to breaking up fights. I didn't do it by myself—I had a chain of command consisting of cadet lieutenants, sergeants, and corporals—but if anything went wrong, the onus was on me.

I'd noticed that when morale in a cadet company went bad, it was typically because the company had divided into hostile cliques. So I set about dissolving the cliques I saw forming in my company. There were three: military zealots who thought we should have harsh discipline, cadets who were indifferent about the company and were off in worlds of their own, and guys like me, in the middle. If I'd said, "I'm company commander and you're gonna do what I tell you," it would have driven the groups apart. Instead I cooked up ways to get all the upperclassmen involved in running the company with me. To be an effective leader, you have to have a manipulative streak—you have to figure out the people working for you and give each tasks that will take advantage of his strengths. That part of the job isn't fun, unless you're a real Machiavellian. The fun is when the person comes back, having done well what you asked of him, and says, "What can I do next?"

One of the indifferent guys had artistic ability, so I asked him to design a company mug—we billed it as a coffee mug, but it was actually a beer mug. When he finished, I asked him to follow up and get it manufactured. Meanwhile I found the perfect outlet for the energy of the zealots—harassing plebes. To me that was a pain, but zealots loved making them stand at attention, hollering at them, and sending them to reshine their shoes. I let the zealots do it only to the degree necessary to support the plebe system, and I'd rein them in if I thought they were getting carried away. Personally I found that I got much better results with plebes by teaching, setting a good example, and helping them along.

———

The culmination of a West Point education from a military standpoint was "branch selection," the day on which each first classman picked which part of the Army he wanted to join. Branch selection came three months before graduation, but the various branches permitted to recruit at West Point—Engineers, Armor, Signal Corps, Artillery, Infantry—started as early as our sophomore year. We could also choose the Air Force, which recruited West Pointers because it didn't yet have a military academy of its own. Each branch had officers on the faculty who tried to win over the best cadets; that's one reason we heard so many wonderful war stories. Then, during the summers after our sophomore and junior years, we were sent on tours of military posts around the country, each one home to a different branch. This was the Army equivalent of fraternity rush.

We were obliged to serve at least three years after graduation, and—with the exception of the small minority of cadets who eventually became generals, or later switched branches—your branch would remain the same during your entire Army career. Each was a distinct Army tribe, a world unto itself, with its own history and traditions and culture. Choosing was as fateful a decision as choosing a wife.

Cadets made their selections in order of their class standing, and since each branch had only a fixed number of slots open, the men near the bottom of the class got stuck with whatever was left. West Point was founded as an engineering school, so traditionally the class leaders went into the Corps of Engineers; the thirty or forty goats typically ended up in the Infantry, the Army's biggest branch. Infantry life was perceived to be the hardest, and cadets who didn't plan to stay in the Army avoided it because there was not much call in the civilian world for people whose specialty was charging up hills with bayonets.

The summer after my sophomore year, in 1954, my classmates and I toured three Air Force bases, and I was seriously tempted to sign up. It was apparent to all of us—even in the ivory-tower world of West Point—that Congress was cutting back the Army and giving the Air Force all the money. The Soviets had just gotten the H-bomb, and the prevailing wisdom was that there would never be another ground war. The Strategic Air Command had captured the imagination of the nation—we were certain that, should the communists ever attack, General Curtis LeMay and his B-52 bombers would fly over to Moscow and wipe them out. The Air Force was expanding so rapidly that lots of young-looking guys were already colonels and generals. The bases I toured were brand-new and had more creature comforts than any Army post I'd ever seen; and our hosts went out of their way to wine and dine us and tell us how welcome we'd be. But two things stopped me from signing up. First, I wanted to lead men in battle, and in the Air Force I'd be in charge of comparatively few. As an Infantry captain, for instance, I'd command a company of two hundred; as the Air Force counterpart I'd command one airplane and its crew. Second, I got airsick: it had happened on my flight to Tehran as a kid and both times I flew in an Air Force trainer. I'd gone to see *The Bridges at Toko-Ri*, and I couldn't imagine myself as William Holden's wingman, swooping in on the attack. I knew I'd be throwing up in my oxygen mask.

Next we spent a month with the Infantry at Fort Benning, Georgia. Here, to my surprise, officers did not fall all over themselves flattering the cadets. They knew they were the *real* Army, the branch that produced great troop commanders like Omar Bradley. And they also knew that the top men in the class would never be theirs. They'd settle for decent officers, figuring that even at the tail end of branch selection they were getting West Pointers, so the men would be good enough. Despite the Infantry's relative lack of status, I found myself drawn to their élan. And I was impressed when I heard that the Infantry had a scheme for winning money away from the Air Force. As the Army's answer to SAC they'd invented STRAC, the Strategic Army Corps: airborne divisions tailored to fight on the atomic battlefield.

The following summer I toured posts belonging to the other Army branches. The Signal Corps at Fort Monmouth, New Jersey, was not very interesting to me, and I'd already dismissed it as too technical. I had just as little affinity for the Artillery, which we visited at Fort Sill, Oklahoma. I kept remembering a remark Hollingsworth had made. He called the Artillery "twelve-mile snipers."

Fort Belvoir, Virginia, was the home of the Engineers, traditionally considered the elite by everyone, even though most of America's famous generals had come from the Armor, Artillery, and Infantry. I tried to keep an open mind. A colonel took us out to a deep gully, presented us with a second lieutenant, and said, "You are now going to see this man's platoon build a bridge. Watch him very carefully, because he bears tremendous responsibility. This could be your job next year if you choose Engineers." Then the colonel turned and said, "All right, Lieutenant, it's yours." And the lieutenant turned and said, "Sergeant! Build the bridge!" The platoon built the bridge while the lieutenant stood without saying a word. I thought, "Wait a minute! There's got to be more to life than this."

Ever since hearing Hollingsworth and Martin tell their stories, I'd fancied myself a budding tank commander. So I was really looking forward to visiting Fort Knox, Kentucky, the home of the Armor. The big day came when we were allowed to try out tanks. But it was scorching hot, and they put us in T-41s, small, light, four-man tanks that were very cramped. One of my classmates drove and I sat in the turret. The tank had a jerky motion, rocking back and forth and from side to side, buffeting me until I felt not only broiled alive, but motion sick again. I climbed out and said to myself, "I don't think I'm going into the Armor."

Senior year began and I'd made up my mind that I was joining the Infantry. Suddath, Horton, and about twenty others made the same choice. We were very close to Major Hal Moore, our senior military instructor, a highly decorated infantryman in World War II and the Korean War. He looked like the Marlboro man, tall and lean with a chiseled jaw, and wove war stories as vivid as Hollingsworth's—but he also had a quiet, serious side that inspired me. He'd often end his war stories by talking about his responsibility for the men he was leading in battle. It reminded us that the cost of an officer's mistake in war can be human lives.

By Christmas, branch selection was on every first classman's mind, and those of us who'd chosen Infantry began looking for ways to boost its prestige in the eyes of our fellow cadets. We finally hit on a scheme to recruit enough people to fill all the Infantry slots, so that the class goat would get ranked into some other branch. Right after the Christmas holiday we launched our campaign. We'd go up to people and say, "Hey, have you made your branch choice yet?"

"No."

"Well, I'm going into the Infantry. Let me tell you why."

As selection day drew near, Major Moore and some of the other infantry officers supplied us with two-foot-long wooden replicas of paratrooper wings and the Combat Infantryman's Badge, the decoration foot soldiers wear after they've proved themselves in combat. We nailed these up in the orderly rooms of all twenty-four companies, and the cadets were happy to have them because orderly rooms were truly bare, depressing places. That created such a stir that the West Point commandant of cadets ordered Major Moore to stop. "This proselytizing has gone too far," he said. Clearly we were gaining ground, and faculty members from other branches were starting to complain.

On the evening of the fateful day, all 480 graduating first classmen assembled in the electrical engineering lecture hall. At the front of the room was a big board displaying all the available slots. Seated nearby were administrators and representatives from the six branches. Cadets were called in order of class rank, and when a man stood up and said, "I pick the Corps of Engineers," they put his name on a tally sheet and reduced by one the number of available slots in the corps.

I was forty-third in the class and wanted to be the first man into the Infantry. Somebody beat me to it; I was the second. But that didn't bother me because I was excited by what was starting to happen in the room. As the polling went on, whenever a cadet said, "I pick the Infantry," our group would yell, "All right!" and cheer. Pretty soon more cadets got into the act, and guys started switching their branch choices. If someone's first choice had been Armor, but all the Armor slots had filled, he might have been thinking of Artillery as his second choice and Infantry third. But when he saw all the emotion he wanted to be part of it, so he chose Infantry over Artillery. This happened increasingly as we worked our way down the list.

Finally we got down to the second-to-last man, and there were two openings left, one in Infantry and one in Artillery. We held our breath as he stood. "I pick the Infantry," he said, a cheer went up—and Artillery got the goat! The casualty of our success was a friend of mine named Jack Sloan, who was the class goat and wanted the Infantry, too. When he saw he'd been ranked into the Artillery, he was devastated. So we went to the front of the hall to talk to the head Artillery officer. I began, "Sir, I hope you don't mind, Jack Sloan feels unhappy about being ranked into the Artillery. Is there any way you think you could let him join the Infantry?"

This guy was so upset that the Artillery had closed last that he snapped, "Goddammit, we don't want anybody in the Artillery who doesn't want to be. If he wants to be in the Infantry, he can be in the Infantry."

"Do you really mean that, sir?"

"You're damn right I mean it!"

So Jack got to join us in the Infantry.

On June 5, 1956, I graduated. At West Point the handing out of diplomas culminates an entire week of parades, speeches, ceremonies, concerts, and dinners—and is immediately followed by dozens of marriages in a cadet chapel. I was proud to wear on my sleeves the four stripes signifying my cadet rank, proud to be awarded my commission as a second lieutenant in the United States Army, proud to be the forty-third man called up on the stage, proud as we all cheered afterward and flung our white caps in the air. But my greatest feeling of accomplishment had to do with my dad. He and Mom were there, of course, and after the ceremony when he gave me a hug, his eyes were brimming with tears. I could see by his happiness that having his boy graduate from West Point had fulfilled his dream. More than any other day of my life, I felt like a good son.

———

To this day it's hard to explain the impact West Point had on me. Somehow, during the four years I spent in that idealized military world, a new system of values came alive in my mind. When I began as a plebe, "Duty, Honor, Country" was just a motto I'd heard from Pop. I loved my country, of course, and I knew how to tell right from wrong, but my conscience was still largely unformed. By the time I left, those values had become my fixed stars. It was a tremendous liberation. The Army, with its emphasis on rank and medals and efficiency reports, is the easiest institution in the world in which to get consumed with ambition. Some officers spend all their time currying favor and worrying about the next promotion—a miserable way to live. But West Point saved me from that by instilling the ideal of service above self—to do my duty for my country regardless of what personal gain it brought, and even if it brought no gain at all. It gave me far more than a military career—it gave me a calling.

Not everybody left West Point with that sense of mission, but many of us did. Thirty years after our graduation, I found myself sitting in a Pentagon office drinking coffee with two of my best friends, Tom Weinstein, a classmate, and Bob Riscassi, who'd entered the Army through ROTC. By this time we were all three-star generals, and we were bemoaning the fact that so many people we dealt with in Washington—both at the Pentagon and on Capitol Hill—had no higher goal than personal advancement.

Tom was a shrewd guy who had become head of Army Intelligence and had a knack for getting to the point. I asked him, "How come you're not a careerist? Why try to live by moral and ethical standards other people don't have?"

He didn't hesitate to answer. He said, "When I entered West Point I was a little Jewish boy from New Jersey and I didn't know a damn thing. During the four years we were there, you remember all that shit they taught us? Well, I really believed it."

So did I.

Little that I learned at West Point prepared me for the shock of serving as a second lieutenant in the United States Army. When I reported for duty at the 101st Airborne Division at Fort Campbell, Kentucky, in early 1957, I was the typical new West Point graduate—eager to serve my country, hungry for glory, filled with the wish to be a leader of men. I'd put in for the 101st because it was part of the vanguard, the Strategic Army Corps, and had lately attracted publicity as America's first "Pentomic" division, specially tailored to fight on the atomic battlefield. It had a magnificent tradition as well, paratroopers from the 101st having won their place in history by jumping behind German lines on D-Day and by holding off Nazi tanks at the Battle of the Bulge.

The Army that I entered was suffering from the aftereffects of Korea. Officers and noncommissioned officers were in short supply and budgets had been cut so severely that there weren't even enough funds for day-to-day operations. In the age of the doctrine of massive retaliation, the Army believed itself in danger of being completely overshadowed by the Air Force. Despite this pessimistic outlook, my friends and I were not discouraged. The political battles at the Pentagon were hundreds of miles away. We couldn't affect the outcomes even if we wanted to, and it was clear to *us* at least that there would always be a need for an Army. Who had ever seized and held territory with an airplane? Our job was to be ready when called upon.

Compared with West Point, Fort Campbell wasn't much to look at: it was located in nondescript, rolling farm country, and most of its buildings were pale yellow, wooden World War II barracks and newer green ones made of cinder block. Lieutenant Colonel Leroy David Brummitt welcomed me; he was acting commander of the 2nd Battle Group of the 187th Airborne Infantry, the 2,000-man unit to which I'd been assigned. I marched into his office anticipating a briefing—on our battle group's role in America's defense and the small but valuable contribution that Second Lieutenant Schwarzkopf was expected to make. Instead he looked me up and down and asked, "You play football, don't you?"

"No, sir."

"What! You're so big. You should play football. You sure you don't play?"

When I told him I hadn't played for years he seemed displeased. I soon learned that the battle group had requested me because I was six feet three inches, weighed 220 pounds, and had played tackle at West Point, according to my personnel file. The battle group was known in the 101st mainly for its athletic teams, so for Colonel Brummitt the main business at hand was not soldiering, but sports. Literally dozens of troops were assigned to "special duty," which meant they did nothing but play football or basketball or box. But now that he had me, it was too late to send me back, so he assigned me to E Company, under Captain John J. Plosay.

I couldn't have asked for a better superior. Plosay was a slim, acerbic Pennsylvanian who had joined the Army after college and earned his commission at Officer Candidate School. Now, at the age of twenty-eight, he was a great example of what a young leader could aspire to. As company commander, he had responsibility for the lives of 250 men and hundreds of thousands of dollars' worth of equipment. He had to follow orders from higher up, of course, but in the day-to-day running of the outfit, he was one hundred percent in charge.

Plosay was delighted to have me, because E Company was seriously understaffed—technically he should have had six lieutenants, but he'd been making do with only one. Though I'd completed basic infantry training and jump school during the eight months since I'd graduated from West Point, I had no experience in the day-to-day duties of a lieutenant in a company and no knowledge of the specialized chores associated with Airborne operations, such as coordinating with the Air Force for the use of their planes, issuing and checking parachutes, and orchestrating the troops' departure. But that didn't bother Plosay. Rather than waste time on explanations, he simply said, "Come with me," and let me learn by watching. He put me in charge of the weapons platoon, fifty soldiers who manned the company's mortars and recoilless rifles, where he knew I'd be in good hands. In general, the Airborne had highly experienced noncommissioned officers, and in the weapons platoon were two tough old sergeants, Calvert and Barney, who had fought in World War II and Korea. They taught me willingly. Calvert had run the platoon before I arrived, and he knew the job so well that I asked myself, "Why should he yield to me?" But he made it clear that he was glad to be relieved of the burden of making decisions—and being responsible when things went wrong.

It didn't take me long to realize that living at West Point had filled my head with unrealistic expectations. When a parade at West Point was scheduled for five o'clock, for example, first call was at 4:55. You could count on all 2,400 cadets to fall out of the barracks at that instant, in the proper uniforms, with their rifles, and to be marching within minutes across the parade ground in a magnificent review. But at an ordinary Army base, if you wanted to have a five o'clock parade with that many soldiers, you could start assembling the men at 11:00 A.M., and even then you'd still be lucky to pull off the review on time.

Army life seemed to operate on the general principle that in any activity involving troops, chaos could erupt at any moment. I discovered this when I led my platoon on a parachute jump the week I arrived. I'd gone to jumpmaster school just before coming to Fort Campbell, and we always used the same precision drill to get the men out of the airplane. The jumpmaster would position himself by the door and when he said, "Get ready!" the men would sit at attention on the edge of their canvas benches and in their right hands hold up their static lines, the long canvas straps that automatically opened the chutes as the paratroopers jumped. On the next order, "Stand up!" the men would stand and face the rear of the plane. With subsequent commands, they'd hook up their static lines, check each other's equipment, sound off an "okay" from the front to the rear of the plane, stand in the door of the aircraft, and finally jump. From the moment of takeoff until we hit the ground on the drop zone, the entire exercise took only fifteen minutes, which was why veteran paratroopers disparagingly called it a "Hollywood jump."

At Fort Campbell, they liked to make the training more realistic: on that first exercise we had to fly a low-altitude circuit for an hour and a half before jumping. The flight was rough, and many of the troops got airsick, and then felt so weak that they lay down on the floor. This didn't seem promising, but I was determined to proceed by the book. When we finally approached the big empty field that was to serve as the drop zone, I stood near the door and called out, "Get ready!" But the cabin was a madhouse of soldiers climbing and falling all over each other, with equipment strewn everywhere. When I shouted, "Stand up!" only about half the platoon was able to stand. Then one kid popped his reserve chute by accident and we had silk ballooning all over and the sergeants were screaming at him. We pulled him out of line so the rest of the men could jump. Out of forty jumpers, eight missed the drop zone, but I considered it an accomplishment just to get them safely out the door.

The troops were almost all draftees, and the company had everything from suburban college kids to farm boys to inner-city dropouts with tattoos on their arms that said things like "Death Before Dishonor" and showed parachutes and skulls with daggers sticking through them. One of the first lessons I learned was that there was no *single* way for the leader of a small unit to command the soldiers' respect: you had to address each person in terms *he* could understand. The college kids were persuaded by logical explanations, the farm boys by common sense, and what the dropouts understood was their leader's size and strength, and the fact that he could be one tough son of a bitch.

In the summer of 1957 we had a huge influx of draftees, and we were working fifteen-hour days to get them properly trained and assimilated into the unit. The worst soldier in the bunch was a guy from upstate New York. He insisted that he'd been in a motorcycle accident and had sustained brain damage that caused him occasionally to become catatonic. Given that he'd passed his draft physical, this seemed improbable, and we soon noticed a close correlation between this private's catatonic fits and the prospect of hard work. We'd be camped fifteen miles from the base, getting ready to march home, and the private would pass out. Or it would be time to run the obstacle course, and he would pass out. Each time we'd carry him to the dispensary, but he always revived just before the doctor examined him.

The doctor was mystified; he couldn't say what the problem was, but he also couldn't say there was no problem. Sergeants Montoya and Gonzales, Korean War veterans who supervised the recruits, did not think very much of this at all. "Sir, that son of a bitch is getting over on us!"

I was concerned that if he did have a medical condition, the man could die: "Look, Sarge, he may be or he may not be. We just don't know and we can't take a chance."

So the sergeants improvised their own cure. The troops lived on the second floor of the barracks, and every Friday night they had what was called a GI party—which entailed scrubbing the floor, waxing it, and buffing it to a high shine. One Friday I heard screaming and raced upstairs and burst into the squad bay. Montoya and Gonzales had the private hanging out the window upside down by his ankles. He was in a panic, and Gonzales was yelling, "You little bastard! It didn't take you long to wake up this time!" After that the private had no more catatonic fits, although the Army discharged him anyway, a few months later, as unfit for military duty.

The toughest NCO in the entire battle group was also the smallest: First Sergeant Carlos Leal, who stood five feet seven inches and weighed 130 pounds. There was a hulking giant of a soldier in his company—he went on to play tackle in the National Football League—who sometimes got ornery and beat up other soldiers. The NCOs would bring him to Leal to be disciplined. I came into the first sergeant's office once and the private was standing in front of Leal's desk, blubbering. Leal was saying, "You son of a bitch, if you ever do that again I am going to *whip your ass*! Do you understand that? Now get out of my sight!" Just by force of will, Leal had the soldier terrified.

After the man left I asked, "Sergeant Leal, what would you do if one of these guys ever decided to take you on?"

He said, "Sir, that would be no problem at all." He reached under his desk and showed me a sawed-off baseball bat. "I'd beat the hell out of the son of a bitch, sir, if he ever dared lay a hand on me."

I enjoyed watching Sergeant Leal with the men. He loved them and they loved him. The summer after I joined the Airborne we got a new colonel who announced that he didn't like profanity. The order came down that there was entirely too much foul language in the Airborne and it should be stopped immediately. I of course went straight to Leal's reveille formation the next morning. He stood on the steps in front of his soldiers and said: "All you fuckers listen to me. We've got a new commanding officer, and he says there's too much fucking swearing going on in the Airborne. So I want all you shitheads to understand, I want the fucking swearing knocked off right away. You got that?"

"Yes, first sergeant!"

"All right. Dismissed." Leal was a loyal NCO. He had no intention of undercutting the colonel or the new rules. He was just putting out the word the only way he knew how, and in terms he knew the troops would understand.

Years later, serving as a military advisor in Thailand, Leal was killed in a free-fall parachuting accident. To this day the thought of him warms my heart and brings a smile to my face.

———

Though I'd have happily spent all my time with the troops and NCOs, by the end of my first year in the Airborne I felt disillusioned and torn. I loved the glamor of the 101st. As far as the public was concerned, we were still the "devils in baggy pants" of World War II fame. Everyone else in the Army wore shoes; we wore big black jump boots with our trousers bloused into them. Our paratrooper wings had brightly colored cloth backgrounds and on our overseas caps were red, white, and blue parachute patches. We had an incredible mystique. People would ask what it was like to jump, and we'd always answer modestly, "Oh, there's really nothing to it," but of course when we said this it was with a small sigh and a faraway look, since we really wanted them to understand otherwise. It was great to be part of such a death-defying unit.

Yet at the same time, the more I saw of my fellow officers, the more I was dismayed. I'd signed up for the Airborne thinking I'd be part of the elite, but good leaders like Plosay were the exception. Most of the senior first lieutenants and captains I encountered were hard-drinking rogues left over from World War II and Korea. Talented wartime commanders had long since ascended to senior positions all over the Army or retired to civilian jobs. The ones still in the junior ranks were too often the dregs— guys who were just marking time, who had no sense of duty or honor, and who saw the world through an alcoholic haze. For the first time in my life I found myself required to answer to men I didn't respect—a dilemma for which I was not prepared.

Nobody at West Point had told me you can learn as much from a lousy leader as from a good one, but in the course of that year I had ample opportunity to find that out for myself. After only three months Captain Plosay got promoted to the battle group staff, the team of officers that assisted the colonel in such matters as personnel, intelligence, training, and logistics planning. Plosay's replacement as company commander was a short, fat, lazy, forty-year-old first lieutenant who'd left the Army after Korea only to come back because he couldn't make it on the outside. He stayed in the Airborne because of money—each officer got a jump bonus of a hundred dollars a month, which was a lot considering that a first lieutenant's regular monthly pay was about two hundred and fifty dollars. But the man was afraid to jump. When a jump was scheduled, the platoon leaders would get the troops out of bed at four in the morning and assemble them for breakfast. The lieutenant would show up at the mess hall and say things like, "I've had a terrible night. I've got the flu. I'm really sorry I can't make the jump this morning. But I'll tell you what: you go ahead and I'll meet you on the drop zone because I don't want to miss today's training."

So we'd take the company through the jump, and as we floated down the lieutenant would be standing right in the middle of the drop zone. If someone from battle group headquarters came by to inspect, he would make a show of brushing dirt off himself. The inspectors bought it, but the troops didn't; they knew he was afraid. If those men had had amoebic dysentery they wouldn't have followed him to the latrine.

The lieutenant ran the company only a couple of months, but I served under his successor for almost a year. He was a forty-four-year-old armor officer who, like the lieutenant, had stayed in the Army because he couldn't hold a civilian job. Our new captain was an alcoholic. Each morning he'd drift in at around nine o'clock, sign the morning report, and say, "I have to take care of something important up at headquarters. Take charge and don't leave until I get back." He often didn't come back, and at six in the evening I'd get a call from the bartender at the base's rod and gun club saying my commander had just passed out. I'd drive out, load the captain in the car, take him home, and turn him over to his wife.

Even by Airborne standards his drinking was extreme. But, to be fair, alcohol was a big part of paratrooper culture. If you didn't show up for happy hour at the officers' club on Friday afternoon, you were regarded as a weak sister. Drinks cost a quarter, and the object was to put away as many as possible before seven o'clock. Then the band would start to play, and officers would dance with other officers' wives, especially senior officers with junior officers' wives who were really good-looking. That often led to fights—you'd see a major or lieutenant colonel brawling with a subordinate in the parking lot. Saturday morning was the time for weekly inspections, and we'd all report out at six A.M. with terrific hangovers. Most of the troops would be in the same condition. We'd stumble through until one P.M., at which point we'd adjourn to the officers' club for a little hair of the dog.

When the captain was drunk, he went out of his way to tell me how much he hated West Pointers. It gave him pleasure to make me do his work—especially after the end of 1957, when I got a routine promotion to first lieutenant and became his executive officer. Normally an executive officer assisted his boss with administrative chores, such as supervising the mess hall and the motor pool, managing unit finances, and preparing routine reports. But the captain simply dumped his responsibilities on me.

For example, whenever battle group headquarters called a meeting to issue orders for upcoming maneuvers, he'd take me along. Each company commander then had twenty-four hours to prepare a plan and brief the colonel on how he would execute his company's portion of the order. The captain would turn to me and say, "All right, Schwarzkopf, this will be a training exercise for you. I want you to come up with a concept and brief me on how you'd execute this order." I'd work for hours, poring over maps and writing up an operations order. The captain would review it and snap, "This is the dumbest thing I've ever seen. Didn't they teach you anything at that goddamn tin school on the Hudson?" Then he'd leave me behind and take the work to battle group headquarters to present it as his own.

In late December, the captain and his drinking landed the entire company in trouble. We failed a practice alert, a drill designed to test the company's readiness for rapid deployment in the event of war. It worked like this: during a designated week, your unit would be on "ready alert," meaning that your weapons were secured for transport, your jeeps loaded, and your troops all on hand with their barracks bags packed. At some point an alert would be called, and you then had two hours to pack the last of your equipment and assemble for an inspection, as if you were about to fly to a distant war zone and fight. The night our alert was called, I was working at battle group headquarters as night duty officer, and our company's only other lieutenant was a newcomer who had no experience in alert procedures. That left only the captain to organize the alert—and the company arrived at the assembly point forty-five minutes late with half its equipment spilling off the jeeps.

Lieutenant Colonel Brummitt, the acting battle group commander, was furious. Even though our ready-alert week was supposed to be up, he called another practice alert for December 30 and warned that if we flunked that, he'd make us do still another on New Year's Eve. The thought that 240 troops might miss their New Year's celebration because their commanding officer was a jerk bothered me. So when the thirtieth came, I busted my tail making sure that this time we'd pass.

Around midday the captain disappeared. That was okay with me, because we could do better without him. I called the sergeants together and said, "We're not gonna blow it. We're going to do this thing in fine style," and by nightfall we had everything squared away. Around nine o'clock the captain stumbled back, and he was slobbering drunk. The first thing he did was demand a meal. Of course, the mess sergeant had packed up his stoves, but I told him to feed the captain because we needed to sober him up. The sergeant cooked a steak and a huge helping of french fries. The captain ate about half the food and suddenly said, "Goddammit, these french fries are greasy!" and flung his mess tray across the room. There were french fries all over. Then he noticed a couple of privates gawking at him and decided to inspect their barracks bags. He started pulling out their uniforms, socks, and drawers and throwing them in the air.

Next he said to the first sergeant, "Call the whole company. I want to have a company meeting now." The company formed up in front of the barracks steps and the captain teetered on top of them. He said, "You sons of bitches! You flunked this alert the other day because you're trying to get me in trouble. I've been getting out of trouble all my Army career and I'm going to get out of it this time."

The men could see he was drunk and laughed at him. That made him furious and he decided to inspect the jeeps that we'd parked in front of the barracks. He started untying loads that we'd spent all day tying, and pulling stuff off. Finally I couldn't stand it. I grabbed him and said, "Sir, come on with me." I took him into his office, inflated an air mattress, put it on the floor, and said, "You lie down and sleep. You need a rest."

"Aw, Norm, you're really taking care of me. You're the only one in the company that really loves me!"

Love him! I wanted to kill him! But what I wanted even more was to pass that alert. He went to sleep, headquarters called the alert at four A.M., and by six we had the entire company standing tall and looking good. I woke the captain up, took him out, and propped him up in front of the formation, thinking, "Now you're gonna get yours, you SOB! The colonel is going to see that this company is ready to go, but he's also going to see that you're drunk."

But it didn't happen that way. Colonel Brummitt drove up in his jeep, stopped in front of the captain, and said, "Let this be a lesson to you. Don't ever let it happen again," and drove off.

Some of the men had had enough and reported to the Army inspector general that their commander had been drunk on duty. But Brummitt did not want the inspector general meddling in battle-group affairs, and the lieutenant colonel he appointed as investigating officer subverted the inquiry by giving the captain the names of the kids who'd offered to testify. The captain called them in, one at a time, and made sure they were so scared that they denied having seen anything. The investigation was dropped.

I was in the office when headquarters telephoned the captain with the news that he was in the clear. He was laughing! At first I was stunned and then I was mad as hell. Something inside me snapped. I called the investigating officer and asked for an appointment. "What's this about?" he said.

"I need to talk to you about an incident that occurred in my company."

"Are you sure you want to do this?"

"Yes, sir. I feel it's my duty."

I knew I was jumping the chain of command, and when I walked into the lieutenant colonel's office *I* was scared. He said, "Lieutenant, I want to tell you something. The single most important value in the Airborne is loyalty to your commanders. That's loyalty no matter what. Any attempt to undermine the authority of your superiors will be viewed in the most dire light by all of us in this headquarters. Now, what is it you want to talk to me about?"

I said, "Sir, I don't want to talk to you about anything." I walked out thinking, "You and your Airborne can go to hell."

For a couple of weeks I seriously considered bailing out. West Point graduates were allowed to change their Army branch after two years of active duty, and I actually went to Washington that March to look into joining the Ordnance Corps, the branch whose primary missions were to manage the Army's ammunition and see to the heavy maintenance of its vehicles. I'd been promised a warm welcome by the head of the Ordnance Department at West Point. But the Ordnance Corps representatives in Washington told me that if I transferred, I'd have to start my career again essentially from scratch, by attending the Ordnance Corps basic course. I gave up and went back to Fort Campbell thinking, "Okay, what now?"

I was stuck with the captain for five more months. The bright side of working for an incompetent commander was that I had far more responsibility than most lieutenants. Everybody knew who was in charge of the company: the first sergeant and the platoon leaders would come to me when they needed answers. Nor was headquarters as oblivious as I thought: Captain Plosay and other officers realized I was doing the commander's work for him, and in July 1958 I was rewarded by being reassigned to the battle group staff.

My new superior, Major Tom Whelan, was smart and blunt, a hard-working midwesterner who had a reputation as a tough taskmaster. Like the captain, he'd come up through the ranks, but he had used the military to really make something of himself. But for his influence, I would probably have left the Army once my three years were up. Many of my West Point classmates actually did leave—fully a quarter of the men who'd been in my cadet company—because they couldn't reconcile the ideals we'd been taught with the realities of the job. One day I discussed my disillusionment with Whelan, who knew exactly what to say to make me stay: "There are two ways to approach it. Number one is to get out; number two is to stick around and someday, when you have more rank, fix the problems. But don't forget, if you get out, *the bad guys win.*" I didn't want the bad guys to win.

We were a small group of young officers, all surprisingly good. Two of my West Point classmates, Ed Valence and Russ Mericle, had also worked their way onto the battle group staff—Ed as training officer and Russ as a planner. We talked often about the Airborne's flaws. The Strategic Army Corps trumpeted itself as a great fighting force, but we knew we really weren't that good. We could see it in our officers, in the way we maneuvered, in the quality of our equipment. We claimed we were able to fight on the plains of Europe against massed formations of Soviet armor. That made no sense! Given the few and relatively ineffective antitank weapons we had, the Soviets would have chewed us to pieces. Nor were we as mobile as we pretended. The rationale for having airborne forces was that we could fly anywhere in a crisis and hit the ground ready to fight. The problem was that, once we parachuted in, all we had besides our feet were the jeeps that had been air dropped with us—our ammunition and mortars moved in jeeps and our recoilless rifles and heavy machine guns were mounted on them— and those jeeps weren't designed to haul such heavy loads. Even in Kentucky, I'd spent half my time as a platoon leader hip-deep in mud, trying to get the jeeps unstuck. The Airborne was deluding itself just as the cold war was getting more intense—the Soviets had just launched *Sputnik* and were massing sophisticated weapons along the NATO border.

But there was no way to admit these shortcomings. Training revolved around a ritual called the "annual training test," and all year we practiced routines we knew would be on that test—at the individual level, the squad level, the platoon level, all the way up to the battle group. Two weeks before the test, we'd rehearse, usually on the same terrain where the test itself would take place. It was really that mickey mouse. Even so, the first time I participated in one, I could see that the battle group did not perform well. The orders did not get out on time, the attack was carried off sloppily— there were problems galore. Yet when we got our final score, it was 99.8! That was our culture—admitting weakness was seen as a failure to manifest the can-do attitude expected of an Airborne officer. To me this seemed not only crazy, but incompatible with the standard of honesty we'd learned at West Point.

At battle group headquarters, we didn't rate our companies on training or equipment readiness—factors that would have saved soldiers' lives if we'd ever had to fight. Our "best company" award, given each month, was based on criteria such as lowest number of soldiers AWOL, lowest number of soldiers with VD, and contributions of money to the Airborne association. The consistent winner was A Company—until the spring of 1958, when the county police discovered a burglary ring involving soldiers operating right out of the A Company barracks. The troops were breaking into stores in nearby Clarksville, Tennessee, stashing the stolen goods in the barracks attic, and getting away with it because the company commander never bothered to make a thorough inspection.

———

Despite these circumstances, there was still a job to be done, and we did our best to accomplish it. We continued to work long days, which was tough on men who had wives and babies at home. I thought being a bachelor was an important advantage. I had girlfriends, but scoffed at the idea that you could be a good junior officer and raise a family at the same time.

I'd also pulled away from my own family almost completely. I saw my parents only once during my first year at Fort Campbell. Pop came to meet me at the airport. On the way home, I told him I'd had my first parachute malfunction on a jump the week before and had had to pull the ripcord on my reserve chute. He was enthralled. He would have liked to know the details of all my Army experiences. I didn't accommodate him: I was a lousy letter writer, preferring phone calls. But they were expensive, so I didn't call often and the conversations were never very long.

Pop was at loose ends. He'd retired after my senior year at West Point and didn't really have anything to do. He planned some do-it-yourself projects around the house—putting up paneling, retiling the basement floor—and bought the tools and materials, but never finished. He wrote—anecdotes that he'd send off to *Reader's Digest*. He'd always thought of himself as a good writer, so he figured they'd get published, but they never did. A company that wanted to use his connections hired him as a consultant to help pioneer automobile seat belts, and one Christmas he gave me a set. I thought they were the dumbest thing I'd ever seen. You had to drill holes in the floor of your car and bolt them in. Whenever we talked he'd ask, "How do you like your seat belts?" and I'd say, "Aw, Pop, I haven't gotten around to installing them."

His health was failing, but I wasn't seeing enough of him to realize it. The first indication that he was sick came in August 1958, when I reported back to Fort Campbell after traveling to the Pacific for several weeks on Army business. I was being welcomed back at a cocktail party at someone's house and the colonel's wife found me, took me into another room, and said, "I hate to tell you this. Your father has died. You need to get home right away."

I drove back to my quarters in a daze and called Mom: Dad hadn't died. She'd evidently phoned to tell me he wasn't well and to find out why I hadn't called. But she had been drinking, and the guy who took the message was sure this was a woman grieving over her husband.

It was always hard to evaluate news from home, because I never knew how much of what Mom told me was the loving wife and registered nurse talking and how much of it was the bourbon. A few weeks later she called again to say that Pop was seriously ill. This time I raced back to New Jersey—but it was a false alarm. Pop wasn't even in bed and seemed surprised to see me. He didn't appear to be sick at all, except that he'd lost weight. But then he told me he had lung cancer and had been operated on a month before. He assured me the tumor had been removed and he was free of cancer. It was very confusing. Mom and Pop had been trying to shield me from the fact that he had cancer, but at the same time they were resentful that I hadn't known what was going on. "If I'd only known, I would have been here," I told them. I was dismayed because they acted as though they didn't know how much I cared.

Mom called again, a week before Thanksgiving, and said Pop was in bed with pneumonia and to come if I could. She did not make it sound as if his life was in danger, and I arranged a plane reservation for a few days later. But when I got there my father was dead. Mom and Sally were with him during his final moments, but until the day I die I will regret not having been there myself. My father was a selfless public servant, a true patriot, a man of honor, and a loving father. To me he was a great man, I loved him dearly, and we never had a proper chance to say good-bye. Alcohol had shattered our family so badly that I'd pulled away just when he needed me.

Pop had left instructions detailing what he wanted done, and I followed his wishes to the letter. Ruth Ann, who had even less to do with our parents than I, drove down from Rhode Island. We gave him a simple service at a funeral home, a moving ceremony, although hardly anybody came—just our family, a few friends, and a handful of men who'd known him in the state police. Ever since I was a small boy he'd told me he wanted to be cremated, and I stayed with his body to see that this happened. We buried his ashes the next day at West Point. The academy gave him full military honors, including an honor guard and a thirteen-gun artillery salute out over the Hudson, because he had risen to the rank of major general in the Army Reserve. As I listened to the booming of those guns under the gray November sky, I realized that no one had ever fired a salute for my father when he was alive, because he'd never commanded a troop unit as a general. It seemed right that he should have a salute at last, and that it should be at West Point.

———

That winter Major Whelan chose me to be the air mobility officer, which meant that when the battle group was on the move, I was the one responsible for arranging the airplanes and supervising the loading of two thousand paratroopers, hundreds of jeeps, trucks, and artillery pieces, and tons of other equipment. Later I became the assistant operations officer. This was a job normally reserved for a senior captain, but Whelan picked me because the battle group's few good captains were commanding companies and the rest were incompetent. Most of them were relieved not to get the job—they didn't want to work for a tough boss. In the spring Whelan left for a four-month stint at the Army's Command and General Staff College and I stood in for him as the battle group operations officer. I was a first lieutenant doing a major's job.

I learned a lot from being able to watch the battle group from the vantage of headquarters. We had seven companies reporting to us, each had roughly the same quality of troops, and yet three of the companies ran well and four poorly. To my surprise, the best company commanders were the ones who could carry out a bad order when necessary, and knew how to do so without ruining the troops' morale. When it was announced, for example, that the four-star general in charge of all Army units in the lower forty-eight states was coming to visit our battle group, every company was ordered to repaint its barracks building whether it needed it or not.

All seven company commanders protested, but as soon as it was clear the colonel wasn't going to change his mind, the commanders of the three good companies went back to their units and executed the order as if they'd thought of it themselves. They told the men, "Okay, guys. We've got a new mission and that is to get our barracks in shape for the general! Let's show him who's the best company at Fort Campbell!" The troops got out their buckets and brushes, and in no time the walls glistened with fresh green paint. Meanwhile the commanders of the other four companies kept trying to change the colonel's mind until he threw them out. Then they told their men, "The general is coming and battle group says we gotta paint the damn building even though it doesn't need it." The troops, in turn, worked lackadaisically; since the commander had wasted so much time fighting the order, they ended up having to spend their weekend slopping on paint while the troops of the good commanders were downtown having fun.

I had ample opportunity to study this effect because battle group was issuing plenty of dumb orders. We'd gotten a new commanding officer who had worked in the Pentagon for seventeen years. Up until then our commanders, for all their flaws, had been seasoned paratroopers, but the colonel was somebody's fair-haired boy and he'd been assigned to run this battle group on his way to a general's star. He'd been awarded his jump wings only the week before he arrived.

To be fair, George Patton himself would have had to work hard to command a unit successfully after seventeen straight years of commanding a desk at the Pentagon. The colonel never stood a chance. The first thing he did was call all the officers to a meeting, where he announced that a parachute was only a means of transportation: "Once you hit the ground, the Airborne is no different from any other infantry outfit." It was not the way to win the hearts of veteran paratroopers. Then he antagonized the NCOs by chewing them out for not knowing technicalities that he'd just looked up himself, such as the latest rule for how often to swab out the barrel of a mortar on the firing range. His personal habits also alienated the men: the first time we went out on maneuvers, he declared that there was no reason a man—meaning himself—should not be comfortable in the field. "We all deserve a good night's sleep," he said. He had a little tent set up next to the operations tent, and each night he'd put on pajamas, a maroon satin dressing gown, and fuzzy slippers made of lamb's wool. He'd sit on his cot where troops walking by in their dirty fatigues could see him. "Look at that candy ass," they said.

We were busy gearing up for the annual training test. On the first day, we were to parachute in and establish a defensive perimeter. Around noon would come a simulated enemy atomic attack—the Army used a smoke pyrotechnic called an "atomic simulator" that produced a mushroom cloud visible for miles around. When we saw that, we were supposed to go through a dispersion routine, jumping into our jeeps and scattering in all directions so we would not be killed by radioactive fallout. Later that day we'd reestablish the perimeter, and on the second night would come an enemy infantry attack. It would continue until the enemy had made a sizable penetration into our perimeter, and then we'd commit our reserve to a counterattack that would eject the enemy. On the third day we'd attack the enemy's position and win, and the test would be over. We'd have exercised our airborne procedures, our dispersion procedures, our defensive procedures, our counterattack procedures, and our offensive procedures.

The test took place in March at Fort Campbell; the umpires and evaluation teams came from our archrival, the 82nd Airborne at Fort Bragg,

North Carolina. We jumped and set up our perimeter, and everything was going fine until the second night. Around 2300 hours the enemy attacked. This was when they always attacked, and in the operations tent we were standing near the map with our counterattack plans ready. We waited a decent interval, then Major Whelan turned to the colonel and said, "Sir, the enemy has penetrated to this point. Recommend we execute counterattack Eagle Claw." We always had great names like that for our operations.

I was holding my Eagle Claw overlay, all ready to slap it on the map. But the colonel said, "Absolutely not! They are trying to get us to commit our reserve and then they're going to attack us someplace else. We're not going to fall for that trick."

"Yes, sir." We'd been through this exact same test the year before, and you could read the scenario in the training manual. But committing the reserve is a major decision, so it didn't seem like such a bad call to let the situation develop a little more.

The umpires allowed the enemy to penetrate another mile. It was now 0100 hours and someone went to wake the colonel, who'd gone to bed. He came into the operations center wearing his dressing gown and fuzzy slippers. The umpires from the 82nd Airborne were too amazed to laugh, and I wanted to crawl in a hole and die.

By this time we had Eagle Claw up on the map. Major Whelan said, "Sir, the enemy has penetrated another mile. They are now deep within the perimeter. I've got the reserve company alerted and we are prepared to execute the counterattack."

The colonel said, "Tom, I told you before, it's a trick! Don't you understand?"

"Sir, given the depth of the penetration—"

"No, no, no! I am not going to do it!" And he stormed out of the tent.

An hour later, we could hear the blanks being fired two hundred meters from our command post. We were about to be overrun. We got the colonel out of bed again, and Whelan said, "Sir, I strongly recommend we commit the reserve at this time."

He threw a fit. "I've already told you! I'm not going to be fooled by this ruse!"

Then one of the umpires from the 82nd said, "Goddammit, Colonel! Commit the fucking reserve so we can all go to bed!"

Our colonel wheeled around and said, "Who are you?"

"I'm your chief umpire, Colonel Withers of the 3rd Airborne Battle Group at Fort Bragg. Now will you just commit your goddamn reserve?" They argued back and forth until finally our colonel said, "All right. I'll commit the reserves. But I've got witnesses here. Tom, Norm, you witness this. If you try anything dirty, these people will testify that you ordered me to commit my reserve." So we committed the reserves, the enemy pulled out, the perimeter was restored, and everybody finally got some sleep.

The next day was attack day and the division commander, Major General William C. Westmoreland, joined us. A division commander had never come to this exercise before, but when Westmoreland heard what had happened the previous night, he decided to attend. This did not improve the colonel's performance. Instead of executing the flanking attack the situation called for, he ordered a full frontal assault. When it became obvious this tactic was a disaster, the colonel came unglued. He started running up behind troops and shaking their canteens, saying, "Soldier, why don't you have any water?"

Westmoreland never said a word. But when we got our critique, the battle group's grade was 80. It was the only time in the history of annual training tests that anyone could remember a grade below 95. The next day the colonel was gone. He might have been a brilliant staff officer, but in looking to push him ahead, somebody had put him in the wrong job. I'd have felt sorry for him, except that if we'd been at war, his brand of leadership would have gotten us all killed.

7

When orders came through in June 1959 instructing me to report for a two-year tour in Berlin, I felt as elated as I had as a kid when I learned I could leave Princeton, New Jersey, for Tehran. I was trading rural Kentucky and Tennessee for the place where war between the United States and the Soviet Union was most likely to break out.

Berlin was a fifteen- by twenty-mile enclave, a hundred and ten miles into East German territory, that had been jointly occupied by U.S., British, French, and Soviet troops ever since World War II. But that winter, Nikita Khrushchev had issued an ultimatum giving the western powers six months to pull out. And although he let the deadline pass when President Eisenhower pressed for negotiations, Berlin was still a powder keg.

When I got there I saw why Khrushchev found the place so annoying. His half of the city was still in ruins from the war, and East Berlin's streets gave a chilling picture of life under totalitarianism. The stores were mostly bare—I once passed a grocery whose window display consisted solely of three dusty cans of condensed milk stacked in a pyramid. Pedestrians in drab coats hurried along furtively, never raising their eyes; I'd look down long avenues and there wouldn't be a single automobile, not one. Along the Stalin-Allee, East Berlin's grand boulevard, the government had built long rows of imposing facades; but when I looked through the archways I saw mounds of rubble behind, and the facades themselves were so shoddy that their marble panels were falling down.

West Berlin, by contrast, was like a glossy advertisement for free enterprise, having benefited from ten years of West German rebuilding. The wartime rubble had been long since bulldozed and planted over to make beautiful hilly parks. Everywhere you looked were neon lights; department stores spilled over with the latest fashions; Volkswagens and Mercedes and Porsches zipped through the streets, and the Kurfürstendamm, the city's main drag, was crowded with sidewalk cafes, restaurants, pastry shops, and nightclubs. Khrushchev denounced all this as decadence and predicted that "West Berlin will fall into our hands like a rotten apple." But as East Germany was shabby and gray and oppressive, and as there was no Berlin Wall yet, East Germans who did not want to live under communism simply came to Berlin and crossed over into a western sector. Each weekend hundreds did, and the constant influx of refugees on their way to a life of freedom made West Berlin feel like one big party.

I found the U.S. Army in Germany far more professional than the Army I'd left behind at Fort Campbell. Units understood their mission, trained hard, and were ready for battle. Whereas at Fort Campbell I'd been pressed into jobs usually reserved for captains and majors, in Berlin I was back to being a rifle platoon leader—ordinary lieutenant's work. But that didn't bother me, because the duty was exciting and the forces here really *were* America's elite. The Army carefully screened everyone assigned to the city, right down to the privates: if you had the slightest blot on your record, you didn't go; one screw-up while you were there and they shipped you out. The Army did not want to detonate the powder keg by mistake.

My platoon patrolled the border, went on maneuvers with the British and French occupying forces, and stood guard at Spandau prison, where Rudolf Hess and two other Nazi war criminals were serving their sentences. We marched in countless parades—a way of broadcasting the American presence—and learned riot control, because of a persistent concern among western planners that communist provocateurs would someday cross over into West Berlin and create civil disturbances in order to give the Soviets a pretext to invade. Under the circumstances, motivating my men was easy— I just took them to the border, pointed to the East Germans and Soviets, and said, "There is your enemy." That's all it took.

After three months I was handed a plum assignment: to command the battle group reconnaissance platoon. In a typical infantry outfit, the recon platoon gets the best troops and operates with far greater autonomy than other platoons. Its primary mission in war is to run patrols and report on enemy activity in front of the battle group and on its flanks, as well as to probe and raid enemy positions. In Berlin we also had an exciting and unique peacetime mission: to conduct actual reconnaissance against East German and Soviet forces.

When we went on patrol in East Berlin, four of us would pile into a couple of Army sedans and cross the border at the Brandenburg Gate armed with nothing more than radios. (We carried no guns, in keeping with the pretense that all four occupying powers were friends.) Sometimes we were to gather intelligence; other times we were simply to exercise our right of free access, supposedly guaranteed to all members of the allied armed forces.

The rules of engagement that governed our conduct at the border seemed surreal. The border was manned by East Germans, but since the United States did not recognize East Germany, we were not supposed to acknowledge or stop for them. So if the East German guards had a barrier down, we'd keep driving, albeit very slowly, until they raised it. If one of them stepped in front of our sedan, we'd act as if he weren't there, and continue to drive slowly, straight toward him, until he stepped aside. Then there were the times that an irritable guard would take aim at us as we drove by. We'd keep our eyes straight ahead, praying he'd stick by the principles of occupation that guaranteed us safe passage, and that machine-gun bullets would not explode through our rear window. It made for an interesting game of chicken. Once through, we'd drive around making notes on troop concentrations, types and locations of military equipment, the location of radar antennas, anything of military interest.

Every year, the Soviets and East Germans staged a big May Day parade in Marx-Engels-Platz, East Berlin's central square, where they would show off their tanks, artillery, and rocket launchers. So as not to tie up the square during the day, they held dress rehearsals the week before at three o'clock in the morning. Our orders were to find out if the parade was going to include any new military hardware.

We crossed at the Brandenburg Gate late at night without any problem. But when we arrived at Marx-Engels-Platz, we made a wrong turn and somehow found ourselves in the middle of the practice parade itself. We went right past their reviewing stand, our two Army sedans mixed in with the Soviet rocket launchers and tanks. The East German and Soviet officials were furious and ran after us, hollering and waving their arms, but at that moment we reached a cross street, screeched around the corner, and took off. Such was the cat-and-mouse game in which we were involved.

Because our platoon was so active, we had seventy-five men, more than twice as many as an ordinary recon platoon. Our troops were handpicked by the battle group personnel officer, and the belief that we were the very best permeated everything we did. We even had a sign on the door of our weapons storage room that read:

RECON WEAPONS
Best Weapons Room in the Battle Group

The men knew that every inspector who saw that would vow, "I'll show these guys." But we *knew* our weapons maintenance was that good. By setting a standard of excellence and keeping to it, we built our pride and morale even higher.

The platoon was so close-knit that the worst punishment was to be excluded from it. If a soldier got out of line, I could chew him out or confine him to quarters. While that might bother him a little, the most fearsome threat I could make was to boot him out, although I'm not sure I fully appreciated that until I actually did it once. We had a superb radio operator, a guy from Alabama named Eiselle, who seemed to have a perverse need to buck authority. Because he knew he had an integral role in the platoon, he figured he could get away with skipping formations, coming back late when on an evening pass—an array of minor infractions. I'd talked the problem over with my NCOs and we'd warned him repeatedly. When I finally told him he had to leave, he couldn't believe it—he broke down. Sergeant First Class Winton, the highest-ranking NCO in my platoon, witnessed the incident and later told me, "Sir, I thought you were gonna give in when he started to cry."

"I almost did."

"I could see that, and I was hoping that you wouldn't. You did the right thing, sir." Coming from a tough old soldier like Winton this was high praise indeed, and he proved to be right. The effect was to make the rest of the men more disciplined. They closed ranks, and their pride in themselves and our platoon grew even fiercer, so the loss of a good radioman was more than offset by the gain in cohesion.

Simply walking around the city was good for morale. Even though we were technically still an army of occupation, the Berliners treated us as heroes. At Christmastime German families would invite American soldiers into their homes. When the Harlem Globetrotters came over, the city's biggest exhibition hall was packed. On weekends at bars along the Kurfürstendamm, the Germans would send over a round of beers and toast the USA. Nobody had forgotten the great airlift of 1949, when the Americans and British rescued the city from Stalin, and they never lost sight of the fact that if the United States pulled out, West Berlin would be crushed.

Bonn had an interesting refugee policy, which resulted in a four-to-one ratio of women to men in West Berlin. When people arrived in the city from the East, only those with certified skills were eligible for immediate resettlement elsewhere in West Germany. Most of the men had trades, but most of the women didn't, so the female population of Berlin soared. Women were easy to meet—including marvelous, well-educated women from good families. It was the best place in the world to be a bachelor. A favorite night spot was the famous Resi, a bar downtown, where each table had a big number on it and a telephone. (It was also a favorite meeting place for spies.) If you spotted somebody you liked across the room, you called her up, and if you were wearing a U.S. Army dress uniform, your phone rang like crazy.

Some officers liked to flaunt their German girlfriends at the officers' club, but I did most of my dating away from the flagpole. I'd take my girlfriend to neighborhood restaurants and quiet local night spots. Nonetheless, I was frequently confronted by one or another of the older officers' wives at cocktail parties. "I understand you're dating a German girl," she'd say. "That's all well and good. But you certainly don't want to marry her. What you want to do is go home and marry a good American girl." I didn't see why marrying an American was so great, given the way many American couples treated each other. Sometimes I'd see a woman who'd spoken to me like that, or her husband, making time with somebody else's spouse at the very same party.

Halfway through my tour in Berlin I was picked to be the aide to General Charles E. Johnson III, a one-star who commanded all the American troops in Berlin. He was a gregarious fellow who laughed a lot and with great gusto—whenever he was at the officers' club people knew he was there. General Johnson was forty-nine years old and had served as a lieutenant colonel in Rome at the same time as my father, but I'd never met him there. Watching him maneuver in the complicated military-diplomatic world of Berlin was a little like watching Pop in Iran. We were running joint exercises with the British and French, dealing with diplomats and West German civil authorities, and, of course, confronting the East Germans and Soviets. I learned a great deal about the flexibility, patience, and professionalism required of a general in an international arena. For instance, Willy Brandt, the mayor of West Berlin, once demanded free use of U.S. Army tents, and troops to set them up, so he could hold a political rally. As commander of an occupying army, General Johnson could simply have said, "Get lost." But in deference to Brandt's international stature, Johnson politely turned him down, diplomatically explaining that he wasn't authorized to spend American taxpayers' money in this way.

I was responsible for the general's schedule and went with him everywhere. If an invitation came for a diplomatic reception or cocktail party, it was automatically assumed I was included. If General Johnson wanted to take his fellow generals to dinner at a German restaurant, I'd set it up and sit right there at the table to make sure nobody's order got lost in translation and that the bill was correct. Ever since my days in Tehran, I'd enjoyed dealing with foreigners, and I understood the need to adapt to them rather than force them to adapt to me. I spoke mostly German with my girlfriend, and my command of the language was so fluent that Berliners had difficulty pegging me as an American if I wasn't in uniform. I was a very effective go-between. By this time I owned a dog, a German shepherd named Troll, and on Sunday afternoons I'd dress in a tweed jacket and lederhosen and take him for a *Spaziergang*, or promenade, in the Grünewald, the local wood, stopping for beer in the little restaurants along the way. I thought I was a pretty dapper fellow.

Even as I enjoyed myself, I knew the good times could end in an instant. This was a period of extreme tension between East and West—that September, Khrushchev had pounded his shoe at the United Nations, and the following summer the Berlin crisis came to a head. The flow of refugees into West Berlin became a flood, with *thousands* of people now crossing each weekend, and the East Germans watched as many of their most talented citizens fled in what became famous as the "brain drain." One week after my tour ended, the Berlin Wall went up.

In the summer of 1961, the Army promoted me to captain and brought me back to Fort Benning, Georgia, for a year of advanced training in infantry tactics. The program was disappointing because it placed little emphasis on troop leadership—a subject I feared not enough Army officers understood, if my experience at Fort Campbell was any indication. Instead, the Army had become obsessed with its hardware, having by this time staked out a role for itself in the cold war arms race by amassing an arsenal of atomic artillery shells and short- and medium-range missiles capable of carrying nuclear warheads. So the course at Fort Benning that got the most attention was on the battlefield use of nuclear weapons—we learned to analyze a target in terms of the type and size of atomic blast needed to destroy it. The lectures were highly technical, very demanding, and naturally based on highly classified material; each man had his own safe and had to lock up his workbooks after class. The school let you know that if you didn't master the subject, you didn't have much of a future in the Army.

I did well at Fort Benning, finishing in the top third of my class, and earning high ratings in speaking and writing. I even walked off with a tennis trophy, playing doubles with my old West Point roommate Leroy Suddath, who had turned up in the same course. I also won something called the George C. Marshall Award for Excellence in Military Writing, with an essay entitled "The Battered Helmet." It recounted a commander's thoughts upon having won a major battle and began:

> The general trudged wearily into his tent and threw his helmet on the bunk. Another large dent was noticeable in the already battered headpiece. He made a mental note that he must see about getting a new one. Obviously, as chief of all the ground forces in the area, he shouldn't be seen wandering around the battlefield with a battered helmet.
>
> He sank into a chair and pulled off his mud-spattered boots. It had been an exhausting day. From the predawn preparations, through the attack and smashing victory, to the relentless pursuit, the general had been on the move. Now, he had won a major battle which would probably spell the end of the campaign and might even bring about the end of the war. He felt a deep sense of accomplishment, but was too tired to be jubilant. Besides, there was still a great deal to be done.

I wrote it to demonstrate the timelessness of the principles of war: after an involved review of the day's attacks, feints, and counterattacks, the reader learned that the general in question was Julius Caesar, and the victory his triumph on the plains of Pharsalus over the rebel Pompey.

I was eager to command soldiers in battle, but there was no war, or at least none I knew about. Reports had surfaced that President Kennedy was sending more and more forces to Vietnam, but all we knew was what we read in the papers, and nobody was calling it a war. Instead I was offered what seemed to be the ideal peacetime assignment: two years at taxpayer expense getting a master's degree at the University of Southern California. Working with the USC School of Engineering, the Army had arranged a specially designed curriculum of mechanical engineering and aeronautical engineering courses that led to a master's degree in guided missile engineering. Only a small number of officers were chosen to attend and the Department of Mechanics at West Point offered to sponsor me if I would agree to serve as an instructor at the academy for three years afterward. That seemed a fair trade for a graduate education that would enhance my ability to serve my country—but I confess my thinking was also influenced by the fact that I was still a bachelor, that the graduate school was in southern California, and that I had never in my adult life lived off a military post.

I did not want to arrive unprepared, so I started work on my suntan right away. It was late spring and the weather in Georgia was hot, so every day at lunch hour I'd lie in the sun outside the Fort Benning officers' club. Just before setting out for California, I traded in my old Renault sedan for a beautiful maroon Oldsmobile F-85 convertible with a powerful 185-horsepower V-8.

I visited Mom in New Jersey in June, and then Troll and I headed west. The interstate to California wasn't built yet, so we went to St. Louis, picked up Route 66, and drove through the southwest, stopping at the Grand Canyon to sightsee and at Las Vegas to gamble. Nobody had told me about the Las Vegas Strip, so I got a room in a hotel downtown and ended up in a seedy gambling parlor nearby thinking, "Gee, Las Vegas isn't as glamorous as I expected." I won two hundred dollars. As I crossed the southwestern deserts, I drove with the top down, wearing nothing but a bathing suit. I endured terrible heat, but by the time I reached Los Angeles, my tan was truly splendid.

On the day I descended into the L.A. basin, I was stunned. The weather was hazy and overcast, and before long I found out it had been that way all spring. I was the only man in Los Angeles with a tan. Everywhere I went people said, "Oh, you must be new here." They kept asking if I was from Arizona.

I rented a small apartment in Redondo Beach. It had an ocean view—if you looked real hard between two buildings across the street you could just see the water—but to me it was like paradise. I saw USC as an opportunity to make up for a terrible gap in my education: I'd never been to a coed college. That led to a second rude shock. On the opening day of school, another bachelor officer and I went to the student union at lunchtime. We strolled up to the entrance, looked through the glass, and spotted three coeds about to come out who looked exactly like the missed cheerleaders of my dreams. I straightened up, sucked in my stomach a little, and gallantly held open the door. They looked at me, then at each other, and said, "Thank you, sir." I suddenly saw myself as they did—a grown-up, obviously pushing thirty—and realized with sorrow that my fantasies of coed college life would remain forever unfulfilled.

The third shock was that I was strapped for cash: Army pay didn't go very far in L.A. Counting my housing allowance and captain's pay, I was taking home four hundred dollars a month, and I needed half of that just to cover my car and rent. The men with families had it especially tough. As a result, we all had to moonlight. One officer worked at an appliance store, another sold shoes at Sears, Roebuck. I found a job teaching calculus and basic engineering at the Northrop Institute. I also taught accounting and business math at South Bay Women's College, a secretarial school. South Bay didn't pay as well as Northrop, but it did wonders for my morale.

There was a place a few blocks from where I lived where the regular piano player was Bobby Troup, who was married to the singer Julie London and gave great renditions of the blues. My tastes in popular music ranged from there all the way to Elvis Presley, but I loved folk music best. I may have been the only captain in the United States Army who listened avidly to The Weavers and Peter, Paul and Mary. I owned every record Joan Baez made and was a great Bob Dylan fan. "The Times They Are a-Changin' " was one of my all-time favorite songs. I liked the folk singers for their sound, but the message of social activism appealed as well. I was a liberal and an admirer of President Kennedy, and Barry Goldwater made me uneasy when he blustered about rolling back the clock on civil rights and challenging the Soviet Union to war.

Getting a master's degree was nowhere near as tough as I'd expected. We spent only a third as much time in the lecture hall as we had at West Point, and our courses were by and large easier. Most of the officers in the program were convinced that the future of the Army lay in missile warfare and atomic weapons, and took the cold war rhetoric about the imminent risk of nuclear war literally. I had trouble believing it. In Berlin I'd lived for two years with the possibility that war could break out any minute. Yet the talk of a massive Soviet attack on the United States just didn't seem plausible. Their bombers had too far to fly; their missiles weren't that good; and we had all kinds of early warning systems, not to mention the ability to retaliate. I didn't approach the subject of guided missile engineering with the same reverence as some of my colleagues did.

The only time my sense of confidence was shaken was during the Cuban missile crisis. During my first October at USC, President Kennedy announced the naval "quarantine" on a Monday, calling it that and not a blockade because a blockade is an act of war; but it was clear to me that we were on the brink. On Tuesday morning I walked down to the beach. The ocean and sky were both gray, and as I looked out over the water, I spotted an airplane in the distance. I suddenly thought, "That could be a Soviet bomber coming to drop a hydrogen bomb on Los Angeles." I knew my mind was playing tricks on me, but for the rest of the day I could not shake the feeling of impending doom. Late that afternoon I went to buy groceries at Fort MacArthur, the Army post in nearby San Pedro, and stopped when they sounded retreat. I stood at attention as the flag was lowered, and told myself that if war came, I was prepared to do whatever had to be done. But at the same time I was uneasy: I wasn't attached to a military unit—at the moment I was out on my own in the civilian world. What if the bomb had gone off in downtown Los Angeles? I had no orders. What would I do? Pick up the telephone and call the Pentagon? The telephone wouldn't be working. And if war began, the Pentagon would have a lot more to worry about than thinking up an assignment for Captain H. Norman Schwarzkopf at the University of Southern California.

The crisis passed, and my fears had long since subsided when my fellow officers and I spent six weeks the following summer touring southern California aerospace plants and R&D facilities. At North American Aviation I met some of the engineers working on the Apollo program and stood under one of the giant Saturn rocket nozzles designed to lift astronauts on their way to the moon. I'd taken a course in astronautics that focused on the engineering theory of spaceflight, and I was in awe of these engineers who were actually making it happen. They were thinking in terms I'd never imagined—I was bound to the earth, while they were opening the doors to the heavens. It was the one time that I regretted not having set my sights higher at grad school. Sure, I'd make a good instructor of engineering at West Point, but that was all I'd be. These men were pioneers, on their way to frontiers I would never explore.

Much as I enjoyed my stint at school, and much as I welcomed the breather, the world darkened that year with the assassination of President Kennedy. The following spring I was shaken by news of a death closer to home. The *Los Angeles Times* landed on the doorstep one morning with a front-page story about a West Point friend named Tom McCarthy who had been killed in Vietnam. Tom had joined the Infantry a couple of years ahead of me. Whatever the politicians were calling it at that point, I realized that there was indeed a war on, and Americans were dying. Yet here I was, finishing two years of soft life in California and committed to three more years of soft life at West Point. My sense of duty told me this wasn't right; Vietnam was where I belonged.

And would they die for it? That's the question one finally has to ask oneself. Would I die for it! And the answer one has to say—is—yes, sir, I would!

That made a tremendous impression on me. It summed up succinctly why I was going to Vietnam. It had nothing to do with careerism. It had to do with ideals.

8

At Travis Air Force Base, north of San Francisco, I met up by chance with a West Point class-mate, John Snodgrass. We sat together on the long flight to Saigon. Our refueling point was Honolulu, where we passengers all tumbled out of the plane and did what we thought soldiers headed for war were supposed to do—went straight to a bar and fortified our courage with exotic tropical drinks. Two hours later we were loaded back into the plane. At takeoff there was a lot of shouting and joking, but before long the merriment gave way to loud snores. Our freshly starched khaki uniforms had long since wilted and wrinkled, and I couldn't help but think that when we finally landed in Saigon, we wouldn't look much like the razor-sharp, steely-eyed warriors we all thought we were.

Later, as the soldiers woke up, the cabin again filled with friendly banter and laughter. John had been specially trained to work with the Vietnamese, and now he took a couple of hours to fill me in on their culture. I asked dozens of questions. Suddenly somebody looking out a window said, "There's land below," and we knew we were over Vietnam. From then until we landed, the cabin was very, very quiet.

We were met at Tan Son Nhut airport outside Saigon by Army buses with wire mesh covering the windows. The mesh, we were told, was to prevent Vietcong from throwing grenades into the buses: the week before, they'd actually set off a bomb in the main terminal. About fifty of us officers filed through the building, where the floor was still strewn with broken glass and debris, and crowded into a hot wooden shack that had been hastily erected next door. There we received a briefing on the dos and don'ts of Vietnam—mostly don'ts: don't congregate in large groups, don't wander around Saigon alone at night, and so on. Then the buses took us downtown to the Hotel Majestic, where we were to stay pending our assignments. The hotel was a five-story white plaster building at the far end of Tu Do Street, right on the Saigon River; the river itself was wide and muddy with numerous sampans and lush vegetation along its banks. It looked like rivers I'd seen in *National Geographic*.

John had a list of Saigon's best restaurants, and he and I planned to celebrate our arrival with a good dinner. But by the time evening came, jet lag was catching up with us, and we agreed to eat in the Majestic's own rooftop dining area instead. We had just placed our orders when *wham!* there was a loud explosion below. John and I leaped up, while everybody else in the restaurant threw themselves to the floor. I asked the waiter, "What was that?"

He said simply, "VC."

We peered over the edge of the roof as sirens started to wail. Directly across the street, moored to the riverbank, was a floating restaurant, and men and women, many of them bloody, were crowding across the gangplank that connected it to shore. Suddenly another explosion blasted them from the gangplank into the water. It was a carefully coordinated Vietcong attack: first the terrorists set off a bomb inside, and then, as panicked diners and employees tried to escape, they detonated an antipersonnel device called a Claymore mine that had been positioned to spray the gangplank with shrapnel. The death toll came to thirty-one and included nine Americans. When the waiter told us the name of the place—the My Canh—we realized with shock that it had been number one on our list of recommended restaurants. That was my welcome to Vietnam.

The next morning I barely avoided a different kind of disaster: I was handed a staff assignment that would have kept me in Saigon for my entire tour of duty, helping create mathematical computer models of the war. I threw myself on the mercy of a lieutenant colonel in the personnel office, pleading for a job in the field. At first he insisted none was available, but finally he relented and asked if I'd be willing to work with the 25th ARVN division. "ARVN" stood for "Army of the Republic of Vietnam"; the 25th was a South Vietnamese division that had seen several of its units nearly annihilated in fights with the VC. The division was notorious for running off in battle, leaving its U.S. advisors behind. I replied, "If that's where the work is, that's where I'll go." At least I wasn't going to be stuck behind a desk.

The next day, I was at the central issue facility drawing my jungle boots and other gear when my old West Point roommate Leroy Suddath showed up in camouflage fatigues and a red beret, the uniform of the Vietnamese airborne and its advisors. "There you are!" he said. "Why didn't you let me know when you got here? Come on. I'll get you an interview with my boss." Colonel Francis Naughton, the senior advisor of the Vietnamese Airborne Brigade, was a tall, lean, veteran paratrooper who didn't seem particularly impressed that I'd gotten good grades at West Point and served in the 101st Airborne and in Berlin. But when I mentioned I'd learned French in high school, he brightened. "Great!" he said. "Not all the Vietnamese understand English, but most of them know French. How would you like a job with the airborne?" He made a call to cancel the job I'd begged for the day before and have me assigned as advisor to a newly formed "task force" of paratroopers. Thanks to Madame Maurette and the École Internationale, I'd landed one of the most coveted advisory assignments in Vietnam.

The Airborne Brigade was South Vietnam's best and most cohesive fighting force, six battalions and five thousand men. The Saigon government used it, along with the Marine Brigade, as a "national reserve," or all-purpose backup: whenever things went to hell in an important province in a battle involving the regular army, the airborne or marines would be sent to the rescue—and this happened often. Many of its officers and NCOs were tough old pros who had been fighting communists since before Dien Bien Phu. While they welcomed our presence and U.S. military aid, they never missed an opportunity to remind us that this was *their* war. On my very first night in the jungle, Captain Hop, the chief of operations for the task force I was assigned to, told me that he'd rather see his children dead than in the hands of the communists, and added without rancor, "You advisors come here and fight, but after a year you can go back to your peaceful homes. But this *is* our home and we're fighting for our survival."

Some of the airborne officers viewed America's entry into the war with a kind of ironic detachment. One night, after I'd been in Vietnam several months, I was sharing a bottle of cognac with a task force commander named Major Hao. Suddenly he grinned and asked if I knew he was a Buddhist.

"Of course," I said, puzzled.

"Well, when I am reincarnated, I want to come back as an American advisor. You have the perfect setup! When we win a battle, the advisor gets a medal. When we lose, the commander gets the blame."

There were thirty-five of us attached to the Vietnamese airborne, and those based in Saigon shared a villa downtown called the Manor BOQ—"bachelor officers' quarters." On the third floor we had a bar and dining room, and we all chipped in to pay Gun, our Chinese cook, who fixed fantastic meals. We lived like soldiers of fortune: we'd go through harrowing experiences with our units in the field, but when the action ended we'd come back to Saigon, where there wasn't much to do but party and stand by for the next crisis. The battalions would return to their bases at Tan Son Nhut airport or outside Saigon, rearming themselves and training new recruits, but their commanders were so skilled and experienced that they didn't need our help. We remained on alert twenty-four hours a day, and when the call came for our units, we'd pack our rucksacks, hop in a jeep, race to airborne headquarters at Tan Son Nhut, and fly into battle. Once in the field we lived as Vietnamese: we ate what they ate, slept where they slept, wore the same uniform, and suffered the same hardships. We were much more involved with our Vietnamese counterparts than many of the U.S. advisors attached to regular units. They typically worked with the Vietnamese only by day; at night they usually returned to the relative safety of American compounds.

I came to Vietnam pumped up for battle, but the enemy I faced in my first outing, in mid-July, was the climate. We were assigned to open up and secure a stretch of Route 19, which was the main road running across Vietnam and through Pleiku, a provincial capital in the central highlands about 230 miles north of Saigon. It was commonly referred to as *la rue sans joie* ("street without joy"). From the air the terrain along the highway looked flat, but once under the triple-canopy vegetation, we encountered one huge ravine after another, coated with slippery mud. We had to probe each ravine to make sure it did not harbor Vietcong. We moved in single file, skidding down into dirty water at the bottom of each slope, then clawing our way up the other side. Huge elephant-eared plants held in the sweltering heat, mosquitoes whined in our ears, and bizarre-looking insects dropped on us from the jungle canopy.

I began to have doubts about how well suited I was to this work. I'd been told that Vietnamese soldiers lacked endurance, but I'd be halfway up a ravine, panting and drenched with sweat, and watch a scrawny paratrooper packing a hundred pounds of mortar ammunition on his back breeze by with a smile. One word I'd learned was *nuoc* ("water"). I'd turn and gasp, *"Nuoc!"* and my driver, Sergeant Hung, would struggle forward with an oversize canteen. Hung had served with the airborne since the days when it had been the French colonial parachute battalions. He thought he'd finally landed a soft job in the rear when he was assigned to be my driver—he didn't realize that Vietnamese drivers were expected to accompany their advisors into the field, carrying their equipment. He and I had gotten off on the wrong foot because I'd insisted on bringing a huge, clumsy rucksack stuffed with regulation U.S. Army gear—a sleeping bag, a jungle hammock, multiple changes of clothing, and so on—and Hung had to carry it. (On *my* back, I carried a heavy radio, since my primary responsibility in battle was to serve as a one-man fire coordination center. Most of the firepower available to support our missions was American, so it was my job to call for artillery barrages, helicopter gunship attacks, and Air Force strikes if we needed them; make sure the pilots or gunners knew where we were; adjust their fire so it rained down on the enemy and not on us; and finally, coordinate the resupply and medevac helicopters during lulls in the fighting.) As we marched, Hung complained constantly in Vietnamese about the vast quantity of water I consumed—I later found out his nickname for me was "water buffalo"—and his buddies were cracking up.

The way the South Vietnamese airborne operated in the field was totally unlike anything I'd seen in the U.S. Army, and I found a lot to admire about it. For one thing, the Vietnamese ate better and more sensibly than U.S. troops. When we set out on a march, each man had live ducks and chickens tied to his belt, with their beaks taped so they couldn't make noise. He also carried in his rucksack pork and beef from freshly slaughtered animals and cans of sardines, and wore across his chest a long brown fabric tube packed with rice. The staple was always rice, but you could gauge how long we'd been in the field by what was served with it for dinner: the first few days we ate pork; the next few days beef; then chicken and duck for several more days. At around the twenty-day mark, when the mission generally ended, we were down to the canned sardines; any longer than that, unless we were resupplied, we would eat only rice and whatever leafy vegetables we could forage from the jungle and boil. We ate sitting cross-legged on the ground around the communal rice bowl and meat dishes, which were seasoned with fermented fish oil called *nuoc mam*. It was standard lore among Americans in Saigon that *nuoc mam* tasted vile, but most of them had never tried it. I thought it was great!

By the end of that first twenty-five-mile march, which took fourteen hours, I was beginning to fit in. We set up our command post in the jungle above the highway and camped for several days, while a South Vietnamese engineer battalion repaired bridges the VC had damaged, and supply trucks began to roll. Sergeant Hung and I had long talks in pidgin French about our families, our countries, and most of all my equipment. Once I had promised to replace it with lighter, Vietnamese-style gear, he and I became friends. Toward the end of our operation, the engineers invited the airborne officers down for a bridge-blessing ceremony. We were each given a glass with a large belt of scotch. We then watched as the engineers slaughtered a pig and filled the glasses the rest of the way with blood, and then made a toast. My year in Tehran had taught me what was expected, so while the engineer battalion's U.S. advisor wouldn't touch his drink, I gulped mine down, toasting the completion of the bridge. My Vietnamese counterparts were surprised and pleased. They later told me that the engineer battalion commander had meant to embarrass the Americans present and that by my action I'd brought great credit to the airborne. Simply by drinking that toast of scotch and blood, I'd begun building ties that would prove vital in battle.

During the last week of July, we were ordered to carry out a mission for Major General Vinh Loc, the commander of II Corps of the South Vietnamese army, headquartered in Pleiku. Vinh Loc wanted us to drive the Vietcong away from a South Vietnamese special forces camp, Duc Co (which we pronounced "*due* koh"), that sat in the so-called 24th tactical zone at the western end of Route 19, where the road crossed into Cambodia. Duc Co had been established to prevent guerrillas from coming across the border, but the camp had been more or less under siege all summer and the guerrillas had gained the upper hand. Nobody knew how many enemy were in the camp's vicinity, but the estimate was two VC battalions—about seven hundred men.

I was impressed when I saw the operation order: it was written in letter-perfect U.S. Army style by the Vietnamese commander of the 24th tactical zone (one of Vinh Loc's subordinates) and his American advisors. They'd seemingly thought of everything—the order called for a twenty-minute air strike to drive back the enemy, then we were to make a mass helicopter landing in a field about seven miles northeast of Duc Co. An air strike was standard procedure before a helicopter assault, because helicopters are like ducks: easiest to shoot just as they get ready to land. So the last thing any helicopter-borne soldier wants is for the landing zone to be "hot," or under fire, when he comes in. From the LZ we were to attack west on foot to the Cambodian border, then south in a wide arc around the camp. The order gave us an "air cap" of fighter-bombers, support from "all available artillery," and, as our reserve, a battalion of Vietnamese rangers stationed at the airfield in Pleiku.

We had forty-eight hours to prepare our men. I spent the night helping the task force commander, Major Nghi (pronounced "knee"), plan the ground operation. The brother of a famous war hero, Nghi was a peculiar character who was horribly scarred from a training accident in which he had mistaken an incendiary grenade for a smoke grenade and set it off in his hand. While he briefed the troops the next morning, I went to the U.S. air section at Vinh Loc's headquarters to double-check on the strike. But the guy at the desk gave me a blank stare and said, "We don't know anything about an operation at Duc Co." When I read him the order—twenty minutes of air strikes—he insisted they'd received no such request. "By the way," he said, "if you're going tomorrow, you won't have any air, because we need forty-eight hours to line up the planes."

I thought, "Holy smoke, I'd better get some artillery." I went to the office of the fire-support coordinator, showed two guys there my order, and asked, "What artillery is in that area?" They laughed!

"Do you know what 'available artillery' is?" said one. "There's one mortar tube inside the special forces camp."

"Yeah, but don't depend too much on that," added his partner, "because *they only have twenty rounds of ammunition left!*" They were a regular comedy team.

It was standard procedure to reconnoiter the LZ with the helicopter flight leader who would command the air portion of the mission. We flew to Duc Co low-level all the way to keep from attracting enemy ground fire, and found out there *was* no LZ—there were too many trees. The staff officers had simply taken a map and picked a spot that looked like a clearing; but in the jungle, yesterday's clearing is today's forest. We found the nearest open field on the other side of Duc Co, about fifteen miles away.

I started to panic. The 24th tactical zone commander and his advisors had issued a textbook order, but apparently no one had bothered to see that it was carried out. When I got back to Pleiku, I stopped for a quick bite at the snack bar and, happily, ran into Captain Paul Leckinger, who was the advisor to the ranger battalion that was scheduled as our reserve, and whom I knew from Fort Benning. I told him how worried I was about the attack and said, "Well, at least you'll be there if we need you."

He gave me a funny look. "What are you talking about? My battalion has just come back from three weeks in the field. We sent them all home to their villages for a break. We couldn't get them back together in less than three or four days."

By now it was seven o'clock at night, and we were supposed to attack early the next morning. I went to find Major Nghi. Nghi's eyes got wider and wider as I told him what I'd discovered. Nghi was not known as a great commander—a couple of my fellow advisors had warned that he owed his job to political connections—but he understood we were in bad shape. "What do you advise?" he asked.

"I advise that we not go! We need a forty-eight-hour delay to sort some of this out." Nghi agreed. He notified his headquarters in Saigon, then reluctantly called General Vinh Loc.

As they talked on the phone, I could hear the general screaming at him all the way across the room. Nghi looked very unhappy as he hung up. He said we'd been ordered to a ten P.M. meeting at the general's house and explained nervously that Vinh Loc was not only an important general, but also a Vietnamese prince who expected unquestioning obedience.

The general lived in a colonial mansion in downtown Pleiku. We were ushered into a large marble-floored hall, at the far end of which was a semicircular elevated platform. Vinh Loc was seated in the middle; next to him was his U.S. advisor, a full colonel; and along the semicircle was an array of Vietnamese generals and colonels and *their* U.S. advisors. It looked very much like a military tribunal. In front of the platform were two chairs—one for Nghi, one for Schwarzkopf.

Vinh Loc started off by demanding, in Vietnamese, "How *dare* you say you're not going to attack tomorrow?" Major Nghi explained that he had requested the postponement on the recommendation of his American advisor. So Vinh Loc turned to his own advisor, the U.S. colonel, who turned to me: "Captain! How *dare* you tell them not to attack!"

I said, "Sir, we do not have air support, we do not have artillery support, we've had to switch to a completely new landing zone—which means we don't have a ground tactical plan—and we don't have a reserve."

"For crying out loud, it's just a couple of VC battalions! And what do you mean, you don't have any air support? If you get in trouble, we'll divert airplanes from someplace else. That's the way we operate."

I kept my voice as steady as I could. "And what about the air strike on the LZ before we go in?"

"You don't *need* it. There's *nobody* out there."

"Sir, I just don't consider that adequate air support."

The colonel was seething. He narrowed his eyes, leaned forward, and said sarcastically, "Well, *Captain*, just what *do* you think would be adequate air support?"

I was pretty angry, too. "Sir, when it's my ass out there on the ground, about a hundred B-52s circling overhead would be just barely adequate. Now, I'm willing to settle for something less, but I'm not willing to settle for nothing."

I had only been in Vietnam a month and a half and had never been in combat. But I knew that what Vinh Loc and the colonel were pressuring us to do was wrong, and if I was really there to advise the Vietnamese, I had to tell the truth. The colonel went on and on, at one point calling me "an embarrassment to the United States of America." But I held my ground. I understood that he and his subordinates had not seen battle in Vietnam, either—they were all rear headquarters types—and, moreover, that it had been their responsibility to see the operation order through. Finally he snapped, "Captain, you're obviously not suited to this job. You're relieved of your duties."

"Sir, I'm sorry. You're not in my chain of command. The only one who can relieve me is my senior advisor."

In an absolute rage, he screamed, "Get me his senior advisor on the telephone!"

It was now 11:30 at night, but they somehow tracked down Colonel Naughton in Saigon. He listened to what we each had to say, then told the colonel, "I support Captain Schwarzkopf, and my Vietnamese counterpart here supports Major Nghi. All we ask is a forty-eight-hour delay."

The next morning Colonel Naughton himself arrived, surveyed the situation, and declared I was right. As it turned out, we needed seventy-two hours to prepare the attack properly. The staff in Pleiku kept saying, "It's only two battalions of VC, for crying out loud." As far as they were concerned, H. Norman Schwarzkopf was the world's biggest pain in the ass. But Naughton did one other classy thing: orders had come through to promote me to major, and he pinned on my new rank, on the spot.

———

On the night before the attack we camped in a huge field halfway between Pleiku and Duc Co. At dawn a massive flight of forty helicopters arrived. As I climbed on a ship with eleven Vietnamese soldiers, my mouth went completely dry—a sign of the adrenaline surging through my system. Soon we lifted off—and our helicopter clipped a tree, the only tree in the entire field, fluttered forward, and crashed into the jungle just off the end of the pickup zone. We were badly banged around but nobody was actually hurt, so we walked back to get a ride on the second lift. Meanwhile, the first lift had arrived at Duc Co—one of the refinements we'd made in the plan was to land on the airstrip right next to the camp—and despite the fact that we'd gotten our advance air strikes, the pilots radioed that they were under mortar fire. The LZ was hot. Now my mouth was *really* dry. As we flew in I could see a sunbaked red clay airstrip surrounded by jungle on three sides, with the camp in a clearing to the south.

Mortar rounds started falling around us as we landed, but no one was hit as we ran up a small incline and into the camp. Duc Co itself wasn't much to look at—a triangular barbed-wire enclosure smaller than a football field. It had obviously taken a pounding. I could see craters and caved-in bunkers everywhere. An American second lieutenant was waiting for me. He introduced himself as the camp advisor—I don't think I'd ever met a happier man. For weeks he'd been out here with fifty South Vietnamese, constantly getting reports that they were about to be overrun; we represented his salvation.

The next day we moved out of the gate on the north side of the camp and began our two-day sweep. The plan was still to work our way west to the Cambodian border, then turn south, and finally circle back to the west side of the camp. By midafternoon we'd covered ten or twelve miles across the same tough jungle terrain we'd encountered in our earlier operation along Route 19. Major Nghi and I walked with the 3rd Battalion, which had three advisors—First Lieutenant Chuck Gorder, a young ROTC graduate, up at the front of the 500-man column; Captain Mike Trinkle in the middle of the battalion with us; and Sergeant Vince Romano, a World War II and Korea veteran who worked the rear. Even farther back was the 8th Battalion, which had its own three-man advisory team headed by Captain George Livingston, Jr.

We were within a few miles of the Cambodian border when I heard firing up front. I radioed the lieutenant and said, "Gorder, what's going on?"

"Sir, it's VC!"

"Gorder, I *know* it's VC. How many VC are there? What's their disposition?"

"Sir, all I know is there's a whole hell of a lot of them! We're getting fire from all sides and we're taking casualties!"

We returned fire and I called in some helicopter gunships that drove the attackers off. Finally we moved up to Gorder's position at the edge of a clearing. Three paratroopers had been killed. Unlike some other South Vietnamese units, the airborne went to great lengths to return soldiers'

My father, Herbert Norman Schwarzkopf, graduated from the United States Military Academy at West Point, New York, in April 1917—three months early because of World War I.
(U.S. MILITARY ARCHIVES)

My graduation from West Point on June 5, 1956. I was commissioned a second lieutenant in the United States Army Infantry.
(U.S. MILITARY ARCHIVES)

At age three and a half in 1937. I had a happy early childhood in Lawrenceville, New Jersey.

Age two, with my mother. She had left her home in West Virginia for a successful nursing career in New Jersey before her marriage.

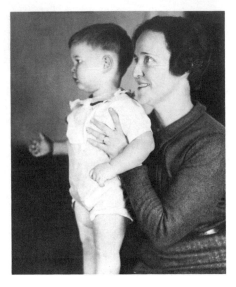

After my father left for Iran in 1941, my mother regularly took pictures so he could see how quickly my sisters and I were growing (Sally is seated, Ruth Ann standing).

Our family home was an old stone house built in 1815. Each Christmas it was decorated with elaborate lights.

I considered myself a typical international scholar, complete with long hair and sandals, after a year of school in Geneva, Switzerland.

My mother and sisters (Sally at left, Ruth Ann at right) joined my dad and me in Tehran in 1946. My sisters were not happy to leave their New Jersey school, and I wasn't particularly happy to have them with us.

My father as a colonel in Iran. This is how I remember him— a great military man, but with a warm smile and a twinkle in his eye.

For an official audience with King Abdulaziz al-Saud in Saudi Arabia in 1945, my father, then a brigadier general, was required to wear full Arab regalia.

Summer 1952. Leroy Suddath was my tentmate at the end of Beast Barracks, and my roommate all four years at West Point. Later he commanded all Army special forces, worldwide.

As a West Point plebe I learned to keep my sense of humor, which made it easier to get through some of the rough challenges there.

Summer 1953. My dad was very proud that I had made it through plebe year.

Duc Co special forces camp, August 1965. When I went to help a wounded Vietnamese paratrooper after a mortar attack, this picture was snapped by a young AP reporter, Peter Arnett. (AP/WIDE WORLD PHOTOS)

After the siege at Duc Co, we had to walk out along Route 19 to friendly-held territory some sixty miles away. The tank in the rear is from the rescue column that relieved us. (UPI / BETTMANN)

Colonel Truong, the chief of staff of the Vietnamese Airborne Brigade, was one of the finest commanders I have ever known. Here, after a major victory in the Ia Drang Valley, November 1965.

Lieutenant Colonel Kha was my South Vietnamese counterpart, the commander of the First Task Force of the Vietnamese Airborne Brigade. His daughter was killed in her home by a rocket fired accidentally from a U.S. helicopter.

On February 14, 1966, at Bong Son, I was wounded in what we later jokingly called the St. Valentine's Day massacre.

Brigade commander (of the 1st Brigade of the American Division) Colonel Joe Clemons, the hero of the battle of Pork Chop Hill in Korea. He was a straightforward, no-nonsense soldier and one of the best bosses I've ever had.
(U.S. ARMY PHOTOGRAPH)

In front of my tactical operations center on Fire Base Dottie, 1970. The metal ammunition cans behind me were filled with sand and piled two deep around the bunker.

I was presented my third Silver Star as the result of a minefield incident in the spring of 1970. It was pinned on by Major General Meloy, the division commander of the American.
(U.S. MILITARY PHOTOGRAPHER)

Brenda Holsinger had left the small town of Timberville in Virginia's Shenandoah Valley to become a flight attendant with TWA. We met in 1967 and were married on July 6, 1968, at West Point. The best man and the ushers formed the saber arch for us to walk through.
(SALVATORE J. PALAZZO, HIGHLAND FALLS, N.Y.)

My thirty-seventh birthday was celebrated with me flat on my back in a body cast after spinal surgery. I had asked Brenda for a tennis racket as incentive to get me back on my feet.

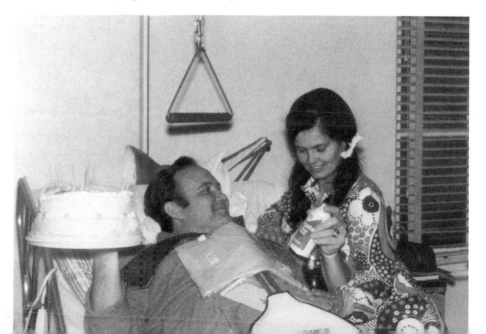

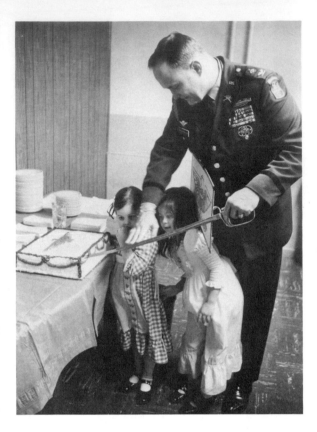

I was promoted to full colonel on November 1, 1975. My daughters, Cindy (age five) and Jessica (three), watched wide-eyed as I cut the promotion cake with an Army saber.

In Mainz, Germany. My daughters and I took weekend *Volksmarsche* through the beautiful countryside. Cindy (age eleven), Jessica (nine), and I are accompanied by our shepherd, Rocky.

My son, Christian, was born on June 20, 1977, while I was stationed at Fort Lewis, Washington, commanding my second brigade.

Christian celebrated his tenth birthday at Fort Lewis, where I had returned as a lieutenant general to command the post and I Corps.

I'm glad I was able to attend Jessica's graduation from high school in June 1990, because the crisis in the Arabian Gulf kept me from being with her when she entered college that fall.

Brenda and I visited Cindy during her freshman year at Auburn University.

Fort Greeley, Alaska, 1975. One of
Brigadier General Will Latham's favorite
training techniques was the long march.
This one was twenty-five miles. Since I was
brigade commander, I got to do it three
times. (U.S. MILITARY PHOTOGRAPHER)

(Top, right) I loved every minute I was
stationed in Alaska. Surrounded by nature's
beauty, I took every opportunity to explore it.
(Center, right) Summer 1976, on the Kenai
River in Alaska. Fishing and rafting are two
of my favorite hobbies.
(Bottom, right) In fall 1989 I spent two
weeks on a float trip north of the Arctic
Circle with Major General Tom Fields. At
the end of the trip Tom said I looked more
like a mountain man than a general.

As a brigade commander at Fort Lewis in 1977, I was happy to be part of the dramatic change taking place in the Army.

Brenda and Major General Dick Cavazos pinned on my brigadier general stars during a ceremony at Fort Lewis in June 1978.
(U.S. MILITARY PHOTOGRAPHER)

As military commander in Mainz, Germany, I placed great emphasis on family activities. In 1980 I served Thanksgiving dinner to Jessica's third-grade class.

Canberra, Australia, 1979. As a member of a military planning group, I met with counterparts Brigadier General Neil Paramour (left), from Australia, and Brigadier General Rob Williams, from New Zealand.
(U.S. MILITARY PHOTOGRAPHER)

My military counterpart in Mainz in 1980 was Major General Hermann Vogt, a strong supporter of German-American relations.
(U.S. MILITARY PHOTOGRAPHER)

Fort Stewart, Georgia, 1984. I congratulated the winner of the pie-eating contest during the annual Family Day that I instituted.
(U.S. MILITARY PHOTOGRAPHER)

I had to give up command of I Corps in 1987, after only one year, and return to Washington. I took my final review with Forces Command commander Joe Palestra and my successor, Lieutenant General Bill Harrison.
(U.S. MILITARY PHOTOGRAPHER)

(*Left*) My first visit to the National Training Center in the California high desert, in 1983. I would return many times with my division.

As commander of Central Command, I visited Kuwait in late 1989. Major General al-Sanii, chief of staff of the Kuwaiti armed forces, invited me to wear Arab clothing at a dinner party in my honor.

While visiting Pakistan in the summer of 1989, I went to the Khyber Pass and inspected an honor guard of the famous Khyber Rifles.

bodies to their families. Several soldiers carefully wrapped each dead man in a poncho; then they tied cords around the neck and ankles, suspended the bodies on poles, and prepared to carry them with us. But when a U.S. Army helicopter landed with the fresh ammunition I'd requested, the Vietnamese soldiers decided to load the corpses on the helicopter for the return flight to Pleiku. "No bodies!" the crew told them, and tried to push the bodies off while the pilot revved his blades. I ran over and climbed on the skid next to the pilot's window. He was a captain. I shouted, "What's going on?"

"We don't take bodies in this helicopter. They get blood and shit all over the flight deck."

"Hey, we've got to get these bodies out of here. If we don't, we have to carry them."

"I don't give a shit. We ain't takin' bodies out." If those had been dead Americans, I knew he wouldn't have thought twice, and that burned me up.

"Let me tell you something, sport. Either you take those bodies or you stay here on the ground, because I'm not gonna get off this skid. If you take off, I'm gonna fall off this airplane and die. Are you willing to take responsibility for that? And second, if you try to take off, I'll shoot your ass!" Either he didn't realize I was bluffing, or the fact that I was a major focused his attention: they loaded the bodies on.

Without knowing it, I'd endeared myself forever to the South Vietnamese troops. They saw an American who cared enough about them to climb up on a helicopter skid and make the pilot accept their dead. Word went all the way back to Saigon and up to Brigadier General Du Quoc Dong, the airborne commander. For weeks after I returned to Saigon, American advisors came up and told me they'd heard about the incident from their South Vietnamese counterparts.

We reached the border, marked by a destroyed roadblock, and spent a couple of hours setting up for the night: arranging our forces in a roughly circular defensive perimeter, posting security, digging foxholes for protection from mortar fire, and planning fields of fire in the event of an attack. The night passed without incident, and the next morning we moved out. This time the 8th Battalion led, the 3rd brought up the rear, and our task force group walked right in the middle. We worked our way south along the border on overgrown jungle trails until around noon.

That's when all hell broke loose. One minute the jungle was quiet. The next we were getting shot at from every direction. A bullet going by doesn't make a bang; it makes a nasty little *crack!* which is actually a small-scale sonic boom. All around, I heard *crack-crack-crack-crack*, but the jungle was so dense we couldn't see a damn thing. Then we heard a hollow thunk—the sound of a round being dropped into a mortar tube—and knew that round was heading toward us. There was no place to hide; the foliage along the trail was so thick that a man could lean against it and not fall. All we could do was stand and wait until *wham!* the round hit. Nobody panicked. I was struck by the paratroopers' almost fatalistic coolness; they'd been under fire many times before. A mortar round would land, someone would mutter in Vietnamese, "That one was close," and then we would move on as though nothing had happened.

But it was an endless, desperate afternoon; we had walked into a major concentration of enemy forces and they were waiting for us. We knew that if we failed to make it back to the special forces camp by nightfall, the enemy would maneuver into position to annihilate us that night or the next day. Five or six times that afternoon, whenever part of the task force got pinned down, I had to stop to call in air strikes, then wait to make sure the planes or helicopters accomplished their task. Major Nghi, desperate to get back to the safety of Duc Co, became increasingly impatient with me. Finally he and his staff simply left me behind. I waited for part of the 3rd Battalion to come up, ran into Sergeant Romano, and proceeded with him. He'd been through two wars, but looked grim. Every time automatic-weapon fire got close he'd look at me and say, "Holy shit."

Half an hour later we came under fire from enemy troops blocking the trail ahead of us. I called for another air strike and popped a smoke grenade to mark our position.

"Okay, I see you," said a pilot. "Where do you want it?"

"I need it about one hundred yards in front of me."

"Jesus, one hundred yards—that's awful close."

"If it's not that close it won't do us any good."

Romano was just ahead of me as the strike came in. We looked up and saw bombs that seemed to be falling straight at us. We panicked and started to run, but collided and fell down. The bombs sailed over our heads and landed in front, exactly as requested.

We finally got back to Duc Co at dark and I caught up with Major Nghi. He was with his staff, building a sandbag bunker. Before I could make an issue of the fact that he'd left me behind, I was confronted with a much more urgent problem. The 8th Battalion had made it back, but Mike Trinkle called on the radio, saying he and parts of the 3rd were still in the jungle, having trouble finding their way in. Meanwhile the troops *in* the camp, fearful of being overrun, were ready to shoot at anything that moved. I looked at Nghi. "Somebody's got to find the 3rd Battalion and guide them in." He just stared at me. "Don't you have somebody you can send?" I asked.

"No," he said.

"Okay, I'll go. Just make sure the camp doesn't open fire on us." He looked stunned. Apparently, he felt no obligation to go out, so he couldn't understand why I did.

As I walked out the gate, I had the same odd sensation that I'd experienced for much of the afternoon: a dissociation from my actions. It was a kind of out-of-body experience, as though I stood watching at a safe remove while Schwarzkopf went back outside the perimeter, at the risk of being blown away. But there was nothing eerie or mystical about it. I was kind of on automatic pilot.

I made my way alone west of the camp across a wide clearing, all the while talking to Trinkle on the radio. It was pitch black, so I fired a little red flare to help the men orient themselves. "I think I saw it," Trinkle said. "Can you pop another?" The enemy was starting to shoot at me, but I did as he asked and moved on quickly. A couple of hundred yards farther into the jungle, I ran across soldiers from Trinkle's unit and pointed them toward the camp. Finally Trinkle and I linked up and I led the way back in.

We were surrounded. In the space of two days, more than forty paratroopers had died and at least twice that number were seriously wounded. We radioed Pleiku and asked for medevac. "We're sorry," the response came back, "we can't fly out there. Too risky." Duc Co was in a basin, and airplanes trying to land had to come in over a high ridge where the enemy was dug in. But an Air Force pilot, Lieutenant Earl S. Van Eiweegen, heard about us that night in a Pleiku bar and volunteered for the job. The next morning we carried our wounded on stretchers to the airstrip and waited.

The instant his four-engine C-130 turboprop appeared, the enemy opened fire. I didn't think Van Eiweegen and his three-man crew would make it. By the time the airplane touched down, it had been shot full of holes and was leaking hydraulic fluid from three or four places. The crew lowered the tail ramp, and Van Eiweegen kept the props turning while we loaded the men on stretchers. Meanwhile the airstrip came under mortar attack. More people were hurt, and we threw them on the airplane, too. Van Eiweegen sat in the cockpit with his copilot, waiting patiently until I gave the signal. Then he turned the airplane around and took off over the same ridge, getting shot up some more. Even though the plane was seriously damaged, he bypassed Pleiku and took the wounded straight to Saigon, where he knew they'd receive more sophisticated care. His flight was the most heroic act I'd ever seen.

Meanwhile, we had no idea how big an enemy force had hemmed us in. We sent out patrols during the day, and no matter which direction they took, they came under fire. We had U.S. Air Force forward air controllers, affectionately called Red Barons, flying around in Cessna 0-1s, to help direct the air strikes. When one checked an area a few miles away, I heard him exclaim, "Jesus! The whole field moved!" He'd seen hundreds of enemy troops with branches tied to their backs as camouflage, running for cover before the bombers arrived.

Peter Arnett, at the time an AP reporter, was in Duc Co for the first three days of the siege. After shooting lots of film, he told me he wanted to leave to file his story. One of the South Vietnamese battalion commanders had been seriously wounded and I persuaded Pleiku to try a medevac flight at night. "You can come in with your lights off and the VC won't see you," I said.

To guide the helicopter in, Pleiku instructed me to position four men with flashlights at the corners of the landing pad. Holding one of those flashlights took nerve: a sniper might shoot you. I told Arnett, "Okay, if you want a ride, you have to hold one of these." We brought the wounded man out to the landing zone and listened as the helicopter began its descent. Over the radio the pilot told us, "I can't see your lights. How about shaking them so I can pick them up?" I called out that instruction to the others around the pad. A voice in the dark replied, "I don't know about you guys, but my flashlight's been shaking ever since we got out here." That was Arnett. The helicopter landed safely and he was able to leave.

Each night we went to bed with the conviction that the camp would be overrun and we would be killed. I learned to sleep with one ear cocked, because I knew that at some point every night there would be a mortar barrage. The thunk of the rounds dropping into the mortar tubes was audible hundreds of yards away, and when I heard that sound I knew I had maybe eight seconds to make it to a foxhole. Many nights I'd find myself sprinting for my foxhole without quite knowing why, but sure enough, explosions would erupt all around. In the morning we would wake up with relief and the realization that we might make it after all.

As the days went by, conditions in the camp became grim. Early on, the mortars destroyed the water tank. Although there was a watering hole outside camp, the enemy knew about it; so when we needed water, we had to send a platoon to fight its way down and back. Food ran low, but when the airborne tried dropping fresh supplies, the planes stayed so high that the wind blew the parachutes outside the perimeter. We asked them to stop, because all they were doing was feeding the enemy. We were soon down to rice and salt. Sometimes Sergeant Hung would crawl out through the wire and come back with a certain kind of root he'd dig up in the jungle. It looked like a big turnip, and could be eaten raw, so we'd sit with our rice and pass the root back and forth, taking bites.

Finally, after about ten days, a task force of South Vietnamese marines arrived from the east to relieve us. The enemy, which had by now been identified as two full *regiments* of North Vietnamese regulars—several times as numerous and much better trained and equipped than the two Vietcong battalions we'd expected to fight—turned to ambush the marines before they reached the camp. A battle erupted and the marines forced the communists back to their sanctuary across the Cambodian border. Our daylight patrols stopped getting shot at, and planes were able to fly low enough to air-drop supplies.

A radio call came from a staff officer in Pleiku, and I was asked for an enemy body count. "I haven't the slightest idea," I told him. "We didn't stop to count, for crissakes. We were fighting through them trying to get back to the camp."

"Well, give us your best estimate, because we're required to report a number."

I called the battalion advisors, who said things like, "I don't have any idea. But my Vietnamese counterpart says maybe fifty." I compiled those guesses and called Pleiku. "Look, I have an estimate. It's one hundred and fifty. But I want you to understand that I have no confidence in that number. We pulled it out of a hat." When the official report went in, it said, "Body Count: 150." I felt like I'd been party to a bureaucratic sham.

Meanwhile, we had about twenty of our own corpses lying by the runway starting to putrefy and the medics were telling me we had to get them out for health reasons. U.S. Army helicopters from Pleiku were crisscrossing the sky above the camp, though still high up because they thought it was too risky to land. That made me crazy and for the first time I lost my temper in public. All the tension and fear of the last two weeks came boiling out and I got on the radio screaming, "You sons of bitches! We gotta get these fucking bodies out! Why won't you come down and help us?" Naturally, it was a violation of radio procedure to use profanity.

A helicopter finally did land—and out climbed Vinh Loc's senior advisor, the colonel who'd wanted us to carry out our assault without support. "Who made that last radio transmission?" he demanded. The answer was obvious—I was the only person with a radio on his back—and I wasn't about to take any crap from him. When he saw me he became very conciliatory, which was lucky for me because otherwise I'd probably have done something that would have gotten me in serious trouble. He said, "Major, I know that in the heat of battle you can get carried away, but you've got to maintain your self-control and not scream at people on the radio."

"Goddammit, sir, I've got to get these bodies out of here."

"Don't worry. We'll take care of it," he said, and ordered two more helicopters in. We had to carry the bodies and load them on ourselves, because they reeked and the crews wouldn't touch them. As we picked up one, a mixture of putrefying body fluids ran out of the poncho and over my arms. When we finished I washed and washed and washed, but the smell seemed impossible to get off.

———

The colonel had an unstated motive for landing in the camp. He'd evidently scheduled a major briefing at Duc Co to review the siege for a high-ranking general and needed to check out the facility. The next morning the colonel came back with his entire Pleiku staff. They descended on us wearing clean, starched uniforms and beautifully shined boots, carrying their map boards and overlays and easels and pointers. When they ousted the camp commander from his building to get ready for their briefing, I sat wondering, "How the hell do *they* know what happened at Duc Co? They weren't here!"

Soon the sky *filled* with helicopters. Only one of them contained the general and his staff—the rest were full of reporters and cameramen, who walked into the camp and ignored us standing there dog-tired and filthy from two weeks of combat. They looked at us, through us, and away from us all at the same time. Then they went inside for their briefing.

Eventually the general and the colonel emerged. The colonel said to him, "Sir, this is Major Schwarzkopf, who was the senior advisor on the ground." The general came over and recoiled a little because I hadn't had a change of clothes in a week and had been handling bodies and stank. Meanwhile, the cameramen had followed and several reporters came up with microphones. "No, no," the general said. "Please get the microphones out of here. I want to talk to this man."

I'm not sure what I expected him to say. Maybe something like, "Are your men all right? How many people did you lose?" or "Good job—we're proud of you." Instead there was an awkward silence, and then he asked, "How's the chow been?"

The chow? For chrissakes, I'd been eating rice and salt and raw jungle turnips that Sergeant Hung had risked his life to get! I was so stunned that all I could say was, "Uh, fine, sir."

"Have you been getting your mail regularly?"

All my mail had been going to my headquarters in Saigon and I assumed it was okay. So I said, "Oh, yes, sir."

"Good, good. Fine job, lad." *Lad?* And with that he walked off. It was an obvious PR stunt. He'd waved off the microphones, but the cameras were still whirring away. At that moment I lost any respect I'd ever had for that general. The next night, back in New Jersey, the local TV station called my mother and told her that her son was going to be on the evening news. She watched the report, and until the day she died, she always spoke glowingly of the wonderful general she'd seen talking to her son in Vietnam and bucking up his morale.

————

I'd gone to Vietnam for God, country, and mom's apple pie. But by September I was fighting for the freedom of my South Vietnamese companions and friends. We airborne advisors often provoked the scorn of other American advisors working in provincial towns like Pleiku and Kontum. They thought we were crazy to decline invitations to sleep inside their safe, air-conditioned compounds.

"No, I'm sorry," I'd say. "We stay with our unit."

"You *what?* You stay out there with the gooks?"

"Yeah, we stay out. And don't call them 'gooks.' They are South Vietnamese military."

"How do you know those little fuckers aren't gonna walk off and leave you at night?"

"They won't. We're members of their unit!" And they never did. The other Americans' disbelief was partly a rationalization for not exposing themselves to danger; but to be fair, some of the units to which they were assigned were not nearly as competent militarily as ours. I was confident staying with the airborne because I had no doubt about their ability to fight and their concern for my well-being.

I felt more fulfilled than I ever had before. I was glad to be in Vietnam and happy at my work, helping men I liked and respected fight for their country and their freedom.

But the war was already changing from a mainly regional conflict to a struggle between North Vietnam and the United States. On General Westmoreland's recommendation, President Johnson was pouring in hundreds of thousands of U.S. troops—at least six divisions during my tour of duty alone—and all over South Vietnam, U.S. Army bulldozers and cement mixers and cranes were carving out roads and building command posts, airfields, helicopter pads, and logistical bases. Brand-new harbors were going in along the coast. While I wasn't involved—it all seemed part of another war—the kind of fighting in which we engaged soon reflected this dramatic shift.

Hanoi's answer to the mass influx of Americans was to increase its own force in the South. The North Vietnamese had never before sent large units into South Vietnam, and the guerrillas in the South generally avoided attacking large concentrations of U.S. or South Vietnamese troops. But in the late summer and autumn of 1965, Hanoi radically changed its tactics. Three army regiments—some seven thousand men—massed in the central highlands (we'd stumbled into two of these units at Duc Co, as they were crossing from Cambodia into South Vietnam). Their plan was to sweep down from the highlands onto the heavily populated coastal plains near Qui Nhon, thereby cutting the country in half. That attack was thwarted in mid-November, when the U.S. 1st Cavalry Division (Airmobile) crushed a large part of the communist force along the Ia Drang River (pronounced "ee drang"), south of Duc Co. In what came to be known as the Ia Drang Valley campaign, helicopters were used for the first time to maneuver large American units in battle. It was a landmark in modern warfare and also a landmark for me, because it introduced me to the most brilliant tactical commander I'd ever known.

Colonel Ngo Quang Truong was General Dong's chief of staff. He did not look like my idea of a military genius: only five feet seven, in his midforties, very skinny, with hunched shoulders and a head that seemed too big for his body. His face was pinched and intense, not at all handsome, and there was always a cigarette hanging from his lips. Yet he was revered by his officers and troops—and feared by those North Vietnamese commanders who knew of his ability. Any time a particularly tricky combat operation came up, Dong put him in command.

The airborne was alerted to prevent the North Vietnamese regiments defeated in the Ia Drang Valley from escaping back into Cambodia. I was half asleep in my room at the Manor BOQ after a big meal of curried chicken and beer when the call came to get out to the airport. Truong had assembled an unusually large task force of some two thousand troops to go to the Ia Drang the following morning, and had chosen me as his advisor.

We flew in transports to the red clay strip at Duc Co, my old stomping ground, then by chopper south to the river valley. From the minute we stepped off our helicopters we were involved in skirmishes and firefights.

The valley was about twelve miles wide at the point where the Ia Drang flowed westward into Cambodia—and somewhere in those miles of dense jungle the main body of the enemy was on the move. We had landed to the north, and Truong ordered the battalions to cross the Ia Drang and take up positions along the Chu Pong Mountains, which formed a series of steep ridges to the south. It was fascinating to watch him operate. As we marched, he would stop to study the map, and every once in a while he'd indicate a position on the map and say, "I want you to fire artillery here." I was skeptical at first, but called in the barrages; when we reached the areas we found bodies. Simply by visualizing the terrain and drawing on his experience fighting the enemy for fifteen years, Truong showed an uncanny ability to predict what they were going to do.

When we set up our command post that night, he opened his map, lit a cigarette, and outlined his battle plan. The strip of jungle between our position on the ridges and the river, he explained, made a natural corridor—the route the NVA would most likely take. He said, "At dawn we will send out one battalion and put it here, on our left, as a blocking force between the ridge and the river. Around eight o'clock tomorrow morning they will make a big enemy contact. Then I will send another battalion here, to our right. They will make contact at about eleven o'clock. I want you to have your artillery ready to fire into this area in front of us," he said, "and then we will attack with our third and fourth battalions down toward the river. The enemy will then be trapped with the river to his back."

I'd never heard anything like this at West Point. I was thinking, "What's all this about eight o'clock and eleven o'clock? How can he schedule a battle that way?" But I also recognized the outline of his plan: Truong had reinvented the tactics Hannibal had used in 217 B.C. when he enveloped and annihilated the Roman legions on the banks of Lake Trasimene.

But, Truong added, we had a problem: the Vietnamese airborne had been called into this campaign because of high-level concern that American forces in pursuit of the enemy might otherwise venture too close to the Cambodian border. He said, "On your map, the Cambodian border is located here, ten kilometers east of where it appears on mine. In order to execute my plan, we must use my map rather than yours, because otherwise we cannot go around deeply enough to set up our first blocking force. So, *Thieu-ta* Schwarzkopf"—*thieu-ta* (pronounced "tia-tah") is Vietnamese for "major"—"what do you advise?"

The prospect of letting an enemy escape into a sanctuary until he was strong enough to attack again galled me as much as it would any soldier. Some of these fellows were the same ones I'd run into four months earlier at

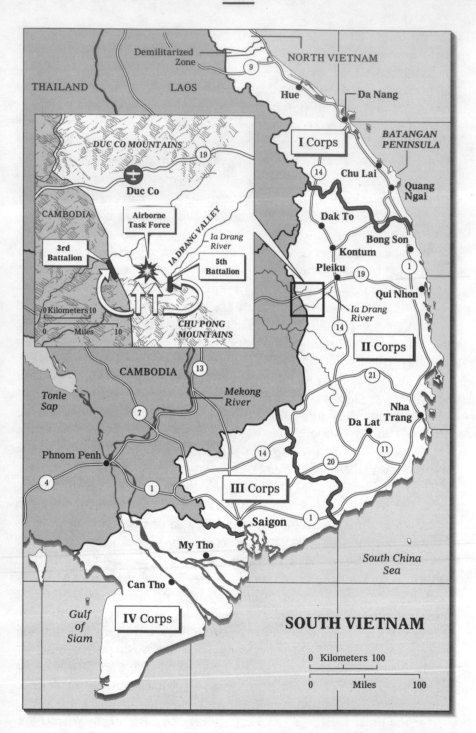

THAILAND

LAOS

Demilitarized
Zone

NORTH VIETNAM

9

Hue

Da Nang

I Corps

*BATANGAN
PENINSULA*

14

Chu Lai

Quang
Ngai

Dak To

Bong Son

DUC CO MOUNTAINS

19

± Duc Co

Airborne
Task Force

*Ia Drang
River*

CAMBODIA

3rd
Battalion

IA DRANG VALLEY

5th
Battalion

*CHU PONG
MOUNTAINS*

0 Kilometers 10

0   Miles   10

Kontum

Pleiku

19

Qui Nhon

*Ia Drang
River*

14

II Corps

21

CAMBODIA

13

*Mekong
River*

*Tonle
Sap*

7

Phnom Penh

4

1

14

20

Da Lat

Nha
Trang

11

III Corps

1

Saigon

My Tho

*South China
Sea*

Can Tho

*Gulf
of
Siam*

IV Corps

SOUTH VIETNAM

0   Kilometers 100

0   Miles   100

Duc Co; I didn't want to fight them again four months from now. So why should I assume that my map was more accurate than Truong's?

"I advise that we use the boundary on your map."

Long after he'd issued his attack orders, Truong sat smoking his cigarettes and studying the map. We went over the plan again and again late into the night, visualizing every step of the battle. At dawn we sent out the 3rd Battalion. They got into position and, sure enough, at eight o'clock they called and reported heavy contact. Truong sent the 5th Battalion to the right. At eleven o'clock they reported heavy contact. As Truong had predicted, in the jungle below us the enemy had run into the 3rd Battalion at the border and decided, "We can't get out that way. We'll double back." That decision violated a basic principle of escape and evasion, which is to take the worst possible route in order to minimize the risk of encountering a waiting enemy. Had they climbed out of the valley up the Chu Pong Mountains, they might have gotten away. Instead they followed the low ground, as Truong had anticipated, and now we'd boxed them in. He looked at me and said, "Fire your artillery." We shelled the area below us for a half hour. Then he ordered his two remaining battalions to attack down the hill; there was a hell of a lot of shooting as we followed them in.

Around one o'clock, Truong announced, "Okay. We'll stop." He picked a lovely little clearing, and we sat down with his staff and had lunch! Halfway through the meal, he put down his rice bowl and issued some commands on the radio. "What are you doing?" I asked. He'd ordered his men to search the battlefield for weapons: "We killed many enemy, and the ones we didn't kill threw down their weapons and ran away."

Now, he hadn't *seen* a damn thing! All the action had been hidden by jungle. But we stayed in that clearing for the remainder of the day, and his troops brought in armful after armful of weapons and piled them in front of us. I was excited—we'd scored a decisive victory! But Truong just sat, smoking his cigarettes.

———

Working as closely as I did with the South Vietnamese airborne, I saw the influx of U.S. combat units partly through their eyes, and I had mixed feelings. On the one hand, I welcomed the added firepower—the 1st Cavalry Division, for example, was wonderful at flying artillery into the jungle and starting to fire right away, which was what enabled our task force to operate as we did at the Ia Drang.

On the other hand, the Americanization of the war disturbed me. We were suddenly going in the wrong direction with the South Vietnamese. It was their country, their battle: eventually they would have to sustain it. I thought we should give them the skills, the confidence, and the equipment they needed, and encourage them to fight. Yet while our official position was that we were sending forces to help South Vietnam fight, the truth was that more and more battles were being fought *exclusively* by Americans, rather than by United States and South Vietnamese units working together. American officers began saying things like, "These guys can't handle the war. None of them are fighters. None of them are worth a damn." (The South Vietnamese Airborne and Marines continued to participate in combined operations with the Americans, but even we could see that supplies and equipment were harder to come by because American units had priority.)

We also tended to lose sight of the fact that we were in somebody else's country. For example, shortly after its arrival the 1st Infantry Division, the famous Big Red One, took up positions north of Saigon and test-fired its artillery. That was standard defensive procedure, but in this case, it also meant dropping shells onto people's rice paddies, which left the peasants terrified and offended.

As Washington abandoned the goals of the advisory effort, South Vietnamese soldiers—and their U.S. advisors—came to be treated as second-class citizens. One Sunday in November, I brought my counterpart into an American compound. He was a devout Catholic lieutenant colonel named Kha who had been to school in the United States and while there had discovered corn, which was impossible to find in Vietnam. I'd been eating out of his cooking pots for months, so when I heard that the officers' club in Kontum, near where we were operating, served canned corn, I immediately invited Kha to lunch, along with a couple of his staff and a couple of my battalion advisors. We were all looking forward to the break in routine. At the gate of the compound I found myself arguing with a military policeman who insisted that Vietnamese were not allowed. I settled that quickly enough (rank), but Kha, who spoke perfect English, knew he was being insulted, and I was embarrassed for both of us. When we got to the officers' club itself, a manager came over and informed us, "We don't serve Vietnamese." Again I settled the matter (size), but throughout the meal my stomach was in knots. I invited Kha to meals after that, but he always politely declined.

Certainly I was not the only American in Vietnam who was impressed by our hosts and sympathetic toward them: there were many others like me who lived with the South Vietnamese, fought by their sides, and learned to regard them with great respect. But we were definitely in the minority. The majority of Americans in Vietnam fell into two groups: members of purely

American headquarters and combat units who had no contact at all with the South Vietnamese military, and members of the U.S. advisory detachment who had no direct South Vietnamese counterparts and spent most of their time in offices with other Americans. Since they didn't know any South Vietnamese, they believed the stories that the South Vietnamese couldn't fight. Our senior commanders might have been able to set matters straight, but they too had a distorted view: there was no shortage of corrupt and incompetent Vietnamese officers at high levels, and while they were not the majority in the South Vietnamese military, they were the ones our leaders saw regularly.

Throughout the winter of 1965 we worked at a harrowing pace. As a task force advisor, I saw twice as much combat as advisors at the battalion level: the battalions took turns going into action, while task force commanders were almost constantly engaged. The communists had stepped up their attacks against the South Vietnamese army, and airborne units were constantly being plunged into extreme situations. In one operation our casualty rate was more than fifty percent. Over those six months, I fought in six major operations, and the constant exposure to jungle conditions took its toll. I had to be hospitalized twice, once in Nha Trang for malaria and once in Qui Nhon for amoebic dysentery. I was exhausted.

In late January the action shifted to the Bong Son plains, a roughly forty-mile stretch of coastal lowlands north of Qui Nhon that the VC had dominated for years. The South Vietnamese airborne, the U.S. 1st Cavalry Division, and American and South Vietnamese marines were sweeping the area in a coordinated maneuver to reclaim it. Under Lieutenant Colonel Kha, we had been in battle for a week—taking a lot of casualties as we attacked across open rice paddies into villages honeycombed with VC tunnels and bunkers. Everybody was jumpy. Then Kha received devastating news from Saigon, 180 miles to the south, where his family lived. A helicopter gunship parked at Tan Son Nhut air base had accidentally fired a rocket that had flown across the city, gone through a window of Kha's house, and exploded, killing his eight-year-old daughter. Kha had endured years of war courageously, but when he learned of her death, he broke. He went back to Saigon, and although he remained in the military, he never fought again.

Losing Kha rattled the entire task force, and as we sat for a day in the grim little village we'd just taken, I felt terribly uneasy. Matters grew worse when the airborne medics became very agitated, talking and waving their arms. I went to see what was wrong. They showed me a half dozen emaciated bodies that had been dragged from a Vietcong tunnel, and said that these men had died of cholera. I suddenly was a boy back in Tehran, where cholera was greatly feared, and the hair on the back of my neck stood up.

That same afternoon I was summoned to Bong Son to meet with Colonel Truong, whom General Dong had wisely sent to take command of the task force. We were to pursue a Vietcong force that was trying to slip away from the coast, westward to the An Lao Valley, long a communist stronghold. The enemy were thought to be in a particular hamlet, and Truong said we would mount an assault the following day, using the task force reinforced with ten armored personnel carriers. Again he pored over his maps late into the night. He'd turn on occasion and say something like: "Look at the terrain here. If we go in from this direction, we run the risk of the enemy being here. What do you think?"

He was still at it when I rolled up in my quilted poncho liner on the ground in the command tent and fell asleep. That night I had a dream. Someone was chasing me through the locker rooms at West Point. I raced down long hallways, one after another, until I came to a dead end. I cringed against the tile wall and whoever had been chasing me whispered, "We are going to wound you." Not "We are going to kill you," but "We are going to wound you." I woke up in a cold sweat. Then I thought, "What a dumb dream," and went back to sleep.

The next morning the armored personnel carriers arrived, and Truong said laughingly, "You've got it easy today. We'll put our command post in this personnel carrier, and you won't have to walk." The APCs were designed so that the top could be opened and troops riding inside could look out, but the Vietnamese were short and had difficulty seeing over the sides. So they'd put down wooden ammunition boxes to raise the level of the floor. My height now became a real disadvantage: standing on those ammo crates, I was exposed nearly to my waist.

The village looked like an island of trees and underbrush in the middle of open rice paddies. Our intelligence had been accurate: the Vietcong were present in great numbers and our battalions came under heavy fire. As we maneuvered forward in the APC, I noticed a tree line on our left. I said to one of the officers, "I sure hope somebody's cleared those trees." He assured me someone had, but as we drew parallel, a machine gun opened fire. Suddenly the air around me was going *crack, crack, crack* and I saw my left arm jerk—I was hit. I squatted down, bleeding heavily. My cheek and eyebrow and eyelid were all lacerated by fragments from bullets that had splattered against the armor plate, and my left eye swelled shut.

Somebody silenced the machine gun. I was in a little bit of shock as a medic bandaged me up. I pried open my eye to make sure I could still see.

"Hey, I'm all right," I thought, even though the wounds hurt like hell. Truong squatted beside me and said, "My friend, if you would like, I will turn the personnel carrier around, and we will go back and get you a medevac. But I don't want to do that. We're in the position we need to be in, and I need your help."

I told him I'd stay. The Vietcong had pinned down our men in the rice paddies and Truong wanted artillery and air strikes to cover our advance. This was standard procedure: the air strike would come first—planes would drop napalm, then bombs, and finally make a couple of strafing runs with their 20-mm Gatling guns; after the planes got out of the way, the artillery would fire; finally, the infantry would charge. But despite all the impressive firepower, we weren't making much progress. The VC would hide in their tunnels during the shelling, and the lulls in between gave them time to pop back into position to fire on us again.

The attack I outlined for Truong was designed to give the VC *no* opportunity to shoot back. It began with an air strike, but I told the pilots, "Give me your napalm and give me your bombs, but don't make strafing runs. The instant you finish bombing, let me know so we can fire our artillery." I said to the artillery officer, "I want fifteen minutes of artillery falling on top of the village after that. But when you finish, I don't want those guns quiet. I want you to shift your fire to the open area behind the village, so we cut off their route of escape." Meanwhile I had helicopter gunships waiting behind our forces, and told them, "The instant the artillery shifts, I want you coming in, straight over our heads, firing to our front directly into the village." And, I said to Truong, "At that instant, we should order the armored personnel carriers to attack, firing their .50-caliber machine guns. The APCs will advance under the gunships and we'll take the village." Truong agreed.

So that's what we did. Firing continuously we rolled into the village. It was a rout. We killed many VC, and when the paratroopers found the body of one very high ranking officer, they slung it on a long pole and paraded it around triumphantly.

We set up a command post in a hut that was, somehow, still standing, and I took some painkillers and rested. Pretty soon Truong walked in, chuckling and shaking his head. "*Thieu-ta* lives a charmed life," he said, repeating what he'd just heard the troops say.

"What are you talking about?" I said.

"Go outside and look at the personnel carrier."

I walked outside to where a bunch of sergeants were pointing to a row of bullet marks three inches below the top edge of the armor plate. The sergeants were saying, "Look, the VC aimed right at him and he only got hit by fragments!" I didn't feel too good about it—if that machine gunner had raised his barrel a single millimeter he'd have cut me in half.

The weather had turned nasty, slowing down the medevac helicopters, and it was night before my turn came. I waited in pouring rain, contemplating the destruction we'd wrought. Trees lay twisted on top of each other in grotesque shapes, flames burned in the background, and as the helicopter came in, its floodlight shined down through sheets of rain flickering with the light of the fires. That surreal scene made me remember my dream. I wondered what I'd do if I dreamed it again, especially if this time the guy in the hallway said, "We are going to kill you."

I fought one more major battle after Bong Son; by then I'd been awarded two Silver Stars and three Bronze Stars, fought in seven major operations, and survived being shot up once and afflicted by tropical diseases twice. But by the middle of March, when I'd been in Vietnam nine months, our new senior advisor, Colonel Jim Bartholomees, decided I'd seen enough combat. He called me in and said, "You've got three months left on your tour, but I don't want you in the field anymore. I want you to stay in Saigon."

I was bone tired and didn't argue. I spent the spring at the Vietnamese airborne division headquarters at Tan Son Nhut air base, still many levels below where major decisions concerning the conduct of the war were being made. While I might have moved from my worm's-eye view, I was now at a bug's-eye view. Never, during my tour of duty, would I have a sparrow's-eye view, much less an eagle's. I saw a lot of Truong and helped manage the expansion of the brigade into a full division.

Saigon itself had been transformed. When I'd arrived the summer before, the city had still been the pearl of the Orient—a quiet place of acacia trees, sidewalk cafes, and a gracious, relaxed pace. Americans were everywhere, but they fit in, and many had close friends among the Vietnamese. I seldom saw anybody in the street dressed for battle. Soldiers would wear khaki uniforms with short-sleeved shirts, or if they did wear battle fatigues, the clothes were clean and starched. The city had its red light district, called Tu Do Street, but even that was fairly subdued, and there were plenty of bars where you could go for female company with no expectation of sex. I'd often wander into such places with my buddies. While we drank our beers, the bar girls would sit with us, sipping tea that was billed to us as whiskey, which was how we paid for their company. We'd joke with them, play gin rummy and tic-tac-toe, and eventually get up and leave.

But in the spring of 1966, less than a year after my arrival, Ambassador Henry Cabot Lodge complained to U.S. troop leaders about the "Dodge City atmosphere" their men had created on Tu Do Street. I'd now take a walk there at night and watch trucks roar in from the boonies, drop their tailgates, and deposit troops in filthy jungle fatigues. Pretty soon those guys would be staggering around the streets, swigging bottles of Ba Muoi Ba and La Rue, the local beers, and brawling. Tu Do Street wasn't fun anymore. And the pearl of the Orient had turned into a bawdy house.

I wanted no part of that scene. I did stay close to the other airborne advisors, but for the most part I was immersed in Vietnamese life. I had a girlfriend named Loan (pronounced "lo-ahn"), a beautiful young woman from a Catholic family in Hue whose father was a professor at the university. My favorite night spot was the Arc-en-Ciel, an establishment that was half fancy nightclub and half Chinese restaurant. It had once been popular with the French Foreign Legion; now the nightclub was filled with American diplomats and reporters, while the restaurant was crowded with Chinese and Vietnamese. I spent my time in the restaurant.

Saigon was still dangerous, with occasional bombings downtown and a lot of violence on the outskirts. That spring the Buddhists rioted and we were ordered to stay home. The only problem was that the main temple was just up the street, and demonstrators clashed with the police right outside our front gate. We breathed tear gas for a week.

I took advantage of my time in the rear to make parachute jumps with the Vietnamese every chance I could. By summer I'd earned my U.S. Master Parachute Wings; I'd also completed three free-fall jumps to qualify for South Vietnamese Jumpmaster Wings, a badge rarely awarded to Americans. (I never liked leaping from aircraft without the reassurance of a static line, but my earning those wings was important to Colonel Truong.)

I was happier than I'd ever been and didn't want to leave. But when I wrote to the Department of the Army requesting an extension of my tour, it was denied, and I got a blistering note from the head of my department at West Point, saying in effect, "What do you think you're doing? Have you forgotten you gave your word that you'd come back here after a year? West Point put you through graduate school so you could teach. For the next two years, you are ours." I had to admit he was right.

The morning I left, when I said good-bye to Sergeant Hung, his eyes filled with tears. I'd never seen a Vietnamese soldier cry. I gave him my pistol, a gesture that violated about a hundred U.S. directives against fraternization with the Vietnamese, but I didn't care. When I arrived at the airport, part of the airborne was being sent into battle north of Hue. Truong was already on the battlefield. As my plane rolled down the runway, the Americans around me cheered, but I had a lump in my throat. Out the window I could see my paratroopers being loaded onto C-130s. It hurt leaving the men I'd fought with. I felt as if I were abandoning them.

9

In the early morning, two days after leaving Tan Son Nhut, I found myself aboard a helicopter, sweating from every pore. Below me was not Vietnam, but New York City. I'd arrived at Kennedy Airport and hopped on the shuttle that flew to Newark, with a stop along the way at the Pan Am Building in midtown Manhattan. Looking down at the city's buildings and streets, I was terrified that *we were flying too high*. I'd ridden helicopters hundreds of times in Vietnam, but never much above treetop level.

At Newark Airport, I climbed into a taxi. Wearing my uniform with all my ribbons and my Vietnamese airborne beret, I kept waiting for the driver to make a big fuss and exclaim, "Hey! You're just back from Vietnam, aren't you!" Nothing. So I fed him hints like, "Gee, I haven't seen Newark for a while." But he dropped me at my mother's place with scarcely a word.

She had moved to a cookie-cutter apartment in a high-rise building after Pop died—a place I didn't think of as home. She cried and hugged me at her door and over the next few days proceeded to stuff me with food as though I'd just been released from a POW camp. I was pretty disoriented. I couldn't think about anything but Vietnam. The war was all over the newspapers, but people seemed not to care. Even when Mom introduced me to a few of her friends, they only said things like, "Well, I guess now you'll be able to get on with your life." No one wanted to know about

Vietnam: the public wasn't caught up in the war, not at all like the spirit I remembered from my boyhood, during World War II. After two days I wanted to run through the streets yelling, "Hey! In Vietnam people are dying! *Americans are dying!* How can you act like nothing is happening?"

I tried to distract myself by buying things—a stereo, a recliner, and a green Mustang fastback coupé with racing tires and four on the floor. There had been no place to spend money in Vietnam, so I had a great deal of accumulated pay. In the three days I visited Mom I spent five thousand dollars. But it didn't help. I took long, solitary walks around the city and felt such pent-up aggression that I almost wished a mugger would try to jump me.

Even though the beginning of the academic year was still weeks away, I quickly returned to West Point. Before I'd left for the war, the school's isolation had bothered me; now West Point seemed like the perfect place in which to decompress. Yet as the familiar rituals went on around me—Beast Barracks, football camp, preparations for the academic year—they seemed inane. I longed for the moral clarity I'd found in Vietnam—life here seemed muddy and slow—and I missed the excitement of combat. One morning I received a long distance phone call from Chuck Gorder, the lieutenant who'd fought at Duc Co. "You know what I almost did last night?" he asked. "I almost went out and drove the wrong way on the freeway because I missed the sense of danger."

"Get a handle on yourself," I said with alarm. "I do not want you driving the wrong way on the freeway." Then I added with a laugh, "That's an order!"

"Yes, sir. Right, sir. I understand. I won't do it."

He wasn't alone: whenever the subject of Vietnam came up, I found it very hard to control my emotions. One afternoon when I'd been back a month I went to Delafield Pond, the academy's swimming hole. I hoped working on a suntan would help me relax. I'd just stretched out on a towel when one of my former social science professors, whom I'd thought highly of as a cadet, stopped to chat. He was on the permanent faculty and would never go to Vietnam. He wanted to discuss my Vietnam experience, but pretty soon was asking questions like, "Don't you think we're wasting our time trying to prop up a corrupt regime?"

Something happened that scared me: I felt an urge to beat him into the ground. It was so strong that I immediately excused myself from the conversation and walked away. I kept telling myself, "Don't lose control. Don't lose touch with reality." When I calmed down, I reminded myself that a lot of Americans were asking the same question and that I might be the guy on the outside who had to fit back in.

———

At war I'd come to envy men with families: the toughest South Vietnamese commanders gained sustenance from theirs, and family ties gave almost every American something to come home to. Even before I returned I'd decided to try to reestablish connections with my mother and sisters, particularly Ruth, from whom I was almost totally estranged. We hadn't seen each other since Pop's funeral, seven years earlier.

Just before the start of the school year, I left West Point and spent a week with her in Oberlin, Ohio. While I was still a cadet at West Point, she'd married a Brown University instructor named Simon Barenbaum—a considerable shock to Pop, since Simon was a French Marxist Jewish intellectual. I'd missed both ceremonies, one in a synagogue and one in a Unitarian church, because I couldn't get leave from West Point, but for years I'd listened to Pop proudly assert that he'd embraced Ruth's choice of a mate and had even worn a yarmulke at the ceremony.

Simon, now a professor at Oberlin, was attending a conference in France when I arrived. I really hit it off with my nieces and nephew: Nicole, fifteen; Miriam, eleven; and Kadia, eight. I don't think they'd ever met a soldier. Kadia was awed by my size, and Nicole and Miriam had deep discussions about the fact that while I could never marry Miriam because we were blood relatives, I could marry Nicole, who was Simon's daughter from a previous marriage. They were bright, affectionate, and fun-loving kids, and I felt myself begin to unwind at last.

Ruth was much as I'd remembered her, still active in the civil rights movement and immersed in what seemed to me weird stuff. She was now a member of Women Strike for Peace, an international organization opposed to the nuclear arms race. Their big issue was the contamination of milk by fallout from atomic tests, and Ruth, who'd inherited some of Pop's genius for management, had organized a march of Ohio mothers and babies that made all the local papers. We wanted to get along, so Ruth and I intuitively understood it was best not to exchange views on the war. But when I described Vietnamese culture and the people I'd met, she was intrigued. She heartily approved of the fact that I'd had a Vietnamese girlfriend and asked: "Why didn't you bring her back?"

Two days before I was supposed to leave, Simon and Ruth's best friend drove down from Michigan. He was a prominent French Marxist named

Raymond Jean. Ruth had told him I was there, yet he insisted on coming anyway and invited himself to stay. "Well," she said to me, "at least you'll have a lot to talk about." Raymond had been a professor in Vietnam before the fall of Dien Bien Phu and France's cultural attaché in Morocco.

He was a rumpled, bespectacled fellow, a lot older than I. We sat up late into the night, talking about what a beautiful country Vietnam was and about the sweetness of its people. Then he began telling me how the glorious Ho Chi Minh, by defeating France on the battlefield, had taught the colonialists the error of their ways. My answer was, "Ho Chi Minh represented only *one* faction in Vietnam. A lot of the men I fought alongside are Vietnamese who belong to families that have been run out of the North and have lost everything they own. They want their country back and they want to be free." We both were very polite and neither of us changed his mind. I later learned that Raymond announced to Simon and Ruth that he'd found me to be an intelligent and sensitive young fellow, but added, "What a tragedy that he would end up doing such deeds."

Ruth had only one guest bed. I'd slept in it all week, but since Raymond was older, I volunteered to sleep on the floor. It was only for two nights and I figured, "Hey, I've been sleeping on the ground for a whole year. Two more nights isn't gonna bother me."

But it did.

Lying on the floor in a sleeping bag I thought about how, not long ago, I'd been lying wrapped in my poncho liner in the damn jungle. Here I was, back in my own country, visiting my own family, and I was relegated to the ground again—*so a French communist could have the bed!* The more I thought about it the madder I got. "This is wrong," I thought. "This is really wrong."

We all spent the next day at Lake Erie, and I swam with the kids and had a good time. But as I drove off on Sunday, I was smoldering with anger. My plans to reestablish family ties weren't working out exactly as I'd hoped. I think I realized that if I was ever to have a close family, it would have to be with a wife and children of my own.

———

I was known at West Point as "a highly decorated Vietnam veteran." Not many instructors had been over, and none had come back with as many awards. Whenever the campus newspaper needed a picture of someone from Vietnam with a lot of ribbons on his chest, they'd trot me out. This got the attention of the cadets in the classroom. I became their Colonel

Hollingsworth or Major Moore, telling war stories when I was supposed to be teaching engineering mechanics.

Each time I was assigned to teach a new group of cadets, I'd start with the same spiel: "My name is Major Schwarzkopf. I want you to feel free to call me by my first name: Major. You'll hear some teachers at West Point call themselves 'academic officers.' I want to make it clear to you I am not an academic officer. I am a TOAD." I'd write on the board T.O.A.D. "Temporarily on academic duty. Don't you *ever* call me an academic officer. I'm a United States Army infantryman and damn proud of it!"

Often, I'd put aside the textbook, sit on the edge of the desk, and talk about what it meant to be an officer, about values and morality and honor. I felt that was my responsibility far more than teaching the principles of friction and why wheels roll down hills. Sure, I wanted the cadets to understand mechanics—but only so they'd graduate and become good Army officers.

Teaching gave me a new sense of mission. I had a unique talent for working with the goats. I knew none of them was ever going to qualify for the Corps of Engineers, but some would make great officers if only I could teach them enough mechanics to squeak by. I kept their attention by force of will, by theatrics, by zinging pieces of chalk against the back wall when they fell asleep in class. There was one cadet, a football player named Keith Harrelson, whose fate hung on being able to pass a makeup exam. Harrelson had great leadership ability; I wasn't going to lose him to numbers and formulas. I coached him every night, hard. I hollered at him, and when he lost his temper and hollered back, I hollered even louder, browbeating him into learning what he needed to know. He passed and eventually graduated. While I lost a few cadets I worked with, I didn't lose many.

Even in the ivory tower world of West Point, we weren't immune to the controversy over Vietnam. In 1967, after I'd been back a year, the admissions office barely found enough candidates to fill the entering class. As cadets became scarce, West Point's attitude toward them changed. I'd spent my four years as a cadet proving I was good enough to stay, but in an uncomfortable reversal, West Point now seemed more concerned with proving *it* was good enough. The admissions office began soft-pedaling the fact that West Point was a military institution. They even considered modifying the official statement of mission, which had always read, "to train the future leaders of the United States Army," so that it would read, "to train future leaders of the United States"—making West Point sound just like Harvard and Yale. One of my Vietnam buddies, Mike McCarthy, was a tactical officer in the new-cadet barracks and told me with concern that he wasn't sure the plebes even understood what the Army was about, let alone Vietnam. He asked me if I'd talk to them. I showed up in my jungle camouflage fatigues and red beret and gave a vivid account of my year in Vietnam, complete with color slides—no blood and gore, just a description of what it was like to soldier in war. The next day Mike called and said, "Great talk, but I think we're in trouble." Five plebes had dropped out that morning, claiming they'd never focused on the fact that they'd be expected to fight.

My mother, meanwhile, had been telling her friends, "Norman has interesting things to say about the war." Her banker, a member of the local Rotary Club, arranged for me to give a speech, which led to invitations from other civic groups. As more Americans were lost in Vietnam, the national mood became more uncertain, and people were asking, "Why are we there?" I had good answers. I could talk about the people I'd known and explain that the South Vietnamese were getting a bad rap when the press portrayed them as cowardly, corrupt, and incompetent. I could vouch for the fact, as I had to Ruth's Marxist friend, that these people were fighting for their country and their freedom. As the public debate increased over the course of the academic year, I built a name for myself as a speaker. I addressed the American Veterans Association regional convention in Atlantic City, New Jersey, the following spring, and their national convention in Hollywood, Florida, in August. There I had an audience of several thousand. It made me feel that at least I was doing something for the war effort, even if I couldn't be in Vietnam.

———

I often imagined myself in the future, surrounded by my adoring children, but I hadn't yet married because I wasn't ready to balance the responsibilities of being an officer with those of being a husband and father. At West Point I dated lots of girls—a beautiful German stewardess for Pan Am, a bunny from the Manhattan Playboy Club, a general's daughter, an Army nurse who went to Vietnam, and several others—but found no one I seriously considered marrying. My chances didn't look good, as I told my friend Russ Parsons, sitting in the crowded officers' club bar one Saturday in November. Russ was a classmate from the master's program at the University of Southern California and a fellow bachelor and we'd just come from an Army football game. I had a season ticket for two, but hadn't taken a date to that afternoon's game.

"The way the chips are falling, I'll probably never get married," I told him.

Army life, I'd decided, gave me little opportunity to meet the right kind of woman. And having grown up in a chaotic household, I wanted a lot: a genuine, kind-hearted, stable person who'd be a faithful wife to me and a great mother to my children.

Five minutes later Walt Gordon, a fellow I'd known as a cadet, spotted me and made his way over. "I've got someone I want you to meet," he said. People were always trying to fix me up, but I thought, "Why not?" Walt had left the military and now worked as a pilot for TWA. Leading me across the room, he explained that his wife, a TWA stewardess, had brought a good friend from work and that the blind date they'd arranged for her had fallen through. We maneuvered through a crowd of bachelors who had gathered around a beautiful brunette with a gorgeous smile, and Walt introduced me to Brenda Holsinger. I had no sooner said hello than friends whisked her off to a round of post–football game parties. I philosophically settled in for the evening at my usual spot at the officers' club bar.

I had a regular Saturday night routine. After the football game I'd socialize at the officers' club till around seven o'clock, go home, change into civilian clothes (we were required to wear uniforms to the games), and come back for dinner. Then I'd sit at the bar. The officers' club bar had no waitresses, so if you wanted a drink, you had to come to the bar. During the course of the evening I'd meet and talk to just about everybody there. Other bachelor officers would join me and we'd end up telling stories—mostly about Vietnam. I liked to think of myself as a great raconteur, like my dad. Late in the evening I'd nurse a bottle of cheap champagne and talk to George, the bartender, who'd previously worked at the Stork Club and was a buddy of us bachelors—he was not only a true philosopher, but a source of free drinks.

Much later that night Brenda and her friends came back looking for Walt, who was supposed to drive them home. But he'd disappeared, and as the search went on Brenda waited at the bar with the patience of someone used to long flight delays. Someone introduced us again, and by the time Walt finally wandered in, laughing sheepishly and brushing dust from the back of his business suit—he'd decided to take a little nap—I'd asked Brenda for her phone number.

When we started dating, I quickly appreciated that here was a warm, sweet person, totally without frills or airs. A little voice in my brain started saying, "Hey, maybe . . ." Brenda was twenty-six years old, an only child, born and raised in the tiny town of Timberville, Virginia, in the Shenandoah Valley. She'd graduated from junior college, gotten engaged to her high-school sweetheart, and had been on the brink of settling down when she realized just barely in time that she didn't want to spend her life in a small town. So she broke the engagement, signed on with TWA, and moved to New York. Leaving took nerve, and what I admired in Brenda was that she'd done it without becoming hard. She cared about people and knew how to bring out the good in them—even in a somewhat ornery combat veteran like me.

Brenda was also the first woman I'd ever dated that my mother liked. I'd always dreaded bringing girlfriends home. Mom was ferociously protective, convinced that some seductress would trap me into a premature marriage that would wreck my military career. Before I turned thirty, she'd always told me, "Get out and live a little before you settle down." After I turned thirty, the message became, "Don't you know there's something peculiar about a man your age who's not married?" But even then, she rejected every woman I was seeing.

On a couple of occasions I'd brought home a girlfriend only to have Mom become intoxicated and insult her. But for Brenda she was on her best behavior. I arranged their first meeting for a Saturday in January 1968—Sally was in town from Washington, and the four of us went to a matinee performance on Broadway of *The Prime of Miss Jean Brodie* and then had an early dinner. Mom and Sally loved Brenda: at one point when she excused herself from the table, they put their heads together like a couple of schoolgirls, whispering, "Isn't she terrific?" I shouldn't have been surprised—Brenda was, after all, a farm girl from the hills of Virginia who had left home to come to the big city, just like Mom. But I felt tremendous relief, because I'd already decided I wanted Brenda to be my wife.

A couple of months later, she came to West Point for a party, and a little before it was scheduled to start we were sitting on my living room couch. Brenda knew I was going to propose, and I knew her answer was going to be yes, which was a good thing, because I made her as unromantic a marriage proposal as any man ever made. "I'm going to ask you to marry me," I said, "but before I do, I want you to understand what you'll be getting into if you say yes. Here is what to expect as an Army wife. There will be times when I'll have to work late into the night. There will be times I'll have to go to the field for maneuvers and not come home for two or three weeks.

"We are going to be transferred all over the world, and no matter how much we like the place where we are living, when orders come to move, we'll pack up and move. That means we'll never be able to put down roots.

"Most important, I may be called upon to go to war. And when the call comes, it may be sudden, and I might not even be able to tell you where I'm going. Before you say you want to be my wife, I want to make sure you understand."

This was not the first time I had tested Brenda's patience. She had obviously figured out all this already and was astounded that I was giving her a lecture right in the middle of proposing. But I knew what wartime separation had done to my own family, and I'd seen too many Army households collapse because the wife had failed to realize she was marrying into an institution. I wasn't going to take any chances.

"All that said," I continued, "I want to ask you to marry me. I'm thirty-three years old and I'm no saint. I've dated a lot of women, and you're bound to hear about some and even meet a few. But remember that although I dated them, you're the one I want to marry. You're the one I want for the rest of my life."

Brenda cried a little and then accepted. I gave her an engagement ring I'd had made—a miniature of my own West Point ring, set with a diamond I'd inherited from Grandma Schwarzkopf.

———

We set the wedding for July 6, 1968, at the West Point chapel. The announcement appeared in the local paper with the headline "Holsinger–Schwarzkopf," which caused Russ Parsons, who'd agreed to be best man, to wisecrack, "This doesn't sound like a wedding to me. It sounds like the opening of a butcher shop."

Brenda's mother, Elsie, visited New York that spring and we got along fine. But I still had to pass muster with Jesse Jefferson Holsinger. Brenda's dad had started out as a farm boy with an eleventh-grade education, trained himself to be an electrician, and built a solid reputation in Washington, D.C., ninety miles from Timberville. He spent each workweek there, coming home only on weekends.

For starters, Jesse wasn't keen on the idea of his daughter marrying a Yankee Army officer, and he seemed quite aloof when we met. I'd traded in my Mustang for a Ford Country Squire station wagon and I saw Jesse eyeing the new car. I asked if he'd like to drive it.

"Yeah, let's take it out and see how it is." Timberville was a town of fewer than a thousand people, and before I knew it we were back in farm country, zooming up and down rutted dirt and gravel roads, with dust pouring in the windows and the car shaking down to its bolts. Eventually we pulled up back at the house and Jesse declared, "Well, I guess it's okay. Ran fine." I was in shock.

As we walked inside he said, "How about a drink before dinner?" That was a surprise because drinking didn't seem to be part of Timberville social life—the town's only beer parlor doubled as a doughnut shop called The Downy Flake. I thought, "This fellow isn't going to be so bad after all. We're finally going to unwind."

Once in the kitchen, he asked, "What do you drink?"

"Scotch."

He said, "What's that?"

"A kind of whiskey."

He pulled out a bottle of bourbon and said, "Is this scotch? Well, it's all we got. How do you take it?" He grabbed a tumbler and dribbled in about a half inch of bourbon. There was no soda, so I went to the sink and added some water. Meanwhile Jesse poured himself a shot, slugged it down, and said, "Okay, let's eat." I trailed him to the table, wondering what to do with the watery bourbon in my hand.

The weekend was spent with the people of Timberville coming by to check out Brenda's fiancé. We'd sit in the parlor, and they'd look at me and then turn to Elsie and ask, "Where does he come from up north?" I talked to the men about hunting and the experiences some had had in the Army; with the ladies the conversation was limited pretty much to gardens and the weather. They were nice people, the salt of the earth, but the tumultuous events of that year—the Tet offensive in January, the assassinations of Martin Luther King, Jr., and Bobby Kennedy—seemed even more remote here than they did at West Point.

Jesse and I didn't get down to serious conversation until breakfast the day before we left. We were eating smoked, salty Virginia-style country ham, and I was gazing out the window toward the Blue Ridge Mountains. I said, "This really is a beautiful place."

"I want to talk to you about that," said Jesse. "You know Brenda is our only child, and Elsie and I have always hoped she'd live here." The Holsingers and Elsie's family, the Hartmans, traced their roots back six generations to the great migration of German farmers into the Pennsylvania and Virginia hills. Jesse was worried I'd take his daughter away and never return to Timberville.

"Sir, don't worry about that. I know that Brenda loves the valley. Sure, in the Army we move around a lot. But we'll always be coming back home." There wasn't much more I could say. Brenda herself had long ago separated from Timberville.

We got married two weeks later. The afternoon was gorgeous and everybody was happy. After the ceremony in the Protestant cadet chapel,

Brenda and I went down to Trophy Point to have our wedding picture taken. Then we went to the officers' club for the reception. Mom was there in a new green dress, again on her best behavior, and beaming as the mother of the groom. Sally was a bridesmaid, and Ruth had been invited but couldn't make it. It was a classic West Point wedding, complete with dress white uniforms and the traditional arch of crossed sabers for the bride and groom coming out of the chapel, but it was also done on the cheap. Brenda had gone down to Manhattan's garment district and bought a stunning satin-and-lace wedding dress off a bare pipe rack. The manager and assistant manager of the officers' club were poker buddies of mine and gave us the lowest possible rates on space, booze, and food. The bill was only fourteen hundred dollars for two hundred people. Even so, the father of the bride blanched when he received a bill for seven hundred dollars, which just shows how far it was from Timberville to West Point: Brenda and I, to ease the culture shock and make sure he had a good time, had secretly kicked in the other half.

———

I had orders to spend the academic year of 1968-69 studying at the Command and General Staff College at Fort Leavenworth, Kansas. Within weeks Brenda and I were heading west in the overloaded station wagon, all ready to set up our first household. I'd gotten a letter from the housing office that said, "Dear Major Schwarzkopf: We are happy to inform you that you will have a three-bedroom house in Pershing Park. Enclosed are floor plans."

"See?" I'd said proudly to Brenda. "You're very lucky you've married a major. Most of my classmates married when they were second lieutenants, and their wives had to live in shabby little apartments."

Then we looked at the floor plans. The rooms seemed awfully small—practically doll-house size—but I declared someone must have made a mistake on the scale. When we reached Fort Leavenworth and pulled up in front of 16 Heintzelman Court, I was all set to carry my bride across the threshold, but took one look and thought, "I'm moving my wife into a crackerbox and she'll hate it!" I was wrong. Brenda *loved* the tiny house and was determined to make it our home.

We spent all day wrestling in our belongings in the sweltering August heat. The queen-sized bed barely fit into the largest bedroom, and once we added a dresser we had to scoot sideways to get around in the room. But there were just two of us, so one of the bedrooms became the repository for the beautiful things from Iran and Germany that had belonged to my parents. At one point Brenda motioned toward a wall that was leaning so badly that the venetian blinds hung out six inches from the bottom of the sill. "I sure hope we don't get a Kansas tornado," she joked. "But it's okay—I'll find some beautiful curtains."

Being married brought me great happiness—Brenda gave me the first stable home I'd had since I was eight years old. Even so, certain adjustments had to be made. People can't spend as many years as we had unmarried—I was thirty-four, Brenda twenty-seven—and shift immediately into wedded bliss. In our cramped little bathroom, for instance, Brenda put a fuzzy pink cover on the lid of the toilet. It was really very pretty, I thought. As a bachelor, I'd never had a pink top on the toilet. The problem was that the lid now would not stay up, so I had to learn to do my thing propping up the lid with one knee. I also learned to eat a lot of something I hadn't eaten since I was a small boy: meatloaf. For all her sophisticated New York ways, Brenda had not learned to cook. We consumed a great deal of catsup. The transition to married life was made easier by the fact that Brenda continued to work: she flew out of Kansas City, twenty-five miles away, and that gave each of us time and space to ourselves.

Pershing Park was jumping with kids. Every family on our little street had them except Brenda and me, and the kids responded by adopting us and spending lots of time at our house. I put on magic shows—I'd been fascinated by magic ever since I'd lived in Princeton. I knew some simple tricks like "Hippity Hoppity Rabbits" and "The Magic Die Box" that never failed to amaze kids. Brenda meanwhile was always baking them cookies and telling stories. They loved her more than they did me. On her twenty-eighth birthday, in March 1969, the kids pooled their resources, came to the door, and with great ceremony gave Brenda a dollar. Talk about weeping! Brenda was overwhelmed.

One of the ancillary benefits of the Army school system was to give officers a breather—they weren't required to rise at the crack of dawn and command troops until late at night. They had time to get to know their families again and to renew ties with old friends in a whirl of cocktail parties, dances, and barbecues. I ran into my West Point classmates Pete Lash and Bill Cody, whose wives, Ginger and Nancy, took Brenda under their wing. My being at the Command and General Staff College made it easier for her to get to know the Army way of life.

I concentrated hard on work. In the view of many military men, Command and General Staff College was the pinnacle of Army education. Eisenhower and Bradley raved about how much it taught them; Colonel Truong's greatest regret was that he'd never had a chance to attend. (I never met anyone who needed Fort Leavenworth *less* than Truong—he could have written the textbooks.) The course was designed to equip an officer with the knowledge and skills he'd need to plan military campaigns and maneuver large formations of troops (divisions and corps) in battle, and the bureaucratic procedures he'd need to maneuver in staff jobs at the Pentagon. I loved studying the art of war and detested studying Pentagonese. I did not visualize myself as a Washington staff officer for many years to come. But I worked diligently enough to stay in the top ten percent of the class.

Around Christmas, I started talking to Brenda about going back to Vietnam. We were eager to start a family, but I knew the war would hang over me until I served another tour. The American buildup had reached a new high—540,000 men—and there was a terrible need for qualified officers. Given my combat experience and my knowledge of how to survive in the jungle, I believed a few more troops might make it back if I commanded them instead of an officer new to Vietnam. An Infantry Branch personnel officer told me that if I wanted to go, I'd have to volunteer. I'd been promoted to lieutenant colonel, and they'd marked me for a three-year tour at the Office of the Chief of Research and Development in Washington, where I'd put to use my knowledge of missile engineering. Once again, a lot of people said I was crazy to volunteer: "Why are you going back when you don't have to?"

I told Brenda I thought it was my duty, and then I argued that we should wait to start our family until I returned. That way she could continue to fly, which would give her something to do while I was gone. And, of course, in the back of my mind was the thought that if I died, it would be easier for her to make a new start. Brenda understood why I felt obliged to go, although we'd been married less than a year and she wished it could have been some other way. The night we made the decision, there were many things she could have said, things I knew other wives had said when their husbands volunteered for war: "If you love me, how can you leave?" or "Go if you want, but don't expect me to wait." Brenda said nothing of the kind: she knew I loved her; she knew I'd come back; and I knew she'd be there when I did.

So I volunteered, and my orders came through in March: to command a battalion in the 9th Infantry Division in the Mekong Delta, south of Saigon, starting in June. I spent the spring preparing myself by focusing on riverine operations in my studies at Fort Leavenworth—units of the 9th Infantry Division were conducting offensive operations along the South Vietnamese rivers and canals using heavily armored patrol boats. After graduation, I took a one-month leave to get Brenda settled in an apartment we'd rented near Washington, where we expected to be based after I came home.

We paid a visit to Timberville the weekend before I was scheduled to leave. As I came down to breakfast on Saturday morning, Jesse greeted me with a big grin. "Guess what, Norm," he said. "You don't have to go back to Vietnam! Look here." The newspaper headline read: "U.S. Division Coming Home." In keeping with its new policy of Vietnamization, or turning the war over to the South Vietnamese, the Nixon administration had started withdrawing U.S. forces. The first division coming back was the 9th Infantry Division, my new outfit.

Jesse was puzzled when I sat down, stunned. He didn't understand how the Army worked. The fact that the 9th Infantry Division was leaving Vietnam didn't relieve me of the obligation to go; it only meant I was no longer assured of commanding a battalion. I could imagine all too well what was waiting for me instead: one of those Saigon desk jobs.

10

I arrived at the Army's headquarters at Long Binh just northeast of Saigon on a steamy July afternoon, changed into the jungle fatigues I'd kept from my first tour, and went directly to the bar in the replacement depot. I was talking to friends and drinking from an oversized can of Foster's beer, which the Australians had introduced me to during my first tour, when a lieutenant tracked me down.

"You're supposed to come with me, sir," he interrupted. "General Mabry wants to interview you to be his executive officer."

"That's bullshit, lieutenant! I did not come over here to work at headquarters. I came over to command a battalion. Now get out of here." It was rude, but it worked: he left. I turned back to my friends and my beer, knowing I hadn't heard the last of General Mabry. Pretty soon the lieutenant came back, only this time he had a full colonel with him who simply said, "Schwarzkopf, come with us." I was seething.

They ushered me into General Mabry's office. Under other circumstances, Major General George Mabry would have been fascinating to meet: a tough little man with glasses who had won the Medal of Honor in World War II. Mabry had an infectious laugh and always joked about his size, saying in his slow South Carolina drawl, "I'm five foot six and three quarters. And don't ever forget the three quarters." He was chief of staff for

Frank Mildren, the general in charge of all U.S. Army combat units in Vietnam. Mildren, in turn, worked for Creighton Abrams, who had succeeded Westmoreland as commanding general for all U.S. forces in Vietnam, including combat units and advisors.

Mabry sat me down and asked what I thought about becoming his executive officer.

"Sir, I don't want the job. I came to Vietnam to command a battalion."

"You think that makes you different?"

"No, sir, I don't. But you asked what I thought and I'm giving you an honest answer."

"Schwarzkopf, let me tell you something. I came over here to command a division, not sit here at headquarters as chief of staff. But this is where the Army needed me."

"Sir, I'm a soldier. Whatever the Army wants me to do, I'll do. But I still want you to know that I came over here to command a battalion."

"Fair enough. We understand each other. If you do a good job I'll try to spring you after six months so you can get that battalion."

With that, I took over one of three desks in General Mabry's outer office; the others belonged to his secretary and his aide, the lieutenant who'd come looking for me. Across my desk, making its way to the general, flowed the paperwork of the entire U.S. Army staff in Vietnam—plans and reports on everything from battles and casualties to budgets and USO shows. The staff's job was to ensure that all the cogs of the giant Army war machine kept turning. Mabry presided over an administrative hierarchy that included numerous large offices: for example, Personnel Management; Deployment and Redeployment Planning; Petroleum, Oil, and Lubricant Distribution; and Finance and Accounting. The staff of these offices did the mundane work necessary to support a force of more than 500,000 soldiers a long way from their supply bases back home.

Even though Mabry was an excellent boss, and many of the staff officers were terrific guys, I hated every day there. Long Binh was a barren two-mile-by-four-mile barbed-wire compound with hundreds of temporary buildings and thousands of men, and it epitomized everything wrong with the U.S. Army in Vietnam. It was a magnified version of the compounds for U.S. advisors I'd tried to avoid years before at Pleiku and Kontum—places designed to keep all the Americans inside and the "gooks" outside. After work each day, the staff adjourned to officers' clubs around the base, dark, grungy dives that served alcohol in unbelievable quantities. Wednesday was steak night, known as "burn-your-own night": each man picked a slab of meat and cooked it himself on the grill. There was always some Japanese or

Filipino rock band on hand, performing loud, perfunctory renditions of American songs. Officers would hunch over their drinks, exchanging phony war stories or boasting about alleged sexual conquests.

The clubs for noncommissioned officers and enlisted men were worse. Some NCOs were lining their pockets by raking off profits from the slot machines, which eventually led to a major scandal. The bars also featured stripteasers of about the same caliber as the officers' club musicians. The steam bath on post was really a whorehouse, as I learned when I innocently asked for a steam bath and the attendant at the desk looked at me like I was weird. Theft and the misuse of equipment were rampant: I spent months requisitioning a new jeep for General Mabry—only to have it vanish without a trace from the PX parking lot one day after it was delivered. Meanwhile, many officers on the base drove jeeps that bore markings such as "1 CAV" (for "1st Cavalry Division") or "5 MD" ("5th Mechanized Division"): vehicles "diverted" from combat units in the field. What was frustrating was that there wasn't much General Mabry—or anybody else— could do: so many units were crammed into Long Binh that the lines of command were confused and accountability had virtually disappeared. No one was really in charge. To me, Long Binh was a cesspool.

I lived in a plywood box—a little one-room hooch twice as wide as my cot. It had a raised wooden roof and open eaves to let out the heat, and when the wind blew, fine brown dust came in and coated everything. I finally understood the awful tedium of war for people in the rear. We simply worked and worked and worked—pushing paper twelve hours a day, six days a week and a half day on Sunday, with no days off. And at night, there was nothing to do but drink or get into trouble. I became a sack rat: rather than go to the officers' clubs, I'd stay in my hooch and eat crackers and cheese, then climb into bed and read myself to sleep.

As the months wore on, I scanned every combat report that came in, noting which units were seeing the most action and wondering where I'd eventually be assigned. From a tactical standpoint, the war was going well, in the sense that wherever U.S. forces were present, the enemy had been suppressed, and whenever the enemy chose to stand and fight, he was soundly defeated. Yet at the same time, there wasn't much combat to speak of—certainly no big battles like the Ia Drang Valley campaign of my first tour. Commanders were under strict orders from Washington to keep casualties to a minimum, and much of the effort at headquarters was devoted to orchestrating the withdrawal of troops. The 9th Infantry Division had gone and two others were leaving, so that by the end of 1969, total U.S. strength in South Vietnam was down by sixty thousand men. At least one more division was scheduled to follow, from near Saigon where the South Vietnamese Army was strongest.

In November some friends in the personnel office told me that a battalion command in the Americal Division (the 23rd Infantry Division) was coming open, and I jumped at the chance. My greatest fear was that I'd get a unit that was just marking time, but from reports I'd been reading the Americal had seen more combat recently than any other division. Even better, it was based in the coastal region between Quang Ngai and Chu Lai—not far from where I'd fought once before. General Mabry generously agreed to let me grab the assignment, even though I hadn't quite finished the six months I'd promised him.

Over Thanksgiving I took a one-week leave and met up with Brenda in Hong Kong. We had a honeymoon all over again—dining, dancing, going on harbor cruises, buying clothes for each other—and in the course of that week I felt as though Brenda's goodness had cleansed me somehow of all the pollution of Long Binh. Away from Vietnam, it was hard to believe the real danger was about to begin. But a few days after we said good-bye and I went back to Saigon, I got on a transport plane to Chu Lai. I was going back to war.

———

I reached the seacoast town of Chu Lai on December 9, two days before officially assuming my command. An aide showed me to the plush trailer where I was to spend the night and announced, "Dinner is at the officers' club at seven, and General Ramsey has invited you to attend." That struck me as an odd way to characterize an officers' mess in a war zone, but I got cleaned up and walked over.

The place was almost worthy of a Club Med—a spacious building with screened porches and low tropical eaves, nestled on a hilltop with a gorgeous view of the South China Sea. We were seated at a long, U-shaped table with white tablecloth, china, and wineglasses—Major General Lloyd B. Ramsey, his deputy commanders, his staff, and me—as soldiers waited on us. At the end of the meal came what I learned was the nightly ritual: a staff officer stood and recited a *poem* he'd written about the day's events at headquarters. Everybody laughed and applauded. Then another officer stood and with a lot of joking asides announced the movie for the evening. I was heartsick. We had men—about eighteen thousand men—out in the mud and the jungle, maybe fighting the enemy, maybe dying at that moment, while their senior officers ate off fine china and recited cutesy little poems.

We adjourned to the movie room, where soldiers came around and served drinks while everyone sat in overstuffed chairs and, to my disbelief, enjoyed the latest war movie out of Hollywood. When the show was over a couple of staff colonels invited me back for the tea dance that weekend. *"Tea dance?"* I asked incredulously.

The tea dances were great, one of the men told me. They were held every Sunday afternoon, and some of the Red Cross girls and nurses from the hospital came over for them.

"Yeah! You can pick up a cute little babe if things are flowing the right way," said the other. "There's real action around here."

The next day I was briefed on my outfit, officially known as the 1st Battalion of the 6th Infantry, or 1/6 ("First of the Sixth") for short. When the assignment had been offered, I hadn't stopped to ask or wonder whether the battalion was any good—that hadn't seemed important so long as it was a command. Now I felt the beginnings of uneasiness. I discovered that the America1's *other* ten battalions occupied fire bases in the jungle or the foothills and spent their time hunting down the enemy. My battalion was based at a compound called LZ Bayonet, right on the main highway barely outside Chu Lai. We were adjacent to the headquarters of the three-battalion brigade to which we were assigned, and our job was to police the "Rocket Pocket," a band of foothills west of town where the VC liked to sneak in and launch rockets into the division rear. The rockets were unsophisticated flying stovepipes about eight feet long, carrying an explosive charge about the size of a large mortar shell. They *kalumped* in Chu Lai at the rate of a few per month, and to my knowledge had never done much damage, although they sure scared the division rear. Our mission, it seemed to me, was little better than sentry duty.

The five staff officers who briefed me were alarmingly vague when I asked for details: "Well, the First of the Sixth . . . um . . . they do a pretty good job, a pretty fair job." When they finished the briefing, a couple of them spoke glowingly of battalions *they* were scheduled to take over in the coming months—causing me to wonder why nobody had grabbed the 1/6. That evening at the officers' club I gulped when I heard the battalion's nickname: the First of the Sixth was known as the "worst of the Sixth."

The change-of-command ceremony took place the following morning on a little mud field under gray skies. As I accepted the battalion colors, I wondered what I'd gotten myself into. Afterward, while punch and cookies were served by my new mess hall, the assistant division commander, a one-star general who'd been cordial up until then, strolled over to inform me that the 1/6 had just flunked its annual equipment-readiness inspection,

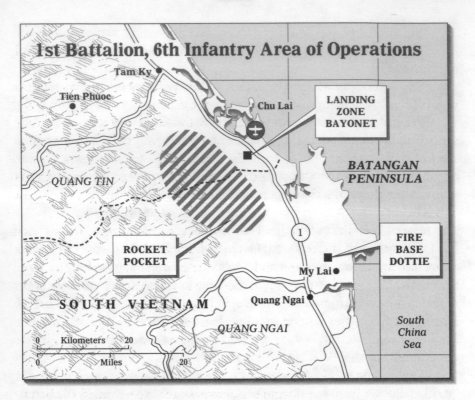

1st Battalion, 6th Infantry Area of Operations

scoring sixteen out of a possible one hundred points. He added, "We'll reinspect in thirty days. That's long enough for you to get your unit in shape. You'll be held responsible for the results."

Then the outgoing battalion commander, an unprepossessing older guy, medium-sized, thin, with a receding chin, sought me out. We'd never met. "Come on back to my hooch," he said. "I need to talk to you a little." We drove about a mile to the battalion base camp, which was at the bottom of a hill, and then walked to a little cabin halfway up the hillside. On the table sat a bottle of Johnnie Walker Black Label scotch. "This is for you," he said. "You're gonna need it." I was expecting a two- or three-hour discussion of the battalion, its officers, its NCOs, its mission—but he only said, "Well, I hope you do better than I did. I tried to lead as best I could, but this is a lousy battalion. It's got lousy morale. It's got a lousy mission. Good luck to you." With that he shook my hand and walked out.

Right next door on the hillside was the battalion tactical operations center and I thought I'd better learn what the hell was going on. I walked in and the battalion executive officer saluted and said, "Sir, we're prepared to give you your briefings."

I said, "I don't want briefings now. I want to visit the companies."

"Sir?"

"I want to visit the companies. Don't we have a command-and-control helicopter?"

"Sir, we do, but Major Lee has it." Major Will Lee was the operations staff officer. "As a matter of fact, sir, he has the helicopter all the time."

"What do you mean? Isn't that a command-and-control helicopter for the battalion commander? Get it back here right now." There was a stunned silence in the operations center. "Sir, may I talk to you for a minute outside?" said the exec. We stepped out and he explained, "I know this is unusual, but the chopper isn't here because your predecessor never went out in the field."

It would require half an hour for the helicopter to return. I went back inside to wait and discovered that there was no place in the operations center for the battalion commander—no desk, no chair, nothing! I went back to my little cabin where I sat desperately trying to figure out what to do next. "How does this outfit function?" I wondered. "Who's in charge?" Finally the helicopter landed. Walking back into the operations center I overheard someone say, "What the hell did you guys call me in for? I've got work to do out there!"

I had visions of this Major Lee as some kind of tin-pot Napoleon who'd taken advantage of his commander's weakness and transformed the battalion into a little empire of his own. I was dead wrong. He was an enthusiastic veteran officer, eager to follow orders, who'd simply been trying to hold the operation together in the absence of any real leadership. When I introduced myself and told him I wanted to go out in the field, he exclaimed: "That's great, sir! Let's go! Which company do you want to see first?"

"Well," I said, "how about A Company?" The battalion had four rifle companies, A through D, and a heavy mortar company, E, and I intended to inspect them all. As we flew out, Lee explained over the intercom that the rifle companies all had the same mission: to intercept the VC rocket teams. They'd set up a camouflaged daytime position, known as a day laager, where the men would eat, rest, clean their weapons, and make plans; then they'd send "ambush patrols" into the countryside at night. Lee said, "Sir, we're about to come up on A Company. As a matter of fact, you can see them."

And I thought, "You sure as hell can," because A Company's day laager looked like a damn gypsy camp. Nothing was camouflaged: as we circled I saw red cloth and white paper everywhere, and to my further consternation most of the men were up and moving around instead of resting for night operations. The guy who guided us in to land wore a pair of bright red shorts, flip-flops, and a yellow bandanna around his head, and had a three-day growth of beard. I jumped off and walked over to a lieutenant standing nearby—he had no helmet and no weapon, even though this was supposedly enemy territory. He did salute.

"Lieutenant, where the hell's your weapon?"

"Sir, it's over there, near my hammock."

"Are you the company commander?"

"No, sir. That's him, in front of the helicopter."

The guy in the red shorts. I motioned him over and ordered him to put on his uniform and get his weapon. That caused a ten-minute delay. Meanwhile the helicopter pilot took off; standard procedure in combat zones was to limit the time helicopters spent on the ground, since they drew fire. With the noise of his turbines gone, I suddenly heard loud rock and roll from transistor radios, echoing out into the hills. The captain came back—still wearing no helmet. "Sir, I don't have one," he explained.

"What do you mean, you don't have one?"

"Sir, we don't use helmets. You've got to understand that our mission . . ."

"Wait a minute. Don't start telling me how to conduct military operations. The first thing I want to do is check your security. Do you have security posted around your perimeter?"

"Uh . . . yes, sir."

"You've got security out, right? You made an analysis of the enemy avenues of approach, and you've put out security to protect your position. Is that right?"

"Yes, sir."

"Okay, take me to it."

We started walking into the bushes. As we moved further and further out, the captain was calling, "Security? Security?"

After a couple of hundred yards I said disgustedly, "We're wasting our time. Let's go back and ask your platoon leaders where security is."

A second lieutenant led us out of the camp in a different direction. No more than ten yards down the trail we almost tripped over a private sitting in the dirt.

"What are you doing here, soldier?" I asked.

"Sir, I'm security." The latrine was probably farther into the bushes than this guy.

"Where's your foxhole?"

"Here, sir." He pointed to a little furrow he'd scraped in the ground, maybe three inches deep. I said, "Okay. Pretend you're under attack. Get in the foxhole." He got down in it—he knew it wasn't big enough for him—and lay there looking up at me sheepishly.

"Let me ask you something, soldier. Does that give you any protection at all? Why even bother digging this much?"

"The lieutenant told me to." So I looked at the lieutenant and said, "Why didn't you make him dig a fighting position?" The bottom line was that they had no security. The enemy could have strolled in, opened fire, and killed dozens of men.

We retraced our steps and I inspected the camp itself. I walked up to a machine gunner whose weapon had no bullets in it and was coated with rust. When I asked why the gun wasn't loaded he hung his head and explained that his ammunition was in his rucksack. I wasn't angry with him—it was his sergeant who was responsible—but I said, "Okay, soldier. Let's do a simulation. You're under attack. Get your ammunition." The guy scrambled over to his rucksack and turned it upside down. Out tumbled a portable radio, cans of food, books, and a hopeless tangle of ammunition belts, all rusty and caked with the crumbs of cookies from home.

I knew I had to put an end to this carelessness before men started dying. I took the company commander, the guy who had been wearing red shorts, aside. "Things are going to start changing around here, Captain, right now. *Right now.* My inclination is to relieve you of your command, but I can't do that because apparently this is the way you've been allowed to operate. But I'm telling you: you know what to do and it had better happen. First, when you stop someplace, you will put out security, and I mean *good* security. Second, I want every portable radio out of the field. Third, I want every weapon in this outfit cleaned, and I'd better never come in again and find anybody without a weapon. Ever! In his hand! With clean ammunition! Fourth, I want every man, starting with you, shaved, cleaned up, and in proper uniform. With a helmet! And fifth, there is no way these men can go on ambush patrol tonight and stay awake, because they're all awake now."

Major Lee, who had been glued to my side during the entire inspection, could barely contain himself as we got in the helicopter: "Goddammit, sir! You're right, sir!"

We next flew to B Company, at the other end of the Rocket Pocket about twenty miles away. With its ragtag uniforms, it looked like Cox's army. They'd arrived at a new position an hour before and immediately lost two men to a booby trap. The entire force was milling around in shock, so we spent an hour talking to the troops and helping the young captain disperse his men, put out security, and make new plans for the night, since the company hadn't reached its intended position. The captain impressed me as a sincere, caring commander. By this time, it was raining and almost dark, so we flew back to LZ Bayonet.

By the time I got to the mess hall there was a long line—troops standing in the rain, NCOs bossing them around. I took my place at the end of the line, which caused a mess sergeant to trot over: "Sir, you don't have to stand in line. We've got a special section for officers."

"Sergeant," I said, "if my troops have to stand in line out here in the rain, I'll stand here, too." He seemed confused by that and went away. Meanwhile the troops were staring at me. They had all sorts of weird crap on their necks—bandannas and beads and gold chains—but they started talking to me and for the first time I felt encouraged.

"You the new battalion commander?" asked one. "You gonna make a lot of changes?" asked another. A third added, "This is the first time we've ever talked to our battalion commander. It's good to talk to you, sir." The line moved along, and once I got inside I discovered that the officers didn't even have the same dinner hour as the men. They waited until the troops were done, then sat down and got served. I sent for the exec and told him that from now on all officers would eat with the troops. Then I had my supper.

That evening I held my first meeting with the twenty-man battalion staff. Their briefings confirmed all my fears: the 1/6 was failing in its mission. The Vietcong were able to wend their way into the Rocket Pocket and launch at will—not surprising, given the way we were advertising our positions. Horribly, we were also losing lives. Two weeks before, a platoon from D Company had wandered casually into a village and been ambushed. Six men had died—without accounting for a single Vietcong. I didn't have to convince the staff that our ways had to change.

I walked out of the operations center and gazed down the hillside. Something had been gnawing at me all day about the operations center and my cabin, and now all of a sudden it hit me. Son of a bitch! The barbed wire and bunkers that made up the LZ Bayonet security perimeter were below where I was standing—the operations center and my cabin were *outside the wire*!

I called the executive officer outside and demanded an explanation. "Sir, the former battalion commander was afraid of rockets. He moved the operations center and his hooch up here because this hill shields us from the launch sites."

I thought, "This layout is absolutely crazy." The odds of a rocket randomly landing on the operations center were minuscule, but if the

Vietcong ever attacked the base on foot, which was not so improbable, my staff and I would have no protection whatever.

For a long time afterward I tried to figure out how the situation could have been allowed to deteriorate so far. Perhaps the answer was ticket punching. In those days all a lieutenant colonel needed to get promoted to colonel was to command a battalion in Vietnam "successfully"—that is, to come back alive with a decent efficiency report. Officers were rotated through battalion command every six months, which enabled the maximum number to punch their battalion-command ticket, but also meant that many unqualified officers were put in charge of men's lives. It was common practice to reward a loyal staff officer at higher headquarters by assigning him a battalion (I was an example). Because officers remained in command for such a brief time, they didn't have to suffer the results of their incompetence. These ills were inherited by the next commander, and even *his* successor. This seemed to be what I was up against in the Worst of the Sixth.

———

The next day I was awakened with the news that a dawn patrol had shot a Vietcong sneaking through the wire along our perimeter. On his body they'd found detailed sketches of LZ Bayonet—the sort of reconnaissance needed for one of the Vietcong's most devastating tactics, called a sapper attack. At night, guerrillas who had memorized the layout of a base would sneak through the wire at one end, sprint across the compound throwing grenades and explosive charges into bunkers and sleeping hooches, and make it out the other end, having inflicted huge casualties. Finding those sketches of our base made everybody's pucker factor increase considerably, mine included—not least because the drawings clearly indicated the locations of the operations center and my hooch.

Ten minutes later, as I finished dressing, there was a knock on my cabin door. It was my brigade commander—a legendary combat infantryman named Joe Clemons, who had become a national hero and won the Distinguished Service Cross in the battle of Pork Chop Hill during the Korean War. The battle had been the subject of a best-seller by S. L. A. Marshall and a Hollywood movie in which Clemons was played by Gregory Peck. Colonel Clemons was also new to the brigade, and I was looking forward to working for him, but we hadn't met because he'd been away on leave. He'd heard about the Vietcong in our wire and wanted to make sure I knew how to protect my base.

I saluted, and he asked me to brief him on the dead Vietcong. Then he said, "Let's go inspect your perimeter."

I hadn't seen the LZ Bayonet perimeter the night before, but I had no illusions about what we'd find. Clemons was furious within fifteen minutes. The bunkers had long since caved in. All along the barbed wire were yawning gaps where anyone could enter. The Claymore mines, which had originally been positioned to cut down enemy soldiers charging the wire, had mostly rusted away from their detonating wires, so they'd have been useless during an attack. Worse, some had been turned around so that if we had set them off, their shrapnel would have blown back into the camp. Joe Clemons chewed me out. I was furious, too, but all I could say was, "Sir, I'll take care of it."

"Didn't you inspect the bunker line yesterday?"

"No, sir."

"Why the hell not?"

"There were a lot of other things I was inspecting, sir."

"This is a disgrace! I've never seen anything this bad in all my years in the Army." We walked the whole perimeter, and the colonel berated me the entire way. I knew he was right: if there had been a sapper attack the night before, a great many of my men would have died.

As soon as he left, I rounded up the officers and NCOs and we spent the entire day making sure sandbags got filled, foxholes dug, and Claymores replaced so we could defend the camp. We extended the perimeter to take in the operations center and my cabin, although I had decided that eventually both would be moved down into the base. Clemons's reproaches kept echoing in my mind. I decided I couldn't work with a commander who doubted my competence. I called and asked if we could meet. He received me at his headquarters that evening but did not offer me a seat.

"Sir, you had every reason to be angry at what you found at my unit today," I said. "But I want you to know that I was angry, too. I was as shocked as you at the state of that perimeter. And I recognize I was at fault not to have inspected it as soon as I took command."

Clemons locked eyes with me as I spoke and didn't say a word. I took a breath and continued, "I don't know what you know about my unit. But on the basis of two days' experience, I can tell you I've probably inherited the worst battalion in the United States Army. I know what's wrong and I will fix it, but that can't happen overnight. And it won't do any good for you to chew my ass every time you come around. You'll just slow me down."

He didn't say anything, just kept staring at me with his icy blue eyes. Finally he said, "Colonel Schwarzkopf, I want to tell you that *I've* inherited the worst *brigade* in the United States Army. I'm willing to believe you know what needs to be done. Now let's do it together." There was no smiling or backslapping—we were both under the gun.

———

In the weeks that followed, disaster piled on disaster. In D Company in late December, a veteran sergeant who had just joined the battalion after a year of advanced training in the United States, and whom I had personally briefed on what I expected of him, led a dozen GIs into the jungle on night ambush patrol. Completely ignoring all the rules, they moved into their position in broad daylight, blew up their air mattresses to get comfortable, and of course all fell asleep. The Vietcong found them within hours and killed them all, except for one private who ran away and was able to tell us what had happened.

A couple of weeks later I received a letter from the sergeant's wife that said in effect, "I demand to know who got my husband killed. I demand a full investigation, and whoever is at fault should be court-martialed." That was the only letter that went unanswered during my time as a battalion commander, because the reply would have been: "It wasn't murder, it was suicide. And your husband took eleven people with him."

I had to be a complete son of a bitch to get any results, which often entailed losing my temper five or six times in a day. Being calm and reasonable just didn't work. For one thing the antiwar protests were mounting in the United States and a lot of our draftees knew they'd been sent to an unpopular war and didn't want to fight. Then there was the Army's policy of keeping Vietnam tours to one year, which meant a constant stream of raw recruits and a constant exodus of experienced men. When these new kids arrived, they'd immediately be exposed to a bogus combat-veteran culture that was in reality no more than an accumulation of bad habits. Some other troops would tell them: "Forget that crap you learned in basic training. This is how we do it around here. This is the real thing."

Because the war had put such strain on the Army personnel system that experienced junior officers and NCOs were scarce, I didn't have enough leaders to set everybody straight. At the rank of sergeant first class or above, for example, our battalion had slots for thirty-five NCOs, but we had only five. Even our lieutenants were mostly draftees—college kids who'd been offered the chance to go to instant officer school and who'd decided that if they had to go to war, they'd rather do it as lieutenants than privates. But psychologically they were unprepared to take responsibility for men's lives. I thought of them as my commissioned Pfc.'s.

We had no choice but to treat troops almost like raw recruits and teach them to wear their helmets and flak jackets and to carry their weapons and keep them clean. After discovering many of the men couldn't shoot straight, I had each company build a little rifle range and required the troops to train there. At the same time we began moving more aggressively in the Rocket Pocket, patrolling areas we'd never entered and pushing the VC farther back into the hills. It was dangerous, uncomfortable work, and to help the troops decompress I set up a rotation system that let units come back from the jungle and spend a week manning bunkers in the rear. That gave the men a chance to relax, shower, wear clean clothes, and eat three square meals a day.

I was flying out every day to supervise my field forces and holding staff meetings every night, pounding on the officers and NCOs about things we needed to fix—all this while LZ Bayonet was still under threat of attack by the VC organization that had sent the scout who carried the map of our base. After a few weeks, the pressure really started getting to me. One afternoon I confided in First Sergeant Walsh, a highly experienced, competent, crusty old NCO who was a big reason B Company had its act together: "Jesus, Top, I have to operate on such a short fuse . . . the battalion's in such lousy shape . . . there's a million things that need to get done. I'm not normally like this."

"But you're right, sir. Everybody knows you're right," he said. Then he paused and studied my face. "Sir, I know you're worried about having to be a son of a bitch. But don't worry about that. I've worked for lots bigger sons of bitches than you." And he smiled and saluted and walked away. I didn't know whether to feel relieved or depressed.

The one day I knew I could be a nice guy was Christmas. I ordered the mess hall to prepare a huge meal for the troops and starting late Christmas morning, we loaded food onto helicopters in insulated cans and flew dinner to each company. A big, corpulent Medical Service Corps officer who was black had agreed to dress up as Santa Claus, and he went with us and waved from the helicopter as we landed. We set up a chow line with Christmas dinner—turkey, dressing, cranberry sauce, the whole nine yards—while Santa wandered around the camp, ho-ho-ho-ing and handing out candy canes to the troops. We'd brought along a minister and a priest, and after the men ate they attended a religious service. Meanwhile the helicopters went back to load up chow for the next company.

That was the way we fed Christmas dinner to the entire battalion. I went through the day with jumbled emotions: the night before, I'd gotten a cassette tape from Brenda telling me I was going to be a father—the result of our wonderful week in Hong Kong. I should have been ecstatic, but instead I felt a huge new sense of responsibility for my wife and soon-to-be-born baby, on top of my concern for this awful battalion in which so many lives depended on me. The sheer magnitude of my task seemed overwhelming to me and I missed home terribly.

We visited D Company last, late in the afternoon. I went looking for the commander, but his executive officer explained that he was at the hospital at the rear, visiting troops who'd been wounded in a firefight. I was planning to compliment him when he came back. But he never showed. Finally we returned to LZ Bayonet. I was exhausted, but the first thing I did was look for the D Company commander. A sergeant pointed and said, "He's in the mess hall. Been there a couple of hours." And there he was, wearing a nice clean uniform and polishing off Christmas dinner with some officer friends.

"Come with me," I told him. I led him to a nearby building where I had a little office and we sat down. He was wary and avoided my eyes. He'd served on my predecessor's battalion staff and had been in command of his company for only a month. I praised him for visiting his men in the hospital and then asked, "Why didn't you go straight back out to your company?"

"Well, sir, I wanted to have Christmas dinner."

"What about your troops? Don't you understand that it was your responsibility to see that they had *their* Christmas dinner?"

He frowned. "Sir, as far as I'm concerned . . . ," he began, but then stopped. "Sir, I knew you were bringing them a Christmas meal, and I thought that as long as I was here, I'd take a shower and put on clean clothes and eat my dinner."

"Captain, do you realize what you've just told your troops? You think they don't know that while they're out in the boonies on Christmas Day, their leader is in the rear? If you're not willing to go through the discomfort of spending Christmas with them in the field, how do you expect them to believe you'll be with them when they go into battle?"

He shrugged, shook his head, then looked me in the eye. "Frankly, sir, I really don't like this company command business. I don't like being responsible for the troops all the time. So sometimes I just take care of myself."

"Then I'll remove you from your command. Is that what you want?" I asked incredulously.

"Yes, sir. That would be wonderful."

One of my staff officers, Captain David Trujillo, really wanted to command a company. I found him and said, "Pack your gear." The D Company commander sat by watching and looking relaxed. When I ordered him to get into the helicopter with Trujillo and me, he finally showed some surprise. We flew out to D Company, and I ordered the commander to assemble his men. I then faced him in front of the formation and said, "I am relieving you of command of this company immediately because you don't care about your troops. You do not deserve to be a company commander in this battalion. Go over and get in the helicopter." I turned to Trujillo. "Captain Trujillo, you are now in command of Delta Company. Take care of these men."

I'd always been taught that the responsibility of a commander is to develop his subordinates, not to relieve them, and I felt conflicted about what I'd done. But I believed those soldiers desperately needed to know that somebody cared about keeping them alive. The message apparently got through: as I walked toward the helicopter, the men cheered. And on the ride back, I realized that relieving the guy had disturbed me more than it had him. Over the intercom he observed with perfect equanimity, "Sir, that was a humiliating experience"—and then proceeded to chat about the lousy weather. The next day I arranged a staff job for him at division headquarters. Whenever I ran into him afterward, he greeted me warmly. There were no hard feelings on his side at all.

Gradually the battalion came around. The thirty days passed and the hard work of cleaning weapons, squaring away equipment, and rebuilding our perimeters paid off when we passed the readiness inspection we'd failed so miserably in early December. In itself, that wasn't such a big deal, but for the first time the men started realizing, "Hey, we can do it right. We can be a success. We're not the 'worst of the Sixth' anymore."

More important, we became increasingly effective at our missions. Our casualty rate dropped and so did the number of rockets falling on Chu Lai. In early January 1970, by plain dumb luck, we even caught a Vietcong rocketeer in the act. In my helicopter one afternoon I saw two rockets shoot off from a densely vegetated hummock surrounded by rice paddies. I quickly radioed the position back to LZ Bayonet. We now had a platoon on twenty-four-hour alert, so the troops flew out, landed on the hummock, and started combing the bushes. When the guy shot at them, they fired back and killed him.

Two rockets he had not had time to fire were still sitting on the hill. We'd never been able to figure out what sort of launchers and launch procedure the VC used. I was stunned to discover that they didn't use launchers at all—the rockets were simply propped up with crossed sticks! From what I could figure, the VC carried the rockets into the area, either by hand or on primitive carts. Keeping the tail on the ground, they'd use branches lashed in the shape of an X to raise the nose for the trajectory needed to reach Chu Lai, then they'd scoot the tail left or right until the rocket was pointing in the right direction. Then everybody would leave except a lone rocketeer, who would fire the rockets electrically.

Our killing the rocketeer must have stymied the VC because there were no more rocket attacks for an entire month. A couple of weeks later, our intelligence people sent us a captured enemy report that warned Vietcong units to stay away from LZ Bayonet. The report said a strong new American battalion had moved in. The enemy had paid me the greatest compliment I ever received as commander of the 1/6.

One of our sister battalions, the 5/46, was assigned to the Batangan Peninsula, a rectangle that protruded into the South China Sea between Chu Lai and Quang Ngai. The Batangan was what the troops called a "bad-ass" place—loaded with booby traps and minefields from one end to the other. One of the peninsula's villages was My Lai, where two years before American forces had killed more than three hundred Vietnamese villagers in an incident that was still under investigation. Supposedly the 5/46 had gone to the Batangan to fight a VC battalion known as the "Phantom 48th"— "phantom" because nobody ever actually found it—but the troops had become so demoralized by the mines and booby traps that they'd lost their will to fight. When patrols were sent out at night, they'd go two hundred yards outside their perimeter and stop, and the next morning they'd come in and report that they'd completed their mission and encountered nothing.

Colonel Clemons called me in and said, "The Fifth of the Forty-sixth isn't cutting it down there. They're scared to death. I want you and your unit to trade places with them." As word got around our battalion, a lot of the kids thought I'd volunteered for the mission. I was a gung-ho commander, but not *that* gung-ho. My feelings weren't much different from many of the men's: while it was a compliment for our unit finally to be handed a real assignment, the Batangan was a horrible, malignant place.

We moved in during the last week of March 1970. From a helicopter the countryside was deceptively pretty—rolling coastal hills and rice paddies. But in fact this land had been fought over for thirty years—the Japanese had seized it during World War II, the French after that, then South Koreans in support of the United States, and finally the Americans themselves, not to mention the Vietcong. That was why it was no longer safe to take a walk. When you stepped on a mine you never knew whose it was—it could be a small French pressure mine that blew off your foot, or a 1940s-vintage U.S. Army Bouncing Betty, a little canister designed to spring out of the ground and explode at groin height, or a dud bomb or artillery shell rewired by the VC.

By that time Major Lee had been reassigned to brigade headquarters and I had a new operations officer, a West Pointer named Slade Johnson. He was big (six feet five, 240 pounds), tough, and smart. We dug through the records of the 5/46 and plotted the sites of mine incidents on the map, trying to make sense of the place. It ended up showing lethal little red dots from one end of the peninsula to the other. But we found patterns—for instance, abandoned night defensive positions, where a force had previously camped, were among the most treacherous spots. So from the minute we arrived we gave mine maps to the troops and preached three rules: Avoid known roads and trails. Avoid ready-made openings in hedgerows between rice paddies. Avoid previous night defensive positions.

At the beginning, despite these precautions, we averaged one mine incident per day. Every time a mine went off, I flew immediately to the site. Mostly I did this to make my helicopter available—it took a medevac half an hour to come down from Chu Lai, and if we could eliminate that delay we could save lives. But I also wanted to talk to the men who'd just lost a buddy. Mines have an insidious effect on morale—the troops are walking along and suddenly somebody is dead or has lost a limb; a helicopter swoops in and takes him away, and there is nothing the men can do to even the score. While I abhorred the massacre at My Lai, I could also imagine how it might have happened. I could read the emotions in the faces of my own men. If I'd said, "The people in that village obviously knew this mine was here; in fact, one of them probably planted it. Go clear the place out," they'd have killed everyone in sight. So I'd move among the troops, asking, "How did it happen?" and saying, "Hey, you know, you can avoid these things if you stay off the roads and trails." I could reduce the tension just by being there, by talking and reassuring and reminding. Our efforts paid off—the men became very good at avoiding mines, and after the first month, if we had one incident in a week that was a lot.

Visiting the wounded was gut wrenching, especially when the casualties came day after day. The hospital at Chu Lai was a cluster of long, low, prefab buildings linked by wooden ramps. I tried to get there while the wounded were still in the recovery room. Unless there was a medevac helicopter on the helipad next to the emergency receiving building, we'd land there and I'd walk in. Both sides of the large room in the receiving building were always lined with wounded soldiers on stretchers set upon what looked like metal sawhorses. Each man had an IV in his arm and medics hovering over him trying to determine how badly he was hurt. The medics welcomed commanders who came to see their troops and would help me find the men I was looking for. If they were in surgery I'd have to wait, but if they were in the emergency room, the recovery room, or the wards I could see them right away.

I'd go up to a kid who'd just lost his leg and was lying there in shock and in pain, and the first thing he'd do would be *apologize*. "Sir, I'm sorry. I fucked up. I knew better than to do that." Then he'd want to know, "Did anybody die because of me?" I'd tell him how proud I was of him and tell him everything would be okay. If he was in good enough shape, I'd try to arrange for him to talk to his parents on the phone, so they could at least have the reassurance of hearing his voice. I'd usually put my hand on his shoulder and silently pray that somehow my strength would flow into his broken body so that he would live and heal quickly. I'd also know it was probably the last time I'd see him—we moved seriously wounded soldiers to Japan as soon as they were stable. I never broke down in front of a wounded man—it would have embarrassed both him and me—but I frequently found myself outside afterward, on one of those wooden ramps, coughing and choking back tears. Once a doctor came by and asked if I was all right. "Hell, yes, I'm all right," I growled. But I wasn't. These were *my* men, and when they got hurt, I was responsible.

I knew I had to give the men a chance to let off steam. Periodically we'd pull each company from the field and send it back to Chu Lai, where the men could lie around on the beach for three days and drink beer. Before returning them to the Batangan, I'd meet with the whole company. I'd sit in a folding chair on a stage in front of them and talk about whatever they wanted to discuss, whether it was the minefields we were facing or how soon they would be going home. I believed that the better informed a soldier was, the better he'd fight.

Those rap sessions were no fun, however. In a better organization the junior officers would have dealt with a lot of the misinformation and grievances that surfaced. The men would ask, "Why do we have to go out in these minefields? Did you volunteer us for this mission?" And, "Why do I have to wear my helmet and flak jacket all the time? It's hot out there." They hated the minefields. They hated the heat. They hated their helmets and flak jackets. Most of the time they hated *me*. But I never made the mistake of confusing their comfort with their welfare. I'd say, "Look, guys, I ain't here to win a popularity contest. My primary concern is keeping you alive. If on the day you leave for the United States your last thought of me is, 'I hate that son of a bitch,' that's fine. Actually, I'll be *happy* if that happens. Because an alternative is for you to go home in a metal casket, and then you won't be thinking anything at all. That's why I make you put on your helmets and flak jackets."

———

When we moved to the Batangan Peninsula we also moved to a new fire base, called FB Dottie, after the wife of the officer who had commanded the battalion at the time of the My Lai massacre and who had later been killed in action. Our tactical operations center at FB Dottie was in a large bunker and next door was another bunker where my staff lived. I slept in a cubicle right in the operations center. I could lie on my cot and hear the radios and know exactly what was going on in the battalion. I'd learned to sleep with one ear cocked during the siege of Duc Co five years before, but now I listened for incoming problems instead of mortar rounds. Working the reins twenty-four hours a day was the only way my staff and I could make sure that the 1/6 kept pulling in the right direction. Though we were now a good battalion, we knew we'd never be a great one because we never had enough seasoned junior officers and NCOs.

The enemy dictated my peculiar schedule. During the dry season, which started in April, they moved at night and attacked at night, a tactic that protected them from our helicopter gunships and air strikes. So generally I'd be up until about 4 A.M.—close enough to dawn so that I could hit my cot reasonably confident that there would be no attack that night. Then I'd sleep three or four hours and try to catch a short nap again in the afternoon. I became quite a student of the communist calendar, because the VC had a penchant for striking on holidays or on the anniversaries of past victories. On those dates, we'd string extra barbed wire willy-nilly through the camp and stage "mad minute" barrages: we'd rake our own perimeter with machine-gun and artillery fire to forestall any sapper attacks.

My view of the Vietcong never changed. I saw them as opportunistic brigands who with guns and encouragement from the North Vietnamese oppressed the peasants, stole their money and crops, and bullied them into cooperation. I'd have loved to fight a full-scale battle against the Phantom 48th. We had a competent battalion staff and I was quite confident we could have outmaneuvered and destroyed them. But the war had degenerated by then into piecemeal engagements that played to our weaknesses: our shortage of capable junior officers and NCOs, and our draftees' reluctance to fight.

On a couple of occasions, troops on ambush patrol simply let the Vietcong walk by. The men had figured out that if they didn't shoot at the VC, the VC wouldn't know they were there and so wouldn't shoot either. Good NCOs never would have let them get away with this, but we couldn't count on ours. So we devised a different solution: we beefed up the ambush patrols to fifteen or twenty men instead of the usual six or eight. That gave the men sufficient confidence to attack. Even so, the figures at division headquarters showed that my battalion wasn't killing as many VC as some of the other battalions. When units of the 1/6 were involved in a firefight, we reported the body count exactly as we knew it. We didn't speculate and we didn't inflate.

We had an assistant division commander in charge of operations, a general, who was convinced we should be killing more Vietcong. He had risen through the Corps of Engineers and then become a helicopter pilot and a commander of aviation units, but in my opinion he never should have been put in charge of combat troops.

One day while Colonel Clemons was visiting my headquarters the general flew in from Chu Lai and announced, "I've figured out why you're not making more enemy contact. The VC have broken up into two- and three-man groups. So I want you to break your battalion into two- and three-man groups as well, and station them all over the area. You'll kill a lot more enemy."

I explained that I'd just found it necessary to *increase* the size of our patrols. "Sir, if you send these men out in two- or three-man groups, they'll be scared to death and won't fight. On top of that, very few know how to read a map. They won't be able to tell us where they are, and we won't be able to fire our artillery without endangering our own men."

This made the general furious: "Well, that just sounds like a leadership problem to me! Obviously you need to exercise firmer control over the men in this battalion."

Stung, I was on the brink of saying, "General, I'm sorry, but I cannot obey your order."

Luckily, Joe Clemons stepped in and said, "Sir, Schwarzkopf's analysis is absolutely correct. What you're suggesting would not be a wise course of action." The general stormed out of the bunker, too angry to speak.

If Clemons hadn't interposed himself, my career might have ended on the spot. The general was just vindictive enough to say, "That's insubordination. Since you refuse to follow my orders, you are relieved of your command." Instead, Clemons took the heat. It was the right thing to do—a commander sticks up for his subordinates when they're right—yet it required tremendous moral courage.

The general moved to a different assignment the following week, but because of that incident and others where Clemons had stood up to him, he wrote an efficiency report that he had to know would effectively ruin Clemons's career. A year and a half later, when I was a personnel officer at Infantry Branch in Washington, Joe Clemons came to check his file. It included the general's report, which by military standards was so lukewarm that Clemons had not been selected for promotion to general. He knew he never would be, and he eventually retired as a colonel—a terrible loss for the Army and its troops.

———

In May we launched an all-American construction project: we brought in an engineer battalion and ran a road straight into the heart of the peninsula. The object was to link a series of hamlets previously accessible only by foot. This drove the VC crazy—at every opportunity they took potshots at the road-building teams, which were guarded by infantry, and tried to figure out where the teams were headed next so they could seed the area with mines. But we prevailed, and the road opened the way for Saigon to bring in doctors and teachers and government representatives to disseminate information against the Vietcong.

Major General Stanley Meloy had taken over from General Ramsey as division commander in Chu Lai. Meloy was not the sort of commander you'd catch attending a tea dance in a war zone. He was a short, stocky, tough graduate of Officer Candidate School who had never finished college. As a commander, he reminded me of Colonel Truong. The first time he came to FB Dottie for a briefing, he looked at my maps as I explained the battalion's operations. When I finished, he studied the maps silently for twenty minutes, every now and then asking a question. I saw he was taking the information I'd provided, weighing it in his mind, comparing it with the situation he saw on the maps, and judging whether it made sense. I was comfortable with that, but apparently the silence drove some battalion commanders wild. As the general scrutinized their maps they'd nervously brief him more. He'd thank them and turn back to the maps, only to be interrupted again. The first memo his new chief of staff issued to the battalions was a classic. It read in its entirety: "The division commander has observed that many battalion commanders seem more interested in his hearing what they have to say than in hearing what he has to say."

Meloy told Clemons that in his judgment, only four of the Americal's eleven battalion commanders were worth a damn, and that I was one of the four. I felt overwhelmed. I was surprised at how much the compliment meant to me—it made me reflect how unhappy this Vietnam tour was compared with my first, during which I'd needed no praise because the work itself had been so fulfilling.

Meloy liked to send touring congressmen and generals to visit FB Dottie. This was partly to prove that the Americal had cleaned up its act in the two years since My Lai. I'd give a two-part briefing to guests, talking first about military operations and then about the civil programs we'd undertaken to help the Saigon government gain more control, such as the road-building and the Medcap program, which provided local villagers with regular medical care.

In early May 1970, General Creighton Abrams, the U.S. commander in Vietnam, showed up to be briefed. I was eager to meet this wise, blunt-talking, cigar-chomping soldier's soldier who had first become famous commanding a tank battalion in the Battle of the Bulge. His grand plan was to turn the war back over to the South Vietnamese military, in whose hands I'd always thought it belonged. I explained that we hadn't made much progress toward that goal in the Batangan, mostly because the local South Vietnamese army units were quite weak, but Abrams was interested in every detail of the efforts we'd undertaken to build up those units.

A general accompanying Abrams tried to move the briefing along and interrupted, calling attention to the civil affairs topics I had yet to cover: "Sir, Schwarzkopf has done a better job at winning hearts and minds than just about any battalion commander in this area."

But Abrams was in no mood to curtail the discussion of military operations. He looked at me with his cigar in his mouth and growled, "My experience has been that if you grab 'em by the balls, their hearts and minds will follow."

On the morning of May 28, 1970, while I was in my helicopter heading for a mortar position we maintained out by the edge of the peninsula, C Company reported that a soldier had tripped a mine and gotten hurt. We flew to the scene and I told my pilot to be prepared to medevac the guy to Chu Lai. As we began to descend, I studied the company's position. They were on top of a large knoll and across the whole area were the outlines of old foxholes and trenches. "Goddammit!" I thought. "Another preventable casualty." They'd let themselves wander into an old night defensive position. The helicopter lifted off with the wounded soldier and I stayed behind with Tom Bratton, my artillery liaison officer, and told Tom Cameron, the company commander, what I'd seen from overhead, adding, "There are probably more mines out here, and we'd better decide how we're going to get these men out. Where's your map?"

Suddenly, *bam!* another mine went off. I turned and twenty yards away a soldier was on the ground, one of his legs grotesquely twisted. He was thrashing and wailing in agony: "Oh, Jesus! Somebody help me! Somebody help me!" I worried that by flopping around he'd sever an artery and end up bleeding to death.

Meanwhile, other guys started to yell: "Oh, my God!" "We're in the middle of a minefield!" "We're never gonna get out!" "We're all gonna die!"

"Knock that bullshit off!" I yelled back. "You're *not* all gonna die. We're going to get you out of here."

But the wounded man kept screaming and I realized I had to get over to him and help him. His cries were causing panic among the troops and the worst thing that could happen would be for them to break and run.

So I said to the company commander, "I've got to take care of that guy. You get on the radio. Start talking to your leaders. Get control of your company. Don't let them panic."

I started through the minefield, one slow step at a time, staring at the ground, looking for telltale bumps or little prongs sticking up from the dirt. My knees were shaking so hard that each time I took a step, I had to grab my leg and steady it with both hands before I could take another. I had to nearly double over to move. It seemed like a thousand years before I reached the kid.

I lay down on top of him because I wanted to stop him from thrashing. I'd been a wrestler at West Point and knew how to pin a guy down; also, I weighed about 240 pounds. I started talking to him: "You're gonna be okay. We're gonna get you out of here. Calm down and quit screaming. You're scaring the shit out of people. You're not gonna die. We want to save your leg, but if you keep on flailing around like that, you're liable to break an artery and kill yourself."

"Yes, sir," he gasped, and before long he quieted down.

"Okay. Now let's get you out of here," I said. I turned and spotted a bush twenty yards away, right where I'd been standing when we came in. "Bratton!" I called. "Grab your knife and cut me a couple of branches to use as a splint." Bratton took one step and *boom!* a mine blew off his right arm and leg and he went down. I felt shrapnel punch into my chest. I looked down and saw blood coursing from several gashes.

The troops started to panic and I shouted, "Nobody moves! Stand where you are until we can get you out!" I removed the kid's belt, lashed his wounded leg to his good leg, and left him there while I ran back to where the company commander and a couple of other guys were bending over Bratton. The blast had taken a chunk out of his skull, and I was sure he was going to die. But we bandaged him as best we could, put him on the medevac helicopter we'd called for the kid, and turned our attention back to the troops.

I radioed my headquarters and told them we needed an engineer team with mine detectors. Twenty minutes later they flew in and I watched the skids of the helicopter touch down, half expecting it to detonate another mine and kill us all. I told the head engineer, "Clear the landing area first, and mark where you find mines."

The guy looked stricken. "Sir, we don't have anything to mark them with. We thought you were just gonna walk behind us and let us lead you out."

"What about all these other guys? We've gotta mark paths." I radioed FB Dottie and said, "Gather up as many cans of shaving cream as you can."

On the other end of the radio, my executive officer must have thought I'd gone crazy—that I was in a minefield and I'd decided to make the men shave. "Sir?" he said. "Are you sure you want shaving cream?"

"Goddammit! Don't argue with me! Get the shaving cream out here *now*! I'll explain why later!"

So we sent the helicopter to fetch shaving cream, and the engineers spent the next couple of hours clearing paths with metal detectors to wherever there were men. The troops slowly made their way to the helicopter, which lifted them off the knoll, ten at a time, to a safe area below. By the time the last man left, the whole hillside was covered with little white circles. How many actually represented mines we'd never know—given the number of bombs and bullets that had fallen in that area over the past thirty years, there was buried metal everywhere.

When the last kid was off the hill, I had them fly me to the hospital. After they dug seven or eight pieces of shrapnel out of my left pectoral muscle and bandaged me up, I bullied the doctor into letting me go back to my battalion right away. I knew they had been working on Bratton in the emergency room and went to check on him. He was lying on a gurney behind a curtain, and amazingly he was conscious and in no apparent pain—which scared the hell out of me: I'd seen badly wounded men rally that way, only to die minutes later. "Hang in there, Bratton," I told him. "Goddammit, you're going to make it."

Then I went down to the recovery room, looking for the other men who'd been hurt. Three black soldiers stopped me in the hallway. "Colonel, we saw what you did for the brother out there," one said. "We'll never forget that, and we'll make sure that all the other brothers in the battalion know what you did." I was stunned. It hadn't registered on me until that moment that the kid in the minefield was black.

My chest had been numbed, but by the time I got back to FB Dottie it had really started to hurt. I lay down on my cot, but in a few minutes the executive officer came by to inform me that Colonel Clemons had flown in to get a report. I went to meet him in the briefing room. I was still buzzing with adrenaline and I must have been a little punchy also: I forgot to button my shirt. Before Clemons had a chance to say anything, I began talking. I talked and talked and couldn't stop. I even started drawing little diagrams. Suddenly he burst out, "For Christ's sake, Schwarzkopf! You don't have to brief me! Go to bed!" He wasn't looking at my face; he was looking at my chest. The wounds had popped open and blood was streaming from under the bandage.

———

I took a few days to recuperate, and then Clemons sent me to Bangkok for R&R. I spent the week in a fleabag hotel, chosen arbitrarily from an Army list. I ordered jewelry to give Brenda when I got home—seven rings, one for each month she'd been pregnant, and a baby ring set with a beautiful cornflower-blue star sapphire. I took tours of the city and loaded up on standard-issue souvenirs—bronzeware and prayer beads and silk scarves. But mostly I cast about, distracted and bored. I'd been in Vietnam just over eleven months. Up to now I hadn't taken time to face the end of my tour. I felt torn: on the one hand I felt the powerful tug of home; on the other hand, I'd worked so hard to put my battalion in shape that I couldn't imagine not running it. But I knew it was time to let go.

Two weeks later I got in my helicopter, flew to each of the five companies, and gave the troops a farewell talk. I joked with them: "I know that when you saw this helicopter, you thought it was the chow coming in. I'm sorry to disappoint you." Then I said I hadn't wanted to leave without telling them thank you. I thanked them for serving their country. I thanked them for serving under my command. I thanked them for the privilege of being their commander. I wished them good luck. Finally I told them that the thing I was most proud of was that they were alive, and I wanted them to stay alive and get home safely.

Some of the men applauded and cheered, and then I went back to the helicopter and took off. I was sitting in the door as we circled the position to gain altitude, and the men stood waving and giving the peace sign. The sight reminded me of my old West Point instructor, Captain Martin, whose men had waved to him from their tanks. I gave them a thumbs-up, which seemed an appropriate way to return their salute.

When I returned to FB Dottie my replacement was waiting—a good friend from West Point and Fort Benning, Lieutenant Colonel Fred Woerner. He was a terrific officer and I was glad he was taking over my battalion, and to make sure he understood the situation fully, I gave him a four-hour briefing. I was determined that there would be no repeat of my predecessor's treatment of me.

I got into Cam Ranh Bay the next afternoon and twenty-four hours later joined the line to board the plane home. A transportation officer, a captain, shoved some papers into my hand. "Sir, here are the manifests," he said. "You've been designated airplane commander."

"What the hell does that mean?" I said.

"You're responsible for the discipline of the troops on the airplane. When you arrive, you must turn over these documents to the officer who meets the flight. If you should land at any location other than your planned destination, you will be responsible for the men."

I realized I was really tired of being a commander.

As we flew out I remembered how hard it had been to leave after my first tour, knowing that my Vietnamese friends had to stay behind and fight. This time my emotions were utterly different. I thought, "Thank God it's over." I'd saved as many lives as I could, and while a lot of those men were still out there, they were no longer my responsibility. I wanted to get home to my family.

11

took the red-eye out of San Francisco to Baltimore/Washington International Airport on Thursday,
July 23, 1970. As we made our final approach early on Friday morning, we
flew straight into a thunderstorm. Wind buffeted the plane, lightning
flashed, and just as we reached the runway I watched the right wing outside
my window dip sickeningly toward the ground. "Great," I thought, "I've
survived two tours in Vietnam and I'm gonna crash here in front of my
wife."

Both Brenda and Sally were waiting at the gate. We hugged and kissed
one another and then Brenda stepped back and I looked at her in all her
eight-months-pregnant glory. She was beautiful. I told her diplomatically
that she looked as if she hadn't even gained a pound. Brenda laughed and
hugged me again. After we collected my bags, Sally had to say good-bye
because she was already late for work at the National Security Agency.
Brenda and I walked alone to the car. "You're tired. Let me drive," she said.
So I settled into the passenger seat for the thirty-mile trip to our modest
two-bedroom apartment in the Virginia suburb of Annandale. It was a
dreary, rainy day, and I worried whether Brenda should be driving in her
condition; but as she talked happily about our baby and our family and all
that had happened while I'd been gone, I felt myself start to relax. The war
was ten thousand miles away.

Over the next few weeks we immersed ourselves in baby preparations, turning the second bedroom of our apartment into a nursery complete with a music-box merry-go-round mobile over the crib, and reading to each other from Dr. Spock. I plotted the route to the hospital with military precision—the fact that there was a drawbridge on the way made me very nervous. On August 23—the day after my thirty-sixth birthday—Cynthia Pauline Schwarzkopf came into the world. I was pacing in the waiting room like a classic 1950s dad when a nurse emerged, announced that we'd had a girl, and told me that I couldn't see Brenda for a few minutes but that the baby was in the nursery. I ran down the hall to the viewing window with my heart in my throat, and there was a tiny, perfect baby with lots of dark hair and big dark eyes. I could almost imagine the "Made in Hong Kong" label on her bottom and loved her from the minute I set eyes on her. I got back to the delivery room just as the orderlies wheeled Brenda out. All I could say was, "She's beautiful!"

"I'm so happy," Brenda smiled. I gave her a kiss and then was ordered home by the nurse and instructed not to come back until tomorrow. I went, phoned everyone I could think of, and finally sat for hours in my big reclining chair wondering how I'd measure up as the father of a daughter.

The next day Brenda's mother Elsie arrived from Timberville and stayed for a week after Brenda and Cindy came home. With her help and that of a formidable babysitter named Mrs. Murphy, Brenda and I realized that Cindy would thrive despite our inexperience and clumsiness.

———

I hate to think what my life would have been like if I hadn't had Brenda to come back to after Vietnam. I'd read about Kent State and the antiwar upheavals that spring—at Oberlin, my sister Ruth had organized a workshop to make placards for demonstrations. I'd also heard about antiwar protesters spitting on soldiers. I'd made up my mind even before coming home that I'd punch out anybody who spit on me. Luckily, no one did. But one day that fall, I stopped at a mall in Virginia after work wearing my green uniform. I walked into a department store, and salespeople and other shoppers glared at me. I paid and left as quickly as possible, but getting into the car I thought, "I am in the nation's capital, wearing the uniform of the United States Army, and the people around me see me as some kind of monster!" The mood of the country had turned ugly.

Ironically, I was now in the business of sending people to Vietnam. My new job was in the personnel office at Infantry Branch, a thirty-man organization that dealt out assignments to more than thirty thousand infantry officers worldwide. To be chosen for this was a compliment, as Branch had its pick of all infantry officers; but you'd never guess that from the working conditions. The Officers Personnel Directorate in Washington across the Potomac from the Pentagon consisted of a cluster of so-called tempo buildings—wooden structures that had been thrown up during World War II. Infantry Branch occupied a large, fluorescent-lit and roach-infested first-floor bay; we'd brought down our file cabinets from the second floor after Army building inspectors had warned that if we left them upstairs, we'd come in some morning to find they'd fallen through the ceiling. I ran a group called the Professional Development Section, which consisted of seven officers and was separated from the Assignment Section by a series of low partitions. Assignment plugged officers into jobs the Army needed filled, while we checked to make sure each assignment made sense for the individual selected.

It was all desk work, twelve to fourteen hours' worth each day because, despite the reduction of forces committed to Vietnam, we were still an army at war. As head of the section, I often dealt with lieutenant colonels who, as they neared the twenty-year mark in their careers, wanted to know if they had a future in the Army. The toughest to face were men who had been misled by their bosses—for example, a battalion commander whose brigade commander had promised him, "You've done a great job and you're gonna be rewarded with a terrific efficiency report."

The fellow had expected to be selected to attend the Army War College, an honor accorded to the top fifteen percent of lieutenant colonels. When his name hadn't appeared on the list, he came to Infantry Branch to find out why and I had to tell him, "You got a bad efficiency report as a battalion commander."

"But my brigade commander said he was going to give me a wonderful report, and I know the assistant division commander also thought I was really good."

"Here's your report."

He looked at it, stunned. "What does this mean?"

"It probably means you aren't going to the War College. Your chances for promotion to colonel are fifty-fifty. And if you do get promoted, you probably won't be selected for brigade command, and you'll retire as a colonel." Colonel Hugh "Pat" Patillo, the chief of Infantry Branch, felt strongly that we ought to level with the men, and I agreed. Once an officer understood that his Army career had probably peaked, he could make other plans. Perhaps he'd always wanted to be a National Guard advisor in Hawaii, move his family there, and start a business once he retired. Rather than wait around for a brigade command that was never going to materialize, he could request a more appropriate assignment now. The frequency with which we saw people who had been lied to was astonishing to me.

That summer of 1970, the Army War College issued a scathing report—commissioned by General William Westmoreland, who was now chief of staff—that explained a great deal of what we were seeing. Based on a confidential survey of 415 officers, the report blasted the Army for rewarding the wrong people. It described how the system had been subverted to condone selfish behavior and tolerate incompetent commanders who sacrificed their subordinates and distorted facts to get ahead. It criticized the Army's obsession with meaningless statistics and was especially damning on the subject of body counts in Vietnam. A young captain had told the investigators a sickening story: he'd been under so much pressure from headquarters to boost his numbers that he'd nearly gotten into a fistfight with a South Vietnamese officer over whose unit would take credit for various enemy body parts. Many officers admitted they had simply inflated their reports to placate headquarters.

To any of us who had served in Vietnam, none of this was news. But what was disconcerting was the extent of unscrupulous behavior right there in Washington. High-ranking officers were pulling strings to prevent favored subordinates from being assigned second tours in Vietnam, even though it meant others would serve a third time. Other officers were tampering with the school selection process. One case was that of a major who was in his last year of eligibility for Command and General Staff College. He'd already been passed over several times because his record wasn't good enough, but his brother-in-law was a long-standing member of the House Appropriations Committee. That fall, Brigadier General John A. Kjellstrom, from the Army Comptroller's Office, came to see the head of the Officers Personnel Directorate and told him we had a problem: the congressman was threatening to stonewall the entire Army budget if we didn't let his brother-in-law into Leavenworth.

My staff and I, naive and idealistic, declared, "Ha! That'll never happen." But sure enough, someone arranged for the guy to occupy a slot that should have gone to a more qualified man. Later the major had the nerve to write us from Leavenworth: "Now that I'm here, my next goal is to attend the Army War College."

I found myself in a quandary: morally and ethically the Army was in as bad shape as when I'd joined, yet my own career was going great. I'd been promoted early to major, been promoted early to lieutenant colonel, and commanded a battalion in combat successfully. When the list for the War

College appeared in November, I was on it—one of only five people from my class to be picked in our first year of eligibility. Without having compromised, I'd become a front-runner in the officer corps of an institution that I felt was tarnished.

I was able to put off my growing ambivalence that winter of 1970–71 because there were more immediate problems to attend to. I was in trouble physically. For years I'd known I had a cracked vertebra in my lower back—a chronic fracture that one doctor suspected had occurred at birth and that I had aggravated by years of jumping out of airplanes. By the end of my tour in Vietnam, simply sitting in the fiber seat of my helicopter had become agony. But I'd ignored it until I'd taken a shower my first day home and, for the first time in a year, looked at myself in a full-length mirror. It was a real shock: the muscles of my right leg had atrophied to the point that the leg appeared markedly scrawnier than my left. I knew this was a symptom of nerve damage and told myself I had to do something about it. But then I'd pushed aside the thought because, with our baby about to be born and a new job to start, I had no intention of going into the hospital.

Since Cindy's birth the pain had worsened—Brenda would rub my back each night to try to alleviate it—and the leg continued to waste away. I finally went to Walter Reed hospital in February, and the doctors presented me with an ultimatum: either undergo major spinal surgery and lengthy rehabilitation, or risk eventual paralysis. Brenda was concerned for my health but left the decision to me. After making sure that I could defer my entry into the War College for a year, I opted for Walter Reed.

———

On June 15, 1971, I checked into Ward 1, the officers' orthopedic ward, which was to be my home for months. I walked through the door into a long hallway crowded with men in wheelchairs and on crutches—all amputees. I was suddenly back in Vietnam. "Hey, Colonel Schwarzkopf!" a familiar voice called. I turned, and limping toward me with a huge grin on his face was Tom Bratton. I hadn't seen or heard from him since the day he had nearly died in the minefield and I'd left him near death in the emergency room at Chu Lai. But this was Bratton all right—a big, dark-haired, jovial southerner. He grabbed my hand. "How are ya, sir? I read your name on the admitting list. It's great to see you!"

"Bratton! Why didn't you let me know you were here?"

"I didn't know where to find you." Bratton explained that he'd been in the ward for more than a year and was now learning to use his artificial arm and leg. "Come on, sir, let me show you around."

The hallway had doors mostly on one side. One opened into a semiprivate room, a second into a long porch ward with seven beds; finally, down at the end, there was a large square bay with beds against three walls. "Here's where I live," Bratton announced as we entered the bay. "Hey guys, this is Colonel Schwarzkopf. He's thinking about moving in." Suddenly he stopped and pointed to the middle of the floor, where someone had inlaid a one-and-a-half-foot mosaic of a rattlesnake into the linoleum. "We call this place the Snake Pit," he explained.

Then he introduced me to some of his pals: Mike Sinclair, who had lost both legs and an arm to a mine; Larry de Meo, whose arm had been blown off at the shoulder; and Henry Schroeder, whose bed was mounted on a huge round frame that the medics rotated to balance his circulation as they tried to save his legs. They all knew I was scheduled for surgery the next day. "Don't worry about a thing," Bratton reassured me. "We know how this place works and we're gonna make goddamn sure you get the kind of care you're supposed to." I was deeply touched. Here were guys who'd lost limbs, and they'd taken it upon themselves to worry about me.

As scheduled, the doctors performed a spinal fusion, which entailed taking bone from my hip, grinding it into paste, and using it to cement together three vertebrae in the small of my back. I spent the first two weeks after surgery strapped to an eight-foot-long metal and canvas device called a "Foster frame"; I had to be turned every four hours like a pig on a barbecue spit. By the end of June I had graduated to a body cast: forty-five pounds of plaster that went from my shoulders to my hips and down one leg to just above the knee. The day it went on, the orderlies brought me back to the ward and literally flopped me onto a bed. All I could think of was a turtle turned on its back. I'd started out in the semiprivate room, but soon they moved me to the porch ward, where Bratton and other guys in wheelchairs and on crutches were constantly wandering in and out.

Brenda visited every day, even though it was an hour's drive each way and she wasn't feeling well—she'd discovered, to our great delight, that she was pregnant again. Apart from her visits, life was measured by mealtimes, which I looked forward to because my arms were free and I could feed myself. I was dependent on nurses for virtually everything else. It wasn't long before the days and nights ran together. I read until my eyes ached. The Red Cross librarian would wheel in a cart twice a week and I'd grab whatever was there—spy novels, historical novels, mysteries, classics, even an occasional book of poetry. But after forty or fifty volumes I didn't want to read anymore. Brenda brought me a little television, and I watched until my brain got numb. I slept whenever I could because sleeping passed time. But as a consequence, I often found myself awake in the middle of the night, staring at the ceiling of the dimly lit ward. I thought constantly about Vietnam.

My mind went back to the spring just past, when it had seemed as though our whole country had gone insane. In April hundreds of Vietnam veterans, some in wheelchairs, had come to Washington to protest the war and had thrown their medals onto the steps of the Capitol; the newspapers reported that the medals included some Silver Stars and Purple Hearts. I couldn't make myself believe that anyone would throw away such decorations—I figured they must be just the administrative medals that were automatically awarded to everyone who served in the war zone. A couple of days later 200,000 people showed up in Washington for an antiwar march, and the week after that the police arrested thousands of protesters who impeded traffic and blocked government buildings in the so-called Mayday demonstrations. Finally, two days before I was admitted to Walter Reed, *The New York Times* started publishing the Pentagon Papers, secret documents from early in the war. Ostensibly, the papers raised questions about whether President Johnson had deceived the public concerning America's growing involvement.

I *hated* what Vietnam was doing to the United States and I *hated* what it was doing to the Army. It was a nightmare that the American public had withdrawn its support: our troops in World War I and World War II had *never* had to doubt for one minute that the people on the home front were fully behind them. We in the military hadn't chosen the enemy or written the orders—our elected leaders had. Nevertheless, we were taking much of the blame. We soldiers, sailors, airmen, and Marines were literally the sons and daughters of America, and to lose public support was akin to being rejected by our own parents.

Bitterly, I recalled an incident that had taken place during my first tour in 1965. My Vietnamese airborne unit had overrun a Vietcong headquarters, and among the documents we'd captured had been a directive from Ho Chi Minh. It said in effect: "I know you're facing more and more Americans right now, but don't worry. We're going to win the war against America the same way we won the war against the French: not on the battlefield, but in the enemy's homeland. All you have to do is hang on. The American people are not tough enough to see this war through and we are. We have fought for twenty years; we can fight another twenty years; before then, they will give up and not support their troops anymore, and we will claim victory."

I'd brought it back to the Manor BOQ and we'd talked about it as a joke. "Look at this crap! Look at the propaganda these people are printing!" But Uncle Ho had known what he was talking about—he was an astute student of the western mind and understood his enemy better than we understood ourselves.

I slowly realized that I'd have to think long and hard before ever going to war again. The Army would get ready to send me and I'd have to stop and ask, "Is it worth it?" I felt stuck: I couldn't imagine refusing to obey orders, yet I also couldn't imagine fighting another war to which my country wasn't fully committed.

I reflected on my military career. I'd been in the Army fifteen years; in five more I could retire. Actually, I probably could arrange a medical discharge and retire right away. I was sure I could get a job on the outside, teaching or maybe working with one of my classmates who had already left and gone into business. But as I imagined leaving, I knew that that wasn't really what I wanted. I was good at being a soldier and what I wanted was to see the Army—and the attitude of the public—change so that I could proudly remain one. But who was going to change it?

Whenever I became depressed and withdrawn, Bratton would shake me back to reality. He'd come over to my bed and say, "Goddammit, sir, if I can walk with just one leg, how come you can't walk with two?"

"You don't have this turtle shell on your back," I'd shoot back. But I was embarrassed because I was eventually going to have a normal life, while Bratton never would. He and his pals were in and out of my ward every day, joking, playing cards, and generally terrorizing the orderlies. I began to understand how the Snake Pit worked. Newcomers just back from Vietnam were often bitter and consumed with self-pity. If a man didn't snap out of it, the doctors would assign him a bed down in the Snake Pit. Like Bratton, most of the guys had been there for months or years and were fighting to overcome terrible injuries. So they were merciless when the newcomer would start moaning. They'd yell, "You fuckin' wimp. Shut up! What are you moaning about? There's a lot of guys here who are hurt worse than you. You're gonna walk again, you little bastard. Shut up, goddammit! We don't want to hear it."

They'd often reduce the new man to tears. But after that, he'd grind his teeth and fight back, which was precisely what they wanted. They knew that mastering artificial limbs required tremendous physical conditioning and mental discipline, particularly for multiple amputees; a man consumed with self-pity simply wasn't going to make it. The guys in the Snake Pit were relentless, but they brought people back to life. In my eyes they were heroes.

Gradually as I recuperated my morale improved. My brightest day was August 22, my thirty-seventh birthday, because the staff bent the rules to let Brenda bring Cindy. The two of them were waiting in a dayroom when the orderlies wheeled me in on a gurney. I was worried that the baby wouldn't remember me—I'd been gone ten weeks and she was just one year old—but the minute she saw me she said "Da-Da" and started climbing happily all over my body cast. I was elated and relieved. Brenda had brought me the birthday present I'd requested: a tennis racquet. I asked an orderly to hang it up opposite my bed.

I started physical therapy, which in my case meant learning to walk in the body cast. They tilted me upright on a giant rotating table—I'd been off my feet so long that my soles hurt like hell when I stood on them—and a tiny, birdlike nurse steadied me as I took my first steps. "You'd better get out of the way if I fall," I warned her. "I'll squash you flat."

In late September the day finally came when the doctors switched me to a body cast that only went from my shoulders to my hips. I could go home! I was still assigned to the hospital and would still have to check in for therapy every other week, so there were no long good-byes with the guys in the Snake Pit. We had a momentary crisis in the hospital driveway when I couldn't fit through the door of the car, but with the help of Brenda and an attendant I was able to slide in and prop myself diagonally across the backseat. It didn't matter—I'd have ridden tied to the roof if that's what it took.

———

Shortly after coming home from the hospital, I got a letter from C. D. B. Bryan, a writer for *The New Yorker* magazine. In it, he explained that he was working on an article about the family of a young sergeant named Michael Mullen who had been killed by so-called friendly fire in the Rocket Pocket while under my command. He wanted to interview me about what had happened.

The soldier's parents had come to see me at the hospital. They were ordinary Iowa farm people trying to absorb not only the death of their son, but the tragedy that he'd been killed by his own side. The Army had made things worse: by being clumsy and evasive about the accident, it had caused the Mullens to become convinced that there was a conspiracy to cover up the truth about Michael's death. Their faith in the government was destroyed and Mrs. Mullen had become an outspoken member of the antiwar movement. Before I left Vietnam, she'd sent me a half-page advertisement she and Mr. Mullen had placed in *The Des Moines Register*. It began: "A silent message to the mothers and fathers of Iowa. We have been dying for nine, long, miserable years in Vietnam in an undeclared war . . . how many more lives do you wish to sacrifice because of your silence?" Printed underneath, in neat rows, were 714 tiny crosses—the number of Iowans who had died in the war. Mrs. Mullen was fiercely proud of that ad: she'd paid for it with Michael's two-thousand-dollar Army death gratuity.

I'd agreed to meet with the Mullens in the hope of setting their minds at rest: I couldn't bring back their son, but they had a right to a straightforward explanation of how he'd died. I'd answered their questions and laid out the facts as clearly as I could. On the night of February 18, 1970, C Company had dug in on a jungle hilltop. They'd made a routine request for our artillery to zero in on the trails near their position in case the Vietcong attacked during the night. One of the test rounds detonated directly above them, spraying the men with shrapnel and killing Michael Mullen and another soldier. A subsequent investigation concluded that a lieutenant at the artillery fire direction center, in calculating trajectories, had forgotten to take into account the vegetation on the hilltop. The round had been meant to sail over C Company; instead it had hit a tree and exploded.

The mood when the Mullens first arrived had been tense, but the conversation had become more cordial as we went along. I'd provided all the information I had and suggested other people for them to talk to, and at the end Michael's father had shaken my hand, which he'd refused to do at the start. But I now saw from Bryan's letter that the Mullens hadn't believed me; Bryan wanted to hear my explanation for himself.

I called the Army public affairs office to notify them of the request. The officer I spoke to quickly said, "You don't have to talk to him."

I thought that was crazy. "But I *want* to talk. I don't have anything to hide."

"Fine. You're on your own." He suggested I use a tape recorder during the interview to make sure nothing was taken out of context, then added, "Be sure to stay within your level of expertise." By that he meant I shouldn't criticize my commanders or the President.

Bryan showed up on the morning of October 6, 1971, a tall, beanpole-thin fellow with combed-back hair, sharp features, intelligent eyes, and a soft, pleasing voice. He explained that the C. D. B. Bryan of his byline stood for Courtlandt Dixon Barnes Bryan, but that everyone called him Courty. We set up at the dining room table and talked—first about what had happened that night in Charlie Company, and later more generally about the 1/6's operations in the Rocket Pocket and on the Batangan Peninsula.

He asked very detailed and precise questions and I think found me more candid and down-to-earth than he'd expected. Whenever he asked, "How can I verify that?" I was able to provide the names of people to corroborate. As the hours passed, I surprised myself by talking about what it meant to be a military officer and voicing many of the doubts I'd wrestled with during those long nights in the hospital. To me the death of Michael Mullen was not just one tragedy but two: the needless death of a young man, and the bitterness that was consuming his parents.

Late in the afternoon Brenda came home—she'd been visiting friends with Cindy—and cooked dinner and we invited Bryan to stay and eat with us. Then I drove him to his hotel. We finished the interview the following morning and corresponded for weeks after that. Bryan's notion was that the story of the Mullen family was a symbol of how Vietnam was tearing America apart. I just hoped I'd finally been able to set the record straight. Bryan ultimately published a book on the subject, *Friendly Fire*. When it came out, in 1976, I found it an honest and moving account of the incident.

By the early spring of 1972 I'd pretty much picked up my life where I'd left off. I'd graduated to a back brace that fit under my uniform and returned to work at Infantry Branch. In March our daughter Jessica was born. What a joy she was—her baby smile could light up a room. Having a toddler and an infant in the house, coupled with my physical condition, limited our ability to socialize—but neither Brenda nor I took much interest in the Washington whirl. We spent most of our social time with classmates and their wives, such as Pete and Ginger Lash, Ward and Judy Le Hardy, and Bill and Nancy Cody, who lived close by. We also managed occasional visits to Brenda's parents in Timberville, one hundred miles south of Washington. We both looked forward to the summer, when we'd move to Pennsylvania to start our year at the Army War College.

One Saturday evening that spring Sally came over for dinner bringing a magnum of Châteauneuf-du-Pape. Sally was practically a part of our household: every Thursday she'd come over to play cards, watch TV, or just talk, and often she'd turn up one evening on the weekend, too. Sally lived right across the Potomac in a hilly, wooded section of Bethesda, Maryland, where she'd rented a wonderful, eccentric log cabin that had once been a summer cottage. She had immersed herself in her career and never married—and while she could tell us very little about her job, we knew she was one of a handful of women to achieve an executive position at the National Security Agency. Sally had also become the glue that held the Schwarzkopf family together. More than the rest of us, she looked after Mom, who, at seventy-one, suffered serious medical problems and had moved to Chevy Chase, Maryland, in order to have access to Walter Reed. Sally also stayed in close touch with Ruth, who in the past year had moved to Middlebury, Vermont, where Simon had a new teaching job. I had grown particularly close to Sally, and though she was older than me—she was now forty—I'd come to think of her as my kid sister.

After cocktails and a long, lively dinner—Brenda hardly drank, so Sally and I polished off the magnum between us—we all settled down in front of the TV. Sally and I were always great talkers and tonight we'd started some desultory discussion about civil liberties when I noticed the screen. There was a Korean War movie on, and a number of soldiers in combat fatigues were moving out across a large open field. The minute I saw that, I knew what was going to happen: they were walking into a minefield. Sure enough, a guy stepped on a mine, and I recoiled in horror. The other guys kept walking and I heard myself saying, "Don't do that. Don't do that. Don't do that." They hit the mines too.

Sally was looking at me in amusement. "Come on, Norman, it's just a movie. It's not even about Vietnam. Aren't you overreacting?"

"I'm not," I said. I was shaking.

"Oh, you are. It's not that bad."

"What the hell are you talking about, not that bad? People died! Arms were blown off! Legs were blown off! You have no idea what you're talking about. How can you tell me it's not that bad!"

"Why worry about it? It's behind us," she insisted.

I deeply resented that. "It's *not* behind us. It's still going on. Goddammit, I can't stand the people in this country who say it's over, who are trying to put it behind us, who are trying to pretend it never happened! Don't tell me I shouldn't react. You sound just like the peaceniks!"

Sally misread how strongly I was reacting. She thought I was just being argumentative and pressed on: "You can't just dismiss everything the peaceniks say. They have some legitimate points."

"You don't know anything about it."

"Oh, yes, I do. I read the newspaper every day." That really burned me up—Sally always believed every word in *The Washington Post*. Before I knew it, she was going on about the South Vietnamese—how their government was corrupt and didn't really represent the people, how they weren't capable of running their own country, and on and on. I couldn't believe my ears. I'd always thought Sally was on my side. But what I was hearing was a dismissal of the war and a willingness to walk away from everything we stood for in Vietnam—an attitude that, to my mind, was contributing to the loss of more American lives. I couldn't tolerate that. "I'm sorry," I interrupted, "but if you honestly believe these things, if you honestly feel that way, then I don't want you in this house."

Sally bristled. "Well, I honestly do feel that way."

"Then get out." I was in tears because I felt so betrayed, and now she was crying, too. "Get out of my house."

"Oh, now, Norman, I . . ."

"There's nothing to talk about! Get out." Sally left.

Brenda had watched in shock as the scene unfolded. "You shouldn't have said that, Norm. Why don't you go after her?"

"Hell, no! I meant every word." I went to bed.

When I woke up the next morning, I remembered what I'd done and some of the things we'd said. I couldn't believe the insane way in which I'd treated my sister. Lying there, I came to two conclusions. Number one, I had to put Vietnam behind me. I would never forget the lessons it had taught me, but I couldn't allow it to consume me and destroy my family. Number two, I reminded myself: "Schwarzkopf, your mother is an alcoholic. What happened last night was largely a result of your having had too much to drink." I'd been a heavy weekend drinker since my days as a second lieutenant at Fort Campbell, and I'd always assumed I could handle it. Now I saw I really couldn't, and made up my mind that I'd never let booze take control of my life.

Then I got up, called Sally, and told her I was sorry. She, in turn, apologized for getting me upset. That ended the fight between us, which was really not where the anger had come from at all. It had come from inside me.

———

The site of the Army War College was a beautiful, sleepy town called Carlisle in Pennsylvania Dutch country about one hundred miles west of Philadelphia. We qualified for a two-bedroom apartment on post, but Brenda and I opted to take the quarters allowance and rent a small, three-bedroom, brick house in town. This effectively took us out of the social mainstream—pickup softball games in the afternoon and spur-of-the-moment parties that seemed to go on at all hours—but for our young family it was just right, and I savored the time spent with Brenda and the girls.

The War College devoted very little time to lessons on waging war. Its aim was to take lieutenant colonels accustomed to seeing the world from the worm's-eye perspective of a battalion commander and whet their appetites for knowledge that had application far beyond the battlefield. Accordingly, the program ranged across contemporary history, world affairs, international relations, U.S. policy-making, and numerous other aspects of national and international thinking—a curriculum that even faculty members frequently described as "a mile wide and an inch deep." My class, which numbered 234 and included a sprinkling of Navy, Air Force, and Marine officers, was segmented into fifteen-person seminar groups. A typical day had the entire class assembling for a lecture in the morning, then breaking for lunch, moving on to our respective seminar rooms for an hour of discussion in the early afternoon, and then heading home, ostensibly to read or work on case studies for the balance of the day. So much latitude was built into the schedule that at first no one could believe it—we kept looking over our shoulder to see if someone was checking on us.

It was a strange time to attend the War College. Not only had Vietnam demoralized our soldiers and wrecked our credibility with the American public, but it had soaked up a huge share of the Army's budget. Meanwhile our fighting equipment had become obsolete, our bases and facilities had fallen into disrepair, and our ability to fight anywhere else in the world—even in Europe against the Warsaw Pact, which was still the Army's number-one mission—had seriously deteriorated. Many officers looked to Creighton Abrams, who had succeeded Westmoreland as chief of staff, to lead the Army to recovery, but we all knew the process would take years.

My class, which consisted almost entirely of Vietnam veterans, didn't hesitate to challenge speakers who tried to paint rosy pictures. One morning that winter, a brigadier general presented a detailed description of how NATO would turn back a Warsaw Pact invasion. In his scenario, the enemy—sustaining terrible losses—would gradually force NATO all the way back across Germany and France to the beaches of Spain. There huge U.S. Air Force C-5A transport planes would swoop in, land on the sand, and unload thousands of fresh troops and hundreds of tons of equipment, thus enabling NATO to launch a counterattack that would repulse the Red horde. There was an embarrassed silence in the lecture hall. Then an Air Force lieutenant colonel stood up: "Sir, I know a lot about the C-5A and the bearing weight of runways. There are no runways in that part of Spain that the aircraft can land on, and it certainly can't land on a sand beach." Another officer rose and asked: "Where are these nonexistent troops and equipment coming from?"

The general looked around, and it finally dawned on him that he was in a roomful of critics. "What I detect here," he said, "is a *non*-can-do attitude."

On Saturday, January 27, 1973, Henry Kissinger, our national security adviser, and Le Duc Tho, the principal negotiator for North Vietnam, signed a cease-fire agreement in Paris and the war officially came to an end.

Nobody felt like celebrating. That same day Secretary of Defense Melvin Laird announced an end to the draft. We would somehow have to attract volunteers at the exact moment when virtually nobody wanted to serve. The Army had an answer to this challenge—its so-called Modern Volunteer Army initiative—which had been in the works for almost two years. It called for us to make military service more attractive by making it more like a civilian job. To kick off the new recruiting strategy, we launched a big advertising campaign built around the theme "The Army Wants to Join You."

I was curious to see how all this was going to work and had my chance on a class field trip to Fort Carson, Colorado, the home of a mechanized division that served as a test-bed for Modern Volunteer Army innovations. We were shown into a large briefing room where a brigade commander was ready with a presentation. I was expecting descriptions of new training programs, improvements in family living quarters, and the like, but the first thing he did was to pull out a multicolored *baseball cap*. "These specially made caps help the troops to relate to the task force they're in," he said. Each color meant something different. If a task force consisted of, say, two infantry battalions and an armor battalion supported by an artillery battalion, the cap would have two blue panels, one yellow, and one red. He went into this in great detail and then moved on to such innovations as beer vending machines in the barracks and topless go-go dancers in the officers' and NCOs clubs. He told us, absolutely straight-faced: "This is the modern era! We in the military have to adjust to the way civilians think."

"This is crazy," one of my classmates muttered. He was right—the entire program we were shown consisted of bells and whistles, with not a single fundamental change that would have meant anything to the troops. It suddenly struck me that the Army was lost and groping to find its way.

Meanwhile, I had known that December 1972 was the first time the Army would consider officers in my year group for early promotion to full colonel. We could expect routine promotions two more years down the road. All autumn everyone had told me they were sure I'd be picked; I'd even gotten feelers from various Army units that wanted me for a colonel's job. Having served in personnel, I knew that only a very small percentage of officers got selected, and while I thought I had a pretty good chance, I believed very strongly that no one had a right to *expect* an early promotion. All the same, being promoted early buoyed an officer's reputation and I'd secretly let myself look forward to it.

The list came out on a January weekend, and by the time I walked into the War College Monday morning and saw several of my classmates patting each other on the back, I knew my name wasn't on it. I was disappointed, confused, and shaken: I'd have another shot at early promotion the next winter, but this was the first time in my career when I was clearly no longer at the front of the pack. People offered condolences, which drove me crazy, as well as theories as to why I'd been bypassed. The main one was that I'd never served on the Army staff at the Pentagon. I found that convincing: at Infantry Branch we'd always advised lieutenant colonels that for early promotion they needed battalion command, the War College, and high-level staff service. We'd considered ourselves high-level staff at Infantry Branch, but maybe we'd been wrong.

Soon I got a call from my friends Bob Riscassi and Dick Larkin, colonels who worked for an assistant secretary of the Army at the Pentagon and knew I'd now be looking for a lieutenant colonel's job. I'd met Dick during my second tour in Vietnam, and Bob when I'd worked at Infantry Branch. "There's an opening here at the Pentagon," they said. "If you take it, you'll be working in the highest circles of the Army. If you're interested, we'll throw your hat in the ring." I asked what the job was; they told me, military assistant to the assistant secretary of the Army for financial management. It wasn't exactly the sort of work I'd aspired to, but I was comfortable with numbers and knew I could handle it.

My alternative was to go to Fort Benning, Georgia, where I was being offered a role in the Army's effort to recover from Vietnam. One of the first major reforms had been the institution of a new four-star command, Training and Doctrine Command, or TRADOC. Its head was General William DePuy, who had proven himself a brilliant, innovative field commander in Vietnam. DePuy's mission was nothing less than to totally rethink the way the Army trained its forces and fought its wars, and my job would have been to help test and refine the new ideas at the Infantry School at Fort Benning. The prospect excited me: not only did I like innovation and enjoy teaching, but I knew I'd have terrific colleagues—DePuy had selected some of the Army's most talented officers to work at the service schools.

The only problem was that TRADOC was new and everyone was advising me to return to Washington, so I reluctantly decided the Pentagon was where I had to be. In early February I asked Riscassi and Larkin to speak up on my behalf, and before long I was invited to Washington to meet Hadlai Hull, the Army's assistant secretary for financial management. The interview went very well; within days the job was mine.

For the first time in my Army career, I'd opted for an assignment not because I wanted it, not because I felt it was where I could make the greatest contribution to the Army or my country, but because I thought it would help me get ahead. I'd decided to ticket punch.

Working in the so-called Army secretariat—the civilian-dominated section of the Pentagon that included the offices of the secretary of the Army, his undersecretary, his assistant secretaries, and their deputies—took some getting used to. On my first afternoon I'd gone to attend to a bureaucratic task elsewhere in the building, and when I came back to our office at five o'clock, I found myself locked out. Everyone had gone home. The Pentagon staff manual stated that business hours were from 8:00 A.M. to 4:30 P.M., and those were the hours the secretariat kept. This was a pleasant change from the fourteen-hour days at Infantry Branch.

The bad news was that Riscassi and Larkin had exaggerated somewhat when they'd implied that my name would be known in the highest circles of the Army: being a military assistant was actually a fairly obscure job. My first inkling of this came early on, when I was assigned to do a lot of work for Deputy Assistant Secretary Ekhard Bennewitz. He was a dark-haired, middle-aged man with a friendly disposition who for some reason got it into his head that my name was Marvin. Whenever we passed each other in the hall, he'd say, "Hi, Marv!" After about two months it really got to me, and I asked his executive officer to discreetly let him know my real name. The next week, whenever Mr. Bennewitz saw me in the hall, he'd grin and say, "Hi, Norm! Good to see you, Norm!" I felt much better.

That Friday I was scheduled to give a briefing on a major study we had in the works that concerned Army-base closures and was known as Project Concise. The meeting was a strategy session and all the deputy assistant secretaries assembled in Mr. Bennewitz's office. When the moment came for me to speak, Mr. Bennewitz called me in and introduced me to his colleagues: "Of course you all know one of Mr. Hull's military assistants. This is Norm Schwarzmueller." Riscassi and Larkin, who thought this was hilarious, promptly nicknamed me Marvin Schwarzmueller.

Project Concise opened my eyes to the inner workings of Washington. Early in 1972 the Army had faced up to the fact that, because of budget cuts, it could no longer sustain all its bases across the United States. The staff had set out to determine objectively which would have to close. During the autumn of 1973, we digested tens of thousands of pages of mission analyses, economic-impact studies, environmental-impact studies, and the like, representing thousands upon thousands of hours of work, to derive a final list. We were confident that this was the best and fairest base-closure list in military history.

Howard "Bo" Calloway, the secretary of the Army, decided that, as a courtesy, we would brief senators from the states involved before we made a public announcement. So he dispatched a team of staff officers to Capitol Hill and I went along as an observer. Our first call was on Senator John J. Sparkman, the powerful Alabama Democrat whose state was home to Fort McClellan—the base we'd identified as the least efficient in the entire U.S. Army. We'd prepared a superb briefing, crystal clear in its evidence and irrefutable in its logic as to why Fort McClellan had to close. The senator, a kindly old gentleman, listened intently as my colleagues laid out our case. Finally, in his deep southern accent, he said, "Young men, ah wanna compliment you on this wonderful briefing. It's obvious that you have gone to a great deal of hard work, and the facts that you have assembled are startling, and I feel quite sure that you think every one of 'em is true." We all started to preen. Smiling, he continued, "There's something else I'd like to say about this wonderful presentation."

We all leaned forward. "Yes, sir? What is it?"

"You go back and tell your bosses in the Pentagon that as long as I am the senator from the great state of Alabama, you ain't *nevuh* gonna close Fort McClellan!" With that he stormed out of the room.

I was in Bennewitz's office on a Saturday morning two weeks later when we made up the final list for public announcement. It was one hundred percent political: "Well, we can't close that base, and we can close this one, and here's another we'll probably get away with, but we won't be able to . . ." Eighteen months of hard work counted for nothing: we could have put together the list without a single day of study. To accomplish anything in Washington meant having to compromise, manipulate, and put in the fix behind the scenes.

Despite my disenchantment with the Pentagon and Washington, my decision to ticket punch now looked as if it were going to pay off. In early November the Army nominated me to serve as a military aide to Vice President Ford—a prestigious Executive Office Building job that would leave me with powerful connections in the event I decided to retire. I was flattered to be chosen out of all the lieutenant colonels in the Army, and didn't even mind when I got a call from my West Point classmate Don O'Shei, a fellow lieutenant colonel who said he'd been nominated too. After I congratulated him, Don remarked, "I hope you know that Jack Walker's name has cropped up also." Walker was a friend from the Army War College and a great officer who had served as a military assistant to Defense Secretary Melvin Laird for years.

"Jeez, I had no idea," I said. I thought about it for a minute and concluded, "Let's not be naive. If Walker is really up for the job, it'll go to him. Melvin Laird is one of the Vice President's best friends. Why should we even consider ourselves in the running?" Don agreed.

Shortly afterward I ran into Walker at a cocktail party and asked about the military aide job. "I'm not interested in that at all," he said. "I want to command a brigade. As a matter of fact, I'm pushing for *you* to work with Ford."

As the selection process went on, I really got my hopes up. I was interviewed by Jack Marsh, the Vice President's assistant for national security affairs—and, as it happened, a former congressman from the Shenandoah Valley. A banker Brenda knew there sent a note on my behalf, and the interview went very well. Then I had an opportunity to meet the Vice President himself. I thought we really hit it off. Ford was famous for having played center during his football days, and I had been a nose guard; he joked that he wouldn't hold it against me that I'd beat up on so many centers. Finally I was interviewed by his chief of staff. All the while, Don O'Shei was going through the same beauty contest—he and I kept comparing notes—and periodically Jack Walker would call to check on how we were doing. November and December passed.

Early January 1974 brought two events in quick succession. First, the Army released its list for early promotion to colonel, and to my utter shock, again I'd not been selected. I sat in my office reading and rereading it in stunned disbelief. On it were the names of several friends and classmates and contemporaries—my West Point roommate Leroy Suddath was on it—but not mine. I felt a wave of revulsion at the manipulations I'd been party to in my eagerness to get picked—the secretariat, for instance, had submitted my efficiency report way ahead of schedule to make sure the promotion board knew that I'd gotten my Pentagon ticket punched.

A few days later Jack Walker called me at work. "Norm, I've just been notified that I've been selected to go to work for Gerald Ford," he said. "But I'm sure it's not the same job that you're competing for."

I couldn't believe what I was hearing. "Jack, *of course* it's the same job. Congratulations. I'm happy that you got the assignment—if that's what you wanted." I got off the phone as quickly as I could and sat at my desk feeling like a total fool. The whole thing had been rigged and I hadn't seen it. Obviously Walker had had the job from the start; O'Shei and I had just been there for show.

I raced downstairs to the Pentagon athletic center, where I worked out every day, and started punching the heavy bag. I didn't even bother to put on gloves. I pounded it and pounded it, angry at the whole damned dumb system. How could I have allowed myself to ticket punch? How could I have gotten caught up in a race to join a political world I detested? I beat that punching bag until it was smeared with blood from the knuckles of both fists. I think I was imagining it to be me.

———

I kept my sanity that year through physical activity. I swam and went running every day, consumed quantities of vitamins, and by the time I turned forty, was in the best physical shape of my life. At home, I played with my kids, immersed myself in hobbies, including wine making and magic, my old favorite, and developed into quite a handyman. When we'd moved back to Annandale from the War College, Brenda and I had bought our first house, a brand-new five-bedroom colonial with a large unfinished basement. I'd promptly boned up on home-repair manuals, spent lots of money on tools and supplies, and set out to build a rec room. I paneled the walls, laid a linoleum floor, hung the ceiling, and installed wiring—all to the amazement of Brenda's dad. Until that moment, I think, Jesse Jefferson Holsinger had honestly believed that his son-in-law was in the military because he wasn't really capable of anything else. The fact that I'd graduated from West Point, earned a master's degree in missile engineering, and commanded a battalion in Vietnam meant virtually nothing to him compared with my being able to finish a rec room with my own two hands. For the first time Jesse seemed persuaded that I would survive in the real world if I ever got out of the Army.

Meanwhile, life at the Pentagon went on. The Army had announced its intention to develop and build a whole new generation of weapon systems over the next ten years—the M-1 tank, the Bradley Fighting Vehicle, the Apache and Black Hawk helicopters, the Sergeant York air-defense gun, and the Patriot and Pershing missiles. A good part of my job was to weave these costly programs into both our annual budget and the five-year plan and then help the Army staff and secretariat figure out how to sell them to Congress. I worked hard and gained a reputation as a team player who knew how to get things done in the bureaucracy—something of which I wasn't entirely proud.

I knew I had to make a change. I had two years left at the Pentagon; three before hitting the twenty-year mark in my career. I could extend my current assignment a year and then retire without ever leaving Washington. But that didn't seem to be a real choice. I asked myself why I was wasting my time as a staff officer and I thought back over the jobs that had made me happy, starting with my earliest days as a second lieutenant commanding a platoon. I realized that even if I were destined to end my career at twenty years, I wanted to get back to the troops. Yet I knew the odds were against that: officers on the Pentagon staff were considered essential and were rarely permitted to leave Washington before their tour was complete.

In November, my name finally appeared on the list for colonel—no cause for celebration, as far as I was concerned, because the promotion was practically automatic for officers with more than six years as a lieutenant colonel who had commanded a battalion and attended the War College.

A few weeks later I got a call from a friend, Brad Johnson, whom I'd met during my first tour in Vietnam—he was the helicopter pilot who medevacked me the day I got shot riding in the armored personnel carrier with Colonel Truong. We'd been drinking buddies afterward as instructors at West Point, and our paths had crossed again during these last few years in Washington. He was now commanding a helicopter battalion in Fairbanks, Alaska. Brad knew how miserable I was at the Pentagon. After congratulating me drily on my promotion he said, "There's something up here that you ought to know about." He launched into an elaborate description of U.S. Army Alaska, the command to which he was attached. He explained that, in addition to an unusually large combat brigade, it included the garrisons of three bases, the Arctic Test Center, and several National Guard and Army Reserve support units, so that it totaled twelve thousand personnel, nearly enough for a full division. As part of a major reorganization of the Army, U.S. Army Alaska was being renamed the 172nd Infantry Brigade (Alaska) and placed under a single brigadier general. He would be swamped with administrative work, so actual command of the combat brigade would fall to the deputy brigade commander, a colonel.

"What's the point of telling me this?" I asked.

"They can't find anybody to take the deputy job. If you grab it, you'll be a brigade commander in everything but title and you'll have one of the largest brigades in the Army. It's perfect!"

Something clicked in my brain: Brigadier General Willard Latham, who was reputedly the most hard-nosed general in the entire Army, had just been assigned the Alaska command. I'd heard friends from Infantry Branch complain that nobody wanted to be his deputy. They'd tried to recruit an experienced brigade commander because the combat unit was so large, but every colonel they'd approached had said in effect, "Are you nuts? I've already got my brigade-command ticket punched. Why should I risk my career to work as a deputy for Will Latham?"

But I was through worrying. Here was my chance to be a troop commander again—in a setting about as far away from the Pentagon as I could get. All week at my desk I could scarcely get Alaska out of my mind. Finally I made an appointment at the Colonels Division of the Officers Personnel Directorate. Since I was now on the promotion list to full colonel, that office would handle my next assignment.

The Assignment officer had been there when I'd run the Professional Development Section. He was happy to see me until I asked whether I could be considered for a new assignment. Then he began to hem and haw: "Well, you're in a very key job. It would have to be something very important for us to try to break you loose."

"How about Alaska?"

His eyebrows shot up. "Are you *interested*?" I thought he was going to leap across the desk and kiss me. He said, "I think we can make this work."

Two weeks later, I had my orders. They read something like this:

THE FOLLOWING NAMED OFFICER IS RELEASED EFFECTIVE 7 DE-CEMBER 1974 FROM ASSIGNMENT AS MILITARY ASSISTANT, OFFICE OF THE ASSISTANT SECRETARY OF THE ARMY (FM) AND WILL RE-PORT NOT LATER THAN 11 DECEMBER 1974 TO REPLACEMENT COMPANY, FORT RICHARDSON, ALASKA, FOR FURTHER ASSIGN-MENT AS DEPUTY COMMANDER, 172ND INFANTRY BRIGADE, FORT RICHARDSON, ALASKA: SCHWARZKOPF, H. NORMAN, LTC(P)

I was free. But while my friends offered congratulations, they couldn't understand why I would give up a plum career assignment in order to command troops in the Arctic in the dead of winter, working for a notoriously fierce boss. The ticket punchers thought I was crazy.

12

Brenda, the kids, and I landed in Alaska on a Wednesday in mid-December. It was 4:30 in the afternoon and already pitch dark. The colonel I was replacing was a fellow named Dan Sharp, who was on hand to greet us along with his wife and a couple of soldiers who collected our bags. As we were leaving the terminal we practically tripped over a team of sled dogs. Brenda turned and looked at me as if to ask, "Where have you brought us?" Sharp, who observed this, chuckled and reassured her that dog sleds were not the conventional means of transportation: in fact, this team had been shipped in from the "lower forty-eight" to practice for the upcoming annual Iditarod race.

Anchorage airport was southeast of town while Fort Richardson was northwest, tucked into the foothills of the Chugach Mountains, rugged ridges that rise abruptly from the glacial plains around Anchorage. As it was now five o'clock, our driver decided to avoid rush hour by going around the city. We kept wiping our frozen breath from the windows to peer out at what seemed to be a total wilderness of snow and mountains and pine trees with every now and then, along the side of the road, a bundled-up figure bouncing along on a snowmobile. After an apparent eternity, we reached the post.

The house we'd been assigned, a medium-sized three-bedroom ranch, had been unoccupied for months, but in anticipation of our arrival, the brigade had bulldozed the accumulated snow off the driveway into huge walls on each side that reached way over the heads of our kids. We straggled in at about midnight Eastern time, totally exhausted. Just as Sharp's men were about to leave, we realized we were low on Pampers. They scratched their heads. "Sir, we're not sure we have any of those up here," said one. "And anyway the PX is closed by now." Brenda and I looked at each other, wondering how we would ever survive in a place with no Pampers. "Well, sir, welcome to Alaska," the men said, and closed the door. Brenda burst into tears.

The next morning I pulled on my olive-drab regulation Arctic parka with its coyote-fur-lined hood and stepped outside to walk to work. Headquarters was only a few hundred yards down the hill. The air was sharp and clean and so cold that the hair inside my nostrils froze. As I made my way along with the snow squeaking under my boots, I surveyed the stark white mountains against the pure blue of the sky and felt a surge of joy. I really had escaped the dismal swamp of Washington.

———

The unit I was about to inherit was a 4,500-man force composed of light infantry, paratroopers, artillerymen, engineers, aviators, and logistical specialists, and nicknamed the Snowhawks. In the winter they trained to fight as ski troops, in the summer as mountain troops. I figured I'd have to learn fast to have any credibility: I hadn't spent any real time in the mountains since my high-school days in Switzerland, and I was a novice at skiing, snowshoeing, and Arctic survival. My long hours at the Pentagon athletic center were about to pay off. Bob Jolley, the brigade operations officer and an expert cross-country skier, took me out to a five-mile-long ski track that ran from the edge of the base back into the wilderness and coached me on the fundamentals. I practiced diligently every day. Another of my staff officers, Lonnie Bartholomew, had grown up in Alaska; he set about teaching me the survival techniques I'd need for Operation Jack Frost, the brigade's winter maneuvers that were scheduled for early February 1975. This year's exercise would involve two weeks of mock combat across a windswept, subzero waste near Fairbanks, one hundred miles from the Arctic Circle. It was barely five weeks away.

Since I had paratroopers under my command, I chose to start parachuting again for the first time since my tour with the Vietnamese airborne. Brenda, who had never seen me jump, brought Cindy and Jessica out to watch the first day, when I was to parachute from a helicopter on the Fort Richardson reservation. It was twenty degrees below zero, with a wind-chill factor of minus 120 degrees as I sat in the helicopter's doorway under the wash of the rotor. But I was so bundled up in parkas and face masks that I barely noticed. When the time came to jump, I practically rolled out the door.

Alaska had a reputation as a military backwater, and after only a couple of weeks on the job, I could see why. Among the headquarters staff and the garrison commanders were at least a dozen colonels who had long since given up any hope of promotion to general and who had come to Alaska to hunt and fish out the remainder of their careers. I was not especially welcome in their midst. For one thing, I had leapfrogged over several of them into the deputy commander's slot; for another, they associated me with General Latham, who they knew was on his way with a mandate to shake things up. When I'd been introduced at a holiday cocktail party a few days after we arrived, one of the old guard had remarked, "So you're the henchman." There was no point in telling him I'd never met Latham, because he simply wouldn't have believed me.

In early January 1975, Latham arrived. He was short, tough, and stocky, and there was nothing about him—at least on the surface—for a good old boy to like. He was a nondrinking, nonsmoking moralist who expected to see his commanders in church every Sunday. "I don't care whether you believe in it or not," he told us. "When you're in combat and you're holding a dying soldier in your arms, you owe it to him to know how to pray." Latham was also a fanatic about fitness: he'd fought in Korea when the Chinese came across the Yalu River, and had seen men die or get captured during the retreat because they couldn't keep up. So one of his rules was that everybody in the command had to be able to run five miles in fifty minutes. That shook up headquarters something terrible, because most of those colonels hadn't exercised in years. But within days they were out there, huffing and puffing and getting in shape. There was no way for them to fake it, either: Latham worked out right alongside them.

He was relentless in his demands and stingy with praise, and when he didn't get results, he could be extremely harsh. Yet I sensed this was a man I could learn from. First off, he pointed out that our brigade lacked a clear mission. We knew we were supposed to defend Alaska, so each year the brigade exercised on different terrain, figuring we would fight the Soviets on the shores of the Bering Strait, or around our Arctic air bases, or wherever they might show up. Latham thought this was an unacceptably vague approach. He had just come from Germany, where each commander down to the level of squad leader knew exactly where his unit was supposed to fight if war broke out. Latham insisted that our plans be just as specific.

The Alaska pipeline was being completed, and Latham recognized it as the perfect strategic objective: if anything in Alaska were to attract a Soviet attack, it would be that pipeline. This made sense to me, even though defending more than eight hundred miles of pipeline winding across two mountain ranges seemed difficult, if not impossible. But oil-company experts were quick to tell us that there was no need to guard every inch. If the Soviets blew a hole in the pipeline, it could easily be repaired. But if they were to destroy the complicated manifold valves that shunted oil from the fields at Prudhoe Bay, or the pump stations along the way that kept the oil moving, then we were in big trouble. As one expert put it, "If you lost two adjacent pump stations in winter, the flow would stop, the oil would freeze, and you'd have the world's longest licorice stick." Defending Prudhoe Bay and those pump stations became the Snowhawks' defining mission.

Latham also brought with him a new approach to training that had been developed by General DePuy at TRADOC. With the advent of modern tank and helicopter warfare, DePuy had envisioned a battlefield that was expanding and becoming more complex. To have any hope of victory, Army units would now have to be prepared to exercise greater intelligence, flexibility, and initiative than could be developed by rote. His solution was to take an army whose grand tradition of drill stretched all the way back to General Friedrich von Steuben at Valley Forge and turn it into an army that could *think*. Commanders were increasingly expected to define their unit's mission, figure out which individual and collective skills were essential to it, and then concentrate their training program on developing them. That was my first encounter with a revolution that was about to sweep the Army.

By the time spring rolled around—the traditional season for company and battalion training tests—we had developed a specific scenario that required the units to march twenty-five miles and defend a string of pumping stations against an attack by mock Soviet commandos. Being given a clear mission had an electrifying effect: the Snowhawks understood that the pipeline was a prize worth fighting for, and the training hardships we asked them to endure now made sense. Morale, which had already been high, got higher, and the brigade's performance improved markedly.

Latham also set me and my staff to work writing standards for our commanders. By summer, we had a single sheet of paper for each type of platoon that spelled out the skills we expected that unit to master. An infantry platoon, for example, had to be able to attack, defend, and fight a delaying action in Arctic and mountain conditions; conduct helicopter operations both by itself and as part of a larger unit; and so on. I could hand that paper to the platoon leader and tell him, "This is how I will measure your unit's performance. I will never grade you on anything that is not on this sheet." Meanwhile, Latham promulgated individual standards for fitness and Arctic and mountaineering skills. His lists enabled us to focus our preparations in a way I'd never imagined possible.

I was excited to play a part in Latham's pioneering effort, and began thinking that the Army and I still had a future together. But on Sunday, April 30, 1975, shortly before the training tests were to start, Saigon fell. I sat motionless in front of the TV listening to reports that the only South Vietnamese forces still putting up any resistance were remnants of the airborne at Tan Son Nhut air base. I knew that the airborne's cause was lost and that men who were my friends, like Hop, Hao, and Hung, were probably fighting to the death, at that moment. I took out a bottle of scotch and got drunk.

I couldn't shake the feeling that America had betrayed the South Vietnamese. We'd promised them a lot of help and given them guns and equipment when we'd put the war back in their hands. But the minute Nixon resigned, Congress had cut off the flow of ammunition and spare parts. After that it was only a matter of time. Never mind that the communists won—geopolitical pros and cons were irrelevant to me—the war never should have been allowed to end that way. I conjured up the countless thousands of lost lives and mutilated bodies and ruined marriages and wondered what we had accomplished. For me, drunk in my living room in Alaska, the answer was nothing.

———

When promotions to major general were announced that spring, Will Latham's name was at the top of the list, and with his new rank came orders to take over the Infantry school at Fort Benning, Georgia. His way of saying good-bye was absolutely in character: he challenged the brigade to the toughest summer field exercise in its history. We'd been scheduled for maneuvers in July near Mount McKinley, and Latham now decided that, rather than ride to the exercise area, we would cover the seventy-five-mile distance in a three-day road march. My commanders and I trooped along with our men, and while the march was arduous for everybody, the sense of unity it produced made it worth every step. We got to the break-off point on schedule at the end of day three; I pushed myself up to the head of the column and was standing at the entrance to the bivouac area as the men came in. They were whooping and hollering and waving, "Hey, sir! The first seventy-five miles was easy! Where do you want us to march next?"

The week of the exercise our new commander, Brigadier General Jim

Boatner, arrived. He was—in manner—Latham's antithesis: a relaxed fellow with a quiet sense of humor who enjoyed seeing his subordinates happy and who preferred persuasion to confrontation. Beneath the genial exterior, however, Boatner had standards every bit as high as Latham's. He adopted Latham's training methods and enforced the physical-fitness regimen he had established. Boatner also recognized the laziness and incompetence that Latham had been up against. But he saw it as his mission to build on Latham's legacy, unifying the brigade and working to motivate as many of the good old boys as he could. The rest he prepared to quietly ease out.

Boatner brought with him another TRADOC innovation that shocked some of my commanders: a new kind of annual training test specifically designed to uncover a unit's weaknesses. Like all of our generation, my commanders had grown up on evaluations that told them how magnificent they were. One of my commanders said plaintively at the end of his first critique: "But we did all sorts of things well."

"You're right," the evaluators told him. "And we mentioned those things. But you did some things poorly too, and our purpose is to pinpoint those so you can fix them."

Boatner continued the mission Latham had defined. The second Jack Frost exercise, in February 1976, involved an oil-pipeline scenario. We designated a series of wilderness locations as pumping stations, and the brigade's mission was to defend them. The Army brought up the 1st Ranger Battalion from Fort Stewart, Georgia, to play the part of the aggressor force. The Rangers were considered to be the Army's best-trained unit, but our guys performed so impressively against them that we soon got an influx of Ranger NCOs who had asked to join us when their tours at Fort Stewart ended.

Alaska was satisfying on so many levels that I almost felt ashamed to collect my pay. I rafted down wilderness rivers, backpacked, went fly-fishing in pristine streams, and hunted Dall sheep, moose, and caribou in the Wrangell Mountains. Brenda and I bought the obligatory second freezer, which was soon jammed with coho, sockeye, and king salmon, caribou steaks, and roasts from moose and mountain sheep—as well as boxes of king crab legs that we bought at the commissary for one dollar a pound.

Many winter nights I would arrive home late from work, put on cross-country skis, and head down the long hillside behind our house to Ship Creek, a stream that drained out of the Chugach Mountains. In the moonlight its frozen bed looked like a highway paved with snow. I'd ski up it toward the mountains, and within ten minutes would be in unspoiled wilderness, wrapped in the utter silence that comes with heavy snow cover.

I'd see moose and fox; sometimes coyotes in their heavy winter pelts would run alongside me on the tops of the banks. After twenty or thirty minutes I'd turn and ski home. I never slept better in my life.

As the summer of 1976 approached, I read in a book put out by the Seattle Mountaineers about the Resurrection Pass trail. It was a forty-mile-long wilderness path on the Kenai Peninsula that climbed from the shores of Cook Inlet through mountain passes to the old gold-rush country north of Seward. Supposedly a hiker in good condition could cover it in three days. I decided to hike the trail alone and planned the trip meticulously. I pored over terrain maps for weeks in advance, assembled the necessary gear, bought food, and calculated how to reduce the weight of my pack. Several Alaskans told me I was crazy to venture into the wilderness on my own: suppose I had a heart attack, or fell into a ravine and broke a leg? So I carefully briefed Brenda and my staff on the schedule I expected to keep and packed a handgun, flares, and a small walkie-talkie for emergencies.

The big moment came on a cloudy Friday afternoon in mid-June. Brenda kissed me good-bye at the trail head and drove off. Pulling on my sixty-pound pack, I started walking, and soon encountered a party of hikers coming the other way. They had rifles and shotguns strapped to their packs. "You going up alone?" one asked. When I nodded, he warned about a lake whose name I didn't catch: "Be careful around there. We saw bears."

As I climbed, I was amazingly content. Ascending from lush coastal rain forests, I entered pine forests filled with rushing streams. Gradually the trees began to thin out and the ground underfoot, at first matted with pine needles, became rocky. I'd come to understand that as a military commander the only time I could completely relax was when no one else was around. At the post, I was constantly on display, being careful to set an example and also being judged—it made no difference whether I was on duty or off. Here I had no standard to live up to but my own.

The afternoon of the second day, it began to pour. I was way up above the tree line nearing Resurrection Pass when I came upon a grizzly-bear paw print smack in the middle of the trail. The animal must have been huge—its paw print looked as though someone had pressed a dinner plate into the mud and drawn claw marks on one side. Suddenly I realized that as hard as it was raining, *the print couldn't be more than ten minutes old*. I felt a surge of adrenaline as I forced myself to look around slowly. I then walked on, resisting the urge to run. An hour passed and I was safely over the pass and back down below the tree line. Toward evening I found a beautiful little lake where I pitched my tent, caught a couple of trout, cooked them for dinner, and went to bed.

I woke at dawn with a jolt: there was noise on the lake right outside my tent. Splash, splash, splash, then silence. Then again, splash, splash, splash, and silence. The hiker's warning came back to me. "Oh, God," I thought, "I've camped in some bear's favorite fishing area. He's wading near my tent and heading this way." The sound came again: splash, splash, splash. I took my pistol in one hand and a grenade simulator—a training device that produces a very loud bang—in the other. My heart pounding, I quietly unzipped the tent and—gathering all my courage—stuck my head out to look for the source of the noise. It was a huge moose—all the way on the other side of the lake, fifty or sixty yards away. She would walk a few steps, then stop to eat water lilies, and the resulting splash, splash, splash was carrying all the way to my tent. I cooked breakfast that morning with a shaky hand, but by the time I was back on the trail, my sense of well-being had returned.

I reached the highway where Brenda was to meet me late that day. She hadn't yet arrived, so I sat down, took off my boots, and waited. I was drenched, bone tired, bleeding from torn blisters on both feet—and a very happy man. I realized that in Alaska I'd found my way back to the troops, I'd reconnected with nature, and I'd freed myself for good of the ticket-punching syndrome. I was beginning to learn to derive my satisfactions from within. Brenda said she'd never forget how I looked as she drove up—sitting there on the gravel in my socks with a beatific smile on my face.

We weren't sure how long our stay in Alaska would last, and even before our first year was out, I got a call at home from the assignment chief at Colonels Division. "You've been selected to command a brigade," he announced. "We'll let you know where you'll be going in a few months, after the assignments have been firmed up. And congratulations." I thanked him and hung up. Brenda, who'd been watching me, asked, "What was that about?" She was extremely adept at reading my expressions, but this time there were too many conflicting emotions for her to make out whether the news was good or bad. Only a minority of colonels were ever chosen for full-fledged brigade command, so the call meant I was back on the fast track. Yet the minute the Army assigned me a unit, we would have to leave Alaska. In July the order finally came: effective December 1, I was to assume command of a brigade of the 9th Infantry Division at Fort Lewis, Washington.

In September, Sally called to say that Mom was going into Walter Reed Army Hospital for gall-bladder surgery. She assured me that the surgery was routine and we agreed that there was no need for me to fly east. But the procedure was a disaster: Mom had a massive heart attack on the operating table and the doctors did not think she would survive. I flew to Washington on emergency leave.

By the time I arrived at the hospital, the immediate crisis had passed and Mom had stabilized. But when I walked into her room, I was stunned to find her talking incoherently. She had always had a sharp mind, even as she aged and even when she drank. The doctors explained that she was suffering from "intensive care syndrome," a result of having been kept on a respirator, and assured us it would pass. Despite their words, I was scared.

Sally was there and Ruth had driven down from Vermont; we spent every day at Walter Reed, holding Mom's hand, talking to her, trying to bring her back. We all stayed at Sally's little cabin, coping with the stress as best we could. One afternoon I came back from my daily three-mile run and looked in the cabin window. Sally was sitting in a chair at one end of the living room doing transcendental meditation; at the other end was Ruth, doing t'ai chi. We all felt pretty desperate.

After a week, Ruth had to return to her family, and Sally and I wrestled with the question of what to do next. Despite what the doctors had said, Mom was recovering physically but not mentally. Sally and I both had to admit that, if she left the hospital, she would no longer be able to take care of herself. I traveled around town looking at nursing homes and found a surprisingly cheerful one on Wisconsin Avenue not far from Sally's house. It cost more than Mom could afford, but Sally and I decided we'd each chip in. Then I had the conversation with Sally that I knew she'd been dreading. "I have to go back," I told her. "I've got a wife and small children and a brigade I'm accountable for. And if I use up all my leave, I can't come back if there's another emergency." Sally said she understood, but I knew it was tough on her to be left with all the responsibility.

Three weeks later, Mom died quite suddenly. I flew back and made arrangements for the cremation and funeral services: a small ceremony in town where her friends could attend and another at West Point, where Ruth and Sally and I would bury her ashes next to Pop's.

It was a dreary, overcast October morning, and as we sat at the quiet graveside, I felt overwhelmed by sorrow and regret. I had loved my mother—in my own way I had managed to separate the woman she was from the alcoholic she became—and now I would never see her again. I grieved for the opportunity we'd lost. We could have been a close, loving family, but alcoholism had driven us apart; and while I'd realized years ago that the warmth I'd longed for would never be, her death put an end to that dream. I desperately missed Brenda and our children, and I missed Mom and Pop.

Our last night in Alaska was October 31, Halloween, and that afternoon it started to snow. I loved it when the winter snows came. For a couple of weeks beforehand Alaskans would study the mountain peaks, where the snow cover would start up high and each morning creep a little lower. They called this "termination dust," because it had been the signal in the old days for prospectors to come in from their claims. Brenda and I had already moved ourselves out of the house and down to Fort Richardson's guest quarters, ready to leave the next morning. We had promised the girls they could trick-or-treat, but all they had was flimsy little ballerina costumes. By the time evening came it was snowing heavily and freezing cold, and I was afraid we were going to have to disappoint them. But Brenda came up with the perfect solution. We wrapped the girls up in bulky coats, drove them to the top of the hill where the general and all the colonels lived, and took them from door to door. When someone answered the doorbell, Cindy and Jessica would yell, "Trick or treat," open their coats just long enough for the person to exclaim over their pretty costumes and to produce candy, then close their coats and run to the next house. We were all in high spirits when the time came to leave.

There were three infantry brigades at Fort Lewis and I was assigned the one nobody wanted. I'd been preceded by a commander who was an ex–White House fellow, a prolific contributor to military journals, and, in the eyes of many at Fort Lewis, a show-off. He'd been great at calling attention to the 1st Brigade with gimmicks, but some felt he had no real grasp of his business as an infantry commander. For example, he'd had a wild notion that if the United States were ever to fight the Soviets, the only way for the Army to conceal its intentions on the battlefield would be to avoid using radios. Therefore, with great fanfare, he revived the use of semaphore flags and couriers. In theory, a commander at war could turn to one of his runners in the middle of the night and say, "Take this order to the 3/33 battalion," and the guy would charge out of the bunker and unerringly do the job. In practice, of course, it wasn't so simple: during one of the brigade's exercises a courier got lost and never delivered his message, with the result that when the brigade moved the next day, it left its artillery behind.

Like Latham, he was obsessed with fitness, but he'd managed to turn that into a show as well. Every Friday morning the brigade's 2,500 troops would turn out at dawn and run five miles. Then they'd pass in review. Finally they'd go to "struggle pits"—sand arenas where the soldiers would take turns jumping in and wrestling. These "Friday morning follies" were a big hit with visiting dignitaries, but caused a great deal of resentment among the other units on base. While the brigade's official nickname was the Recondo Brigade (short for "Reconnaissance/Commando"), everybody else had another name for it. They called it the "circus brigade."

I'd come across the brigade twice during my time in Alaska, after the Army introduced a program in which units from the lower forty-eight states rotated up for a month of training. One of the Recondo battalions was among the first that came, and its performance was a disgrace. The officers and enlisted men bitched nonstop about the cold, and the day they left not a single vehicle we'd loaned them was still running. Even though we'd carefully explained Arctic maintenance procedures—keeping engine block heaters plugged in, starting engines several times at night, and so on—they simply hadn't bothered. A Recondo company showed up during the next summer's training. We put them out on a glacier, where they promptly violated a cardinal rule of Arctic survival: they snacked on their emergency rations. A couple of days into the exercise, the weather turned foul and they had to hole up in their tents. We let them go hungry for a while, but when the weather didn't clear we had to undertake a risky helicopter mission to resupply them.

I had a couple of weeks at Fort Lewis before assuming command, so I spent a great deal of time interviewing the staff and studying the brigade's records at division headquarters. On the day I took command, I called in my key officers—the staff chiefs, the battalion commanders, the company commanders, and the sergeant major—twenty-two officers in all. "I am trying to assess this organization," I told them. "I've made some observations on my own and I've talked to a lot of the division staff. Now I'd like to know what *you* think. Over the weekend I want you to take a piece of paper and answer the following questions anonymously. Number one, what are the commanders of this brigade supposed to be doing? Number two, how well are we doing it? Number three, if you could start something, stop something, and continue something in this brigade, what would those things be?"

Twenty-two responses, some typed, some handwritten, were waiting for me on Monday morning. I read them with increasing fascination. In response to the first question, all but one of the officers had answered as I would have. They said in effect: "Our job is to prepare this brigade to go to war if necessary." The remaining man's answer was so incoherent that I'd frankly have considered removing him if I could have figured out who he was.

To the question: "How well are we doing it?" five officers responded, "Not very well." Sixteen said, "We aren't doing our job *at all*."

In response to "What practices should we stop?" they all replied, "Stop the mickey mouse—the semaphore flags and runners and wrestling matches and so on."

To "What should we start doing?" they replied, "Let's go out to the field and do some real training."

And to "What should we continue?" they answered, "We like the emphasis on physical fitness."

All through December we worked on the nitty-gritty changes: revamping the vehicle-maintenance program, learning how to establish communications in the field, writing standard operating procedures for our units, and putting together long-term training programs for units and individuals.

Meanwhile my family and I settled into a large, comfortable two-story brick house on a quiet, tree-lined street. It was part of a housing area built by the Civilian Conservation Corps during the New Deal. The transition from Fort Richardson was much smoother than Brenda and I had anticipated. Not only were the people at Fort Lewis open and welcoming, but in terms of natural beauty, which we'd feared losing, the base more than held its own. Our house was near one end of the parade ground; at the other, rising majestically forty miles to the east, was Mount Rainier. Its presence influenced the entire base: on days when Rainier was obscured by clouds, people seemed subdued, while on days when the mountain was "out," they seemed happy and vibrant.

After the holidays I invited Major General Volney Warner, our division commander and a veteran of both Korea and Vietnam, to visit the brigade. I admired Warner enormously: the day I'd arrived at Fort Lewis he'd laid out what he called his "big four"—the four types of training exercise he expected every unit to do well. He'd explained in his quiet way, "That is how I will grade you, and beyond that, I'll not tell you how to do your job." He gave his commanders tremendous latitude.

Warner knew the condition of the 1st Brigade, but he listened intently, nodding every now and then, as I presented my own assessment. I then told him that I had a specific request. In analyzing the records at division headquarters, I'd discovered that my unit had spent much less time in the field than the other two brigades: we'd been assigned primarily to "post support"—guarding the base, supplying manpower for housekeeping chores, marching in parades, and similar tasks. "We can fix our problems through training," I said, "but it would help a whole lot to have a goal. I'd like the 1st Brigade to represent this division in next summer's maneuvers." The maneuvers I was referring to were annual major exercises code-named Brave Shield. The next was to take place at Twentynine Palms Marine Corps

Base in the Mojave Desert, where our troops would play an enemy force defending against an entire division of U.S. Marines. I was asking a lot: Warner would be staking the division's reputation on us, along with a substantial chunk of his annual training budget. He didn't miss a beat. "Fine," he said. "I know you'll represent the division and the Army well."

The troops were galvanized by the news. We trained hard all winter and spring, and the brigade's real potential soon became apparent. Thanks to the Army's newly adopted centralized command-selection process, we had superb battalion commanders. The company commanders were highly competent as well, and happy to get back to no-nonsense soldiering. By the time we began our final preparations, spirits were running high.

My own spirits were running high as well. On June 20, 1977, Brenda gave birth to our son, Christian, and this time I actually witnessed the birth. I'd brought Brenda to the hospital with no intention of going into the delivery room. But after Brenda had been in labor for several hours, things suddenly happened very fast. A doctor declared, "We've got to get her in there right away," and before I knew it the nurses had dressed me in a gown and mask and pushed me through the door, too. I felt triumphant when it was over. Later I kidded Brenda: "The first two times I sent you in there by yourself, and you brought out girls. This time I wanted to make sure it was a boy." Soon after Brenda brought Christian home, he—unlike his sisters—developed colic. When the brigade finally left for Brave Shield three weeks later, I welcomed the trip because I knew that, even in simulated war, I'd probably get more sleep than I'd been getting at home.

Brave Shield pitted our three battalions against *thirteen* battalions of Marines. The war game's scenario called for us to establish initial defenses along a line of desert bluffs and, once the Marines dislodged us, to fight a delaying action—alternately resisting and withdrawing—until, after ten days, we finally succumbed. Instead, we practically *won*. We held our positions along the bluffs so effectively that we repulsed the Marine attack twice. The umpires finally had to order us off the bluffs because the exercise was running so far behind schedule.

We'd played strictly by the rules, but the Marine two-star general wouldn't even speak to me when the exercise ended. My only regret was that I didn't immediately get to thank General Warner for showing faith in us—he'd been promoted to lieutenant general and moved to an assignment at Fort Bragg, North Carolina, while we were still in the desert.

Major General Richard Cavazos was his replacement, a Korean War hero who was as outgoing as Warner had been quiet. He had a reputation as an inspiring leader and trainer, but on his arrival in September, none of us knew exactly what to expect because his background was in Armor, not Infantry. Cavazos got our attention right away: on the morning of his first commanders' conference, I pulled up to division headquarters in my jeep and noticed a commotion in the parking lot. The general had intercepted the commander of the Army hospital, had ordered him to raise his jeep's hood, and was under there checking the engine for grime. I beat it into the building as fast as I could, before he decided to inspect *my* jeep. Overnight, the equipment maintenance in the 9th Division took a quantum jump.

Cavazos *was* a great commander of troops. He was superb at rallying the men: he'd give a morale-building speech that would bring tears to their eyes, then move through the ranks joking, backslapping, pretending to be gruff. If he knew a battalion was out on a road march in the middle of the night and it started to rain, he would drive to where the troops would pass and stand out there in the downpour and wave. His concern for the soldiers wasn't just show: he constantly looked for and found ways to improve the troops' lives. For example, he hated seeing soldiers forced to work on weekends, and if a commander scheduled a task for a Saturday or Sunday, Cavazos would challenge him: "This is peacetime! Why are you running your unit as if we're at war?"

I'd also never met a better trainer. The primary mission of the 9th Division in the event of war was to fly to Europe and reinforce NATO—a daunting assignment that meant our light infantry force might have to confront Soviet tanks. Cavazos showed us how to take the training practices that hadn't changed since my days as a second lieutenant and tailor them specifically to that mission. The traditional battalion field exercise called for a unit to practice delaying, defending, and counterattacking, all in a single week. But Cavazos's idea was that we'd do better concentrating on one element: digging in against armored attack. Over the next several months we learned a great deal about stringing barbed wire, laying minefields, establishing fighting positions, putting up camouflage—fundamentals that we'd all studied years before but had never had time to practice. If the division had ever gone to war, Cavazos's approach would have saved a lot of lives.

My unit thrived. After Brave Shield nobody dared call us the circus brigade; the troops knew they were good, and that made them confident. We led the division that winter in every measure of brigade performance, from maintenance statistics to the number of troops volunteering for the Red Cross blood drive. And Cavazos came to rely on us: in March 1978, when the Army called upon him and his staff to participate in two major exercises simultaneously, he chose me and my staff to serve as the division's proxy in one.

I'd been back from the headquarters exercise only two days when Cavazos's executive officer called: "The general is on his way over to see you. He wants to talk about your maintenance program." I thought that was odd, because our maintenance program was fine. I hung up the phone, went to the window, and saw a couple of jeeps pull up. With Cavazos were both of his assistant division commanders, a sergeant major, and a couple of other officers. He burst into the office and said loudly, "Norm, the Army has really screwed it up this time."

"Sir?" I said.

"Would you believe that the United States Army has selected you to be a brigadier general?" He laughed, pulled out the official promotion list that would be published the following day, and pumped my hand. Meanwhile a couple of my officers brought in a cake decorated with a big red star. I was moved by the celebration and congratulations—but all I could think of was going home to tell Brenda.

The minute I opened the door, I saw from her face that she already knew: the wife of one of the assistant division commanders had come by with a bottle of champagne and two glasses. I took Brenda in my arms and said, "I guess we did it." After we put the kids to bed, I called to congratulate Cavazos's chief of staff, who was also on the list. I could hear a noisy party going on in the background. But our mood was more one of quiet reflection. I'd always wanted to be a general, my dad had been one. And while I would not have left the Army brokenhearted if I'd never made it, I felt very proud to have been awarded that star.

Later in the evening, Cavazos stopped by. He'd just come from the party at his chief of staff's house and I suspect was surprised not to find one at ours. But he sat down and we talked and shared some champagne. Finally I said, "There's one favor I'd like to ask." He gave me a quizzical look. "I'd like to give my brigade the day off tomorrow."

He broke into a broad grin. "Absolutely," he said. He understood the impulse to share good fortune with the troops. I called my night duty officer and announced that we would hold a formation in the morning.

At 6:30 A.M. the entire brigade assembled on the parade ground. I clambered up onto the raised platform that commanders used to direct calisthenics. "This afternoon, at fourteen hundred hours, the Department of the Army is going to announce that I have been promoted to brigadier general," I told them. The whole brigade started to *cheer*. I hadn't expected that and got all choked up. Then I said, "Any commander worth his salt knows that when a good thing happens to him, it happens because of the soldiers under his command. I am proud of this brigade. I am proud of the great work you guys have done. When I get that star, a little piece of it is going to belong to each one of *you*. While I can't actually give you each a piece, there *is* something I can do to say thank you: I want you all to take the day off. Now get out of here and I'll see you on Monday!" They cheered even louder than before and ran off in every direction.

―――――

Three weeks later, in April, I—along with thirty-five other new general-officer designees—reported to the Pentagon. We'd been summoned for a ten-day orientation known as "charm school." The theory went that being made a general entailed rising to an entirely new sphere of responsibility. Until now we'd each belonged to a particular Army branch, but as generals we would have to command soldiers from many branches. To do our jobs well, we would therefore need a much broader view of what was going on in the Army. That was charm school's official purpose. The joke was that its *real* purpose was to reveal the secret handshake. Classmates would kid each other, "Did you get the secret handshake yet?"

"Yup, I got mine. Did you get yours?"

The first item on the agenda was to pose for a class photo with General Bernard Rogers, the Army chief of staff, who would then give a welcoming speech. At nine in the morning, we arranged ourselves in the grassy central courtyard of the Pentagon, but General Rogers was nowhere to be seen. We waited and waited; finally word came that we should take the photo without him and proceed with the day's schedule—he'd join us when he could.

We assembled in an auditorium where the director of the Army staff previewed the week's events. We'd be hearing a very impressive roster: the secretary of the Army, the chairman of the Joint Chiefs of Staff, the heads of other armed services, and several of the Army's four-star commanders. We'd go to Capitol Hill and call on senators and congressmen. We'd even spend four days at a conference center outside Washington participating in an organizational-effectiveness seminar. And there would be a cocktail hour and dinner party almost every night. I was fully prepared for the latter: before leaving Fort Lewis, I'd gone to Tacoma and bought my first good suit, a Hart Schaffner & Marx pinstripe, and a tie to go with it. The bill had come to a hundred and ninety dollars, a painful amount to spend on clothes. Then the preview ended and we launched right into intensive briefings given by various senior members of the Army staff.

Late that morning, General Rogers finally appeared. As he strode to the front of the auditorium, gray haired, handsome, square jawed, and ramrod straight, there was a ripple of excitement. After all, here was the man who'd approved our promotions and who would now congratulate us and tell us we were a credit to the Army, describe the fine careers we'd go on to have, and let us in on problems he'd need our help to solve. He reached the podium and studied us for a moment. "If all of you had taken the same airplane to Washington, and that airplane had crashed and you had all been killed, we could go right back into the ranks of colonels and find thirty-six more just as good as you." There was a stunned silence. "Now," he said, "let me tell you what I *didn't* promote you to do. I didn't promote you to abuse your power. I didn't promote you to chase every skirt that's walking down the street. I didn't promote you to have your wife browbeat everybody on your staff and run the base for you when you're out of town." I glanced around; my classmates seemed to have sunk down into their seats. He went on to give us a tough lecture that felt as if it went on for an hour. At the end, he did offer congratulations. We later found out that President Carter had just announced that the United States was pulling its Army forces out of South Korea, catching General Rogers—who was responsible for those troops—completely unawares. That was why he had missed the photo session, and why he was in not too good a mood when he gave us our welcome.

One other speaker made a deep impression that week: Dick Trefry, the Army inspector general. He was a big, lumbering guy who dominated a room the moment he walked in. "Okay, guys, pay attention, because this is probably the most important class you're going to have. I'm here to tell you all the ways you can get in trouble as a general. And I'm here to promise that if you do any of these things, *I'm going to come after you.*" We knew that the Army was fierce about policing its ranks: it investigated *every* complaint against a general officer, even anonymous ones, and if any wrongdoing turned up, whether related to the complaint or not, the general's career was swiftly terminated.

Trefry then proceeded down the list of transgressions that had oc-curred over the past year: misspent funds, personal trips in Army aircraft, misuse of aides—the list seemed endless. What perplexed me was that all those generals had presumably gotten the very same lecture we were get-ting, yet they had broken the rules all the same. The most common breach was moral turpitude—generals getting mixed up with younger men's wives or with the women soldiers under their command. I remembered an ironic remark General Boatner had once made: "It's amazing. The minute I got promoted to brigadier general, my sense of humor improved dramatically. Now every time I tell a joke, everyone laughs." Having been around gen-erals all my life, from the time I was a teenager in Germany with my dad, I'd always been surprised by how many men actually *did* think they'd become funnier, or smarter, or more attractive to twenty-two-year-old women the moment they pinned on stars.

Between lectures, most of my classmates spent much of their time at the General Officer Management Office (GOMO) arranging their first jobs. For seven of us, there were strings attached to our stars: for some reason, the Pentagon had decided to enforce an old regulation that officers had to serve at least one tour in a joint command with the other armed services before qualifying as generals. I was one of the "filthy seven," as we were called, who hadn't fulfilled that requirement. Our promotions came with the stipulation that our first tour had to be in a joint headquarters.

I had a great job lined up: General Alexander Haig, the supreme allied commander in Europe, wanted me to join his staff. But just as charm school ended, the officer in the job was granted permission to extend for a year because of a family problem. I made a panicky call to GOMO. "We don't have any joint assignments available at the moment," the officer said. "Your classmates have been in here for days lining things up, and I'm afraid all the good jobs are taken."

I allowed as how I was scheduled to give up my brigade in a few weeks, and asked what the Army wanted me to do.

"I don't know. Sign yourself out on leave and we'll call."

So I returned to Fort Lewis, had a change of command at the end of May, and waited. I refused to believe that the Army was going to hold me to the joint-assignment requirement if none were available. Here I was, the Army's most experienced brigade commander. I figured maybe they'd end up making me an assistant division commander—maybe even right there at Fort Lewis, where a slot was about to open up. While I waited, General Cavazos held a promotion ceremony for me, and he and Brenda pinned on my stars.

Finally, after letting me vegetate for three weeks, GOMO called. I was to be assigned as an assistant staff officer for plans and policy at Pacific Command in Hawaii. Not just a staff job, but an assistant staff job! I was dismayed. Five minutes later the phone rang again. It was Pacific Command, asking how soon I could get there because they needed me right away. "Jeez," I said, "can you give me two weeks? I've got to move my family."

"Okay," they said. "But no later than July 2." Five minutes later the phone rang yet again. This time it was General Cavazos. "I just heard about your assignment," he growled. "Whoever made that decision is a dumb bastard."

We rushed to pack, sold our camping trailer, and gave away our cat. Brenda made a quick trip to Timberville to tell her parents good-bye. In two weeks flat, we got ourselves moved to Hawaii, arriving at two o'clock on the afternoon of July 2, 1978. Waiting for us at the airport was Brigadier General Jack Sadler, the man I was replacing. "Glad to meet you," I said. "As soon as we drop off my family, I'll be ready to start work."

He gave me a puzzled look. "No need for that. Headquarters is closed. It's the Fourth of July holiday. It won't really open again until the sixth."

13

Pacific Command was situated in the hills west of Honolulu at a Marine base named Camp Smith. The three-story stucco headquarters had been built originally as a hospital and wasn't much to look at. But the setting was spectacular: palm trees, banyan trees, elephant ear plants, mango trees laden with ripe fruit, and lovely tropical flowers in every shade of red imaginable. A jogging course circled the building, and each day at lunchtime it would fill up with suntanned Marines who were in training for the Honolulu marathon. Nearby, set in a beautiful natural bowl, were the camp's tennis courts and a parade field with a stunning view of Pearl Harbor.

Jack Sadler was about to retire. On my first morning he introduced me to my new boss, Rear Admiral Don Shelton, the chief of plans and policy for the command. Next, Sadler led me to a conference room where Admiral Maurice F. Weisner, the commander in chief of Pacific Command and Shelton's boss, was about to start the morning's staff meeting. The room was dominated by a large U-shaped table where Weisner presided, flanked by the generals and admirals who headed various sections of the staff. I followed Sadler to a row of movie-theater-style chairs behind the table as more officers filed in. "Here's where the deputies sit," he explained, and we each took a place. When the meeting began, I looked up and down the row and realized with a start that every other deputy was either a colonel or a

Navy captain. Sadler and I were *the only general officers not at the table.* I reassured myself by remembering that, seated at the table or not, I was about to be privy to the inner workings of one of America's most important headquarters. Pacific Command's area of responsibility extended from the west coast of the United States to the east coast of Africa—covering literally almost half the world. On sea, it spanned the entire Pacific Ocean and the entire Indian Ocean; on land, it was responsible for everything east of the Iran-Pakistan border including India, Indochina, Australia, New Zealand, Indonesia, the Philippines, Japan, and South Korea.

But I was to be disappointed. Before long, I realized that these morning meetings were largely a formality. Whenever something important came up, Admiral Weisner would discuss the issue at the table, but would then adjourn with his chief of staff and his staff admirals to his office, where the real decisions would be made.

A few days later, just before his retirement ceremony, Sadler invited me into what was about to become my office for a private talk. He pointedly mentioned that not only was he retiring as a brigadier general, but his predecessor had too. He warned: "Get out of the Pacific as soon as you can. This place means everything to the Navy, but the Army doesn't take it seriously. It'll ruin your career."

Matters didn't improve when I discovered that Shelton—who was the second most senior two-star admiral in the Navy—was bitter that *his* career hadn't advanced further. Moreover, he viewed me with absolute disdain: I was an Army officer, and he didn't like the Army; I was a West Pointer, and, as a graduate of Annapolis, he didn't like West Point; and to add insult to injury, I was big and he was five foot seven. Whenever I'd stand near him to show him something, he'd make a point of stepping away.

For months I was relegated to message-writing and other paperwork tasks that normally would have been jobs for lower-ranking action officers. I told myself over and over that I'd been lucky with bosses in the past and that I'd be lucky again. Still, I kept hoping that the Army would move me. Though my assignment was officially for two years, the officers at GOMO had said that I'd probably be transferred after just six months. But six months came and went, and I finally faced the fact that I wasn't going to get a reprieve.

Shelton paid a great deal of attention to naval base negotiations in the Philippines, where he had formerly been U.S. commander. But he was less interested in the political-military work—maintaining relations with governments and military leaders—in the rest of the Pacific Basin. In time, as he realized that I was a team player loyal to the goals of Pacific Command, he seemed content to leave that responsibility to me. I traveled extensively and found myself conducting planning and base negotiations with Koreans, Taiwanese, Australians, and New Zealanders. We were in the initial stages of military planning with the Japanese, wrestling with such questions as what role Japan would play if the United States and the Soviet Union were to go to war, what would happen if the Soviets were to attack Japan, and so on. In those days bilateral planning between the United States and Japan was so politically sensitive because of the Japanese people's antimilitarism that neither government would admit it was going on. When I visited my counterparts in Tokyo, we'd meet in absolute secrecy in my hotel room and lay our maps out on the floor.

The other side of our business was planning how America's own forces would deploy and fight in various contingencies. Admiral Shelton liked to concentrate on grand strategy. Everybody understood that, in the event of World War III, the Navy didn't have enough ships to confront the Soviets simultaneously in both the Atlantic and the Pacific. So the Pentagon had adopted a "swing strategy," stipulating that if war were to break out, the Navy would steam most of its forces to the defense of NATO first, then come back and fight in the Pacific, much as it had in World War II. But Admirals Weisner and Shelton were convinced that times had changed and strenuously argued that the Pacific Basin had outstripped Europe as the area of long-term strategic interest to the United States and therefore should be defended first. Our strategy division advanced that view by churning out report after report; I learned more about economic growth and trade in the Pacific Basin than I'd ever have thought possible. But beyond grand strategy, Shelton was completely uninterested in such specific plans as, say, how Pacific Command would deploy its forces if another war broke out in Korea. The staff and I found it impossible to get into his office to brief him. After a couple of months and without his actually ordering me to, I just took over the planning operation and ran it. The work brought me into close contact with officers from all the services, and I came to understand that the Navy in particular did business differently: decision-making power was concentrated at the top, while middle-ranking officers had much less autonomy than did their counterparts in the Army, Air Force, and Marine Corps.

The more independence Shelton allowed me, the happier I was. In April 1979, both he and Weisner announced that they were going to retire, and Shelton cut back the number of hours he worked and transferred more responsibility to me. He retired late that summer. By the time the new commander in chief, Admiral Robert L. G. Long, took over in early November, I'd been the acting plans and policy chief for two months and had moved up to a seat at the table at the morning meeting. I admired Bob Long tremendously—he was a nuclear submariner who had a reputation both as an intellectual and as a tough, able commander.

Long had been at Pacific Command only a few days when we were drawn into a maelstrom of events in the Middle East. On November 4, right after the deposed shah of Iran was admitted to the United States for medical treatment, followers of the Ayatollah Khomeini stormed the U.S. embassy in Tehran and took more than sixty people hostage. Iran was the headache of European Command, but our headquarters was responsible for neighboring Afghanistan and Pakistan as well as the Persian Gulf, so we were called upon to help outline military options for President Jimmy Carter. I was astounded to learn that our military could offer him almost none. Our Army had almost no forces ready to fight in the Middle East; our Air Force had no access to the region's airfields and only limited use of its airspace; and our Navy insisted that the waters of the Persian Gulf were too constricted to accommodate its big aircraft carriers. In desperation, we asked the Strategic Air Command about dispatching a massive B-52 strike, figuring that we could attack Tehran from our air base in Guam. But SAC advised us that it would have such difficulty positioning tankers for aerial refueling that the maximum number of B-52s we could launch against Iran simultaneously was *two*.

On November 21, Islamic radicals in Islamabad, Pakistan, burned that U.S. embassy to the ground, and the tension at headquarters increased considerably. Pakistan *was* part of Pacific Command, and if it became necessary to rescue the embassy staff, the mission would be ours. We were hamstrung not only by a lack of plans but by a total lack of knowledge: we literally had to get out a world atlas to find out exactly where Islamabad was. For twenty-four hours we worked frantically to cobble together an evacuation plan; fortunately, the government of Pakistan restored order and we never had to act. A similar crisis came and went a month later, when the Soviets invaded Afghanistan but allowed U.S. citizens safe passage out. We were lucky: again, we had no contingency plans.

Within two weeks of the Soviet invasion, President Carter decided that protecting the oil fields of the Middle East was in the strategic interest of the United States. He enunciated what came to be known as the Carter Doctrine: that any attempt by an "outside force" to gain control of the Persian Gulf would be repelled "by any means necessary." Meanwhile, the Tehran crisis had made the Defense Department realize that it might be called upon to take action in "remote" regions, and it had responded by creating the Rapid Deployment Joint Task Force. The new force was based in the

United States, but its appearance, in conjunction with the advent of the Carter Doctrine, made European Command and Pacific Command very nervous: they worried that chunks of their territory would soon get carved away to create a new four-star command responsible for the Middle East. Lieutenant General P. X. Kelley, the tough, blunt-spoken Marine who ran the Rapid Deployment Force, did nothing to allay their concerns. When he visited Pacific Command that spring, he sat at the big table answering questions. Finally Admiral Long asked point-blank: "So what do you see as your role?"

"I see myself as a commander in chief in waiting," Kelley replied. People gasped. But privately I thought he might be right—establishing a new command might be the only way to give the Middle East the attention it deserved.

March 28, 1980, was my happiest day in Hawaii. Not only was it Brenda's birthday—we were invited to Admiral Long's house for dinner that evening to celebrate—but I finally got my orders to leave. We were headed for Germany, where I was to serve as an assistant division commander of the 8th Mechanized Infantry, a top-notch division that was part of NATO's front-line defense. I was excited. I was going back—to the Army, to the troops, to the same part of Germany where I'd lived as a kid, and to friends. The division commander, Major General Bill Livsey, was someone I'd known ever since I'd been a second lieutenant; my fellow assistant division commanders, both brigadier generals, would be Bob Riscassi, my friend from Infantry Branch, and Rick Brown, a classmate from West Point.

We had several months to plan our departure because I had to wait for my replacement. He arrived in July, precisely two years after I had, on the same date, at the same hour, aboard exactly the same flight from the United States—and I was there waiting for him just as Jack Sadler had waited for me. But unlike Jack, I was able to tell him that my job in Long's headquarters had been fulfilling, that I'd gained great experience working with the other armed forces, and that serving in the Pacific would *not* be the end of his Army career.

The 8th Mech, one of the Army's largest divisions, comprised four brigades and twenty-four thousand soldiers. Its mission in the event of war was to help defend the Fulda Gap, a broad, flat corridor in Germany's central hills that provided a natural invasion route for the Warsaw Pact's tanks, right into the heavily industrialized Rhineland. I was keen to work with an armored unit—having come up through the light infantry, I knew I had everything to learn about mechanized warfare—and I wondered how Livsey would handle my education.

I was also very curious about the *other* job I'd been given. The 8th Mech, like most U.S. divisions in Germany, did not mass its forces in one place. Headquarters was in the sleepy little town of Bad Kreuznach, about forty miles southwest of Frankfurt, and the brigades were spread among four cities spanning an eighty-mile-by-sixty-mile area of the Rhineland: Wiesbaden, Mainz, Baumholder, and Mannheim. The Army designated brigadier generals as so-called community commanders to administer these American enclaves and help maintain friendly relations with the local German government. I was to be the community commander of Mainz—responsible for five thousand soldiers and their families, their housing, the post office, the stores, the clubs, and the elementary school where my own daughters would be attending third and fifth grades. There was also the Army's giant tank-repair depot downtown, as well as Finthen Army Air Field outside town, where the division's helicopter battalion was based.

Mainz fascinated me from the moment we arrived. The city was actually an ancient river port situated at the point where the Main River flowed into the Rhine. In medieval times, it had been one of the free cities of Germany that swore allegiance only to the Pope; Gutenberg had produced the first printed Bible there. Brenda and I took the kids through the narrow cobblestone streets of the old town, past quaint shops and into the great open central marketplace dominated by the cathedral. We then walked the promenade along the Rhine, watching the procession of paddlewheel steamers loaded with families and couples on summer outings.

Residential neighborhoods radiated from the city center along trolley lines to the north, south, and west. Mainz was a blue-collar town, many of whose residents earned their living in the huge belt of factories along the Main. The American military community bordered working-class neighborhoods such as Gansenheim and Wakenheim six miles west of the city center. We moved into a housing area built by the French when they'd occupied the city immediately after the war. Our small, stucco three-bedroom house was unprepossessing and had originally been intended for a lieutenant colonel—it would never prompt anyone to say, "Wow, a general must live there." My friend Riscassi, who had us to dinner the night of our arrival, *did* have such a house—he was the community commander of white-collar Wiesbaden, just across the Rhine, and he and his wife, Virginia, lived in a virtual palace that the U.S. Air Force had built for one of its four-star generals.

My first day at work was to be taken up by a full-fledged change-of-command ceremony that installed me as the community commander. This turned out to be a surprisingly big deal. Livsey's boss, Lieutenant General Will Scott, commander of the Army's V Corps, presided. A representative of the lord mayor of Mainz was present, along with the mayors of the city's eight neighborhoods and the county commissioner, plus a dozen other local officials. Representing the Army were Livsey, the Mainz 1st Brigade commander, and at least fifty other officers. They all brought their wives. Afterward I worked my way around the room, exchanging pleasantries with the German officials, who complimented my fluency in their language, told me how closely they'd worked with my predecessor, and invited me to call upon them at their offices as soon as I got settled. I said I would be honored. Finally General Scott sought me out. "I need to talk to you about your duties," he said, and led me off to a quiet corner. I figured that we'd done our bit for German-American relations and that Scott would now impress upon me the importance of keeping the 8th Mech ready for battle.

"The Pope is coming to Germany this fall," he began.

"Sir, I didn't know that."

"It will be the first time a pope has visited Germany in centuries. He's only going to visit four places, and one of them is Mainz. It's a very important event." He paused and looked at me.

"That should be wonderful for Mainz," I replied, feeling as though I were missing something.

The general continued, "They're expecting five hundred thousand people to hear him say Mass. The only place that can take care of that big a crowd is Finthen Army Air Field. I've told the Bishop of Mainz that we'd be delighted to host the Holy Father's visit." It finally dawned on me that I would have to oversee this event. I gulped. General Scott nodded approvingly and added, "It's very important for German-American relations that this come off smoothly." Then he smiled.

I didn't make it to Livsey's office until the following day. He greeted me warmly, offered me a seat, and then leaned back in his chair and grinned at me across his desk. "I've been thinking about your assignment," he said. "You've never been in a mechanized outfit before. You don't know very much about tanks or armored personnel carriers or self-propelled artillery. So I'm gonna help you learn fast—I'm gonna make you the assistant division commander for support." I was stunned. As ADCS I would be in charge of the *maintenance* of all that equipment I didn't understand—not to mention the division's transportation and supplies. This was a much bigger dose of mechanized warfare than I'd bargained for. The look on my face made Livsey laugh. "I know you can handle it, Norm," he said, and then added, "I started out as an ADCS myself—and I want you to know that I was the *best* ADCS I've ever met. So you've got a lot to live up to." It was his backhanded way of promising to show me the ropes.

He leaned over and handed me a piece of paper. "This is your charter. It's to keep you and Riscassi and Brown from stepping on each other's toes," he said, referring to my fellow assistant division commanders. It was a detailed description of my responsibilities under the headings

COMMAND MAINZ MILITARY COMMUNITY

OVERSEE 1ST BRIGADE, DIVISION SUPPORT COMMAND, AVIATION BATTALION, SIGNAL BATTALION, ENGINEER BATTALION

RESPONSIBLE FOR DIVISION MAINTENANCE

RESPONSIBLE FOR LOGISTICAL OPERATIONS

OVERSEE AMMUNITION STORAGE AND DISTRIBUTION

SUPERVISE DIVISION TRANSPORTATION PLANNING TO INCLUDE RAIL, ROAD, AIR

Livsey reviewed each task, outlining for me what he thought needed to be done. "Make sure everything's working in these areas that should be. If you find something that needs fixing, don't ask my permission. Just fix it. You've got free rein."

Once back at my office, I called in Colonel Jack Rozier, the head of Division Support Command, which included our supply, maintenance, and transportation units. "I need to go to school on you," I told him. "Talk to me about what the problems are and what needs to be done." I then summoned Lieutenant Colonel Paul Vanderploog, who ran the division logistics staff. "I need every bit of information you can give me on our plans to supply and maintain this division. Tell me how we will distribute ammo if we go to war. I want you to walk me through your plans in detail." By the end of the week, I'd accumulated a stack of maintenance and supply manuals four feet high, piled next to my desk.

I visited the division's combat units and was amazed at the degree to which the Army had changed during the two years I'd been away. For one thing, TRADOC had completely rewritten our battle doctrine so we could take advantage of the new generation of high-tech weapon systems—the

M-1 tank, the Apache helicopter, the Bradley Fighting Vehicle, the Pershing missile, and so on—that were finally nearing production. The new doctrine abolished the traditional concept of head-on, grind-the-enemy-down warfare. TRADOC assumed that we'd be facing the Warsaw Pact, a force that had us outnumbered and outgunned, but that tended to fight in rigid, predictable formations and echelons. The way to win, therefore, was to use our new technology to offset their numerical superiority; synchronize our combat power; and encourage commanders at every level to exercise initiative, flexibility, and ingenuity on the battlefield.

Meanwhile, the new training philosophy had really come into its own. The techniques I'd seen implemented piecemeal in Alaska and Washington—such as training to standards, training to accomplish a specific mission, training to overcome weaknesses, and so on—had been integrated into a comprehensive system that every commander followed. What's more, TRADOC had begun to test high-tech training aids and often used the 8th Mech as its proving ground. One such innovation was a battle-simulation system, called MILES, that employed lasers and made our training much more realistic. In the old days we'd used blanks, so when a soldier during field exercises claimed to have shot an enemy soldier, the enemy could argue, "No, you missed me," and go on fighting. Now the troops had lasers on their weapons and detectors on their equipment, and if a soldier got hit, his beeper would sound, signaling that he was a casualty. I was amazed by how this increase in realism inspired soldiers to work harder at training. Other systems allowed tank crews to simulate firing their main guns at moving enemy tanks projected on a screen. Stop-action replays then showed exactly where their anti-tank rounds had "hit." Our gunnery proficiency increased dramatically, and when the crews went to ranges to work with live ammunition, their frequency of first-round hits was impressive.

Like Cavazos, Livsey ran a happy division. The soldiers worshipped him, and he'd built the commanders and staff into a compatible group that worked hard yet knew when to knock off and have fun. He set the tone, constantly laughing and joking, yet challenging and teaching all the time. I'd only been in Germany a month when he called me in one afternoon and declared theatrically, "I'm at my wits' end." He handed me a computer printout that indicated the combat readiness of each battalion. The Army rated units on a scale of C1 (fully combat ready) to C5 (not combat ready), and took into account a whole range of factors such as the kinds of training a battalion had completed, the state of its equipment, whether it was fully manned, and so on. "Look at the Aviation Battalion," he said. It was one of the few units in the division that wasn't C1. In fact, as I scrutinized the printout I could see that it had *never* been C1—and that the criterion on which it always fell down was helicopter maintenance. I said, "I think I see what you're getting at."

"I want you to study that maintenance program, find out what's wrong, and fix it." As I walked from his office I had a feeling of impending doom. I had barely begun to learn about *tank* maintenance—I hadn't even had time to open the manuals on helicopters.

I did some fast reading and found that to be classified C1, a battalion had to have at least seventy-five percent of its helicopters flying every day. Then I went over to the airfield and started asking questions. I talked to the battalion commander, the maintenance officer, the platoon leaders, and the technicians and mechanics, trying to fathom why more aircraft weren't flying. After a couple of hours, I realized that several people had mentioned hitting the seventy-percent mark. "Why is everybody talking about seventy percent?" I asked the battalion commander.

He gave me a puzzled look and said, "Sir, that's the maintenance standard."

It turned out that for the Huey helicopters the battalion had, a Department of the Army regulation stated that seventy percent should be kept flying for an operation to be considered "acceptable." Apparently, no one had called the Army's attention to the higher combat-readiness requirement established elsewhere in the Pentagon.

I said to the battalion commander, "We're changing the standard. Don't let your troops talk about seventy percent anymore. I want you to shoot for seventy-five percent. The only standard we're interested in in this division is combat readiness." His initial reaction was that maintaining even seventy percent had been difficult. But in less than a month he had his unit operating at C1.

Livsey thought I was Albert Einstein. He imagined that I'd delved deep into the maintenance practices of the Aviation Battalion, uncovered a subtle error in the way our technicians were adjusting the turbines or some such, and taught them how to do their jobs right. When I confessed that all I'd actually done was raise the passing grade, he laughed.

The most challenging part of my work turned out to be community command, which was unique to Germany. We'd only been in Mainz a month when Brenda got a call from a neighbor, a captain's wife, who'd picked up a young Pfc. hitchhiking. The young man was in tears. She'd asked what was wrong and he'd explained that his wife and baby daughter were due to arrive at the Frankfurt international airport that night, and that he had no money and no place for them to stay. Brenda called me at work and I immediately got on the phone with the 1st Brigade commander. "I'll check into it," he said, "but chances are that they're nonsponsored dependents."

"What difference does that make?" I asked.

"That means they're not our responsibility."

"Colonel, one of your men is standing by the side of the road in tears because he can't take care of his wife and his baby, and you're telling me it's not our responsibility? You get that man's battalion and company commanders on the phone and solve that soldier's problem. Then get back to me and let me know what you've done."

They arranged for the man to get an emergency loan, found his family a hotel room, and helped him rent an inexpensive apartment downtown. After I cooled off, I started asking questions of the community command staff. The Army, it turned out, had created a gigantic problem for itself because it couldn't afford to bring over every soldier's family. Only the dependents of officers, NCOs, and enlisted men who were willing to commit to extended tours abroad were "sponsored"—which meant the Army paid their way over and provided housing and all the usual amenities of an American military base. Most Pfc.'s and Spec-4's were not authorized to bring their wives and kids.

The families came anyway. A young wife would fly into Frankfurt with one or two small kids so she could be with her husband. He'd find some cheap, run-down apartment, usually in downtown Mainz. And there they'd be—uprooted from everything they knew, with no access to English-language schools or stores or clinics or services, struggling to get by in the high-priced German economy on skimpy soldier's pay. That weekend I visited some of these homes and found them to be tiny, cramped apartments with only the barest essentials for a family.

We did the obvious first, which was to open the Mainz community commissary, clinic, and day-care center to nonsponsored dependents. But that didn't help enough, because we'd failed to take into account that for young mothers in downtown Mainz those services were hopelessly far away. Even if the family had a car, the husband took it in the morning to get to work, which left the wife and children stranded downtown. There was the streetcar, of course, but if the wife came from a little town in, say,

Alabama and didn't speak a word of German, she probably couldn't manage. So we converted small vans from our motor pool into shuttle buses.

Although the official Army position never changed, I told our unit commanders point-blank that they were responsible not only for their troops, but for the troops' families—sponsored or not. Many of them did not like hearing that. One battalion commander bristled: "My job is to get these guys ready to go to war, not waste time on this family stuff."

"That's shortsighted," I argued. "You can train your men all you want, but what do you think will happen if war breaks out and these guys think nobody is here to look after their families? They're not going to fight very well, that's what." Before long I was up to my neck in the administrative details of the child-care center, the enlisted men's clubs, the elementary school, and other services essential to the well-being of troops and families both on and off the base.

Any attempt to make a change was complicated by the fact that the Modern Volunteer Army campaign was still having trouble attracting first-rate recruits. The summer before, there had been a big scandal when the Army had discovered that recruiters, under pressure to make their quotas, had been cutting corners for years—coaching applicants, giving out copies of the entrance exams, even helping people hide the kinds of felony convictions that would have made them ineligible for service. Hundreds of recruiters had been fired, but our ranks were still full of troops they'd signed up. To exacerbate the situation, the recruiting program itself had backfired. To attract candidates, we had allowed them to enlist, if qualified, for the specialty of their choice. The smart ones generally wanted to learn technical skills that they could use later in civilian life, so they picked branches of the Army that allowed them to do so. Meanwhile a large number of the *less* qualified were placed in the Infantry, the Armor, and the Artillery: nearly two-thirds of the Infantry's new recruits were "category four"—soldiers with IQs of sixty to eighty. This not only slowed training—commanders would find themselves forced to repeat simple instructions five or six times—but also made it difficult for us to defuse culture clashes with the German community. Boom boxes were a big fad among the troops, for example, and off-duty soldiers took to wandering the streets of Mainz playing the latest rock-and-roll tapes full blast. The Germans, who revere peace and quiet, were incensed, but we could not make the troops understand that loud music was considered offensive in the local culture. We finally solved the problem by forbidding them to carry their boom boxes off post.

I involved myself in the German community. I joined a *Volksmarsch-verein*, or walking club, and on weekends Cindy and Jessica and I would participate in ten-kilometer hikes that attracted many Americans and hundreds of German families. As we tramped across the countryside and chatted with the Germans, I felt as if I'd picked up my connection where I'd left off in Berlin twenty years before. At work, I met once a month with a panel of city officials to identify and resolve German-American frictions such as the boom-box problem before they got out of hand. And in preparation for the Pope's visit, my staff and I also met with the cardinal's committee—weekly at first, then every few days, and finally daily as autumn arrived.

On Sunday, November 16, the Vatican helicopter touched down at Finthen and out stepped His Holiness Pope John Paul II to the cheers of a huge throng of faithful. The cardinal—the Bishop of Mainz—the lord mayor, General Scott, and I greeted him and then sat bundled in our greatcoats as he said Mass. It was a blowing, freezing, drizzling day, and the crowd numbered only three hundred thousand rather than the five hundred thousand we'd expected, but the event came off without a hitch. Or so I thought until Monday morning, when I discovered that my deputy commander had, without authorization, allowed a financial guarantee to be given to the main concessionaire. Thanks to the cold weather and unexpectedly small turnout, the Mainz community command now owned one hundred thousand leftover ham-and-cheese sandwiches at a cost to us of $1.25 each. We hawked them to field kitchens and snack bars all over Germany, trying to unload as many as we could before they went bad.

By the time the Pope visited, we were into Fasching, the Rhineland carnival season. Fasching stretched from "11-11-11"—eleven o'clock on November 11—all the way to Ash Wednesday in late February. Brenda and I were invited to an amazing round of dances, parades, and wine parties, which, of course, the community commander and his wife were always expected to attend. Not many other Americans went—the entertainment always centered on satirical skits in a difficult-to-understand dialect—but nonetheless we found the parties great fun and the Germans were pleased that we came. We socialized with the lord mayor of Mainz, the county commissioner, my military counterpart the commander of the local defense force, Major General Hermann Vogt, the eight neighborhood mayors, the police commissioner, and other city leaders. Many invited us to dinner parties at their homes as well—and we broke precedent by hosting dinner parties at our small house in return.

I also accepted invitations to join German hunting circles. The German

Forstmeister, or game wardens, expressed concern that the wild animals on Army-controlled land—where the wardens were not allowed—were vulnerable to starvation and disease because they had been permitted to multiply unchecked. After long and careful discussion, we decided not only to open the land to German hunters, but to put the animal population under *Forstmeister* supervision.

On a Saturday in February Brenda met me at the door when I came home from a pheasant hunt. "Congratulations, Norm," she said and gave me a big hug. "You're going to be a major general." A friend had phoned to tell us I was on the promotion list that would be published that week. General Livsey was in the United States on Army business, but called an hour or so later. "I guess you've heard the good news," he said, sounding happier than I'd ever heard him. He'd scored a coup: not only was I on the list, but so were Riscassi and Brown, making Livsey the only division commander in memory to see three of his assistants advance simultaneously.

I was elated. Two-star was the highest rank in the Army decided upon by a promotion board that weighed all eligible candidates in open competition, and only half of all one-stars ever made the cut. It gave me the right to extend my Army career to thirty-five years rather than being required to retire at thirty. We joked that being promoted to major general was the Army's way of saying it hadn't screwed up when it made you a brigadier general.

In June 1981 the Army added another star to Livsey's collar as well, ordering him to Stuttgart to take command of VII Corps. His successor at the 8th Mech was Carl Vuono, whom I'd known longer than anybody else in the Army: we'd met on a train in June 1952, on our way to West Point to take an entrance exam. He'd served the first part of his career in the Artillery; our paths had crossed again at the Army War College. And when I'd opted for ticket punching at the Pentagon, he'd gone straight to work for General DePuy. He was recognized as one of the hottest young generals out of TRADOC.

I'd never met anyone with greater energy. Vuono was big-hearted, gregarious, happy in his work—and work he did, twenty-four hours a day, 365 days a year. He came to the 8th Mech determined to implement and hone to perfection the Army's new training techniques. Vuono began by instituting a teaching device called the "training management review." Vuono would arrive at the headquarters of a brigade accompanied by his entire staff and the assistant division commander to whom that brigade was assigned, and would set up shop in a conference room. He would then call in the first battalion commander, asking him to lay out his entire training schedule and programs for the next six months. Vuono would scrutinize every detail, which required the commander to either justify his plans on the basis of the battalion's mission and strengths and weaknesses, or rework the plans on the spot. These sessions would go on for what seemed like endless hours: they started at seven-thirty in the morning and often did not end until seven or eight at night. Within six months the 8th Mech looked sharper on almost every aspect of readiness.

We also started to feel the benefits of reforms in the Army's recruiting system. After the scandals, Congress had decided to raise soldiers' pay and benefits, and gave us funds to offer big bonuses to people who enlisted in the Infantry and Armor. Just as important, Recruiting Command had replaced its wimpy recruiting slogan of the 1970s, "Join the people who have joined the Army," with one that grabbed kids who wanted to make something of themselves—"Be all that you can be." It was advertising genius. All of a sudden we started seeing young soldiers who learned more quickly and adapted more readily to military life and German culture.

Vuono and I worked together very closely. He made me his assistant division commander for operations, responsible for the division's war plans and fighting units, and I began to see the limitations—as well as the strengths—inherent in his approach. The rigorous training was terrific, but our troops also needed to learn flexibility, because unexpected things happen in war. This lesson was brought home when our division played the role of a defending force in Reforger, the annual fall exercise of the Army in Europe. It was a big deal: Lieutenant General Scott, the commander of V Corps, was the exercise director, and Dick Cavazos, who was now a lieutenant general and commander of III Corps at Fort Hood, Texas, came to observe. Some of Cavazos's forces were also participating. Lieutenant General Paul "Bo" Williams, who was to be the new commander of V Corps, was also an observer. I couldn't help run the 8th Mech's operation: General Scott had designated me chief umpire for the exercise.

The 3rd Armored Division, our sister unit in V Corps, was to play the Warsaw Pact force. In the war game scenario, they would attack and we would fall back and fight a delaying action until we'd blunted their assault. Then we'd switch to offense, regain the lost ground, restore the mock German border—and the war would be over. Vuono carefully laid out his plans weeks in advance and then drilled the battalion commanders on their parts, until each man was able to recite in great detail, day by day, exactly how his unit would first fall back and later advance.

The "war" started and the 3rd Armored Division didn't follow the script. Rather than attack all across the front, it attacked in only one sector, driving a wedge deep into our positions. Technically, this violated the game's rules—which prescribed limits to the enemy's daily advances—but General Scott wanted to see what the 8th Mech would do and decided to allow it. To my dismay, the 8th Mech ignored all battlefield intelligence flowing into its headquarters and continued to execute by rote the plan that Vuono had drilled. We retreated in sectors where we hadn't even been attacked, and milled around in chaos in the one sector where the enemy had penetrated too far. At Reforger headquarters, I was forced to listen while Williams and Cavazos and their staffs complained throughout the first day, "For chrissakes, they've got this giant penetration right here; why aren't they counterattacking?" *I* knew why but couldn't say: our plan had no provision for a deep penetration—it was just fall back, fall back, fall back, as called for by the exercise scenario.

On the second day, General Scott *ordered* the 8th Mech to counterattack. One of my colleagues in the division called me in a panic: "What's going on? What's going on?"

"Read your intelligence reports! I'm not *allowed* to tell you what's going on." But I knew I would—I couldn't stand the idea of our troops being humiliated.

The 8th Mech performed much better during the offensive phase of the exercise—that was something we'd drilled on, and it allowed our superior training to show. By the end of the exercise the division staff was saying things like, "Well, we got off to a little bit of a bumpy start, but then we really turned it around." All the same, the staff seemed rather hangdog when we came back to our home bases, and the 3rd Armored guys kidded us for months about the whupping they'd given us. As for me, I'd learned a major lesson about staying flexible enough on the battlefield to react to unexpected enemy actions.

That winter, even as the training performance of the 8th Mech hit new highs, the officers and troops seemed worn out. Just before Easter I went out to a training area to visit one of the battalions from the Mainz brigade. I complimented a company commander, "You guys have been working hard. I'll bet you'll be glad to get back to Mainz for Easter."

"Sir, we're not going back for Easter," he said wearily.

"What do you mean?"

He looked at me as if I was crazy. "Sir, except for Christmas, the men in this battalion have not been home for a long weekend in six months."

I went back, did some checking, and discovered that to maximize training time, the 8th Mech had been grabbing extra days in the exercise areas that other units didn't want—with the result that the troops were usually in the field on weekends and holidays. I remembered Cavazos's remark about training on weekends—"This is peacetime!"—and suggested to Vuono that we ease up. He listened carefully, but finally shook his head. "As long as my soldiers are training well and training hard, their morale will stay high." I didn't agree, but he was the boss.

My tour in Mainz was almost up and, in spite of our differences on this subject, Vuono and I worked well together throughout the spring. Just before I left, he even arranged to hold my promotion ceremony to major general a few days before the official date, so that he could pin the stars on me himself.

I'd been ordered back to Washington that June of 1982 to serve as director of military personnel management in the office of the deputy chief of staff for personnel. I never would have believed I'd look forward to another job at the Pentagon, yet all of us were excited as we packed for the move. Cindy, now almost twelve, and Jessica, ten, welcomed the chance to return to the world of malls, hamburger stands, and TV in time to become teenagers. Brenda was looking forward to reclaiming our house in Annandale, which had been rented out for seven and a half years, and living once again close to her mom (Jesse had died of a heart attack in October 1981, on the way home from visiting us in Mainz). And I was delighted with my new assignment. Not only was I returning to the personnel business, which I enjoyed, but I was about to work for one of the most interesting characters in the Army.

———

I'd met Max Thurman when I'd first taught at West Point, almost twenty years before, and we'd shared many dinners at the officers' club. Even then he'd been considered eccentric by Army standards: a rail-thin, intense, aggressive artilleryman who'd been commissioned in the Army through the ROTC after graduating from North Carolina State with a degree in chemical engineering—which he liked to refer to as "comical engineering." As a tactical officer in charge of one of the cadet companies, he had become legendary for his unrelenting approach to discipline. No cadet felt safe from the eyes of Max Thurman anywhere on the military reservation. He had a way of turning up at odd hours, even in the middle of the night, to check on his charges.

Thurman had hit it big in the Army in 1979 when General Edward C. "Shy" Meyer, the new chief of staff, had pulled him out of a job at

TRADOC to clean up Recruiting Command. He was the one who completely rewrote the rules under which the recruiters worked, and the "Be all that you can be" advertising campaign was his baby. We had Max to thank for the first-rate soldiers streaming into the ranks. Meyer wasted no time in jumping Thurman up to three stars as deputy chief of staff for personnel—the Army's number-one personnel man. He had been in that spot about a year, overhauling the systems that governed enlistment, reenlistment, pay, bonuses, testing, promotion, and retirement for a million and a half people, everyone from privates to generals.

A lot of officers loved Thurman and a lot of officers hated him. Some warrior types in the Pentagon called him a lightweight, complaining that he'd never commanded any unit larger than a brigade and therefore didn't deserve to be chief of personnel. The criticism stung, and Thurman asked Meyer for an experienced division commander to be his assistant deputy to give the office more credibility. This led to a stalemate: Meyer needed his division commanders for other jobs, and Thurman rejected every less-qualified candidate Meyer proposed. So the number-two spot was sitting open when I arrived. A week later, Thurman came into my office and said, "Pack your files and move into the assistant's office. You're going to be my acting assistant until I can get a permanent one. Of course, you'll also keep your current responsibilities." So I now had *two* major general's jobs, one of them clearly intended for an officer with several years' more experience than me.

Thurman was an exciting guy to work for, and it was an exciting time to be in Army personnel. After years of failed experiments and false starts, we were finally on a roll. More than eighty-five percent of our recruits now were high school graduates, the highest proportion ever, and the reenlistment rate was the highest since before Vietnam: we actually had more soldiers *asking* to stay in the Army than we needed. Thurman jumped on the opportunity, instituting programs to weed out lazy and incompetent NCOs and crack down on drinking and drug abuse. Under the new regime, the alcoholic bums I'd served under in the late 1950s would never have survived.

Thurman also was planning to ratchet up our physical-fitness standards. Before leaving Mainz I'd put myself on a diet—the director of military personnel management supervised the Army weight-control program, and I'd felt obliged to get down to well under the 220-pound maximum for people my height. I practically had to starve myself and I was not happy. So when Thurman asked me to critique the old standards, I saw my chance to strike a blow for large people everywhere. I got a copy of the

Washington Redskins' roster and pointed out that not a single one of those athletes could qualify under the existing height-and-weight rules. They'd all have gotten kicked out of the Army. "You can't say these guys are out of condition," I argued. "These aren't so much fitness standards as beauty requirements. Whoever wrote them just wanted us to look pretty in our uniforms!" Thurman agreed. After careful research, we junked the height-weight rules and substituted a regulation that set a limit on the percentage of body fat.

One of Thurman's big campaigns was to make the Army more accessible to women. Women accounted for only eight percent of recruits, and our hundreds of military occupational specialties were still almost entirely reserved for men. Thurman's first step was to commission a study called "Women in the Army," to reassess our policies on women soldiers. The study recommended that we immediately ease gender restrictions in non-combat specialties and, at the same time, continue to exclude women from direct combat. Both conclusions were controversial. But Thurman had the drive to make them Army policy. To speed the change, he put me in charge of a review process in which each branch sent a general to Washington to explain how it would apply the new gender rules to its military specialties. I was to judge whether they were doing what Thurman wanted.

Before I knew it, I gained a reputation as the guy at Army headquarters who was carrying the banner for the women's cause. Some branches really didn't want women and would present all sorts of specious arguments about how this or that job would put a female soldier in danger of direct combat. The military police, for instance, argued against allowing women in units whose wartime mission was to guard shipping terminals and airports: "The port-security company is a direct-combat organization because spies and saboteurs try to sneak through and we have to fight them." They were quite upset when I opened that unit to women, but the no-women policy applied only where there was *routinely* a high probability of direct combat.

We launched a half-dozen other major reforms over the course of the first six months, tightening criteria for enlistment and reenlistment, revamping the procedures for commissioning graduates of the ROTC, completely revising the promotion standards for NCOs, and putting real teeth in the officer-retention standards. When mulling over some new policy, Thurman would use me as a sounding board because I'd had so much experience at troop command. "I know what *I* think about this," he'd say, "but how would you feel as a brigade commander if this were foisted upon you?" Carrying two jobs bothered me less than it might have, because Thurman allowed me a degree of latitude practically unheard-of in the military. I represented him in numerous high-level forums where he gave me complete authority to speak in his name. His guidance to me beforehand always consisted of a single sentence: "Do what's right."

Late one Friday in March 1983 he walked into my office and gave me a huge grin. "I've got a surprise for you," he announced. "How would you like to go out and command one of this great Army's divisions?"

I was stunned. I'd only been in my job nine months and had no idea I was up for another command. But I managed to say, "Just tell me which one. I'm ready."

He laughed. "I've just talked to Shy Meyer and we're gonna send you to Camp Swampy, Georgia, where you and the alligators will be in charge of the 24th Mech." Dick Cavazos, who was now the four-star general in command of all Army forces in the United States, had evidently asked for me.

I started to stammer out a thank-you, but I noticed that Thurman was still grinning expectantly. "Okay," I said. "Come on. What else do you have to tell me?"

"What do you think *I'm* gonna do?" Thurman allowed that he was being reassigned as well, as vice chief of staff of the Army. That was a stunning promotion: in the space of two years he had rocketed from two stars to the Army's second-highest four-star job.

We congratulated each other, and I left the building euphoric. Division command was the pinnacle of success for a combat arms officer. The Army had only sixteen active-duty divisions, and each command turned over every two years, so that, of the fifty or more major generals who might have been qualified, only eight would get a division in a given year. I felt like one of God's children.

I drove home, careful not to speed, but with my mind racing. I suddenly remembered the words my old boss Tom Whelan had spoken twenty-five years earlier, when I was a disillusioned young first lieutenant at Fort Campbell: "Stick around and someday, when you have more rank, you may be able to fix the problems." So now I had my chance: this would be my opportunity to apply everything I'd learned in my military career.

———

As I walked in the front door, Brenda took one look at my face and said, "Oh, my. Where are we going?"

I took her into my arms and told her my news. Cindy and Jessica were swept up in our enthusiasm, and though Christian was too young to understand completely what was going on, both he and our dog Rocky knew it must be something good because the rest of us were so excited.

Within half an hour, in the highest tradition of the Army wife, Brenda was researching our move. She called Mary Ann Soyster, a good friend who lived around the corner and whose husband had been an artillery commander with the 24th Mech. Mary Ann came over that evening and loaded us up with advice about Fort Stewart, the surrounding towns of Hinesville, Glennville, and Claxton, the nearby city of Savannah, and, of course, the alligators.

That night, long after the house had fallen quiet and my family was asleep, I lay awake wondering, "What does a division commander *do*?" I conjured up my role models—Latham, Boatner, Warner, Cavazos, Livsey, Vuono—and remembered how Warner in particular had started me off when I'd arrived at Fort Lewis with his "big four" list of goals. I would come up with a list of my own.

Number one was obvious: to make sure my division was combat ready. I knew that the 24th was already damned good—it had a terrific reputation and its current commander was Major General Jack Galvin, the guy I'd succeeded in Mainz. My job would be to keep it sharp.

Number two was the principle I'd learned from Cavazos and Livsey: to take care of the soldiers.

Number three was something I'd learned on my own in Mainz: to take care of the soldiers' families.

Number four was based on what I'd learned in war: that loyalty to one another was what motivated soldiers to fight. Camaraderie and cohesion at every level of the 24th had to be encouraged.

Finally I recognized that I would have a responsibility to teach my subordinates, just as my mentors had taught me. That gave me my "big five."

Every other goal I could think of fit somewhere within that list. Clearing dead wood, for example, fell under maintaining combat readiness; setting high ethical standards was part of teaching my subordinates. I finally drifted into a sound sleep around four in the morning, satisfied that I knew what kind of division commander I wanted to be.

On Monday, June 20, 1983, Brenda and I piled our family—Cindy, Jessica, Christian, Rocky, two parakeets, and a horned toad—into two cars and headed south. We worked our way down the coastline of Virginia and the Carolinas at a leisurely pace, spending several nights at beach motels and visiting friends. The afternoon before my change-of-command ceremony, we got off Interstate 95 at the Fort Stewart exit just south of Savannah. The road seemed to lead straight into a swamp, but immediately we encountered a large black-and-white sign with a division crest that said "Welcome to Ft.

Stewart." We all peered ahead eagerly, expecting to see the base that would be our home for the next two years, but instead we drove for a full half hour, across twenty-five miles of scrub pine and swampland, before the road finally hooked left into the post. Meanwhile the sky had darkened in the late-afternoon heat, and just as we turned in, there was a gigantic thunderclap. Cindy, the family comedian, announced from the backseat, "Watch out, Fort Stewart. He's here."

To anyone who walked around Fort Stewart, the mission of the 24th Mech was obvious. Instead of the standard olive drab, every vehicle—every tank, supply truck, armored personnel carrier, and jeep—was painted in desert camouflage. We were the first armor-equipped division in U.S. Army history earmarked to fight in the Middle East.

It had been three years since I'd left my plans and policy job in Hawaii, and in that time the Carter Doctrine had become a cornerstone of U.S. foreign policy. To ensure that we had the military wherewithal to protect the United States's interests in the Persian Gulf, Washington had expanded the Rapid Deployment Force, effective January 1, 1983, into a full-fledged four-star command. In the event of war, Central Command, as it was called, had an impressive array of forces at its disposal, including the Ninth Air Force, headquartered at Shaw Air Force Base, South Carolina, the First Marine Expeditionary Force, at Camp Pendleton, California, and the Army's XVIII Airborne Corps, at Fort Bragg, North Carolina. We were part of the XVIII Airborne Corps.

The Army's role in Central Command's war plan was to prevent the Soviet Army from swooping down out of the Caucasus and seizing the oil fields in Iran. Should such an invasion seem imminent, our two sister divisions, the 82nd Airborne and the 101st Air Assault, would rush to the

Middle East aboard giant Air Force C-5A and C-141 transport planes. Then our division's troops would fly in while our tanks and heavy equipment followed aboard high-speed cargo ships. Everyone knew that the coordination of light infantry and heavy armor in battle would be a tricky undertaking for the XVIII Airborne Corps commander, Lieutenant General Jack Mackmull, the bulk of whose experience was in Army aviation and the Airborne. That was the main reason Cavazos had recommended me: I was one of the few major generals with extensive experience in light infantry and airborne, as well as armor. The assignment required that I understand the strengths and weaknesses of the airborne units we'd have to fight alongside.

Now that I finally had my own division, I was eager to introduce everything I'd learned—Vuono-style training management reviews, Cavazos-style maintenance programs, Schwarzkopf-style family programs, you name it. I had to keep reminding myself that the 24th Mech was *already* a good division with no need of emergency repairs; it would be a mistake to disrupt it by moving too fast. So instead, I blocked out the first six months for the organization to adjust to the change of command—I figured I could put the time to good use by understanding how the division worked, thinking through our mission, educating my commanders and staff on my priorities, and simply getting to know the hundreds of people I'd be working with inside and outside the unit. A modern division is big and complex: the 24th Mech consisted of three tank battalions, three mechanized infantry battalions, three field artillery battalions, a cavalry squadron, an aviation battalion, an engineer battalion, an air-defense artillery battalion, and two brigades of support troops. We also had a roundout brigade of reservists, the 48th Brigade of the Georgia Army National Guard, which consisted of a tank battalion and two mechanized infantry battalions and was supplemented by another tank battalion from the South Carolina National Guard. Finally, we were responsible for Fort Stewart itself and Hunter Army Airfield in Savannah. Hunter was home to the 1st Ranger Battalion, which I did not command but for which we provided supplies, transportation, housing, and administrative support.

Although I'd delayed any sweeping changes, I *was* on the lookout for ways to establish myself as the leader from the moment I set foot on the base. The morning after we arrived I went out for a run. As I came up on the barracks area, a formation of troops raced by me, led by a guy who looked as if he belonged in the Olympics. I turned around, and stretching back into the distance were the soldiers who hadn't been able to keep pace. The leaders stopped in front of their barracks and were catching their breath as I jogged up. They saluted and I could see they knew I was the incoming division commander. So I stopped and asked the company commander what they were doing. "Sir, we've just completed our five-mile run."

"That's terrific. But what about all those people back there?" I asked, pointing down the road.

"Sir, those are guys who couldn't keep up."

"But you've run off and left them." The captain gave me a puzzled look. "Think of it this way," I said. "Suppose you're a new recruit. You come to your new unit, you're just out of basic training, and you're feeling great about being a soldier. But then you find out that your new unit does a lot more running than you're used to. And the very first day you're out with them, you run and you run until your legs give out and your lungs give out—but your unit keeps going and leaves you. What kind of unit cohesion does that build?"

The light dawned on the captain's face. After suggesting ways he might reorganize the morning run so that nobody was ever left behind, I jogged off, satisfied that I'd just taught a young officer number four of my big five—that cohesion at every level be developed. I knew the episode would get talked about around the base.

I made it a point never to pass by a mistake and tried to instill that principle in all my leaders. I'd be all dressed up in a coat and tie, heading someplace with my family, and I'd see one of my troops walking along the street with his uniform shirt improperly buttoned. I'd stop the car.

Brenda would say, "Here he goes again."

"Dad, this is so *embarrassing*," Cindy and Jessica would moan. But I'd get out, identify myself, and ask calmly, "How come your shirt's unbuttoned?" The morale of the 24th was so strong that the soldier generally would not become defensive, but would simply say something like, "Aw, sir, I just came out of the gym and I was hot, sir, and I screwed up," and button his shirt.

Now that I had the authority to make the rules, I determined to do away with unnecessary weekend training. My first Saturday on post I was driving along one of Fort Stewart's many back roads, checking out bass lakes, when I came upon a company of troops sitting under pine trees by the side of the road. I stopped the car and asked, "What's up, guys?"

"Sir, we have training," one private answered glumly. I looked out across the flats and spotted a couple of squads moving into position along a tree line. But most of the men involved were just being made to sit and wait.

Within minutes, the company commander arrived and gave a smart salute. I took him aside. "Why are your men training on Saturday?" I asked.

"Sir, we didn't accomplish all our training objectives this week, so we're making it up today." He said it proudly—from his point of view, he and his unit were showing real dedication.

"When did you let your troops know they were going to have to train today?" I continued.

"Yesterday, sir."

"What about the fact that your troops might have had weekend plans with their families?"

"Yes, sir, but we hadn't met our training objectives."

As soon as I got to headquarters Monday morning I called in my assistant division commanders and chief of staff and described what I'd seen. I told them, "This is not why these kids enlisted in the Army. I just finished a tour as assistant deputy chief of staff for personnel and I know for a fact that this isn't what the recruiters promise when they sign them up. The recruiters tell them it's a five-day-a-week job, and unless we're at war or on field exercises, that's the way it's gonna be. Weekend training is going to stop, as of now." I laid out a set of rules: "First, if a commander wants to train on a weekend, he has to let his troops know six weeks in advance. Second, it had better be *good* training—not soldiers twiddling their thumbs under pine trees—because I'm gonna be out there personally inspecting it. And third, any commander who makes his men train on weekends has to give them comp time—and I'm going to monitor that too."

They were incredulous—no division commander had ever issued such an order. Colonel Pete Taylor, my chief of staff, said bleakly, "Sir, I've gotta warn you, our combat readiness is really going to suffer."

"No, it's not," I said. "It's gonna get better."

———

The Army's new National Training Center, at Fort Irwin, California, was the most sophisticated practice range ever devised. It occupied a thousand-square-mile tract of the Mojave Desert not far from the Twenty-nine Palms reservation where my Fort Lewis brigade had given the Marines such a hard time. Its crumbling shale mountains and scrubby plateaus were hospitable only to horned toads, rattlesnakes, and scrawny jackrabbits—but the terrain was particularly well suited to our purposes because it so closely resembled that of northern Iran. Thurman had let me go out to see the NTC as soon as I'd been named a division commander, and I'd come away convinced that it gave us an advantage over every other army in the world.

We could now teach and evaluate our armored forces under circumstances so closely resembling battle that the only absent elements were actual wounds and death.

The NTC was designed to accommodate two visiting battalions at a time, along with a supporting artillery battalion and the supply and transportation companies, signal companies, engineer companies, and other units also needed for support. The battalions arrived and took three days to attach lasers, transmitters, and monitors to their equipment. They were then thrown immediately into two weeks of simulated combat, twenty-four hours a day, against a world-class "enemy" force that had them greatly outnumbered. This was a unit known as the OPFOR (short for "opposing forces") that had been organized and equipped to fight like Soviets—OPFOR prided itself on trouncing the visiting team with great regularity.

The training consisted of a rapid-fire sequence: as soon as a battalion finished one mission, it would be thrust into the next, just as in combat at its most intense. Evaluators accompanied the unit at every level—squad, platoon, company, and battalion—and the battlefield itself was fully automated: all the tanks and troops were equipped with the same laser detection system we'd used in Germany, and the heavy weapons and communications systems were linked into central computers that recorded the action. When a battle ended, the evaluators would gather the unit's commanders for an immediate and detailed critique. I'd sat in on one of those sessions, in a van in the middle of the desert, and it had been fierce. The evaluators had asked the battalion commander: "Why did you shift Bravo Company at 0900 hours so that it was backed up against a canyon with no ability to maneuver?"

"I didn't do that."

"Yes, you did," the evaluators persisted—and punched up a computer display that showed exactly where he'd positioned his force. Next they turned to a captain and said, "Alpha Company commander, at 1500 hours your battalion headquarters ordered you to advance. It took you an hour to move. Why?" They were relentless.

Meanwhile the unit's NCOs remained in the field, replenishing supplies, feeding the troops, dragging "shot-up" tanks off the battlefield to a maintenance tent where their support units could "fix" them, just as they'd have to do in a real war. Traditionally, armies on field exercises hadn't bothered to exercise their wartime supply and maintenance procedures, but those skills were crucial and had to be practiced. Battle conditions were mimicked in every detail: for example, the blanks fired by tanks during the exercises didn't weigh much, so battalions were required to haul boxes of dirt to simulate the weight and bulk of real ammunition. If they failed to thus "resupply" their tanks, they were prohibited from using them in the next battle.

Two of my battalions were slated to go to the NTC in September 1983, and we had been preparing for months. Ten days before the exercise, I stood and watched as they loaded their tanks and equipment onto railcars for the long trip west. I'd been thinking how important it was that the battalion and company commanders approach the NTC in the proper frame of mind. Just before they left, I called them in. "There's something I want you to remember," I told them. "The NTC is the National *Training* Center—not the National *Testing* Center. I *expect* you to make mistakes. I want you to use your initiative. I'd rather have you fall on your ass in peacetime than in war, because in peacetime it doesn't cost lives." I needed them to understand that the most important thing to me was that they learn from their experiences and that, if they failed, I wasn't going to hold it against them.

I also knew better than to be hovering over my units during their first few days at the NTC. Visiting battalions fared miserably against the OP-FOR at first—sometimes they even failed to accomplish their mission and got "wiped out." After two or three days of nonstop pounding, the commanders and troops would be hot, filthy, and exhausted, and their performance and morale would plunge. But then they'd grit their teeth, find ways to fight more effectively, and begin to rebound. I timed my visit for the *second* week.

Meanwhile the division staff and I prepared for a high-level exercise of our own: a two-day secret conference at XVIII Airborne Corps headquarters to walk through our part of Central Command's Middle East war plan. We convened in mid-October in a wooden, one-story building at Fort Bragg, set apart by razor-wire barricades. Each of more than a dozen commanders delivered a detailed account of how his unit would fight its part of the Iran campaign, after which we compiled a list of what we thought were shortcomings that the Pentagon needed to address. A primary concern was the need for stockpiles of weapons, machinery, and supplies, specialized ships, and cranes and other cargo-handling equipment for the rapid resupply of operations in the Middle East.

———

I went fishing the weekend after I got home, caught a whole bunch of bass, and on Sunday afternoon was in the kitchen. I'd long been promising my family a dinner of bass cooked in a beer batter by Dad. I had the bass in a paper bag and was shaking it to coat it with salt and pepper and flour when the phone rang. It was Major General Dick Graves, the director of operations at Forces Command. "What have you got lined up for the next few weeks?" he asked.

"What's this all about?"

"I need to know. You're being considered for a very important mission, and General Cavazos asked me to find out your plans."

I outlined the division's program—we had no major exercises scheduled and I planned to be on base—and he said, "Okay. I'll call you back around six o'clock."

I felt both curious and anxious: the day before, terrorists had bombed the U.S. Marine barracks in Beirut, and I guessed we were about to launch some kind of military response. I tried to get my mind back on cooking, but the meal was far from what I'd planned—instead of enjoying a relaxed dinner, I gulped down the food.

At exactly six o'clock Graves called again. "How quickly can you get up here to Atlanta?"

I told him I could be there in a few hours. "All right. You're going on a military operation. You'll be away for about three weeks." Since my home phone was not secure, I knew better than to ask questions. I called my division duty officer, lined up a plane, and started packing. Not knowing what the mission was, I laid out both summer and winter uniforms. Then I drove over to headquarters and got hold of Graves on a secure phone. The connection was awful—it kept garbling his voice—but I found out the mission had nothing to do with the Middle East. I was being sent to Grenada. After placing the division in the hands of my assistant division commanders, I went back home and stuffed my summer battle dress uniforms into a bag.

At nine o'clock a car pulled up to take me to the airfield. I kissed my children good-bye and took Brenda's hands. She looked scared. "Are you going to be in any danger?" she asked in a small voice.

"I'm not going to Beirut," I reassured her, "but I can't tell you any more than that." She shook her head with relief and kissed me good-bye.

When we landed at Charlie Brown Airport in Atlanta, we taxied up to the small Army terminal where Dick Graves greeted me at the door. His briefing was sketchy. the government of Grenada had been overthrown by a military junta and hundreds of American medical students were being detained in their dormitories. "The Navy is preparing to launch a major operation in which we will go ashore to liberate the students and put the legitimate government back in. A lot of Army forces are going to be involved—the 82nd Airborne and Special Operations units and the 1st Ranger Battalion—and Washington wants to make sure that the Navy uses them correctly. That's where you come in. General Cavazos wants you to go along as an advisor to the Navy."

"Hold it," I said. "It doesn't sound as if I'm exactly going to be welcome."

Graves, who was a dour fellow, winced. "As a matter of fact, you're not. The Navy doesn't like the fact that you're being sent. But," he added, holding up a finger, "you have the support of the highest people in Washington. If the Navy gives you a hard time, just let us know and we'll get it straightened out."

"Okay," I said dubiously. "Now fill me in on the operation."

"I've told you all I know. There's a meeting at seven o'clock tomorrow morning at Atlantic Command in Norfolk. You should be there."

I climbed back aboard my airplane. As we flew up the coast, I realized I wasn't even sure where Grenada *was*. Neither were the two planners I'd brought with me. I knew it was a Caribbean island, but I'd have been hard pressed to find it on a map.

I walked into Atlantic Command the following morning, October 24, and felt about as welcome as a case of mumps. Vice Admiral Joseph Metcalf, a wiry, feisty three-star with a sharp New England accent, immediately started peppering me with questions about what I expected to contribute to the operation. Then Admiral Wes McDonald, the commander in chief of Atlantic Command, arrived, and we all went upstairs to the briefing room. A couple of other Army generals were present—Major General Ed Trobaugh, commander of the 82nd Airborne, and Major General Dick Scholtes, the Special Operations commander—but Admiral McDonald singled me out. He walked up and said roughly, "Now, for chrissakes, try and be helpful, would you? We've got a tough job to do and we don't need the Army giving us a hard time."

I replied, "Sir, I'm here to help in any way I can. I served two years at Pacific Command under Admiral Weisner and Admiral Long, and I understand how the Navy works. I have no intention of being disruptive." That seemed to mollify him somewhat.

The invasion was scheduled for two o'clock the following morning—only nineteen hours away—and this was the final planning conference. At the end of the long table was a large map that showed an island shaped like a football. Grenada was about ten miles wide and twenty-five miles long; part of the coast was sandy beach, but the island consisted mostly of mountainous jungle terrain that came straight up out of the sea. Admiral McDonald opened the briefing by saying, "Before we get into the operational plan, everyone should bear in mind the strong possibility that we won't have to carry it out. The crisis is still being handled through diplomatic channels, and we are told it is very likely that the rebels will back down." A State Department representative, seated across the conference table from the admiral, nodded his agreement.

The operation was conceived as what military planners called a "coup de main," a one-punch knockout. While the Navy cordoned off the island with ships and planes, the Marines would make an amphibious assault on Grenada's eastern shore. Their objectives were Pearls Airfield, the island's only operating airport, and the town of Grenville, which housed a military garrison. Simultaneously, the Rangers would fly in and seize the Point Salines airfield, a very large installation under construction at the island's southern tip, as well as the True Blue campus of the medical school, where it was reported that the American students were being detained. As soon as the airfield was secured, two battalions of the 82nd Airborne would relieve the Rangers. Meanwhile, our Special Operations forces were to fly their helicopters into St. George's, the capital, on the island's west coast. There they were to rescue Sir Paul Scoon, the British-appointed governor general, who was being held at his residence, and capture the radio station, Fort Rupert downtown, and Fort Frederick and Richmond Hill Prison above the city. The prison was where the rebels had allegedly incarcerated Prime Minister Maurice Bishop and various other government officials. As the day progressed, our units would fan out from the airfields and assert control of the rest of the island.

The Grenadian army consisted of two thousand active-duty troops and a few thousand more in reserve. But the briefers assured us, "Don't worry. When the army sees we're Americans, they'll give up." There were antiaircraft emplacements around Point Salines and St. George's, but the briefers told us, "Don't worry. The gunners are poorly trained and don't represent a real threat." Finally there was the question of the Cuban construction workers at Point Salines airfield—six hundred to eight hundred men who had had military training and were armed. "Don't worry," said the briefers again. "They're not going to fight." The plan, in fact, called for the Rangers to drive to the Cuban compound and announce, "We are here to reinstall the legitimate government of Grenada. You will not be hurt. Please stay here while we get this thing over with." The thought that kept running through my mind was, *"How do we know the Cubans aren't going to fight?"*

Major General Dick Scholtes, the Special Operations commander, expressed concern about how the Rangers would get on the ground. They could parachute in if necessary, but the operation would be more effective if they could simply land their transport planes at Point Salines. The night before, a Navy SEAL team had been dispatched to sneak onto Point Salines beach and climb up to check the condition of the runway. But the water had been so rough when the SEALs parachuted in that they'd been swept out to sea and were now missing in action. Given that we still didn't know the condition of the runway, Scholtes recommended we postpone the invasion for twenty-four hours. There was a flurry of discussion, until Admiral McDonald burst out, "I can't *believe* what I'm hearing around this table. All you're going to face is a bunch of Grenadians. They're going to fall apart the minute they see our combat power. Why are we making such a big deal of this?"

In the sudden silence, the State Department representative added: "I would not recommend that we delay. The Organization of Eastern Caribbean States, which asked us to intervene, is a shaky coalition at best. There's no telling how long it's going to support this thing."

"That's it," McDonald said. "We go on the twenty-fifth as planned."

"Okay," answered Scholtes unhappily. "But at the very least we should try to do some reconnaissance tonight. Can we delay the operation by two hours?" McDonald agreed, and H-hour was pushed back to four o'clock.

As the meeting closed, somebody raised the question of the press. We agreed that we would open Grenada to reporters at five o'clock the next afternoon, because by then Grenada would be ours.

———

The next thing I knew I was on an airplane bound for Barbados. The task force staff that filled the cabin were all Navy and Marine Corps officers—the entire Army contingent consisted of me, my two assistants, and a junior liaison officer from the 82nd Airborne. We reached Barbados in midafternoon and it was obvious that word had gotten out about the possibility of U.S. military action: the press was at the airport in force. Admiral Metcalf ordered us to stay in the airplane as we waited for helicopters to take us to the fleet. After about thirty minutes two big Navy helicopters showed up. We climbed aboard and headed out to sea.

Soon there was nothing but ocean in every direction, which made me very uneasy: if the helicopter had suddenly lost power, it would have been just us and the fish. The officers in the cabin did not seem like men on their way to war—no one really believed we'd fight, and the trip felt more like an excursion. After about an hour I spotted a little postage stamp way ahead on the ocean. It turned out to be the helicopter carrier *Guam*, which would be

Admiral Metcalf's flagship. The minute I set foot on the gently rolling deck, I sent one of my officers inside to find me some seasickness pills.

By now it was 5:30 in the afternoon. We went below and got cleaned up, and almost immediately dinner was announced. The admiral's mess turned out to be a large room with a single long table and a spanking white tablecloth. We ate a soup appetizer and had just started on the turkey main course when Admiral Metcalf's chief of staff came in and announced, "It's a go." There was a stunned silence. "It's a go," he repeated. "We're going. H-hour has been bumped back one hour. It's a go at 0500."

Everyone sat for a moment, poking at their food. "Jeez, I'd better get busy," somebody said. One by one, people got up and left, until I was the only person in the room. I didn't have anything to do, so I just sat in front of my half-finished meal, trying to take in what was happening. After a while I climbed the stairs to the command center behind the bridge, where directives were streaming in from Norfolk and Marine commanders were issuing terse last-minute orders to their units. I felt in the way and finally stepped outside to the platform that ran around the bridge. It was now pitch dark, and I realized that by this time tomorrow, we'd be at war. I had misgivings about whether we should be sending troops to Grenada. Were we being committed to another war that the American public wouldn't support? The question wasn't strategic or political; it was personal. I had to remind myself that I'd thought this all through when I'd come home from Vietnam and decided to remain in the military. My job now was not to question the judgment of our leaders or the wisdom of our mission. My duty was to help make sure it got carried out with a minimum loss of American lives. I said a prayer and went below to get some rest.

The room I'd been assigned was right under the carrier's flight deck, and at four o'clock in the morning I woke to the whine of turbines and the clamor of shouts and running feet. I went up to the bridge and watched dozens of helicopters load up with Marines and take off. One of the operations officers told me that during the night a SEAL team had reconned the beaches near Pearls Airfield and Grenville and reported them unsuitable for an amphibious landing. So Admiral Metcalf had revised his plans and the attack on that side of Grenada would be by helicopter. As a result, the *Guam* and its escort ships had steamed to within about five miles of the island, which loomed like a great black hump to our north. SEALs had also tried to scout Point Salines again, but the seas were still too rough, their boats had gotten swamped, and the mission had been aborted. That meant the Ranger battalions now en route from Savannah still did not know what they'd find.

Meanwhile, because of a navigation-equipment failure, the Rangers were going to be a half hour late; but the Marine helicopters were already in the air, ready to attack. The question was, should we go at 0500 or delay? Metcalf asked my advice. "You've got to attack now," I said. "They can hear our helicopters on the island and if we wait even another half hour, we'll totally lose the element of surprise." Metcalf agreed, gave the go-ahead order, and at 0500 hours the Marines landed at Pearls Airfield and took it almost without a fight. At 0630 the Marines launched another wave of helicopters and took the town of Grenville, also without a fight.

However, at 0535 when the Rangers arrived at Point Salines, the enemy was waiting for them. Worse, it was now daybreak and the Rangers, forced to parachute in, were in plain sight of the enemy gunners. From the bridge of the *Guam* we could see the parachutes coming down and the green tracers of antiaircraft fire reaching up past them. As the Rangers hit the ground, they reported that the Cuban construction workers were not only heavily armed but dug in: they occupied sandbag bunkers on the hills all along the airfield. At first we got only fragmentary reports, but it was clear that this was no cakewalk. People were getting killed.

In St. George's, the Special Operations helicopters had run into anti-aircraft fire so intense that they couldn't even reach Fort Rupert, Richmond Hill Prison, or Fort Frederick. Troops did manage to land at the governor general's house—only to find themselves surrounded and trapped. It was total chaos and confusion. From the bridge of the *Guam* we could see Army helicopters on their way back from the island. Two crashed into the ocean. Others set down on our flight deck shot full of holes and leaking hydraulic fluid all over. In the midst of this, Admiral Metcalf received an urgent message from the office of the Navy's comptroller in Washington warning that he should not refuel Army helicopters because the funds-transfer arrangements with the Army had not yet been worked out. I watched Metcalf read the message and hand it back to his chief of staff. "This is bullshit," he said. "Give them fuel."

Our intelligence people, monitoring radio traffic, had identified Fort Frederick as the headquarters of the rebel force. "I want to bomb it," Metcalf told me. "What do you advise?" It was a tough call because the fort was close to the town and we were under orders to minimize damage and civilian casualties; Metcalf knew that a decision to bomb might be second-guessed. I was pleased he'd asked me—he'd realized I was there to offer expertise.

"Bomb it," I seconded him. "If we let them keep up an organized resistance, we'll take a lot more casualties and eventually have to bomb it

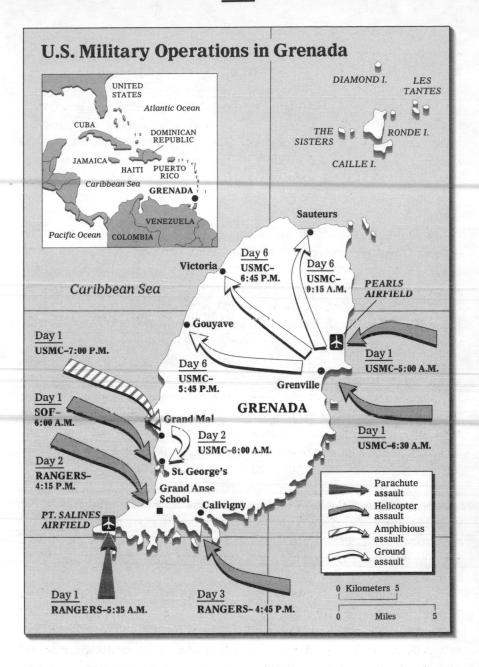

U.S. Military Operations in Grenada

DIAMOND I.

LES TANTES

THE SISTERS

RONDE I.

CAILLE I.

UNITED STATES

Atlantic Ocean

CUBA

DOMINICAN REPUBLIC

JAMAICA

HAITI

PUERTO RICO

Caribbean Sea

GRENADA

VENEZUELA

Pacific Ocean COLOMBIA

Caribbean Sea

Sauteurs

Victoria

Day 6
USMC–
6:45 P.M.

Day 6
USMC–
9:15 A.M.

PEARLS AIRFIELD

Day 1
USMC–7:00 P.M.

Gouyave

Day 6
USMC–
5:45 P.M.

Day 1
USMC–5:00 A.M.

Grenville

GRENADA

Day 1
SOF–
6:00 A.M.

Grand Mal

Day 2
USMC–8:00 A.M.

Day 1
USMC–6:30 A.M.

Day 2
RANGERS–
4:15 P.M.

St. George's

Grand Anse
School

Calivigny

PT. SALINES
AIRFIELD

Day 1
RANGERS–5:35 A.M.

Day 3
RANGERS– 4:45 P.M.

Parachute assault

Helicopter assault

Amphibious assault

Ground assault

0 Kilometers 5

0 Miles 5

anyhow." So Metcalf ordered an air strike and Fort Frederick was destroyed. We later learned that the bombing also wrecked a mental hospital next door that we hadn't known was there.

At ten o'clock came the biggest shock of the day. The Rangers, having finally secured the runway at Point Salines so that our airplanes could land, moved on to their next objective: rescuing the students. They burst into the dormitory at the True Blue campus and told the students they were now safe. The students replied, in effect, "Great! But what about the rest of us?" The bulk of the student body wasn't at True Blue at all, but two miles away in a beachfront hotel near a campus we hadn't even known about called Grand Anse.

By noon we could also see that because of the antiaircraft defenses, the Special Operations forces wouldn't be able to secure St. George's. We'd have to take the city some other way. I reminded Metcalf that our amphibious force was sitting at sea off Grenville and Pearls, where it had been unable to land: "Suppose we bring that force around and land it north of St. George's?" Metcalf asked his commanders how long it would take to reposition the ships, and dispatched a SEAL team to reconnoiter the beach. Within a couple of hours the SEALs reported that a landing was feasible, and we scheduled it for late afternoon.

Toward evening, Metcalf and I sat down to take stock. Measured against our objectives, the first day's results were pretty dismal. Though we'd secured the airfields and sealed off the island, the rebels were still in power, the government buildings were still theirs, Governor General Scoon and our Special Operations forces team were surrounded, and most of the American students were still in enemy hands. One bit of good news came in just before sunset: the Marines had landed successfully on a western beach called Grand Mal and taken up positions to begin a drive on St. George's in the morning. But the coup de main had failed utterly. Metcalf and I agreed that the Army and Marines would have to fight their way cross-country to rescue the students and take St. George's from the ground. He took a deep breath and looked at me. "I will confess that I know very little about ground operations. Would you make up the plans for tomorrow and write the orders that we should give to the forces?"

"Of course," I said. I sat down with my planners, and Metcalf—who had been working thirty-six hours straight—got ready to knock off for the night. But as he turned to leave the command center, a call came in from Atlantic Command in Norfolk. "What's your enemy body count for today?" an officer wanted to know.

I looked at Metcalf darkly, "We need to stay away from this body-count business. It caused terrible trouble in Vietnam and it'll cause terrible trouble here. Let's just concentrate on accomplishing the mission."

"You're right," he said, and so instructed his staff and left. A half hour later the phone rang again and Atlantic Command *ordered* us to provide a body count.

Soon, having dutifully collected estimates from the various commanders in the field, Metcalf's staff showed me the reply they were about to send: "Body Count: Army 13; Marines 133."

I couldn't contain myself. "This is the biggest bunch of bullshit I've ever seen! The Marines weren't even in battle today. Where did they get this hundred and thirty-three?" I burst out. Seeing the shock on their faces, I said, "Guys, don't you realize how much grief there was over body counts in Vietnam? We can't send in numbers that make no sense." The staff went back to the Marines, who explained that the 133 enemy had been "killed by helicopters." I told the staff: "I find that impossible to believe, but if you want to send it in, fine. But *please* aggregate the reports into one number, so we don't start a body-count competition between the Army and the Marines. And be sure to call it an estimate." I could sense from their demeanor that they thought I was concerned about the Marines' showing up the Army, but that wasn't it at all. I just thought the whole thing was insane.

At daybreak Wednesday, the Marines drove their armored vehicles from Grand Mal south to the heights above St. George's. They first relieved the Special Operations unit at the governor general's residence, put Governor General Scoon and his wife onto a helicopter, and flew them out to the *Guam*. By ten o'clock they were sipping tea in Admiral Metcalf's mess.

Our forces at Point Salines, however, weren't making any progress toward rescuing the students at Grand Anse. The problem certainly wasn't a shortage of troops: the day before, the 82nd Airborne had landed two full battalions at Point Salines, and although Admiral Metcalf had told Trobaugh that that was enough, the division had poured in men all night. So now the Army had *four* battalions of paratroopers on the ground—in addition to the 82nd Airborne artillery—to back up its original two battalions of Rangers. But they were making no progress because reconnaissance reports that morning indicated that a large enemy force was blocking the way to Grand Anse, and the 82nd was still consolidating its units at Point Salines. At the same time, we were getting bombarded with messages from Atlantic Command saying Washington wanted to know why we hadn't rescued the students. The atmosphere in our command center became more and more tense.

During the night the *Guam* had moved down the Grenadian coast, and we could look off the bridge and actually see the students' dormitory. Late in the morning, I stepped outside for a moment of peace. Standing on the bridge, I looked straight across at the students' building, which was fronted by a long stretch of white, sandy beach. Then I looked directly down onto the flight deck and focused on the dozens of Marine helicopters just sitting there. *Why were we fixated on attacking over land?* I went back inside, where Metcalf was talking with his staff. "I want to show you something," I told him, and brought him back out on the bridge. "Listen, that's where the enemy is, right over there. Look at that beach. It's a perfect landing zone! We've got all these helicopters here, and all those Rangers and Airborne troops down at Port Salines. Why not pick up the troops, fly in from the sea, and rescue the students?"

"Great!" Metcalf exclaimed. "Make it happen."

So I called Trobaugh at the airfield and told him to get his soldiers ready. Then I asked the Marine colonel in command of the entire battalion landing team to come to the bridge. He listened impassively as I sketched out the plan. Finally he said, "I'm not going to do that."

"What do you mean?" I asked.

"We don't fly Army soldiers in Marine helicopters."

I looked at him incredulously. "Colonel, you don't understand. We've got a mission, and that mission is to rescue these students *now*. Your Marines are way up in Grenville securing that area, and your helicopters are right here. The way to get the job done is to put Army troops in those helicopters."

"If we have to do it, I want to use my Marines. They'll rescue the hostages," he maintained stubbornly.

"How long would that take?"

He looked me straight in the eye and said, "At least twenty-four hours."

"Listen to me very carefully, Colonel. This is a direct order from me, a major general, to you, a colonel, to do something that Admiral Metcalf wants done. If you disobey that order, I'll see to it that you're court-martialed."

A couple of the colonel's subordinates who had been listening to this conversation turned to him. One said, "Sir, can we talk to you outside?"

After a few minutes he came back and said, "Well, all right. I guess we'll do it."

The raid took only a few hours to prepare—and was simplified by the fact that our forces were actually in touch with the students. One young fellow, on hearing the shooting the day before, had simply called the Point Salines airfield and gotten the Army on the phone. They raised the students now, explained that we were about to shell the Grenadian positions in preparation for the raid, and gave them instructions: "Tie on white armbands. Put mattresses against your windows and lie on the floor until you hear the shelling stop. When the helicopters land and unload their troops, run outside and climb on." Our forces went in at 4:15 in the afternoon and the plan worked beautifully. The Marines flew a regular shuttle—delivering Rangers to Grand Anse and students to Point Salines—and within thirty minutes we'd rescued all two hundred and twenty-four students, with only two Rangers slightly injured. The situation now looked much better than it had on day one.

At sunset Metcalf and I reviewed the day's results and he again asked me to work up plans and orders for the following day. As I finished the orders, I thought about my lack of formal authority. "Here are your plans," I said to Metcalf in his office. "But let me tell you what happened this afternoon." His eyebrows went up as I recounted the incident. I looked at him and concluded, "I'm more than happy to run your ground campaign, but I've got to have some authority."

Metcalf said quietly, "I can fix that." He called in the entire senior staff and said, "As of now, Schwarzkopf is the deputy commander of this task force. He is my second-in-command. In my absence, he is in charge, and when he gives an order, you should consider that that order comes from me." I was gratified to see him act swiftly and decisively on my behalf.

The following morning, the Marines finished sweeping the high ground above St. George's and encircled the town. Meanwhile the 82nd Airborne—which now had *six* battalions on the ground—had finally taken over from the Rangers and begun working its way north and east from the air base. Metcalf and I flew into Point Salines to visit Army headquarters around noon. We had just sat down for a briefing when the *Guam* relayed an urgent message from Atlantic Command: the Joint Chiefs of Staff wanted us to take the Calivigny barracks by the end of the day. Calivigny was a garrison situated on a peninsula about five miles east of the air base; intelligence sources reported it to be a Cuban-run terrorist training camp. We'd been planning to secure it in the final phase of our operation. The 82nd Airborne was headed in that direction, but was moving very slowly because Trobaugh had ordered his men to clear out each pocket of enemy resistance as it was discovered.

We sent a message back to Atlantic Command that said something like, "The 82nd Airborne is moving that way and will take the Calivigny barracks by the end of the day tomorrow." But Atlantic Command responded, in effect, "Absolutely not. JCS orders you to take the Calivigny barracks by tonight."

We hurriedly ordered another helicopter assault. The task force bombarded the Calivigny barracks for almost an hour with air strikes and naval gunfire; finally, at 4:45, the Rangers went in. The operation was a disaster. Two helicopters collided in the crowded landing zone, and shattered rotor blades flew in every direction, mowing down almost two dozen of our men. Meanwhile, no enemy were there at all—we'd been chasing ghosts.

I was back on the *Guam* when they brought in the wounded, and I hurried down to the hospital bay. The scene was awful, with blood splashed everywhere from horrible wounds. A Ranger lieutenant who had lost his leg tried to get out of bed and stand at attention when he saw me walk in. I gently pushed him back. "Sir, how did my troops do?" he asked anxiously. "Did we accomplish our mission?" I assured him that they'd done well. Then I told him how proud I was of him. He smiled and recited his motto: "Rangers lead the way—*hoo-ah*!"

I was angry as I climbed back up to the bridge. Soldiers had died, this kid was lying there mutilated, and there had been no military reason that we had to take the Calivigny barracks that day. I wondered which son of a bitch had ordered the attack.

The battle for Grenada was now pretty much over. The next day, Marines moved into St. George's where the townspeople welcomed them and led them to some of the rebels' hiding places. Hudson Austin, the coup leader, had vanished and was rumored to be trying to flee the island. Maurice Bishop, the prime minister whom he had overthrown, was missing and presumed dead, as were other members of his government. Richmond Hill Prison, where they supposedly had been locked up, was empty when the Marines arrived. We loaded the Cubans we had captured onto airplanes and sent them home.

Admiral Metcalf left early that morning for Barbados to meet with the Organization of Eastern Caribbean States. Right after lunch his chief of staff and his operations officer came to me, seemingly concerned. Evidently, the Navy had been shadowing a Cuban ship, the *Vietnam Heroica*, that had been moored in St. George's Harbor at the beginning of our operation. We'd suspected that its purpose was intelligence gathering and had ordered it to stand at least twelve miles off Grenada, but instead it had turned and steamed away toward Trinidad. Admiral Metcalf's last order had been for our ships to stop tracking the vessel as soon as it put in at Trinidad. But the staff reported that Port of Spain, Trinidad, had just refused the *Vietnam Heroica* entry. "It's continuing to steam," they said. "Do you want us to keep following it?"

They knew I didn't have a clue, but were playing to the hilt the fact that Metcalf had named me deputy commander and that, therefore, I had to make this naval decision. So I did what all great commanders do. I asked, "What does my staff recommend?" Fortunately, the Trinidad authorities reversed themselves and allowed the ship to enter.

In Barbados, Metcalf had finished his meeting with the Organization of Eastern Caribbean States and was holding a press conference on our action in Grenada. Since we'd blocked reporters from covering the invasion, the twenty or thirty he faced were not entirely friendly.

We hadn't introduced them on the first day as originally intended because chaos had reigned. But on day two, a couple of reporters who were already on the island had actually succeeded in getting flown out to the *Guam*. When I saw two civilians sprint across the flight deck and leap into a helicopter as we prepared to launch the raid on Grand Anse, I ran down to the deck and told them, "Get off. You're interfering with a military operation." Metcalf then ordered the captain of the *Guam* to see that they stayed off the flight deck. The reporters spent the rest of the afternoon sitting in the officers' wardroom drinking coffee and eating sweet rolls. The incident showed up in *The Washington Post* as a story about journalists being "held incommunicado" on the *Guam*.

The reporters quizzed Metcalf about that and then moved on to another incident on day two. We had Grenada completely cordoned off—we were concerned that Cuba would send reinforcements and we wanted to prevent Hudson Austin from slipping away. The Navy had been warning all ships: "Stay away from the island. If you approach, you are going to get shot at." But around eleven o'clock in the morning, we'd received an urgent report in the command center from an observation plane: "High-powered speedboat headed straight for Grenada." The Navy had dispatched a fighter that made some low passes, but the speedboat showed no sign of changing course. "Who could be doing this?" we'd wondered. "Is someone trying to pick up Hudson Austin?" After consulting Metcalf, the Navy instructed the fighter pilot to fire warning shots. The boat didn't turn. Finally Metcalf ordered, "Fire one more burst of warning shots. If it doesn't turn around then, sink it." But after the second set of warning shots, the boat turned and left the area. Later we learned that the boat had been chartered by reporters—one of whom was now present at Metcalf's press conference. He identified himself and asked, "Admiral, what would have happened if we hadn't turned around?"

Metcalf didn't miss a beat. "We would have blown your ass right out of the water," he growled.

On Wednesday, November 2, Admiral Metcalf officially declared that hostilities had ceased. The next day, we climbed aboard his airplane in Barbados and made our way back to Norfolk. A cheering crowd and a Navy band greeted us at the airfield, Metcalf and I shook hands and said a warm good-bye, and then I hopped into the little airplane that was to take me back to my division.

As we landed at the Fort Stewart airstrip, I was astounded to spot another crowd of people waiting. Fifty or sixty people cheered and waved American flags as we taxied up. I could see Brenda, Cindy, Jessica, Christian, and even Rocky, as well as the 24th Mech band. I was moved almost to tears. I'd come home from war twice before, but I'd never received a welcome. I hadn't expected one now, and it made me feel like a million dollars.

My own emotions about the operation were complicated. Above all I was proud that we'd gotten the job done and elated that the American public—at least from my observation—had come out in support of its troops. At the same time, we had lost more lives than we needed to, and the brief war had revealed a lot of shortcomings—an abysmal lack of accurate intelligence, major deficiencies in communications, flareups of interservice rivalry, interference by higher headquarters in battlefield decisions, our alienation of the press, and more. Yet I was heartened that these deficiencies had come to light in our *own* after-action reports. We were through trying to paper over problems as we had in Vietnam; for me, this was the best evidence that the military had changed.

I picked up running the 24th Mech where I'd left off. Our training regimen really started to click. We sent two more battalions to the National Training Center in January, and by coupling the NTC desert war games with the array of training techniques that TRADOC had introduced over the last ten years, we managed to hone the 24th Mech into a superb fighting division. Simply put, we trained smart and with purpose, instead of dumb and by rote.

I knew that the more battalions we sent through the NTC the better we'd be, and I snapped up every rotation we could get. Instead of the standard two per year we did four. The commanders and troops of the

Opposing Force would psych themselves up whenever our battalions were coming because they knew they'd be in for a hell of a fight. My young commanders relished the challenge, but—more to the point—always kept sight of the fact that they were out there to learn. That fall one of my lieutenant colonels had been assigned to defend a sector against an OPFOR advance. I visited his command center and asked him to explain his tactical plan. "May I tell you something, sir?" he said. "This is my second rotation out here, and I know how to defeat the OPFOR. I could kick their butts and really make them look bad. But I've never managed my unit successfully through a defense-in-sector, and this is a chance for me to give it another try." He was referring to a complicated, hard-to-control maneuver that called for a battalion to simultaneously fight and fall back by echelon. I felt terrific—by his willingness to concentrate on learning and not worry about the outcome or my reaction to it, the lieutenant colonel had paid me an enormous compliment.

I'd always known that taking care of soldiers' families would be the trickiest of my big five to implement, because it was the least traditional. I began by making small improvements—such as extending the hours of the commissary so families could shop on Sundays and requiring the finance office to stay open at lunch hour. We set up a bus tour of the post for young wives after we discovered that many didn't realize that the stores on the base were for them. They were buying disposable diapers at the local grocery for more than twice what the PX charged. We also made them aware of the programs the Red Cross and Army Emergency Relief offered to Army families in trouble. For families looking for housing off base, we offered a referral service that steered them away from landlords known for ripping off the troops. When we found that the local phone company had been requiring soldiers living off base to pay a huge deposit—money most soldiers simply didn't have—before they could have a phone, we guaranteed the soldiers' payments. The phone company soon dropped the deposit requirement.

I became more aggressive as time passed. I declared August 3, 1984, Family Day, and we put out word that soldiers could have the day off as long as they brought their families to the base. We held open house in our offices, barracks, mess halls, and motor pools so families could see where their spouses, fathers, and mothers worked. We had games and rides, a pie-eating contest with trophies for winners, a mock jump tower that kids could leap from, a raffle in which we gave away microwaves, bicycles, and other items donated by local merchants, and a giant barbecue on the parade ground. For the few thousand dollars it cost the division, the payoff was enormous.

Some of the unit commanders soon caught on. Battalions ran picnics and Easter egg hunts; some units started putting out newsletters when they were about to leave on maneuvers, telling families how to get help if problems came up while the head of the household was away. But many commanders still saw family programs as extraneous to their Army duties, and no amount of subtle—or even unsubtle—proselytizing was going to change their minds. So that fall I summoned all the brigade and battalion commanders to a meeting of the Family Action Council—the central committee for all the dependents' support organizations on the base. There, with great ceremony, I made each commander responsible for something besides his unit. I handed each one a charter—"You're now in charge of the daycare-center"; "You're now in charge of the Cub Scouts"; "You're now in charge of the kids' soccer league." Some of the commanders liked it and had previously volunteered for their activities; some didn't. But within a few months we had dynamite family programs, because the battalion and brigade commanders were also the division's movers and shakers.

My concern for the troops didn't always endear me to the locals. While the division had very friendly relations with the towns of Glennville and Claxton, the guys who controlled Hinesville seemed to think Fort Stewart existed only to make them rich. One of the most disturbing scams involved the local gin mills, which were all clustered along the highway that led southwest out of Hinesville. In order to drive from those places back to the main gate of Fort Stewart, the troops had to pass through three police jurisdictions; and every payday, the police would lie in wait for them, haul them in, and book them for driving under the influence. The Army dealt very severely with DUI charges, and soldiers were desperate not to have one on their record. So they'd go to the local court, where the standard procedure for getting a DUI reduced to speeding was to pay $200 for the lawyer, $200 for the fine, and another $100 that was never quite accounted for. This made me furious. So we started encouraging troops to stay on base by booking big-name entertainment at the enlisted men's clubs, installing Nautilus equipment at the gym, and sponsoring parties in individual units. Soon the number of DUI fines dropped and some of the locals were incensed: one bar owner even accused us of scheduling maneuvers on payday so the troops couldn't go drinking.

Then there was the time I brought a Burger King to Fort Stewart— one of the first ever on an Army base. I'd been invited to join the board of directors of the Army and Air Force Exchange Service, a huge organization that ran PXs all over the world. AAFES was having a terrible time getting troops to buy the hamburgers at PX snack bars: despite the fact that

AAFES-burgers, as they were called, were made of the finest ground round steak, a survey revealed that the troops wanted McDonald's or Burger King hamburgers instead. When I heard AAFES was negotiating with Burger King, I volunteered the 24th as a pilot test site. The deal was unbeatable: we'd provide a location on the base, Burger King would set up the stand, and Fort Stewart and Burger King would split the profits fifty-fifty. The stand, which opened in April 1985, was mobbed with troops every day. Hinesville was in an uproar, and even though the town's fast-food outlets were still heavily patronized by soldiers and their families, the local merchants decided we were stealing their business.

I was invited to a breakfast at the chamber of commerce, ostensibly to explain the schedule for the next year's training exercises, but the minute I went to the podium the owner of the local Baskin-Robbins stood up and said, "I know you're planning to open a Baskin-Robbins franchise next. You're taking the food out of my children's mouths!" Other businessmen stood and accused the Army of restraint of trade. Soon the story was in all the local papers and the controversy grew so fierce that it ended up on the floor of the United States Senate, which put on hold the construction of Burger Kings on military bases pending a full investigation. Since ours was open already it was excepted, however—and to my great satisfaction, I was able to take our share of the profits and earmark it for construction of a swimming pool in the family housing area.

As summer approached, I recalled a conversation I'd had with Gene Anderson at Forces Command soon after I'd taken over at Fort Stewart. Gene, who had been a division commander himself, had asked whether I liked the experience.

"I *love* it," I'd answered.

He'd said, in a gloomy way, "Well, just remember one thing."

"What's that?"

"The sand is running out of the hourglass even as we speak. Before you know it, you're going to be sitting in a staff job like me, so enjoy it while you can."

Now that my twenty-four months were almost up, I felt a twinge of regret with every passing day. I did not want to leave command.

A lot of generals retired as soon as their division command tours ended, because if you wanted to lead troops, virtually any other job in the Army was an anticlimax. And on top of that, there was very little financial incentive to stay. A major general like me, with twenty-nine years' active service, was already making as much as the law allowed: we worked under the same $68,700-a-year wage cap as did civil servants. So no matter how many stars got added to my collar or how much additional responsibility I was given, I would never earn a nickel more. And *whenever* I retired, I would start collecting an annual pension equal to three fourths of that wage. So my actual compensation for staying on active duty worked out to something like $18,000 a year, plus, of course, free housing.

Though Cavazos's successor, General Bob Sennewald, had rated me the overall best division leader under his command, my expectations for my next assignment were not high. I was not a favorite of General John Wickham, the new chief of staff; in fact, two corps command slots had come up for which Cavazos had pushed me, but I hadn't been picked. Still, I felt indebted to the Army for having given me the opportunity to command a division, and I made up my mind to serve at least one more tour in whatever job I was assigned.

Tradition dictated that division commanders learn their next assignment while attending a two-day commanders' conference in Washington in the spring. At some point the chief of staff would take each man aside and say, "This is what I have in mind for you." I went to the conference that April of 1986; on the first evening, General Wickham invited us all to his quarters for dinner. Sure enough, during the cocktail hour, he asked me to step into the hallway. "Norm," he said, "I just want to tell you what your next assignment's going to be."

"Thank you very much, sir."

"I'm going to make you the assistant deputy chief of staff for personnel." I'm sure my jaw dropped. Wickham had assigned me the very same job I'd had under Max Thurman two years earlier.

"Yes, sir," I managed to say. "You know I had that job before I became a division commander."

"Yes, and I want to explain that to you. My intention is to make you the deputy chief of staff for personnel, but right now *that* job is filled." This was no consolation: the man in that spot had started two years before, and the job wouldn't open up again for at least another year. The same evening I learned that Wickham was promoting three of my colleagues to lieutenant general and giving them three-star jobs.

I went back to Fort Stewart feeling as though I'd been kicked in the stomach. I told Brenda, "It's like being told I have to go back and do third grade all over again." But we dutifully packed up our household, and on a muggy Friday morning in June came the ceremony in which I relinquished command of my beloved 24th Mech.

Three days later we were in Washington, trying to shoehorn our possessions into the tiny house we'd been assigned at Fort Myer, which sits on the Potomac next to Arlington Cemetery. The moving van was at the curb and we had boxes all over the lawn when a military policeman drove up and said, "You have to call GOMO right away."

Brenda turned to one of the movers, who had just emerged from the van carrying an overstuffed chair. "Stop!" she said. "Put that chair here on the sidewalk and *don't move another thing* until we know what this is about." Then she sat in the chair.

Sure enough, my assignment had changed. Carl Vuono, my old friend, had just been appointed the Army's deputy chief of staff for operations and plans, an enormously important and prestigious assignment. He wanted me as his assistant. That was the good news. The bad news was that it was a notoriously time-consuming job, even when the boss wasn't an obsessive worker like Vuono. I told Brenda we'd be lucky to see each other on weekends.

———

Vuono was responsible for a huge staff that oversaw every aspect of Army operations—from monitoring day-to-day activity all over the world to writing regulations, preparing war plans, and looking ahead to the weapons and organizations of the future. But he was also General Wickham's chief deputy on the Joint Chiefs of Staff—a job that kept him so busy that he delegated many of the Army duties to me. So on top of my own responsibility, which was to supervise the daily activity of the huge operations staff, I filled in for him in meetings with Defense Department officials, testimony before Congress, routine staff conferences, parades to greet foreign dignitaries, meetings of the Army Reserve Forces Policy Council, presentations for and roundtable discussions with visiting foreign generals, and even speaking engagements at Fort Leavenworth, the War College, and other service schools.

But the most important duty he turned over to me was figuring out how to divvy up the Army's $73-billion annual budget. Vuono knew of my experience at this crucial but tedious work, so to him the arrangement made sense. The budgeting process began each fall when the directors of the Army's programs—research and development, logistics, training, the National Guard, and so on—met to revise the five-year spending program. As a young lieutenant colonel, I'd sat along the back wall at such meetings during my first Pentagon tour; now I not only held a place at the big table, but I played a key role with the director of the Army budget and the director of program analysis and evaluation.

I also participated in the meetings where we made major decisions on

weapon procurements. By this time the Army's post-Vietnam modernization program was well under way—all of our units in Europe and many in
the States had their new M-1s, Bradleys, Apaches, and Black Hawks. We
had turned our attention to applying advanced electronics to the battlefield.
The latest field radios, for example, were equipped with scramblers so
sophisticated that commanders no longer had to bother putting secret
orders into code. Meanwhile, a newly developed rocket system called
MLRS had revolutionized our field artillery, and more sophisticated ver-
sions were in the final stages of development. And we were looking into
exciting possibilities such as stealth technology and battlefield robots.

Vuono and I were as different in style as two generals could be. I liked
to speak my mind and sometimes antagonized people by being too blunt; he
had a reputation as an accommodator who won bureaucratic battles by
wearing down his opponents with friendliness. Our approaches were com-
plementary, and Vuono had sought me out because I was a loyal, effective
assistant; but over time I suspect I got on his nerves by telling him—
privately—when I thought he was wrong. The year was pretty much as
grueling as I'd predicted to Brenda. There was no going on leave, no getting
away for three-day weekends to take Christian camping or Cindy and Jessica
to visit their grandmother's farm in the Shenandoah Valley, and barely time
to make it to the kids' school plays.

By spring, when people on the Army staff started speculating about
imminent reassignments, we were all ready for a change. One of the most
prevalent rumors was that Vuono would be promoted to commander in
chief of TRADOC and that I would succeed him. But I felt I'd had enough
of the Pentagon, and after several years in which my relationship with
General Wickham had been formal and cool, I couldn't imagine working
with him as his chief deputy. After some late nights and long talks with
Brenda, I concluded that I'd had a full career and that I'd accomplished
everything that I'd stayed in the Army to do. So I decided to look for a
civilian job.

But before anything could happen, Wickham offered me an assignment
I didn't even know I was in the running for: command of I Corps at Fort
Lewis, Washington. As expected, Vuono was promoted to four-star general
and became the TRADOC commander. The job of deputy chief of staff for
operations and plans went to my friend Bob Riscassi, who'd been commanding the Combined Arms Center at Fort Leavenworth for only a year. I
was happy for both of them and ecstatic for myself. I was going back to
commanding troops in a part of the country that I loved. I Corps was
responsible for three divisions: the 7th Infantry Division at Fort Ord on

California's Monterey Bay, the 9th Infantry Division there at Fort Lewis, and the 6th Infantry Division, the successor to my old brigade in my favorite place of all, Alaska.

Assuming a corps command meant that I would become a three-star general, and all three-star and four-star generals were presidential appointees. Before my promotion could be forwarded to the Senate for confirmation, I had to be interviewed by Caspar Weinberger, the secretary of defense, who was acting on President Reagan's behalf. After ten minutes or so he smiled and said, "Well, I find you completely qualified." So in early June, Brenda and I loaded up our cars and set out with Christian for the Pacific Northwest—leaving Cindy and Jessica behind with friends to finish the school year. We drove the northern route and went sightseeing at Mount Rushmore and Yellowstone. Finally, late in the afternoon of June 8, 1986, we set our eyes again on Mount Rainier.

I found corps command to be just like division command, only on a grander scale. I was in charge of seventy thousand active-duty troops and almost eighty thousand reservists, the largest reserve contingent of any Army corps. In addition I had responsibility for the entire Fort Lewis installation, which included Madigan Army Medical Center, the 1st Special Forces Group, the 2nd Ranger Battalion, and a separate support brigade, as well as the 9th Division and my own headquarters. All told, it was a community of seventy-five thousand soldiers and dependents with an annual operating budget of well over one hundred forty million dollars.

Within six months after I arrived, I'd launched my family programs, established a welcome center on the base, and replicated many other programs I'd run successfully at Fort Stewart and in Mainz. Militarily, our primary wartime mission was to fight in Korea, and in the spring of 1987 I brought my headquarters staff and several active and reserve units to Seoul for the annual Team Spirit military exercise with Combined Forces Command Korea. The four-star general in charge there was my old friend and mentor Bill Livsey.

I'd been at Fort Lewis less than a year when I was unexpectedly ordered back to Washington, where there had been another personnel shuffle at the Pentagon. Admiral William Crowe, the chairman of the Joint Chiefs of Staff, had grabbed my friend Bob Riscassi to serve as director of the Joint Staff. That left vacant once again the job of deputy chief of staff for operations and plans, for which General Wickham now picked me. Wickham was due to retire and Carl Vuono had just been named to succeed him as Army chief of staff.

Although the prospect of returning to the Pentagon depressed me, I reminded myself that being chosen the Army's chief operations officer carried enormous prestige and virtually guaranteed that I'd move on to a four-star assignment. Still, I'd already endured four stints in Washington— more than was healthy for anybody but a politician. Moreover, at fifty-two, I'd now been in the military thirty years and had reached the age when most generals retire. Having made it back to the Pacific Northwest, I felt ready to put down roots. If the Army had let me serve out my three years at I Corps and then said it had nothing more for me to do, I'm sure I'd have retired happily. I'd probably be living in Oregon or Washington state to this day, catching a hell of a lot of salmon.

15

I reported dutifully to the Pentagon in mid-August, 1987, shortly after Vuono was installed as Army chief of staff. As I knew from having served with him during *his* tenure as deputy chief of staff for operations and plans, I now held the Army's toughest job. On a typical day, I'd hit the office at 6:30 A.M. and, if I was lucky, manage to get home fourteen hours later. I was responsible for the policies and regulations that governed the day-to-day operations of the entire Army—an organization roughly the size of General Motors. My most important duty was to serve as the Army's prioritizer, advising Vuono on how the annual budget—$75.3 billion for 1987—should be spent and which operations and procurements should have precedence. This explained why the deputy chief of staff for operations was first among equals on the Army staff. Unlike the other three-star deputies, who reported to the vice chief of staff, I usually worked directly with Vuono and could walk into his office any time.

Reporting to me were the heads of five huge "directorates," staffs that oversaw essential Army functions. The director of plans and strategy presided over not only long-range planning but every action the Army undertook in conjunction with the other services as well as hundreds of plans to cover wars and other contingencies anywhere in the world. The director of operations ran the Army Operations Center, the war room and communications complex that monitored Army activities worldwide; when the Army had to mobilize for war or help cope with a natural disaster or urban riot, he was the man who cut the orders. The director of requirements shaped the Army of the future, defining the weapons and organizations we would need to win on twenty-first-century battlefields, and at the same time constantly reshaped the Army of the present in response both to changes in enemy threats and to personnel and budget limitations imposed by Congress. The fourth directorate governed training policies and regulations Army-wide, and the fifth set Army policy for nuclear and chemical weapons, as well as weapons in space.

That was half the job. I also served as Vuono's so-called operations deputy in the Joint Chiefs of Staff—a position whose responsibilities included accompanying Vuono to every Joint Chiefs meeting, as well as representing the Army in meetings of my peers, the operations deputies from the Navy, Air Force, and Marines. Vuono and the other Joint Chiefs convened twice a week in a soundproofed conference room known as the Tank. Located on the Pentagon's first floor just inside the River Entrance, the Tank was sacrosanct. I'd never set foot there in ten years as a general. The first time I walked in with Vuono, I was somewhat disappointed. I'd imagined something out of *Dr. Strangelove*—a sinister, dimly lit briefing room crammed with flashing electronic maps and displays (such setups did exist elsewhere in the building). But the Tank was simply a large, elegant conference room dominated by a big mahogany table. Oil paintings decorated the walls—images of the armed forces in action and a magnificent rendering of Westminster Abbey on the occasion of Eisenhower's being knighted. Each chief sat in a designated place with his deputy by his side; the chairman, vice chairman, and director of the Joint Staff sat next to each other. Additional chairs were set along two walls for visiting briefers, executive officers, stenographers, and other horse-holders. The meetings were informal but followed a strict protocol: when the Joint Chiefs were in session, only they could speak. I'd sit silently next to Vuono, keeping a detailed record of the discussion and slipping him notes whenever I thought there was something he should know or say.

The Middle East was at the top of the agenda that summer. The previous fall, Iran, in the eighth year of its bloody border war against Iraq, was launching cruise missiles at ships in the Arabian Gulf.* In response, the Reagan administration offered to escort Kuwaiti supertankers under the American flag in order to safeguard the flow of oil. Eventually this escort operation,

* The body of water also referred to as the Persian Gulf.

code-named Earnest Will, involved twenty-four major warships and sixteen thousand personnel. The week I arrived in Washington, one of the super-tankers, the *Bridgeton*, struck a mine that we suspected the Iranians had put in its path. By international convention, this was an act of war, but there was no proof Iran had done it. The United States limited itself to dispatching special night-vision-equipped Army helicopters, which ultimately detected and helped capture the *Iran Ajr*, an Iranian ship sowing mines.

Our responses to Iranian attacks subsequently became more violent. We launched retaliatory strikes twice during my almost eighteen months in the Tank. In October, after an Iranian cruise missile struck a tanker flying the American flag in Kuwait City harbor, we attacked two Iranian oil platforms in the gulf; to avoid civilian casualties, we gave workers a chance to evacuate beforehand. Operation Praying Mantis, our second and larger retaliation, came in April, after an Iranian mine nearly sank the U.S. Navy frigate *Samuel B. Roberts*. We destroyed three of their warships, and when the Iranians tried to strike back, an intense naval battle cost them several more ships and airplanes.

The role of the Joint Chiefs in such crises was to recommend military options from which the President, the National Security Council, and the secretary of defense could choose; as the Joint Chiefs reviewed the possibilities, I was startled to learn how limited our capabilities were in the gulf. Little had changed since my days at Pacific Command. Because of America's standoffish relations with Arab nations, the Air Force still had no access to the region's airfields; the Navy was still insisting that it couldn't put its carriers in the constricted waters of the gulf.

The Soviet Union also consumed endless hours of the Joint Chiefs's time. The newspapers were full of *glasnost* and *perestroika*, and we were constantly being briefed on the dramatic changes taking place. At one point in 1988, no fewer than four sets of arms-reduction talks were under way: talks on the Strategic Arms Reduction Treaty and the Intermediate-Range Ballistic Missile Treaty; the weapons-in-space negotiations; and the mutual balanced force reduction talks, aimed at shrinking the armies facing one another in Europe. Even a short time ago, none of us would have believed that a Soviet general would someday be welcome in the Tank, but Marshal Sergei Akhromeyev, the highest-ranking officer in the Soviet military, entered the room for the second time, on July 6, 1988, as part of an exchange of visits with Admiral Crowe.

I watched as the cold warriors around the table gradually became convinced that the struggle with the Soviets was ending, and I found myself wondering how the armed forces would adapt to the new reality. From the time I'd joined the Army more than thirty years before, our entire raison d'être had been to fend off communism. With the diminution of that threat, money for defense was going to be short, and the Pentagon would have to face the challenge of radically rethinking its mission.

Not all meetings in the Tank were so compelling. It was the responsibility of the Joint Chiefs to guarantee the "military sufficiency" of any arms agreement—to be able to tell Congress, "This treaty has the necessary safeguards. We're not leaving the country defenseless." We monitored U.S. negotiating positions in minute detail. When the briefings got really dull, my eyes would stray to the wall behind Admiral Crowe and fasten on two paintings of Vietnam: the Marine artillery at Khe Sanh and an Army patrol making its way through a jungle swamp. Whenever I worked in the Pentagon, I began itching for a new command.

Vuono's office was on the third floor of the Pentagon's outer ring, the "E" ring, where the highest-ranking Defense Department civilians as well as the military's top brass reside. From his window he could look out over the Potomac toward the Capitol. He often held his most important meetings late in the afternoon—after he'd finished the day's ceremonies and routines—and he'd usually keep me behind after the other attendees had gone and ask my opinion about what had transpired. We both liked to talk, and the conversation would sometimes stretch into the night.

It was on one of those evenings in late June 1988, after I'd been back at the Pentagon almost a year, that Vuono observed that the four-star job was coming open at Central Command, which bore responsibility for all U.S. military operations in Southwest Asia, parts of the Middle East, and the Horn of Africa. "I have to send up a nomination," he said. "Are you interested?" Technically any of the armed services could put up candidates for commander-in-chief jobs; the choice ultimately belonged to the secretary of defense and the President. But Central Command had traditionally alternated between the Army and the Marines, and since the current commander, General George Crist, was a Marine, his successor would almost certainly be the man Vuono chose.

He continued, "Of course, there are two *other* jobs coming open next summer. Which would you prefer?" I knew the positions he meant: Forces Command, which was in charge of all Army combat units in the United States; and Combined Forces Command Korea, in charge of all U.S. units and the United Nations peacekeeping force in Korea, as well as South Korea's own military in the event of war. I asked for twenty-four hours to think it over.

I actually knew what my choice would be. I'd thought about Central

Command, in one form or another, all my life. The Middle East had always fascinated and compelled me: a great deal of Schwarzkopf family life had been invested in that part of the world. I could also foresee the region's increasing strategic importance—after all, we had just engaged in a shooting war to protect the flow of Middle Eastern oil.

I also knew Vuono would not line up the options the way I did. Though almost any general would leap at the chance for a four-star assignment, Central Command was not one of the most desirable—it included too many so-called political-military responsibilities. In the event of war, of course, an impressive array of forces was earmarked for Central Command that now included the Ninth Air Force, the First Marine Expeditionary Force, and the Third Army at Fort McPherson, Georgia. (This was the newly activated planning headquarters for the XVIII Airborne Corps and Central Command's other Army elements.) But in peacetime, while Central Command directed planning for all those forces, the only combat force under its day-to-day operational control was the Navy task force in the gulf—about to shrink because the Iran-Iraq war was ending. The commander in chief was also in charge of a headquarters staff of nearly a thousand, many of whom shuttled between the command's new three-story building at MacDill Air Force Base in Tampa, Florida, and the command's area of responsibility, seven thousand miles away. In that area, an additional three hundred personnel in ten countries served as "security assistance" officers and liaison officers. (Security assistance encompasses military aid, military exchange and training programs, and the supervision and technical support of arms sales.) One of my principal peacetime duties could be to act as a kind of military ombudsman in that part of the world—overseeing the advisors' work, administering $1.6 billion a year in military programs, and solidifying relations with rulers and generals. Most Army officers perceived the diplomatic aspect of the job as distasteful, but I'd always relished the opportunity to be among people of other countries, whether in Iran, Germany, or Vietnam.

To be sure, the other two assignments that Vuono had mentioned involved commanding many more troops. Forces Command would have been a lot of fun: traveling all over the United States, visiting soldiers, inspecting Reserve and National Guard units on the weekends, having people fawn all over me. But the command's direction had been pretty much set, so I didn't see a lot of challenge in the job. I also wondered if it would really be open when the present chief retired in 1989; by then the Reagan administration would be gone, and General Colin Powell, the national security advisor, would be back in the Army looking for a position. Forces

Command seemed the natural choice for him—if only as a way to mark time until Admiral Crowe retired and the new administration picked the next chairman of the Joint Chiefs, a job most people thought would go to Powell because of his political connections.

That left Combined Forces Command Korea, an assignment I found problematic. Theoretically the entire South Korean military was supposed to obey the U.S. commander in chief in the event of another invasion of their country, yet America had less than one division there. I'd participated in military exercises in Korea a number of times, and while their generals always treated me marvelously, I had strongly suspected that their deference to the commander in chief was mainly show. I didn't think I'd be happy in such a situation.

The next day I told Vuono, "I'd like to go to Central Command."

He gave me a startled look. "Would you mind telling me why?"

I explained that while I loved commanding troops, the real challenge seemed to be in the Middle East. Here was a complex region, important enough to us that we were already at war there, tumultuous enough that no one knew what would happen next—a region where much could be and needed to be done to strengthen American ties. After giving him my analysis of the other two jobs, I came back to the point that Central Command was the most exciting and unpredictable, and concluded emphatically, "Of the three assignments, Central Command is where you can make history."

Vuono was skeptical—I could almost hear him thinking, "There goes Schwarzkopf again"—but he promised to send my name up to the chairman of the Joint Chiefs.

As it turned out, I got the job only after an ugly fight. The Navy unexpectedly put up its own candidate, an admiral and fellow operations deputy named Hank Mustin. When the Joint Chiefs voted on the nominations, they deadlocked along traditional lines—Army and Air Force for me, Navy and Marines for Mustin. Admiral Crowe sent *both* names to the secretary of defense, with a note of personal support for the admiral.

The turf battle reminded me once more why I hated Washington. The Navy had *never* been interested in the Middle East (it had always maintained that its Pacific fleet, headquartered in Hawaii, could adequately protect America's interests there) and I was convinced it would dismantle Central Command if it could. Almost as aggravating, somebody leaked word of Crowe's recommendation to *The Washington Post*, which ran a story saying Admiral Mustin had gotten the job. People were coming up to me in the halls of the Pentagon, laughingly making remarks like, "Too bad the Navy screwed you. But don't worry, sooner or later you'll get your fourth star."

The commotion went on for a full two weeks, until Frank Carlucci, the secretary of defense, had interviewed us both and made his choice, which the President promptly approved. I never knew what went into his picking me, but I doubted that the premature announcement in the *Post* had helped the Navy's case.

My appointment was announced in late July 1988, so that fall I signed up for an intensive course on the Middle East at the Foreign Service Institute in Arlington, Virginia, which is where the State Department sends its diplomats before dispatching them abroad. When I'd tell people in the Pentagon how I was preparing for Central Command, they'd look at me and ask, "Why?" To them, the Middle East consisted only of sea-lanes, strategic assets, and colored blobs on the map. The Foreign Service Institute program was taught by Peter Bechtold, a German-born expert on the Sudan; eight hours a day for two weeks in October, I sat in the front row, taking copious notes on cultures, customs, oil issues, water issues, and religious conflicts. I came home to Fort Myer every night exhilarated.

On November 18, Brenda helped Carl Vuono pin on my shoulders the four stars of a general, the highest rank in the U.S. Army. Jessica, by now a blossoming sixteen-year-old, and Christian, a rough-and-tumble eleven-year-old, witnessed the ceremony in the Pentagon's Hall of Heroes, where the walls are hung with pictures of men who have earned the Congressional Medal of Honor. Cindy couldn't be there—she'd just started her freshman year at Auburn—but my sister Sally was, as were many of my classmates and close friends such as General Tom Weinstein and General Bob Riscassi. I wished Mom and Pop could have been present; I wished Ruth were there, too.

I took over Central Command on November 23, at my new headquarters in Tampa. *That* ceremony almost didn't happen. The night before, MacDill Air Force Base had taken the full brunt of a tropical storm. Uprooted palm trees littered the landscape, and Cindy, who had driven from Auburn through torrential rain, wisecracked, "I hope this isn't a sign of things to come."

———

Less than two weeks later, I found myself standing on the balcony of a Cairo hotel room, looking out across the Nile and listening to the nighttime call to prayer. This was my first trip to the Middle East since 1947, and my mind was flooded by memories. In the moonlight, I could make out the domes and minarets, familiar shapes from my boyhood. Back then the muezzins had climbed the minarets five times each day to sing out their haunting call; now the towers were equipped with loudspeakers that saved them the steps. I could smell the fetid stench of the Nile and the odors of the donkeys and oxen that pulled carts through the city's streets. I could smell the aroma of Turkish tobacco and the lingering scents of brewed coffee and tea—all day men walked the streets of Cairo with huge urns on their shoulders, selling cupfuls to passersby. And underneath all the other scents was a peculiar mustiness—the smell of great age. I was back. As a fourteen-year-old schoolboy in Switzerland I'd promised myself that I'd return, and now, after forty years, I had.

I hadn't yet gotten used to the trappings of being a commander in chief. A six-man detail of crack U.S. bodyguards and a twenty-man detail of Egyptian security men were posted in the hotel, assigned to me full-time; next door was a radio operator responsible for maintaining round-the-clock satellite contact with my headquarters in Tampa; and parked at the Cairo airport was my Air Force jet, a windowless, military version of a Boeing 707 outfitted as a flying command post. It had delivered my staff and me from Florida that afternoon after a seventeen-hour nonstop flight with aerial refueling. I was obliged to ride from the airport in an armored limousine with a noisy police and military escort. I'd forgotten that careening was the custom on the roads of the Middle East—we constantly seemed within a hairsbreadth of a fatal crash. Downtown, we immediately found ourselves in a traffic jam. With our sirens wailing and the Egyptian security men leaning out hollering and pounding on the sides of their cars, the other drivers just turned in their seats and looked at us; none of them moved. The cause of the tie-up was a donkey cart.

I thought about how the Defense Department had defined the boundaries of my new area of responsibility. In 1982, when Congress and the Reagan administration ordered the Joint Chiefs to establish Central Command, responsibility for the region was divided between European Command in Stuttgart, Germany, and Pacific Command in Hawaii. Even though neither had paid the Middle East much attention—a neglect I'd witnessed when I'd served in Hawaii—their commanders protested vehemently when their worst fears came to pass and nations for which they had had responsibility were now assigned to Central Command.

This explained why Syria, Lebanon, Libya, Tunisia, Algeria, and Morocco were not included in Central Command, even though the Arabs saw those countries as part of the Arab world. European Command had argued that since its Sixth Fleet patrolled the Mediterranean, it should retain responsibility for countries with Mediterranean ports. European Command also kept Israel, which from my viewpoint was a help: I'd have had difficulty impressing the Arabs with Central Command's grasp of geopolitical nuance if one of the stops on my itinerary had been Tel Aviv. Geographically my new command centered on the Arabian Peninsula and the crucial fingers of water along its sides: the Arabian Gulf, the Gulf of Aden, and the Red Sea. But it spanned an oval much larger than that: from Egypt, the Sudan, and the Horn of Africa all the way northeast to Afghanistan and Pakistan, some four thousand miles.

I intended as soon as possible to visit as many of my countries as I could; at the time, we didn't have military-to-military relations with Iran, Iraq, Afghanistan, Ethiopia, or the People's Democratic Republic of Yemen. For my first trip I'd scheduled Saudi Arabia, Egypt, and Pakistan, the Saudis being the gulf region's most important stabilizing force, and the Egyptians and Pakistanis the second- and third-largest recipients (after Israel) of U.S. military aid. In Cairo and Islamabad, Pakistan's capital, the meetings were genial and direct. I spent hours talking and dining with Lieutenant General Safy Abu Shanaf, the Egyptian chief of staff, and Major General Ahmad Abdul Rahman, his chief of military intelligence. In Pakistan I was hosted by Admiral Iftikhar Ahmed Sirohey, the chairman of the Pakistani joint chiefs of staff, and briefed by General Mirza Aslam Beg, the strongman who'd taken command of the army after the assassination of General Mohammad Zia Ul-Haq in August. I then had long meetings with President Ghulam Ishaq Khan and Prime Minister Benazir Bhutto.

In Riyadh my reception was cooler. For years Congress had strictly limited the Saudis' freedom to buy American arms, on the theory that any weapon sold to Arabs, even moderate Arabs, would end up being used against Israel. Not surprisingly the Saudis, though they preferred American equipment, had taken their business elsewhere, outfitting their force with British fighter planes, French air-defense radars, Brazilian artillery, and Chinese missiles. Whatever U.S. security assistance they needed was negotiated for directly in Washington by their skillful ambassador, Prince Bandar Bin Sultan al-Saud. Adding insult to injury, in October 1987, early in the "tanker war," Central Command had sent a two-star general to Riyadh *uninvited* to direct a joint force of Saudi and U.S. planes. When General Mohammed al-Hamad, the Saudi chief of staff, learned of the American's presence, he'd quite rightly kicked him out of the kingdom.

So when I arrived I found Prince Sultan Bin Abdulaziz al-Saud, the minister of defense and aviation, "unavailable." I did have brief, formal sessions with General Hamad and the heads of the armed forces. Hamad, standoffish at first, warmed up when I said I hoped the relationship between

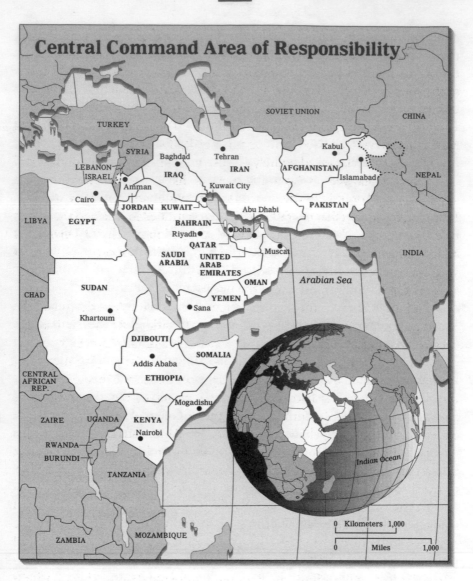

Central Command Area of Responsibility

our countries would improve and be of *equal* benefit to both. Finally I had a twenty-minute audience with Prince Abdul Rahman Bin Abdulaziz al-Saud, the deputy minister of defense and aviation. The prince was one of the forty-seven sons of King Abdulaziz al-Saud, the great Bedouin chieftain who unified Saudi Arabia in the 1930s, and one of the six full brothers of King Fahd (the remaining forty were half brothers). The prince was an engaging man, tall, heavyset, and about my age, and spoke fluent English. He gave me my opening when he asked politely, "Is this your first visit to Saudi Arabia?"

When I allowed as how I'd been in his country before, he was surprised—and doubly so when I told him my visit had taken place in 1947. I went on to explain that my father had been stationed in Iran and that when he'd taken me to school in Europe, we'd stopped in the city of Dhahran. I added rather formally: "It is wonderful to have this opportunity to meet you, because history is repeating itself."

"What do you mean?" asked the prince.

I reminded him of the warm relations between the Americans and the Saudis after World War II, during which President Roosevelt had befriended King Abdulaziz. "As a result," I continued, "my father came here to Riyadh in 1946 and had an audience with your father. He met King Abdulaziz al-Saud, and now I am meeting you. I consider this a renewal of the ties my family has had with yours." I meant it, but the prince was amused to hear an Arab sentiment from the lips of an American general. He ended our meeting by chiding me gently for Americans' ignorance of his country: "When you Americans come to Saudi Arabia, you never take the time to get to know it. The next time you visit, I will put a helicopter at your disposal so you can see the kingdom." I said I'd be delighted.

I took naturally to the courtly style of Arab conversation. When I'd studied at the Foreign Service Institute, Peter Bechtold had said, "In the Arab world, your position gets you through the door, but your personal relationships get you commitments from the Arabs." That way of conducting affairs had evolved from the Bedouin tent in the desert, where business discussions were followed by long hours of storytelling at night. When an Arab host asks, "How was your flight?" it is uncouth to reply, "Fine, thanks." A polite guest would say something like, "The trip took seventeen hours, and during that time it became difficult to tell night from day and my body was in turmoil. But now I am better, because I landed in your beautiful capital, and driving here from the airport I was able to see the sights and hear the sounds of your city, and I feel as though I'm home again." It was a form of diplomacy I genuinely enjoyed.

By the spring of 1989, I'd made three trips to the Middle East and was surprised by some of the things I'd learned. The previous July, when Defense Secretary Carlucci had interviewed me for the Central Command job, I'd told him I thought we should be concerned about Iraq's military might. I wanted to gauge how Iraq's victory in its war against Iran had changed the balance of power in the Arabian Gulf. The United Nations-sponsored cease-fire in August had left Iraq with a million-man army and an economy too weak to absorb the soldiers back into civilian life. "I've been thinking the same thing," Carlucci had replied.

As I traveled around the gulf, however, I was amazed to find that most countries—Saudi Arabia, Jordan, the United Arab Emirates, Bahrain, Qatar—were leery of Iran, not Iraq. The prevailing wisdom was that the cease-fire was merely a lull and that as soon as Iran had rearmed, it would go back to fighting Iraq and menacing its other Arab neighbors. As for Iraq, Jordan's King Hussein articulated the majority view when he had me to lunch in January 1989. "Don't worry about the Iraqis," he said. "They are war weary and have no aggressive intentions toward their Arab brothers." He reminded me that Jordan, Egypt, Yemen, and Iraq had just formed the Arab Cooperation Council, and he assured me that Jordan and Egypt would persuade Iraq to moderate its militaristic behavior.

My second surprise was to discover that many Arab leaders both anticipated and welcomed greater U.S. military involvement in the gulf region. America's intervention in the tanker war had made a dramatic impression. As Major General Mizyad al-Sanii, the Kuwaiti chief of staff, put it, "We never thought you Americans would come, but you did. When you came, we thought you'd leave as soon as you took casualties, but you didn't. You stayed and defended us. We now believe the United States is a friend of the Arab world."

Until then, only the tiny island emirate of Bahrain had favored a U.S. presence in the gulf. It had hosted the headquarters of the Navy's Middle East Force since the Truman era. Despite criticism from other gulf nations, the emir of Bahrain had remained steadfast in his commitment, and his kingdom was without doubt America's best friend in the Middle East. Some of its neighbors now realized that, had Bahrain barred the U.S. Navy from its port, the outcome of the tanker war would have been quite different.

I had taken over Central Command with orders from Admiral Crowe to scale back America's forces in the gulf to their pre–tanker war level. ("Get 'em back down to normal," he'd said.) But "normal" meant a token force of only four warships whose real job was to show the flag. I came to believe that was the wrong approach. If anything, we needed to *increase* our commitment to the gulf. In April 1989, I flew to Washington, where I urged the members of the Senate Armed Services Committee to ease strictures against arms sales to Arab moderates such as the Bahrainis, Saudis, and Kuwaitis. I emphasized that American technicians and advisors would go with the weapons and exert a powerful influence on how the arms were ultimately used. I didn't get very far, but the minor concessions I won helped boost Central Command's credibility in the region.

The Arabs always wanted to discuss our positions on Israel and the Palestinians. Here I had to walk a tightrope: the United States wasn't about to reduce its support for Israel, yet I wanted them to know that Americans could appreciate the Arab point of view also. The question came up, for example, in the fall of 1989 when I met the alternate deputy commander of the Saudi Arabian national guard, Sheikh Abdulaziz Bin Abdul Mohsen al-Tuwaijri, a Bedouin sage. I'd sought him out in part because he was a confidant of Abdullah Bin Abdulaziz al-Saud, the crown prince, whose consent was important to cooperation between our countries. We met at his home in Riyadh. A small, wispy man who loved to banter, al-Tuwaijri began the conversation by looking me up and down and exclaiming, "It is a great honor to be in the presence of such a magnificent American general!"

"It is an even greater honor for this general to be in the presence of a man of your wisdom," I replied.

He pressed me almost immediately about Israel, listening closely as I explained America's moral and emotional commitment. "Isn't it true that if the United States had to choose between Saudi Arabia and Israel, you would always choose Israel?" he finally asked.

"Why must it ever come to a choice?" I replied. "I can't imagine it. The United States is friends with *both* Saudi Arabia and Israel. Isn't a man entitled to have more than one friend, or must he have only one?"

The sheikh laughed and said, "That's very good! I like that!" As we walked out of the palace he was holding my hand—an Arab expression of friendship I was still trying to get used to.

———

I'd stumbled upon a neglected frontier. The American ambassadors in the region—shrewd diplomats like Chas Freeman in Saudi Arabia, Frank Wisner in Egypt, and Bob Oakley in Pakistan—understood and supported my need to cement military friendships. But what I encountered in Washington scared me. Arabists did not rise to the highest places in the State Department and the CIA, and at the Pentagon they were downright scarce. When I talked about the Arabs with my fellow generals and admirals, their only question was, "What treaty obligations do we have with them?"—

meaning that since there were no treaties, the United States had no responsibilities. They were totally focused on fulfilling America's commitments to NATO, Japan, and Korea, but they weren't looking toward what I saw as the future.

I couldn't imagine a more important region. Oil imported from the Arabian Gulf already accounted for two thirds of Japan's annual consumption, thirty percent of Western Europe's, and a tenth of the USA's. The region held sixty-five percent of the world's proven oil reserves, so it stood to reason that its importance to industrialized countries would only increase. One estimate I ran across at the Foreign Service Institute showed that the gulf region would be pumping oil for at least two centuries, while America's economically exploitable reserves might be used up in as little as two decades. Assuming no other practical energy sources came into existence—and our record in developing them had been poor—we would find ourselves competing for oil in the Middle East, not right away, but perhaps in twenty-five years. And some of our current best friends—Japan, England, France, and Germany—were the nations we would have to compete against.

Between trips to the Middle East, my staff and I rebuilt Central Command from the bottom up. For close to two years, it had been focused almost entirely on war: not only on the tanker war, but also on America's clandestine support for the war in Afghanistan. Meanwhile, the peacetime elements of Central Command's work—cultivating military relationships with Middle Eastern governments—had been allowed to atrophy. Pressed by events, my predecessor, General Crist, had simply stopped visiting several countries, such as Jordan, crossing them off as unimportant. Central Command's staff section for plans and policy had become purely a war-planning shop: when I asked what our peacetime objectives were, country by country, I discovered we had none.

Reestablishing a political-military branch within the plans and policy section was the first step; within six months we had defined objectives and a program for each country. We also started conducting seminars for Central Command staff, where visiting professors and government officials discussed the region. Though several of my senior staff had joined Central Command at the same time I had, and with no prior experience in the Middle East, they quickly became enthralled.

My deputy commander in chief was Lieutenant General Craven C. "Buck" Rogers, a veteran fighter pilot who was at home in the international arena, having served most recently as U.S. Air Force commander in Korea. My chief of staff, Major General Joe Hoar, was a wiry Marine combat veteran from New England. I knew from the start that I could count on him for his expertise in marine and amphibious operations, but as we reorganized the command, I learned to count on Joe for *everything*. Brilliant, aggressive, charismatic, and cool under pressure, Joe was the man I held responsible for every piece of work that came out of the headquarters. He always delivered results that exceeded my expectations.

The rest of the staff was also strong. My director of intelligence, Major General Hank Drewfs, had just arrived from the Defense Intelligence Agency bringing an insider's knowledge of the Washington intelligence community. Major General Jim Record was a Central Command veteran— he'd served as director of operations throughout the tanker war. Like many fighter pilots Jim was a hard charger. I found I sometimes had to hold him back but never had to prod him forward. I liked that. Brigadier General Dan Cougill, my director of communications, was reputed to be the best man in the Air Force in that technical specialty. Major General Chris Patte, my director of logistics, was a friend from my lieutenant days at Fort Campbell; he'd been at Central Command two years and was a recognized expert in the security-assistance field. Another of the old guard was Rear Admiral Bill Fogarty, chief of plans and policy. He had earned high marks in Washington for his investigation of the tragic incident in which the cruiser U.S.S. *Vincennes* shot down an Iranian airliner, and was about to assume command of the Middle East Force and the Joint Task Force, Middle East. His replacement, Rear Admiral Grant Sharp, was a tough leader with a keen intellect who would soon face the mammoth task of remaking Central Command's war plan. Finally, Brigadier General Norm Ehlert, my inspector general, played a far more important role than his title implied. As Central Command began very quietly conducting bilateral military planning with several nations in our region, he was the general I sent to work out the details. He soon developed a better understanding of the military in the Middle East than anyone else in Central Command.

I had a host of advisors from Washington agencies—the CIA, the Defense Intelligence Agency, the National Security Agency, the Defense Communications Agency—among whom the most important was our man from the State Department, political advisor Stanley Escudero. It wasn't hard to pick him out at Central Command headquarters: not only did he dress in three-piece pin-striped suits, but he wore a beard. We called him our State Department spy. But Stan was a first-class diplomat with great insights into the politics of the gulf region; I came to rely on his advice completely.

Within about six months, word got around Washington that Central Command had focused on its region in a new and interesting way. When we testified on Capitol Hill, Central Command's strongest longtime supporters—senators Sam Nunn, John W. Warner, Ted Stevens, and Daniel K. Inouye—seemed proud, as though the command had finally come into its own. Our colleagues at the State Department began complimenting us on our growing understanding of the Arab world. The only ones not pleased by our progress were Pentagon insiders who had a vested interest in reducing America's forces in the Middle East.

We did not expect to establish military bases in the region—Arab governments, in particular, were too protective of their sovereignty to let American forces stay on their soil. Rather, we defined Central Command's goal as arranging access to crucial airfields, harbors, and military bases in the event of war. I didn't expect to achieve even that during my tenure. We were committed to gradual progress, such as sending teams to Pakistan to teach Afghan refugees how to protect themselves against Soviet mines, digging wells for villages in Somalia, and persuading Congress to grant a $500,000 increase in military aid to Jordan to pay for runway repairs and other expenses associated with joint military operations. Our greatest successes took the form of military exercises—from a small joint training exercise of U.S. and Saudi special forces on a postage-stamp-sized island in the gulf, to a major desert maneuver in Egypt involving paratroopers from the 82nd Airborne Division and tank units from the 24th Mechanized Infantry Division. Such exercises demonstrated that other nations had become willing to accept Central Command's presence, even if temporarily and on a small scale.

———

By the fall of 1989, during my second round of visits to the Middle East, I found doors starting to open. Now that they knew of my fascination with their culture, my Arab counterparts welcomed me into some of their palaces, museums, and mosques. They were also willing to share military secrets. During my first visit to Kuwait, for example, General al-Sanii had refrained from going into specifics about his defense plans and, like other gulf Arabs, had downplayed the idea of a possible threat from Saddam Hussein. But when I returned that October, he took me on a tour of his military installations. I couldn't help noticing that all of Kuwait's guns were pointed north, toward *Iraq*. Al-Sanii now told me point-blank that Iraq was the number-one threat to Kuwait. He explained that Saddam had failed to achieve one of the major objectives of his war with Iran: regaining Iraq's access to the Arabian Gulf. In its recapture of the Al Faw Peninsula, Iraq had completed the destruction of the very prize it sought. The Shatt al-Arab waterway had not been dredged for the entire course of the war and was so full of silt, sunken ships, and unexploded artillery shells and bombs that it would be unusable for years to come. Now, al-Sanii said grimly, Iraq was more dependent than ever on Umm Qasr, its military port near Kuwait's Bubiyan Island, which Saddam Hussein would very likely try to seize.

As if to underscore the danger, April Glaspie, the U.S. ambassador to Baghdad, sought me out the second day of that visit to Kuwait. She had a very tough job. Not only were relations between the United States and Iraq strained, but she was a woman doing what in the eyes of the Arabs was man's work. This would have discouraged someone of lesser character, but it didn't bother Glaspie a bit. She spoke with the bluntness some diplomats manifest when they know they don't have to negotiate. Describing Iraq as a bleak, repressive regime in which she was barred from moving around freely, she said it was nevertheless too powerful a nation for the United States to ignore: "It would be like denying cancer." I agreed. Since Iraq was a military state, she continued, perhaps military-to-military contact through Central Command would be an effective way to promote communications between the two governments. I said I'd be willing to meet with Iraqi generals if she could find a suitable opportunity.

Glaspie had to return to Baghdad right away, but Central Command business kept me and my staff in Kuwait City several more days. General al-Sanii found a way to lighten the atmosphere considerably before we left, by arranging a dinner for me and both our staffs at a famous restaurant, a replica of a large dhow, or sailing vessel of the sort that in earlier years had plied the waters of the gulf. Stopping by my hotel room a day in advance to tell me about the restaurant, he then asked casually, "Would you prefer to wear western clothes or Kuwaiti clothes?"

The thought of wearing Arab robes had never crossed my mind, but I figured he wouldn't have raised the question if he hadn't wanted me to choose them. "I'd like to wear Kuwaiti clothes, if that wouldn't offend you."

His face lit up. "It wouldn't offend me at all! We'd be delighted. I'll get them for you."

"I've never seen westerners here wear Kuwaiti clothes," I observed.

He looked at me and replied quite pointedly, "No, you haven't. But in the United States you see many Arabs wearing western clothes." I got the message: we expected them to adapt when they did business in our country, yet did not feel our corresponding obligation in theirs.

That afternoon, my *thaub*, a long-sleeved, high-necked white cotton garment, and my *bisht*, a long black outer cloak made of yards of fine, soft, loosely woven wool bordered by gold thread, were delivered. I also received the traditional head covering—a square white cotton *ghutrah* and a black corded *iqal* to hold it in place. I put the robes on and stood in front of the mirror. They felt pretty good. Turning self-consciously this way and that, I couldn't help but think of the film *Lawrence of Arabia*, in which Peter O'Toole, dressed in Arab garb for the first time, twirls slowly around on the sand dunes admiring himself.

Al-Sanii and his entourage came to fetch me, and we rode the elevator downstairs where my unsuspecting staff waited. Norm Ehlert saw al-Sanii come across the lobby with all those other Arabs and wondered, "Where's General Schwarzkopf?" He told me later that, for all the time he'd spent in the Middle East, it had never occurred to him that an American might put on Arab robes.

At the restaurant al-Sanii had arranged his officers in a long receiving line to greet us. Each man broke into a wide grin as I shook his hand, and made a point of telling me how pleased and honored he felt to see me wearing their clothing. Before sitting down to eat, we strolled around the main deck of the dhow chatting, sipping fruit juice, and gazing out across the gulf. It was a clear, windy evening, and as I stood amid the Kuwaitis in the ship's bow, my robes flying, I wondered what my West Point classmates would think of me now.

Central Command's new approach also paid off in the United Arab Emirates. In late 1988, our governments had been practically estranged. President Sheikh Zayed Bin Sultan al-Nahyan, the shrewd old Bedouin who had unified the UAE, had declared many times, "The United States is no friend of the Arabs because it is a friend of Israel." And Central Command itself had further soured relations with an arms deal a few years before. We had overseen the sale to Zayed's government of tens of millions of dollars worth of Hawk Mod. 2 ("modification two") air-defense missiles—without mentioning that the Pentagon was about to declare them obsolete and shift to Hawk Mod. 3s. The UAE felt cheated.

The deputy chief of staff of their armed forces, Sheikh Zayed's third son, Sheikh Mohammed Bin Zayed al-Nahyan, was dissatisfied with this state of affairs. Hearing from General Ehlert that a new crew had taken over Central Command, he invited me to the UAE's National Day parade in December 1989. I had to make a special trip to the Middle East to attend, but it seemed worthwhile: the UAE was in a strategically crucial location. Also, I was fascinated by the country's rapid modernization under Zayed's leadership and wanted to see for myself. Mohammed, who had learned I loved the outdoors, had made the invitation doubly difficult to refuse: he'd offered to take me falcon hunting in the desert the following day.

The evening we met, Mohammed and I hit it off immediately. We agreed our countries needed to make a new start, and I promised to assign Colonel Jack McGuinness, one of the best officers in my headquarters, as chief of the U.S. military mission. The next day we went to the parade.

Military from all nations had been invited. There were many other generals in the section of the reviewing stand where I sat with Hoar and Ehlert, but as I was the highest ranking, the others came over and shook hands as they arrived—all except two. Seated right next to us were a pair of Iraqis who didn't give us the time of day. When I smiled and said good morning, they didn't acknowledge me—it was as though I weren't even there. Mindful of my conversation with Ambassador Glaspie a few weeks before, I thought, "We sure have a ways to go before we're friends with these guys."

———

From its inception in 1983, Central Command had been defined as a rapid-deployment force whose wartime mission was to stop the Red Army from seizing the precious oil fields of Iran. That scenario was the rationale for Central Command's so-called operating plan, the master scheme we employed in organizing units, conducting maneuvers, and stockpiling supplies, and in competing against other commands for Pentagon budget dollars. I knew the plan inside out—having commanded the 24th Mechanized Infantry Division, which was assigned to fight as part of Central Command if war broke out. In fact, the only tanks in the Army camouflaged desert brown rather than forest green had been ours.

We'd used the operating plan for years, but most generals knew it made no sense and would eventually be junked. For one thing, it was suicidal. It called for Central Command to rush forces to the Zagros Mountains in northern Iran. The narrow passes and forbidding terrain greatly favored the defense, but we knew that no matter how well we fought, we would be seriously outnumbered, seven thousand miles from home, and destined to run out of supplies and troops in a matter of weeks. When we practiced the plan during our biannual war games, the umpires always stopped us before the battle reached that point, declaring vaguely, "The diplomats have just negotiated a cease-fire." The plan did not inspire great confidence.

Nonetheless, Central Command used it for years to justify spending millions of dollars of taxpayers' money on specialized supplies and equipment. By the time I took over, we had stockpiled hundreds of miles of custom-made pipe to build a fuel system in Iran; rather than have us count on Iranian refineries, the plan called for Central Command to *ship petroleum to the Middle East* and pump it to the front lines. We had also made plans to buy large numbers of hovercraft, amphibious barges, and other specialized equipment so we'd be able to move all of our supplies and gear over the beach—the rationale being that, given the Iranian government's hostility to the United States, we couldn't assume we'd have access to the ports. Unless we could define a valid purpose for my new command, I was prepared to recommend to the secretary of defense that we shut it down.

One night in July 1989, eight months after becoming commander in chief and after my initial visits to the Middle East, I lay in bed staring at the ceiling and let a new plan begin to take shape. I ran through my mind what I'd concluded. I was confident of the Middle East's strategic importance and, therefore, of Central Command's reason for existence. Nobody except a few stubborn hard-liners believed that we'd go to war against the Soviets in the Middle East: each day brought confirmation of arms-control talks succeeding and cold war tensions easing. In Central Command's own region, the Soviet military had actually retreated from Afghanistan after eight years of fighting.

So I asked myself, what was most likely? Another confrontation like the tanker war, one that had the United States intervening in a regional conflict that had gotten out of control and was threatening the flow of oil to the rest of the world. I counted up no fewer than thirteen current conflicts in the region—border wars, civil wars, tribal wars, religious wars—and any one of several could endanger our interests. Therefore Central Command had to develop an operating plan to cope with the worst of these conflicts. Then, I figured, we'd be able to take any other regional crisis in stride.

What was the worst case? Iraq as the aggressor: the world's fourth-largest army was sitting just north of oil fields whose output was essential to the industrialized world. I thought of the many Arabs who had said I shouldn't worry about Iraq, and the few who'd said I should. I decided worrying was the prudent course, partly because Saddam Hussein had done nothing to reduce his army's size in the year that had elapsed since the cease-fire with Iran.

I knew my next step was to work my way through the Pentagon bureaucracy so we could officially forgo further preparations for the Soviet invasion of Iran. A regional commander can't simply promulgate any war plan he pleases: the Joint Chiefs of Staff dictate his mission in accordance with the stated national strategy. This comes in the form of a slim secret document, the Defense Planning Guidance, handed down by the secretary of defense. Pentagon strategists use the DPG to develop an illustrative planning scenario, another secret document, which envisions the various sequences of events most likely to lead the United States to war. This in turn serves as the basis for the Joint Strategic Capabilities Plan, which directs the various commands to start detailed war planning and earmarks the forces with which each command is to work. Clearly, we had to get those documents revised.

I anticipated real resistance—not because the Zagros Mountains plan had many fans, but because the Pentagon was under enormous pressure to cut its budget concurrently with the end of the cold war. Admiral Crowe was preparing recommendations on national military strategy to deliver to Congress before his retirement in September. His first draft, which the Pentagon circulated to the commanders in chief for comment, *made no provision whatever* for the Middle East: he thought the Defense Department should reserve its resources for the continental United States, NATO, and the Pacific. Subsequent drafts said exactly the same thing, despite repeated formal and informal attempts by Central Command to get the Pentagon to acknowledge the growing strategic importance of the Middle East. I argued our case on several occasions to Vice Admiral Jon Howe, Crowe's assistant, who always thanked me but did nothing. (Crowe himself was impossible to get hold of in his busy final weeks as chairman.) I tried persuading the generals and colonels at the Joint Chiefs, pointing out, "What the hell is the Pacific without Middle Eastern oil?" and, "For chrissakes we just went to war with the Iranians over the free flow of oil!"

Many of them agreed that what I was saying made sense. But they told me, "You don't understand. Admiral Crowe wrote this himself."

I considered my options. Having been stuck behind a desk in Washington five times, I knew enough bureaucratic kung fu to fight back. If necessary, I could appeal to Central Command's backers on Capitol Hill—I knew I wouldn't have to convince Senator Nunn, for example, of the importance of the Middle East. But I didn't like the idea of working outside the Defense Department chain of command. As it turned out, I didn't have to. In the normal course of business I'd already presented my plan for redefining Central Command to Defense Secretary Dick Cheney's top civilian strategists, Paul Wolfowitz, the undersecretary of defense for policy, and Henry Rowen, the assistant secretary for international security affairs. So when Admiral Crowe submitted his strategy for Secretary Cheney to review, Wolfowitz and Rowen called me and asked incredulously, "Do you agree with this?"

"Of course not!" I growled, explaining how I'd been stonewalled.

They took the problem directly to Cheney—who immediately ordered that the Middle East be written in.

One ally I'd found in the interim was Colin Powell. As expected, he had returned to the Army and taken over Forces Command. I called on him at his headquarters at Fort McPherson, where I'd gone to visit the planners who were responsible for the Third Army's portion of our war plan.

At that point, Powell's reputation in the military was mixed. A lot of people thought of him as half general, half politician. In his rise through the ranks, he'd never commanded a division—an important proving ground. Instead, as a two-star, he'd been Secretary of Defense Caspar Weinberger's military assistant, a job with tremendous clout. From there he'd been promoted to three stars and assigned command of the V Corps in Germany. Before he had a chance to prove himself in that job, he was pulled back to Washington to serve in President Reagan's White House, eventually as national security advisor. So he'd been essentially out of the military for several years—and now he'd come back as a four-star in a very prestigious command. Despite the fact that he had served twice in Vietnam and that many officers who had worked with him in other assignments vouched for his ability to soldier, his rapid rise caused a lot of generals whom he had leapfrogged to grumble about his relative lack of military experience.

I didn't know Powell well enough to form a judgment. My only dealings with him had been in groups at senior generals' conferences, where he'd struck me as smart, insightful, and of the same mind as I was on many key issues. In discussions about the future of the Army, it was often Powell and Schwarzkopf against many of our colleagues. We argued that, because the Army could no longer expect to go to war against the Soviets, we should rethink the way we were structured and equipped—before Congress did it for us. But many generals believed that reforms were premature.

Our discussion at Fort McPherson started out as a courtesy call: it is Army custom for a visiting general officer to say hello to the senior general on post. The Third Army was one of the major forces under Powell's authority, and he took the opportunity to tell me he was concerned that Central Command had troops training for an unrealistic scenario—the war in the Zagros Mountains. He also thought that stockpiling equipment for that war was a gigantic waste of money.

"Don't worry," I told him. "I'm in the process of drastically revising our strategy and war plans. I think we can make major cuts in our spending." Then I outlined the changes I wanted to make. Powell was enthusiastic and volunteered to help in any way he could.

If we'd gone by the book, reorienting Central Command as I intended would have taken two full years. Each of the services had to flesh out its portion of the new war plan, and Central Command had to assess the feasibility of delivering the necessary forces and supplies to the war zone. Then a companion logistical plan had to be prepared, consisting of thousands of pages of computer printouts that would specify how and in what order troops, pieces of equipment, and supplies would actually be shipped. (Pentagoners call this plan a "tipfiddle," short for "time-phased force deployment list.") Normally a command could not adopt an operating plan until all of these time-consuming steps were complete. I now had to figure out a way to get the people of Central Command thinking in terms of the new scheme as quickly as possible.

Our annual war game, code-named Internal Look, was scheduled for the following summer. Known as a "command post exercise," it involved eight grueling twenty-hour days in which Central Command's staff, as well as the staffs of our Army, Navy, Air Force, and Marine components, would practice running a war—developing and issuing orders, sorting out battlefield reports, directing flows of ammunition and supplies, and coordinating the maneuvers of air forces, armies, and fleets—by using computer programs instead of actual forces in the field. It was the headquarters equivalent of training a pilot in a flight simulator.

My operations staff had already begun work on Internal Look for 1990, preparing an exercise premised on the Soviets' coming through Iran—the discredited Zagros Mountains scenario. "Why should we knock ourselves out for a week on a plan that's being junked?" I asked Jim Record. He explained that since the new plan hadn't been officially approved, they'd dutifully followed the old one. I told him to forget the Zagros Mountains and to test the plan we had in the making. I wanted to learn its strengths and weaknesses and to force our component units to think through their new roles. I was determined that the scenario we'd rehearse that summer would be one in which the enemy was not the Soviet Union, but Iraq.

16

e played Internal Look in late July 1990, setting up a mock headquarters complete with computers and communication gear at Eglin Air Force Base in the Florida panhandle. As the exercise got under way, the movements of Iraq's real-world ground and air forces eerily paralleled the imaginary scenario in our game. We had envisioned a huge force—some 300,000 men, 3,200 tanks, and 640 combat planes—which would mass in southern Iraq and attack the Arabian Peninsula. Central Command's much smaller force was supposed to stop the invasion before it seized crucial Saudi oil fields, refineries, and ports. To make the drill more realistic, several weeks in advance I'd asked our message center to start sending a stream of fictional dispatches about military and political developments in Iraq to the headquarters of the Army, Navy, Air Force, and Marine units scheduled to participate. As the war game began, the message center also passed along routine intelligence bulletins about the *real* Middle East. Those concerning Iraq were so similar to the game dispatches that the message center ended up having to stamp the fictional reports with a prominent disclaimer: "Exercise Only."

I spent the week uneasily, with one foot in the realm of the exercise and the other in the realm of fact, where the real crisis had started to build. On July 17, Saddam Hussein angrily and publicly threatened Kuwait and the United Arab Emirates with war. He accused them of shoving a "poisoned dagger" into Iraq's back by exceeding production quotas set by OPEC, thereby driving down the price of oil. Their greed, he went on, had prompted them to conspire with the American and Israeli imperialists to sabotage Iraq; they had stopped acting like Arab brothers. That same day, the first reports of unusual Iraqi troop movements just north of Kuwait came in.

The quarrel over OPEC quotas was old hat. Saddam, with his eighty-billion-dollar war debt, had long wanted to jack up prices, but the other gulf leaders had consistently refused to go along. Highly cultured men such as King Fahd of Saudi Arabia and Sultan Qaboos Bin Said of Oman saw Saddam as a thug, but weren't particularly worried by him. After all, he had run Iraq as a military state for eleven years without turning on his Arab neighbors (Iranians are Aryans, not Arabs). And they held to the belief that Arabs would continue to settle rivalries peaceably among themselves, as they liked to say they had for centuries. But in his speech, Saddam overstepped: blunt threats were almost unheard of in the Arab world, and I knew we'd see quick reactions from other Arab states.

The United Arab Emirates was the first to ask for help. Sheikh Mohammed, with his father's consent, approached us with a request for a pair of tanker planes for aerial refueling. Mohammed wanted to keep his air force continually in the air, ready to defend instantly against an Iraqi attack. He also asked if we could provide early warning if the Iraqis launched a raid. Both requests were defensive and both made sense—and I realized the UAE saw this as an acid test of the new relationship I had promised. I also knew that asking for American help took courage, because the UAE was exposing itself to the scorn of every other Arab nation. I said, "Of course."

The UAE then made a formal request to Washington—and the State Department recommended we *turn it down;* they dismissed Mohammed as a "playboy prince." That judgment came from an expert on Egypt who knew little about the UAE. He had the wrong man: Mohammed was a pious Moslem, a competent military officer, a patriot, and a loyal, devoted son. My protests fell on deaf ears, so finally I turned to Colin Powell, who by now, as expected, had become chairman of the Joint Chiefs of Staff. I told him, "This one is very important to us. They're not asking much, and we have to support this if we expect to have any military relationship with the UAE." He strongly agreed, as did Secretary Cheney, but it took a couple of days to get the State Department to reverse itself. Meanwhile Mohammed called and said, "Are you going to support this or not?" And the U.S. ambassador to the UAE, who had also promised help and was really out on a limb, was complaining to the State Department: "For crying out loud, why aren't we supporting this? What's the commitment? Just two tankers! We stand to win the goodwill of these people forever." It was typical of the way we did business in the Middle East. Nothing was ever simple. Finally, near the end of July, we quietly sent over the tankers for what we called joint exercises with the UAE air force. We also spread three of the five ships of our Middle East Force in a picket line across the gulf, so that if Iraq launched an air raid, we would pick it up on radar in time to alert the UAE.

In Kuwait, my friends Major General al-Sanii and Major General Jaber al-Khaled al-Sabah put their forces on full alert and deployed them in the defensive positions north of Kuwait City that I'd been briefed on the year before. But the emir, Sheikh Jaber al-Ahmed al-Sabah, overruled them and ordered the troops back to their garrisons. Based on experience, the emir assumed Saddam could be placated with money: Kuwait had contributed billions of dollars to the war against Iran, and Saddam was now claiming that Kuwait had stolen $2.5 billion worth of oil from the Rumaila field that both countries shared. American diplomats agreed that Saddam would not attack. During the last week of July at Central Command, we received analyses from both the State Department and the international diplomatic community saying things like "Saddam is merely saber rattling to gain leverage over Kuwait in the oil-pricing debate" and "No Arab nation will ever attack another."

But I was blessed with an intelligence staff whose work was so good that the military intelligence community in Washington usually let Central Command take the lead, seconding our assessments of developments in the Middle East. Each morning the staff briefed me on the Iraqi military's latest moves. We had extraordinary data to draw on: ever since the tanker war, the United States had kept the region under stepped-up surveillance, both human and high-tech, so each day brought a huge haul of fresh information. We tracked convoys of troops and trainloads of tanks as they moved south from Baghdad to Basra in southern Iraq, and from there to assembly.

Iraq had used the desert near Basra for military training before and at first we thought this might be merely another exercise. Their troops were sitting around in tents, and their armor, equipment, and supplies were way back at the rear. But by the end of July, the Iraqis were no longer confined to the exercise area; they had fanned out southeast and southwest of Basra and pointed themselves toward the Kuwait border. Now the tents had disappeared, the armor had moved forward, and equipment was deployed near units that could use it: helicopters alongside special-forces units and pontoon-bridging equipment next to marines. There was no way to mistake what we were seeing for a mere show of force: this was a battle plan taking shape.

When we returned to Tampa my staff shifted without a break from the artificial intensity of the war game to the real intensity of the crisis. Among the officers I depended on most there had been major personnel changes. Joe Hoar, my chief of staff, had been promoted to a three-star assignment at the Pentagon that put him on the fast track for a four-star command. I was proud to see him rise—and delighted when his replacement, Major General Bob Johnston, turned out equally strong. I'd heard other generals describe Johnston as a future commandant of the Marine Corps, and his performance in Internal Look showed me why. The chief of staff plays a pivotal role in a command-post exercise—just as in a real crisis—and though Johnston had been at Central Command for only a month, he did the job as well as I'd ever seen it done.

Major General Burt Moore, a seasoned Air Force man, came in as my new director of operations—a no-win assignment when the commander in chief is an old warhorse like me who thinks of himself as the best operations man around. Burt, who had just spent four relatively placid years as Air Force congressional liaison in Washington, found himself on the hot seat from the start, first in Internal Look, then in the real crisis; his experience as a combat pilot was what pulled him through. Meanwhile our intelligence section—already the best in the Middle East business—got a brain boost with the arrival of its new chief, Brigadier General Jack Leide. A Far East specialist who had been America's military attaché in China at the time of the Tiananmen Square massacre, Leide had come to Central Command expecting a well-deserved respite. But when the crisis broke, he jumped in and taught our young staff how to be effective under a crushing work load.

In response to a Kuwaiti request for information on the Iraqi threat, we dispatched one of Leide's experts, Major John F. Feeley, to Kuwait City with a briefcase of top-secret photos. Shortly after noon on the last day of July, we notified Washington that war between Iraq and Kuwait appeared imminent. Analysts at the Defense Intelligence Agency, who had been following the same data, supported our conclusion. That afternoon Colin Powell ordered me to come to Washington to brief Secretary of Defense Cheney and the Joint Chiefs of Staff on what our options would be if the shooting started.

The following afternoon I entered the now-familiar confines of the Tank, handed out diagrams and surveillance photos of Iraqi troop dispositions, and gave a ninety-minute spiel. Pointing to a map of Kuwait that was on the projection screen, Cheney asked what I thought the Iraqis would do. I made a prediction that turned out to be half right and half wrong. "There's no doubt that this is a military plan. I think they're going to attack," I said, but added that I didn't believe Saddam would grab the entire country. I anticipated he'd move to positions just south of the 30th parallel, taking Kuwait's part of the Rumaila oil field, as well as Bubiyan Island, which controlled the sea-lane to Iraq's new port, Umm Qasr, and then he would stop.

I presented the detailed plans we'd worked up for air and sea strikes we could launch against Iraq. I ticked off lists of so-called high-value targets—military headquarters, power plants, factories—that we could quickly destroy. At the end, and almost as an afterthought, I outlined our contingency plan to send troops to defend Saudi Arabia, even though none of us thought Saddam would threaten to invade Saudi territory. The meeting ended with no sense of urgency. In the hierarchy of world crises, this one was still a minor blip.

On the way back to Tampa, I phoned ahead, reported that the briefing had gone well, and ordered my staff to stand down, leaving only a "crisis action team" on duty. It was the staff's first break in two weeks. I was satisfied that we'd done all we could until Saddam made another move, and when we landed late that afternoon, I headed home.

———

An hour later, just as I was climbing on my exercise bike ready to banish the Iraqis from my mind, the phone rang. It was Colin Powell, who said matter-of-factly, "You were right. They've crossed the border."

I hurried to the command center still wearing my warm-up suit. The crisis action team officers briefed me on the initial intelligence reports, which indicated that the main Iraqi attack had bypassed the Rumaila oil field and struck deep into Kuwait—Saddam seemed to be going further than I'd expected. Then, for a couple of hours, no news. We waited to hear from our security-assistance team in Kuwait or from Major Feeley. Finally, a little after nine P.M.—four A.M. Kuwait time—Feeley called. He'd awakened in his hotel room to the sound of distant explosions and run across the street to the American embassy, where Central Command kept a satellite radio that could link directly with Tampa. Now he was on the line with General Leide, who relayed his report: "The Iraqis are in downtown Kuwait City."

This was obviously not the limited incursion I'd predicted that morning. I reached for the red phone, my high-security line to Washington, to alert General Powell, but it rang before I could pick it up. Powell had heard the same news through the State Department, from Ambassador Nat

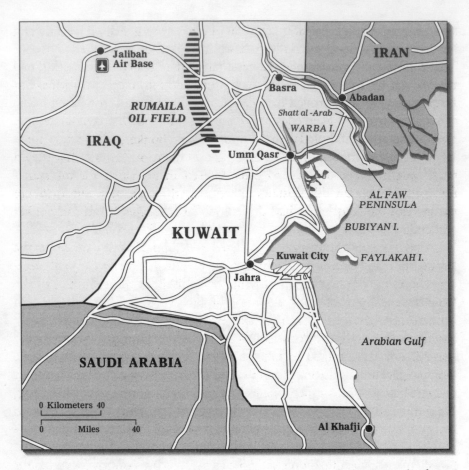

Howell in Kuwait, and was calling to tell me. Everybody was surprised—an Arab had attacked a brother Arab. Powell added: "I'll probably need you here tomorrow morning to brief the President."

Meanwhile, Major Feeley climbed up on the embassy roof and provided a running commentary on the morning battle for Kuwait City. The embassy was perfectly situated—only a quarter mile from the main palace, a key objective for the Iraqis. Feeley described the Iraqi tanks, fighter planes, and helicopters he could see attacking. The helicopters, he said, were delivering special-forces troops to strategic locations throughout the city; he spotted men in civilian clothes signaling them to their landing zones. The Iraqis had thoroughly prepared—they'd gone so far as to plant agents to act as ground controllers for incoming forces.

Over the next hours, a picture of the invasion emerged. The offensive consisted of little more than a drive down Kuwait's north-south superhighway until the Iraqis reached Kuwait City. There they ran into resistance and slowed; meanwhile, a separate column of tanks swung around the city and headed south, toward the military bases and oil fields of southern Kuwait. That morning, I later learned, General Jaber, the deputy chief of staff, had tried to get his troops out of their garrisons and into battle positions. But Iraqi commandos destroyed his headquarters, so he spent the dawn hours driving around in a Mercedes, directing the forces with a cellular phone. Later he and his staff holed up in an underground bunker, only to have three Republican Guard tanks pull up and park on the roof. Certain that they'd been caught, Jaber decided to offer himself in exchange for his staff's freedom. He sent an aide upstairs to negotiate the surrender, but luckily in the interim the Iraqi tanks had driven off. Jaber escaped from the bunker and ended up directing the remnants of the army for several more weeks.

Early the next morning I reported to Colin Powell's office in the Pentagon, ready to accompany him to the National Security Council meeting where, for the first time in my life, I would brief the President of the United States. Powell took one look at the expression on my face and warned me not to expect much: "National Security Council meetings are basically a forum for the President to gather information. Everybody in the Cabinet will feel obliged to talk, so you might hear some dumb things. Don't expect any decision. When the President has to make one, he does it in consultation with a much smaller group." Flipping through the briefing slides my staff had labored most of the night to prepare, he directed me to limit my presentation to what Central Command could do right away—specifically, the air strikes and sea strikes I'd described to the Joint Chiefs. Powell made it clear he didn't want me to get into our contingency plan for sending troops until we knew better what Saddam was up to. Whether the United States would intervene militarily, he continued, would depend on how far the Iraqis went. Then he surmised, "I think we'd go to war over Saudi Arabia, but I doubt we'd go to war over Kuwait." Finally, he advised me that I was a guest and as such would be expected to stay on the sidelines and not speak until invited to do so. I took it all in—as a former national security advisor, Powell knew what he was talking about—and the protocol he described sounded much like the Tank's. With that, we climbed into a sedan and drove across the Potomac to the White House.

Powell's predictions were right on target. Judge William Webster, the head of the CIA, led off with an intelligence update. Though the agency had access to exactly the same information as Central Command, what he presented was a warmed-over description of the Iraqi forces a few days *before* the invasion. He offered only skimpy data about the attack itself—not a word, for example, about the battle for the palace the previous night.

Lieutenant General Brent Scowcroft, the national security advisor, Tom Pickering, the ambassador to the United Nations, and Secretary Cheney made interesting contributions, but other Cabinet officers who should have helped assess the new developments seemed quite unprepared.

President Bush wanted to look at every facet of the crisis. Was there any possibility Iran would side with Iraq? Could we cut off the flow of oil from Iraq and Kuwait? What would be the effect of that on the world economy? Why had Yemen abstained from the United Nations Security Council vote to condemn the invasion? What could we do to prevent American citizens from being taken hostage? I was impressed by his willingness to listen to what everyone had to say and not make snap judgments or decisions before he had the complete picture. He went around the table, searching for specific information but not getting very much. I fought the urge to leap to my feet and lecture. I *knew* the simple answer to the question about Yemen: its role in the Security Council was to represent the Arab League, and in this crisis Arab leaders had reached no consensus. I successfully contained myself until Webster announced that all contact had been lost with the U.S. embassy in Kuwait.

"I don't think that's right," I said, explaining that we'd talked to Major Feeley by radio all night. My speaking up didn't seem to offend the participants. I suspected Webster only meant that the CIA had been unable to communicate with its station chief. I thought it important to reassure the President that the embassy hadn't been blown off the face of the earth.

When Powell introduced me, I stood and laid out the options as he had instructed. While we could do nothing to stop the invasion, I cautioned, we could make certain moves with our air and sea power to demonstrate U.S. determination and, if necessary, punish Iraq.

Although the invasion of Kuwait was barely fourteen hours old, it was clear that President Bush had already determined that Saddam's aggression had to be checked. He instructed us to be prepared to fight if Iraq took the American embassy staff hostage. Then Powell asked, "Should we look at laying down a red line with regard to Saudi Arabia?" The President said yes. He considered an attack on the Saudis to be cause for war.

———

Two days later Powell brought me back to brief the President again. "This meeting will be different," he told me. "We're going to Camp David. We'll talk to the President and a very small group. It'll be your show: take as much of the morning as you need and lay out your operating plan." The President was ready to consider sending troops.

The worst-case scenario I'd imagined had materialized. The conquest of all of Kuwait had taken less than three days and it looked as if the Iraqis weren't planning to stop there. On Friday, attempting to cool the crisis, Egypt, Jordan, and Saudi Arabia moved to arrange an Arab League summit. But the same three divisions of the Republican Guard that had led the initial attack into Kuwait began massing tanks and artillery along the border of Saudi Arabia and bringing supplies forward. We had to assume they were getting ready to cross.

Central Command headquarters was a pressure cooker. We had warships in the gulf forming a radar picket line as we'd promised the UAE; our security-assistance teams in Saudi Arabia and Egypt were readying airplanes to pluck civilians out of Kuwait if we got the opportunity; and we were preparing to take command of the aircraft carrier *Independence* and her six-warship battle group, which before the crisis had been steaming toward the island of Diego Garcia in the Indian Ocean and had now been diverted north toward the gulf. At the same time we were working with the Navy to plan a maritime embargo of Iraq and asking the Air Force to put on alert units around the United States that might have to fly to the war zone. Lcide's intelligence officers were bringing me hourly updates not only on Iraq but also on Iran and other Middle Eastern countries whose intentions were still unclear. Finally, we had to cope with questions from Washington. These most often took the form of calls from Colin Powell. He called several times a day. "How long would it take us to mount a rescue operation for the embassy staff?" he'd ask. Or, "What do you think the Arab League is going to do?"

Though my staff rose magnificently to the occasion, I was not an easy commander. I drove them mercilessly, admonishing them over and over, "This is no exercise. This is the real thing. When we tell the President of the United States that Central Command can do something militarily, he is very likely to turn around and say, 'Okay, do it.' I don't want us winging it, and I don't want any false bravado." The U.S. military in Vietnam had been accused of regularly sugarcoating the truth in an effort to please the President, and on the basis of bad information the President had made some disastrous decisions. We were not going to repeat that mistake. Every shred of information we gave the President would be the most accurate we had, even if it reflected unfavorably. If we told him we *could* do something, we *would* be able to deliver on our promise.

Early on Saturday, August 4, I met Powell and Cheney at the Pentagon and outlined my presentation during the twenty-minute helicopter flight into the Maryland hills. I'd brought along Lieutenant General Chuck

Horner, my Air Force commander. I wanted him to brief the President on air capabilities, and since air power was the option most immediately available, I felt Chuck should hear everything that was said. As we came in to land, I saw a complex of beautiful red-oak buildings on a low wooded mountaintop, about as different from the desert battlefields of the Middle East as I could imagine.

We rode in golf carts, the primary mode of transportation at Camp David, from the helipad to the main lodge, a quarter mile up the hill. In a comfortable conference room, President Bush had convened his inner circle: Vice President Dan Quayle, Secretary of State Baker, Secretary Cheney, General Scowcroft, White House chief of staff John Sununu, and Judge Webster of the CIA. Baker had returned early that morning from a trip to the Soviet Union, where he and Foreign Minister Eduard Schevardnadze had issued an historic joint condemnation of the Iraqi invasion. Powell, Horner, and I were in uniform, but everybody else was casually dressed—the President wore a sport shirt and a windbreaker to keep off the chill of the air conditioning. It hardly looked like a council of war.

The President was very much in charge. He repeatedly expressed his concern for Kuwait and the plight of Americans trapped there. He also argued that Iraqi aggression could not be allowed to go unchallenged by the United States and the rest of the world. When it was my turn to speak, I stood, looked around the table, and explained what we were up against. Among the world's standing armies, Saddam's ranked in size behind only those of China, the Soviet Union, and Vietnam. (The United States ranked seventh.) The Iraqi military machine consisted of 900,000 men organized into sixty-three divisions, including eight elite Republican Guard forces. Saddam had approximately double the number of troops needed for his country's defense against its neighbors. His arsenal included some of the best weapons the international arms bazaar had to offer: Soviet T-72 tanks, South African 155-mm heavy artillery, Chinese and Soviet multiple rocket launchers, Chinese Silkworm and French Exocet antiship missiles, Soviet MiG-29 fighters and Su-24 long-range fighter-bombers, French M-1 Mirage fighters—the list went on and on. I spent a little time highlighting what I saw as Iraq's military strengths, such as its ability, evinced in the second Al Faw campaign of the Iran-Iraq war, to wage an offensive with chemical weapons; and its weaknesses, primarily feeble logistics and a centralized system of command and control in which important decisions, even in the heat of battle, could be made only by Saddam personally.

I went back over the air-power and sea-power alternatives I'd offered two days before and then turned to a possibility we hadn't discussed:

sending ground forces. The defensive plan was the same one we'd practiced in Central Command's Internal Look war game just one week before, but now included a troop-deployment timetable that we'd sweated over until I could confidently offer the entire package to the President with a *guarantee* that this was what we could accomplish.

I pointed out that we would need Saudi Arabia's cooperation to execute such a plan, since it depended on the use of their airfields and harbors. Then if the President gave the order, we could put a brigade of the 82nd Airborne Division—four thousand soldiers—on the ground right away. Their job would be to assert a U.S. presence—a dangerous mission, because if Iraq attacked, the 82nd Airborne's light weapons would be no match for Saddam's tanks. Within two weeks, we could more than triple that ground force with a brigade of Marines, a special-forces group, and more airborne troops. By the end of the first month, our so-called "heavy" units would start to arrive: an air-assault brigade with its Apache helicopters and a brigade of mechanized infantry with its Abrams tanks. "This is the tank-killing equipment we would really need to stop the Iraqis dead in their tracks," I noted. To protect the forces as they flowed in, the Air Force would deploy hundreds of warplanes to Saudi airfields, and the Navy would begin to steam two more aircraft-carrier battle groups to within striking distance of the gulf. We would need three months to mass enough combat power to be absolutely assured of fending off a full-scale Iraqi attack.

The President had already been warned that deploying troops was not an instant solution. In the context of a crisis only three days old, three months seemed almost an eternity. Still, I wanted to make absolutely certain that the civilians around the table understood how powerful an enemy we would face.

"What I've discussed so far is a contingency plan for the *defense* of Saudi Arabia," I went on. "If we ever wanted to kick the Iraqis out of Kuwait, we'd have to go on the *offense*—and that would take a whole lot more troops and a whole lot more time." I put up a slide that showed my back-of-the-envelope calculation: we'd have to more than double the size of the projected force, pulling at least six additional divisions out of the United States and Europe and transporting them and additional support units to the gulf. The earliest such an army would be ready to fight was the slide's bottom line. It read, "Time frame: 8–10 months."

I heard a few people around the table gasp. This was a much larger commitment of forces than they had ever imagined making in the Middle East. It was also much more time than they thought would be needed to solve the crisis by force. Both Cheney and Powell completely supported my position.

I'd come to assure the President that Central Command was prepared, but if he'd asked my opinion that morning, I'd have said I didn't think the situation would lead to war. I felt very concerned for the safety of the people in Kuwait—not only my many Arab friends, but also Nat Howell, the American ambassador and a former political advisor at Central Command, and the members of my security-assistance team. But as long as the Iraqis went no further, it seemed to me that the diplomatic community and the Arab nations would figure out a way to resolve the crisis peacefully.

———

Almost the minute I returned to Tampa on Saturday afternoon, Colin Powell phoned again. "King Fahd is asking for someone to brief him on the threat to his kingdom. We want you to join the delegation and explain to the king what we are ready to do. Bring as many people as you need to give detailed briefings to the Saudi military as well."

When I landed in Washington the following morning with my hastily assembled team, I discovered Powell now wanted me to head the delegation. "Secretary Cheney was supposed to go," he explained when I reported to him at the Pentagon, "but the Saudis haven't cleared him because they want to keep the meeting low-key." He added almost as an afterthought: "When you get there, you'll have to play it by ear."

I was halfway out the door when I thought, "Play it by ear?" I wasn't worried about meeting King Fahd, but if I was going to discuss military action with the Saudis, I had to know what we actually proposed to deliver.

"Is the U.S. government saying we're prepared to commit forces?" I asked.

Powell said tersely, "Yes. If King Fahd gives his permission."

I was stunned. A lot must have happened after I left Camp David that Powell wasn't talking about. President Bush had made up his mind to send troops.

We waited at the airport for Chas Freeman, the U.S. ambassador to Saudi Arabia, a brilliant diplomat and Far East scholar who had been deputy chief of mission in China and served as President Nixon's translator on his historic first trip to Beijing. Because of the crisis, Freeman had decided to cut short his home leave in New England and accompany our delegation.

Less than an hour before we were due to take off, I found myself demoted—the Saudis had cleared Secretary Cheney to lead the delegation after all. We switched to his airplane—one of the Air Force's "special-mission" airliners fitted out with conference rooms and a VIP suite—for the long flight east. The party also included Paul Wolfowitz, civilian strategist for the Pentagon; Pete Williams, its public-affairs chief; Art Hughes, a Pentagon expert on Middle Eastern affairs; Major General Marty Brandtner, the vice-director of operations for the Joint Staff; and Bob Gates, the deputy national security advisor. A CIA analyst was on hand with a folder of the latest satellite photos to show the king. I'd brought along the commanders and staff officers I would need to brief the Saudis and, if necessary, to put forces on the ground. All had been to the Middle East before: Lieutenant General Chuck Horner, a fighter pilot and commander of the Ninth Air Force; Lieutenant General John Yeosock, an old friend and commander of the Third Army; Major General Dane Starling, the head of Central Command's logistics staff and the best logistics planner I'd ever met; and Rear Admiral Grant Sharp, my top planner and strategist. I also brought my executive officer, a smart, aggressive Army Cavalry colonel from Tennessee by the name of Burwell Baxter Bell (we called him "B.B."). I made it his responsibility to keep my personal logbook during the crisis—a complete record of actions and decisions that eventually filled more than three thousand typewritten, single-spaced pages.

Secretary Cheney had been at the Pentagon just over a year and he'd unnerved a lot of generals by replacing one four-star and giving warnings to others he felt were acting with too much autonomy. Yet as I watched and listened to him during the flight, he impressed me as smart, attentive, and easy to work with. He was curious about every nuance of Arab protocol. As the delegation discussed how to handle the presentation to the king, he wondered at one point how the Saudis would react to an offer of American troops. I warned that Arabs tended to approach major decisions with great caution: "If they run true to form, you're not going to get an immediate answer. They'll ask questions and then say, 'Thank you very much. Now we would like to study the information you've provided and will let you know our decision.' "

King Fahd awaited us not in Riyadh, but in Jidda on the shore of the Red Sea, not far from Mecca. The Saudis said that the king "summered" in Jidda; in fact he spent more than half of each year there. Ostensibly the reason was that Jidda's climate was cooler and more comfortable than Riyadh's. Rumor had it, however, that the king's motive was to avoid the capital, because a soothsayer had once told him he would be assassinated there. I suspected the simple truth was that, having been raised in Jidda, the king felt more at home there than in the formal atmosphere of the capital.

The Saudis had provided us with a convoy of Mercedeses. We drove to the guest palace, a splendid building fitted out like a five-star hotel and decorated with priceless Middle Eastern artifacts. It was late afternoon and we spent an hour conferring in Secretary Cheney's suite. Then we climbed back in our convoy for the five-minute drive to the royal palace.

As we were ushered through the halls, I had only a brief glimpse of greens and golds and silk carpets as far as the eye could see. We arrived at a huge room with seats all the way around the perimeter, where the king holds his formal audiences. A big, heavyset man with hawklike features but kind eyes, King Fahd was seated in the far left-hand corner. He stood as our delegation approached. After Ambassador Freeman introduced us one by one, members of the court showed us to our places along the wall, with Secretary Cheney just to the right of the king.

I recognized Abdullah, the crown prince; Prince Saud al-Faisal, the foreign minister; Prince Bandar, the ambassador to the United States; Prince Abdul Rahman, the deputy defense and aviation minister; and one or two other members of the royal family. King Fahd understood some English, but all official business was conducted in Arabic, so Bandar acted as interpreter. Our delegation included Secretary Cheney, Gates, Wolfowitz, Williams, Hughes, Horner, Brandtner, and me; only Cheney and I were to speak. When everyone had settled down, Cheney conveyed a greeting from President Bush, spoke briefly about our concern for the situation in Kuwait, and then gestured toward me saying, "General Schwarzkopf is going to brief you on the intelligence situation as we see it and on the military options we have available."

Since I had photographs and charts to show the king, I walked over to him. There was no place to sit, so I got down on one knee. This embarrassed the king, who quickly said something in Arabic, and a servant immediately ran over with a chair. Now I was sitting to King Fahd's left, with Prince Abdullah on my other side looking over my shoulder, and Prince Bandar standing behind us, interpreting.

I showed the king a series of photos of Iraqi tanks at the Saudi border. Actually, a couple of the photos showed tanks that were *across* the Saudi border. At that point, the king muttered something to Prince Abdullah that Bandar didn't translate. I explained that while we didn't know whether the Iraqis intended to attack Saudi Arabia, we judged from their deployment and from similar Iraqi actions during the Iran-Iraq war that they were in what we called a strategic pause, busy rearming and reequipping before continuing offensive operations. They had their best units forward, poised to attack; their posture was certainly not defensive.

Then I outlined our plan to defend the kingdom. I flipped through a series of charts that showed, week by week, the forces we could provide. I didn't elaborate as to how such a deployment could actually defeat an attack—my main message was the scale of the operation, to make sure the king understood that we were talking about flooding his airfields, harbors, and military bases with tens of thousands more Americans than Saudi Arabia had ever seen.

I returned to my seat and Cheney spoke again. He made a few remarks about the gravity of the situation and then said, "Here is the message that President Bush has instructed me to convey: We are prepared to deploy these forces to defend the kingdom of Saudi Arabia. If you ask us, we will come. We will seek no permanent bases. And when you ask us to go home, we will leave." He then fell silent.

The king and his advisors began debating among themselves the pros and cons of bringing us in. I knew enough to sense what was at stake in King Fahd's decision. If he did nothing, he risked losing his kingdom to Iraq. But if he invited the Americans, even with a presidential assurance that we would respect Saudi sovereignty, Saddam and other Arab leaders would denounce him for toadying to the West. Simply put, he risked undermining the authority of his throne. There were also huge risks inherent in inviting an army of foreigners into a xenophobic kingdom fiercely devoted to keeping itself religiously and culturally pure. I felt sure that Fahd would need days to discuss these risks with other members of the royal family before making up his mind, and that he would ultimately choose to involve us as little as possible.

The discussion among the members of the royal family present was very brief. One by one, the princes spoke, but Bandar didn't translate. King Fahd responded sharply to one of them and then turned to Cheney and said in English simply, "Okay."

If someone had snapped a picture at that moment, it would have shown me with my mouth wide open. Fahd had made one of the most courageous decisions I'd ever witnessed. Until now, the giant deployment we'd prepared had seemed like just another drill. Now I realized, "In about five minutes I am going to push that boulder over the top of the hill, and it will start to roll."

We were all quiet as we walked back to our cars. I turned to Cheney and asked, "Do you want me to start the forces moving?" He said yes. I looked over to General Horner, who had four tactical fighter squadrons at Shaw and Langley Air Force bases standing by to fly to Saudi Arabia. "Chuck, start them moving," I said.

We held a short meeting to review what had taken place. Ambassador

Freeman, who had followed the royal family's conversation in Arabic, told us that the princes had mostly counseled caution. The turning point had come when one remarked, "We must be careful not to rush into a decision." This had caused King Fahd to retort, "The Kuwaitis did not rush into a decision, and today they are all guests in our hotels!"

Cheney excused himself to inform the President, after which we discussed what to do next. Cheney and I would go on the next morning to brief President Hosni Mubarak in Egypt before heading back to Washington. Then I gathered my senior officers in my room. There weren't enough chairs, so with Admiral Sharp and General Starling sitting on the bed and Colonel Bell taking notes in the corner I announced: "We're committing forces *now*." Not a man present had packed for more than a three-day trip, and I had to break the news that I'd be leaving them behind for at least a few weeks. Speaking in a quiet, steady voice, I dealt out their assignments. "Chuck, since you're the senior man present, you're going to be acting CENTCOM commander, forward. At the same time, you need to make arrangements to bed down the airplanes that are on their way and those that will follow."

I turned to General Yeosock, who was sitting in a chair by the window. "John, since the 82nd Airborne is going to be here right away, I need you to get together with the Saudis and arrange for us to position our forces according to the plan. Then you'll organize the ground units as they flow in."

General Starling had to make arrangements to absorb the mammoth flow of troops, weapons, and supplies. I told him, "Dane, you know what the logistical challenges are going to be. I need you to lay the groundwork, and I particularly want you to make sure the ports are ready to receive our first supply ships. The ones in the Indian Ocean will be arriving any day."

And I turned to Admiral Sharp. "Grant, Paul Wolfowitz has asked that you travel with him while he visits the other gulf nations to brief them on our deployment."

Finally I laughed. "I know none of you expected to stay over here. I'll try to get you back to the States in about three weeks, so you can pack your bags. Meanwhile, I promise that I'll call each of your wives and explain why you had to stay."

As they left to carry out my orders, I had Colonel Bell place the call I'd never expected to make. Using the secure telephone linking us to Central Command in Tampa, where it was about noon on Monday, August 6, I told General Rogers, my deputy commander in chief, that we were going to commit troops, and instructed him to have the Joint Chiefs of Staff give orders to deploy the first unit, the Division Ready Brigade of the 82nd Airborne, from Fort Bragg.

The next day, after meeting with the Saudi minister of defense and aviation, Prince Sultan, who hadn't been present the night before, Cheney and I flew to Alexandria, Egypt, to brief President Mubarak on our deployment and to seek his help; we needed rapid transit through the Suez Canal for our warships, as well as use of Egypt's airfields and airspace, if we were to meet our schedules. Mubarak had long since established himself as a strong leader with a major voice in Arab decision making. He was confident enough of his power to have publicly condemned the Iraqi aggression while at the same time actively seeking a negotiated settlement. He received us on a balcony of the Alexandria palace overlooking the Mediterranean and, after hearing what Cheney and I had to tell him, readily granted each request, until I said, "We might also like to use Egypt as a base for military aircraft."

"What kind?" he asked.

"Well, we may want to use it for B-52s," I said. Mubarak's eyebrows shot up—angry as he was at Iraq's aggression, he was not ready to let U.S. bombers operate from his soil. He said quietly, "I don't think we need to decide that right now."

We were on our way back across the Atlantic that evening when the White House informed us our mission wasn't yet complete: we had to detour to Morocco. Belatedly, the State Department had realized that, having met with King Fahd and President Mubarak, we would risk alienating the North African Arabs unless we also briefed King Hassan and asked his support. Arriving at his non-air-conditioned Casablanca palace late that evening, we waited in a sweltering antechamber for an hour while skeptical government officials asked questions. We couldn't disclose the nature of our mission, but given the rate at which news traveled in the Arab world, I felt sure they already knew. Finally we were summoned into the presence of the king, who turned out to be quite cordial and, in a private session with Cheney, promised his support.

Finally, seven hours later, our plane touched down at Andrews Air Force Base in Washington. It was well after midnight on Wednesday, August 8; a smaller jet waited nearby to take me back to Tampa. We stood for a moment in the muggy Washington night, at the base of the ramp next to Cheney's sedan. Thanking me for the briefings I'd given, he remarked, "We're involved in an historic event."

"Yes, sir. I know." I felt somewhat awed. We'd set in motion the largest U.S. deployment since Vietnam, an action that could easily lead to war—and I was commander in chief. I was also the person who had formulated the defense plan on which we were now staking soldiers' lives and the prestige of the United States. I prayed I had it right.

Cheney shook my hand and said, "Good luck, Norm." Then he got in his car and I headed back to Central Command. The next time we met would be in Riyadh.

17

7 AUG 90 C-DAY

0745 Called Mrs. Schwarzkopf and notified her of security at residence. Informed her they are there as a precaution and will ID all visitors as well as check grounds. Also thanked her for brownies she sent over last evening.

8 AUG 90 C + 1

1030 CINC [commander in chief] recommended to JCS this operation be called Peninsula Shield. Subsequently rejected—other names submitted.

—*from Colonel Bell's log*

Wednesday morning the first planeloads of American soldiers were touching down at the military air base outside Dhahran as I returned to the war room in Tampa. President Bush appeared on television at nine A.M., Eastern Standard Time, and declared that the United States was drawing a "line in the sand" against Iraq's aggression. At Central Command we finally came up with the name

Desert Shield, which reflected the order to defend the Arabian Peninsula, and we designated Tuesday, August 7, the day we got the go-ahead from the Joint Chiefs of Staff, as "C-day" (commencement day) for the deployment.

Saudi Arabia's oil wealth is concentrated on the gulf coast within two hundred miles of Kuwait, so I was concerned about Saddam Hussein's next move. My main worry was that a ground war would come to us. While "Pentagon sources" were telling journalists that our forces would be "impregnable" by the first weekend, I knew that the Iraqis could overrun the Saudi oil region in a week. Our soldiers knew it too: paratroopers from the 82nd Airborne Division at Dhahran nicknamed themselves "Iraqi speed bumps." In an attack their only option would be to pull back to an enclave on the coast and hope we could either reinforce them or get them out. It would have been something like the U.S. retreat to the Pusan perimeter in the early days of the Korean War—a very disturbing thought.

We had all the force we needed to prevent such a disaster. There was only one small problem: the force was still in the United States. We had a squadron of two dozen Cobras—helicopters bristling with antitank missiles—at Fort Bliss, Texas. We had a brigade of Apache attack helicopters in Major General Binney Peay's 101st Air Assault Division at Fort Campbell, Kentucky. We had four battalions of desert-camouflaged heavy tanks in Major General Barry McCaffrey's 24th Mechanized Infantry Division at Fort Stewart, Georgia. We had over a hundred A-10s—warplanes designed for attacking tanks—in Chuck Horner's Ninth Air Force, sitting on aprons at bases around the country. All we had to do was move the forces to the crisis. On the timetable we'd promised the President, that would mean a seven-thousand-mile shift of five and one third divisions, or 120,000 troops, in four months.

The science of logistics had come so far since World War II's IBM punch cards and clipboard-toting clerks that the Pentagon now possessed a computer system capable of producing an individual itinerary for every single piece of equipment we needed, from tanks to mess tents. In theory, all I had to do was push a button. Hours after Desert Shield began, our divisions should have been inundated with thousands of pages of printouts saying things like, "Send tank number 123 from the X Battalion of your Y Brigade by rail to Norfolk, Virginia, to be loaded on ship Z, which will sail for 20 days, to arrive at Dhahran harbor by August 30."

However, there was a big problem. Since we'd been in the middle of revising Central Command's battle plan when the crisis broke, we hadn't yet entered the data into the computer banks—a painstaking process that under normal circumstances takes a full year. Our only alternative was to schedule the airlift and sealift by hand. Moving even a single division is a horrendously complex task; for example, when fully reinforced, the 24th Mechanized Infantry—Central Command's first armored unit scheduled to deploy—consisted of four tank battalions, five mechanized infantry battalions, and three artillery battalions, plus ordnance battalions, transportation battalions, medical battalions, signal battalions, and helicopter squadrons, each with its own particular transportation needs. For the 24th to arrive in Saudi Arabia in fighting form, the movement of all those units had to be carefully synchronized: what was the sense in sending tanks if they arrived without ammunition, maintenance teams, and spare parts?

Central Command had three Army divisions of different types traveling, plus our Air Force units, plus elements of two Marine expeditionary forces (reinforced divisions of Marines). Naturally, all were competing for space in the same airplanes and cargo ships, and an enormous amount of my time was devoted to untangling snafus. The first question the transportation planners needed answered was: "What are your priorities?"

"Combat troops and tank-killing airplanes and helicopters!" I'd say. Then, in coordination with the various services, the planners would make up long lists of the forces that had to be deployed and then notify the U.S. Transportation Command, which was responsible for carrying out the airlift and sealift. Transportation Command in turn would rush its giant cargo planes, which were in short supply, to the appropriate bases to pick up the forces. That's when human nature would take over. Some high-ranking officer on the ground would decide that, just to be on the safe side, his unit really needed to bring more people and equipment than originally planned. So airplanes would take off carrying loads they weren't scheduled to carry. I was stunned when I learned that the first unit landing in Saudi Arabia was the airborne corps *headquarters staff.* I'd been imagining infantrymen—fighters!—coming off those airplanes, not a bunch of generals and staff officers and clerks. What if Saddam *had* attacked?

It soon became clear that we were going to come up short on our first week's goal of deploying a full reinforced airborne brigade. I kept calling in my staff, brandishing the charts we'd shown the President, and demanding, "This is the force we guaranteed! Why isn't it there?" The inevitable finger pointing started. Officers at Transportation Command told us: "We keep sending airplanes down to Fort Bragg and they keep loading on the wrong stuff!" The Airborne commander at Fort Bragg insisted, "I'm sitting here looking at an empty airfield. I've got troops lined up waiting and there isn't a single airplane anywhere!"

We were in danger of losing it. I called each of the generals whose subordinates were squabbling: General H. T. Johnson, commander in chief of Transportation Command and of Military Airlift Command; General Ed Burba, who'd succeeded Powell as chief of Forces Command; and Lieutenant General Gary Luck, commander of the XVIII Airborne Corps. After explaining the difficulty we'd encountered, I said, "Let's quit finger pointing. Nobody's trying to fix blame here. What we're trying to do is fix the problem. It's time to get the forces moving." Each of the generals was a good friend and a solid professional, so I knew the response I'd get. They put out the word and from then on, the Army's transportation turmoil started to sort itself out.

The Air Force was a whole different matter. The squadrons of F-15 and F-16 fighter planes it had promised flowed to Saudi Arabia wonderfully—a little *too* wonderfully, it turned out, because at the end of the first week we had not the five squadrons I'd expected, but ten. In a way, that was terrific: the safety of our arriving forces depended heavily on those fighters, which, along with the Saudi air force's own F-15s and British-made Tornados, were supposed to turn away any Iraqi air attacks and strike any invading tank columns. But each twenty-four-plane squadron also required more than fifteen hundred engineers, technicians, and armorers. Moving all those people and their equipment tied up dozens of flights we had allocated for other units.

I'd never dealt with anything so complex, nor had to make so many key decisions so quickly, in my life. Problems were coming at us from Washington, from Riyadh, from units and bases across the United States, and from our admirals who were preparing a blockade to enforce the United Nations trade embargo of Iraq, passed on August 6. I was accustomed to conferring with my staff on matters of importance but there was no time for that now. I just gave orders, one after another. The staff did a superb job of disseminating and interpreting the orders to other headquarters that weren't very familiar with the Middle East and our plan. Though this wasn't the way I preferred to work, I felt the urgency of the situation demanded it. I was there long enough to know plenty of the mistakes we had to avoid. One of the first orders I gave was that no alcohol or pornography was to be brought into Saudi Arabia. ("Pornography" meant girlie magazines as well as X-rated stuff.) I knew some of the troops—along with their congressmen—would complain, but liquor and pornography were against the law in Saudi Arabia, and nothing would have ruined our welcome sooner than for us to let it all hang out the way some Americans had in Vietnam.

As soon as our forces started touching down, I got worried calls from General Horner and General Yeosock. They reported that the Saudi military had taken the position, "Your soldiers are on our soil, so of course we're in charge of everything." We knew full well that the response of Americans would be, "Bull. *We're* sending most of the forces; *we* should be in charge of everything." Horner, Yeosock, and I agreed that for the alliance to have a prayer of working, we needed a hybrid system like the one we'd used in Vietnam, where Americans had fought under American commanders, South Vietnamese under South Vietnamese commanders, and the actions of the armies were coordinated at the very top. Though this approach violated an age-old principle of warfare called unity of command, I'd seen it in action, and I knew I could make it work even better in the gulf than it had in Vietnam. I presented the idea to Washington while Horner and Yeosock pitched it to the Saudis, and within a few days both sides had agreed. Egypt, Great Britain, and other nations were also talking about sending troops, but for the moment we left open the question of who would command them.

Such progress would have pleased me if Saddam hadn't seemed so hell-bent on raising the stakes. He kept pouring forces into Kuwait: in their border outposts the Saudis now found themselves looking down the gun barrels of nine Iraqi divisions (130,000 soldiers, 1,200 tanks, and 800 artillery pieces, many capable of firing toxic-chemical shells). To defend adequately against such a force we needed at least five weeks' buildup, and I was gravely concerned that the Iraqis would figure that out and attack now. My standing order to Chuck Horner was: "Before you go to bed at night, make absolutely sure that every one of your commanders—on the ground and at sea—knows what to do in the event of an attack."

On August 9, Saddam ordered the borders of Iraq and Kuwait closed, trapping more than thirteen thousand westerners and other foreigners and changing the entire nature of the crisis. The taking of American hostages could be cause for war and I felt sick to my stomach at the news. By the time we'd opted for Desert Shield, we'd completed our planning for symbolic air strikes, but symbolic is all they were. If the Iraqis started executing U.S. embassy employees, say, and the President wanted to retaliate, Central Command had little to offer short of a nuclear strike on Baghdad. I would never have recommended such a course of action, and even if I had, I am certain the President would never have approved it.

The following morning I called Colin Powell and asked that the Air Force put planners to work on a strategic bombing campaign aimed at Iraq's military, which would provide the retaliatory options we needed. The plan they came up with was code-named Instant Thunder; it would ultimately become the first phase of Desert Storm.

Meanwhile an Iraqi defector turned up in Egypt bearing a map that purported to show the plan for the Iraqi invasion of Saudi Arabia. There was no knowing whether it was genuine, but as I studied it, I immediately knew that if I'd been commanding the other side and had been ordered to take over Saudi Arabia, this was the precise plan I'd have laid out. It involved a three-pronged attack to be launched from Kuwait: one thrust down the coastal highway that led to Saudi oil fields and refineries and to the port of Al Jubayl; a second far to the west, along the highway to the sprawling Saudi base at King Khalid Military City; and a third across the desert straight toward Riyadh, 280 miles to the south. To mount such an attack Saddam would need to more than double his force in Kuwait, which would take several weeks. But if such an invasion began to take shape, we'd have to scramble to rearrange and expand our defense. I ordered my forward commanders to set up battle positions as a precaution on all three invasion routes.

14 AUG 90 C+7

1007 CINC cautioned Lieutenant General Horner on housing situation for U.S. troops. Reminded General Horner of Beirut Marine barracks terrorist attack and cautioned him against setting U.S. troops up for a similar situation.

Exactly one week into Desert Shield, Colin Powell arrived in Tampa and found me champing at the bit. Now that the initial snafus of the airlift and sealift had been resolved, I was anxious to get to Saudi Arabia. Yet I'd just learned I'd be stuck in Tampa for another week. I had to wait for my communications network to be installed over there. From my Tampa war room I could readily contact any commander and, for that matter, any of Central Command's planes in the air, ships at sea, and units on the ground in the Middle East; but in Saudi Arabia the available U.S. military communications systems were so anemic that we had to build a redundant, secure satellite-communications network from scratch.

Though Powell and I conferred by phone many times each day, we hadn't seen each other since Desert Shield had begun. The minute we sat down in my office, I raised a concern I'd been brooding about all week: I couldn't see where the operation was supposed to lead. I told Powell that the longer Saddam waited to launch his invasion, the more certain we were of being able to defend Saudi Arabia. But suppose the invasion never came? I couldn't imagine the United States simply pulling out while Iraq still occupied Kuwait. Nor could I imagine waiting a year or more for diplo-

matic or economic pressure to convince Saddam to withdraw—the mothers
and fathers of America would never put up with the idea of their sons and
daughters roasting in the hot sun all that time. Nor was I sure how long the
soldiers themselves would tolerate such an assignment. The only alternative,
I told Powell, would be to attack—a course of action I'd warned the
President would involve a much larger military commitment than we'd
made. Powell replied that he was as worried as I about where Desert Shield
would lead, but that nothing more had been decided by the White House.
When he left, I thought at least he and I were in basic agreement.

Two days later I was called to the Pentagon to help the Joint Chiefs
brief President Bush on the progress of Desert Shield. When the meeting in
the Tank broke up, the President and Secretary Cheney went upstairs to
Cheney's office while Powell invited me into his. I knew that later that
morning the President was scheduled to make a speech to Pentagon employees, which Powell and I were supposed to attend.

As soon as we sat down Powell asked, "If you had to kick the Iraqis out
of Kuwait right now, how would you do it?"

"What? I wouldn't. I couldn't! I've made it clear to everyone that we
aren't sending enough forces to do that."

"Suppose you were ordered to."

I went cold. I actually had asked my planners to look into conducting
an offensive using only the forces we were sending for Desert Shield. They'd
studied the problem and come back with, "It can't be done." The one
possibility they'd offered was a plan to attack straight into Kuwait, thereby
cutting the Iraqi supply lines. But we all knew that was a high-risk mission
that could waste thousands of American lives.

"I'll show you," I told Powell grimly, sketching a map of Kuwait on a
piece of paper and indicating where the attack could take place. "We could
seize this crucial road junction near Jahra northwest of Kuwait City and
block the flow of supplies to their front lines. If we could hold it, they would
be forced to withdraw. But it would be crazy as hell and we'd probably end
up losing the entire force."

He nodded, and we went on to other business. When I got up to leave
he said, "Would you mind if I kept the sketch?"

Twenty minutes later he called me back to his office and told me that
he'd met with Bush and Cheney. "I've shown your offensive plan to the
President," he added.

I was thunderstruck. "Wait a minute! Jesus! That's not my recommendation!" In the chain of command, Powell was my link to the top, and I was
worried that he'd volunteered us for a course of action that could lead to

disaster. But he reassured me: "Don't worry, Norm. I just used it as an illustration." We walked outside to where the President was about to speak. We both still felt that America's show of force in Saudi Arabia would probably cause Iraq to back down and offer some sort of compromise. "I don't see us going to war over Kuwait," Powell said again. "Saudi Arabia, yes, if we had to; but not Kuwait." I agreed.

A throng of Pentagon employees and reporters had by now gathered outside the River Entrance. Powell took his place on the dais with Secretary Cheney; I sat in the front row. Soon President Bush appeared—and launched into a fiery speech calling for "the immediate, complete, and unconditional withdrawal of all Iraqi forces from Kuwait." He went on to label Saddam Hussein a liar and to compare him to Adolf Hitler. I gave Powell a glance—this did not sound like a leader bent on compromise—and he met my eyes impassively. The United States's response to the crisis was still escalating.

As President Bush continued, I was swept up by his words in spite of myself. I was inspired to hear the President of the United States speak of making a stand "not simply to protect resources or real estate, but to protect the freedom of nations." He looked right at me a couple of times, and at the end, when he said, "There is no substitute for American leadership, and American leadership cannot be effective in the absence of America's strength," and told us he was relying on us and was honored to be our commander in chief, I felt very proud that I was part of this momentous undertaking.

Afterward, as the President started to get into his car, he stopped, straightened up, came over to me, and shook my hand. Everybody got that on videotape. "Good luck, Norm. We're with you all the way," he said.

I answered, echoing his speech, "I'm proud that you're our commander in chief."

On the way back to Tampa that afternoon, I had the front cabin of the Air Force jet to myself—my first time alone since the start of the crisis. I gazed out the window at a brilliant, sunny day and felt euphoric that the briefing to the President had gone so well, that I'd had a front-row seat at his speech, and that he'd personally recognized me on national television—it all went to my head. For the moment I forgot all about the worries waiting for me back at Central Command and thought, "If this thing turns out right, maybe I should reconsider my retirement plans. I've been thrust into the limelight—I could end up chief of staff of the Army!" Other people, most significantly Colin Powell, had told me I was a contender for the Army's top job; suddenly it seemed like a real and appealing possibility.

But only for a few minutes. As we flew on, I reminded myself, "Schwarzkopf, you've *never* wanted to be chief of staff." For one thing, it would mean living and working in Washington for four more years. More important, I realized that during this crisis I didn't want my judgment clouded by concern with how my decisions would affect my chances for a job. I'd been down the careerism road before, during the dark phase of my life that followed my service in Vietnam, and I wasn't going to make the same mistake. So I decided again, this time irrevocably, that in August 1991, I would retire. Or if Desert Shield went on longer than that, I'd stay until the job was done right, or until I got fired.

18 AUG 90 C + 11

1710 Conversation with General Denny Reimer, Army deputy chief of staff for operations. It is clearer today that what they are doing in Kuwait is digging in.

21 AUG 90 C + 14

0715 CINC wanted General Horner. Abu Nidal has committed to Iraq to strike U.S. targets in Saudi Arabia. I want a sense of urgency about getting people out of hotels. Use U.S. Military Training Mission, three or four to a room, tents in athletic field, etc. This is not business as usual. I don't want this handled routinely. I want a response within twenty-four hours on what you are doing.

Saddam replied to the President's speech at the Pentagon with a rhetorical blast of his own: "You, the President of the United States . . . have lied to your people. . . . You are going to be defeated." He didn't actually deliver the speech himself—it came in the form of an "open letter" read by a government spokesman on Iraqi TV. In the war room we monitored the broadcast, listening as the Iraqi leader threatened our troops: "Thousands of Americans whom you have pushed into this dark tunnel will go home shrouded in sad coffins."

I knew the speech was mostly propaganda: I could see the reality, there in the war room, on a huge graphic display board that gave an up-to-the-minute picture of how Iraq's forces were deployed. What it showed forty-eight hours later was the Republican Guard divisions *pulling back* a bit from the Saudi-Kuwait border. Though my intelligence experts warned that other armored units had moved into the front lines and that the Republican

Guard could return to an attack formation with as little as twenty-four hours' notice, it seemed that the Iraqis had blinked and that, for the first time, the likelihood of an immediate invasion had decreased. I was grateful for any breathing room we could get. Next to the display devoted to Iraq's troops was a map of our own deployment: it showed the Saudi oil fields still exposed and our positions limited to defensive perimeters around key airfields and ports. Desert Shield had barely begun to take shape.

What was most on my mind was the threat Saddam *hadn't* talked about: terrorist bombings. Our forces were now pouring in so fast that in Riyadh alone the Air Force had three thousand people billeted in high-rise luxury hotels. We kept receiving intelligence reports that the hotels had been singled out as targets. I browbeat my forward commanders to get those people spread out—into tents, if necessary—so they weren't piled on top of each other in a "vertical target" that a single bomb could destroy. I was desperate to avoid a repetition of the events of October 23, 1983, when a truck bomb killed 241 U.S. Marines in their barracks in Beirut.

On Thursday, August 16, Colonel John Warden and a team of Air Force officers showed up from Washington to brief me on their plan for Instant Thunder, our retaliatory air campaign. I was leery of Warden, who was from the Curtis LeMay school of Air Force planners—guys who think strategic bombing can do it all and that armies are obsolete. In 1988 he'd published a book called *The Air Campaign: Planning for Combat*, which had a section headed, "War Can Be Won from the Air." But to my delight he turned out to be a flexible thinker who was just as knowledgeable about close air support—the kind of air strike used to support soldiers on the battlefield—as he was about strategic bombing.

Warden had brought along a couple of young planners; with me were Bob Johnston, Burt Moore, and B. B. Bell. We'd scheduled the briefing for nine o'clock at night—four A.M. in the war zone—because that was usually the quietest period of the day, and we met in a small, bare, fluorescent-lit conference room down the hall from the war room.

Less than a week had passed since I'd called the Pentagon for help, yet Warden and his team had put together a remarkably good plan. Though no one had told us, "We don't want you to destroy Iraq as a nation," my assumption in directing the planners had been that the United States would continue to need Iraq as a regional counterbalance to Iran. Warden had come up with a strategy designed to cripple Iraq's military without laying waste to the country.

The targets were grouped into categories, the first being Iraq's leadership. After the shooting started we repeatedly asserted that the United

States was not trying to kill Saddam Hussein—President Bush said so himself—and that was true, to a point. But at the very top of our target list were the bunkers where we knew he and his senior commanders were likely to be working. Because of Iraq's highly centralized system of command and control, Saddam was what military theorists call an enemy center of gravity—an aspect of the opposing force that, if destroyed, will cause the enemy to lose its will to fight. (Clausewitz, the great Prussian philosopher of war, defined the concept of a center of gravity in his 1832 book, *Vom Kriege*.) For our purposes, it was sufficient to *silence* Saddam—to destroy his ability to command the forces arrayed against ours. If he'd been killed in the process, I wouldn't have shed any tears. We also targeted communications facilities and television and radio transmitters to keep Saddam from passing orders to his soldiers.

Warden then laid out how the Air Force proposed to knock out Saddam's antiaircraft installations, airfields, missile storage sites, munitions plants, weapons labs, oil refineries, bridges, and railroads. The planners had come up with *hundreds* of major targets, and I was again struck by the degree to which Saddam had transformed his country into an armed camp.

I asked how long the Air Force would need to do all this bombing. "Six days," Warden replied—assuming Central Command had at its disposal thirty-five squadrons of airplanes, or roughly double the number we'd thus far been assigned. Even with double the air power, his estimate seemed to me optimistic. But I now had something else on my mind.

"If we flesh this out, we'll have the retaliatory package we're looking for," I said. "Now let's talk about what happens if we have to extend this into an offensive campaign." I looked around the table; nobody batted an eye. "What would you have to do if we wanted our airplanes to operate freely over the battlefield in Kuwait?"

"Immediately destroy their air defenses," Warden replied, adding that doing so in Kuwait would be tough. The air defense system in Iraq consisted of fixed installations—easy to pinpoint and therefore easy to target—while those in Kuwait were mobile weapons that had been brought in by the invading troops. These included radar-guided Soviet SA-8 and SA-13 missiles and radar-controlled ZSU-23 and ZSU-24 flak guns. "We *can* do it," he concluded, "but it would take another two to four days."

"Good enough," I said. "Now, after that, what if I wanted you to pound and weaken their army so we could attack successfully?" Pulling a number out of the air, I said I'd need fifty percent of the Iraqi occupying forces destroyed before launching whatever ground offensive we might eventually plan.

As we talked I'd been scribbling notes, laying out the concept for a four-phase campaign:

1. Instant Thunder.
2. Suppression of air defenses over Kuwait.
3. Attrition of enemy force by fifty percent.
4. Ground attack. (?)

I showed the notes to Warden and said, "Here's how an offense might look. But there's one more thing: the Republican Guard is another center of gravity of Iraq's army. While you're running your phase-one campaign over Iraq, why can't you be bombing the Republican Guard in Kuwait?"

He shook his head. "Too dangerous. We won't have suppressed the air defenses in Kuwait yet."

"What about B-52s? Can the Iraqis hit B-52s?"

"No," he acknowledged. Flying at thirty thousand feet and equipped with the latest jamming devices, the B-52s would be invulnerable.

"Okay. If it comes to this, I want the Republican Guard bombed the very first day, and I want them bombed every day after that. They're the heart and soul of his army and therefore they will pay the price."

As we ended the meeting, I parceled out assignments. I sent Warden and his men to Saudi Arabia to hand off further stages of the air-campaign planning to General Horner and his staff. Horner had not been happy that I'd asked the Pentagon for planning help. Actually, he'd been furious: "Sir, the last thing we want is a repeat of Vietnam, where Washington picked the targets! This is the job of your Air Force commander." I'd reminded him that as my forward commander in Riyadh he had his hands full, and promised he could take over once the preliminary work was done.

I then told General Johnston to explain the concept for a four-phase campaign to our senior staff. Now that we had defined a framework, we could embark on the lengthy planning process needed to turn the concept into something we could execute. Finally I handed my notes to Colonel Bell to add to my log. "What are we going to call this thing?" Bell asked.

"We don't want it mixed up with Desert Shield," I said. "Why not call it 'Desert Storm'?" Everybody approved; we also agreed to keep Instant Thunder as the code name for phase one.

The next morning I reported to Colin Powell that I'd come up with a concept for an offensive campaign, and described the four phases I'd scribbled down. We had no ground-attack operation to propose for phase four, I said, and I doubted we could come up with a satisfactory one without a whole lot more troops. But I intended to turn my planners loose on the problem once I reached Riyadh. Then I told him the new code name. He seemed pleased and said he'd pass the information on to Secretary Cheney.

———

Within a few days of the President's Pentagon speech events had begun to move very fast. The White House proceeded with a naval blockade, despite the fact that the United Nations Security Council had not yet granted permission to reinforce the embargo by military means. That raised the tension at Central Command considerably. Under international law, a blockade is an act of war; if we were to sink one of Saddam's supertankers, he would have a pretext to launch an invasion or retaliate in some other way. Once people start shooting at each other, it is never easy to remain just a little bit at war.

The following evening in the gulf, we picked up the presence of the first Iraqi ships: two small, beat-up intercoastal tankers, heading home empty. Our ships were ready to blow them out of the water. Vice Admiral Hank Mauz, my Navy commander, radioed, "What do we do?"

Our orders said nothing about empty ships. I tried to phone General Powell but he wasn't in. We asked his staff, but they had no additional instructions for us. Finally I dug out a copy of the United Nations resolution. It stated that the embargo's purpose was to block all exports and imports; that seemed to mean that Iraq should be able neither to sell its ill-gotten gains from Kuwait, nor to obtain supplies for its war effort. It seemed to me that empty tankers violated neither condition. So I called Admiral Mauz and said, "Let them go. There's no use starting World War Three over empty tankers."

A few hours later, Powell was on the phone telling me that Secretary Cheney felt I was not obeying orders. Powell himself was on edge—we were all working under tremendous pressure. I burst out, "For chrissakes, I didn't have any guidance! I tried to call you. I got no help from the Joint Staff. You're paying us to exercise good judgment. The only thing I had to go on was the language of the United Nations resolution."

"Well, you made the wrong decision."

"Okay. Now that you've made it clear what you want, the next tanker that comes through, we'll blow it away."

Fourteen hours later, on Saturday afternoon in the Middle East, another Iraqi ship came along—a fully loaded oil tanker on its way out of the gulf. The U.S.S. *Reid*, a Navy frigate, fired two sets of warning shots across the bow, but the tanker didn't stop. Meanwhile we received a frantic call from the Joint Staff revising our orders: we were not to sink the ship without a go-ahead from the White House. So we fired a third set of warning shots. The Iraqi captain radioed that he would not stop, adding cryptically that he had an international crew on board. We called the Pentagon again and said, "We're ready. Awaiting permission to shoot." At the same time, the Iraqi ship notified Baghdad that it had been fired on by Americans. I called General Horner in Riyadh to warn that an Iraqi attack might be imminent, and put my naval and air forces on high alert, ready to launch retaliatory strikes.

The President was on vacation in Kennebunkport, so it took a while for Washington to confer with him and General Scowcroft. An hour and a half later the decision came down: "Give the Iraqi one more warning, by radio. Tell him if he doesn't stop, we will shoot at the bridge and stern of his ship to disable the steering. If he still doesn't stop, warn him to move his crew forward. Give them time to evacuate the stern. Then fire a shot over the stern as a final warning. Tell him, 'This is your last chance—the next one will hit you.' Then fire to disable the ship. But don't sink it."

By the time the orders got back out to the gulf, it was dusk. Admiral Mauz said, "Jeez, we can't see well enough to do that." So we were off the hook until daybreak, having been treated to a classic illustration of what happens when Washington tries to direct combat operations from afar. Under most circumstances, being "micromanaged" would have made me furious, but in this case I didn't mind. Obviously someone in Washington had belatedly realized that sinking an Iraqi ship would be a major escalation and had decided that the United States should make every effort to turn back the tanker before attacking it. That was fine with me—and it made me doubly glad I'd decided to spare the empty tankers the day before.

During the night, cooler heads prevailed. Powell called and revised our orders for the fourth time in twenty-four hours: "Don't engage that ship. Continue tracking it, but the UN ambassador is making progress getting approval for the blockade from the Security Council and we don't want to precipitate anything." Until the Security Council finally authorized the blockade a week later, we restricted ourselves to shadowing Iraq's ships.

The tanker we'd almost attacked chugged onward to Yemen, where the Yemenis declared they would observe the embargo and not unload the oil. That Iraqi captain knew how close he'd come to getting blown out of the water—we'd been listening to him radioing Baghdad in a panic and being told things like, "Press on, my friend, and when you become a martyr, you will be posthumously decorated by Saddam himself." When the fellow reached Yemen, he contracted a mysterious illness and had to be evacuated back to Iraq. We took bets that his ailment had to do with the fact that he did not want to come back out and face the guns of the United States Navy.

———

The President's next move was to call up the reserves. He had the authority to activate up to 200,000 reserves for up to 180 days without asking Congress, and by doing so he gave a powerful signal to the people of the United States that we had a job to do as a nation. I was in favor of this move: I'd always been convinced that one of the terrible mistakes we'd made during the Vietnam War was *not* mobilizing—Washington sent our soldiers into battle without calling on the American people to support them.

The call-up, not surprisingly, touched off a bureaucratic free-for-all at the Pentagon that involved the chiefs of the Army, Navy, Air Force, and Marine Corps, the commanding general of Forces Command, and the generals in charge of various elements of the National Guard. Everybody was arguing about which reserve units ought to go to the gulf. Because the Central Command war plan was only half complete, we hadn't gotten to the point of earmarking specific reserve units. So the chiefs of the Army, Navy, Air Force, and Marine Corps produced estimates of how many reservists *they* thought were required. The total—more than 300,000 people—was bigger than all of Desert Shield and many times what the President had in mind. Powell finally called in desperation and quite correctly dumped the problem into my lap: "The services are out of control. *You* sort it out, and I'll okay only the units you request."

I knew precisely what we needed: truck drivers, stevedores, ammunition handlers, telephone installers, mechanics—workers to take on the nitty-gritty tasks of supporting a deployment in a combat zone. The hard part was getting that message through to some of the people in Washington. I had heated discussions with my old boss General Vuono and his staff about National Guard combat units known as "roundout brigades." A creation of the past twenty years, these were designed to be activated in wartime to complete divisions that we normally maintained at two-thirds strength to save personnel and money. Vuono wanted to prove the concept worked, and congressmen from the states where the Guard units were based were clamoring to have them join Desert Shield. But the roundout brigades made no sense for the 180-day call-up the President was talking about. Once activated, these troops would need months of training to be ready for combat; by the time we sent them to the Middle East, I'd have to worry about bringing them home. I ended up telling Vuono, "I understand your political problem but goddammit, we're fighting a war now."

Powell backed me, as did the commander of Forces Command, General Ed Burba, and the roundout brigades were removed from the call-up list. Since the readiness of the National Guard was one of Burba's responsibilities, he knew better than anyone whether the units were prepared to deploy. To his great credit and at some risk to his own career, he spoke against their use, preferring to acknowledge the units' limitations rather than send men to war unprepared. Even after the decision was made, the controversy went on and on in Congress and the newspapers until, in September, a roundout brigade from Georgia was sent to the National Training Center in the Mojave Desert to see how long it would actually take to bring it to combat readiness. After sixty days, it still wasn't ready. At that point even some of the congressmen who had been vocal on the issue had to admit that roundout brigades might be better suited to a longer war.

The call-up question was the last big one I had to resolve before leaving Tampa. By this time the airlift and sealift were working so effectively that, on August 21, General Johnson of Transportation Command and Military Airlift Command gave a triumphant news conference at which he boasted that his airplanes and ships had carried a huge number of people and that one billion pounds of weapons, ammunition, and other supplies had arrived at or were en route to the gulf. He compared this to moving all the men, women, and children in Jefferson City, Missouri, to Saudi Arabia—along with their cars, trucks, household goods, food, and water supply. The effort by then was so huge that controllers at the Military Airlift Command were tracking as many as eighty planes at a time winging their way across the Atlantic. (They nicknamed the airlift their "aluminum bridge to the Middle East.") Meanwhile, huge loads of tanks and other heavy equipment were closing in on Saudi ports on board the Military Sealift Command's "Fast Sealift Ships," souped-up freighters that steamed at more than thirty knots (equivalent to thirty-five miles per hour); dozens of other cargo ships were scheduled to follow.

Finally the communications networks in Saudi Arabia were installed, and on August 23 I notified Colin Powell that I was ready to move my headquarters to Riyadh. I told him that Buck Rogers, my deputy commander in chief, had agreed to stay in Tampa and hold the fort; I knew I could count on him to keep the forces flowing smoothly from stateside. Powell recognized that I had to go, but admitted he liked having me within easy reach of Washington, and was concerned that I'd become inaccessible once I left the States. In our day-to-day communications, Powell and I had developed an unusual modus operandi that would continue through Desert Storm. We conferred by secure telephone, usually several times a day, and when we had to exchange written information, we did so outside normal Pentagon channels. We each had a fax machine hooked to a secure telephone line; if I had an important document or diagram I wanted him to see, I'd hand it to Colonel Bell, who would notify Powell's office it was on its way and then stand by the machine until the fax went through. At the other end Powell's executive officer would be waiting by his machine to catch the message and put it directly into Powell's hands.

We figured that was the only way we could be sure of maintaining secrecy. During the year and a half I'd worked in the Tank I'd heard Powell's predecessor, Admiral Crowe, say over and over, "Once something is put in writing in Washington, D.C., you can consider it compromised." When messages came to the Joint Staff—top-secret messages to the Pentagon's inner sanctum—they would be logged, reproduced, and distributed to various staff directors, who would in turn make copies for their deputies, their deputies' deputies, and so on—until before you knew it the information showed up in *The Washington Post*. Handling everything by secure phone and secure fax ensured that nothing ever leaked; of course, it also meant there was no official record of many of our communications.

Officially, as a commander in chief, I reported to Secretary Cheney, but Colin Powell was virtually my sole point of contact with the Administration. "It's my job to keep the President and the White House and the secretary of defense informed," Powell would say. "You worry about your theater and let me worry about Washington." This arrangement was efficient: I'd tell Powell we needed to get something done in Washington and he'd make sure it happened. And there is no doubt in my mind that General Powell was the best man for the job during this crisis. Not since General George Marshall during World War II had a military officer enjoyed such direct access to White House inner circles—not to mention the confidence of the President. Powell could get decisions in hours that would have taken another man days or weeks. But I also found the arrangement unnerving at times, because it kept me in the dark. Often, after White House meetings, Powell would call with questions that made me wonder whether our civilian superiors had grasped military realities.

For example, when Saddam announced on August 19 that he would use westerners as human shields to keep the United States from bombing Iraq, Powell called right away and wanted to know: "What are you going to do about the human shields?" I'd kept him briefed all along and thought he knew the unhappy answer as well as I. We'd been weighing hostage-rescue possibilities since the crisis began, and what had quickly become apparent was that the United States couldn't do much about captives in Iraq; for starters, our "human intelligence" sources were poor, and it was difficult even to pinpoint where the hostages were.

I had to tell Powell, "That's not my call. We can't get most of them out. We'll make every effort to find out where they are, but if we go to war and they're on essential targets, the President will have to make a very tough decision." Central Command couldn't solve the problem Saddam was giving us: it was a moral and political choice.

When I called Powell at the Pentagon to say I was ready to leave for Riyadh, he quizzed me closely about whether he'd still be able to reach me by phone. "Are you sure the communications are in? I can't afford not to be able to get hold of you." Then he added, almost as an afterthought, "On your way, I'd like you to stop here in Washington and give me a full briefing on your offensive-campaign plan—air and ground both."

It took me about five minutes to register what he'd said. I told my staff I needed to talk to the chairman in private and asked them to clear the war room. Then I got Powell back on the line. "I want to make sure of something that I thought we'd decided before," I said, trying to keep my voice steady. "I briefed a defensive plan to the President, I'm following orders to put a defensive force in place, and all of a sudden you guys in Washington are asking me to prepare an offense using that defensive force. Something is wrong here. I can give you my conceptual analysis, but that's all it is—apart from the phase-one air attack, it's nothing I'd recommend, nothing we've actually planned, nothing I'd act on. I'm afraid somebody who doesn't understand that is going to turn around and say 'execute this offensive.'"

"Norman! Trust me. You've got to trust me," Powell exclaimed. "Do you think I'd ever let that happen? My problem is that I've got all these hawks in the National Security Council who keep saying we ought to kick Saddam out of Kuwait now. I've got to have something to keep them under control."

Powell seemed to be gambling that if he could convince the White House that the military had the crisis under control and was making progress toward developing contingency war plans, we wouldn't be ordered to do anything rash. I decided that he was right—not that it mattered, because I had no choice but to go along. On Saturday morning, August 25, I met Powell in the nearly deserted Pentagon, brought him up to date on our strategic bombing plans, and discussed how such an air campaign might serve as a prelude to a ground offensive. But I emphasized again and again that the idea of launching our existing ground forces into Kuwait seemed no less foolish than it had before.

24 AUG 90 C + 17

1300 CINC spoke with General Reimer, Army deputy chief of staff for operations. What I need are some voices in Washington to stand up and be counted and say that's dumb— we shouldn't be pushed into doing something we are not ready and capable of doing. People in Washington are anxious to push us into doing something but we may not be ready and if it all goes to shit we, the military commanders, are left holding the bag.

———

I'd waited until I was sure of my departure date to tell my family I was leaving. Before Iraq had invaded Kuwait, we'd been looking forward to the third week of August in the Schwarzkopf household: Cindy and I were going to celebrate our birthdays and Jessica was starting college at the University of Tampa, where Brenda and I had planned to attend family orientation day. Now I was going to miss it all. When I finally gathered Brenda and the children to tell them I was about to leave, I gave a little speech. "I want you to understand that there is no place I would rather be than here with you, but I'm a soldier. And when a soldier is called to go, he has to go. But I don't want you ever to think that means I don't love you."

Brenda knew I would be gone for the duration of the crisis. She'd heard me talk this way once before—early in our marriage, when I'd left for my second tour in Vietnam. But that was before our children were born, and although they'd spent their entire lives adjusting to my military comings and goings—Cindy was now almost twenty, Jessica eighteen, and Christian thirteen—I'd never been away for more than a month, even during the Grenada crisis. Now I was telling them that I was about to pick up my headquarters and move seven thousand miles.

They said they understood, but they really didn't. Five days later, as I stood by the door hugging everyone good-bye, I murmured to Brenda, "I wish I could tell you when I'm going to see you again." Cindy stared at me, shocked.

"You're going to be home for *Christmas*, aren't you? It just wouldn't be Christmas without you."

"Cindy, I don't know." I took one look at her face and rushed to add that in every war America had ever fought, the commander had always been called to Washington for periodic consultations. I promised I would visit home whenever I came back to the States. I never imagined that I wouldn't be back at all.

stepped out of the airplane into a blast of desert heat. The temperature at the Riyadh military airport was 115 degrees in the shade, and it was only midmorning. Waiting for me at the base of the stairs were the senior commanders I'd left behind, Chuck Horner and John Yeosock, and a burly Saudi military man I didn't recognize. Horner quickly introduced him as Lieutenant General Prince Khalid Bin Sultan al-Saud, commander of the kingdom's air-defense forces and the man King Fahd had appointed as my counterpart. It struck me that the prince had inherited his size from his grandfather King Abdulaziz al-Saud, the founder of Saudi Arabia. He was as big as me.

Khalid's appointment was Horner's and Yeosock's first victory. Initially they had tried working with the various other Saudi generals, only to find that, while they were friendly and cooperative, nothing got done. King Fahd had pledged fuel, water, and transportation for the incoming American forces, but even on such simple matters as leasing supply trucks, the generals would say with embarrassment, "We want to help, but we're not authorized to spend the money."

After ten days of this, Horner and Yeosock had appealed in frustration to Prince Sultan, the minister of defense and aviation. Prince Sultan, in turn, had conferred with his brother the king, and their response had been to put Khalid, Sultan's eldest son, in charge. Khalid was ideal: he'd been educated at Sandhurst, the British military school, had attended the U.S. Air Force Air War College at Maxwell Air Force Base in Alabama, held a master's degree in political science from Auburn University, and was the highest-ranking prince in the Saudi armed forces. His military credentials were nowhere near as important as his princely blood, since almost all power in Saudi Arabia resides in an inner circle of the royal family. Simply put, unlike the other generals, Khalid had the authority to write checks. Now, when Horner and Yeosock needed trucks, all they had to do was ask the prince and they got trucks. Our forces also started getting the promised fuel and water.

To welcome me, Khalid had arranged a traditional coffee ceremony in a reception hall at the base. A huge Persian carpet covered the floor (I later learned the rug was so heavy that the Saudis had knocked out a wall and brought it in by crane). Khalid and I sat on a sofa at the hall's far end, Chuck and John sat to my left, and the air-base commander and members of Khalid's staff were to his right. As the strong, cardamom-laced coffee was being served, the prince and I exchanged pleasantries. Khalid came on as a bluff, genial, hail-fellow-well-met sort, but Horner and Yeosock had cautioned me that he was actually very concerned about this meeting. Though the prince had been comfortable working with them—fellow three-stars—when he found out that I was coming he'd asked a lot of questions and become very wary. Horner and Yeosock had guessed he was worried that with my higher rank and broad experience as a commander I'd try to bulldoze him or order him around. I had no such intention, and as Khalid recognized this in the days that followed, we became true friends and effective colleagues. He concluded our brief welcome by saying, "My staff will contact your staff about when we can meet."

We drove in heavily armored Mercedeses downtown to the Ministry of Defense building—headquarters for Desert Shield. The Saudis had given me an imperial-sized second-floor office hung with large oil portraits of King Fahd, Crown Prince Abdullah, and Prince Sultan. At one end was a big, modern wooden desk with my red high-security phone to Washington on a shelf behind it. Along the other three walls were white brocade overstuffed chairs and large marble cubes that served as coffee tables. Adjoining the office were a bedroom and a small bathroom with a shower, all very plain. The bedroom looked out onto a concrete courtyard where pigeons were roosting.

Horner had called a few days before to pass on an invitation from the Saudi government: "The Saudis have picked out a *palace* for you. You've gotta see it to believe it—when you go in the front door you walk through an arch of elephant tusks!" I'd politely declined—as Horner had known I would. Meanwhile, my staff had reserved a suite for me directly across the street from the ministry at the luxury Hyatt, where several of my senior officers were already staying. But as I'd been the one harping about getting people *out* of hotels, I could hardly check into one. A third possibility was a suite in the Saudi officers' club, more than three miles away.

"I'll just sleep here tonight," I announced. It was where I ended up living for nine months.

The first thing I wanted to do was visit the war rooms: down two elevators, through a heavily guarded long hallway, down a flight of stairs, and finally through heavy doors. In the subbasement, five stories below ground, the Saudis had made provision for a major command post that they'd never gotten around to completing. Three weeks before, this space had been empty; now it was the nerve center for Desert Shield.

Yeosock's deputy commander, Major General Paul Schwartz, led me into a huge room, two stories high, crowded with military men and desks. I'd been delighted when the Army assigned Schwartz to Desert Shield; having earlier served as project manager for the Saudi national guard, Paul liked the Saudis and worked well with them. This room was his creation, a coordination center where Saudi and U.S. liaison officers from every military branch and specialty worked side by side: air force men with air force men, coast guardsmen with coast guardsmen, air-defense planners with air-defense planners, and so on. High on one wall overlooking everything was a glassed-in mezzanine conference room that served as the U.S. command post while our technicians built a full-fledged command-and-control facility down the hall. This facility replicated as fully as possible our command center in Tampa. Eventually it would consist of an intelligence center, a communications room, offices for the staff, a small auditorium that could seat forty for briefings, and most important, a war room that would be my command post if a war started. The Saudis, meanwhile, had equipped their own command center one floor above.

Paul introduced me to the Saudi and U.S. colonels responsible for operating the coordination center. I asked for a progress report on our deployment of forces, and they directed my attention to a giant map on the wall behind me. It reflected a plan prepared by Horner, Khalid, and their staffs that positioned U.S. and Saudi forces along the Saudi-Kuwaiti border in the initial defense of the kingdom. Immediately I saw a big problem. We'd faxed them the Iraqi battle plan obtained from the defector two weeks before—the one calling for a massive three-pronged invasion—and yet, because of a shortage of forces, *they'd left one of the avenues of approach wide open!* The coastal highway leading from Kuwait to Al Jubayl was defended, as was the western highway leading to King Khalid Military City. But in the middle of the border—where the Iraqis had drawn their third prong—was a yawning, unguarded gap at least forty miles wide. If Saddam wanted, he could launch a thousand tanks on that axis and nobody would notice until they were deep in our rear.

I decided not to raise a ruckus in the presence of our Saudi counterparts. "This is a good start," was all I could manage. We walked away from the map and I said quietly to Colonel Bell, "Make sure you take a picture of that and save it. It'll remind us where we started."

———

When I hit Riyadh, I was prepared to work around the clock if necessary to deliver on our promises to the President and to make sure—to the extent possible—that our troops returned unhurt. Intelligence estimates now said that Saddam Hussein could throw 150,000 troops and 1,200 tanks against us in a heartbeat. I worried about getting kicked back into the sea and losing thousands and thousands of lives, and knew that my first priority was to eliminate that danger as fast as I could.

But I had to mask my sense of urgency in my dealings with the Saudis. To my consternation, their most pressing concern was neither the threat from Saddam nor the enormous joint military enterprise on which we were embarked. What loomed largest for them was the cultural crisis triggered by the sudden flood of Americans into their kingdom. We'd done what we could to forestall problems before the troops arrived: we'd banned alcohol and sexy magazines, lectured the troops on cultural sensitivity, and distributed a primer called *The Military Guide to Arab Culture* that had been hastily put together by the Central Command staff (one section began: "Men and women cannot touch each other in public, but there is a lot of touching between individuals of the same sex . . ."). But nothing we did was going to eliminate the culture shock completely. For example, merchants in downtown Dhahran were appalled when off-duty women soldiers started browsing in their stores: troops in a war zone take their weapons with them wherever they go, so these women had assault rifles slung over their shoulders! At a warehouse we'd rented, women soldiers unloading boxes of medical supplies took off their fatigue jackets and worked in their T-shirts. We got angry complaints about women disrobing in public; Saudi women never show their arms in public. Most of these incidents took place around the air base and port city of Dhahran, where foreigners were an everyday sight. What I really worried about was touching off a much bigger backlash in Riyadh, a city that until the late seventies had been practically

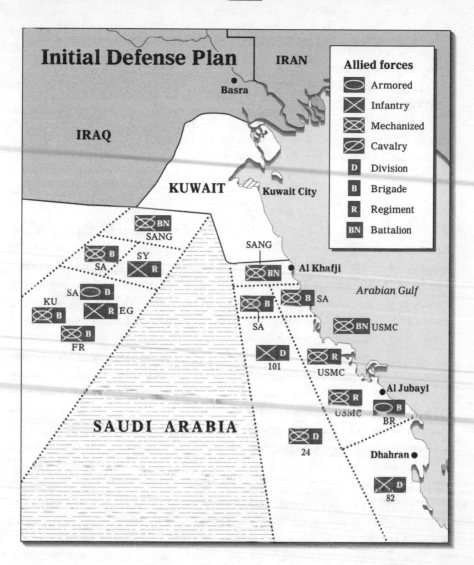

The initial defense plan was predicated on the use of all forces that were available or promised. These included Saudi Arabian National Guard battalions (SANG); Saudi (SA), Kuwaiti (KU), Egyptian (EG), Syrian (SY), French (FR), and British (BR) brigades; and U.S. Marine (USMC) and Army (24, 82, and 101) divisions.

closed to foreigners. When I'd taken over Central Command in 1988, the two-star general in charge of our military training mission was permitted to enter Riyadh on official business, but always had to depart for his quarters in Dhahran before dark. Now we had thousands of personnel in Riyadh.

I kept reminding myself that I had a lot of guys who could do the military planning, but I was the only one who could assure the Saudis that the Dallas Cowgirls were not going to come over and corrupt the kingdom that was the guardian of Islam's holiest cities, Mecca and Medina. So every night at ten o'clock I went to Prince Khalid's office at the Ministry of Defense. The conversation would frequently stretch past midnight—not at all unusual in Saudi Arabia, where King Fahd himself worked through the night until sunrise prayers. Khalid and I would sit in his big maroon overstuffed chairs, while his aide served fancy fruit juices, coffee, and cappuccino. I'm not known for being patient, but to do the job there, that's just what I was. Decisions that would require fifteen minutes in Tampa or Washington would often consume three hours in Riyadh, as we sipped coffee, told stories, and philosophized.

It was often hard to tell right off the bat what Khalid had on his mind. Saudi culture does not emphasize directness. I knew from long experience to listen until I was sure I understood the point, and then to be willing to compromise. One night Khalid handed me a bag and said, "There are souvenir T-shirts being sold at your stores that are very offensive to us. Here is a whole bag of samples. You must stop your troops from buying them."

I thought, "Uh-oh," because I knew the things some T-shirts in the States had printed on them. I was imagining obscene mottoes, jokes about getting drunk, and pictures of marijuana plants.

"No problem," I said. "I'll just put out an order that no more T-shirts be sold."

Two hours later, I carried the bag back to my office and took out the offending shirts. They were nothing! One showed a palm tree, a camel, and a tank in the desert. So I went right back and asked, "What's offensive about this?"

"We don't like the image of a tank in our desert."

"But there are tanks all over your desert!"

"Yes, but we don't want this advertised to our people."

Then I pulled out another shirt that showed a map of Saudi Arabia with some of the major cities marked. "The location of our cities is classified," Khalid explained.

"But every atlas has maps of . . ."

"We don't allow them inside Saudi Arabia."

It turned out that the shirts weren't being sold in our PXs: entrepreneurial Pakistanis had opened souvenir stands in the souk, or marketplace, catering to the Americans. When I informed Khalid he insisted, "Norm, you must make your troops stop buying them."

"I can't do that. If you don't want these shirts sold in your country, you must make your merchants stop selling them."

I realized that Khalid had known all along that we weren't supplying the T-shirts. Rather, this all had to do with maneuvering by Moslem right-wingers who wanted to use the American presence as a pretext to undermine the king. A member of this faction had probably seen an American soldier buy a T-shirt and taken a sample to his religious leader, who in turn took it to the palace and complained: "This is another example of what happens when you bring foreigners into our country!" Prince Khalid was reluctant to close down the souvenir stands, and he had hoped I could make the problem quietly disappear. I couldn't; eventually the Saudis came to accept that these T-shirts were not offensive.

The touchiest issues almost always involved religion. Within days of my arrival, Khalid called with his hair on fire: "You have brought a rabbi into this country who is saying that for the first time in history, the ram's horn will be blown on Islamic soil!" Jews blow the ram's horn as part of their observance of the new year, the holiday of Rosh Hashanah. I very much doubted that a U.S. Army chaplain would say anything that inflammatory, but I sent my staff chaplain scrambling. We eventually discovered that the rabbi in question was neither connected to Central Command nor present in the Middle East—he was an Army chaplain in the United States who'd been quoted in an Israeli newspaper. Someone had clipped the story and sent it to the king.

The Iraqis also used the American presence to play on the fears of the more unsophisticated Saudis, beaming messages into the country over Baghdad radio that Americans were going to defile their shrines. One story had it that a group of U.S. soldiers had gone to Mecca (a city closed to infidels), entered the Kaaba (Islam's most sacred shrine), and gotten drunk on beer (forbidden by the Koran).

The Saudi concern about religious pollution seemed overblown to me but understandable, and on a few occasions I agreed they really did have a gripe. There was a fundamentalist Christian group in North Carolina called Samaritan's Purse that had the bright idea of sending unsolicited copies of the New Testament *in Arabic* to our troops. A little note with each book read: "Enclosed is a copy of the New Testament in the Arab language. You may want to get a Saudi friend to help you read it." One day, Khalid handed me a copy. "What is this all about?" he asked mildly. This time he didn't need to protest—he knew how dismayed I'd be.

Their insistence on religious purity notwithstanding, the Saudis recognized that our troops could not be denied the right to practice their own religions, as long as they did so discreetly. After discussing the matter with Khalid, I called together representatives of the American chaplains and made a short speech. "We all want the troops to have freedom of worship," I told them, "but to do that we have to use a little judgment. You chaplains who are assigned to Riyadh and other cities already know how sensitive the local people are. The very sight of a cross is offensive to them. So I'm asking those of you in the cities to take the Christian or Jewish insignia off your uniforms, or to wear them in such a way that they can't be seen. Chaplains with combat units in the field will continue to wear their insignia. I know some of you won't like this, but it seems to me a small price to pay." I added with a mock growl, "Besides, if you're worth a damn as chaplains, your troops already know who you are. You don't need insignia."

Next I talked about the ceremonies themselves. "We will continue to conduct services just as we always have. But we don't want to wave a red flag in the face of religious extremists. Therefore, we won't advertise them, publicize them, or let them be filmed—we don't want them broadcast on TV for the whole Moslem world to see. Let's not put the Saudis in a position where they'd feel obliged to say, 'No religious services'—that would be unacceptable to us, to our troops, and to the American people." I'd expected protests, particularly on the issue of taking off the insignia, but to my surprise the chaplains readily agreed, and even went a step further: they started calling themselves "morale officers."

I'd also promised Khalid that we would not bring female entertainers into Saudi Arabia. But one evening after I'd been in Riyadh only a couple of weeks, I received a frantic call from him: "I must see you right away!" I hurried to his office, wondering if there had been a terrorist attack in the kingdom. "You've got dancing girls entertaining your troops in Dhahran! It's on CNN!"

"We don't *have* any dancing girls. What are you talking about?"

Khalid was nearly beside himself: "You brought female entertainers into the country!" I could only imagine what his uncle the king had said to him.

"I can *guarantee* you that no female entertainers have been brought in."

"Well, these pictures are being shown, and you must order them taken off the TV!"

I was about to launch into a lecture about freedom of the press when the telephone rang. Khalid answered, listened for a minute, and turned pale. "That was His Majesty—they're showing it again."

The king was being besieged by the religious activists.

"I know what it must be," said Khalid suddenly. "In your military, you put on talent shows. This must be a talent show where female soldiers are dancing for the men."

I went back and sought out my public-affairs staff. "Would you please find out what the hell this is all about? And get me a videotape of whatever's being shown."

They finally brought me a tape. The clip had been shot so that you could only see the dancers' legs, but they were clearly women and were obviously doing bumps and grinds. Right in front of the camera were American soldiers—from the 82nd Airborne, naturally—hollering, waving their arms, and going bananas. The tape was as bad as it could possibly be. And CNN was regularly beaming it all over the world.

"Find out what this is all about!" I ordered.

The dancers weren't female entertainers at all; nor were they female soldiers. They were American employees of Aramco, the *Saudi-owned* oil company in Dhahran, and members of their families. An unwritten rule applied to the Aramco compound: the Saudis knew that a bunch of wild foreigners lived in there and suspected that alcoholic beverages were served, but they tolerated the conduct as long as it stayed behind closed doors.

Some Aramco employees had worked up an amateur show for their own entertainment. When the troops arrived from the States, they thought it would be wonderful to put it on again to make the soldiers feel at home, and someone in the American consulate came up with the not-so-bright idea of inviting CNN. The military's error had been to accept the invitation.

There were two more shows scheduled for the following evening, which I immediately canceled. Two days later I assembled my senior commanders and used the Aramco incident as an example of what had to be avoided. "Now listen to this," I told them. "Number one, Aramco puts on a girlie show. Can't do that culturally. Number two, the U.S. consulate invites the television cameras in. Stupid! And number three, you dumb bastards go and attend." Hearing me put it that way, they had to laugh.

I then read them excerpts from a book called *The Arabs* by a journalist named David Lamb. I explained that the Middle East had a culture developed over thousands of years, yet we'd come flying in, thoughtlessly expecting to operate the same way we had in Hinesville, Georgia, or Fort

Campbell, Kentucky. I repeated what I'd told the chaplains about religious insignia and the publicizing of religious services.

One commander objected to my ban on sexy magazines, claiming the troops had a "constitutional right" to the same reading matter they enjoyed in the States. I rejoined: "I hope you recognize that the Constitution of the United States applies only on U.S. soil, and therefore we don't *have* any constitutional rights in Saudi Arabia. The law of the land here happens to be Saudi law. So just like we require them to obey our laws in the United States, they have every right to require us to obey their laws here." That made an impression.

I also decided we needed a system to resolve cultural problems before they boiled up all the way to the king. We instituted a community-relations program similar to the one we used in Europe. Designating the senior officer in each major town as community commander, I said to them, "Talk to the Saudis. Identify your town's civilian leader and its military leader. Get them organized in a council and meet on a regular basis so that you can solve these problems when they arise." It worked. Once the local councils got established, the number of problems that made it to the level of the palace and Khalid dropped dramatically, despite the continued influx of U.S. troops.

Khalid, in the meantime, had been working on a way to accommodate our forces and relieve the pressure of too many Americans in Riyadh. "Why don't you move into the Escan Village?" he suggested. It turned out that back in the glory days of OPEC, when petrodollars were pouring into the kingdom, the Saudis had decided that every Bedouin should have a home and so they'd built sprawling compounds of town houses and high-rise buildings some fifteen miles outside Riyadh. The town houses were bright, marble-floored, stucco buildings, air-conditioned, outfitted with modern conveniences, and separated by high walls from the outside world. The government had moved the Bedouins in; the Bedouins had left a week later. "We don't like living with neighbors right next door. We don't like living with roofs over our heads," they'd said, and had promptly gone back to the desert. So we took over one of these vacant villages to house our personnel, busing them into town each day for work and to the souk when they wanted to shop. The arrangement made the Saudis happy, because the foreigners were no longer a constant and overwhelming presence in Riyadh; it made the troops happy, because behind those walls they could dress and live pretty much as they did back home; and it made me happy, because it enabled me at last to clear people out of the downtown hotels where I was scared they'd get blown up.

Riyadh air base, 1991, with a Patriot battery just after a Scud alert.
My visits with the troops in the gulf always raised my spirits.
(DAVID TURNLEY/DETROIT FREE PRESS)

When troops flew into Dhahran air base, they were taken into large tents, where they were sheltered from the burning sun while waiting for transportation to their units. (U.S. MILITARY PHOTOGRAPHER)

Enormous tent cities were set up as initial bases for arriving Army units. (U.S. MILITARY PHOTOGRAPHER)

The congestion at our air base caused me great concern. Had a single enemy aircraft broken through our air-defense screen, it could have wreaked havoc. (U.S. MILITARY PHOTOGRAPHER)

In September 1990 I was relieved to see the armored elements of the
24th Mechanized Infantry Division arrive in Saudi Arabia. Colonel
Paul Kern briefed me at his command post in the desert.
(© 1990 HARRY BENSON)

President Bush
visited Saudi Arabia at
Thanksgiving, and
I was able to brief him
thoroughly on upcoming
operations while flying
in *Air Force One* from
Jidda to Dhahran.
(DAVID VALDEZ/WHITE
HOUSE PRESS OFFICE)

An announcement of the
Bob Hope Christmas
show. In the background
is Escan Village—villas
originally built for
Bedouin tribesmen and
used to house U.S.
personnel in Riyadh.
(U.S. MILITARY
PHOTOGRAPHER)

Sheikh Mohammed Bin Zayed al-Nahyan, deputy chief of staff of the
United Arab Emirates' armed forces and third son of President Sheikh
Zayed Bin Sultan al-Nahyan, was host to French minister of defense
Jean-Pierre Chevènement and me at lunch in the desert.

I enjoyed many hours with my friend Sheikh Mohammed, falconing
in the deserts of the UAE.

Allied commanders sat with royal princes, sheltered from the hot sun by tents, while King Fahd addressed the assembled troops on December 27, 1990. (OFFICIAL DEPT. OF DEFENSE PHOTOGRAPH)

King Fahd reviewed United States troops from the back of a jeep on December 27, 1990. (U.S. MILITARY PHOTOGRAPHER)

Lieutenant General Prince Khalid Bin Sultan al-Saud, commander of the Multinational Joint Combat Group. We worked side by side in the subbasement command center throughout the war. (U.S. MILITARY PHOTOGRAPHER)

Crown Prince Hamad Bin Isa al-Khalifa of Bahrain. He and his father, Sheikh Isa Bin Sulman al-Khalifa, were among our strongest supporters during the war.

In April 1991, I was able to visit with the emir of Kuwait, Jaber al-Ahmed al-Sabah, after his return to his country.

The coalition commanders: *(seated, left to right)* Major General Modani, Saudi chief of plans; Major General Halaby, Egypt; Lieutenant General de la Billière, United Kingdom; Lieutenant General Khalid, Saudi Arabia; General Schwarzkopf, United States; Lieutenant General Roquejeoffre, France;

(Below, left) Lieutenant General Michel Roquejeoffre, commander of French forces and trusted friend. (E.C.P. ARMEES-FRANCE) *(Below, right)* Lieutenant General Sir Peter de la Billière. Peter was a superb soldier, advisor, confidant, and friend. (U.S. MILITARY PHOTOGRAPHER)

Lieutenant General Waller, deputy, United States; Major General Habib, Syria; and Major General al-Shaikh, deputy, Saudi Arabia. Behind Waller is Rear Admiral Sharp, U.S. chief of plans. (U.S. MILITARY PHOTOGRAPHER)

(Below, left) Lieutenant General John Yeosock, commander of all U.S. Army forces in Desert Storm and Desert Shield. (U.S. MILITARY PHOTOGRAPHER)
(Below, right) Vice Admiral Stan Arthur, commander of U.S. naval forces in the gulf. He orchestrated an airtight blockade of ports supplying Iraq, and his forces dominated the sea and air over the gulf. (U.S. MILITARY PHOTOGRAPHER.)

Major General Barry McCaffrey, commander of the 24th Mechanized Infantry Division. He was the most aggressive and successful ground commander of the war.
(U.S. MILITARY PHOTOGRAPHER)

Colonel Jesse Johnson, commander of all U.S. special forces in the gulf. A great soldier and an unsung hero.
(U.S. MILITARY PHOTOGRAPHER)

General Waller, General Powell, Defense Secretary Cheney, General Schwarzkopf, and Undersecretary of Defense Wolfowitz in the war room. In the background are *(left to right)* General Horner, General Yeosock, Admiral Arthur, General Boomer, Colonel Johnson, and my chief of staff, General Bob Johnston.
(OFFICIAL DEPT. OF DEFENSE PHOTOGRAPH)

Lieutenant General Chuck Horner, commander of U.S. Air Force in the gulf, was the man who planned and executed our successful air campaign. (OFFICIAL DEPT. OF DEFENSE PHOTOGRAPH)

Lieutenant General Walt Boomer, commander of all U.S. Marines in Desert Storm and Desert Shield. He and his Marines conducted a daring attack into the toughest part of the enemy defenses. (U.S. MILITARY PHOTOGRAPHER)

At Safwan I did not come to negotiate. I came to tell the Iraqis what was expected of them if we continued our cessation of offensive operations. (U.S. MILITARY PHOTOGRAPHER)

April 20, 1991—one of the happiest days of my life. I was reunited
with my family after eight months in the gulf.
(U.S. MILITARY PHOTOGRAPHER)

(*Opposite*) It seemed as though the entire
city of New York turned out to welcome us
home in a ticker tape parade.
(U.S. MILITARY PHOTOGRAPHER)

When I relinquished command of Central Command on August 9, 1991, Secretary Cheney presented me with the Defense Distinguished Service Medal, as well as the Distinguished Service Medals of the Army, Navy, Air Force, and Coast Guard. (U.S. MILITARY PHOTOGRAPHER)

Queen Elizabeth II traveled to Tampa, Florida, to bestow on me an honorary knighthood: Knight Commander in the Military Division of the Most Honorable Order of the Bath. (JOCK FISTICK/ TAMPA TRIBUNE/SIPA)

On July 3, 1991, President Bush, assisted by Mrs. Bush, awarded me the Presidential Medal of Freedom. Among my fellow recipients were Secretary Dick Cheney and General Colin Powell. (DAVID VALDEZ/ WHITE HOUSE PRESS OFFICE)

(Opposite) On May 15, 1991, I returned to West Point, where the Corps of Cadets honored me with a full dress review. (© 1991 C. RUSSELL, ACADEMY PHOTO, WEST POINT, N.Y.)

H. Norman Schwarzkopf, General U.S. Army, Retired, and Bear.
(MICHAEL A. GORENFLO)

It was a credit to both sides that these cultural crises never got so out of hand that they endangered our mission. The bright young men and women of our armed forces quickly understood their obligation to respect the customs of their hosts, while the Saudis discovered that Americans were not the sex-crazed, alcohol- and drug-addicted atheists they'd feared; most came to regard us as friends who were there to help.

22 SEP 90 C + 46 CINC TRIP TO DHAHRAN

1230 CINC met with the governor, Prince Mohammed Bin Fahd al-Saud. The CINC explained to the governor how he had appointed one commander in each area to be responsible for the actions of the troops and the cultural sensitivities. The CINC said we are not going to win the war and lose the peace. The governor said he has seen the Saudi people waving to the troops in the streets and that they are very happy we are here.

I continued to be troubled that I could not convey to the Saudis my sense of urgency about the military situation. The Iraqis could attack tomorrow, but our hosts on some level still didn't believe they could be overrun—after all, their land had not been invaded for twelve hundred years. Invasion was the furthest thing from their minds, even though it had happened to Kuwait. King Fahd had understood, of course, when he invited us to come, but his decision was never translated into a similar sense of urgency within his government or among his people. They were awed by the number of airplanes, tanks, helicopters, and ships we brought to their country, and felt that no one could attack in the face of such might. They weren't taking into account Iraq's military power or the fact that Saddam had done crazy things before.

I said to Khalid at one of our midnight meetings, "Look at your headquarters. If the Iraqi special forces landed in Riyadh right now, you wouldn't be able to defend the building." He looked blank. "The guards are all standing at the gates, but there are no bunkers out there," I explained. "In Saigon, even as early as 1963, they had sandbag bunkers outside the ministries."

The prince almost choked. "*Sandbags?* We can't put sandbags in the streets! It would alarm the people."

"What's wrong with the people getting alarmed?"

"Oh, no, you don't understand, my friend. We've never done anything like that, and the people would be afraid." Despite his reaction, he did pay attention to what I'd said. Several weeks and many consultations later, the Saudis built fortifications—made of concrete, not sandbags, and *within* the ministry gates—and the national guard positioned armored cars with heavy machine guns in nearby streets.

Militarily, the Saudi air force had meshed neatly with our own—something not unexpected, since we'd sold the Saudis some of their planes and had helped train their pilots, commanders, and air controllers. But their small 66,000-man army was another story. The week we met, Khalid said frankly, "You must help with my ground forces. They are in terrible shape." Well paid, well fed, and wonderfully equipped—with modern American, French, and British tanks, artillery, and armored personnel carriers—the Saudi forces were absolutely tied to their bases, because they had no organization to do the nitty-gritty work of sustaining them in the field. A typical U.S. Army division carried its support systems with it: among its soldiers were hundreds of mechanics, technicians, truck drivers, medics, and cooks. But the Saudis ran their army like their civilian society, hiring contractors to do the manual work. When they bought tanks, for example, they bought maintenance contracts too, so that if a tank broke, rather than climb around in the engine compartment and fix it, the soldiers would call General Motors. Such arrangements worked fine on base, where there were civilian technicians. But there was no Mr. Goodwrench on the battlefield.

This became an issue during Desert Shield. At one point a Saudi battalion commander on the Kuwaiti border complained, "The Americans have sold us defective equipment. All my tanks are broken." We were puzzled, because the battalion had M-60s—a hell of a good medium tank, the same type as used by our Marines. We sent a team of experts to find out what was wrong. The problem, it turned out, was nothing more than dirty air filters. In the M-60, when the filters clog, the driver gets a warning light that indicates the engine is overheating. He is supposed to get out, change the filters, climb back in, and drive on. But what the Saudi commander did was simply park the tank. Of the battalion's twenty-eight tanks, twenty-four had been declared out of order.

Khalid recognized the problem and was determined to fix it. "Where can we buy field kitchens?" he asked in early September. "We need to be able to feed our troops." Although we helped as much as we could, not only was it impossible to create maintenance and logistical systems instantly, but I began to see that the Saudi military hierarchy was encumbered with rivalries and conflicts that Khalid had to resolve before he could be sure his orders would be carried out. How were we supposed to integrate this organization and our own into a coherent defense overnight? I kept muttering to myself in early September, "We can't get there from here."

2 SEP 90 C + 26

2015 At the evening update, the CINC told everybody of observing troops in the area, particularly Dhahran, who were dressing like Rambos. This was unsatisfactory. He told them to get the chain of command working.

By late August Saudi Arabia had absorbed more of our troops and military hardware than it had in its own armed forces, and our deployment was still picking up speed. My hands were mostly filled with administrative matters, but I wanted to see for myself how we were taking care of our soldiers as they hit the ground. A few days after I arrived, I went out to the air base at Dhahran, which was serving as the main entry point for U.S. Army troops. Elements of the 82nd Airborne Division, the 101st Air Assault Division, and the 24th Mechanized Infantry Division were streaming in aboard civilian airliners on loan to the Pentagon.

The Saudis had practically vacated the base to make room for our operation. I looked up and could see—stretching way out into the distance—at least a half dozen large aircraft stacked up in holding patterns awaiting their turn to land. I looked out along the runways at eight or ten mammoth transport planes, their noses and tail doors yawning open, disgorging all kinds of gear, from attack helicopters to crates of rations. Near where I stood, a Northwest Airlines 747 had pulled up, and I watched soldiers from the 24th Mechanized Infantry Division stumbling out into the 130-degree heat. They were shouldering heavy packs and clutching their weapons and the water bottles that had just been handed to them. Reception officers stood by and singled out the officers and senior NCOs, who were sent to be briefed, while the soldiers fell in line and made their way to the large reception tents at the edge of the runway apron. That got them out of the sun, though the tents themselves were hotter than four hundred hells.

Had they arrived two weeks before, they wouldn't even have had the benefit of shade. The fellow who'd come up with the tents—and who was responsible for making sure the soldiers had food, clothing, shelter, transportation, equipment, and bullets—was Major General Gus Pagonis, the chief of logistics for the ground forces of Desert Shield, and the man showing me around the base. Pagonis was a short guy from Pennsylvania whose parents ran a restaurant; he was also an Einstein at making things happen. He had landed at Dhahran airport on the first day of Desert Shield, and when he'd found there was no place to stay, he'd simply curled up in a poncho on the concrete. By the time I saw him he had gotten a building from the Saudi base commander, Prince Turki Bin Nassar al-Saud, and surrounded it with large Bedouin tents.

The Saudis had promised to help with fuel, water, and transportation but hadn't fully appreciated what they were in for; nor had any arrangements been made for accommodations. With tens of thousands of Americans streaming in, both we and our hosts were at a loss as to where to put them until Pagonis discovered that the kingdom had huge numbers of tents in storage—for the hajj, the annual pilgrimage to Mecca. Each year, hundreds of thousands of Moslems come to Saudi Arabia from all over the world to worship, and they set up on the outskirts of the city in tents. The hajj wasn't until late spring or early summer, so Pagonis was able to acquire the tents and create villages for the troops. Each village had long rows of two-person tents and four-person tents, a few beautifully embroidered with garden scenes inside, as well as tents large enough for twenty or thirty people. For the central briefing areas, there would eventually be huge *fest* tents shipped from Germany, where they'd been used for beer festivals— another Pagonis inspiration.

Pagonis and I drove to a back corner of the base, where he pointed out dozens of foreign workers who were nailing together pieces of plywood. He'd hired a Saudi contractor to build gravity-feed portable showers and latrines like the ones we'd used in Vietnam. He proudly explained that the troops would have hot water whenever they wanted because the sun would heat the silver-colored tank on top. As it turned out, the system worked a little too well: the desert sun heated the water so hot that the troops could take showers only at night.

During subsequent weeks I would watch Pagonis pull it all together from scratch: post offices, field clinics, phone booths for calling home, recreation facilities, and mobile hamburger stands. He even improvised his own organization: at the peak of Desert Shield, he had ninety-four different Reserve and National Guard units under his command. Pagonis was the commander of the outfits I'd asked the Pentagon to call up from all over America—the truck drivers, telephone installers, mechanics, and others whose expertise we needed in the war zone. Somehow he managed to integrate them all into his system. If a stevedore unit showed up when he didn't need any more stevedores, he'd say, "I hereby dub this a transportation outfit. You guys go out and drive trucks." The reservists would grumble, "I didn't come over to drive a truck." But Pagonis's attitude was, "We'll talk about that when the war's over. Right now we don't have time."

The same afternoon that I inspected the air base, I flew to the port of Al Jubayl, where part of the First Marine Expeditionary Force was unloading its gear from a half-dozen large U.S. Navy combat-support ships (technically, maritime prepositioning ships) anchored in the harbor. Each squadron of ships was crammed with enough weapons, equipment, food, and supplies to keep 16,500 Marines fighting for thirty days. The ships had been stationed for years at Diego Garcia, a tiny British island in the Indian Ocean, loaded with brand-new equipment and ready for just such an emergency. Their deployment had been part of a controversial program after the Vietnam War. While some members of Congress had objected to the idea of letting tens of millions of dollars of military gear float around unused, we were certainly glad to have it now. I watched with Lieutenant General Walt Boomer, my Marine commander, as a procession of M-60 medium tanks rolled off one of the ships, and seeing them made me feel great.

The 7th Marine Expeditionary Brigade— 15,000 people—had made the 10,000-mile flight from its base at Twentynine Palms, California, to "marry up" with its equipment here. Some of the Marines had already moved out to fighting positions north of Al Jubayl, where they relieved paratroopers from the 82nd Airborne who had manned the perimeter since the start of Desert Shield. I visited one of the forwardmost companies. The troops had been working and training mostly at night and sitting on the ground under camouflage nets during the heat of the day, sleeping or just staring at the empty desert. Some of the young Marines gathered around me to talk. They could have bitched about any number of things—the heat, the lack of recreational facilities, their rations—but to my surprise, what they wanted to hear about was the news. United Nations Secretary General Javier Perez de Cuellar had announced on August 27 that he was going to Jordan to meet with the Iraqi foreign minister—the troops wanted to know if he had made any progress in resolving the crisis. I said to myself, "Hey, dummy, what about radio stations?" In Vietnam we'd always been able to hear the news on the Armed Forces Radio Network, but it hadn't occurred to me that we'd need to set up transmitters for Desert Shield. I promised the troops we'd provide newspapers and radios right away.

Late in the day I returned for a press conference at the Dhahran International Hotel. Though I'd been in Saudi Arabia less than a week, I felt it was crucial not to repeat the mistake we'd made in Grenada, where the military had stonewalled. I had a few minutes beforehand to sit in a little suite of rooms and collect myself—I'd been among troops in the 130-degree heat all day and this was my first moment alone. I wasn't expecting a particularly friendly reception—though the media had had unprecedented access to Saudi Arabia and reasonable access to our forces since the beginning of the crisis, I'd seen complaints about the inaccessibility of U.S. commanders. (A little-known fact: at one point in August the Saudis had decided to ask all reporters to leave, but Central Command had interceded successfully on their behalf.)

Sipping a Coke, I steeled myself for their questions. "Don't let them intimidate you," I told myself. "You know a hell of a lot more about what's going on than they do." I decided I'd make that rule number one for dealing with the press. Rule number two became, "There's no law that says you have to answer all their questions." Rule number three was its corollary, "Don't answer any question that in your judgment would help the enemy." That was in line with an order I'd already given my staff: never to discuss the locations, capabilities, or plans of our forces.

Suddenly it struck me that all three rules were negative in nature. "Wait a minute, Schwarzkopf," I thought, "before you get carried away, think back to the lessons of the past. Think back to what caused the disenchantment of the American public with Vietnam: they felt that they were constantly being misled with false body counts and optimistic talk about the light at the end of the tunnel." So I added rule number four, the most important of all: "Don't ever lie to the American people."

I knew there would be times when I'd be asked questions whose answers I didn't know; I was not going to make up answers. Instead, I'd simply say, "I don't know." There would be times when my information would be incomplete; I had to resist the temptation to draw rosy conclusions and report them as fact. I also understood that any attempt to cover up bad news would lead to disaster. As General Creighton Abrams was fond of saying, "Bad news does not get better with age." I had faith that if I stuck to the truth the American public would know how to weigh what they heard and keep the news in perspective.

Over the years I'd conducted press conferences, but involving at most ten reporters and a single videocamera making a tape. It wasn't until I stepped into the conference room that I realized the ball game had changed. The space was packed with about two hundred reporters—mainly American and British—and there were a half-dozen TV cameras arrayed along the back wall, some of them broadcasting live all over the world. I fielded questions for almost an hour and my rules held me in good stead, particularly when an American asked point-blank if it was true we were still weeks away from being able to defend against a ground attack. I gave the strongest answer I could: "If the Iraqis are dumb enough to attack, they are going to pay a terrible price." With those cameras grinding away, I knew I wasn't talking just to friendly audiences, but that Saddam and his bully boys were watching me on CNN in their headquarters. I wanted to make sure they got that message. But—rule number four—I carefully added, "I'm not prepared to give one hundred percent assurance of any outcome at this time. I may be later on." I couldn't say we were prepared to defend the kingdom. I didn't yet have enough forces in place to make that guarantee. In fact, the oil fields were still there for the taking, although their cost to the attacker was going up every day.

15 SEP 90 C + 39

0900 Qatar trip—Emir Sheikh Khalifa Bin Hamad al-Thani told the CINC he was very impressed with our rapid response and said those who help their friends in this crisis will be remembered in times to come. The emir talked about the Arab image with the American people. The CINC said that 80 percent of the American people supported our efforts in the gulf and that you couldn't get 80 percent of them to say they liked ice cream.

I didn't think Saddam would be reckless enough to start a war with the United States, but I wasn't prepared to bet my troops' lives on it. He was a tyrant surrounded by a bunch of yes-men, and since nobody on our side knew his intent, we had to assume that if he was militarily *capable* of something, he might do it.

We monitored his forces very closely. Every night I had my intelligence officers give me an update, and every night the Iraqi troop disposition looked slightly different. We watched them move forces around and extend roads from their territory into Kuwait. By analyzing such activity we were hoping to guess their plans, but during my first few weeks in Riyadh this seemed about as useful as reading tea leaves—the Iraqis were deployed so that they could have shifted from defending to attacking in as little as twenty-four hours. What *was* clear was that troops were still pouring into Kuwait and the neighboring parts of Iraq. My intelligence officers were constantly drawing circles on their photos around concentrations of soldiers and equipment that represented new units, and the numbers spiraled alarmingly. When I'd briefed President Bush at Camp David, we'd talked about an Iraqi force of 100,000 soldiers and 850 tanks in Kuwait, but we soon found ourselves facing more than *one third of a million* soldiers and

2,750 tanks. The Iraqis had also wheeled in nearly 1,500 artillery pieces capable, we knew, of firing toxic-chemical shells.*

Not until mid-September did we see a clear indication that Iraq was abandoning the idea of invading Saudi Arabia and assuming a defensive posture. Earlier, their Republican Guard divisions had pulled back slightly from the Saudi border; now their other armored units backed away from the border as well. In their place, tens of thousands of infantry moved in, digging trenches and building barricades, evidently preparing for a long siege. Some of the armored units took up reinforcing positions immediately behind the infantry; meanwhile, the Republican Guard units shifted even further to the rear, leaving Kuwait entirely and positioning themselves just inside Iraq. (The Iraqi commanders may have believed that, even if we tried to retake Kuwait, we would never attack them on their own soil; this deployment gave them the option, therefore, of swooping into Kuwait in a counterattack or, if that seemed too risky, staying safely on their side of the border, like the North Vietnamese troops that hid in Cambodia.)

If Saddam could have spied on us during early September he'd have seen how right he was to shy away from an attack. (One of Iraq's great disadvantages, of course, was its lack of modern surveillance technology.) Militarily, Desert Shield took shape exactly as we'd envisioned in our plan. By mid-September Chuck Horner's combat planes were flying more than seven hundred patrols and training missions per day from twenty-one fully equipped air bases, some of which had been little more than bare runways a month before. If the Iraqis had attacked on the ground, Horner would have taken them on with a massive force of F-15s, F-16s, and A-10s. The A-10 was an ugly, heavily armored jet nicknamed "the Warthog" because of its bizarre shape. Armed with Hellfire missiles and a Gatling gun powerful enough to rip through heavy armor, it had just one purpose—to fly low and slow over the battlefield, blasting tanks.

We'd also built a steel curtain against Iraqi air attacks; if an Iraqi bomber had ventured over Saudi territory, Horner's F-15 and F-16 fighters would have gunned it down within ten miles of the border. High in the Saudi sky, controllers in big AWACS (airborne warning and control system) surveillance aircraft monitored everything that flew on either side and coordinated U.S. air operations with those of at least seven of our allies. The more countries that committed combat forces, the less likely Saddam would

---

* As of September 14, the Iraqi force in Kuwait consisted of ten divisions with 155,000 troops, 1,350 tanks, 900 armored personnel carriers, and 650 artillery pieces; another twelve divisions of reinforcements and reserves had massed in neighboring parts of Iraq.

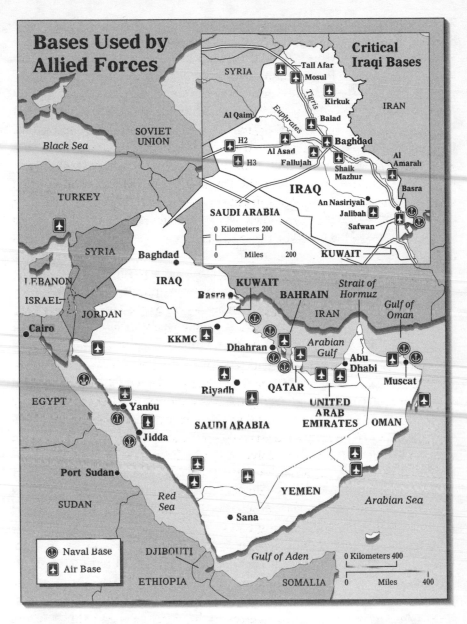

Bases Used by Allied Forces

Critical Iraqi Bases

SYRIA
Tall Afar
Mosul
Al Qaim
Kirkuk
Balad
IRAN
H2
Al Asad
Baghdad
H3
Fallujah
Shaik Mazhur
Al Amarah
IRAQ
An Nasiriyah
Basra
SAUDI ARABIA
Jalibah
Safwan

0 Kilometers 200

0 Miles 200

KUWAIT

Black Sea
SOVIET UNION
TURKEY
SYRIA
Baghdad
IRAQ
KUWAIT
BAHRAIN
Strait of Hormuz
Gulf of Oman
LEBANON
ISRAEL
JORDAN
Basra
IRAN
Cairo
KKMC
Dhahran
Arabian Gulf
Abu Dhabi
Muscat
Riyadh
QATAR
UNITED ARAB EMIRATES
OMAN
EGYPT
Yanbu
SAUDI ARABIA
Jidda
Port Sudan
Red Sea
YEMEN
Arabian Sea
SUDAN
Sana

Naval Base
Air Base

DJIBOUTI
Gulf of Aden
0 Kilometers 400

ETHIOPIA
SOMALIA
0 Miles 400

By the time we completed our deployments of forces to the gulf, we were using every airfield available. Even locations that consisted of incomplete facilities were pressed into service and saturated with aircraft. The same could be said about ports. Eventually we had to turn back offers of additional aircraft. We simply ran out of space to park them.

be to attack Saudi Arabia. My spirits were buoyed as I saw our numbers grow. The coalition air force—from the United States, Great Britain, France, Kuwait, Saudi Arabia, Bahrain, the UAE, and Qatar—already outnumbered Iraq's three to one.

In Ad Dammam harbor near Dhahran, our Fast Sealift Ships had arrived jammed with millions of tons of combat equipment and supplies. Convoys of trucks and armored vehicles streamed from the docks to the nearby staging areas of Major General Barry McCaffrey's 24th Mechanized Infantry Division, where his combat brigades linked up with their tanks and armored personnel carriers. At King Fahd air base, north of Dhahran, the combat brigades of General Peay's 101st Air Assault Division linked up with their helicopters. These included scores of missile-carrying, night-vision-equipped Apaches that could blow up enemy tanks in pitch darkness from five miles away.

As these units assembled their ammunition and supplies and moved into the field, General McCaffrey's mission was to leapfrog his units three hundred miles north and to occupy an eighty-mile-by-sixty-mile zone west of the Marines digging in around Al Jubayl. General Peay was to establish bases along McCaffrey's left flank, from which his helicopters and troops could defend a hundred-mile arc of desert to the north and west. A brigade of the 101st would also serve temporarily as a screen, ranging forward of the U.S. positions to detect, delay, and disrupt any enemy attack. Eventually, Colonel Doug Starr's 3rd Armored Cavalry Regiment would arrive to take over that mission.

Meanwhile the Saudis had pushed their forces all the way up to the border of Kuwait. To them it was a point of honor that the first blood shed in defense of the kingdom should be their own. So Khalid had deployed two mechanized brigades and an infantry brigade along the coastal corridor leading to Al Jubayl, and another brigade, composed mostly of fighting units from other gulf countries, along the western highway leading to King Khalid Military City. Though these forces were far too thin to withstand an Iraqi attack, they'd been ordered to defend their positions to the death.

I breathed a little easier each day as our units moved into place. I knew there was still an enormous amount of work to do to strengthen our defense—another American division was scheduled to arrive, and we had to determine how to weave combat forces from Egypt, Syria, Great Britain, and France into the battle plan. But by mid-September—coincidentally, just as the Iraqis shifted into defensive formations—I was able to tell Colin Powell, "We don't have to worry about the attack anymore. No way they're gonna seize the oil fields." Even if Iraq were to launch its entire 2,750-tank

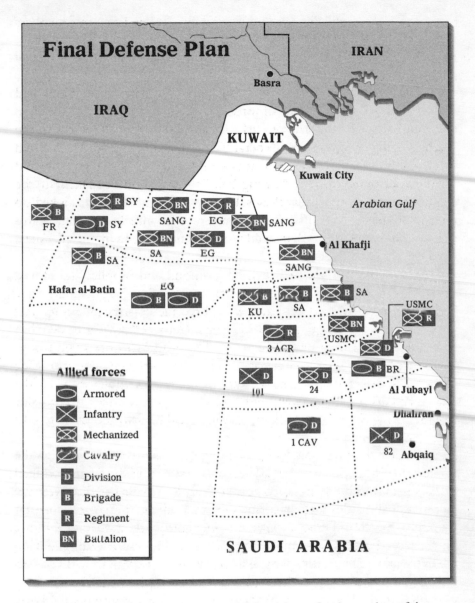

Final Defense Plan

Although we were eventually to receive additional forces for the conduct of the offense, the final defense plan utilized only the U.S. forces originally earmarked for Desert Shield, plus those committed early on by other nations of the coalition. These units, together with air and naval forces, could have stopped any attempt by Iraq to invade Saudi Arabia.

force down the middle approach into the kingdom—the unguarded gap that had flabbergasted me the day I arrived—I could guarantee we'd stop it. As a temporary measure until we built up more combat power in Saudi Arabia, I'd had John Yeosock work up a contingency plan to swing elements of the 82nd and 101st into the gap before the Iraqis advanced too far. Those units, coupled with our air forces, could have done the job.

Our tactics in the event of an Iraqi invasion would have involved yielding to the initial attack, drawing the enemy columns into the Saudi desert, raiding them with Apaches and A-10s as they advanced, and bombing their supply lines. By the time the Iraqis ran up against the main defensive positions of Generals McCaffrey, Peay, and Boomer, about 125 miles south of the Kuwaiti border, they wouldn't have enough force left to prevail. That was the war envisioned in our original operating plan, and we'd have handed Saddam a crushing defeat.

19 SEP 90 C + 43

> 1345 CINC meeting with Kuwaiti minister of defense, Sheikh Nawaf al-Ahmad al-Jaber al-Sabah. The CINC told the minister that we have brought more forces in six weeks than in seven months in Vietnam. The CINC and minister looked over maps, at places in Kuwait where the Iraqis were dug in. The minister said, "When?" The CINC said his orders were only to deter and defend.

Toward the end of September, tensions increased again. Saddam threatened to launch a preemptive strike against Israel and to harm some of his hostages, and his ruling council told the Iraqi people to prepare for the "mother of all battles." The fatalistic rhetoric bothered me a lot less than it would have before the Republican Guard pulled back and we moved our first armored forces into place. When Charlayne Hunter-Gault of the *MacNeil/Lehrer NewsHour* asked in an interview if I thought Saddam was trying to trigger war, I told her no. "I think he is getting desperate. I think the sanctions are starting to pinch him." He was turning up the rhetoric to intimidate us, I said, because that was about all he had left.

The only defeat I now had to worry about was symbolic: if Saddam had been able to sneak a few airplanes through our defenses, he could have caused great embarrassment to the United States. We'd jammed so many aircraft into the Riyadh air base, for example, that it looked like the deck of an aircraft carrier: we had about a billion dollars' worth of AWACS just lined up on the apron, not to mention dozens of other jets. There was no way to solve the overcrowding—we had no other place to put the planes—but every time I flew into or out of that airport I'd think, "If one enemy aircraft were to get through and hit this place . . ." The secondary explosions alone would have destroyed the entire fleet. I would call Chuck Horner and say, "Guarantee me that not one airplane is going to get through your air defense net."

"Not one airplane will get through," he'd say. "You don't have to worry about that."

27 SEP 90 C + 51

0900 CINC traveled to the northern border area. At his first stop, the CINC not only viewed the terrain but also had an unexpected encounter with two Iraqi soldiers who were hungry and thirsty. These soldiers had just come over to the Saudi police post to ask for food and water. They were taken to an isolated room and the CINC inspected their truck and equipment. The truck was in poor maintenance condition and their gas masks had internal packing matter, indicating the soldiers never had the masks fitted for use.

Central Command could have boasted about its great success. We'd moved more forces farther and faster than ever before in history, and we'd carried out our orders to the letter by deterring Iraq's aggression and building Saudi Arabia an impregnable defense. Yet I couldn't help wondering what we were supposed to do next.

Soon after arriving in Riyadh, I'd gone around to visit the smaller countries of the gulf that had opened their borders to American forces — Bahrain, Qatar, Oman, and the United Arab Emirates. I wanted to thank their leaders personally for having provided us with much-needed airfields and ports, and I wanted to make sure that the massive influx of American combat power hadn't overwhelmed them. Bahrain, for example, was a tiny island; its entire air force consisted of eighteen planes. Now hundreds of aircraft were using its runways, and dozens of U.S. warships were patrolling its waters.

What I found surprised me greatly. Though the gulf Arabs are not usually hawkish people, every leader I spoke with wanted to attack and destroy the Iraqis in Kuwait. Sheikh Hamad Bin Isa al-Khalifa, Bahrain's crown prince, put it very simply: "Our war with Iraq has already begun." I heard the same view echoed up and down the gulf. Nobody was shedding tears that the ruling al-Sabah family of Kuwait had suffered a devastating setback—rightly or wrongly, their neighbors saw the Kuwaitis as arrogant in their wealth, and arrogance is a trait frowned upon in the Arab world. But Saddam had attacked a brother Arab, unprovoked, and now sat poised to threaten their countries with the same kind of attack—none of them could live with that. Not only did Sheikh Hamad want the United States to kick the living hell out of Iraq, but he promised that his own forces would fight by our side: "America should lead," he said, "and we are ready to follow."

This unnerved me for two reasons. First, the Saudis themselves showed little interest in going on the offense, so attacking the Iraqis from Saudi territory seemed out of the question. Khalid's attitude reflected that of King Fahd, Prince Sultan, and the rest of the royal family. Sometimes Khalid would say, "Saddam has got to be destroyed," or, "We can't let him get away with this," but his next sentence was always, "But we can't attack our Arab brothers."

I also knew that the United States military had not come to the Middle East to kick Iraq out of Kuwait. Our orders were simply to deter and defend, and Washington was working very hard to find a diplomatic solution to the crisis. In my heart I wanted a negotiated settlement that would spare the lives of our troops. But now that I saw what the gulf Arabs' expectations were, I got a little glimmer of how we could really screw this up. If Saddam agreed to withdraw, the United Nations and the United States would claim a diplomatic triumph for having averted war and returned Kuwait to its rightful owners. Probably somebody would get a Nobel Peace Prize. But as far as the gulf Arabs were concerned, a negotiated settlement would be a disaster. Saddam would still be sitting there with his arsenal, waiting for an opportunity to make his neighbors pay for having cooperated with the West. The gulf Arabs clearly realized something Washington hadn't yet: strategically speaking, anything short of an Iraqi defeat in Kuwait was a losing proposition.

28 SEP 90 C + 52

1700 The CINC received a call from the chairman. The chairman told the CINC that the mood is changing in the U.S. and is becoming less bellicose. *The Civil War* series on TV has had a sobering effect on many.

19

1 OCT 90 C + 55

1000 The public affairs officer briefed the CINC that Major General Pagonis was opening an R&R center for the 82nd Airborne. The CINC was disturbed by this report because there was no provision for facilities for other Army troops deployed deeper in the desert.

2 OCT 90 C + 56

1000 During the update, the CINC was briefed on a plan to build numerous base camps throughout Saudi Arabia and was informed that the staff had approved six for construction. The CINC informed the staff that they did not have authority to approve construction of base camps and he wanted a full briefing on this base camps business before one nickel was spent.

Instant Thunder had been ready since early September. Brigadier General Buster Glosson, Chuck Horner's top planner, had expanded the retaliatory scheme of the Pentagon air staff into the best air campaign I'd ever seen. It gave us a broad range of attack options and could be conducted as a stand-alone operation or as part of a larger war. They'd briefed me on it right after my arrival in Riyadh, and I'd told Powell enthusiastically on the phone, "Have we got a bombing plan now. If you want to execute an air attack by itself, we're ready."

But Saddam's forces were becoming more and more entrenched, and you didn't have to be Clausewitz to realize we needed a plan for a ground offensive. Not only were the gulf nations urging us to kick Iraq out of Kuwait, but Powell had made it clear—although without issuing a formal order—that Washington was impatiently awaiting an "offensive option" from Central Command. My staff and I were completely stumped: no matter how many times we looked at it, we saw no way to stretch the force we had available into a winning offense. Not satisfied that we were thinking creatively enough, I sent a message in early September to the Army requesting a fresh team of planners. A four-man team of graduates from the School of Advanced Military Studies (SAMS), the elite year-long program at Command and General Staff College that concentrated on campaign planning, arrived in the middle of the month. We briefed them on our thinking to date and then I instructed: "Assume a ground attack will follow an air campaign. I want you to study the enemy dispositions and the terrain and tell me the best way to drive Iraq out of Kuwait given the forces we have available." I gave them two weeks to come up with an answer.

A few days later I had a call from our ambassador, Chas Freeman, who said he needed to talk. The following day I made my way to the U.S. embassy. The modern, multistory office building was on a long, palm-tree-lined boulevard in the outskirts of Riyadh, in a section of the city that the Saudis had set aside for embassies, to reduce the number of foreigners downtown. Chas's modest top-floor office was filled with Arabian and Chinese artifacts. In the sitting area there was a framed photograph showing Franklin Roosevelt and King Abdulaziz al-Saud meeting on the deck of an American cruiser in the Suez Canal Zone in February 1945.

Chas was medium-sized, in his late forties, with shrewd eyes, a pleasant smile, and a steady, soft voice. He was one of the few people in the kingdom who'd known from the beginning that Central Command was working on an offensive option. The Saudis didn't know yet, though clearly we'd need their permission to launch any attack from the kingdom; nor had we informed our other allies. Even within Central Command, only a handful of people were privy to the secret.

"I'm concerned about your offensive planning," Chas began. "Before you get too far down that road, I've got to ask: are you satisfied that you understand what we're trying to accomplish strategically?"

"No. I'm working in the dark," I said. "My only orders are to deter and defend, and I *assume* the goal of an offensive would be to free Kuwait and destroy Iraq's ability to threaten the gulf states. But no one has told me that that's what we're trying to do."

"If the United States goes to war against Iraq, it could cause a heck of a backlash in the Arab world. I'm not sure anyone in Washington has given that enough thought," he said.

"Well, we'd better start looking at it," I responded. Chas was echoing a concern that had gnawed at me since my arrival in Riyadh: I wanted to make absolutely sure that if we took on Saddam, we would win not only on the battlefield but in the history books—and that included *Arab* history books. This was not strictly speaking a military concern. But we had to avoid giving the impression that western "colonialists" had unilaterally imposed their will, and I was determined to plan smart. So Central Command organized what we called an "Arab reaction seminar." In a small briefing room a dozen experts from the embassy and Central Command—diplomats and Army, Navy, and Air Force officers who had spent years in the Arab world—assembled. I sat at one end of the big table; at the other end, Gordon Brown, who'd succeeded Stan Escudero as Central Command's political advisor, ran the discussion. The agenda was to look at a long list of possible military actions the United States could take against Iraq and to figure out which—if any—would be acceptable to Arab governments and populations. If we were to launch a full-scale air attack alone, say, would the gulf nations maintain ties with the United States and Central Command afterward? Or would there be a public uproar that would oblige the Arab governments to distance themselves from the United States? What about a ground attack forcing Iraq to withdraw from Kuwait but leaving its vast military machine intact?

After weighing various schemes for more than four hours, I realized I'd asked the question the wrong way. Virtually *any* offensive would be acceptable, as long as two conditions were met: first, Arab forces in significant numbers had to fight by our side; second, we had to win. The war would then be remembered as western nations *and* Arab nations against Saddam Hussein. From there, it was only a short step to what became an inviolable principle of our planning: in any ground war against Iraq, I told my staff, Arab forces must be the ones to liberate Kuwait City.

3 OCT 90 C + 57

> 0800 CINC departed for visit to U.S.S. *Independence* in the gulf. This was an historic cruise in that we had not put a carrier in the gulf since 1974.

5 OCT 90 C+59

1630 CINC departed for tour of Escan Village housing area. During the visit the CINC was not satisfied with the level of morale, welfare, and recreation facilities, or the fact that the pool was not operational. He directed the Air Force to fix the problem.

6 OCT 90 C+60

1730 The CINC received a base camp briefing. The staff and components recommended the completion of six base camps already contracted for, and a plan to finally construct twenty-four camps. The CINC cautioned the staff against allowing our forces to "hunker down" in Vietnam-style base camps. He said that not only does this make them lucrative targets, but also makes them less ready for action. In the end, he gave the go-ahead for the first six camps and directed that we go slowly on any more.

On October 6, the planning wizards delivered their proposed battle plan. It turned out to be exactly what I'd sketched on scrap paper almost two months before: attack straight into Kuwait and seize and hold the crucial highway junction northwest of the capital. Hearing the planners' presentation, I became certain that, unless the President sent more forces, this was the best possible approach—and I liked it now even less than when I'd thought of it myself. For one thing, the offensive lacked any element of surprise: it was a straight-up-the-middle charge right into the teeth of the Iraqi defenses. And even assuming things went well, casualties would be substantial: the SAMS team had predicted (rather optimistically, I thought) eight thousand wounded and two thousand dead for the U.S. forces, and that didn't include possible mass casualties from chemical weapons, which were impossible to estimate. I sat there imagining a half-dozen scenarios in which the attack might bog down. If a division got in trouble, for example, there would be no help available: the plan called for the commitment of all U.S. and allied armored units, with none in reserve. Even if we succeeded in seizing the highway junction, Iraq could throw its huge army north of Kuwait against us in a counterattack. A battle of attrition would follow, in which Iraq's numerical superiority would give it a decided advantage.

I also mistrusted that the forces our allies had promised would all show up in the theater in time, or that their governments would allow them to

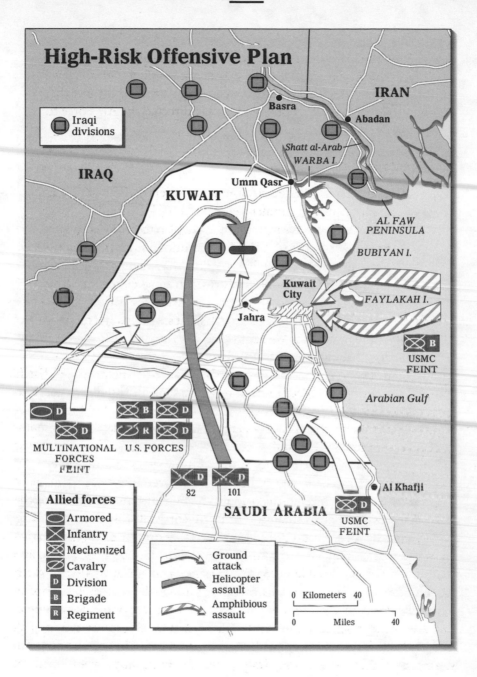

High-Risk Offensive Plan

Iraqi divisions

IRAN

Basra

Abadan

Shatt al-Arab

WARBA I.

IRAQ

KUWAIT

Umm Qasr

AL FAW PENINSULA

BUBIYAN I.

Kuwait City

FAYLAKAH I.

Jahra

USMC FEINT

Arabian Gulf

MULTINATIONAL FORCES FEINT

U.S. FORCES

82   101

Al Khafji

SAUDI ARABIA

USMC FEINT

Allied forces

- Armored
- Infantry
- Mechanized
- Cavalry
- **D** Division
- **B** Brigade
- **R** Regiment

Ground attack

Helicopter assault

Amphibious assault

0 Kilometers 40

0 Miles 40

participate in an attack. The British 7th Armored Brigade (the Desert Rats of World War II fame) wasn't due until mid-November; the French 6th Light Armored Division had arrived but had not yet deployed; the Egyptian 3rd Mechanized Division had arrived but was only half deployed; the Egyptian 4th Armored Division was still in Egypt, awaiting the Saudis' permission to come; and the Syrian 9th Armored Division was supposedly on its way but the arrival date was unknown. I figured it would be December at the earliest before the forces were in place.

Colin Powell called that afternoon to order me to send a team to brief the Joint Chiefs, Secretary Cheney, "and possibly the President" on Desert Storm.

"I gotta tell you, as far as a ground offensive is concerned, we've still got nothing," I warned. I outlined what the SAMS team had come up with.

"Well, your air offensive plan is so good that I want these people to hear it," he replied. "But you can't just brief the air plan. You have to brief the ground plan too."

I got a sinking feeling in the pit of my stomach. With Iraq showing no sign of responding to the UN embargo, and with more than 200,000 young Americans now baking in the Saudi desert, I suspected Washington was finally about to confront the question of what came next. My old fear returned that we'd be ordered to do something foolish. "I'd like to conduct the briefing myself," I said tensely.

"No, you stay there. If you come to Washington it'll cause too many rumors."

"How about Chuck Horner?"

"No. Same problem."

"At least let me send my chief of staff," I urged. Powell finally agreed.

I got off the phone seething and ordered Bob Johnston to get a briefing team ready to leave in twenty-four hours. To my mind Powell's refusal to let me come to Washington made no sense; in every war, the theater commander had been called home periodically for consultations. Eisenhower was called back; MacArthur was called back; Westmoreland and Abrams were called back all the time. Worse, I was now under orders to send in a plan I believed could result in a bloodbath.

The following morning Carl Vuono showed up on a long-planned visit to the theater. I cornered him and vented my frustration: "Goddammit, Carl, you guys on the Joint Chiefs are supposed to be the President's principal advisors on warfare. Why am I being required to send back an offensive plan I don't believe in? These are our Army troops we're talking about! You, the chief of staff of the Army, ought to be telling the President we're in no position to go on the offense unless we have more forces." Vuono, who hated confrontations, smiled and said simply, "Norm, you're doing a wonderful job and we're all behind you one hundred percent." It was later reported that afterward he'd complained that our one-hour meeting had lasted four-and-a-half hours and had been like a psychotherapy session.

Since I couldn't be in Washington myself, I coached my staff and planned their briefing as carefully as I would a major battle. Buster Glosson would present the air attacks of phases one, two, and three; then Lieutenant Colonel Joe Purvis, the head of the SAMS team, would present their phase-four ground attack. After listening to their presentations, I looked at each one of the men: "One of the things we have going for us is that we don't bullshit the President. You should explain our capabilities, but do not tell the President we're capable of something we're not. This is no time for a 'can do' attitude. Do not speculate when you answer questions: confine your responses strictly to what we've analyzed. And do not give personal opinions. If I hear that any one of you has done so, you will be relieved of your duties and sent home. I do not want anybody saying anything that could result in thousands of Americans getting killed unnecessarily." I was pretty sure everybody understood me clearly. Johnston and Glosson had heard me talk this way before, and they simply nodded; the young SAMS officers turned pale.

But I wasn't finished yet. I asked Johnston to come to my office, where I prepared three slides for him to display, summarizing my reservations— about allied participation, about the absence of a reserve, about the fact that we had yet to sell the Saudis on an attack, and about the risk of underestimating the Iraqis' ability to fight. I then wrote out a final slide pointing out that Central Command had accomplished the mission the President had given us—to defend Saudi Arabia. I went back to the point I'd made at Camp David days before we'd launched Desert Shield: that to plan an offensive that did not court military disaster required another "heavy corps" of two armored divisions. The slide read, in part:

CINC'S ASSESSMENT

OFFENSIVE GROUND PLAN NOT SOLID. WE DO NOT HAVE THE CAPABILITY TO ATTACK ON GROUND AT THIS TIME.

NEED ADDITIONAL HEAVY CORPS TO *GUARANTEE* SUCCESSFUL OUTCOME.

DEFENSIVE PLAN SOLID—AS PROMISED THE PRESIDENT DURING THE FIRST WEEK OF AUGUST, UNITED STATES MILITARY FORCES ARE NOW CAPABLE OF DEFENDING SAUDI ARABIA AND EXECUTING A WIDE RANGE OF RETALIATORY ATTACKS AGAINST IRAQ.

I turned to Johnston and said, "When Purvis finishes explaining the ground offensive, I want you to stand up and close the briefing with these slides." Bob nodded, looking grim: he shared my reservations about the plan but it was highly unorthodox for a commander to end a military briefing by impeaching his own presentation. "I don't know what you're going to run into in Washington," I continued. "You can tell them General Schwarzkopf says if this plan is presented, it must be presented with these slides. I want them presented by you personally, not some officer from the Joint Staff. I don't care what orders you get from anybody else. You're working for me and I'm counting on you to speak on my behalf." Johnston understood all too clearly what was at stake; not only was he a veteran commander, but his twenty-four-year-old son was in a Marine unit ultimately headed for the gulf.

---

9 OCT 90 C + 63

1600 In the morning we were informed that the Israelis had killed twenty-one Palestinians during a riot in Old Jerusalem. At the same time we had just suffered the day before ten Americans killed in fixed-wing and helo accidents. In discussions with Lieutenant General Khalid, the CINC cautioned General Khalid not to be too quick to condemn America's historic support of Israel, particularly just after the American people have absorbed ten accidental deaths incurred while defending Saudi Arabia.

12 OCT 90 C + 66

1530 CINC received a briefing on rotation policy. The proposal recommended that ground combat units be rotated every six to eight months and that headquarters staffs also be rotated each six months "to achieve equity." The CINC disapproved the proposal. He informed the staff that any suggestion that a staff in Riyadh should rotate at the same time as a unit living in the desert is crazy. The CINC offered the staff an opportunity to live in a foxhole under a poncho liner for six months and then they would be in a position to discuss equity. The CINC directed them to review the proposal again.

The team briefed the President at the White House on the afternoon of Thursday, October 11. My first call was from Powell: "Your briefers did a nice job. The White House is very comfortable with the air plan, but there was a lot of criticism of the ground attack." He added obscurely, "A couple of people wanted to know why you hadn't come up with anything more imaginative."

"I've been telling you guys all along that we don't have sufficient force to do a ground campaign," I said as calmly as I could.

"I pointed that out." There was a little silence and suddenly he asked, "How much would you really need to do it right?"

"I've been saying an additional heavy corps, but let us make a thorough analysis," I urged, and we agreed to pursue the discussion as soon as my staff had studied the question. Until then we had been required to plan on the assumption that no more troops would be available. Powell also asked us to assess the opposite course of action: "Let me know the minimum force you'd need to defend Saudi Arabia indefinitely." As I hung up the phone I felt somewhat reassured.

On Saturday morning Bob Johnston, having flown all night, added a few details that Powell had skipped. Along with President Bush, those present at the briefing had included Vice President Quayle, secretaries Baker and Cheney, John Sununu, General Scowcroft, and Bob Gates, the deputy national security adviser. "Judging from their questions during the briefing," Johnston told me, "people could see big problems with the ground-attack plan. By the time I gave your assessment, most of your objections had already been raised."

Johnston hesitated. "You're not gonna believe this," he said, shaking his head. "When I put up the last slide—the one that shows we'd need an additional corps—one of the President's advisors says, 'My God, he's already got all the force he needs. Why won't he attack?'"

I wasn't about to let that rest. When Powell called that afternoon, I asked about the criticism. "That's right," he told me. "Somebody even said, 'Schwarzkopf is just another McClellan.'" The man who'd made this comparison was a civilian who knew next to nothing about military affairs, but he'd been watching the Civil War documentary on public television and was now an expert. He'd learned how George McClellan had sat outside

Richmond in the spring of 1862 and refused to attack the army of Robert E. Lee. In his comparison he had overlooked one small fact: while McClellan's army had vastly outnumbered Lee's, our force in Saudi Arabia was vastly outnumbered by Iraq's. This advisor was one of the White House hawks Powell was always complaining about. In fact, according to Powell, after the meeting the advisor began suggesting that we'd intentionally sent in a high-casualty attack plan to scare the President away from launching a ground war.

If the White House wanted a bold offensive plan, I knew how to deliver one. On an easel to the left of my big desk at the Ministry of Defense was an "enemy situation" map that pinpointed every Iraqi unit in and near Kuwait. My intelligence staff updated it three times a day, starting at four-thirty in the morning, and it was the first thing I looked at when I emerged from my bedroom at six. Bright red stickers represented Iraqi divisions, and while Saddam continually shifted individual units in an attempt to keep us guessing, the overall alignment in the Kuwaiti theater had remained constant for a month: the infantry divisions were dug in along the southern border and the gulf coast with armored divisions in reinforcing positions behind them. The Republican Guard was arrayed along the Iraq-Kuwait border up north. The Iraqis were positioned to bring their full weight to bear against any attack from the south or east. By now their buildup had put in place twice as many soldiers and three times as much armor as we'd originally designed Desert Shield to face.

The textbook way to defeat such a force would have been to hold it in place with a frontal attack while sending an even bigger army to outflank it, envelop it, and crush it against the sea. I looked at the bright red stickers representing the army occupying Kuwait; along its western flank was a slab of Iraqi territory three times Kuwait's size, and except for a handful of small towns and air bases, it was desert. More important for my purposes, it was largely *unguarded*. We'd earlier discussed the possibility of launching armored units through that sector but had shelved the idea because our forces would be spread too thin and because we weren't sure we could keep our units supplied with ammunition and gas across such distances. But Washington now appeared willing to consider sending more divisions, and that changed everything. True, it would require the largest maneuver of armor in the desert in U.S. military history—but it seemed the most likely way to end a ground war decisively and fast. On October 15, I told Central Command's planners to assume another armored corps and to develop a flanking attack.

18 OCT 90 C + 72

TIME UNKNOWN The CINC asked the chairman if he would clamp
down on the number of visits. We have eighteen major
delegations scheduled to visit the AOR in the next few
weeks. The CINC also discussed this issue with the ambassador, who not only agreed with the CINC but suggested
that Central Command and the embassy issue a joint message
requesting a halt to the avalanche of unnecessary visits.

19 OCT 90 C + 73

TIME UNKNOWN The CINC approved a dispatch of the proposed
rotation policy. It focused on a six-to-eight-month rotation
for combat units and other units whose personnel are living
in austere or primitive conditions. The policy allowed for
twelve-month rotation for personnel living in conditions not
dissimilar to the U.S.

Even though we hadn't fired a shot, Desert Shield began to take on the
tedium of war. I found myself mired in administrative chores: briefing
congressional delegations, giving press interviews, heading off cultural
problems with the Saudis, and fielding bureaucratic questions from Washington. When I was able to break away from headquarters to visit the
troops, I found them worrying, as I was, about what would happen next.

The day after I'd directed our planners on the new offensive and
defensive options—work that could shape the outcome of the entire
campaign—General Starling, my director of logistics, announced for what
seemed like the one hundredth time at the morning briefing, "The Saudis
still aren't paying any of our bills."

"But we have commitments from King Fahd, Prince Sultan, and
Khalid," I countered.

"Yes, sir. I know, sir. But it doesn't seem to make any difference."

Commanders in chief are not supposed to have to worry about running
out of money, particularly when war might break out any day. When time
allows, the State Department works out financial arrangements anywhere
the United States has a military presence and well in advance of any crisis.
But while Secretary of State Baker had been touring the world lining up
financial backing for Desert Shield, Central Command wasn't seeing much
cash. In short, we had no "host-nation-support agreements" with Saudi
Arabia. Yet I had troops to feed and house, plus supplies to transport.

I went to see Chas Freeman and said, "I think this one is yours."

"I think so too," the ambassador replied in that soft voice of his, "but I confess I have no idea how to do it." So he and I asked Washington to send a host-nation-support expert. Meanwhile I'd try to jury-rig a payment system with Khalid.

One of my earliest conversations with Khalid had been about rental cars in Riyadh. When the Air Force first arrived in August, each unit that needed cars simply rented them from local Saudi agencies. Within weeks, the United States had snapped up every rental car in Riyadh—an excess we eventually cracked down on. But some of those rentals had been necessary, and I'd gone to Khalid and said, "You know, the king offered to pay for transportation. Rental cars are a transportation expense."

"Of course we'll pay for it."

"Who should we give the bills to?"

"No, no." He looked at me in horror. "Don't give me bills. Give me a list of what you need. My staff will find a single contractor, I will make the deal with him, and we will administer the contract from my headquarters."

I tried to explain why that wasn't going to work; U.S. logistics officers in the field could never tolerate an unresponsive centralized decision-making process. Every unit, I told Khalid, had its own mini-version of Gus Pagonis whose job was to take care of his troops. Pretty soon, I predicted, Americans would be wheeling and dealing all over the kingdom. I was right: in Riyadh, for example, the logistics officer went to the Saudi water author-ity and contracted for a huge amount of desalinated water; in Al Jubayl the Marine logistics chief signed a ten-million-dollar lease for a compound to house his men.

Each time Khalid would say, "I could have gotten that for you for five million! Don't sign any more contracts!" But the guys in the field would tell us, "Hey, we gotta sign these contracts because we've got more and more people coming in. We gotta put 'em somewhere."

"The only way this can work," I told Khalid, "is for you to designate officers who can work with us and sign these contracts on the spot." Khalid thought that was reasonable, but then, to his embarrassment, was unable to break the bureaucratic gridlock in his own headquarters. Even when he *ordered* his logistics staff to make payments to Starling and his team, they avoided the necessary decisions, and not a penny changed hands.

Washington's system was no less centralized and tightfisted. Though we were signing contracts left and right, we had no cash to pay for them. The Defense Department operated under a strict rule that, except in time of national emergency, most expenditures of $200,000 or more had to have congressional approval. Given the size of the force we were sending and the high prices in the Middle East, you could assume that *every* lease or contract in Saudi Arabia cost more than $200,000.

Had it not been for the Japanese, Desert Shield would have gone broke in August. While western newspapers were complaining about Tokyo's reluctance to increase its pledge of one billion dollars to safeguard Saudi Arabia, the Japanese embassy in Riyadh quietly transferred tens of millions of dollars into Central Command's accounts. We were able to cover our day-to-day operations before anybody in Washington could lay claim to the money.

Meanwhile Dane Starling's shop had become a giant clearinghouse for receipts, as we documented every dollar that the Saudis had promised to reimburse. It really added up; between mid-August and mid-October, we spent $760 million. When the host-nation-support negotiator from Washington, Major General Bill Ray, finally arrived on October 19, he brought with him the Defense Department's tally of airlift and sealift expenses to add on—almost $1.9 *billion*. This represented wishful thinking on the part of Pentagon budgeteers: from what I knew, King Fahd had promised to pay our transportation costs *within* the kingdom, not *to* it.

When I advised Khalid of General Ray's arrival with a comprehensive bill, he seemed relieved. I did not attend their meeting; Ray reported that the Saudis had readily agreed to reimburse Central Command's $760 million, but, as I expected, not the Pentagon's airlift and sealift expenses. More important, the Saudis had tentatively agreed to a mechanism for paying future bills as they came in. "It sounds like we're finally on the same wavelength," I remarked to my staff—and felt as reassured as you can when someone says the check is in the mail.

------

20 OCT 90 C + 74

1830 The CINC met with Major General Jaber of Kuwait. Jaber requested assistance in outfitting three light infantry brigades. Jaber was concerned that if he did not get together the remnants of disparate Kuwaiti units, they might take action on their own and inadvertently start hostilities. He added that a day would come when Kuwait is freed and a trained and ready force would be necessary to restore order and public service. The CINC agreed wholeheartedly.

22 OCT 90 C + 76

1000 During the update, the CINC was briefed that numerous donated items continue to arrive from the United States and around the world. The CINC reminded the entire staff of the bloody nose that we received in Vietnam over the emergence of illegal enterprises that pilfered equipment and sold items on the black market. We cannot let that happen during Operation Desert Shield. The CINC directed the judge advocate general to prepare a message for the CINC's release that all donated items would be properly accounted for in accordance with service procedures and that commanders would be held accountable for enforcing these procedures.

Colin Powell came to Riyadh on October 22 and once again acknowledged that the forces we had weren't adequate for pushing Iraq out of Kuwait. My staff ran through the various military options, including the plan he'd requested for a minimum force to safeguard Saudi Arabia indefinitely. Finally we unveiled our new plan to envelop and crush the Iraqi army with a huge flanking movement west of Kuwait—possible, we emphasized, only if the United States were willing to send an additional armored corps. This came as no surprise to Powell, since he and I had been trading ideas on the phone all week about possible routes for the envelopment.

He quickly zeroed in on the obvious and unspoken question: could we move enough supplies to sustain the attack? "Logistics could be your Achilles heel," he said. Tanks and armored personnel carriers can readily traverse soft sand, but the huge 5,000-gallon gasoline trucks that follow them into battle need roads or hard ground. So until we knew more about the deserts of southeastern Iraq, our scheme for the world's largest flanking attack could turn out to be a chimera. Powell didn't voice the political risks of expanding the U.S. commitment in Saudi Arabia to a force almost as big as the one we'd sent to Vietnam. I knew that had to be on his mind.

Powell then thanked us for our work, but cautioned that President Bush would take his time making a decision. "The mood in Washington shifts every week," he explained. "Ten days ago it was hawkish; in the past four or five days people have been talking about giving the economic sanctions time to work. But nobody is ready to make a decision: they're preoccupied with the budget crisis and next month's election." He went on to posit that, after the November elections, the President would either settle for military containment or seek the permission of the UN and Congress to launch an attack.

He asked how much time would be required to bring in the armored forces we'd requested. I estimated three months, and we wrapped up the session by agreeing that February was a possible date for a ground attack.

Though Powell had focused on supplying additional forces, he hadn't said what I most wanted to hear: that we could scrap the high-risk, go-with-what-you've-got offensive plan. That meant he hadn't yet crossed it off the list of possibilities and I wasn't surprised the following morning when he asked to be briefed again on that option. I asked my staff to leave the war room. "Let's drop this attack plan," I urged, when we were alone. "You have misgivings about it and so do I." I pointed out that the risks grew every day as Iraq moved more and more forces into Kuwait. "If we have to go on the offensive, I need more forces."

"I'm not sure we can bring more troops to the gulf without a clear mandate from Congress and the American public," he countered. I nodded. Nobody wanted another Vietnam, and I understood Powell's determination to avoid political as well as military mistakes. Unless we were confident of public support, it would be better not to launch an offensive at all.

In the course of that conversation, he made up his mind. "If we go to war," he promised, "we will not do it halfway. The United States military will give you whatever you need to do it right." He'd finally crossed the bridge, and as he left Riyadh with our troop request, I felt as though he'd lifted a great load from my shoulders.

---

29 OCT 90 C + 83

1000 The CINC directed the intelligence staff to conduct a detailed study of the impact of weather on military operations, particularly trafficability, in Kuwait and southeast Iraq. The CINC wanted everything from rain, sandstorms, temperatures, etc. covered, from now through the March-April period. The CINC said that we should use all available resources including debriefing people who have traveled in the affected areas.

1215 The CINC responded to a request by Lieutenant General Khalid for an impromptu meeting. General Khalid asked that at least one week in advance of any entertainer's arriving in the kingdom, we provide a detailed description of the visit, to include the number of days in-country, locations of shows, and the content of what the entertainer will do.

My sense of well-being didn't last long. That Saturday, Powell got back to Washington and called with a bombshell. "I better not go out of town anymore," he began.

"Why not?"

"Well, while I was away, Secretary Cheney came back from his trip to Russia with his own idea for an offensive plan. He had some of the guys on the Joint Staff work it up and went over and briefed the President."

"Would you mind telling me what it is?"

The plan was as bad as it could possibly be. Cheney, it turned out, had also been frustrated by Bob Johnston's presentation at the White House and had decided to come up with something bolder on his own. On his map of Iraq, he'd picked out two major missile-launching sites in the far western part of the country, fully five hundred miles from Kuwait. His proposal was to have the 82nd Airborne Division parachute in, link up with helicopter brigades from the 101st Air Assault Division and tank companies from the 3rd Armored Cavalry Regiment, seize the missile sites, and then head down Iraq's main east-west highway to threaten Baghdad.

"Didn't the Joint Staff point out the fallacies of this thing?" I said incredulously, ticking off a few, such as the impossibility of supplying a major operation so distant from friendly lines, and the fact that the heart of Iraq's military power was to the east. Powell observed drily that the secretary was a hard man to say no to if you were a career-minded young officer on the Joint Staff. "I need you to assess this thing," he said, "and give me something I can use to get the situation back under control."

I was rattled when I hung up the phone. Up to now, unlike the way things had gone in Vietnam, the U.S. chain of command had worked as it should. We'd had no repeat performance of Lyndon Johnson getting on the radio during the *Pueblo* incident and issuing orders to the tail gunner in a bomber. The President had been presidential; the secretary of defense had concentrated on setting military policy; the chairman of the Joint Chiefs had served as the facilitator between civilian and military leadership; and as theater commander I'd been given full authority to carry out my mission. But now I wondered whether Cheney had succumbed to the phenomenon I'd observed among some secretaries of the Army: put a civilian in charge of professional military men and before long he's no longer satisfied with setting policy but wants to outgeneral the generals.

We called this new scheme the "western excursion." I told my planning staff to examine it fairly. They did a masterful job; forty-eight hours later we faxed Powell their scathing analysis, which declared the plan "a bridge too far," comparing it to an overambitious scheme in World War II that cost the

American and British armies a defeat at Nijmegen, Holland. But despite our criticism, the western excursion wouldn't die: three times in that week alone Powell called with new variations from Cheney's staff. The most bizarre involved capturing a town in western Iraq and offering it to Saddam in exchange for Kuwait. Eventually we convinced Washington that these excursions were logistically unsupportable and would do nothing to advance our cause.

I could sense that Washington was groping for an instant solution, and I had no power to stop them. "We can't keep developing new sets of plans overnight," I chided Powell. One day he'd be talking offense, the next day containment, and the next withdrawal of all but a deterrent force. I'd been ordered to develop a troop-rotation plan, but no sooner had I delivered my recommendation than I was ordered to withdraw it, because it might give people the impression that America was making a long-term commitment of forces to the gulf. I began to feel as though Central Command had been sent to compete in an important athletic event without being told what the sport was. We'd run onto the field dressed in helmets and shoulder pads, all set for football, only to have Washington hand out baseball gloves. So we'd dutifully taken off the helmets and pads and gotten ready to play baseball— only to have Washington roll us a soccer ball. Except that this was no game. This was a deadly serious undertaking, with human lives on the line. On Monday, October 29, ten sailors on board the amphibious assault ship U.S.S. *Iwo Jima* in the gulf died when a steam pipe leak resulted in a release of pressure at 850 degrees Fahrenheit.

Our allies were also beginning to question where we were headed now that the coalition had built up sufficient force to defend Saudi Arabia. Saddam Hussein had made it clear that he would never forgive the Arab leaders who had invited western forces into the gulf. In speeches on Baghdad radio he called King Fahd and President Mubarak traitors to the Arab cause. They now sought assurances that America would not withdraw before the Iraqi threat had been eliminated. Meanwhile the British raised the question of timing. Sir David Craig, Powell's counterpart, who was in Riyadh that week, told me that the window of opportunity for an attack would slam shut in March, when Ramadan, the Moslem holy month, began. If the coalition intended to attack, we needed to define our goals and plan the offensive soon, he said. Khalid had made the same point. Furthermore, we had to think about the weather: it would do our troops and equipment no good if we dawdled until summer returned.

As I fretted about this, I realized my misgivings were the same as those expressed by far more illustrious theater commanders. Eisenhower and

MacArthur had each worried that decisions in Washington would be motivated more by politics than by military reality. I didn't want to inflict my doubts on my staff; and to discuss them with my allied counterparts would have been disloyal. But I felt I owed it to our leaders in Washington to voice my concerns. I decided it was time to go on the record. At noon on Wednesday, October 31, I dictated a long memorandum to Powell, detailing the success of Desert Shield to date and again asking, "Where do we go from here?" I hoped that by putting my request for further direction on paper I could get Washington to budge. The memo ended:

> We continue to try to plan for offensive operations, but to be perfectly honest with you, we are doing it in a total vacuum of guidance, with assumptions that change every time someone in Washington gets another brilliant idea. The end result is a staff that is working very hard and has done a very fine job to date, working under increasing pressure and continuous short-term deadlines to the point of great frustration with very little outside appreciation. Perhaps that is the way it has always been, but I don't recall any time in military history when a theater commander has been asked to put together offensive plans for a force of three hundred thousand or four hundred thousand, been told to do it in a matter of a few days with no strategic guidance, and then been asked to defend that plan in detail. I know this isn't a perfect world, and we in Centcom will continue to do what is asked of us, but in a matter of such great importance that involves not only the lives of thousands of American service men and women, but also the prestige of the United States of America and the future of the free world in the Middle East, we should at least be able to do it right.

While the memo was being typed, I left headquarters to visit one of our troop compounds. When I came back, Powell was on the phone. "The President has made a decision. Next weekend Secretary Baker will come to ask King Fahd and our other allies to agree to offensive operations. Then we'll take the idea to the UN and ask for an ultimatum for Iraq to leave Kuwait. You should be prepared to build up the force and go to war."

"How big a buildup do you mean?" I asked carefully.

"It will be dramatic. You're gonna get everything you asked for and more." Naming a half-dozen major units the Joint Chiefs had earmarked, Powell explained that the decision had been to nearly *double* the force of Desert Shield. He promised that we would discuss specifics later.

I had never believed I'd feel reassured to see the United States move toward war. But now, as much as I continued to wish for peace, I was relieved to have a clear mission. I alerted my senior commanders and sent various staff officers scrambling to accelerate our offensive planning, start preparations for the coming influx of troops, and formulate requests for Secretary Baker to discuss with King Fahd.

That evening I went downstairs to the war room for the nightly briefing and found Dane Starling, my logistics chief, and Bill Ray, the bill collector from the Pentagon, outside in the hallway grinning like the Cheshire cat.

"We have something for you," Starling said, handing me a piece of paper.

It was a check, drawn on an account at the Morgan Guaranty Trust and made out to the "The Government of the United States," for *$760 million*. The signature at the bottom was Khalid's. "The Saudis kept their word," observed Ray.

"What are we gonna do with this?" I gasped. Starling and Ray had it all figured out. First they made a photocopy to serve as a memento; then they handed the check to a courier, who raced to the airport, flew on one of Central Command's jets to Paris, switched to the Concorde, and made it back to New York in time to deposit the check before the banks closed on Thursday. That enabled the U.S. Treasury to earn interest on the money over the weekend—which Ray estimated at more than $300,000. We had a good time at the evening briefing looking at the photocopy and speculating about how much *we* could have made by holding onto the money and investing it for a week before turning it over to Washington.

After the meeting B.B. Bell asked, "Sir, what about your message to General Powell?" He held up the desperate request for orders that I'd dictated earlier in the day. I looked at the memo; it was no longer necessary. "File it," I said. In the space of a few hours everything had changed. I kept it as a souvenir—and to remind myself that while our leaders didn't always respond to requests as quickly or decisively as I liked, they had never let us down.

———

I NOV 90 C + 86

1445   In a short phoncon, the chairman told the CINC that the President had confirmed his intent to travel to Saudi Arabia for Thanksgiving. He would arrive in Jidda on the twenty-first and then go to Dhahran on the twenty-second, where he would spend the day touring units and eating multiple Thanksgiving meals with the troops.

1915 At the evening update the CINC was briefed on an incident in which an Iraqi MiG-25 crossed the Saudi border some six to ten miles. Our aircraft in response were locked on and prepared to fire when the MiG-25 turned and flew back across the border. The CINC reminded the operations officer that we do not want to start the war over a single aircraft and that we should carefully review our rules of engagement.

2 NOV 90 C + 87

1530 The CINC told the chairman that he was going over to Bahrain to have dinner with the crown prince and to get a little rest.

As soon as Secretary of State Baker had come to Saudi Arabia and asked King Fahd's permission to proceed, President Bush would announce the new buildup. It was the second difficult decision that the king would have to make in the crisis, but this time we were more certain of the outcome. Saddam had gone too far in his rhetoric: he had accused Fahd, the custodian of the two holy mosques, of betraying Islam, and had proclaimed himself a direct descendant of the prophet Muhammad. Arab consensus had shifted to the belief that Iraq must be punished. I flew down to Jidda to brief Baker beforehand, but that was my only role. Unlike the first meeting in August this was completely a State Department show. I stayed behind at the guest palace as Baker and Chas Freeman went to see the king.

When Baker explained that the United States would like to prepare an offensive to be launched from Saudi soil, the king was expecting the request and did not hesitate. "While we all still want peace, if we must go to war, Saudi Arabia's armed forces will fight side by side with yours," he said. Baker then indicated that we'd need to deploy at least 140,000 more troops. King Fahd did not even blink: "I've never set a limit on troop strength." Baker raised the question of how to approach the other Arab states; the king promised that his government would help sell the idea.

Next, Baker had to ask a potentially explosive question: suppose Israel became involved as the result of an Iraqi attack? King Fahd gave a long explanation of the difficulties this would cause in the Arab world. It would be better for everyone, he said, if Israel stayed out; under no circumstances would Arab forces allow themselves to be perceived as *allied* with Israelis. But then, to Baker's and Freeman's amazement, King Fahd added that he could not expect Israel to stand by idly if attacked. If Israel were to defend itself, he said, the Saudi armed forces would still fight by our side. This stand by King Fahd was an act of extraordinary courage and leadership. He was aware that such a decision could provoke the wrath of the entire Arab world, and yet he took the position he felt was necessary to protect his country and preserve the coalition.

Baker turned to the last two important matters. Number one was money: we needed King Fahd to spell out precisely what Saudi Arabia would pay for. That afternoon I'd alerted the secretary that in addition to fuel, water, and transportation, the Saudis had been supplying accommodations and fresh food. "If we're making a formal request," I said, "we ought to roll those in." Baker did, and King Fahd agreed.

Second was the question of who would be in command if we went on the attack. Washington wanted a stipulation that the United States could call the shots, but having worked so hard to build a collaborative relationship, I was uneasy about Baker's telling the Saudis, "Schwarzkopf's got to be in charge."

"So tell me what you need," Baker had responded.

I took a sheet of paper and wrote, "Command and control: should military operations commence, a joint command as currently exists will continue; however, the commander of the U.S. forces will have final approval authority for all military operations." The first bit was in deference to Saudi sovereignty: it ensured that Khalid and I would continue to be seen as equals. The second clause ensured that I could keep the offensive planning on track. We had it typed up, and when Baker met with King Fahd that evening, he read the statement and said, "This is the command relationship that the United States would like to see."

"Please give me that paper, and it will happen," said the king.

Despite King Fahd's agreement, this shift toward American control made others uneasy. As a result, when I met a few days later with Prince Sultan and Khalid, Sultan pointedly asked, "What does this mean?" He held up the piece of paper Secretary Baker had handed the king.

"It means business as usual," I was able to tell him. "Our joint command will remain in effect. But because I have experience in making offensive plans, my government wants the final decision on such plans to rest with me." Then, in the Arab style, I repeated the explanation in personal terms: "I give you my assurance as your friend that I won't do anything you or Khalid disagree with. We will talk everything over, and I will continue to work with you as we have worked until now, with full consultation on every decision."

Sultan immediately brightened. "That's fine," he said. "You are a good friend of Saudi Arabia."

Each side now had what it needed. Shortly afterward the Saudis promoted Khalid to commander, joint force/theater of operations, their equivalent of commander in chief.

7 NOV 90 C + 92

1415 Trafficability analysis of Kuwait and southeastern Iraq briefing from the intelligence staff and the 513th Military Intelligence Brigade. The briefing covered a terrain analysis, assessment of avenues of approach, the effects of weather to include rain and wind, and light data for the winter months. The bottom line was that mid-February is an extremely advantageous time for U.S. forces to attack.

20

By late October the desert had grown a little cooler and somewhat more bearable—most days the thermometer only hit one hundred. But at isolated base camps with names like All-American and Victory, there was little to take soldiers' minds off the sand, the flies, and the constant conversation about whether we'd go to war or go home. Nobody was telling them what to expect, so when rumors spread that we had a rotation plan in the works, a lot of men and women were hoping they'd be home for Christmas.

I didn't blame them. While we'd provided as many comforts as possible in the course of eleven weeks—scores of post offices, PXs, phone exchanges, and radio and TV transmitters—the troops were forced to tolerate bad boots and terrible-tasting food, both the result of shortsighted decisions made by the Army years before. Since taking over Central Command, I'd continually pointed out that our soldiers had no desert combat boots, and now they were wearing Vietnam-era jungle boots, black ones that became furnaces on hot sand. They had holes along the bottom designed to let water run out when the soldier was in a swamp—in the desert, of course, the holes let sand in. The Army's main chow problems were a lack of cooks and the MRE—Meal Ready to Eat, or as the troops usually put it, Meal Rejected by Ethiopians. The successor to the C-ration, the MRE was an unappetizing glob of irradiated food in a plastic pouch that was supposedly palatable either hot or cold. I'd eaten MREs on training exercises and rejected them, too—they looked and tasted like paste—yet we were asking our soldiers to be happy with one meager hot meal and two MREs a day.

So I wasn't surprised that Secretary Baker found some testy young men and women when he arrived at the desert base of the 1st Cavalry Division on November 4. He made a short speech, taking pains to thank the troops for the sacrifice they were making for their country, and then started shaking hands with officers in the front of the formation. Suddenly, a few soldiers in the back began shouting things like "Have some hot water!" referring to the bottled water they had to drink, and "Eat an MRE!" Later, when Baker moved among the soldiers, a woman sergeant asked point-blank, "When are we going home?"

Four days later she had her answer: not any time soon. President Bush had given the order for the further buildup of U.S. forces in the gulf. It was even more massive than what Powell had described. Where I'd requested two armored divisions, Washington had decided to send *three*, plus an extra brigade, each outfitted with the Army's most modern tank, the M1A1. Beyond that, Central Command was to get a second Marine division plus an additional Marine brigade, two more aircraft-carrier battle groups, a second battleship, and three hundred more Air Force planes. The President had doubled our ground force, tripled our number of tanks, boosted our air power by thirty percent, and doubled our naval force—all to ensure what he termed "an adequate offensive military option."

The news reached soldiers in the desert simultaneously with an announcement from Secretary Cheney that no one would be rotated for the duration. At first some reacted with dismay, but at least the uncertainty had been removed: the soldiers realized, "Well, that's it. We ain't goin' home for Christmas." Commanders got their units out in the desert for offensive training and a new sense of determination took over. I'd hear things like: "All right, let's get this show on the road, kick their ass, and go home—so we don't have to be here *next* Christmas."

I I NOV 90 C+96

> 1745 Phoncon with the chairman. The CINC discussed the visit of the delegation led by Congressman Murtha and noted that it was very successful. They pressed the CINC on the necessity of the Congress to declare war. The CINC said politics was not his purview, but his biggest concern was that premature declaration of war would alert the enemy.

He said a declaration of war at 1455 hours to go to war at 1500 was okay, but not to declare war four weeks prior to an attack. The CINC stated that the delegation was surprised by this comment and said that it was very worthwhile. From the CINC's standpoint they went away with their questions answered and pretty well defanged.

President Bush arrived to spend Thanksgiving with the troops, and they greeted him with overwhelming enthusiasm rather than complaints. King Fahd welcomed him Wednesday afternoon at the airport at Jidda, and the visit started with a state dinner. We spent Thanksgiving crisscrossing eastern Saudi Arabia and paying separate calls to the Army, Navy, Air Force, and Marines.

On the way from Jidda to the first stop at Dhahran air base, the President sat at his desk on *Air Force One* and questioned me closely about our coalition partners, the safety of the embassy in Kuwait City, and other subjects. While he had shown me around the airplane and gone out of his way to make me feel at home, I was still a little awed to find myself one-on-one with the President of the United States. He listened attentively as I explained the battle plan for the ground campaign. After a moment, he looked at me and asked pointedly, "What is the shortest ground war you can visualize?"

I told him there were so many variables and unknowns that I couldn't give him a single answer. But he persisted: "Give me a best-case and worst-case scenario."

"The best case would be about three days, which assumes that the Iraqis quickly fold and surrender en masse. The worst would be a situation in which we fight to a stalemate. That could go on for months."

"Isn't there some scenario in between?"

Since the question was from the President, I felt duty-bound to answer if I could; yet I worried that he'd take anything I said as a promise. I chose a very circumspect response: "I can imagine a campaign lasting three to four weeks, where we encountered tough resistance but were able to seize all our objectives and destroy the Republican Guard."

"Three weeks," he mused.

"That's just speculation," I emphasized. Seeing him fasten on the number made me nervous.

We touched down at Dhahran where a big crowd of U.S., British, Saudi, and Kuwaiti air force personnel surrounded a platform truck that had been parked in front of three warplanes and hung with red, white, and blue bunting. Colonel John McBroom, the U.S. Air Force squadron commander, introduced the President, who then made a big point of bringing on stage George Mitchell, the Senate majority leader, and Tom Foley, the speaker of the House of Representatives, who had accompanied him on the trip. After addressing the cheering troops he hopped down, and he and Mrs. Bush signed autographs and shook hundreds of hands.

The President was buoyed as we got back in the helicopter. But once on board, John Sununu handed him his daily news digest—which included reports that Congress might convene a special session to debate Desert Shield, plus the results of the latest polls, showing his popularity at an all-time low. The President was disappointed.

"I truly don't understand how anyone could be against the stand we've taken," he complained. He held up the digest and pointed to a summary of interviews with Saddam Hussein conducted by British and American TV correspondents. "Look at this. Can you imagine anyone interviewing Hitler in World War Two the way they do Saddam?" He compared Iraq's invasion of Kuwait to Nazi Germany's invasion of Czechoslovakia. I tensed as he added, "If we could whip the Iraqis in three to four weeks, all these critics would suddenly change their minds." The President continued, as much to himself as to the other people in the aircraft, that he wasn't going to be intimidated by poll results or by Congress. He knew that by law he didn't need congressional approval to proceed. In his own mind, he was persuaded that the United States had set upon the moral course. He was certain the civilized world would agree.

We landed deep in the desert where troops from the XVIII Airborne Corps had been assembled, and the President gave another brief speech to cheers from the soldiers. At the end he presented them with a set of horseshoes and challenged their champions to a match on the White House lawn after they came home. The troops loved it. As we waited in the chow line for turkey roll and mashed potatoes, he joked with the soldiers. The presidential party spread out to eat with them at sandbag-and-plywood tables in the sun. Spirits were high despite the heat.

Next on the itinerary was a Thanksgiving religious service seventy-five miles away aboard the Navy helicopter carrier U.S.S. *Nassau*—which, in deference to Saudi sensibilities, had been positioned outside the kingdom's territorial waters. Sailors mobbed the President and Mrs. Bush afterward, and they lingered so long shaking hands that they had to skip a tour of the ship that the Navy had arranged.

No sooner had the President climbed back into the helicopter than Sununu handed him a cable with the news that British prime minister

Margaret Thatcher had resigned. He was stunned—Thatcher was his closest friend and his staunchest ally among the world's heads of state and had helped him the most in the early days of the gulf crisis. The President made arrangements to place a call to her as soon as possible and then quizzed his staff about her successor, John Major.

The last stop was a Marine Corps outpost, only sixty-five miles from the border of occupied Kuwait, where the assembly included U.S. Marines and soldiers from Great Britain's 1st Armored Division, the Desert Rats. The President stood on a hillside and gave his toughest speech of the day: "We won't pull any punches. We are not here on some exercise. And we are not walking away until the invader is out of Kuwait." As they cheered, he added, "That may well be where you come in."

He fell asleep on the flight back to Dhahran—I felt exhausted just from watching him buffeted by the day's highs and lows. I also felt the emotional impact that his visit had had on my troops: there had been no Republicans or Democrats in the crowd that day—only Americans, young and middle-aged, thrilled by the contact with their President. He sensed it too and at one point actually turned to Sununu and said, "Where are Foley and Mitchell? I hope they're seeing this."

The visit from the President was a boost, but what sustained the men and women of Desert Shield as war drew near was the overwhelming support from home. By late November, as the holiday season began, mail was pouring into Saudi Arabia at the rate of three hundred tons a day. It included not only letters and packages from families and friends, but also hundreds of thousands of pieces addressed to "Any Serviceman"—messages and gifts and cookies from individuals, schools, labor unions, offices, churches, civic groups, and old people's homes. Most of the letters were from Americans who approved of Desert Shield and said things like, "God bless you for fighting for freedom and protecting our national interest." But some came from people who thought the United States had no business sending troops and who wrote messages like, "I disagree with the decision that put you there, but you never have to worry about my support as long as you are there. Thank you for the sacrifice you're making for our country."

Something basic had changed since Vietnam, when we had drafted young Americans, ordered them to fight, and then blamed them for the war when they came home. We had matured as a nation to the point where we could separate the political debate from our concern for the safety of the men and women who were being sent off to war.

Almost every general in Desert Shield had fought in Vietnam and we all remembered feeling abandoned by our countrymen. So for me and the other Vietnam vets, the mail that reached us in Saudi Arabia had an impact that was hard to put into words. One letter in particular brought that home to me: it was from my sister Ruth. I'd never gotten over her fierce opposition to the Vietnam War and we hadn't seen each other or even talked to each other much since our mother's funeral fifteen years before. The letter ended, "Please forgive me for not writing you all those years in Vietnam." I read it at my desk in the Ministry of Defense building and burst into tears.

———

Once we knew we'd have the units we needed, the plan for the ground war took shape quickly. On November 14, less than a week after the President announced the further buildup of U.S. forces in the gulf, I was able to call my senior commanders to Dhahran to outline how we were going to defeat Iraq. I knew this would be my most important meeting of the war: these were the men who would have to execute the plan in battle. I stood before a fifteen-foot-wide map of Kuwait and Iraq in the "Desert Inn," a run-down building that the Army had converted to a dining hall, and watched as they took their seats. Of the twenty-two generals and admirals present, almost all wore two or three stars. Many had already played key roles in Desert Shield: my component commanders Horner, Yeosock, Boomer, and Mauz; Gary Luck, the commander of the XVIII Airborne Corps; his division commanders, McCaffrey, Peay, and Jim Johnson; and John H. Tilelli, Jr., commander of the 1st Cavalry Division. Boomer had brought major generals Mike Myatt and Royal Moore, commanders of the 1st Marine Division and 3rd Marine Aircraft Wing, respectively. The newcomers were the heads of the major fighting units that had been added to Desert Shield. Lieutenant General Fred Franks, commander of the Army's VII Corps, had flown down from his headquarters in Stuttgart, Germany, along with major generals Ronald Griffith and Paul E. "Butch" Funk, the commanders of his 1st and 3rd armored divisions, respectively. Major General Tom Rhame, commander of the 1st Infantry Division, the famous Big Red One, had come all the way from Fort Riley, Kansas, for the meeting. Of course Major General Pagonis was present. And in the corner, Colonel Bell stood ready with his tape recorder. As I looked at their faces I felt that no theater commander in history had ever been blessed with such an array of talent.

I'd worked myself up into a ferocious state. Only a few of the commanders had any idea of the plan I was about to present or of the tough assignments I was going to mete out. I needed every man in the room to embrace his mission and be breathing fire by the time he went out the door.

I began by emphasizing the necessity of maintaining the secrecy of what we were about to discuss. I described how a Washington press leak about an upcoming amphibious exercise in the gulf had prompted Iraq to load a bomber with Silkworm antiship missiles. "You are going to be bombarded with questions by the press. I do not want you to discuss military operations. Period. I do not want you to discuss your capabilities. Period. And you should teach every one of your officers the same thing. I don't care what Pfc. Snuffy says, but I do care when some officer gets so enamored of the press that he has to shoot off his mouth. I'm telling you I am going to deal absolutely brutally, *brutally*, with anyone I feel compromises classified information." I was harsh, but I was also convinced that our own newspaper and TV reports had become Iraq's best source of military intelligence. We had already cut off all other sources.

I recounted Central Command's long struggle to get Washington to acknowledge that kicking Iraq out of Kuwait was going to require more troops. Now that VII Corps was here, I said, "My written orders from Washington are still to deter Iraq from attacking Saudi Arabia. But there is no doubt about the fact that we are getting ready to go on the offensive. That's what we are here to talk about today. Forget the defensive bullshit, we are now talking offensive. And we're going to talk offense from now until the day we go home."

I walked them through my analysis of Iraq's forces and our own, curtly noting what we were up against: "There are a whole hell of a lot of them — 450,000 right now in the Kuwaiti theater, twenty-six divisions' worth, and their divisions are the same size as ours. So they've got mass on their side. Another strength I would say is their chemical capability. They have used it in the past and there is no doubt in my mind they're going to use it on us." I pointed to the weaknesses that would be Iraq's undoing and reminded the commanders of our military strengths. Finally I laid out our battlefield goals. "The first thing that we're going to have to do is, I don't like to use the word 'decapitate,' so I think I'll use the word 'attack,' leadership, and go after his command and control. Number two, we've got to gain and maintain air superiority. Number three, we need to cut totally his supply lines. We also need to destroy his chemical, biological, and nuclear capability. And finally, all you tankers, listen to this. We need to destroy—not attack, not damage, not surround—I want you to *destroy* the Republican Guard. When you're done with them, I don't want them to be an effective fighting force anymore. I don't want them to exist as a military organization." For the benefit of the Vietnam vets—practically the whole room—I emphasized that "we're not going into this with one arm tied behind our backs. We're not gonna say we want to be as nice as we possibly can, and if they draw back across the border that's fine with us. That's bullshit! We are going to destroy the Republican Guard." If we were ordered to go on the offensive, we would be free to use our full military strength and attack across the border into Iraq.

"I'm now going to tell you all some stuff that not very many people know about, in Washington particularly," I said, and described the four phases of attack we'd mapped out for Desert Storm: strategic bombing first; then gaining control of the Kuwaiti skies; then bombing Iraqi artillery positions, trench lines, and troops. At last I turned to the plan for the ground offensive—a fully realized version of the envelopment I'd proposed to Powell three weeks before. Using the map, I showed the commanders where I wanted them to maneuver their units. The plan covered a huge area: in order to make sure we fought the campaign on our own terms, we had extended the boundary of the battlefield westward so that it encompassed a rectangle roughly the size of Pennsylvania. Saddam's forces were concentrated at the eastern end, in and around Kuwait. Desert Shield forces would keep them from moving south; to their east was the natural barrier of the gulf; to their north was the Euphrates, which would become a natural barrier once Chuck Horner's air force dropped the bridges that crossed it; and to the west were hundreds of miles of desert that would become our main avenue of attack.

I anticipated, I said, a four-pronged ground assault. Along the Saudi-Kuwaiti border near the gulf, I wanted two divisions of U.S. Marines and a Saudi task force to thrust straight into Kuwait, with the objective of tying up Saddam's forces and eventually encircling Kuwait City. Nodding in Boomer's direction, I said, "I'll leave it to Walt Boomer to figure out how he wants to do that, but it also gives him the capability to come in from the sea with his amphibious forces." I'd reserved a second corridor, in the western part of Kuwait, for a parallel attack by the pan-Arab forces led by two armored divisions from Egypt and another Saudi task force. Their objective would be the road junction northwest of Kuwait City that controlled Iraqi supply lines. Eventually they would enter Kuwait City and have the dirty job of fighting the Iraqis house to house if necessary.

Meanwhile from the west would come the U.S. Army's power punch. Looking at Gary Luck, I indicated a section of Saudi-Iraqi border more than three hundred and fifty miles inland. "I am probably going to send the XVIII Airborne Corps very deep," I said, showing how I wanted Luck's divisions to race north from that area to the Euphrates, blocking the Republican Guard's last route of retreat. Once that sector was secured, I told him, he would hook his forces east, ready to join the attack on the main body of the Iraqi army. Finally I turned to Fred Franks. "I think it's pretty obvious what your mission is going to be," I said, moving my hand along the desert corridor just to the west of Kuwait, "attack through here and destroy the Republican Guard." I wanted to pin them with their backs against the sea, then go in and wipe them out. I couldn't resist adding, "Once they're gone, be prepared to continue the attack to Baghdad. Because there isn't going to be anything else out there." I allowed that taking Baghdad would probably be unnecessary, because by then the war would have ended.

The effect was electric. When we broke for coffee, the commanders rushed up and were climbing all over the map. Peay and McCaffrey, who had been handed challenging missions far out on the flank, told me: "You know, sir, we thought we were still going to use that ho-hum plan of slogging into Kuwait. This is fantastic!" Walt Boomer, whose Marines were being called upon to do some of that very slogging in order to free up the Army for the flanking attack, accepted the assignment because he knew it had to be done. The only dissonant note was from Freddie Franks: "The plan looks good, but I don't have enough force to accomplish my mission." He argued that I should give him the 1st Cavalry Division, which I was holding in reserve. I said I'd consider it when the time came.

When we reconvened I told them to expect D-day sometime in mid-February. That immediately focused everybody's attention on two huge logistical challenges. The first was that the bulk of our armor was still in Germany and the United States: we still had to transport more than three divisions to the gulf, give the soldiers time to acclimate, and then move them and their equipment hundreds of miles north to the Saudi border. The second was a decision I'd made to wait on moving into position for the flanking attack until we launched the air campaign. I didn't want the Iraqis to learn of our battle plan and then be able to shift their defenses. I knew that once our Air Force stopped the Iraqis' reconnaissance flights, they would be blind, and even if they did finally figure out our plan, the Air Force would make it impossible for them to shift enough forces to counter it. So I insisted Franks and Luck keep their corps in staging areas near Kuwait. "You'll be allowed to move as soon as we launch the air campaign," I promised. "You have to trust me that I'll give you enough time." That mollified them somewhat. But we all knew that shifting two corps and all their supplies and ammunition two hundred miles or more laterally across the desert would be a mammoth undertaking. I told them, "I'm going to be drilling you guys unmercifully between now and D-day to convince me that you are logistically prepared."

After a question-and-answer session I tried to set a tone for the coming months. "Let me leave you with one thought, guys. In order for this to succeed—because the enemy is still going to outnumber us—it is going to take, for lack of a better word, killer instinct on the part of all of our leaders out there." I pointed again at the map. "What I'm saying is when the Marines hit the wire right here and when the Army forces hit the wire over here, there's going to be none of this bullshit, 'Well, I think we're going to go in and probe a little bit and see if we can get through.' We need commanders in the lead who absolutely, clearly understand that they *will get through*. And that once they're through they're not going to stop and discuss it. They are going to go up there and destroy the Republican Guard. I cannot afford to have commanders who do not understand that it is attack, attack, attack, attack, and destroy every step of the way. If you have somebody who doesn't understand it, I would strongly recommend that you consider removing him from command and putting in somebody that can do the job.

"Because, let's face it, the prestige of the United States military is on our shoulders. But more importantly, the prestige of the entire United States of America rests on our shoulders. There isn't going to be anybody else in this thing except us. There are no more forces coming. What we got is what's going to do the job. And for our country we dare not fail. We cannot fail, and we will not fail. Anybody in here who doesn't understand that, get out of the way. Any questions? Okay, good luck to you. You know what needs to be done."

———

I was still riding high from the commanders' conference when I went to brief Khalid two days later. He was initially shocked by how deeply we intended to invade Iraq, but soon embraced the concept enthusiastically. I hadn't left this to chance: I'd heard him speak often of his wish that Saudi forces liberate Kuwait, so we'd scripted his troops into both prongs of the attack into the emirate. Two Saudi armored brigades would fight alongside the Egyptians and Syrians on the western thrust and two more would attack in the east, up the coastal highway toward Kuwait City, parallel with Boomer's Marines. Khalid expressed concern about the border barriers Iraq had thrown up—high sand embankments, minefields, razor-wire fences, and other obstacles. I promised advisors who would teach the Saudis the tactics they'd need to breach the enemy lines, as well as armored excavators, mine plows, and other breaching equipment.

Now I faced the ticklish business of enlisting the support of our coalition partners. Even though the United States was supplying two thirds of Desert Storm's ground force, for the plan to work I needed the combat power of the entire coalition. When Iraq declared on November 19 that it was deploying 250,000 more soldiers "as defensive measures in southern Iraq, the provinces of Kuwait and Basra," I felt even greater urgency to get everyone on board. If Saddam went through with the buildup, his force in the theater would number 680,000. My intelligence staff was skeptical of the announcement, but soon we were picking up a frenzy of military construction along the Kuwaiti border, as the Iraqis added to the defenses they'd already built. More troops flowed in too, though not as many as advertised: the Iraqis ended up with 545,000.

20 NOV 90 C + 105

1500 The CINC discussed the recent raid by Saudi clerics on a French home. This particularly brutal raid was a matter of concern for the CINC even though no U.S. servicemembers were involved. The CINC noted that he intended to discuss that issue with General Khalid.

23 NOV 90 C + 108

1500 At the executive update, the CINC noted for the staff that he had discussed with General Khalid the Saudi clerical raid on a French embassy party several nights ago. The CINC relayed that he had emphatically told Khalid that he would not stand by for any of this type of activity with American female soldiers. Khalid became quite energized and assured the CINC that if any such incident did happen, swift and immediate action would be taken.

Just after Thanksgiving I approached the British, presenting our battle plan to Lieutenant General Sir Peter de la Billière, their commander in the gulf. A legendary soldier and adventurer, Sir Peter was former chief of the Special Air Service and the most decorated officer in the British armed services. It was no coincidence that I'd gone to him first: Great Britain had been our closest western ally in the crisis, and he and I had become good friends. I trusted his brains and judgment so much that I asked his advice on even the most sensitive military issues. I wanted de la Billière's newly arrived 1st Armored Division, the Desert Rats, to attack with Walt Boomer into Kuwait. He nodded approvingly as I laid out the details of the offensive plan, but finally remarked bluntly that British voters would object to seeing their boys relegated to the supporting attack; could I reassign his force to the main attack with VII Corps? As I would later tell Powell, I didn't see how we could refuse that kind of request from a close ally, even if it was purely political and not military in intent. So we made the change—over the strenuous objection of Boomer, who was impressed with the Desert Rats and wanted the combat power of their tanks. To compensate him, I had to assign the Tiger Brigade from the 2nd Armored Division in Germany, plus extra air support, to his attack.

The British government also sent a request directly to Secretary Cheney: they still wanted a clear definition of the coalition's strategic and political war aims. When Tom King, the British secretary of state for defense, informed me of this during a visit to Central Command, I assumed the query would cause some consternation in Washington. So I gave an order to Grant Sharp, my plans and policy chief: "Draft a strategic directive that we can recommend to General Powell if he asks."

Sure enough, within a week Powell called seeking Central Command's input, and Sharp handed me three typewritten pages. It was a textbook-perfect strategic directive, and small wonder: he had modeled it on the Allies' historic order to Dwight Eisenhower in February 1944, authorizing D-Day. Sharp's text read in part:

DRAFT PROPOSED STRATEGIC DIRECTIVE
TO COMBINED COMMANDER

1. TASK. Undertake operations to seek the complete withdrawal of Iraqi forces from Kuwait in accordance with the terms of UN resolutions and sanctions. If necessary and when directed, conduct military operations to destroy Iraqi armed forces, liberate and secure Kuwait to permit the restoration of its legitimate government, and make every reasonable effort to repatriate foreign nationals held against their will in Iraq and Kuwait. Promote the security and stability of the Arabian/ Persian Gulf region.

2. AUTHORIZATION. When directed, you are authorized to conduct air operations throughout Iraq and land and sea operations into Iraqi territory and waters as necessary to liberate and secure Kuwait and destroy Iraqi forces threatening the territory of Kuwait and other coalition states. Forces should be prepared to initiate offensive operations no later than February 1991.

At any time, you are authorized to take advantage of the full or partial withdrawal of Iraqi forces from Kuwait by introducing forces under your command to secure Kuwaiti territory and waters, defend against renewed aggression, and permit the restoration of the legitimate government in Kuwait.

Pending authority to execute operations to destroy Iraqi forces and liberate Kuwait, defend Saudi Arabia. Should Iraqi forces attack Saudi Arabia, you are authorized to conduct air, land, and sea operations throughout Kuwait and Iraq, their airspace, and territorial waters.

3. OPERATIONAL GUIDANCE. The objectives of your offensive campaign will be to destroy Iraqi nuclear, biological, and chemical production facilities and weapons of mass destruction; occupy southeast Iraq until combined strategic objectives are met; destroy or neutralize the Republican Guard Forces Command; destroy, neutralize or disconnect the Iraqi national command authority; safeguard, to the extent practicable, foreign nationals being detained in Iraq and Kuwait; and degrade or disrupt Iraqi strategic air defenses.

On November 18 we faxed this draft recommendation to Powell. It disappeared without a trace, and to my knowledge Washington never gave London a formal response. After a couple of days I offered a copy of the draft to de la Billière, saying, "At least this will show you what we *think* we're supposed to prepare for."

---

27 NOV 90 C+112

1510 Executive session with the congressional delegation led by Congressman Mavroules. The bottom line to this session was that the delegation demonstrated that the members of the House were quite likely to fall into one of two categories. The first would be those who want military action now, and the second would be those who want to give the sanctions an opportunity to work, perhaps for as long as two years. The CINC noted that the congressmen were so divided that they actually began a debate amongst themselves in the middle of his presentation to them.

2010 The CINC informed the chairman that the congressional delegation was unaware that Arabs were occupying positions in front of Americans. They believed that the Arabs were not participating.

2 DEC 90 C + 117

0900 CINC met with Secretary of Energy James Watkins. The purpose of Sec. Watkins' visit with the CINC was to seek assurances that an attack on Saudi Arabia would not result in significant damage to oil facilities. Sec. Watkins' focus was to present a speech in hopes that if war broke out oil prices would not skyrocket.

4 DEC 90 C + 119

1000 Two CIA analysts provided a psychological profile of Saddam Hussein. The CINC viewed their presentation as disjointed, allowing the listener to draw any conclusions that he desires.

5 DEC 90 C + 120

2000 General Khalid informed the CINC that he had no idea that Brooke Shields had been denied a visa and he did not think Prince Sultan knew of it either. Khalid informed the CINC that he would call Prince Bandar and find out what is going on. The CINC reminded Gen. Khalid that the Saudis ran the risk of "winning the war and losing the peace" with the U.S. and cautioned Khalid not to allow the same type of thing to happen with the Bob Hope tour.

On November 29, at U.S. urging, the United Nations Security Council lit the fuse of war, authorizing the use of force if Iraq did not leave Kuwait by January 15. Written orders or no, it was clear we were running out of time: only six weeks remained to prepare the coalition for attack.

While I was gratified that Khalid had so readily come on board, I knew the Egyptians were the real key to Arab participation in Desert Storm. Militarily they were indispensable: I needed them to spearhead the second prong of the attack and pin the Iraqis in western Kuwait, a tough mission for which I had no other units to spare. Their two armored divisions, well trained and outfitted with modern American equipment, constituted the largest ground attack force after ours, and what's more we knew they could fight—the Egyptians had been exercising with Central Command forces for years. Politically they were the acid test of my plan: the entire Arab world was watching to see whether Cairo would join the offensive. President Mubarak had evidently taken the position that, while Egypt was willing to fight to liberate Kuwait, it did not want its army to attack into Iraq. I thought I'd hit upon a way to assure Egypt that Arabs would fight in Kuwait while the United States, Great Britain, and France would fight in Iraq—but I didn't know whether Mubarak would buy it.

On December 8, on the pretext of inspecting an M-1 tank factory that was jointly operated by the United States and Egypt, I flew to Cairo. I gave a very detailed briefing to three officers I'd counted as friends since my earliest days at Central Command: General Youssef Sabri Abu Taleb, the minister of defense; Lieutenant General Abu Shanaf, the chief of staff of Egypt's armed forces; and Major General Omar Soliman, the chief of military intelligence. They all immediately recognized the political logic of what I was asking them to do, but they just as quickly picked out the military difficulties.

"Look at these minefields and obstacles," said Abu Taleb, pointing to a map showing the position of the Iraqi front lines. Breaching was a military operation at which the Egyptians had long excelled: in the 1973 Yom Kippur War (called the Ramadan War by Arabs), they had made short work of Israel's vaunted Bar Lev line east of the Suez Canal. Abu Taleb knew what he was talking about.

I emphasized that our phase-three bombing campaign was designed to support the breaching operation by destroying Iraqi artillery, damaging the obstacles, and pinning down Iraq's front-line troops. I showed the Egyptian officers a sampling of the sort of aerial photos we'd provide just before the attack, which would reveal lanes through the Iraqi minefields. I then described the breaching equipment and air support we would supply for the battle itself. They questioned me closely for nearly an hour and were finally satisfied. Abu Taleb said he would recommend to President Mubarak that he accept the plan.

———

9 DEC 90 C + 124

2100   Phoncon with the chairman. The two leaders discussed the issue of a declaratory policy with regard to retaliation against biological or chemical attack. The chairman said he was pressing the White House to inform Tariq Aziz that we would use our unconventional weapons if the Iraqis use chemicals on us. The chairman believed that Secretary Baker would deliver this message to the Iraqi foreign minister.

10 DEC 90 C + 125

1533 Phoncon with the chairman. The leaders entered into a conversation regarding attacking biological warfare storage plants, with the CINC pointing out that General Horner assured him that when we attack the plants we have selected munitions that will kill the bugs. The CINC followed this up by reminding the chairman that if we do not attack these plants, we cannot guarantee that these agents won't be used on U.S. troops. This would be an unforgivable sin.

Meanwhile the French were having difficulty deciding what role they wanted to play in the coalition. Part of their dilemma had to do with conflicting commercial interests: France was a major seller of arms to both Saudi Arabia and Iraq. On a more personal level, Jean-Pierre Chevènement, their defense minister, was a member of an organization called the French-Iraqi Friendship Society and was adamantly against sending forces. Initially the French had insisted on having their own sector to defend and on reporting to no one. When the Saudis rejected this, they'd agreed to place their forces under Khalid's command. Now it was unclear whether they'd participate in the offense at all.

Lieutenant General Michel Roquejeoffre, their commander in the gulf, whom I respected and counted as a friend, kept getting mixed signals from Paris; I sympathized, but needed to know whether we could count on the French to fight. Finally, in December, General Maurice Schmitt, the chief of their armed forces, informed me that France did want to be in on the offensive, but that he was concerned that in a head-on battle, his soldiers' lightly armored vehicles would be no match for the Iraqis' heavy Soviet tanks. Therefore, could his forces be assigned the mission of protecting our far western flank? I agreed immediately. I'd been searching for a force to do the job and the French units fit the ticket exactly.

That left the Syrians. By mid-December President Hafez al-Assad had sent a full armored division to Saudi Arabia. The Syrians would report to Khalid; their assignment was to join the Egyptian attack into Kuwait. Still, their presence in the theater made me uneasy—Syria had long been a Soviet arms client and was on the State Department's list of countries that sponsored terrorism. They were the only major coalition partner I did not consult with personally in planning Desert Storm; I felt more comfortable relying on Khalid to keep me informed of their intentions. But I was not at all sure that when the shooting started the Syrians would come through, because their commander continued to make conflicting statements about whether they would fight.

13 DEC 90 C + 128

1600 Phoncon with the chairman. The CINC reported on the Inouye congressional delegation session, which had just concluded. He informed the chairman that the session had gone very well and was positive and friendly. He stated that the delegation discussed at length a congressional declaration of war, but noted that it had not happened in Korea, Vietnam, or Panama and that it probably would not happen in this case either.

———

By December 22, practically every dock and airfield in the kingdom was overflowing with American equipment, ammunition, and supplies, all of which had to be moved to the front. Remote desert roads experienced their first traffic jams. Moving the gear required thousands and thousands of trucks, and Gus Pagonis and his transportation officers must have leased every truck in the kingdom. Pagonis called it his "gypsy caravan"—the damnedest array of vehicles and civilian drivers I'd ever seen. I'd be out on some road and would marvel at the convoys going by: East German trucks, Czech trucks, and Polish trucks, some so old they didn't look as if they'd run. A lot of the drivers were hired men from Pakistan, India, and Bangladesh who had come to Saudi Arabia to find work. They had a penchant for decorating the trucks with vividly painted designs, little stick-on reflectors, and mirrors.

The number of U.S. personnel in the gulf had hit 300,000—and our reinforcements from Germany were only starting to arrive. Desert Shield had long since grown beyond the most ambitious computer scenarios of five months before. By the time we were through, we'd have as many people in the gulf as we'd sent to Vietnam at the height of the war. Only there the buildup had taken four years; here we were doing it in six months.

With a deadline, Desert Storm took on a powerful momentum. Overhead the coalition air forces flew a thousand training missions a day, while in the desert engineers built full-scale mock-ups of Iraqi trench lines so combat units could practice their assaults. The attack plan matured as field commanders pored over maps, studied the terrain and enemy dispositions, and plotted out their maneuvers in painstaking detail. At headquarters, my preparations for the ground war speeded up. In mid-November Lieutenant General Cal Waller had reported to Riyadh as my deputy commander in chief: now I had someone to help me ride herd. Cal was a friend who had worked for me in two previous commands. Shrewd, soft-spoken, and given to quoting sayings he'd learned from his grandmother in Louisiana, he was also tough and effective. He'd been my first choice for the job: he'd come up through the Army as an armor officer and understood logistics; also I knew I didn't intimidate him at all. We trusted each other to such an extent that he could walk into my office and say point-blank, "Hey, something's all screwed up, it's your fault, and you need to know about it."

As the buildup increased, Cal and I rode our Army logistics experts hard to determine whether they could pull off the giant lateral movement of combat forces and supplies in time for the offensive. For weeks we went around in circles. First we'd ask John Yeosock, who was overseeing the logisticians, "If we don't let you move the forces until the air campaign starts—say on the twentieth of January—how long will it take to get them to their jumping-off points for the attack?"

"Two to three weeks."

So then we'd turn to the corps commanders and repeat, "We've checked with Yeosock and there's no reason for you to move until we launch the air campaign."

The commanders hated that—particularly because they wanted their fuel and ammunition positioned in advance. So they'd pressure *their* staff logisticians, who would start to waffle, and pretty soon Yeosock would come back with a new estimate, saying, "I don't know if we can make it after all."

Meanwhile some of our forces from Germany were delayed—railcars to haul tanks and armored personnel carriers to the docks were scarce; ships broke down or ran into winter storms. About twenty percent of our reinforcements were not going to arrive until after January 15. In particular, the 3rd Armored Division's M1A1 tanks would still be on the high seas. And even once they'd arrived, the 3rd would be far from battle ready: we'd need days to get the equipment off the ships, repaint its camouflage from forest green to desert khaki, marry it up with the troops, move the units to their forward positions 330 miles away, and give them desert training. This last was no small matter: in Europe, soldiers had been able to orient themselves in relation to roads, towns, forests, and other landmarks; in the desert, there were no landmarks—and even the sand dunes moved. So we had to quickly teach the use of satellite navigation equipment, celestial navigation, and dead reckoning.

Every time a ship broke down or ran into heavy weather, Yeosock would come back and say the Army needed to revise the estimate of when it would be ready.

"Okay," I'd say. "We'll adjust the plan; just let us know what you *can* do." So then he'd come back, give us a new date certain—and without fail want to change it again. This went on all through December.

On December 6, Saddam suddenly announced that Iraq would immediately free all its remaining foreign hostages; he called this a humanitarian gesture to promote peace—and added that Iraq had built up its defenses to the point where human shields were no longer necessary. As soon as the Americans were released the following week, Washington pulled the rest of its personnel out of the embassy in Kuwait City. These moves did little to defuse the crisis, but they simplified our war planning—we no longer had to worry about bombing human shields or mounting risky rescue operations in Iraq or Kuwait. At the same time, the latest peace initiative—President Bush's proposal to send Secretary of State Baker to meet with Saddam while inviting Tariq Aziz to the White House—bogged down in a disagreement over when the meetings would occur.

Washington was signaling us to be ready to attack sooner rather than later. "I was over at the White House yesterday talking about possible D-day dates," Powell told me on December 11. "When I mentioned February 10 to February 20 as a possible window, everybody gulped." He told me that if the crisis weren't resolved before January 15, there was going to be real pressure for immediate military action. I replied that, if that were the case, we might have to launch the air attack and just keep bombing until the ground offensive was ready.

17 DEC 90 C + 132

1700 Phoncon with the chairman. The discussion turned to the visitor load facing Central Command. The CINC assured the chairman that he would take every visitor currently on the list, but that it was vital to turn off the visitors after 15 January. The chairman assured the CINC that he would clamp down on visitors and would require the director of the Joint Staff to review all requests. The CINC thanked him, noting that the staff is very tired, saying that some of our knees are buckling now.

18 DEC 90 C + 133

> [from a message to Washington by Ambassador Freeman on the subject of visitor load] "We understand the need to build and maintain congressional support. . . . It does not necessarily follow that Washington should treat Saudi Arabia as if it were an exotic game park with a four-star general and an ambassador as park rangers. . . . There must be a pause in trekking to Saudi Arabia. . . . Give us a break."

On the afternoon of December 19, Secretary Cheney arrived in Riyadh, accompanied by Powell. Cheney's mission was to assess our status and report back to the President. We were ready with detailed briefings on every aspect of our deployment to date, our preparations for Desert Storm, and even an occupation plan in the event Iraq unilaterally withdrew from Kuwait. I hadn't seen the secretary since August and wanted to impress upon him the complexity of our operation and the huge amount we'd accomplished. I also had another motive: to deter him from coming up with any more schemes.

Things got off to a bumpy start. Pete Williams, the Pentagon press chief, had called ahead to ask me to hold a news conference for reporters who would be traveling with the secretary. "That's crazy. I'm gonna be busy with Cheney and Powell," I'd replied. Williams had insisted that we produce someone in authority. So I'd asked Cal Waller to stand in—without thinking much about the fact that he had been in the theater only a month and had little experience with the press. When the reporters repeatedly pressed him about Central Command's readiness, Cal, in an effort to be forthcoming, told them that our ground forces wouldn't be fully prepared to attack until possibly mid-February—headline news because it contradicted the President's posture of putting pressure on Iraq in advance of the UN deadline. Pete Williams and most of the public-affairs staff stayed up all night exercising damage control, and by morning had issued a statement that drew attention to the fact that the Air Force and Navy were poised for immediate attack.

Waller knew he'd screwed up and came to me the first thing in the morning to say so. I felt responsible for having gotten him into this mess and worried he'd be punished. Early in Desert Shield, Cheney had fired

General Mike Dugan, the Air Force chief of staff, for giving reporters classified information. So when Cheney and Powell arrived at headquarters an hour later, I asked them into my office.

"General Waller feels terrible about this flap he's created. But I'm the one to blame, for throwing him into a press conference when he's so new to the theater," I said.

To my surprise, Cheney and Powell responded that they weren't that concerned about his remarks. Cheney even quipped, "It's not always bad to send the enemy mixed signals."

As far as we were concerned the matter was resolved, but both Waller and his family back in the States suffered through a miserable week as news commentators, many of them retired military men who had never carried one tenth the responsibility Cal now bore, labeled him disloyal, dishonorable, and stupid. I saw how these attacks hurt him and wished there were some way to make them stop. "You've just got to ride it out," was all I could say. "You're going to be the center of attention until some new story comes along."

We got on with the morning briefings. Cheney peppered us with questions on everything from the truck shortage to possible terrorist threats, but I needn't have worried: it was clear both he and Powell were completely on board. To my relief, and to some extent due to the Waller blow-up, Cheney acknowledged that the timing of the ground attack *was* subject to logistical constraints. "We can't try to force it too early," he said.

When they left after two full days of briefings, Cheney carried in his briefcase a map overlay we'd produced to help him explain the Desert Storm ground attack plan to the President. As he left he told me, "The sheer magnitude of this is a tribute to all of your officers and troops." Then he added, "We're all proud of what you've done and we know you'll be ready to do whatever is necessary in the future"—leaving no doubt in my mind that unless Saddam knuckled under, the President would order us to bomb the hell out of Iraq's military shortly after January 15.

Secretary Cheney left us a Christmas present: a complete set of videotapes of Ken Burns's PBS series, *The Civil War*. The programs, with their chilling portrayal of wartime death and destruction, had an enormous impact on everybody at headquarters. Though we were in the final stages of preparing for war, none of us wanted it to come. Watching those tapes renewed my conviction that if I had to send my troops into battle, I would find a way to minimize the loss of life.

23 DEC 90 C + 138

2150 Phoncon with the ambassador. The CINC informed the
ambassador about a brewing controversy between the
French and the Saudis over the Saudis' refusal to let a
French rock group with go-go dancers perform for the
troops. Apparently, the king's comment about this was that
the United States was sensitive to Saudi sovereignty issues
and even had the President of the United States attend a
religious service on a ship at sea. It was unconscionable that
the French want to have this rock concert complete with
dancing girls.

Not only did I have to make plans for war; I also had to plan for
Christmas in a war zone—an especially interesting challenge in a strict
Moslem kingdom. Khalid started worrying about religious offenses more
than a month in advance. In mid-November he told me, "You're going to
have to turn off your radio transmitters."

"But we just got them set up. What's the problem?" It turned out the
problem was the broadcasting of Christmas carols.

"I can solve that," I said.

"How?"

"Christmas carols come in two forms. One form is instrumentals. We'll
just broadcast the music without the words."

Khalid was relieved. I also assured him that our religious observances
would stay as discreet as they'd been up to now—no advertising or broadcasting of services, no display of religious symbols, no outdoor Nativity
scenes—and that the ban on female entertainers would extend to holiday
USO shows.

That satisfied Khalid, but some of the religious zealots were still uptight. At their insistence Saudi government censors tried to enforce a ban
against Christmas cards coming into the kingdom. We didn't have to worry
about that: we simply gave them access to the several hundred tons a day of
letters and packages pouring in from home, and before long they gave up.
As the holidays drew near, you could see signs of Christmas popping up in
the U.S. camps. Nearly every tent had spray snow and wreaths and little
aluminum Christmas trees, complete with tinsel and battery-powered flashing lights, that had been sent from home.

I still had to contend with the American media—in particular, dozens
of TV people and photographers eager to record religious services in Saudi

Arabia. Katie Couric of NBC, for instance, had pleaded after an interview, "Oh, General Schwarzkopf, it would really be a great scoop if I could just film *one* of them." I told her no. I knew it would have been a good story, but a single news report of, say, a rabbi conducting a Hanukkah observance on Saudi soil would have left King Fahd no choice politically but to enforce the law of the land and bar all further religious ceremonies. Some reporters found our policy hard to accept even after it had been carefully explained, and a few even tried to get in and film in defiance of the rules.

On December 24, Bob Hope arrived. He and I chatted a little in my office, and then I escorted him out to the Escan Village on loan from the Saudis, where he and his troupe were scheduled to do the first of two days of shows in the region. After introducing him, I went to sit in the audience— more than nine hundred Americans, mainly Air Force personnel who had been among the first to arrive in Desert Shield. The show wasn't very long— some of the equipment had failed to arrive, and he'd been forced to leave the actresses and dancing girls out of performances in Saudi Arabia— but it didn't need to be. Bob Hope and Johnny Bench told jokes; Aaron Tippin sang country-music songs; finally Hope's wife, Dolores, got up and led the troops in singing "White Christmas." There was almost overwhelming emotion in the air. Here we were in a theater of war. It was Christmas. We were missing our families. And we were seeing a Bob Hope show—just like the troops in World War II, just like the troops in Korea, just like the troops in Vietnam. The young men and women in that audience suddenly felt linked to all the American soldiers who had gone off to war and been away from home and those they loved during the holidays. Bob Hope's company went on to make more appearances at camps in Saudi Arabia and then headed for the island of Bahrain, where they were joined by Ann Jillian, Marie Osmond, and the Pointer Sisters. For the eight thousand airmen, Marines, and sailors based on the island, and the thousands of soldiers there on R&R, they staged a couple of performances that I heard were a whole lot less austere than the one I saw.

I wanted to go to church that evening, so I asked an aide to find out where a communion service would be held. The answer was Escan Village and around seven-thirty we drove back out, to where a huge tent had been set up as a church. The service turned out to be nondenominational, so there was no communion, but I didn't mind. Knowing I was likely to shed a few tears—Christmas always affected me that way, and this one was doubly charged because I missed my family so much—I was hoping to find a seat in back. But the tent was packed and someone had reserved me a spot in the very front, right under a row of bare light bulbs. That was probably a good thing, because when the service commenced and we lifted our voices to sing "Oh, Come, All Ye Faithful," being where the troops could see me helped me keep my emotions under control.

Afterward the chaplain's assistants served cookies and cake and coffee at the back of the tent. Officers and enlisted people crowded around me to talk. A young airman asked me to sign his chapel program, saying, "Sir, when I send this home to my parents, they're gonna feel wonderful that you were here with us on Christmas Eve." Everybody had seen Bob Hope perform that afternoon, and several talked about how glad they were that he had come over, and how the show had made them feel part of American military tradition.

I went back to my room at the Ministry of Defense. Brenda had sent a little Christmas tree with lights. I switched it on, put a cassette of Christmas music on the tape machine, and was nearly asleep when I heard the red phone to Washington ring in my office. It was President Bush. "I couldn't let this day go by without calling to wish you and all the men and women under your command a Merry Christmas," he said. "I know that you are far away from your loved ones, but I want you to know that our thoughts and prayers are with you. You now know the course we are on. Our prayers will stay with you during the coming days." I told him how much we appreciated his call and thanked him on behalf of all Central Command.

After we hung up I turned on my Christmas music again and listened long into the night until I fell asleep.

———

25 DEC 90 C + 140

0930 CINC got up and opened Christmas presents. Chief Petty Officer Rick Rieger served two glasses of orange juice, one Swiss mocha and one bowl of grapefruit sections. Christmas music was playing.

When I woke up the next morning, God, did I miss my family! They'd all sent presents—small, personal things—including a gift on behalf of our dog, Bear. Cindy had sent the poem "You Are My Hero," Jessica a video of her rowing team, along with a big button she'd had made up with her and Cindy's photograph on it. Christian had sent a videotape of a wildlife show. From Bear came a box of shortbread cookies. And from Brenda I got the latest book by outdoor writer Gene Hill.

I opened the presents by myself. It was the most desolate hour I'd spent in Saudi Arabia. At other times I'd felt harassed, exhausted, brow-beaten, burdened—now I simply missed my family. I reminded myself that more than three hundred thousand Americans in Desert Shield were experiencing exactly the same hardship.

Then I put on battle fatigues, went down to the war room, and shook hands with every officer and enlisted person on duty, wishing them Merry Christmas and thanking them for serving their country. Next I did what U.S. troop commanders traditionally do on Christmas: inspected the mess halls. The purpose of this exercise was to make sure that the troops were going to have a great meal and to thank the cooks who had been up since three in the morning cooking turkeys.

It was a clear, windy day, not sweltering hot, but blowing a little sand. I started at Lockheed Village, a housing compound in Riyadh that had been taken over by U.S. troops. Some had already sat down to dinner, though it was only noon, because they were eating in shifts. I shook a lot of hands. Next I went back out to the Escan Village, where there were three huge mess halls in tents. At the first a long line of troops stretched out the entryway. I shook hands with everyone in the line, went behind the serving counter to greet the cooks and helpers, and worked my way through the mess hall, hitting every table, wishing everyone Merry Christmas. Then I went into the second and third dining facilities and did the same thing. I came back to the first mess tent and repeated the exercise, because by this time there was an entirely new set of faces. Then I sat down with some of the troops and had my dinner.

In the course of four hours, I must have shaken four thousand hands. As had happened many times before in my Army career, I'd set out to make my troops feel good, and they'd responded by making me feel good. Leaving Escan I went back to Lockheed Village and did the rounds again. Finally, late in the afternoon, in great spirits, I returned to the Ministry of Defense to telephone home. It was morning in Tampa and I knew my family would all be together by the Christmas tree. I told them I missed them terribly. I let them know how much I loved them and how proud I was of each of them. And I said that next Christmas, though I didn't know exactly where we would be, I intended to make sure we all were together, on vacation, and hip deep in snow.

———

26 DEC 90 C + 141

1000 Morning update. The CINC relayed General Powell's description of Secretary Cheney's and his meeting with the

President following their Saudi Arabia visit. The President will probably launch the air campaign as soon as possible after 15 January. The prep time is almost over; we are nearly at war. The President announced that he felt we were ready and that we had our act together. Further, he endorsed our plan one hundred percent. The President said that he did not care if he had the support of a single member of Congress; he would see this thing through to a successful conclusion.

28 DEC 90 C + 143

2000 Phoncon with the chairman. The two leaders discussed the latest news-media speculation on D-day. Reacting to press reports that the air campaign might start on 15 January, the CINC stated we might as well tell Saddam D-day so he can get his gunners ready.

The week after Christmas brought word of more transportation delays—the last ships carrying the 3rd Armored Division were late leaving Germany because the holidays had slowed work at the docks. On the twenty-eighth, the Army came in to reschedule D-day for the ground offensive yet again. A worried Yeosock proposed, among other things, that I let the Army start construction immediately on Log Base Charlie, a huge supply dump it would need to support the flanking attack.

"You already know the answer," I insisted. "Not until the air campaign starts."

Meanwhile Gus Pagonis put up charts showing his latest revised timetable. "Assuming the air war starts around January fifteenth," he said, "we can have everything in place within a month."

"A month! Goddammit, Gus, this is the fourth time we've met on this same subject, and we're now talking brand-new dates." In fact, I wasn't entirely displeased: allowing for an additional three or four days to assemble our battle formations after our forces were in place on the Iraqi border, we'd still be ready to launch the ground attack before February 20—within the window I'd been promising Powell.

"Sir, there won't be any more changes after this."

"Are you willing to *guarantee* that?" I asked.

Pagonis looked me in the eye and drew himself up to his full five feet seven inches. "Yes sir, I am."

"Will you *sign your name* to that chart?"

"Yes, sir. If you want me to."

"I want you to, Gus." He signed it, and I knew we had an attack date we could count on.

---

30 DEC 90 C + 145

0035 Phoncon with the chairman. The chairman told the CINC that British air chief marshal Hine had a meeting with Prime Minister Major to brief him on the operation. After the briefing, Air Chief Marshal Hine turned his briefcases and laptop computer over to his executive officer. The executive officer decided to go shopping and left the classi- fied material in the car. The briefcases and laptop were stolen from the car. The briefcases have been recovered, but the laptop is still missing and the hard disk drive may contain the entire battle plan. The London tabloids have got hold of the story, so if it is a common thief rather than an Iraqi, he will now find out he has something of much more potential value than a computer and try to sell it to the highest bidder.

I reminded my fellow officers every day that we were in a countdown to war. I wanted to get them on a war footing psychologically and emotionally—ready to think in terms of refugee problems, incoming air and missile strikes, and Iraqi commando attacks. The Americans responded well, but I was worried about the Saudis. The closer we moved to war, the more ambivalent they sometimes seemed. I made allowances for the fact that their military had never gone to war before and tried to encourage a sense of urgency at Saudi headquarters. It had been reported to me that the Arab field commanders still did not have the information they desperately needed to complete their units' attack plans.

On New Year's Eve I was ready to explode. In conversation the night before, Khalid had informed me that the Syrians had decided they would not attack. Since their Desert Shield force was under his operational control, technically this headache was his. But the more I thought about it, the more disturbed I became. Not only did a Syrian refusal to fight represent a major crack in the coalition, but it jeopardized the entire offensive plan—*my* responsibility. Without the support of the Syrian tanks, the Egyptians attacking into Kuwait could be badly outgunned. Around noontime on the thirty-first came another shock: Paul Schwartz, the chief of the coordination center at headquarters, brought word that Khalid had stated publicly that, all things considered, the best approach to war would be an offensive launched out of Turkey. He was voicing the old Saudi unease at attacking fellow Arabs (the Turks are Ottomans, not Arabs), but under the circumstances, such a remark had nothing to do with military or political reality. Khalid wasn't at his office; I left word that I needed to see him right away.

About an hour later, he appeared at my door. I ordered my staff to leave the room; then I turned to the prince. "What about this attack out of Turkey?" I demanded. "Where did this come from? How can you possibly make a public statement to that effect, when the king himself has agreed that the attack is to come from Saudi soil? What do you think we're doing this huge buildup for? Why do you think all these additional troops have been flowing in here for two months?"

Khalid was taken aback. This was no way to address a Saudi prince and we both knew it. "Furthermore," I continued, "you and I had better talk about the Syrians. How can you possibly let them get away with not going on the offensive?"

"I was planning to bring you up to date on that," he said, and started to describe what was going on behind the scenes—Prince Saud al-Faisal, the Saudi foreign minister, was arranging a trip to Damascus to talk to President Assad.

I was too angry to listen to news of diplomatic maneuverings. "It's very clear to *me* what is going on," I interrupted rudely. "The Syrians have been enemies of Iraq for thirty years, yet now, when the time finally comes to fight, they don't have the stomach to go to war themselves. Maybe they are cowards, or maybe they just want somebody else to do their dirty work."

Now Khalid became angry too: I'd insulted fellow Arabs. "I do not have to listen to this," he said coldly, and left.

We did not speak for twenty-four hours. But after the evening briefing on New Year's Day, Khalid turned to me and said, "We must meet. We must talk." I went to his office. We chatted, sipped cappuccino, and apologized to each other for the first half hour, until our friendship had been repaired. Khalid then assured me that his government would abide by the plan for Desert Storm. Next we turned to the question of the Syrians.

"I've been thinking about that," I said. "What if I give you an approach that enables Syria to attack but not attack, to go on the offensive but not go on the offensive?"

"How do you do that?"

"Here's what your government could propose. You, General Khalid, the commander of the Arab forces, wish to make the Syrians your reserve. You want the Syrians to follow the Egyptians through the breach. This way the Syrians are, in fact, participating in the offensive, yet they won't be called into battle unless the Egyptians get in trouble. They will not need to fight fellow Arabs unless they are coming to the aid of fellow Arabs."

Khalid was delighted with the idea. Shortly thereafter, Saudi Arabia presented the plan to the Syrians, the Syrians bought it, and harmony was restored to Operation Desert Storm.

---

3 JAN 91 C+149

1545 Office call by Air Chief Marshal Hine. Air Chief Marshal Hine made this almost-no-notice call on the CINC to explain that in the British's best judgment, no material of real significance was compromised during the theft of his executive assistant's briefcase and laptop computer. A mental reconstruction of the laptop indicated no campaign plan data was contained therein.

A few days after Khalid and I resolved our differences, King Fahd came to the desert to review the coalition forces. It was a moment of great symbolic importance to the Saudis and had long been in the works. The king began by visiting a formation representing all the American forces in the kingdom, at King Khalid Military City air base. On the apron the Saudis had constructed a reviewing area by laying down magnificent oriental rugs; facing the area we'd assembled a row of Apache helicopters and a formation of one thousand troops. I'd attended a rehearsal earlier that morning and explained to the troops the meaning of the king's visit: "Earlier, President Bush visited you. Now King Fahd is coming to pay his respects and thank you for defending Saudi Arabia. You are here representing every American soldier, sailor, airman, Marine, and Coast Guardsman in this theater. You look great! I'm proud of you and your country is proud of you. When the king comes, stand tall and be proud of yourselves. And thanks for standing out here in the hot sun!"

We all came to attention as King Fahd arrived in a convoy of at least thirty limousines and security vehicles and stepped out onto a red carpet. I walked to him, saluted, and said, "Welcome, Your Majesty. My troops are prepared for your inspection." Then we took our places in the reviewing area and stood as an Army band played the Saudi national anthem and "The Star-Spangled Banner."

In a traditional U.S. military review, the next step would be for the visiting leader to "troop the line," or inspect the soldiers up close. Saudi royal protocol made absolutely no provision for such a procedure, but King Fahd had agreed to it. We didn't expect him to make the inspection on foot; instead, he and I stood in the back of a specially prepared jeep and slowly drove the length of the formation. Another jeep preceded us, with what seemed like a dozen photographers and TV cameramen hanging off its back and sides to record the event.

During the ride the king said in English that the troops looked good, asked if I had any problems, and finally thanked us. He then climbed back in his Mercedes for the trip to the desert base about twenty miles away where Khalid had assembled a formation of coalition forces. I got into my own car and we joined the convoy as it snaked its way out of the air base. Soon the pavement ended and the cars in back were blanketed with dust and dirt kicked up by the sedans of the king and his immediate entourage. After a few miles, the drivers in back broke ranks, veering off the road and fanning out into the desert to drive abreast of the convoy. I stared out the window, amazed: it looked like a cavalry charge of black and white Mercedeses and Lexuses racing across the desert. My driver had pulled out on the flank with the rest, causing my bodyguards in the car behind us to go crazy on the radio, trying to get us back on the road.

There before us in the middle of the desert I saw a huge formation of troops. Khalid had assembled thousands and thousands of men from every country: Saudis, Syrians, Egyptians, Kuwaitis, Moroccans, Nigerians, Omanis, Qataris, Pakistanis, Senegalese, British, and French. There was even a contingent of Czechoslovakian chemical-warfare experts and a Polish medical team. All of these troops were standing in the hot sunlight as we pulled up, and, as the desert breeze was at our backs, they got covered with the convoy's dust.

Nobody expected King Fahd to troop *this* line. Opposite the formation was a row of black wool tents, open to one side so that they looked out on the ranks. We got out of the cars and went into their shade. The central tent had beautiful carpets, a row of overstuffed chairs, and in the center, a big couch for the king, with a table and microphone in front of it.

Khalid reported to King Fahd: "All my troops are present for duty." The king sat down at the table and gave a long talk in Arabic to the troops, in which he reviewed the entire history of the region's problems with Saddam Hussein and the reasons the coalition had come to Saudi Arabia. Prince Sultan, the minister of defense and aviation, sat next to the king; I was four or five places down the line, with Peter de la Billière to my immediate right. We sat in our soft chairs in the splendor of the tent, sipping fruit juices and listening to the king, and even though this was an historic event, I was concerned about the thousands of soldiers baking in the sun. The king's talk lasted more than an hour.

Finally we got back in the cars and crossed the desert again, to a site near King Khalid Military City where we were to have lunch. The Saudis had erected a huge complex of tents for the occasion. But when we arrived, it was prayer time. The westerners were asked to wait in a big assembly tent, where dozens of chairs had been arranged in a U. The king disappeared into a private tent to pray, but the rest of the Arabs broke into small groups, walked a few yards into the desert, and knelt on the sand. I watched this pious scene feeling quite moved. Less than a half hour before, the Arabs had been part of a frenetic charge of luxury automobiles across the desert. Now there was utter tranquillity. They simply walked out, knelt in the desert facing Mecca, and said their prayers to Allah.

We westerners sat on our chairs. We waited and waited. In the meantime, dusty British, French, Czechoslovakian, and Polish officers came in, having just been released from formation, and some U.S. officers arrived from the earlier assembly at the air base. At last it was time to eat. The Saudis led us to a tent with more oriental carpets, and we sat cross legged on the ground; I was directly opposite King Fahd, and by my sides were Peter de la Billière and Michel Roquejeoffre. Aides started bringing in the food— whole roasted lambs on platters and huge dishes of rice and vegetables— and laying it out before us. I was back in the tribal tent of my boyhood, sitting cross-legged on the ground in the middle of the desert, being served this sumptuous meal, and eating with my right hand. As we ate, we chatted with the king, who struck me as pleasant although most of his conversation was with those who spoke Arabic.

When King Fahd finished eating, he rose and left the tent. As we followed, I noticed that the second shift of lunch guests was waiting outside: lieutenants and noncommissioned officers who had stood in the formation. But that was the end of the ceremony as far as the leaders were concerned. There was no formal meeting. We commanders climbed into our vehicles, returned to the airfield, flew back to headquarters, and proceeded with our preparations for war.

7 JAN 91 C + 153

1000 Morning update. Intelligence noted that Iraqi strength in the Kuwaiti theater was now 542,000, with 35 divisions committed.

21

8 JAN 91 C + 154

1500 Phoncon with the chairman. The chairman passed a verbal warning order to the CINC for launching the air campaign at 0300, 17 January 1991.

9 JAN 91 C + 155

1400 Commander's conference, Dhahran. The CINC gave the commanders the 0300, 17 January D-day for the beginning of phase one.

Late at night on January 9, I sat alone in my office in Riyadh watching TV. In Geneva, Secretary of State Baker and Iraqi foreign minister Tariq Aziz had just wrapped up their talks—the last-ditch effort to keep our respective nations from going to war. When Baker stepped up to the podium, I thought he looked grim. He told the press and the television audience that Aziz had given him no indication that Iraq was willing to withdraw from Kuwait. Somebody asked what the Iraqis *were* willing to do; Baker replied that he'd prefer to let them speak for themselves.

Baker left the room; shortly afterward Aziz entered, walked to the microphones, and droned on for forty-five minutes—without once mentioning Kuwait. I realized this was it: we were going to war. The UN deadline was less than a week away and although I'd already passed on preliminary attack orders to my senior commanders, we'd all still hoped for peace. I felt sick at heart as I conjured the terrible risks we were about to face. We knew we would win, but we had no idea what our casualties would be, how the American public would react, or even whether the coalition would hold together.

I was facing a week of solving last-minute problems. We had been debating with Washington about the best way to inform our coalition partners of the date and time of attack and still keep the information from Iraq. We were particularly concerned about King Fahd, who made it a practice to discuss everything, including state secrets, openly with his princes. We finally worked out an arrangement in which Washington would notify Prince Bandar several hours in advance; he would then alert the king by telephoning and using the code phrase, "How is my favorite uncle?" The leader of each nation whose forces were to participate in the attack would be informed at the same time.

I put myself on a kind of mental countdown. As soon as I woke up each morning, I'd study the enemy situation map next to my desk—hoping against hope that there had been no shifting of Iraq's forces to the west. The map now displayed no fewer than thirty-eight red stickers, each one representing an Iraqi division—together they made up a vast army of 545,000 men, 4,300 tanks, and 3,100 pieces of artillery. I imagined the enemy out there, methodically constructing formidable barriers, miles deep in places, along the border. I could almost see the minefields, tank traps, high sandbanks, razor wire, trenches, and forts. The "Saddam line" it was dubbed by the intelligence people, and it extended along the entire southern border of Kuwait and forty miles farther along the southern border of Iraq—175 miles in all. It had been built on the assumption that we would attack head-on. Saddam and his generals still seemed oblivious of their exposed flank. I knew that if they didn't shift west now, our air force would make sure they never did—for them to try to maneuver forces under our bombing would give us an easy target. Day by day, Iraq's best chance for a successful defense was slipping away.

15 JAN 91 C + 161

1330 At the request of Lieutenant General Khalid, the CINC accompanied Lieutenant General Khalid to visit Prince Sultan, the minister of defense. Prince Sultan expressed his hope that Iraq would withdraw from Kuwait. However, he was not optimistic. The CINC agreed, saying that we have done just about everything we can do before hostilities break out. Sultan then asked bluntly whether Iraq's missiles can reach Riyadh. The CINC stated that the missiles could reach Riyadh, but are very inaccurate. The chances of their hitting anything of value are very small. The CINC reminded Sultan we have Patriot missiles guarding the city. Sultan asked if King Fahd's palace was protected by the Patriots. The CINC responded he was almost sure that it was. Sultan then expressed a desire to strike first and not allow Saddam to start.

2330 Phoncon with the chairman. The chairman told the CINC that the secretary of defense and he had just signed the execution order and that the attack was on for 0300, 17 January. He told the CINC that a single copy would be faxed immediately.

TIME UNKNOWN The judge advocate general forwarded for the CINC's approval a blood chit to be carried by pilots in the event of their capture during upcoming hostilities. This was a sheet printed in Arabic offering a reward for the pilot's safekeeping.

On the surface, the day before the attack passed much like any other. My staff and I attended to dozens of routine questions of finances, visitors, housing, and the like for which there would be no time once the shooting started. Despite the activity, headquarters seemed hushed; there was little conversation. A few of my most senior officers knew we were about to go to war, but most of the principal staff had been told only that there would be a meeting in the war room at 2:15 A.M. I figured they all realized what that meant.

At midnight I went back to my office. I felt as if I were standing at a craps table in some kind of dream—I'd bet my fortune, thrown the dice, and

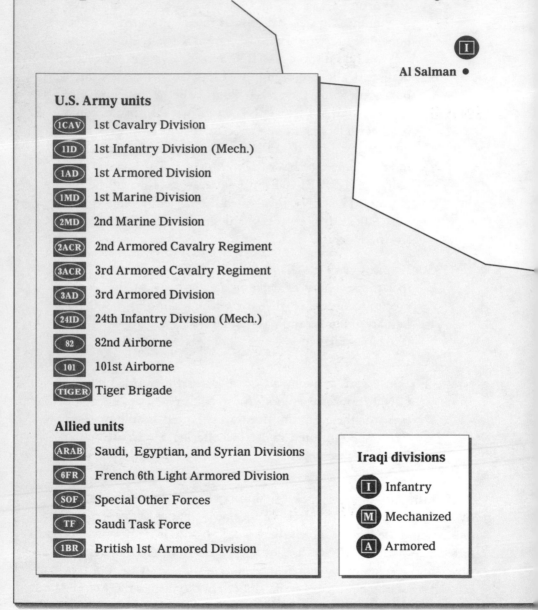

Iraqi and Allied Positions on January 17

Al Salman •

U.S. Army units

1CAV	1st Cavalry Division
1ID	1st Infantry Division (Mech.)
1AD	1st Armored Division
1MD	1st Marine Division
2MD	2nd Marine Division
2ACR	2nd Armored Cavalry Regiment
3ACR	3rd Armored Cavalry Regiment
3AD	3rd Armored Division
24ID	24th Infantry Division (Mech.)
82	82nd Airborne
101	101st Airborne
TIGER	Tiger Brigade

Allied units

ARAB	Saudi, Egyptian, and Syrian Divisions
6FR	French 6th Light Armored Division
SOF	Special Other Forces
TF	Saudi Task Force
1BR	British 1st Armored Division

Iraqi divisions

I	Infantry
M	Mechanized
A	Armored

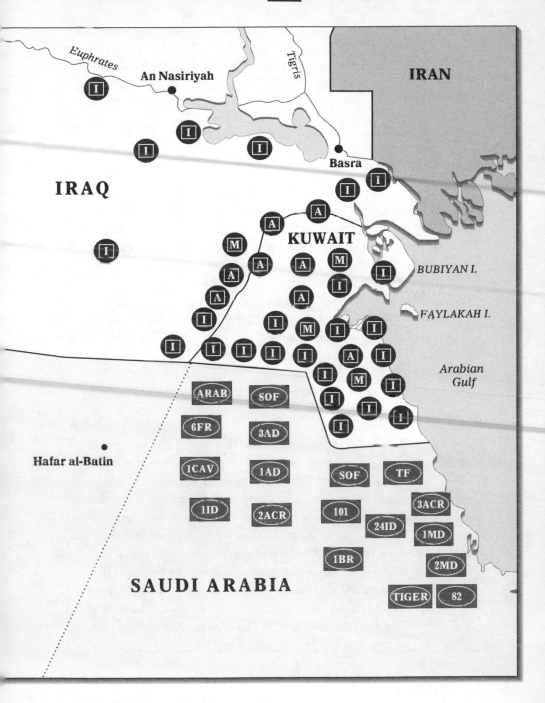

now watched as they tumbled through the air in slow motion onto the green felt. Nothing I could do would change the way they landed. I sat down and did what soldiers going to war do: I wrote my family, saying how much I loved them.

17 January 1991
15 minutes after 12 A.M.

My dearest Wife and Children,

The war clouds have gathered on the horizon and I have already issued the terrible orders that will let the monster loose. I wish with every fiber of my body that I would never have had to issue those commands. But it is now too late and for whatever purpose God has, we will soon be at war.

As a soldier who has had to go to war three times before, I want you to know that I am not afraid. I know that I might face death but you should know that I am far safer than most of the fine young men and women under my command. Some will die; many could die. I pray to God that this will not happen but if it does and if I am one of those chosen by God to sacrifice my life, I wanted you to know that my last thoughts before this terrible beginning are of you, my beloved family.

Brenda, I have never been very eloquent with words and far too guarded in expressing my love for you. I truly regret this but it is the way I am. That is why I wanted more than anything else to write to you tonight and tell you how much you mean to me. I cannot tell you how many times I have thanked God that I married you, nor can I adequately tell you how many times you have made me so proud that you are my wife. Especially during these past difficult five months it has given me great strength to know that you were there, always there, taking care of our family and so many others. Thank you for that and so many other things: the loving, the understanding, the forgiving, the helping, the caring, the supporting—just being my Brenda Pauline.

Cindy, Jessica, Christian, I hope you know how much I love you. The three of you have become the most important reason to me for my being on this earth. I could lose everything I possess and if I still had you, life would be worth living; I could be rich and famous and have everything I desire but without you my life would be meaningless, my heart would be empty, and I would not want to live. The three of you are my immortality! You are the best thing I will leave behind when I leave this world. And you have each returned that love to me. I am a father who knows his children love him and that makes me a very lucky man! As I told you at Christmas, I am so proud of each of you for what each of you are. Be proud of yourselves for you are fine human beings. Thank you for being my children; thank you for letting me be your father; thank you for loving me!

Take care of each other, love each other, and if it be God's will, we shall be together soon. If that should not happen, then know that wherever I am I will be with each of you every day, always!

Your loving husband and father,
H. Norman & DAD

I sealed the letter and told my aide to make sure it got in the mail. Then I wrote a short message to the troops. Finally it was time to go downstairs.

About thirty generals and colonels had gathered in the war room. As I entered someone announced, "Gentlemen, the commander in chief." They all came to attention. I walked to the front and stood before the large map of Iraq, Kuwait, and Saudi Arabia. "I want to read you a message that I have just released to the men and women of Central Command," I said:

DESERT STORM MESSAGE TO OUR TROOPS

Soldiers, sailors, airmen, and Marines of United States Central Command: This morning at 0300 we launched Operation Desert Storm, an offensive campaign that will enforce United Nations resolutions that Iraq must cease its rape and pillage of its weaker neighbor and withdraw its forces from Kuwait. The President, the Congress, the American people, and indeed the world stand united in their support for your actions. You are a member of the most powerful force our country, in coalition with our allies, has ever assembled in a single theater to face such an aggressor. You have trained hard for this battle and you are ready. During my visits with you, I have seen in your eyes a fire of determination to get this job done and done quickly so that we may return to the shores of our great nation. My confidence in you is total. Our cause is just! Now you must be the thunder and lightning of Desert Storm. May God be with you, your loved ones at home, and our country.

—H. Norman Schwarzkopf,
Commander in Chief, U.S. Central Command

I asked Dave Peterson, our command chaplain, to say a prayer. When he was finished, Colonel Bell played a tape of Lee Greenwood's song "God Bless the U.S.A." Every member of the staff stood a little taller and I could see tears glisten in more than one eye. It was now 2:30 A.M. and Burt Moore, my operations director, reported that our airplanes and cruise missiles were airborne. "Okay," I said, "let's go to work."

I had asked the other commanders to let me speak to my staff alone. After I finished, Khalid, Peter de la Billière, and Michel Roquejeoffre joined us in the war room. They looked solemn.

———

The first shots of Desert Storm were to be fired at precisely 2:40 A.M. In preparation, weapons crews had labored since the previous afternoon at airfields across Saudi Arabia, Bahrain, the United Arab Emirates, and Qatar, loading warplanes from six nations with hundreds of tons of missiles, rockets, and bombs. American aircraft carriers in the gulf and the Red Sea had steamed northward, putting Iraq within range of their planes. Cruisers and the battleship *Wisconsin* had positioned scores of Tomahawk missiles in their armored box launchers for firing. Meanwhile flights of B-52s, some armed with ultrasophisticated cruise missiles originally designed to fly nuclear warheads into the Soviet Union, were closing in on Iraq from bases as distant as Barksdale, Louisiana.

A dozen high-tech Army and Air Force special-operations helicopters would start the attack. Flying in almost total darkness only thirty feet above the sand, they were to take out two key early-warning radar installations on the Saudi-Iraqi border. Behind the helicopters, eight F-15 fighter-bombers would streak into Iraqi airspace and destroy the nearest air-defense command center. That hit would, in effect, spring the gate into Iraq by opening a corridor for hundreds more airplanes headed toward targets throughout Iraq. Meanwhile, F-117 Stealth fighters were beginning bomb runs in the night sky over Baghdad.

Sitting in headquarters there was no way for us to tell at first what was going on. As each scrap of information came in, I scrawled it down on a yellow pad.

"0247: SOF TARGETS DESTROYED": Colonel Jesse Johnson, head of Central Command's special-operations forces, called from his headquarters outside Dhahran to say the two Iraqi radar installations had been destroyed; he called again a little later to announce that all the helicopters had returned safely to base. Three o'clock ticked by—H-hour, the official beginning of the attack. By this time, I knew, the F-117s would be pounding numerous targets in Baghdad, and generally all hell should be breaking loose at dozens of sites across enemy territory.

"0310: PHONES OUT BAG": General Leide, whose intelligence staff monitored western TV and radio broadcasts, reported that most correspondents in Baghdad were off the air, which indicated to us that the telephone exchange had been destroyed. An hour later Baghdad's lights went out: the Navy's Tomahawks had done the job on Saddam's power plants. Meanwhile, British Tornado fighter-bombers were blasting Iraqi airfields, French and Italian jets were preparing to go after missile sites, and even the tiny Kuwaiti air force was attacking Iraqi targets inside Kuwait.

"0415: NO FEEDBACK ON AIR TO AIR / NO BEEPERS ON SHOOTDOWN": Chuck Horner was in his command post in the basement of Saudi air force headquarters in Riyadh. He reported that the attack appeared to be on track. So far there were no reports of any real opposition by the Iraqi air force and no radio beacons to indicate downed pilots. We had carefully staggered the attacks. Bombers went in first; when they lifted from their targets and left the area, Tomahawks would arrive. As that onslaught abated, yet another wave of aircraft would be on its way in. For the first forty-eight hours, our objective was to give the Iraqis no rest: we wanted to maximize the shock that relentless bombardment can produce.

Horner called throughout the morning with updates as pilots and crews returned to base. By early afternoon I was able to tell Powell in Washington that we'd completed fully 850 missions. We'd clobbered many of the 240 targets on our list: Saddam's heavily defended lakeside palace in Baghdad had been annihilated; the ITT Building downtown was reportedly "glowing"; two major Scud missile sites in western Iraq had been severely damaged; the key suspected biological and nuclear weapons bunkers had been destroyed. Meanwhile squadrons of A-10 attack jets were shooting up supply dumps along the Iraqi front lines: "They can't get reloaded fast enough," the Air Force told us. The Air Force advised that although flight crews' accuracy had been initially less than predicted—F-117s in the first wave had dropped just fifty-five percent of their bombs on target, and F-111s about seventy percent—their accuracy had been steadily improving throughout the day.

Most important, only two airplanes had gone down—an astoundingly low number, considering that we'd feared losses as high as seventy-five the first day. Horner and his planners had clearly succeeded brilliantly at undoing Iraq's high-tech defense network. By jamming and bombing its radars, they'd blinded it; by striking at its command centers, they'd paralyzed it. While pilots described how the skies over Baghdad were filled with surface-to-air missiles and antiaircraft shells, the Iraqis were firing at random with very little chance of hitting our planes. Meanwhile we shot down six Iraqi MiG and Mirage fighters. Scores more Iraqi aircraft took off from their bases, but then simply flew around avoiding our planes. We couldn't figure out what to make of that: were they under orders not to fight? Leery of being hit by their own ground fire? Cowards? Horner speculated that Iraq was husbanding its air force to strike at us later. I was inclined to agree. "We keep waiting for the other shoe to drop," I told Powell.

At the evening briefing Burt Moore brought the news I'd been waiting all day to hear: the Army was on the move, relocating in preparation for the ground attack. On Tapline Road, the desolate two-lane highway stretching west toward Jordan from the Saudi town of Hafar al-Batin near the southwestern corner of Kuwait, the heavy trucks of the XVIII Airborne Corps and VII Corps had begun moving supplies and equipment west. By the end of the first day of the war, the convoy stretched 120 miles.

17 JAN 91 D-DAY

1830 Phoncon with the chairman. CINC discussed our current embargo on mail. The CINC said we need to put out a worldwide public appeal that explains that troops are on the move and will most likely not receive large mail. We need to ask the public not to send bulk packages.

At three o'clock Friday morning—we'd been in the command center just over twenty-four hours—seven Scud missiles were fired from western Iraq toward Israel. The Air Force scrambled F-15s to bomb the launching sites; meanwhile reports started filtering in of explosions in Tel Aviv. Powell called to advise us that Washington was in an uproar at the prospect that Israel would jump into the war. It was nine P.M. on the East Coast, and the networks were carrying live reports from their correspondents in Tel Aviv wearing gas masks. The Israelis quickly ascertained that these Scuds carried conventional warheads, not poison gas. But that fact gave little comfort: the whole world was conscious of the threat Saddam had made months before—that he would burn half of Israel with chemical weapons.

Within an hour came another launch—this time a lone Scud from southern Iraq aimed at Dhahran. The Army fired four Patriot missiles from batteries that had been set up around Dhahran air base. To our delight, the Patriots—originally designed as antiaircraft weapons, only recently modified to intercept incoming missiles, and never battle tested—knocked the Scud from the sky. Then, just before five o'clock, dozens of Israeli jets took off from their bases. We waited grimly for them to strike Iraq in retaliation, but they remained in Israeli airspace. As Friday dawned with no more Scud attacks, a tired-sounding Powell reported that Washington had persuaded Tel Aviv—at least for now—to call back its jets.

The Scud was a clumsy, obsolete Soviet missile which had been originally designed to lob a half-ton warhead 190 miles and be able to hit within a half mile of its target—close enough for Soviet purposes because their Scuds could carry nuclear warheads. The Iraqis had learned to roughly double the missile's range by welding two Scuds end to end, or adding a section to the original framework, but in doing so they had to drastically reduce the payload. So in essence what they had was a weapon that could fly 300 miles and miss the target by a couple of miles with a warhead of only 160 pounds. Militarily, that was the equivalent of a single airplane flying over, haphazardly dropping one small bomb, and flying away—terrible for anyone it happened to land on, but in the grand scheme of warfare, a mosquito. However, the Scud *was* effective as a terror weapon against civilian populations: in the Iran-Iraq war, the Iraqis had fired Scuds at Tehran in much the same way the Nazis had showered London with V-2s.

By now, our bombers had obliterated every known Scud site in western Iraq, destroying thirty-six fixed launchers and ten mobile ones. But I knew we had a big problem with any remaining mobile launchers—the squat, eight-wheeled vehicles, roughly the size of large gasoline tanker trucks, would be devilishly hard to find.

Three more Scuds hit Israel (Tel Aviv got two, Jerusalem one), and on Saturday morning my operations director handed me a message forwarded by the Joint Staff. The Israelis wanted to launch their own massive counterstrike into western Iraq: one hundred planes the following morning, one hundred more planes the following afternoon, attacks by Apache helicopters the following night, and commando raids—all to enter Iraq *through Saudi Arabian airspace*. I immediately called Powell: "The Saudis will never buy this, and you can't sneak it by them. They have people up in our AWACS and they're gonna know."

Later that morning Powell reported that Prince Bandar, at Washington's request, had called King Fahd to ask about the possibility of overflight rights for the Israeli strike. The king had swiftly replied with the Arabic equivalent of "no way." Powell now told me that President Bush was about to call Israeli prime minister Yitzhak Shamir to try to dissuade him. He would use three arguments: we had already knocked out all known Scud sites; we were continuing our attack with more aircraft and more firepower than the Israelis could muster; and Israeli intervention would strain and perhaps fracture the coalition we had worked so hard to build. At Central Command we'd already made plans to clear our planes out of western Iraq to avoid accidental engagements in the event of an Israeli strike when Powell called and said Israel had again agreed to hold off.

We could feel the pressure Israel was putting on Washington, because Washington was turning around and putting it on us. First the Joint Staff proposed that we let Israel send planners who would sit in my headquarters in Riyadh and tell our Air Force what targets to hit. I told them it was a dumb idea: "How can anybody think the Israelis have better target information than our Air Force? We've been studying that part of Iraq with the most sophisticated intelligence-gathering technology ever invented." Besides, after six months of preaching cultural sensitivity, I couldn't believe I had to explain that the presence of Israeli officers would wreck Central Command's credibility with the Arabs—assuming the Saudis would even let them into the kingdom.

Then we received orders from the Joint Staff to bomb targets on a list the Israelis had supplied to Secretary Cheney. Most were targets we'd already hit; we proceeded to attack the others and found nothing there. Horner had had enough: "Sir, this is insane. We can't have a bunch of Israelis who have no idea of our overall campaign plan telling us where to put bombs. We're throwing bombs into dunes. We're starting to endanger pilots' lives." I found myself lobbying with Powell: "We'll do what you tell us, but just to have bombs falling out of the sky defies military logic."

We reacted to the pressure by diverting fully one third of the more than two thousand combat and support missions scheduled each day for the strategic air campaign to the Scud hunt. F-15s and F-16s repeatedly braved their way through concentrations of antiaircraft missiles to bomb Scud storage bunkers and suspected launch sites in western Iraq. On January 19 a Scud-busting mission ran into four Iraqi MiGs and a Mirage that tried to block their attack. The U.S. jets shot them all down. We had already sent coalition special-operations teams deep into Iraq to watch the roads and report sightings of mobile launchers. Those missions were extremely dangerous: the entire country was an armed camp—even areas that looked empty on the map turned out to be heavily patrolled by military units sent out to capture downed flyers. We'd also underestimated the severity of the weather in Iraq's mountainous northwest. This was winter, and it was alternately freezing and wet. One team actually had two men die of exposure. Finally, each morning as soon as the ground fog cleared, heavily armored A-10 attack jets screamed up the roads and canyons of western Iraq, hoping to catch Scud launchers on the move.

19 JAN 91 D+2

1631 Phoncon with the chairman. The CINC pointed out that the first bomb we dropped on Baghdad equaled the explosive power of all the Scuds (ten) they have launched.

2055 Lieutenant General Khalid asked the CINC to make up charts for him to show Prince Sultan all of the targets we have hit so far. The CINC said no. We will give them info, but cannot divert staff to do the work for them.

The launchers turned out to be even more elusive than we'd expected. We picked off a few, but just as often bombers would streak to a site where a missile had been launched only to find empty desert. We were puzzled. Then Khalid came up with an explanation. In chatting with the Egyptians under his command—the Egyptians being expert in Soviet equipment because they'd formerly owned a great deal of it—he'd discovered that a mobile launcher could drive away as soon as six minutes after firing. We had been told thirty minutes by our intelligence agencies. Now it made sense: by the time we detected a launch and were able to relay the coordinates to our pilots, who then flew to the target, the Iraqis had scrammed.

Shortly after midnight on Monday, January 21, my staff and I were briefly exposed to what the Israelis had been going through: Riyadh was attacked by Scuds. We picked up six missiles heading our way, due to hit in under three minutes. Sirens sounded throughout the city and Patriot batteries went on full alert; in our basement war room we made sure our gas masks were handy. Within a minute the door burst open and in came Khalid and his entire staff, clutching gas masks. We all had our hearts in our throats: the Ministry of Defense wasn't airtight, and while we didn't *think* Iraq had chemical warheads for its Scuds—in years of observing their missile tests we'd never detected any—in those minutes we all cast nervous glances at the air-conditioning vents.

The missiles, unsurprisingly, landed miles away, and we were back at work by the time the reports trickled in: nobody killed, nobody hurt, and *eleven* interceptions claimed by Patriot batteries (they'd shot the same Scuds repeatedly—the system still had a few bugs). Technical reconnaissance teams that examined the Scud impact sites reported no evidence of chemicals.

More Scuds fell in subsequent days and King Fahd summoned me to the palace. He asked what we were doing to suppress the attacks, and I explained why Scuds posed little real threat. The king seemed satisfied. With Khalid acting as interpreter, he asked what other weapons Saddam might have up his sleeve: "On the radio today, Saddam said a prayer for the people of Riyadh. He said in two days he will employ his 'special weapon' that will hit all the people here." I'd just started to tell him why I discounted Saddam's threat when sirens sounded. Khalid ran out of the room to find out what was happening. King Fahd asked in English: "Is this a Scud attack?"

"Yes, Your Majesty, it is."

Khalid came back and suggested that the king take cover. "As a precaution," I agreed, "His Majesty should go to an air raid shelter. I don't feel there is any danger, but there's always the remote possibility of an errant warhead striking the palace."

The king stood, thanked me calmly, and left with his aides. This left Khalid and me sitting by ourselves. I knew we were statistically safer here than we would have been crossing a street in Manhattan. But for lack of anything better to do as we waited for the end of the alert, I asked the prince, "Have you ever fitted your gas mask?"

"Am I supposed to?"

"Yes, masks have to be fitted. While we're sitting here, why don't I show you how?"

I put on my gas mask, Khalid put on his, and I started to demonstrate how to adjust the straps. Just then four members of the palace staff entered the room. When they saw us they gasped and, tearing their own masks from their cases, frantically pulled them on.

———

The frequency of Scud launches began to drop: in Desert Storm's first week, the Iraqis fired thirty-five; in the second week, eighteen; thereafter all they could manage was an average of one Scud a day. These last firings were almost totally haphazard: a missile crew would race from their hiding place, put up the launcher, fire without completing the standard aiming procedure, and drive off as fast as they could. In fairness, there wasn't much else they could do: by that time the Air Force had fighter-bombers patrolling western Iraq around the clock.

Horner had done an extraordinary job. In less than two weeks the coalition had flown thirty thousand missions. And though Iraq claimed to have shot down more than 180 planes, the actual number lost was eighteen.

Horner had systematically destroyed Iraq's air defenses, so it was unlikely we'd lose many more; Iraq's antiaircraft batteries had been attacked and most of its surface-to-air missiles had been expended or bombed. While only fifteen percent of its air force had been confirmed destroyed, the rest was either hunkered down in bunkers that we were attacking regularly, fleeing to bases in Iran, or dispersed in fields, mountains, or residential areas. Chuck's first-phase strategic bombing campaign had taken longer than the six days he'd originally estimated because of bad weather and the diversion of airplanes for Scud hunts. But the bombing was so effective that the delays didn't hurt much.

By the last week in January, the skies over Iraq belonged to the coalition. We were accomplishing exactly what we had set out to do: cripple Iraq's military system while leaving its agriculture and commerce intact and its civilian population largely unharmed.

———

Most nights I stayed awake to see if there'd be a Scud launch—they typically came between two and four in the morning. Since Washington was eight hours behind Riyadh, I could count on a rash of late-night phone calls as afternoon activity there peaked. I also spent those nighttime hours doing business with Khalid, helping to get the Arab coalition and his own forces geared up for war. I'd go to bed just before dawn—my staff had standing orders to wake me if anything important happened—and catch four hours' sleep before the morning briefings. In the middle of the day, crises permitting, I'd take a two-hour nap. I'd moved my quarters to a small room in the basement, right down the corridor from the war room. I'd remembered my experience in Vietnam: I wanted to sleep near the radios that linked me to my troops.

I wasn't eating regular meals. Staff Sergeant Wayne "Smitty" Smith, my enlisted aide, would ask, "Sir, what do you want for supper?" I usually had a choice of instant Cup O' Noodles (Brenda had sent a case of assorted flavors) or a microwaved hot dog. A few nights a week some of the staff would go over to the Saudi officers' club for dinner and bring back a sandwich.

This is not to say, however, that Desert Storm caused me to lose weight. Whenever I could, I got out to see the troops, but most of the time I simply sat on my butt, talking on telephones and over radios, or peering at maps and computer displays. Somebody was always wandering around the war room with a box of cookies from home. We would stuff ourselves to the gills and then groan, "Ugh! No more! Get those out of our sight!"

I called home twice a week, trying to time the calls for when the kids were home. Hearing about Cindy's college term paper or Jessica's rowing team victories or Christian's latest math test brought a note of normalcy to the unreal world I found myself in. Brenda would fill me in on her activities: she and the wives of other generals at MacDill Air Force Base had organized a support group for families whose husbands or wives were in the gulf, and the spouses of young officers or enlisted people often came to them for help with problems.

Some of those conversations were unexpectedly poignant. The night of the first Scud attack on Riyadh happened to be a night I called. Christian answered, and when I asked, "How are you doing?" he responded, "Not too well, Dad." That wasn't like him. Then Brenda came on the line and explained that they'd just heard on TV that Riyadh was under Scud attack. "Don't worry," I reassured them. "Those have already landed. I'm eighty feet below ground. I'm not in any danger." It was a vivid reminder that war touched those on the home front.

Another night Brenda answered the phone crying. "God, Brenda, what's the matter? What's wrong?" I instantly thought that something had happened to one of our kids.

She blurted out, "I just got your letter." The letter I'd written on the eve of the war had taken two weeks to reach Tampa. She said, "Norm Schwarzkopf, if you get killed, I'll never speak to you again."

The only time I saw daylight was when I went into the field. While the air war progressed, I continued to work like crazy on the ground campaign plan, monitoring preparations and visiting commanders and units all over the war zone. Morale was high. The troops knew they were ready to attack and were glad the long hours of sitting in the desert were about to end. At an artillery unit of the 3rd Armored Cavalry Regiment at the front, I found the kids laughing and joking. They asked me to autograph an artillery shell and promised it would be the first they fired when we launched the offensive. I visited Marines dug in near the Saudi-Kuwaiti border. Their attitude was: "We're not going to war, sir, we're going home—and the direction of home happens to be through Kuwait."

We had moved entire divisions so far forward that it took a long time even by airplane and helicopter to get to them. Flying along Tapline Road, I marveled at what the Army had accomplished. We were actually beating the transportation schedule Pagonis had set. Where two weeks before there had been nothing but desert, a pipeline, and an occasional Bedouin tent, there now were seas of camouflage netting that sprawled for miles and that I knew concealed thousands of tons of food, spare parts, fuel, water, and munitions for the offensive. The road itself was a dusty caravan of trucks, fuel tankers, humvees, and heavy transports hauling tanks and armored personnel carriers—thousands of vehicles, stretching from horizon to horizon. What I saw banished any doubt that we'd make it into position for a mid-February ground attack.

None of this had happened by magic; a lot depended on American ingenuity. Yeosock, Pagonis, and their people had solved all kinds of problems that were never taught at West Point. Take the great trucker crisis. We depended on trucks leased from civilian contractors and driven by Pakistanis, Bangladeshis, Filipinos, and Bengalis to haul our ammunition and supplies. We'd prepared sleeping quarters for the drivers, but they were used to sleeping at home. So when they finished hauling a load of howitzer shells to the front—work they didn't relish in the first place—they more often than not would drive back to their company garage and go home. We'd then have to ask their employer to dispatch them again, a process that could take days given the distances involved and the roundabout manner in which Saudis did business. One day, somebody noticed that the drivers were fascinated by videotapes of American professional wrestling—Hulk Hogan versus Macho Man Randy Savage, Andre the Giant versus Jake the Snake, and so on. So Pagonis's transportation officers set up a huge tent at our main supply base near Dhahran with a projection TV. Every morning, as the drivers set out, the officers would announce that night's bouts. At the end of the day, the drivers would race back to watch and we would have them on hand for the next day's runs.

There were some problems even Gus Pagonis couldn't solve. Our corps and division commanders were determined—and rightly so—to get their forces into position and poised for attack as ordered. But if a general didn't get as many trucks, say, as he thought he needed, he would complain to Third Army headquarters or chew Pagonis out. This happened so often that I finally had to ask Gus what the trouble was. "Sir, these guys think we've got a logistical system like the one in Europe, and they're asking for more than their fair share of trucks and supplies." Rather than try to arbitrate, I had a better solution. Powell and I had already agreed that Pagonis was carrying as much responsibility as any commander in the theater and should be promoted. So I asked Powell to expedite his nomination for a third star. The President approved the request on January 28; it was the only battlefield promotion we made during Desert Storm. Now Gus was equal in rank or superior to the other field commanders, and he could tell them to get stuffed if he needed to. Their attitude toward him improved dramatically.

For the first ten days of the war, the front had been quiet except for the occasional artillery duel. But on the night of Tuesday, January 29, Iraq's 5th Mechanized Division launched tank attacks at three points along the Saudi-Kuwaiti border. One of the columns ran into a battalion of U.S. Marines and was quickly repulsed. But the other two hit only scattered resistance from forward reconnaissance units and made their way toward Al Khafji, an oil-processing center on the Saudi coast about eight miles south of Kuwait.

The only Saudi settlement within range of Iraqi artillery, Al Khafji was a ghost town. Its twenty thousand residents had fled after it came under fire on the first night of the war. And Al Khafji had no military garrison because, very early in Desert Shield, I'd pointed out to Khalid that Al Khafji was indefensible: "The enemy can shell you from his side of the border anytime he wants." Khalid had wrestled with that—his directive from King Fahd was to defend every square inch of the kingdom—but finally he'd agreed and pulled his forces out.

As fate would have it, Khalid had gone to the eastern province that night to inspect his troops. He phoned me just as we received a report that Iraqi armored personnel carriers had been spotted in the city. "No problem," I reassured him. "If they're still there in the morning, you'll be able to go in and clear them out. In the meantime we'll pound them with air strikes." Soon Major General Abdulaziz al-Shaikh, his deputy, appeared and informed me that General Khalid would direct a counterattack to retake Al Khafji the following day. "That's great," I said. "That's exactly what your forces should be doing. We'll give you all the air support you need."

In the morning, the action heated up considerably. The Saudis tried to send a tank battalion around north of the city to cut off the invading force. But they ran into a whole lot more enemy armor than they expected. To our amazement, the entire Iraqi 5th Mechanized Division—nearly four hundred tanks and armored personnel carriers—was trying to drive down the coast highway into Al Khafji. The Saudis were forced to pull back and we sent in the Air Force and Marine Air. Our airplanes and helicopters pounded the living hell out of the column all day long, until pilots were complaining they couldn't find targets because of smoke from ones they'd already hit.

My staff and I were perplexed. There was no evidence that Iraq was getting ready to launch a major offensive, yet to attack Saudi Arabia with a single division defied military logic. One analyst tried to make sense of the move by calling it a "spoiling attack"—a thrust by defenders to disrupt an expected attack by their opponent. But we finally decided it must be a propaganda ploy: Saddam wanted to show the world that despite the coalition bombing, Iraq remained unbowed. But it was another blunder. Now his division was trapped: if they decided to retreat, they'd have to drive back through more air attacks; south of town, U.S. Marines and Qatari forces blocked them from advancing any farther. Khalid and his staff prepared a much larger counterattack for the following morning.

But when the day ended with Al Khafji still in Iraqi hands, King Fahd became furious: the thought of Iraqis holding any piece of the kingdom was intolerable. I had been so satisfied with our tactical position that I had ignored Saudi sensibilities. Abdulaziz sought me out in the war room and announced that General Khalid might be in a lot of trouble—Prince Sultan had been in the building looking for me and had left in frustration after being told I was at the Hyatt Hotel across the street, holding a press conference. Abdulaziz reminded me of my Vietnamese friend Truong—he was a thin man who seldom smiled and seemed to carry the weight of the world on his shoulders. Now he was in the unhappy position of serving as a go-between in an explosive situation. "General Khalid has explained to Prince Sultan that he was acting on your advice. Therefore, Prince Sultan asks that you prepare a letter to the king explaining why the Iraqis were permitted to take Al Khafji."

It dawned on me that Khalid might not have informed his father or the king about his decision to remove the Al Khafji garrison. "I'll be glad to," I said. "General Khalid acted absolutely properly."

Abdulaziz left. No sooner had I started dictating the letter when he came back looking even more somber and sat down next to me. "King Fahd wants to know if you can destroy Al Khafji."

"I beg your pardon?"

"The king wants to know if you can send bombers and destroy Al Khafji now." Rather than let another day go by with the city in enemy hands, the king was going to level it. I thought of biblical passages about sowing the fields with salt.

"I'm sorry, we don't conduct ourselves that way," I said. "Can you imagine how it would look in the eyes of the world if the United States of America bombed a Saudi town into rubble just because a few Iraqis were there?"

I could see Abdulaziz worrying about how to take my answer back. But I was skeptical that the request had actually come from the king—more likely some member of the royal court, anxious to anticipate the king's wishes, was asking hypothetical questions in his name. "Let's think this thing through," I said reassuringly. "Tomorrow morning you will possess Al Khafji. You don't have it now only because you've withdrawn. The coalition controls Saudi Arabian territory, and tomorrow morning we'll occupy Al Khafji." I then added a section to my letter:

I would not recommend that we use coalition military forces to destroy the city of Al Khafji for the following reasons:

(a) As I have argued above, militarily it is unimportant that a few Iraqi troops are in Al Khafji.

(b) To destroy the city would take large amounts of ammunition and we would be wasting valuable resources for no military purpose.

(c) World public opinion would never accept that there was sufficient reason for the kingdom of Saudi Arabia to completely destroy one of its own cities.

(d) The Iraqis have had unbelievable damage done to their entire nation and a great deal more will occur in the future. We must expect that they will do something to try to retaliate against the kingdom. There are many other border towns and it will be impossible for them all to be defended; however, even if another border town falls it will be liberated very soon. I know it is very hard for any of us to accept the loss of one centimeter of our sovereign soil, but history will record that we did not save our country by destroying it. Instead, we saved it by liberating it.

The letter concluded, "I very respectfully submit to you that Prince Khalid made a correct military decision when he did not put forces in Al Khafji to defend it." We sealed it in an envelope, and Abdulaziz carried it to Prince Sultan.

If the king had really wanted Al Khafji destroyed, I doubt the letter by itself would have worked. But time was on our side. At daybreak the Saudis counterattacked with an armored brigade, elements of their national guard, and a unit from Qatar. In the afternoon Khalid called, jubilant with victory. He said they'd blown up fifteen tanks and captured hundreds of Iraqis, with minimal casualties to their own force. From Iraq's standpoint, the battle for Al Khafji was a debacle. The 5th Mechanized Division, which had been rated one of their finest armored units, just a notch below the Republican Guard, was almost entirely destroyed—we monitored Iraqi reports afterward that indicated that only twenty percent of that division made it back. During the battle, Iraq's highly vaunted artillery had proved ineffective—they had fired hundreds of rounds but never succeeded in zeroing in on our troops.

I concluded with great relief that the Iraqi army wasn't half as skilled or highly trained as it had been portrayed, and all we should really worry about in the future was their use of unconventional weapons. The battle also marked a major turning point in Saudi morale: Khalid's soldiers had gone into the battle with little confidence in their ability to fight, and Saddam had turned them into victors. Finally, King Fahd was satisfied: by the end of the day the royal press agency had issued a triumphant statement that Al Khafji "has been cleansed completely of aggressive forces."

22

31 JAN 91 D+14

1830 The CINC informed the chairman that we had two troops missing in action from an XVIII Airborne Corps transportation company (one male, one female). Apparently, two heavy-equipment transports had missed a turn on the Tapline Road and gone north to the Kuwait border. Realizing they were near enemy territory, one turned around to return to a Marine checkpoint to seek help because the other one had become stuck. When the Marines returned, the transport was still in place, the two soldiers were missing, and Iraqi troops were in the area. The CINC informed the chairman that we are conducting a search and this was indeed the first female MIA (Baghdad has been claiming that they captured numerous females during the border incursion at Al Khafji).

1 FEB 91 D+15

0250 Following a B-52 raid on the Kuwaiti "national forest" in southwest Kuwait, numerous enemy vehicles were running from the woods. A-10s reported the following kills: twenty tanks, eleven armored personnel carriers, twenty wheeled vehicles, and three multiple rocket launchers. Pilots reported that the battlefield was like "turning on the lights in a cockroach-infested apartment."

I copied out a quote from the *Memoirs of General William T. Sherman* and taped it to my desk: "War is the remedy our enemies have chosen. And I say let us give them all they want." As our warplanes shifted to the fiercest stage of the air campaign, I knew that Saddam's soldiers were no longer getting much sleep in their bunkers and foxholes: day and night our B-52s, fighter-bombers, and attack jets were pounding their positions along the front. Our first priority was to knock out the Iraqis' heavy weaponry—particularly artillery that could be used to fire chemical rounds at our troops. But at the same time we also wanted to erode the enemy's morale. In the lulls between air raids we dropped millions of leaflets that had been written with the assistance of the Saudis. A typical leaflet had a drawing on one side of smiling Saudis seated around a desert fire and serving coffee to a guest, while on the other, Saddam was shown viciously attacking a fellow Arab with a knife. The message in Arabic said something like: "See what Saddam has done. You are occupying your neighbor's land. If you come to us, we will treat you as an Arab brother."

After two weeks of war, my instincts and experience told me that we'd bombed most of our strategic targets enough to accomplish our campaign objectives; it was now time, I thought, to shift most of our air power onto the army we were about to face in battle. But our experts, a team of "battle damage assessment" specialists from the intelligence agencies in Washington who had been assigned to Central Command, disagreed. Their job was to analyze bombing results and tell us which targets we had to restrike, and from the first day of Desert Storm, they had us going in circles. They'd say things like, "You failed to destroy the power plant in Baghdad"; yet we knew that in Baghdad *the lights were out*. Early in the Scud hunt, they told us that the fixed missile launchers in western Iraq were only "twenty-five percent damaged." Even though those launchers never again fired a Scud, we couldn't take chances and so sent dozens of warplanes to hit them again.

Battle damage assessment had traditionally been an art: analysts pieced together pilot reports, bombsight photos, reports from follow-up aerial reconnaissance, and the bits of information that trickled in from behind enemy lines. But the intelligence community had been trying to turn it into a science for years, primarily by spending billions of dollars on surveillance technology. Analysts had accordingly been trained to depend largely on "hard" evidence collected by reconnaissance planes and satellites. So if a pilot came back and said, "The bunker blew up before my eyes," they gave it no credence: pilot reports, they maintained, were always exaggerated. But their equipment wasn't as all-seeing as they thought, and they'd left themselves no leeway to exercise military judgment. So while their analyses were sometimes superb, just as often they made no sense in terms of the criteria I'd defined for assessing damage to enemy installations, units, and equipment. We couldn't afford distorted assessments: too much optimism could prompt us to launch the ground war too soon, at the cost of many lives; too much pessimism could cause us to sit wringing our hands and moaning that the enemy was still too strong.

I let them know how I felt. Colonel Chuck Thomas, our principal advisor on the current intelligence situation, had been my senior intelligence staff officer when I'd commanded the 24th Mechanized Infantry Division, and I knew him to be a brilliant, dedicated professional. Every evening he would brief me on the intelligence community's latest bomb damage assessment and have to listen to me make facetious remarks like: "Well, if we knocked out one span of a four-span bridge so that anything that tried to cross it fell into the Euphrates, you intelligence guys would tell me the bridge was only twenty-five percent damaged."

As we shifted our bombing from strategic targets to the Iraqi forces, these headaches were becoming worse. It was a lot easier to tell whether we'd knocked out a munitions factory or biological weapons site than a battalion of forty tanks dug into the desert, and the Republican Guard had literally gone underground: they'd built bunkers for both their men *and* their tanks. So even though we were hitting them with as many as thirty B-52 sorties every day, it was hard to quantify the results. To solve the problem, we invented a tactic we called "tank plinking": we sent individual airplanes to spot individual bunkers and demolish them with laser-guided bombs. Pilots would return reporting direct hits. Even so, not much damage was visible aboveground, and the analysts stubbornly maintained that the Republican Guard units were still close to one hundred percent strength. It didn't take long for our disputes to become headline news. One story in *The New York Times* (datelined Washington) carried the headline "Best Iraqi Troops Not Badly Hurt by Bombs, Pentagon Officials Say," while another (datelined Dhahran) averred: "Elite Iraqi Forces Hurt by Bombings, Allied Aides Insist."

Thomas was getting as frustrated as I was. Finally I told him, "We have to invent a methodology that makes sense." He retreated to his office for a couple of days, and, to my delight, came back with a method that managed to combine the old art and new science in a way that made sense to everybody. For each category of target—say, enemy airfields—he would take a single sheet of paper and juxtapose the photo analysts' "objective" damage assessment and our own intelligence section's "subjective" evaluation of enemy capability with regard to the overall criterion I had set: "establish air supremacy." The photo analysts in this case characterized airfield damage as moderate to light: "Runways are only twenty percent destroyed and fields are still operational." But we also knew that the Iraqi air force wasn't flying—planes that took off were either shot down or their pilots fled to Iran—so our intelligence personnel subjectively rated the criterion as ninety-five percent met. Integrating the evidence in this way helped us come to the obvious conclusion: we'd bombed the airfields enough and could move on to other targets.

Thomas's breakthrough saved lives—pilots were spared the risks of carrying out needless air strikes—and relieved the pressure from most of the agencies in Washington. Finally I had him explain the technique to Cheney and Powell who, after quizzing us about it closely, agreed that Central Command knew what it was doing. The CIA was the only agency to dissent: on the eve of the ground war, it was still telling the President that we were grossly exaggerating the damage inflicted on the Iraqis. If we'd waited to convince the CIA, we'd still be in Saudi Arabia.

––––––––

4 FEB 91 D + 18

1845 The CINC pointed out to the chairman that the press remains upset and is growing increasingly hostile. Their problem is that there are a thousand people over here yet only 75 or so out on pools at any given time. The other 925 are sitting around with nothing to do except complain. Curiously, most of the press is upset with CNN, mainly because CNN reports inaccurately in trying to get scoops.

8 FEB 91 D + 22

0900 At the close of the morning update, public affairs told the CINC that a couple of journalists had crossed the border, picked up some fully armed Iraqis, snuck them by border checkpoints, and handed them over as POWs to the Egyptians, all to get an interview. The CINC's comment was that someone is going to get killed. When our troops see fully armed Iraqis, before they ask questions, they will simply open fire.

On February 8, Cheney and Powell arrived on behalf of President Bush to assess whether the United States was ready to launch a ground war. In my opinion, we were ready. On the eastern end of the Saudi-Kuwaiti border, our Marines and the Saudis were awaiting orders to move to jumping-off points for the attack. On the western end the pan-Arab corps, spearheaded by the Egyptians, was already poised. The VII Corps under Fred Franks had just about completed its long move from Germany to tactical assembly areas near the front and in a few days would be able to move into attack positions. And far out on the western flank, Gary Luck had already moved his XVIII Airborne Corps into attack positions.

We had planned a full eight hours of briefings for Cheney and Powell and prior to their arrival, John Yeosock came in to give me a detailed preview of the Third Army's presentations. My only major concern after sitting through his brief was VII Corps. There was no doubt in my mind that the corps would make it to the starting line, and its plan of maneuver carried out the mission I'd assigned, but the plan seemed plodding and overly cautious: VII Corps was to advance, stop, regroup, advance again, and so on. Its commander, General Franks, was also still insisting that he needed the reserve division to succeed. The more I thought about this, the more concerned I got. When the time came for crucial decisions to be made on the battlefield, I wasn't going to be there. I was absolutely dependent on the individual skills, temperaments, and judgments of my generals. But I could establish a clear framework and convey my intentions and the spirit in which I wanted the campaign carried out. I reminded Yeosock that VII Corps wasn't fighting the well-trained, well-equipped Soviet army it expected to take on in Europe. "I do not want a slow, ponderous pachyderm mentality. This is not a deliberate attack. I want VII Corps to *slam* into the Republican Guard. The enemy is not worth shit. Go after them with audacity, shock action, and surprise."

When Yeosock explained that Franks was worried that VII Corps did not have enough men or combat power to succeed in the attack, I reminded him that our air campaign was pounding the enemy ground forces and eroding the Iraqis' will to fight. I reiterated: "Let me make it clear, John. I do not want a mechanical grind-it-out operation. We must be flexible enough to capitalize on things as they occur. The idea is *not* to get to intermediate objectives and then stop to rearm and refuel. If you have divisions sitting around, you will present a huge target for chemicals, and you will lose. You cannot have VII Corps stopping for *anything*."

Yeosock said he understood and agreed.

I went out to meet Cheney and Powell when they landed at Riyadh air base on Friday evening. Early the next morning we started the briefings. Horner, Yeosock, Walt Boomer, and Vice Admiral Stan Arthur, who had succeeded Hank Mauz as our Navy commander, led off with assessments of their respective commands. Each confirmed that his force was ready to attack. Then Burt Moore, my operations director, explained that the Army would need a twelve-day countdown to move the remainder of its forces into attack position, run reconnaissance into Iraq, and check out lanes through minefields and obstacles. "What that means, sir," he said to Cheney, "is that if you give us the go-ahead today, the earliest we can attack is the twenty-first." Powell cast an amused glance in my direction—we'd missed by one day the attack window I'd given him back in December.

As the day went on, Pagonis gave a presentation showing that we'd accomplished our giant shift of forces to the west in the allotted three weeks. Cheney was full of praise. Then Franks, Griffith of the 1st Armored Division, and McCaffrey of the 24th Mechanized Infantry Division gave detailed briefings on how they would accomplish their missions—all very impressive, I thought, except for Franks, whose plan was still too deliberate and who insisted on telling the secretary and the chairman that he was going to need the reserve.

Cheney asked if he could speak with Powell and me privately. We went into a small office. "Norm, I've listened to what your men have to say. Now tell me your recommendation."

"I think we should go with the ground attack now. We'll never be more ready—our guys are honed to a fine edge and if we wait much longer we'll degrade their preparedness. Also, at the rate we're consuming munitions, I'm not sure how much longer we could keep up the air attack. Assuming that our bombing has worn down the enemy to the extent we need, the optimum time has always been the middle of February."

Cheney sat quietly, writing on a small notepad. Then he looked at me and asked, "What day do you think we should go?"

"The twenty-first. But I'll need three or four days of latitude because we've got to have clear weather to kick off the campaign." I repeated a point Boomer had made: good weather was especially crucial to the Marines, who had limited heavy artillery and were thus very dependent on air support.

"Start your preparations," Cheney said quietly. "I'll take those dates to the President."

We walked back to the auditorium where the commanders were waiting. "There has never been a time in the history of our nation when the United States military has conducted a more successful or professional operation," said the secretary. Powell echoed that thought and went on, "I cannot believe the lift that this crisis and our response to it have given our country. This is the way the world's only remaining superpower is supposed to behave."

They left. On Tuesday, Powell called from the Pentagon to say that President Bush had accepted our dates. If the United States and its allies decided to launch the ground attack, he said, the precise timing would be left to us: "You can go anytime after twenty-one February. It'll be your call."

---

13 FEB 91 D+27

0900 Morning update. Air priorities continue to be armor and artillery in the Kuwaiti theater of operations, the Hammurabi Division of the Republican Guard, Scud caps, tank-busting sorties, and targets in Baghdad. Tank-killer missions last night report knocking out eighty-five armored vehicles. Overnight, nine enemy prisoners of war crossed the line. A group of Bedouins and a thousand sheep entered the XVIII Airborne Corps sector.

1800 The chairman informed the CINC that there was intensive media interest in our overnight bombing of a command-and-control bunker in Baghdad. While this facility had been on our target list for a long time and had been validated repeatedly by CIA and DIA, it was apparently packed with civilians when we struck it with two bombs at about 0400. The CINC assured the chairman that we had hit the correct target and that we would explain the details of this event to the press at our briefing this evening. (Brigadier General Neal briefed this to the press and while it in no way calmed their inquiries, it appeared as though this was in fact a legitimate military target.)

Boomer started to have second thoughts about his plan, and I didn't blame him. Along most of the Kuwaiti border the Iraqis had built barriers thousands of yards deep that Boomer's Marines would have to breach while under fire. First they'd encounter minefields—a lethal mix of antitank and antipersonnel mines. Next would be huge rows of barbed wire—coils and coils strung atop one another, entangled so they couldn't be pulled apart, and rigged with booby traps and mines. Next, more minefields. Then tank traps (deep ditches that tanks would need bridging equipment to cross), berms (twenty-foot-high barriers of hard-to-climb sand), and so-called fire trenches (ditches flooded with oil and designed to confront the attacker with a wall of flame). Interspersed throughout would be forts consisting of dug-in tanks and trenches from which Iraqi infantry would shoot. The entire barrier complex might be miles deep; and in most parts of Boomer's sector, there was a second complex behind it. The idea was to slow our attack and cause the Marines to bunch up, thereby allowing the Iraqi artillery in the rear to shell them as they tried to complete their breach. Boomer's solution was to insist we redouble our air strikes on Iraqi artillery and frontline positions.

He kept revising his battle plan to take advantage of weaknesses and gaps discovered by reconnaissance patrols sneaking behind enemy lines. By Thursday, February 14, he'd decided to entirely shift his main point of attack some twenty miles to the west. He'd chosen a sector where the Iraqis had moved back their front line just before the air war began, so that the barrier complex nearest the border had been largely abandoned, and a second barrier complex, ten miles back, was still incomplete. I went over his maps and agreed that the change made tactical sense, even though it would cost a few days—we would have to relocate support bases and rearrange lines of supply. I tentatively rescheduled G-day for the twenty-fourth.

When I called Powell to let him know, he balked. "I hate to wait that long. The President wants to get on with this." He explained that with Soviet envoy Yevgeny Primakov having just visited Baghdad to try to negotiate a last-minute withdrawal by Iraq, we did not want to give Saddam any extra time to wheel and deal. Happily, Powell's concern turned out to be a nonissue: the next day, Iraq made a "withdrawal offer" that was nothing more than a litany of old demands, and the coalition quickly rejected it out of hand. The Soviet-Iraqi talks continued, but President Bush agreed to give the Marines the time they needed.

14 FEB 91 D+28

1520 Phoncon with the chairman. One thing we have tried to convey to the Iraqis through our leafletting and broadcasts is the direction of march to defect. Most of the prisoners did not know where the front lines were, but once we started announcing "March toward Mecca" it seemed to help.

15 FEB 91 D+29

0900 Morning update. Intelligence briefed enemy prisoner of war trends as follows: most are veterans of the Iran-Iraq war and tired of war. They are providing unit size, locations of minefields, bunkers, and battle damage assessments. They all say the number of line crossers would be greater if not for the minefields, the Republican Guard, and fear of retaliation against their families. They all say as soon as the ground war begins their compatriots will surrender in large numbers. They prefer to surrender to Arabs but will surrender to the United States.

Meanwhile, Stan Arthur, who was one of the most aggressive admirals I'd ever met, had run three aircraft carriers up into the shallow and constricted waters of the gulf, where the Navy had always refused to allow even one. Now Arthur wanted to mount an amphibious attack on Kuwait's Faylakah Island as a kind of prelude to the ground war. He'd briefed me on his proposal, explaining that the Navy would need ten days to position the necessary ships. While such an attack would distract the Iraqis, I also knew that the island was well defended and casualties might be high—so I'd told him to begin preparations and await further instructions. The week after Cheney and Powell's visit, an order from Arthur crossed my desk directing ships into position for the attack. That would have been fine except that the paperwork was labeled "execution order," which in Army parlance means "we will attack." I called Stan in a hurry: "Neither I nor the White House has given you permission to proceed. What makes you think you can override your orders?"

"It's really just a movement order," he protested.

"Then that's what you should have labeled it." Confusion could get people killed, I told him. "You can position your ships, but you cannot launch an amphibious assault without my permission."

Yeosock, in the meantime, was diagnosed with pneumonia. He went into the hospital in the early hours of the fourteenth, but three days later Doctor Robert Belihar, Central Command's chief surgeon, came to the war room. "Bad news," he said. "Besides the pneumonia, General Yeosock has a serious gall bladder condition." The doctors were recommending immediate surgery.

I asked a few questions. Doc Belihar said that at a minimum Yeosock would need three or four days in the hospital. I proposed that we medevac John to Germany because I knew that his wife, Betta, was there—she was staying with their daughter, whose husband, a captain in the 3rd Armored Division, was now in the gulf. Then I thought for a moment and turned to Waller, who'd been listening to the conversation. "Cal," I said, "I want you to take over as commander of the Third Army, effective today. You'll be acting commander until further notice. When John gets back on his feet, if circumstances warrant it, he'll go back in command."

He said, "Yes, sir," and left the war room. Knowing Cal, I was certain that by the end of the day he'd be out in the field, getting briefings from his corps commanders, changing anything he didn't like, and generally making things jump. I was confident the substitution wouldn't delay our attack plans.

I then went to see Yeosock. He was flat on his back in an immaculate private room at The Saudi Ministry of Defense and Aviation Hospital, an ultramodern facility where U.S. medical personnel had been added to the staff to help handle combat casualties. "The doctors say you have to have surgery, John," I began. We talked about his condition and the fact that he'd be out of commission for a while. Then I broke the news: "I've put Cal Waller down there in your place. He'll be the Third Army commander until you get back." Yeosock didn't say a word. Tears ran down his cheeks. I knew what he was going through—he'd been here since August, we were about to kick off a major military campaign, he was supposed to command the whole thing, and all of a sudden he couldn't be there at all. I continued, as gently as I could: "I want you to consider going to Germany for the surgery. You owe that to Betta. We'll get you back here as quickly as possible." Yeosock reluctantly agreed. He was medevacked out on my airplane that afternoon.

———

In between crises, I constantly studied the maps and displays in the war room, visualizing how the campaign might unfold. We finally had some indications that the Iraqi front-line forces were near collapse: the number of soldiers sneaking across to surrender rose every day; even officers had begun to give up. Our planes were still out day and night, bombing and strafing Iraqi positions at the rate of more than eight hundred missions every twenty-four hours. A tally board on the wall of the war room showed that we had destroyed thirty-five percent of Iraq's tanks, thirty-one percent of its other armored vehicles, and fully forty-four percent of its artillery. On the enemy situation board next to the tally board, the stickers that represented Iraqi units along the front lines had almost all been changed from red to green, which indicated that the units had been bombed to fifty percent strength or less; the units on the second line of defense almost all showed up amber, which meant seventy-five percent strength or less.

I knew we'd defeat them—but I didn't know how bloody the ground war might be. I could conjure up a dozen scenarios in which the Iraqis would make victory extremely costly, and I often reminded my staff: "You can take the most beat-up army in the world, and if they choose to stand and fight, you're going to take casualties; if they choose to dump chemicals on you, they might even win." In the past Saddam had used nerve gas, mustard gas, and blood-poisoning agents in battle; and even though he hadn't fired chemicals on Al Khafji, I was still expecting them when we launched our offensive. My nightmare was that our units would reach the barriers in the very first hours of the attack, be unable to get through, and then be hit with a chemical barrage. We'd equipped our troops with protective gear and trained them to fight through a chemical attack, but there was always the danger that they'd end up milling around in confusion—or worse, that they'd panic. The United States had not fought in a gas attack since World War I. The possibility of mass casualties from chemical weapons was the main reason we had sixty-three hospitals, two hospital ships, and eighteen thousand beds ready in the war zone.

I also worried about the great empty area of southern Iraq where the Army would launch its attack. I kept asking myself, "What does Saddam know about that flank that I don't? Why doesn't he have any forces out there?" The intelligence people suggested offhandedly, "Maybe he plans to pop a nuke out there." They then nicknamed the sector the "chemical killing sack." I'd flinch every time I heard it. I had a nightmare vision of Fred Franks and Gary Luck hitting that area only to have the Iraqis dump massive quantities of chemicals while the Republican Guard counterattacked and fought us to a stalemate. I became increasingly jumpy.

To complicate matters, we now had to contend with more than 1,300 reporters in the war zone; there were always 180 of them out in pools on the front lines. One night early in February, we'd turned on CNN to watch a White House press conference. A live report from a pool correspondent with the troops preceded it. She said breathlessly, "There has just been a major artillery duel in my location between the 82nd Airborne and the Iraqis."

"Son of a bitch!" I exclaimed. The 82nd Airborne was the American division farthest to the west, and any halfway competent Iraqi intelligence officer watching CNN could easily note the time and then canvass his forces to find out precisely where the exchange of fire had taken place. He would then discover that the 82nd was positioned for a flanking attack, a fact we had taken great pains to conceal for the past three weeks. Captain Ron Wildermuth, the Central Command public affairs chief, called the division public affairs officer and said, "You guys are supposed to be screening these reports!"

"We had an escort officer standing right there. He was just as shocked as everybody else. But by the time she said it, it was out over the satellite. You can't pull it back in."

A few days later an issue of *Newsweek* showed up with a map almost exactly depicting our flanking plan. I called Powell: "This stinks! *Newsweek* just printed our entire battle plan. Now the Iraqis could put chemical weapons in that area and completely reorient their defenses."

"Don't overreact," Powell cautioned. "That magazine has been on the newsstands for a week. Other magazines are full of maps showing other battle plans. They're all just speculating." He was right; intelligence reports over subsequent days indicated no change in the Iraqi disposition of forces.

18 FEB 91 D + 32

0900 Morning update. The following accidents occurred in the past twenty-four hours:
—One Marine in critical condition due to a gunshot wound to the head; accidental discharge 500 meters away.
—One UH-1 helo crashed; aircraft destroyed.
—One accidental M-16 firing; two wounded.
—One Army truck wreck; one fatality.
—One Army five-ton truck wreck; one fatality.
—One Army pickup truck wreck; two fatalities.
—One gunshot wound to the head with fatality. (This accident was described as a lieutenant demonstrating the soundness of the safety mechanism on the .45 pistol to those gathered. He put the weapon to his head and it discharged, killing him.)
—Navy forklift fell off a pier, drowning one.

> 1720 Phoncon with the chairman. The CINC stated we had a
> terrible day yesterday with regard to accidents—all the way
> from a Medical Corps major losing control of a five-ton
> truck, resulting in two fatalities, to an MP lieutenant put-
> ting a .45-caliber pistol to his head demonstrating the
> safety mechanism and killing himself. It's like the whole
> command has gone insane.

The tension really started to build late Monday, February 18. First Powell called. "The National Security Council is saying we may need to attack a little early. Can you let me know by tomorrow if you can manage it?" He spoke in the terse tone that signaled he was under pressure from the hawks. Then my staff and I watched news reports of the latest Soviet peace initiative: Iraqi foreign minister Tariq Aziz had met with Mikhail Gorbachev in Moscow and taken a peace proposal back to Baghdad.

I could feel another confrontation with Washington brewing and wanted to give Powell as much support as I could. The following morning I asked my commanders if we could advance the attack by two days. By this time Boomer had reconnaissance teams in no-man's-land, scouting paths through the barriers. "We can if you need us to," he replied. "But we'll sustain a whole lot more casualties." Heavier casualties made no sense, and the other commanders said they needed the time they'd been promised. So I decided to tell Powell: "I'm sorry, the twenty-second is out. We're continuing to plan for the twenty-fourth."

But when he phoned he seemed to have something entirely different on his mind. "This peace initiative may be for real," he said, and described the behind-the-scenes maneuvering that had taken place. Aziz had carried to Baghdad the proposal that Iraq withdraw from Kuwait immediately and unconditionally. The pullout would start the day after a cease-fire so the retreating Iraqis would have the assurance that they would not be shot at. It would be completed in a set period of time still to be negotiated. Powell said Washington had told the Soviets that the plan was constructive but that it failed to satisfy a number of the UN resolutions, such as an annulment of the annexation of Kuwait—and that for now Desert Storm would continue. Meanwhile, according to Powell, the State Department was pushing an even harder line: "They want to demand unconditional surrender."

"You need an Arabist to look at this," I said. "It sounds like the State Department guys are thinking like Americans. That kind of ultimatum does not work with Arabs: they will die first."

We talked about the military implications of a withdrawal and I expressed mixed feelings. I knew that any settlement that left Saddam's armed forces intact would be unsatisfactory to our Arab allies; yet if we could force Saddam to accept a humiliating withdrawal, we could probably sell our allies on the plan. "It comes down to a question of lives," I told Powell. "We have probably inflicted a hundred thousand casualties on the Iraqis at the cost of one hundred for us. Why should we inflict a hundred and fifty thousand casualties at a cost of five thousand for us? We could lose that many in the first two days of the attack." I reminded him that we'd already done heavy damage to Iraq's war machine, and that if required to pull out quickly, Saddam would be forced to leave behind a lot of armor and other equipment.

He agreed. "If they withdraw from Kuwait, it is a victory." Abruptly he changed the subject and asked about launching the offensive early.

"I know this isn't what you're looking for," I began, and told him we were continuing to plan for the twenty-fourth. Moreover, I said, we were worried about the weather: the long-range forecast predicted storms for that day. "So the date might even slip a little."

Powell was disappointed: "I'll take that message back, but we may be ordered to attack anyway."

When I hung up the phone I stewed and then called together my entire staff. "I want you all to know what's going on," I said, and outlined the Soviet initiative. If it had been up to the veteran military men in that war room, they'd have been thrilled to see Saddam accept a cease-fire and walk off the battlefield—not that anyone believed he would. People winced when I described Washington's response; Bob Johnston, whose son was on the front lines, shook his head: "The Soviets are talking about getting us exactly what we asked for, and we summarily turned them down."

The next twenty-four hours brought four more calls from Powell for further details as to why we couldn't launch all or part of our attack right away. At one point he and I and Cheney had a conference call, in which I again argued that militarily there was nothing to gain: "His army is unraveling and time is on our side." Cheney had been one of the fiercest cold warriors while in Congress, and I could sense that Moscow's intervention was not making him happy. "I don't see why the Soviets have to be involved at all," he growled.

"For what it's worth," I replied, "Saddam has to work through a middleman because that's the way Arabs do business. He will never negotiate directly. By working through a broker he saves face. And then afterward, of course, no matter what he has agreed to, he can make any claim he wants because he never talked to his enemy."

20 FEB 91 D+34

> 1900 Evening update. When the provost marshal briefed that several of our POW camps were deficient because they did not have one latrine for every twenty-five personnel in accordance with the Geneva convention, the CINC responded that, much as he hated to admit it, we should invite the International Red Cross to our headquarters because there is no way that our headquarters meets these requirements either.

The increasing pressure to launch the ground war early was making me crazy. I could guess what was going on and figured Cheney and Powell were caught in the middle. There had to be a contingent of hawks in Washington who did not want to stop until we'd punished Saddam. We'd been bombing Iraq for more than a month, but that wasn't good enough. These were guys who had seen John Wayne in *The Green Berets*, they'd seen *Rambo*, they'd seen *Patton*, and it was very easy for them to pound their desks and say, "By God, we've got to go in there and kick ass! Gotta punish that son of a bitch!" Of course, none of them was going to get shot at. None of them would have to answer to the mothers and fathers of dead soldiers and Marines.

Late Wednesday we received another weather forecast: lousy on the twenty-fourth, lousy on the twenty-fifth, with a stretch of clear weather beginning the twenty-sixth. My commanders argued that we should postpone the attack—not only Boomer this time, but also Peay, whose 101st Air Assault Division needed good weather for its helicopters. I had to convince Powell, and that would be a conversation I preferred not to have in front of my staff. It was neither fair nor appropriate to expose them to what I was sure would be real disagreement between their leaders. So I left the command post and phoned from my little bedroom down the hall. The minute I began with, "We're having a problem with the weather," Powell became exercised.

"I've already told the President the twenty-fourth. How am I supposed to go back now and tell him the twenty-sixth? You don't appreciate the pressure I'm under. I've got a whole bunch of people here looking at this Russian proposal and they're all upset. My President wants to get on with this thing. My secretary wants to get on with it. *We need to get on with this.*"

I got pretty exercised too. "I'm not trying to be a smart-ass, but what if we attack on the twenty-fourth and the Iraqis counterattack and we take a lot of casualties because we don't have adequate air support? And you're telling me that for political reasons you don't want to go in and tell the President he shouldn't do something that's militarily unsound? For chrissakes, Colin, don't you understand? My Marine commander has come to me and said we need to wait. We're talking about Marines' lives!"

"Don't *patronize* me with talk about human lives!" he shouted. It was the first time I'd ever heard him lose his temper, and he was livid. "What are you doing? Sitting there in front of all your officers putting on a big show while you talk to me this way!"

I got hot too, because I'd gone out of my way to make sure the conversation was private. "I'm not doing that at all and I'm not being disloyal to you. What I'm trying to say is that I'm under pressure too. My commanders are telling me to wait. Secretary Cheney was sitting right here when General Boomer said he needed four days of air support for his attack to succeed. But you are pressuring me to put aside my military judgment for political expediency. I've felt this way for a long time." I was trying to keep my voice steady but was not having much luck. "Sometimes I feel like I'm in a vise—like my head is being squeezed in a vise. Maybe I'm losing it. Maybe I'm losing my objectivity. But I don't think so."

By this time Powell had calmed down. "No, no, you're not losing it," he told me. "You haven't lost anything. I have great confidence in you."

I said, "I understand where you're coming from, but I want you to understand where *I'm* coming from. I'll continue to watch the situation here, and I'll continue to talk to you about it." We agreed it was important that we keep working together. Then I added, more formally, "And of course I am standing by to do what is necessary."

"I'll take your recommendation to the secretary," he replied.

"Thank you, sir. That is all I can ask for. In fact, it is more than I can ask for."

Half an hour later, naturally, the weather forecasters changed their minds: the weather on the twenty-fourth and twenty-fifth wasn't going to be so bad after all. I called Boomer, who had received the same forecast. "I'd just as soon go on the twenty-fourth," he said. I checked with Waller, who said simply, "We're ready." I called Powell back. "I've got good news. The weather has shifted. Tell everybody the twenty-fourth is a go."

The peace initiative never stood much of a chance. The version of the Soviet proposal Saddam had accepted called for an immediate cease-fire and a lifting of the UN sanctions as soon as Iraq had withdrawn two thirds of its forces from Kuwait—and it gave Iraq fully six weeks to withdraw. Powell faxed a copy of the terms at two in the morning Friday.

"What do you think?" he asked, knowing full well how I'd respond.

"It's bullshit! Give him six weeks to pull out, and he packs up his weapons, goes home, and tells everybody he defied the United States. And he still has enough force to threaten his neighbors. It's the Arabs' nightmare."

The National Security Council was about to meet, and Powell and I hammered out a recommendation. We suggested the United States offer a cease-fire of one week: enough time for Saddam to withdraw his soldiers but not his supplies or the bulk of his equipment, most of which was dug in or disabled. As the Iraqis withdrew, we proposed, our forces would pull right into Kuwait behind them, capture the arsenal, and destroy it. "This would work," I told Powell, "but I doubt Iraq will buy it."

At bottom, neither Powell nor I wanted a ground war. We agreed that if the United States could get a rapid withdrawal we would urge our leaders to take it. Though we hadn't literally defeated Saddam on the battlefield, in the eyes of the world—including the Arab world—under the circumstances a rapid withdrawal would be a defeat for Iraq. And we'd have accomplished it without any additional loss of life on our side.

22 FEB 91 D + 36

1900 Evening update. Iraq's leaders are telling their troops to prepare for chemical warfare because the Americans are going to use chemicals against them. This is the same technique they used in the Iran war when they used chemicals.

On hearing that the final artillery brigade had closed into VII Corps, the CINC said that the enemy is fully out of position and we are in position to attack and destroy him. We have clearly outpositioned him. Everyone in this room should be very proud. One hundred percent of our combat forces are not only in theater but in place.

Friday evening, February 22, we switched on the TV in the war room to watch President Bush issue an ultimatum: by noon Saturday, Iraq would either begin a massive unconditional withdrawal from Kuwait or face a ground war.

We all knew by then which it would be. While I'd instructed my commanders to make sure they could stop short if necessary ("We can't afford to have B-52s hit them if they're pulling out," I'd told Horner), we were marching toward a Sunday morning attack.

Bob Johnston's chair was empty—I'd given him permission to fly to the front lines to spend the night with his son—but sitting next to me was John Yeosock, who to everybody's amazement had walked into the war room the night before. "Reporting for duty, sir," he'd said, and insisted he was ready to resume command of the Third Army. I'd been skeptical that a man could be back on his feet three days after major surgery, and I'd looked at him closely: he'd seemed pale. "You sit right in here," I'd said. "I want to observe you for a couple of days." So now he was in Waller's old slot, as my acting deputy commander in chief, and he'd been bugging me about once an hour about going back to his command. "Shit, boss, when are you gonna let me go back? I'm fine!"

Out of the corner of my eye I'd watch him when he stood up. "See, you grimaced! You're still in pain."

"No, I'm not. I can do my job."

On Saturday morning, with less than twenty-four hours to go before the offensive, I decided Yeosock was right. Besides, he was driving me crazy. John was a somber-looking fellow in the best of circumstances, and now he looked as if he'd lost his last friend. "All right, quit buggin' me," I said. "Go back down and take your command."

I called Cal Waller and told him. Cal knew putting Yeosock back in was the right thing to do—after all, it was his command and his staff. But Cal had gotten himself all fired up to command our three hundred thousand Army troops in the attack and was really disappointed. When he got back to headquarters I saw I'd exchanged one long face for another.

Meanwhile, now that G-day was upon us, I'd canceled the Navy's amphibious assault on Faylakah Island. Plans called for it to precede the ground war by two days, but the helicopter carrier U.S.S. *Tripoli* and the Aegis guided missile cruiser U.S.S. *Princeton* had struck mines, U.S. and British minesweepers had been unable to clear the area, and as a result the Navy hadn't made it into position to launch the attack in time.

23 FEB 91 D + 37

1100 Meeting with General Abu Shanaf, chief of staff of the Egyptian armed forces. Abu Shanaf told the CINC that the

Egyptians are ready to attack and we should have full confidence in their ability. The CINC assured Abu Shanaf that if they get into trouble he has both the 1st Cavalry and the 1st British Armor at his disposal.

Thousands of tanks and armored vehicles—U.S., Arab, British, and French—were now pressed against the border in battle formation, the men catching whatever sleep they could in their vehicles or on the sand outside, and eating MREs if they had any appetite. In places where we needed to breach barriers, combat engineers had moved all the way forward with their armored excavators and bulldozer tanks. Behind the battle formations, convoys of fuel and ammunition trucks had pulled up, ready to follow the columns into battle. Our artillery had moved forward—thousands of howitzers and guns with millions of pounds of stockpiled ammunition—ready for a massive preparatory barrage that would pound Iraqi positions throughout the night. Far to the west, the 101st Air Assault Division was flying helicopter patrols deep into Iraq, reconnoitering landing zones for the assault. To the east, the battleship *Missouri* had worked its way up the Kuwaiti coast and trained its huge sixteen-inch guns on Iraqi units in anticipation of the attacking Saudis and Marines. All along the Iraqi lines, coalition air strikes reached their maximum fury—on the eve of the offensive Chuck Horner sent out nine hundred sorties. The weather in the battle zone was clear, except in eastern Kuwait, where Iraqi troops had begun pillaging the city and setting fire to the oil fields. There a hellish black cloud darkened the sky and obscured the crescent moon, as though Saddam were stoking the fires of war.

The deadline for the President's ultimatum came and went on Saturday night. Everybody in the war room felt the same way: we were ready to get it over with.

23 FEB 91 D+37

1500 Phoncon with Major General Peay, 101st Air Assault Division. The CINC wished him Godspeed in the upcoming attack.

1530 Phoncon with Brigadier General Tilelli, 1st Cavalry Division. The CINC wished him Godspeed in the upcoming attack.

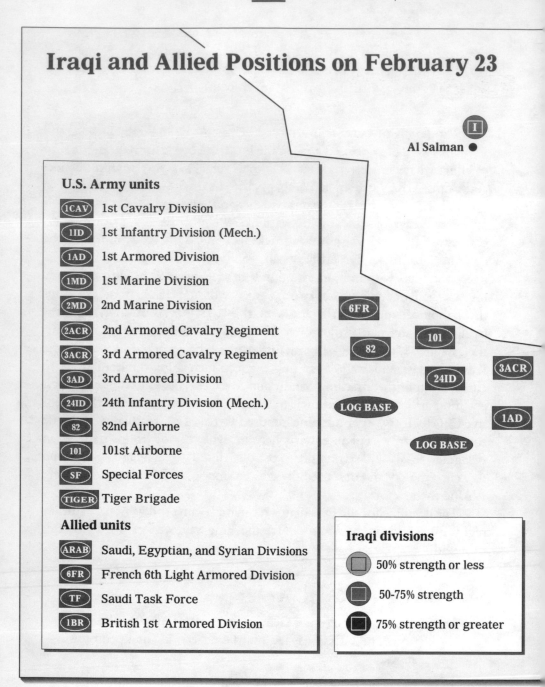

Iraqi and Allied Positions on February 23

Al Salman ●

U.S. Army units

1CAV	1st Cavalry Division
1ID	1st Infantry Division (Mech.)
1AD	1st Armored Division
1MD	1st Marine Division
2MD	2nd Marine Division
2ACR	2nd Armored Cavalry Regiment
3ACR	3rd Armored Cavalry Regiment
3AD	3rd Armored Division
24ID	24th Infantry Division (Mech.)
82	82nd Airborne
101	101st Airborne
SF	Special Forces
TIGER	Tiger Brigade

Allied units

ARAB	Saudi, Egyptian, and Syrian Divisions
6FR	French 6th Light Armored Division
TF	Saudi Task Force
1BR	British 1st Armored Division

6FR
82
101
24ID
3ACR
1AD
LOG BASE
LOG BASE

Iraqi divisions

- 50% strength or less
- 50-75% strength
- 75% strength or greater

1550 Phoncon with Major General McCaffrey, 24th Mechanized Infantry Division. The CINC wished him Godspeed
in the upcoming attack.

1703 Phoncon with Major General Johnson, 82nd Airborne
Division. The CINC wished him Godspeed in the upcoming attack.

1720 Phoncon with Major General Funk, 3rd Armored Division. The CINC wished him Godspeed in the upcoming
attack.

1750 Phoncon with Major General Rhame, 1st Infantry Division. The CINC wished him Godspeed in the upcoming
attack.

1945 Phoncon with Major General Griffith, 1st Armored Division. The CINC wished him Godspeed in the upcoming
attack.

23

24 FEB 91 G-DAY/D + 38

0400 At G-day, H-hour, the following senior officers were present in the war room: the CINC, deputy CINC, chief of
staff, Major General Moore, Brigadier General Leide,
Major General Starling, Brigadier General Neal, and
Mr. Gordon Brown. The war room was extremely quiet,
with a sense that everything that could be done had been
done. Brigadier General Leide moved around the room
visiting with the CINC and other staff officers, sharing
intel reports. One, from the Kuwaiti resistance, was that
the destruction of Kuwait City by the Iraqis had begun.
Explosions had been reported throughout the city and in
major office buildings.

I n cold rain and darkness and under
the covering fire of 155-mm howitzers, the first Marines crossed into
Kuwait—M-60 tanks and Cobra helicopters in the lead, followed by thousands of troops in armored personnel carriers and humvees. The troops
wore clumsy charcoal-lined suits to protect them from chemical weapons,

and carried gas masks on their belts. By the time President Bush went on TV at six A.M. Saudi time to declare "the liberation of Kuwait has now entered a final phase," the Marines had already penetrated the first line of border defenses. As they continued to advance, two brigades of Saudi armor and a combined brigade of Arabs from other gulf countries—the same units that had repelled the Iraqis at Al Khafji—made their way across the border and headed north on the coast road toward Kuwait City.

Nearly three hundred miles to the west, the armored cars of the French 6th Light Armored Division were bouncing across thirty miles of rocky desert into Iraq. Along with a brigade of paratroopers from the 82nd Airborne, they were to seize the Al Salman air base and the surrounding area. This was where Scuds had been fired at Riyadh and was the westernmost objective of our attack. Thirty miles east of the French and 82nd Airborne advance, the 101st Air Assault had been delayed by rain and fog but was about to launch the largest helicopter assault in history. More than three hundred Apache, Cobra, Black Hawk, Huey, and Chinook helicopters, piloted by men and women, were transporting an entire brigade with its humvees, howitzers, and tons of fuel and ammunition fifty miles into Iraq. They were to set up a huge fire base from which attack helicopters could easily strike the Euphrates valley.

Back at the war room in Riyadh, we were so removed from the action that all we knew was that our forces were finally on their way across the border. It might take the entire day to piece together an accurate picture of how the attack was progressing. I desperately wanted to do something, *anything*, other than wait, yet the best thing I could do was stay out of the way. If I pestered my generals, I'd just distract them: I knew as well as anyone that commanders on the battlefield have more important things to worry about than keeping higher headquarters informed. But I would have given anything to be with Barry McCaffrey and my old unit, the 24th Mechanized Infantry Division, which was about to mount a tank charge into Iraq.

My job was to stay in the basement with our radios and telephones, assessing the offensive as it developed, keeping the senior commanders apprised of one another's progress, and making sure we accomplished three strategic goals: to kick Iraq out of Kuwait, to support our Arab allies in the liberation of Kuwait City, and to destroy the invading forces so Saddam could never use them again.

When reports did start trickling in, they were better than we'd dared hope. Making their way through the first line of barriers, the Marines had encountered no impassable minefields, no walls of flame, no murderous gas barrages, and very little resistance. Boomer had chosen his point of attack well. As his units streamed north toward the second line of barriers, they were reporting only minor firefights and few casualties and by midmorning they were taking hundreds of prisoners: after firing a few shots the Iraqis just climbed out of trenches and gave themselves up. The Saudis on the beach road were making remarkable progress. They drove past miles of abandoned bunkers and trenches before running into any resistance at all, and they also reported hundreds of Iraqis waving white flags. Meanwhile, far out to the west, the French and U.S. forces were advancing, as expected, almost unopposed.

I thought about speeding up the schedule of the offensive. Our primary force of heavy tanks—sixteen hundred of them—was waiting at the Saudi border to launch the main attack. It would have three key objectives: to free Kuwait City (the job of the pan-Arab corps of Egyptians, Syrians, Saudis, Kuwaitis, and other Arabs), to outflank and destroy the Republican Guard (the job of VII Corps), and to block the Iraqis' getaway routes in the Euphrates valley (the job of McCaffrey's division in the XVIII Airborne Corps). My battle plan called for this attack to be held off until dawn of the second day, in order to allow Boomer twenty-four hours to breach the barriers and engage the defenders along the border. But Iraqi resistance seemed to be crumbling. I didn't want to stop the Marines, yet I worried that if they drove too far ahead of the rest of the offensive, they ran the risk of opening themselves to a massive counterattack on their exposed western flank.

Just before noon a crucial bit of news came in: the Kuwaiti resistance radioed that the Iraqis had blown up Kuwait City's desalinization plant. Since Kuwait City had no other source of drinking water, this could only mean that the Iraqis were about to leave. And if they intended to pull out of Kuwait City, I reasoned, they intended to pull out of Kuwait.

At that point I knew I had to act. Timing is everything in battle, and unless we adjusted the plan, we stood to lose the momentum of the initial gains. I'd fought this campaign a thousand times in my mind, visualizing all the ways it might unfold, and from the fragmentary reports coming into the war room I could discern that the Iraqis were reeling. If we moved fast, we could force them to fight at a huge disadvantage; if we stayed with the original timetable, they might escape relatively intact.

Hours earlier I'd alerted both Yeosock and Khalid that I might decide to speed up the main attack. I got Yeosock back on the line; he told me that he and his corps commanders—based on their assessment of the battle reports and despite the bad weather—wanted to go *now*. I called Khalid; he confirmed that the Egyptian, Saudi, and other Arab commanders had agreed, after some debate about the weather, that they, too, were ready to go. So I gave the order to my forces, Khalid gave the order to his, and at three that afternoon we let loose the main attack of Desert Storm.

Our soldiers put the few remaining hours of daylight to good use. The huge battle map that dominated the war room showed the XVIII Airborne Corps accomplishing all of its first-day objectives. By early evening the French and the 82nd were closing in on Al Salman; the 101st had established its fire base and already had Apache helicopters blowing up Iraqi trucks on Highway 8, the main road up the Euphrates valley. McCaffrey's 24th Mechanized Infantry was maneuvering across rough hills and gulches that could turn muddy and treacherous in the wet weather. Amazingly, he was already thirty-five miles deep into Iraq.

A little to the east of where McCaffrey was advancing, where the landscape flattened into scrubby desert, VII Corps had moved huge formations of the 1st Armored Division and the 3rd Armored Division fifteen miles into Iraq. Up ahead, the 2nd Armored Cavalry Regiment, with its scout helicopters and vehicles, roamed the desert. Further east, where the enemy border fortifications began, VII Corps's 1st Infantry Division had opened more than a dozen breaches for its tanks and those of the British 1st Armored Division to pour through. General Moore reported that both VII Corps and the 24th were expecting to make good progress during the night.

Across the Wadi al-Batin, the dry riverbed that marked the western border of Kuwait, the pan-Arab corps had advanced to the barrier line. Two brigades of Saudis had taken the lead and begun to make their breach; alongside them, the larger Egyptian force was moving more deliberately and did not expect to begin their breaching operation until morning.

The Marines had hit some stiffer resistance late in the day, fighting an hour-long tank battle at the second line of barriers. But by nightfall they'd captured Al Jaber air base—the hastily abandoned headquarters of Iraq's IV Corps, which commanded a dozen enemy divisions in southern Kuwait—and had covered nearly half the distance to Kuwait City. Our casualties were remarkably light—fourteen killed in action. Meanwhile, Boomer's units were inundated with prisoners of war. The rules of warfare required us to keep the prisoners safe by speeding them to the rear. The Marines filled all the available trucks, but finally had to resort to taking the Iraqis' weapons, pointing south, and saying, "Walk that way." In the rear, we set up checkpoints where we collected the Iraqis as they came wandering back. The Saudis, now ten miles up the coast road, were also overwhelmed with prisoners. I realized the problem was probably a blessing in disguise: without it I'd have had difficulty slowing the Marines enough to get our offensive in sync. I called Boomer later on to congratulate him on a great day's work and he told me his casualty figures had been revised from fourteen killed in action to *one*. Yet neither of us was euphoric: we both knew the next day could bring a chemical attack or a counterattack by Iraqi armor.

I had spoken to Powell regularly throughout the day. His reaction to its events, like mine, was guarded. We both knew better than to make assumptions based on a jumble of disjointed early-battle reports. At ten P.M., I called to give him a final update. I was tired; at the end of the conversation I heard myself say how much I'd like to blow up the giant Saddam statue and the Victory Arch in downtown Baghdad. The Victory Arch, a monument to the war against Iran, was a huge sculpture of two hands, said to be Saddam's, holding two swords crossed. We'd spared both the statue and the Victory Arch during the air campaign because they weren't military targets. To my surprise, Powell was all for it—although he suggested we check with the President first Pentagon lawyers vetoed the idea a couple of days later, but that night, about twenty hours into the ground war, I went to bed content.

———

I came into the war room early the next morning and hurried to the battle map to see how far we'd advanced during the night. "What the hell's going on with VII Corps?" I burst out. Its lines had shifted *backward*.

"Our information yesterday wasn't entirely accurate, sir," said Moore. He explained that while *elements* of VII Corps namely, cavalry scouts— had indeed ranged fifteen miles inside Iraq, the tank force had slowed after crossing the border the day before. That still didn't explain what I was seeing. I had been told that General Franks and his corps would be moving all night and, since there was no enemy to their front, had expected to find them closing in on Objective Collins. This was a ten-mile-wide oval of flat, gravelly desert west of the main Republican Guard positions that was to serve as the jumping-off point for VII Corps's attack. There General Franks was supposed to turn his formations east to hit the Republican Guard. I looked at the map again; what made VII Corps's lack of progress especially hard to understand was the dramatic advance of the 24th Mech farther west. McCaffrey obviously *had* pushed all night, over much tougher terrain, and was already sixty miles into Iraq.

I called Yeosock. "Did VII Corps stop for the night?" I asked. "Look, I don't want them to do anything stupid, but they haven't had a shot fired at them as far as I know. They seem to be just sitting around. What's going on?" Yeosock said only that he'd get back to me.

As I hung up I shook my head and looked at Cal Waller. "I thought they'd be halfway to Collins by now."

"Hell, sir, I thought they'd be *on* Collins!"

A few minutes later Gary Luck called with a better report. "Sir, we accomplished all our objectives yesterday, and we've already accomplished our objectives today." He ticked off the positions of his units and added, "We've captured thirty-two hundred prisoners as of last night and we're still counting."

"That's terrific, Gary." I paused. "Now give me the rest of your report." The final item of a battlefield report is the casualty count.

"So far, sir, we have one wounded in action."

I'd known the day before that we were succeeding beyond our expectations, but suddenly my relief at not having lost large numbers of people hit me. I was overwhelmed. I thanked Luck, quickly got off the phone, and took a few deep breaths to collect myself. The morning briefing showed that our good fortune extended across the entire theater: after a day of ground warfare, we had eight dead and twenty-seven wounded, and while there was no way to gauge the number of Iraqi casualties, we had taken more than thirteen thousand prisoners.

By the time Yeosock and I spoke again at noon, I was determined to turn up the heat. The campaign had shifted from deliberate attack to what tacticians call an exploitation, in which an army pursues a faltering enemy, forcing it to fight in hopes of precipitating a total collapse. Yeosock and I didn't waste time discussing the inaction of VII Corps the night before. He simply confirmed that Franks had cautiously chosen to stick to his original plan, even though it was based on the assumption that the Iraqis would fight a lot harder. Franks had insisted on getting all his divisions past the barrier and then stopping to regroup on the other side. That process was now almost complete, Yeosock said, and soon VII Corps would move north. If all went well, it would be in position to attack the Republican Guard the next day. While this pace was nowhere near as fast as I'd have liked, it was acceptable. Our intelligence showed that the Republican Guard was still holding its positions along Kuwait's northern border; as long as VII Corps moved out aggressively that day, it could still accomplish its mission. But its delay meant I had to slow down McCaffrey, whose tank brigades were nearing the Euphrates valley: I didn't want them to face a Republican Guard counterattack by themselves. I began to feel as if I were trying to drive a wagon pulled by racehorses and mules.

The Marines and the Saudis on the coast were involved in the heaviest fighting on Monday. Both forces seemed bent on liberating Kuwait almost as rapidly as the Iraqis had conquered it. The Marines fought off three Iraqi counterattacks in a series of battles that lasted most of the day and wiped out scores of Iraqi tanks, took prisoners in huge numbers, and suffered only one dead and eighteen wounded. On the coast road, the Saudis and gulf Arabs had seized all the objectives assigned them in the original battle plan and were moving so well that Khalid and I lifted their limit of advance, allowing them to proceed north toward Kuwait City. When they finally hit heavy resistance in the afternoon, they fought well and took lots of prisoners.

While the Marines and Saudis were closing in on Kuwait City, the pan-Arab corps—the force *supposed* to take Kuwait City in our plan—was still back at the border. The Egyptians had spent most of Monday making their breaches through the barrier line. This was partly their military style: they were tough, methodical fighters who—like Franks—preferred to stick to a preordained plan. But I also sensed politics at work: the idea of attacking fellow Arabs was so controversial at home that I suspected the commanders might have been ordered by Cairo to keep casualties to an absolute minimum. Through Khalid and General Schwartz and the coordination center staff, I urged Major General Abdulrahman al-Kammi, the Saudi in charge of that sector, and Major General Salah Mohamed Attia Halaby, the Egyptian corps commander, to get a move on.

25 FEB 91 G + 1/D + 39

1510 Phoncon with the chairman. The chairman gave the CINC permission to blow up the statue of Saddam and the Victory Arch.

1815 The chairman called the CINC and told him to hold up on hitting the statue and Victory Arch.

The tension in the war room rose the minute the evening weather report arrived. We'd counted on clear skies for Tuesday, but instead found ourselves facing thirty-six hours of heavy rain, wind, sandstorms, and a cloud cover so dense that it would hide the battlefield from our overhead cameras. I was terribly frustrated: we needed to watch the Republican Guard. Up until now, the three armored divisions we were gunning for—the Tawakalna, Medina, and Hammurabi—hadn't moved from their bunkers along the northern border of Kuwait. But VII Corps scouts had already exchanged shots with outlying elements of the Tawakalna, so some Iraqis knew we were on their flank. If they realized that this was the vanguard of our main attack, they might try to escape. I told Powell: "If they spend

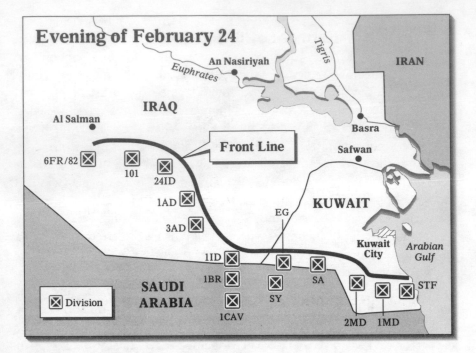

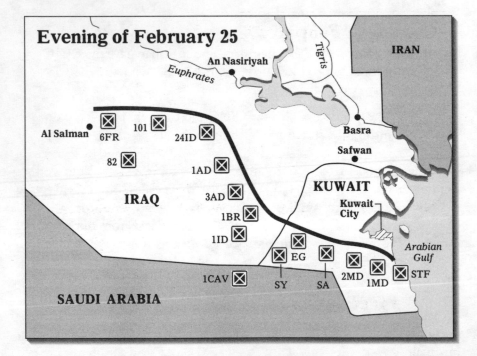

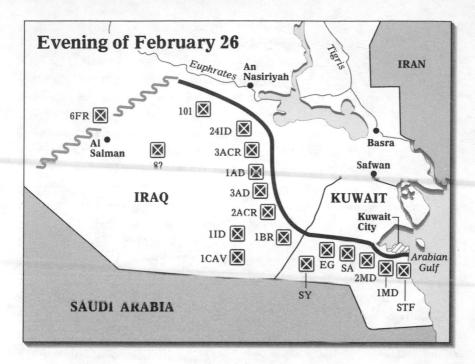

Evening of February 26

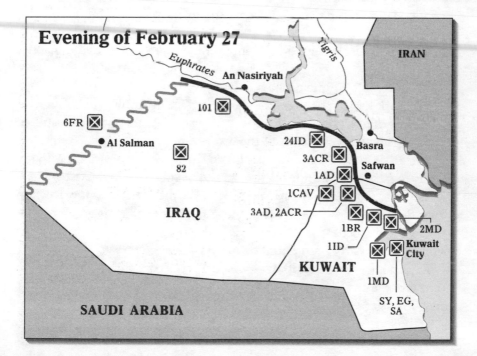

Evening of February 27

tonight in their holes, we have them. If not, it will be a race back to the Euphrates." The timing couldn't have been worse.

President Bush called shortly before eight P.M.—the first time we'd spoken since Christmas Eve. He listened carefully to my five-minute synopsis of the campaign, then quizzed me for several more minutes about our handling of POWs, about reports of Iraqi atrocities in Kuwait City (we'd received many, but none had been confirmed), and about how we were getting along with our allies in the campaign. I predicted, "Tomorrow or the next day will be the big battle with the Republican Guard." Finally I thanked him for his leadership. As I hung up the phone, I was struck by what the President had chosen *not* to say: he'd given me no orders and hadn't second-guessed the decisions I'd made, and the detailed questions he'd asked had been purely for clarification. His confidence in the military's ability to do its job was so unlike what we'd seen in Vietnam that the conversation meant the world to me.

An hour later Yeosock reported that while VII Corps's columns were still unopposed, rain and sandstorms were slowing them down, and they were twenty miles short of Collins. "I'm glad I told the President 'tomorrow *or the next day*,'" I said sarcastically to Waller after hanging up. Cal was practically beside himself.

"Goddammit, sir, we gotta make them move out!" He grabbed a phone.

"Cal," I said sharply, "don't interfere. You're not the commander anymore."

"But, sir, we've gotta do it. It's the right thing!"

"Yeosock knows the pressure is on. The Third Army is his command and you've got to let him run it the way he wants." Waller was so frustrated that he got up and walked out of the war room.

Later that night I went upstairs to see Khalid. He was pleased with the overall progress of the ground campaign and delighted with the victories his brigades were scoring on the Kuwaiti coast. We then turned to the question of the pan-Arab corps. "Unless they move faster, the battle is going to pass them by," I warned. "The Marines are already asking for permission to liberate Kuwait City. I can't hold them very long."

Khalid knew I was bluffing—we both understood that the coalition had to take the city. But he also knew that, militarily, I had a point. "Don't worry, I will get them moving," he promised. The sooner we could force an end to the war the better. Within the hour, we received a report that a Scud fired at Dhahran had struck a U.S. barracks. The explosion killed twenty-eight of our troops and wounded many more. It was a terrible tragedy—this terror weapon launched into the sky that by sheer fate happened to fall where we had a concentration of troops—and it brought home once again to our side the profanity of war. I was sick at heart.

———

At 2:15 that morning Brigadier General Butch Neal, the night operations chief, nudged me awake. "Sir, we picked up a public broadcast on Baghdad radio. They're ordering their troops out of Kuwait."

I went into the war room, shaking my head to clear it. We were only forty-six hours into the campaign, but the days and nights were starting to blur. Waller was back at his desk. "It looks like this might be for real," he remarked. We'd intercepted radio messages from III Corps, the Iraqi force occupying Kuwait City, ordering its units to pull out, and JSTARS, our high-tech observation plane that monitored activity on the battlefield, had picked up a convoy of 150 vehicles moving rapidly north out of the city.

Powell called almost immediately. I told him we were monitoring the roads and would bomb any military target that presented itself. He confirmed we were to continue with the attack—Iraq had given no indication that it was willing to accept the UN resolutions. But he speculated, "This could very quickly lead to a cease-fire."

"If it happens in less than a day or two, we could have a big problem with the Republican Guard," I said. Since their positions were in Iraq, not Kuwait, an immediate cease-fire would mean they'd probably escape. On that worrisome note, I went back to my room for a few more hours' sleep.

When I returned to the war room just after sunrise, I immediately asked, "Where is the Republican Guard?"

Leide said that storms were still hampering our reconnaissance. "We're not sure, but we think they haven't moved." That news, if true, was encouraging. But then Burt Moore, my operations chief, informed me that *VII Corps hadn't moved either*—only a few lead elements had reached Objective Collins. "Get me Yeosock," I ordered.

On the phone, Yeosock confirmed the report. "John," I said bluntly, "no more excuses. Get your forces moving. We have got the entire goddamn Iraqi army on the run. Light a fire under VII Corps. I want you to find out what they intend to do and get back to me." Before ending the conversation, I brought up the XVIII Airborne Corps. I'd been restraining the 24th Mech since noon the day before. "We need to seal off the Euphrates valley now," I told Yeosock. "Do you think McCaffrey can make it all the way to the river?"

"I'm sure he can."

"Okay. Release them now. We can't wait around for VII Corps anymore. But make sure the 24th has plenty of protection from the air, and helicopter support from the 101st. They're gonna be out there all by themselves."

Gary Luck, the XVIII Airborne Corps commander, called a little later, and I repeated my instructions about McCaffrey and the 24th. "You guys are doing a great job," I continued. "Now I want to make sure you understand your mission from here on out. It is to inflict maximum destruction, *maximum destruction*, on the Iraqi military machine. You are to destroy all war-fighting equipment. Do not just pass it on the battlefield. We don't want the Iraqis coming at us again five years from now."

While I waited for Yeosock to report back, I called Boomer at his mobile command post, a group of amphibious armored communications vehicles he'd used to follow his combat units through their two-day advance. "We went through a whole field of burning Iraqi tanks this morning," he said. "It would have done an old tanker's heart good." That morning the 1st Marine Division was attacking Iraqi strongholds at Kuwait International Airport on the city's southern edge, while the 2nd Marine Division, along with the Tiger Brigade, was fighting its way west toward the main highway junction at Jahra linking the road from Kuwait City with the road to Iraq. That junction would be the bottleneck through which the Iraqis in the capital would try to run. It had been assigned to the pan-Arab corps in the original battle plan, but now Boomer asked if his force could take it. "If you can get there without undue risk, go ahead," I told him.

I began to worry that the weather would bog down VII Corps still more. It was raining hard in that part of the theater and the wadis, or riverbeds, were filling up. Meanwhile, it became clear that the Republican Guard was no longer sitting still. Their commanders—using the cover of the storm—were organizing a classic battlefield retreat. Intercepted radio messages indicated that the Tawakalna Division was to stay in place and fight a delaying action while the Medina and Hammurabi pulled back in stages toward Basra. Finally, Yeosock called. Franks's advance force was on Objective Collins, he reported, and Franks was now in the process of bringing his tank divisions forward. "He'll attack once everything is lined up," Yeosock said.

"When?"

"Dawn tomorrow at the latest."

I let out a breath. We could scarcely afford to lose another day. I didn't like it, but I had no choice: given the units' location, there was no way I could get them there faster. "Okay, we'll have to do it his way," I said. "But there can be no question about his attacking tomorrow morning." In an effort to speed things up, I told Yeosock to give Franks the 1st Cavalry Division, the theater reserve he had been lobbying for since November. There was no longer any reason to hold it back: I didn't need it elsewhere in the theater and the long-term success of Desert Storm was now riding on VII Corps. I was confident they could destroy the Republican Guard—if only they could get there before the war ended.

At noon we heard that Moscow, still operating as Baghdad's intermediary, had called for a meeting of the UN Security Council to discuss a possible cease-fire. That prompted a phone call from Powell, who, after listening to my description of our progress across the front, asked, "Can't you get VII Corps moving faster?" I explained the timetable Yeosock and I had agreed on for attacking the Republican Guard, and suggested that, if a cease-fire seemed imminent, "You might have to buy us some time."

Things got very quiet on the other end of the phone. Then Powell said evenly, "Call General Yeosock. Tell him the chairman is on the ceiling about this entire matter of VII Corps. I want to know why they're not moving and why they can't attack an enemy that has been bombed continually for thirty days. They've been maneuvering for more than two days and still don't even have contact with the enemy. It's very hard to justify VII Corps's actions to anyone in Washington. I know I shouldn't be second-guessing anyone in the field, but we should be fighting the enemy now."

I relayed the message willingly—I hoped it would further encourage VII Corps to move—but the pressure from headquarters had already galvanized Franks. Within half an hour Yeosock reported that the 2nd Armored Cavalry Regiment had attacked the westernmost elements of the Tawakalna. He also indicated that the 1st Infantry Division, with its heavy tanks, would take over the attack at the end of the day. "Does that mean that if we can attack tonight we will?" I asked.

"You bet," said Yeosock.

A little while later—by now it was late afternoon—Franks himself called. "General Yeosock told me that a report to you would be in order," he began stiffly. The first thing he brought up was his concern that some Iraqi units he'd bypassed might come up to hit him on the flank. He wanted them destroyed before his forces turned to the Republican Guard, and therefore was about to order an attack toward the *south*.

"Fred," I interrupted, "for chrissakes, don't turn south! Turn *east*. Go after 'em!" Waller, sitting nearby, overheard my end of the conversation; he had his fists clenched and was staring at his desk. I reminded Franks that he had the powerful British 1st Armored Division on his right and he could use that to protect his southern flank. He immediately agreed. I didn't need to browbeat the man—I recognized he was going through the usual last-minute jitters that precede a crucial battle.

Then he told me what I'd been waiting to hear: that he intended to attack the Republican Guard throughout the night. "Great!" I said. "You should have good shooting tonight. Keep up the pressure. Don't let them break contact. Keep 'em on the run. If we can get in under the weather we'll have the Air Force pound them as they pull back in front of you."

We'd finally set the stage for the largest tank battle in military history. The massive force assembled under Franks—the 1st Armored Division, the 3rd Armored Division, the 1st Infantry Division, the 1st Cavalry Division, and the British 1st Armored Division—would confront the elite Iraqi armored units that had spearheaded the invasion of Kuwait. Seven months after they'd invaded Kuwait, the hour of reckoning was upon the Republican Guard.

On the eastern portion of the battlefield, the Iraqi retreat was disintegrating into chaos. Large units from the Iraqi II, III, IV, and VII corps were all trying to make it to Basra but were finding the Euphrates bridges down, and as we'd anticipated, convoys were bunching up in the extreme southeast corner of Iraq. A JSTARS plane, peering through the clouds with radar, was picking out dozens of Iraqi columns for our bombers.

I spent the rest of the day orchestrating the liberation of Kuwait City. The Marines had encircled the capital completely, and though there were still fierce firefights taking place on the outskirts of the city, there were also numerous reports that the Iraqis in the center of town had abandoned their positions and fled. Khalid assured me his forces would be ready to enter the city in the morning: the pan-Arab corps, which was now advancing fast, would catch up with the Marines west of the city by sunset, while the Arab brigades on the coast road would be poised to occupy the city from the east. I called Boomer to caution him that as the Arab units linked up with his Marines, his troops had to be careful not to shoot at them by mistake. We had designed the ground campaign so that forces that spoke different languages had been kept separate on the battlefield, but there was increasing danger of so-called blue-on-blue, or friendly fire, incidents now as they converged.

Our plan was for the Marines to hold their positions while a vanguard of Kuwaitis, Saudis, Egyptians, and other Arab forces made the first entry into the capital. I reviewed the details with Colonel Jesse Johnson, Central Command's special-forces chief. His advisors had been attached to the Arab units throughout the campaign and would accompany them into the city. One of their responsibilities was to remind our allies, the Kuwaitis in particular, not to retaliate against Iraqi prisoners for atrocities committed during the occupation. We didn't want any war crimes on our hands. Johnson had also put together a special-forces team that would retake our embassy, as British and French units retook theirs. "I want a simultaneous reoccupation of all three," I cautioned. "No mad dashes. No one-upsmanship."

Johnson was one of Desert Storm's unsung heroes. Since his arrival in the gulf six months earlier he'd worked close to the front lines helping to hold the coalition together. I complimented him on the performance of his troops: they had run reconnaissance and made raids behind enemy lines, taught the Saudis, reorganized and equipped the Kuwaitis, and, during the fighting, served as military advisors to Arab units. "They're good men, and they've got a good, aggressive commander," I told him. "Now, one other thing."

"Sir?"

"I know you're probably itching to get in on the action. But when your guys retake the embassy tomorrow morning, I am relying on you to be a commander, not a point man."

Johnson laughed. "Don't worry. I have three Purple Hearts and I don't want another one."

We had a hundred things to be overjoyed about, but the atmosphere in the war room was still extremely tense. We still hadn't accomplished what we'd set out to do—eliminate Iraq's ability to threaten the Arab world. Until we'd destroyed the Republican Guard, our job was only half done, and all of us felt the window of opportunity rapidly slamming shut.

---

26 FEB 91 G + 2/D + 40

2030 Meeting with Lieutenant General Khalid. Khalid told the CINC that the emir of Kuwait has summarily announced that the crown prince has been appointed military governor of Kuwait and is now in command of all friendly forces operating in his country. In response to this Khalid, at the direction of his father and the king, was going to move Saudi forces toward Kuwait City at 2400. The CINC suggested that units from all the Arab forces could link up in the city, and Khalid agreed to that. Later the CINC ordered Major General Schwartz to help the Saudis coordinate this.

2125 Phoncon with Skip Gnehm, U.S. ambassador to Kuwait. The CINC relayed the Saudis' problem with the Kuwaiti announcement. They have insulted the king by using the term "friendly" units instead of "brother" units. The Saudis are livid and are thinking about canceling all kinds of support they were preparing to provide the Kuwaitis. The CINC said Khalid had nonetheless issued the order that combined forces would go in tomorrow morning. The CINC then told the ambassador that while he would take care of the military situation, the business of who's in charge of Kuwait City he would leave in the ambassador's capable hands.

VII Corps did attack the Republican Guard all night. Not surprisingly, the Republican Guard fought hard to hold their ground. But we overwhelmed them and by dawn our reports showed that the Tawakalna Division had been almost completely destroyed while we hadn't lost a single tank. The Medina and Hammurabi divisions, confused by the discovery of a massive coalition force closing in on them from the west, tried to hurry their retreat toward Basra. Meanwhile on Highway 8 the XVIII Airborne Corps had destroyed a large convoy of Iraqi heavy-equipment transports trying to haul tanks out of the war zone.

As I studied the lines on the battle map, I felt confident that this war was going to end very soon. Central Command's Army corps were now moving inexorably east, like the piston in an enormous cider press. We were driving the enemy into the pocket across the Euphrates from Basra, which our Air Force had begun referring to matter-of-factly as the "kill box." We bombed the hell out of every convoy we could find—but between air strikes we flew over the battlefield with Black Hawk helicopters equipped with loudspeakers. We kept telling the Iraqis in Arabic, "Get out of your vehicles, leave them behind, and you will not die. We will let you go home." A lot of them had already figured that out for themselves. A tank battalion commander who surrendered eventually told our intelligence officers: "During the Iran-Iraq war I loved my tank because it was the one thing that protected me. But during this war I hated my tank because it could kill me. It was drawing fire. I stayed out of it as much as I could and slept as far away as possible."

In Kuwait City joyous crowds filled the streets as Kuwaiti, Saudi, Egyptian, and other Arab forces rolled in just after daybreak. Back in Riyadh, despite the realization that there was still tough fighting ahead, it was hard not to share in the elation. That morning's briefing seemed almost like a celebration as my staff reviewed the events of the past twenty-four hours. Of the forty-two Iraqi divisions in the theater at the beginning of the war, intelligence estimates now rated twenty-seven as overrun or destroyed. At least six more were considered "combat ineffective," or no longer able to offer real resistance. Iraq's II Corps, north of Kuwait City, was in full retreat; III Corps, which had occupied Kuwait City, had been destroyed; all the front-line divisions of IV Corps, south of the city, had been destroyed; and the infantry divisions of VII Corps, to the west, had collapsed. There was no longer any communication between Baghdad or Basra and the remaining divisions in the field—each had to fend for itself. We'd captured 38,000 prisoners. Of the 400,000 or so troops we'd sent across the border in the ground campaign, our reported combat casualties numbered twenty-eight dead, eighty-nine wounded, and five missing. Finally Ron Wildermuth, my public-affairs chief, advised us that the media pools we'd set up to handle coverage of the war had disbanded: "All the reporters are heading for Kuwait City. It's the symbol they need for their stories and they're totally out of control." As the briefing ended I ordered the staff to work on plans to speed troops home as soon as we declared a cease-fire ("Combat units first," I told Dane Starling).

Then I sat back to watch the victory unfold. In the press reports flowing in, the President was now a hero, Cheney was a hero, and Powell was a hero, while the politicians and military experts who had warned that dire things would happen if we went to war were eating their words. Everybody at headquarters felt very proud. I was happy as hell.

I spent the rest of the day monitoring reports of the fighting along Kuwait's northern border, where Yeosock and his generals were tightening their grip on the remainder of Saddam's army. Even though the weather remained foul—pelting rain, which I called infantryman's weather because foot soldiers take living in the mud for granted—VII Corps made steady progress. Yeosock called in the middle of the afternoon to let me know that our 1st Armored Division had broken through the positions of the Medina Division and at least two entire battalions of Iraqi tanks had been destroyed. He said the Hammurabi Division was now on the run, hiding in and behind an oil field, with our 1st Armored Division in pursuit.

"How much longer do you need to finish off the Republican Guard?" I asked.

"One more day," he answered promptly. "They'll be done for by tomorrow night."

The only upsetting development was a blue-on-blue incident in VII Corps. One of our aircraft had mistakenly attacked two British vehicles, causing numerous casualties. I asked Horner and Yeosock to take extra precautions against such accidents, which would become increasingly likely as our forces converged on the Basra pocket.

27 FEB 91 G + 3/D + 41

1545 Phoncon with Lieutenant General Horner. The CINC told General Horner that this was not a cover-your-ass phone call even though it may sound like one. As the kill box gets smaller, we cannot afford a blue-on-blue. "I am not asking you to do anything you are not already doing, but I am concerned. By the way, save me one bomb for the Saddam Hussein statue. I intend to make a personal request to the President."

Soon Powell called in a relaxed and happy mood and said, "We ought to be talking about a cease-fire. The doves are starting to complain about all the damage you're doing."

"What do you mean?" I said. What had happened, of course, was that journalists were now interviewing Air Force pilots who'd been hitting the convoys fleeing Kuwait. And as soon as we'd liberated the area around Kuwait City, reporters who had once been part of the media pools had taken pictures of Highway 6, where we'd bombed a convoy Monday night. It was a scene of utter devastation that they named the "Highway of Death"—a four-lane road strewn with the burned-out wreckage of more than a thousand military vehicles and stolen civilian trucks, buses, and cars. That was what people saw when they sat down Monday evening and turned on their TV sets. Powell informed me that the White House was getting nervous: "The reports make it look like wanton killing."

He and I both knew that wasn't the case. Though many Iraqis in the convoy had died, most had jumped out of their vehicles and run away. I felt irritated—Washington was ready to overreact, as usual, to the slightest ripple in public opinion. I thought, but didn't say, that the best thing the White House could do would be to turn off the damned TV in the situation room. Powell, for his part, didn't seem perturbed—he was accustomed to the political ebb and flow.

"So tell me what you want to do," he said. I walked him through the current battle maps and relayed what Yeosock had said he needed to finish off the Republican Guard. By the end of the day, while we'd be able to declare Iraq no longer militarily capable of threatening its neighbors, there would still be a hell of a lot of military equipment moving in the Basra pocket. "So here's what I propose," I said. "I want the Air Force to keep bombing those convoys backed up at the Euphrates where the bridges are blown. I want to continue the ground attack tomorrow, drive to the sea, and totally destroy everything in our path. That's the way I wrote the plan for Desert Storm, and in one more day we'll be done." I paused: "Do you realize if we stop tomorrow night, the ground campaign will have lasted five days? How does that sound to you: the 'Five-Day War'?"

Powell chuckled. "That has a nice ring to it. I'll pass it along." He added that we would need a media update at the end of the day. I suggested that the briefing be given in Riyadh rather than Washington because our information would be more timely, and he agreed. When I hung up the phone I put our two enlisted draftsmen to work on a series of schematic diagrams of the ground campaign that I made sketches for.

For the remainder of the afternoon I busied myself monitoring the battle. The charts were ready at seven P.M., and I took them upstairs to review them for an hour before heading across the street to the Hyatt Hotel for the media briefing. The presentation came off even better than I'd hoped. By the time I came out of the hotel I was in a fantastic mood. Looking up at the streetlights I realized this was only the second time I'd been outside the Ministry of Defense in more than a week. (The other had also been to brief the press.)

Powell called again, at 10:30 P.M. "I'm at the White House. We've been batting around your idea about ending the war at five days." He told me that in Washington the controversy over wanton killing had become uncomfortably intense—even the French and the British had begun asking how long we intended to continue the war. "The President is thinking about going on the air tonight at nine o'clock and announcing we're cutting it off. Would you have any problem with that?"

Nine in Washington meant five in the morning in Riyadh—only six and a half hours from now. He waited as I took a minute to think. My gut reaction was that a quick cease-fire would save lives. If we continued to attack through Thursday, more of our troops would get killed, probably not many, but some. What was more, we'd accomplished our mission: I'd just finished telling the American people that there wasn't enough left of Iraq's army for it to be a regional military threat. Of course, Yeosock had asked for another day, and I'd have been happy to keep on destroying the Iraqi military for the next six months. Yet we'd kicked this guy's butt, leaving no doubt in anybody's mind that we'd won decisively, and we'd done it with very few casualties. Why not end it? Why get somebody else killed tomorrow? That made up my mind.

"I don't have any problem with it," I finally answered. "Our objective was the destruction of the enemy forces, and for all intents and purposes we've accomplished that objective. I'll check with my commanders, but unless they've hit some snag I don't know about, we can stop."

Powell explained that the President would make the cease-fire contingent on an end to Iraqi fighting and Scud missile attacks, the immediate release of military prisoners and Kuwaiti civilian hostages, compliance with all the UN resolutions, and other conditions. I asked that the statement also make clear that this was a suspension of offensive operations, not an absolute cease-fire, and that our forces would be free to destroy any Iraqis who fired on us. Then Powell told me that the President would ask for a meeting of generals from both sides within forty-eight hours to work out the military particulars of the cessation of hostilities. That caught me by surprise—it had never crossed my mind that I'd have to sit down opposite Iraqi generals—and we spent a couple of minutes discussing how this might be arranged. Suddenly I looked at my watch. "Colin, I gotta get off the phone. We're talking about stopping this war six hours and twenty minutes from now, and I've got to get word to the guys who are fighting."

I hung up, called Horner immediately, and told him to keep reloading his bombers but to make sure they'd be able to stop at five o'clock. "This isn't definite," I said. "Washington still has to work it out with our allies. But don't launch anything you can't call back."

I called Yeosock and gave him the word. "Until five o'clock it's business as usual. I encourage you to do as much damage as you can with your Apaches right up till then," I added. I called Admiral Arthur, General Boomer, and Major General Wayne Downing, who was running the U.S. special operations deep behind enemy lines. Nobody seemed surprised that a cease-fire might be declared.

———

A few hours later Powell called to confirm: "We'll cease offensive operations, but there's been a change. The President will make his announcement at nine o'clock, but we won't actually stop until midnight. That makes it a hundred-hour war." I had to hand it to them: they really knew how to package an historic event.

President Bush and Secretary Cheney each came on the line to offer congratulations. Finally Powell came back on and said, "Okay, that's it. Cease fire at eight o'clock local tomorrow morning."

I'd gone to my private quarters to take the call; now I went back into the war room and explained the terms of the cessation of operations to the staff. "Our forces will stay where they are in Iraq," I ordered. "I want them to destroy all abandoned military equipment and supplies in their vicinity."

The White House, I told the staff, had added a stipulation that Iraqis in the war zone must leave their equipment and walk north—a stipulation I liked because it would allow us to finish the job of eliminating their weapons. But Johnston interjected that this would be impossible to enforce fully: "Sir, we can block a lot of the roads, but we'll never be able to stop the Iraqis who are already at the river from repairing the bridges and taking their equipment north unless we attack them."

He was right, of course. There was a considerable amount of armored equipment—perhaps two divisions' worth—pushed up against the pontoon bridges at Basra: a mishmash of everything from 1950s-vintage T-55 tanks and BTR armored personnel carriers to several dozen top-of-the-line T-72s that had pulled back when VII Corps was slow to engage the Republican Guard. We'd been attacking that equipment all night, and by the end of the following day we'd have destroyed it all, bombing the traffic jams and sending Apaches along the river to ambush any tanks that tried to cross.

We discussed the implications. We hated the idea of sparing *any* Iraqi equipment, particularly Republican Guard T-72s: sooner or later those tanks would be put to malicious use. But from a purely military standpoint, and from the standpoint of our Arab allies, we weren't concerned. To reconstitute even a single effective division from what was left would take Iraq a long time. The equipment was a mess: much of it was poorly maintained and missing spare parts (the Soviets had stopped supplying them), and some of it was broken or shot up. Moreover, the Iraqis couldn't simply throw together men and tanks and say, "We've got two divisions." They'd need years to assemble and train small units, then companies, then battalions, and so on—probably as many as five or six years, given the chaos they faced.

The decision was too big for Central Command: we had to bring it to Washington's attention. So I called Powell, repeated Johnston's point, and warned, "If we call this cease-fire we're going to see Republican Guard T-72s driving across pontoon bridges."

"Can you hit them tonight?" he wanted to know. I said I'd already ordered Yeosock to redouble his helicopter attacks; we had Apaches flying under orders to destroy every tank they could find.

"Okay," Powell said. "I'll get back to you." Twenty minutes later he called and said the White House now understood that some tanks would get away and had decided to accept it. Since we couldn't force the Iraqis to abandon their equipment without more shooting, the stipulation had been removed from the President's statement.

Yeosock and I still had a crucial matter to resolve: where to halt the ground advance. The XVIII Airborne Corps by this time had captured a large piece of Iraq; VII Corps was chasing remnants of the Republican Guard across northern Kuwait. Looking at the map, I could see only one problem: the main road junction three miles north of the Kuwaiti border, where Highway 6 from Kuwait City and the Umm Qasr highway from the Kuwaiti coast converged on the way to Basra. Unless we blocked that junction, even more Iraqi equipment would escape. I also wanted to secure nearby Safwan Mountain, because the Iraqis had launched many Scuds toward Dhahran from that area. VII Corps's nearest unit, the 1st Infantry Division, was within fifteen miles; Yeosock thought they could easily reach the junction before the cease-fire. "Great!" I said. "Take it, as long as you don't start a big fight that you can't finish in time. It would be the perfect place to set up camp."

I double-checked to make sure all my field commanders knew of the cease-fire. Finally I went to bed, exhausted. When President Bush went on TV two hours later to declare that the Gulf War was at an end, I was sound asleep.

24

1145 The CINC reentered the war room. While there was no formal update, the CINC was told that the cease-fire had gone into effect on schedule. The 1st Infantry Division had gone north out of Kuwait and was now in Iraq, and the 24th Mech had attacked east, ending up at a road junction just south of Basra. Attack helos ran missions last night, but did not kill many tanks.

owell and I had discussed using the deck of the battleship *Missouri* as the site for the cease-fire talks. Douglas MacArthur had accepted the surrender of the Japanese on that deck in 1945 and I wanted to make it obvious that this meeting was a surrender ceremony in everything but name. But in the end the idea turned out to be impractical: the President had given us only forty-eight hours—until Saturday morning—in which to start the talks. Bringing the Iraqi delegation to a warship in the middle of the gulf—not to mention transporting military representatives from every coalition nation and the scores of reporters we wanted to witness the scene—would be a complicated if not impossible undertaking on such short notice.

Our next choice was Jalibah air base—a large Iraqi military installation about thirty miles south of the Euphrates that had been captured by the XVIII Airborne Corps on the third day of the ground war. I liked Jalibah because it was ninety-five miles deep in Iraqi territory, so that it, too, would symbolize defeat, while logistically it would be easy for the Iraqi delegation to reach—they could drive eighty miles west from Basra on Highway 8. Powell concurred, and after we obtained White House approval, the State Department set out to notify Baghdad in a roundabout process in which the United States relayed its messages back and forth through the Soviets.

28 FEB 91 G + 4/D + 42

> 1900 Evening update. The CINC told Lieutenant General Horner that we needed to maintain an obvious presence in the skies over Baghdad, with General Horner quipping, "We have two options, subsonic or supersonic." The CINC said to make sure the patrols were both day and night and picked the supersonic option. They may not see the aircraft but the sonic booms will let them know we're there.
>
> The CINC told the staff that we will be under pressure to get the troops home. The first contingent will be symbolic and we will then shift to a full-blown redeployment. The CINC discussed safety. He wanted everyone to adopt the slogan, "Not one more life." We must not have the accident rate we had when we first arrived. I want the commanders held accountable. Get this down to the lowest level.

I waited in the war room as hours ticked by, aware that there would inevitably be problems to solve, but feeling confident that in the end things would fall into place. When the phone finally rang at two A.M. on Friday, it was Yeosock calling from his headquarters. "There's a problem with Jalibah air base. Gary Luck says it's too dangerous. There's unexploded ordnance all over."

"Oh, great," I said. "I wish we'd known that yesterday." I looked at my map. "Okay. Let's go with Safwan airfield." Safwan was the Iraqi military landing strip just north of the Kuwaiti border and only two miles from the road junction I'd ordered VII Corps to take the morning before.

Minutes later Yeosock called back. "We don't have any forces there."

I stared hard at the situation map. The entire sector around the airfield was clearly marked as being held by the 1st Infantry Division. I'd also personally been given confirmation reports to that effect by Burt Moore when I'd arrived in the war room that morning. "If we're not on the airfield itself, we must have units nearby, right? Just move some troops into that area." Yeosock said he would. Meanwhile I alerted Powell that we'd have to switch the meeting from Jalibah and were thinking of somewhere around Safwan. Barely twenty-four hours remained before the cease-fire talks were supposed to begin.

I replayed the conversation with Yeosock in my mind and became uneasy. Safwan airfield was just an asphalt strip in the desert, but—apart from its use as a meeting site—the whole sector was crucial to our ability to block the escape of Iraqi heavy equipment from Kuwait and root out any remaining Scud storage bunkers. I'd assumed our forces had spent the time since the shooting stopped doing just that. Now I wasn't so sure. On the other hand, there seemed to be no cause for alarm: I had received so many reports that our troops were in the area that a minor shift of forces would rectify the situation.

But Yeosock called back just before dawn and confirmed my worst fears: we had nobody at Safwan—not at the airfield and not at the nearby mountain where the Scuds were reportedly hidden, let alone at the road junction I'd explicitly ordered the Army to take. The Big Red One's helicopters *had* flown combat patrols along the highway and had reported no enemy forces, he said, but its troops had never set foot in the sector. I felt as though I'd been punched in the gut. "Why did they send in reports that they'd occupied it?" I demanded.

"I don't know. We got the same reports, sir," he said helplessly. "I'll have to check with VII Corps."

I finally came completely unglued. "I *ordered* you to send VII Corps to that road junction," I shouted. "I want to know *in writing* why my order was violated and why this mission was reported carried out when it wasn't." I knew there could be legitimate reasons for not taking the sector, but it was absolutely unacceptable that erroneous "mission accomplished" reports had been forwarded to my headquarters. The fact that two days had passed and no correction had been made only made matters worse. I felt as if I'd been lied to. All my accumulated frustration and anger with VII Corps came boiling out. "I want Safwan airfield and Safwan Mountain occupied and thoroughly reconned," I ordered, "and I want all enemy equipment destroyed. I have to depend on you to set up a meeting site that is secure.

Don't get into a major firefight. If there is a large enemy force you'll have to back off. Do you understand your orders?"

"Yes, sir."

"Do you think you are capable of carrying out this mission?"

"Yes, sir."

I couldn't let it go. "If not, let me know, and I will send the Marine Corps up there."

"We can handle it," he said tersely.

"That's good, John. Make sure you do it smart. I don't want any troops put at risk to cover the asses of officers who failed to do the job in the first place." I was being tough on Yeosock but I knew that he understood why. John was a great commander who had been my assistant deputy chief of staff for operations at the Pentagon, and when command of the Third Army had come open, I'd worked hard to get him promoted and assigned there. I knew that he was tough enough to separate my emotionalism from my intent and orders and that he'd get the job done.

I went to bed.

I came back into the war room at noon and found Waller and Moore waiting. "Not only do we not own Safwan," Waller said, shaking his head, "but there is an Iraqi unit occupying the airfield. And the Iraqis have *tanks* at the main road junction." I could see the notion of Safwan as a plausible site for cease-fire talks fast disappearing: if the Iraqis had the airfield, it would mean us coming to them, not them coming to us. And militarily, the thought that the enemy still held that sector was intolerable.

I immediately got Yeosock back on the phone. He related that VII Corps's 1st Infantry Division had gone up to the road junction that morning, but they'd found fifteen Republican Guard tanks and a brigade commander. I said evenly, "We've got to take that road junction, John."

"There's a cease-fire!"

"There is no cease-fire. It's a temporary suspension of offensive operations on our terms. I want you to tell the Iraqis to withdraw. If they attack, return the fire. In the meantime, find us a place to hold the meeting. Start checking Jalibah air base again."

I MAR 9I G + 5/D + 43

1255 Phoncon with Egyptian minister of defense Abu Taleb. After being thanked for the great victory, the CINC responded that it happened quicker than we ever expected. It was a good team effort on the part of everyone. Your forces did a fine job. They are in Kuwait City which is very good. We will be careful that we have a good peace.

By now it was dawn in Washington. I put in an urgent call to Powell, who immediately phoned back from his house. "What's wrong?" he asked.

I quickly outlined the dilemma at Safwan. "The bottom line is that I doubt we'll be ready for the meeting tomorrow."

Despite the fact that it was only five o'clock in the morning, Powell was in a relaxed mood. "You don't need to worry about that," he said, and explained that communications through Moscow between Iraq, the United States, and the United Nations were so slow that Washington was already anticipating a one-day delay. Turning back to Safwan, he asked to hear the entire sequence of events and, after ten minutes' discussion, approved the orders I'd given Yeosock and the plan I proposed.

I called Yeosock again, who grimly announced, "The Iraqi commander says he's not going to leave."

"Fine. I've discussed this matter with the chairman. Here's what you'll do. You've got the entire 1st Infantry Division there. Dispatch overwhelming force and surround the guy completely, and make sure he sees. Then tell him, 'We cannot tolerate Iraqi units this close to our forces. You must leave this area or we will take you prisoner. We are doing this for the protection of our troops. If you fight, we will destroy you.'"

Yeosock asked, "If he won't move . . . ?"

"We're bluffing. I don't want you to attack. If he says no, tell me and we'll go back to the drawing board. But he's only got one company of tanks. There should be no problem getting him to leave without firing a shot."

1 MAR 91 G + 5/D + 43

1407 Phoncon with Ambassador Freeman. The CINC brought the ambassador up to date on the cease-fire meeting. The CINC also noted that Crown Prince Abdullah has warned that the Iraqis will try to assassinate the CINC at the meeting. The CINC emphasized that we would search everyone before they enter the negotiation area.

1540 Phoncon with the chairman. The CINC told the chairman that we had had several members of the coalition demanding a chance to "sign the paper." The CINC had assured them that there would be no paper. The CINC told the chairman of the assassination threat and noted that peace is a hell of a lot harder than war.

I closely monitored the action at Safwan, hoping to avoid a major international incident. I kept Powell informed at every step. By late afternoon a brigade commander from the 1st Infantry Division had encircled the road junction with fifty tanks. For good measure he'd also brought three companies of soldiers in Bradley Fighting Vehicles, and had heavily armed Apaches crisscrossing the skies. At that point he approached the Iraqi commander. After delivering our pitch as directed, he gestured toward his tanks and added, "My men are eager to fight." It didn't take long for the Iraqi to order his tanks to leave.

We also moved troops onto the airstrip, and that night I ordered Pagonis to prepare the meeting site. Then I called Tom Rhame, the commander of the 1st Infantry Division, whose troops would meet the Iraqi delegation at the road junction and escort them to the airfield. I first complimented him on the bloodless capture of Safwan and then described how I wanted to orchestrate the Iraqis' arrival. "I'd like to make sure they come in the proper frame of mind. Therefore, I want you to position a great deal of combat equipment along the airfield access road. Don't just park it— put it in fighting positions—but make sure it is clearly visible. I want the Iraqis to see fresh, undamaged, first-rate U.S. tanks and armored personnel carriers all over the place."

"That's a roger," he said. "We know exactly what to do." I could almost hear him grinning over the phone.

———

In the meantime, Baghdad had been unable to communicate with the remnants of its army still in the Basra pocket, so as those units tried to make their way north, the battle zone remained a dangerous place. On Saturday morning, March 2, two days after the shooting supposedly had stopped, I came into the war room to discover that we'd just fought a major battle in the Euphrates valley. Evidently, two battalions of the Republican Guard had gotten tired of waiting to cross the pontoon bridge at Basra the night before and had headed west on Highway 8. Twice they'd encountered Bradley Fighting Vehicles operating as scouts for the 24th Mech and both times had opened fire with antitank missiles. At dawn they'd run into a U.S. blocking position and had opened fire again. McCaffrey had replied with a full-scale tank and helicopter counterattack, smashing the Iraqi column and taking three thousand prisoners without suffering a single casualty. To me this wasn't altogether bad news—the Republican Guard had shown characteristic arrogance by spotting what looked like a weak U.S. force—not suspecting that an entire U.S. Army division was in the way—and deciding, "Let's shoot 'em up." I was glad that the President's cease-fire statement had reserved our forces the right to shoot back if attacked. Yet the incident underscored the urgency of setting cease-fire terms that would definitively separate the two sides.

The Iraqi delegation was now due to show up at Safwan at eleven A.M. on Sunday. Their chief representatives would be a pair of three-star generals I'd never heard of: Lieutenant General Sultan Hashim Ahmad, the deputy chief of staff of their Ministry of Defense, and Lieutenant General Salah Abud Mahmud, commander of the now-defunct III Corps. On our side it would be Khalid and me, along with observers from many of the coalition countries that had taken part in the war. The agenda would be confined to military issues, but the meeting would have enormous symbolic importance—it would be the first time the two sides would literally face each other across a negotiating table.

Two days before, Powell had asked us to draft a set of military conditions that Iraq would have to meet for the cease-fire to become permanent. These were to be relayed to Baghdad in preparation for the meeting. I'd spent an hour pacing the tile floor of the war room, dictating these so-called terms of reference. Number one was the immediate release of all coalition prisoners of war, as well as a complete exchange of information on troops listed as missing in action and the return of any remains. While not many of our troops were in these categories, it was essential to account for every one: there was no way I wanted a repetition of the POW and MIA agony of the Vietnam War.

Next I'd spelled out the measures necessary to make the battle zone safe. For instance, the Iraqis had to tell us where they'd planted mines and booby traps in Kuwait, as well as indicate any storage sites they'd established for chemical, biological, or nuclear weapons. The last thing we needed was for our troops to stumble onto such sites unawares. Equally important, we had to draw a demarcation line and physically separate the two armies, to keep trigger-happy soldiers from touching off more incidents like the Euphrates valley battle.

My stenographer, Chief Petty Officer Rick Rieger, had patiently taken it all down, and we'd faxed Powell a four-page typescript. "This looks pretty close to what we want," had been his reaction. "I'll pass it along."

We'd as yet received no written instructions from Washington, and when Saturday evening rolled around, I joked that it would be interesting to see which came first: authorization to conduct the talks, or the talks themselves. More to the point, the terms of reference seemed to have disappeared without a trace. Each time I talked to Powell I'd ask, "Is the document okay? Is there something else you guys want me to cover?"

"It's being coordinated," he'd reply. It turned out that the cease-fire terms had to be reviewed by the Defense Department, the State Department, and the White House, and their various bureaucracies were having trouble keeping up with the pace of events.

While we waited, I conferred with Khalid. His government was happy for me to take the lead in the discussion, he said, except for a few Arab issues he wished to raise personally. At the top of his list was the fate of civilian detainees: the Iraqi army had taken hostage some three thousand Kuwaiti young men as they'd pulled out, and the Saudis wanted them included in the prisoner-of-war release. Khalid also planned to insist that Iraq formally affirm the sovereignty of Saudi Arabia: "They must promise that their military personnel will never cross the border into our kingdom."

2 MAR 91 G+6/D+44

1510 Phoncon with the chairman. The CINC told the chairman that we had recently received a report from the CIA that it now agrees with our estimate of the number of tanks destroyed in the offensive. The CINC told the chairman that General Leide and Colonel Thomas had taken the report and had it framed.

If need be, I would go to Safwan and wing it. For one thing, the talks would be limited to military matters, and I understood what needed to be done; for another, our side had *won*, so we were in a position to dictate terms. Even so, I knew I'd feel better walking into that meeting tent with the full authority to speak for the United States. If I had to take a hard line, I'd be much more convincing if I could say, "the United States insists" rather than "Schwarzkopf insists."

It was late Saturday night when Powell finally confirmed that the terms of reference had been approved and sent via Moscow to Baghdad. The State Department had accepted our draft with only one change: every place where I had said in effect, "the participants for the coalition will *negotiate* . . . ," the State Department had substituted, "the participants for the coalition will *discuss* . . ." Their position was that only the State Department was allowed to negotiate for the United States of America. The military was not.

3 MAR 91 G + 7/D + 45

0700 The CINC received a final update from the staff prior to departure for Safwan. It was pointed out that during the night there was agreement by the Iraqis through Washington to attend the meeting, but great discussion about the appropriateness of the level of representatives by D.C. officials. Washington had finally agreed that if Lieutenant General Ahmad headed the delegation and had appropriate authority from Baghdad, this was acceptable.

I climbed aboard my airplane early the next morning for the first leg of the trip to Safwan, accompanied by Michel Roquejeoffre, the French commander, and a half dozen of my staff. Nobody talked much. I gazed out the window thinking about the upcoming negotiation. I wanted the meeting to be a straightforward military discussion with no crowing, no posturing, and no humiliation of the Iraqis. But by the same token, I didn't want them thinking we'd just forgive and forget. The night before I'd told Khalid, "Please, none of this 'Arab brother' business when the Iraqis arrive. No embracing or kissing each other on both cheeks."

Khalid had given me a startled look. "I'm not even going to shake their hand!"

"Good, because I don't plan to either."

As we began our descent into Kuwait City, I rehearsed the points of discussion once again in my mind. Everything seemed in order, yet I felt unsettled. I couldn't put my finger on it—was there some contradiction I'd missed? Some loophole the Iraqis could take advantage of?

Our plane was flying in brilliant morning sunlight, with blue sky above and around us as far as the eye could see. Yet beneath the plane was an eerie and total darkness. This must be the smoke from burning oil fields I'd heard about in battlefield reports, I suddenly realized. Descending, we passed first through light brown clouds; then the air outside the windows became pitch black. I looked at Roquejeoffre; he stared back wide-eyed and shocked. As we made our final approach, I saw huge fireballs in the blackness. The thought flashed through my mind: "This must be what hell looks like." My uneasiness had had nothing to do with the meeting.

We landed, taxied, and stopped. It was 9:30 in the morning, but outside it looked like twilight in winter. Cars were driving with their lights on. There were oil fields surrounding the airport, and as I stepped out I stared at the blazing wells all along the horizon.

At the edge of the apron, Fred Franks was waiting with some of his staff. Since Safwan now belonged to VII Corps, he had chosen to escort me the rest of the way. His Black Hawk helicopter, equipped as a flying command post, stood ready nearby. As we saluted, he seemed tense; I guessed he was wondering whether I'd bring up the seizure of Safwan. On my desk back in Riyadh was the five-page explanation he had provided Yeosock. It boiled down to a claim that VII Corps had taken the road junction "with helicopters from the air." Franks had attributed the erroneous report that VII Corps had physically occupied the road to a misunderstanding. Though his argument was specious—every officer knows he can't seize an objective just by flying over it—I concluded that I had been neither intentionally disobeyed nor deliberately deceived. Besides, we now had Safwan and no one had been hurt taking it.

After making sure Powell knew the details, I'd told him I'd decided to let the matter drop. I had also decided that I'd been too harsh in my criticism of VII Corps's slow progress during the ground battle. It is easy to second guess in the isolation of a war room deep underground where you are not faced with the enormous task of moving huge forces over strange terrain in foul weather against an unknown enemy. I knew that there wasn't only one right way to fight a battle. Franks was a fine commander who had carried out his assigned mission as he had seen it and, just like me, he'd been faced with the challenge of accomplishing that mission while sparing the lives of as many of his troops as possible. We would probably never know whether attacking the Republican Guard one or two days sooner would have made much difference in the outcome. What I did know was that we had inflicted a crushing defeat on Saddam's forces and accomplished every one of our military objectives. That was good enough for me.

We took off and flew north along the so-called Highway of Death. In every direction we could see the burnt wrecks of military and civilian vehicles that the Iraqis had used to try to flee with their booty from Kuwait City. Part of my brain began naming the various pieces of Soviet equipment that I'd learned to identify many years before—T-55 and T-62 tanks, BTRs and BRDM armored personnel carriers, and so on. It was all down there on the ground, totally destroyed.

About ten miles north of Kuwait City we came clear of the smoke and the sky was blue again. But burning oil wells remained visible on the horizon. Suddenly I was overtaken with anger. This was an ecological disaster that the Iraqis had perpetrated, not just on Kuwait but on the entire region, and that smoke was eventually going to drift across the entire world. I'd left Riyadh determined to conduct the cease-fire talks in a calm, level-headed, professional way. But by the time we set down at Safwan, I was just plain mad.

We parked at the end of the runway, where Tom Brokaw and a handful of other journalists met me as I got out. Brokaw asked something like, "General Schwarzkopf, what do you plan to negotiate with the Iraqis?"

"This isn't a negotiation," I snapped. "I don't plan to give them anything. I'm here to tell them exactly what we expect them to do."

Pagonis, who was in charge of setting up the site, and Brigadier General Billy Carter, who was responsible for security, showed me around. The airfield sat in a natural bowl rimmed by sandy hills, and on those hills I counted at least forty tanks and Bradley Fighting Vehicles, their guns pointing our way. The 1st Infantry Division had carried out my instructions with a vengeance. "How much equipment is out there?" I asked Carter.

"Sir, we have positions extending all the way back to the road junction."

We had instructed that the Iraqis drive from Basra to the road junction flying white flags. Our forces would meet them there and transfer them to humvees driven by American troops, then bring them directly to the airfield. As they reached the meeting area the Iraqis would have to pass by dozens of parked Apache helicopters that lined both sides of the runway for two hundred yards, bristling with 30-mm cannon and Hellfire antitank missiles.

Pagonis had worked his usual miracles on the meeting site. Two days before, Safwan field had been a strip of empty asphalt; now there were a helicopter landing zone and a well-organized cluster of canvas tents: one where coalition observers and interpreters were searched as they arrived, another to accommodate them as they waited for the meeting, and a third filled with communications gear that was to serve as my headquarters. There was also an assembly area for journalists and an outdoor podium, flanked by the U.S. and Saudi flags, for a postmeeting press conference. Finally, at the very center of the site, was the twelve-foot-high olive drab meeting tent itself.

Carter ushered me inside. He and Pagonis had arranged things just right: there was a simple rectangular wooden table at the center, with three chairs on our side for Khalid, me, and our interpreter, three chairs on the Iraqis' side for generals Ahmad and Mahmud and their interpreter, an extra row behind those places for the members of the Iraqi party, and a large seating area behind ours for the coalition observers and their interpreters. Pagonis had chosen the table personally and allowed as how, after the talks, he intended to donate it to the Smithsonian Institution in case they ever wanted to re-create the Safwan negotiation scene.

It was eleven A.M. The radios crackled: the Iraqis were at the road junction. Suddenly I looked around. "Where's Khalid?" I asked.

"He's in his helicopter down at the end of the field," somebody said.

"What!" I turned to Pagonis. "Tell him if he doesn't get here right away, we're going to have to stall the Iraqis."

"I'll get him, sir." Pagonis started down the field just as we saw a huge white helicopter with a crown painted on the side taxiing up. The king had loaned Khalid the royal helicopter. It stopped at the tent area, and Khalid, wearing a Kevlar combat helmet and oversized desert goggles, stood in the doorway surveying the scene. I hurried over. "Let's go! They're almost here!"

We made it to the search tent seconds before the Iraqis. Their escort convoy raced onto the airfield—two M1A1 tanks, two Bradley Fighting Vehicles, then eight humvees, each driven by an American soldier with an Iraqi in the passenger seat. A pair of Apache helicopters, flying just ten feet off the ground, brought up the rear.

I stood at the door of the search tent and watched the Iraqis walk up. I'd worn my battle-dress fatigues and a field cap; they had on their green dress uniforms and black berets. General Ahmad, the leader, was a stocky fellow with a heavy Saddam-style mustache. I recognized him with a start— he had been one of the Iraqis who had snubbed us at the UAE National Day parade more than a year before. He now looked extremely uptight.

I turned to the Central Command interpreter standing beside me and said, "I want you to translate what I say." He nodded. "The procedure will be that we will enter this tent, and everyone will be searched before we go into the meeting place."

Ahmad stuck out his chin. "There is no need to search us. We left our weapons in our vehicles."

"Tell the general this is not a negotiation. Everyone who goes into that tent will be searched."

"I refuse to be searched unless the senior participant on the U.S. side is searched as well."

"I *am* the senior participant of the U.S. side."

He stepped back and looked me up and down in some disbelief. "Who are you?"

"I'm General Schwarzkopf."

He said curtly, "All right." We went in and I stood and was thoroughly searched by the military police. They had already collected a whole tableful of weapons from the coalition observers. Next Ahmad submitted to a search. While it was going on, I noticed some of his subordinates snickering at the sight and bantering among themselves. I thought grimly that we were not getting off to a very good start.

We entered the meeting tent and I showed the Iraqis where to sit. The press was allowed in briefly to photograph us facing each other across the table. Ahmad wore an uncertain little smile, probably thinking this was the beginning of a public show trial. But before starting the meeting, we cleared out the photographers and reporters.

I opened by reminding the Iraqis that our purpose was to lay out the military conditions for a cease-fire and informed them that we would tape the conversation so that each side would have a permanent record. As my words were interpreted, Ahmad listened, nodded, and indicated that he was ready to address each of the points raised in our terms of reference.

I expected the Iraqis would pretty much take notes from this point on—any agreement, we all figured, would come only after they'd had a chance to confer with Saddam. "The first thing that we would like to discuss is prisoners of war," I said. I made my first request—that the Red Cross be allowed immediate access to POWs held by Iraq—and Ahmad promptly declared, "This will be accomplished."

"This will be accomplished?" I echoed, surprised.

"Yes."

"That's good." Next I said that we wanted to discuss the release of prisoners of war. He immediately asserted, "We are ready to return all POWs at once, in any way convenient for the Red Cross."

Ahmad had clearly been given authority to come to terms on the spot. I proceeded to work my way down the list of conditions—the identification of coalition MIAs, the return of bodily remains, the disclosure of minefields and unconventional-weapons bunkers in Kuwait, and so on. The Iraqis agreed to all.

The only argument came when Khalid asked Ahmad about the thousands of Kuwaiti civilians who had been taken to Iraq against their will. We wanted them counted as prisoners of war and returned; Ahmad stonily denied that anyone had been abducted. "Once the war started, many Kuwaitis of Iraqi origin *chose* to go to Iraq," he insisted.

"We have the names of Kuwaitis that were taken by force," Khalid replied. He pressed until Ahmad acknowledged grudgingly, "We have not taken anybody against his will, but if there is a case like that, he will be treated as a POW."

"Then we must know of *all* Kuwaitis residing in Iraq," Khalid said. Ahmad never did admit there were civilian detainees and we settled for his

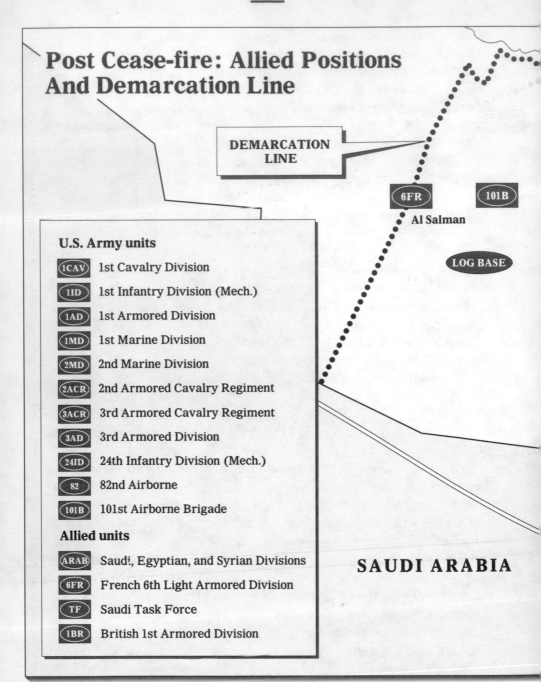

Post Cease-fire: Allied Positions And Demarcation Line

DEMARCATION LINE

6FR 101B

Al Salman

LOG BASE

U.S. Army units

1CAV	1st Cavalry Division
1ID	1st Infantry Division (Mech.)
1AD	1st Armored Division
1MD	1st Marine Division
2MD	2nd Marine Division
2ACR	2nd Armored Cavalry Regiment
3ACR	3rd Armored Cavalry Regiment
3AD	3rd Armored Division
24ID	24th Infantry Division (Mech.)
82	82nd Airborne
101B	101st Airborne Brigade

Allied units

ARAB	Saudi, Egyptian, and Syrian Divisions
6FR	French 6th Light Armored Division
TF	Saudi Task Force
1BR	British 1st Armored Division

SAUDI ARABIA

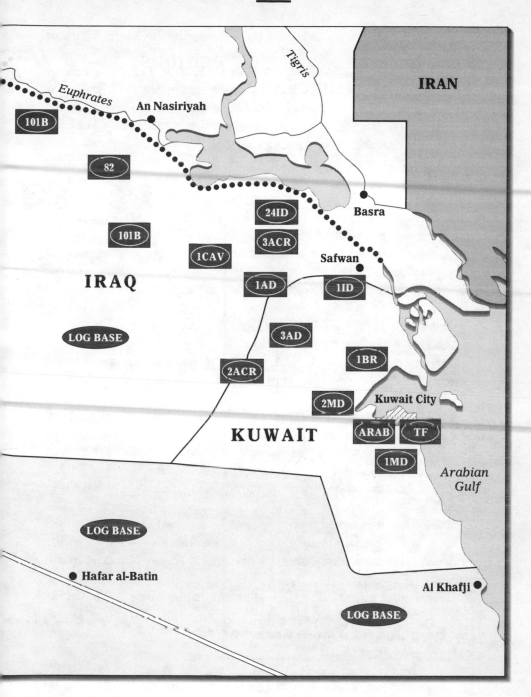

assurance that anyone who had come to Iraq since the invasion of Kuwait would be free to approach the Red Cross and leave if he wanted.

Finally I raised the issue of drawing a cease-fire line. "We had an unfortunate incident yesterday where our troops got in one more battle that we did not need," I began. Ahmad bristled and demanded to know why we had destroyed the Iraqi armored column in the Euphrates valley. "The ones you shot were drawing back," he claimed.

"Well, unfortunately, they shot first." He disputed that, so I interjected, "This is something we could argue about until the sun sets and we would never agree. What is important is to make sure it doesn't happen again."

I knew what was on Ahmad's mind: he had been ordered not to concede any territory, and the cease-fire line we were proposing was deep within Iraq's borders. The atmosphere had become tense. When I said we had prepared a map, he interrupted: "We have agreed that this is not a permanent line?"

"It is absolutely not a permanent line," I reassured him.

"And it has nothing to do with borders?"

"It has nothing to do with borders. It is only a safety measure. We have no intention of leaving our forces permanently in Iraqi territory once the cease-fire is signed."

But Ahmad wasn't finished. He wanted to know why the coalition had launched ground forces into his country in the first place, "after we had withdrawn from Kuwait and announced it on the television and radio."

I was determined not to get sidetracked. "Again, it is a subject I think the general and I could discuss for many hours. I think we will leave it to history."

"I have just mentioned it for history," he retorted. There was a brief silence. At last he seemed ready to continue the discussions, and regarding measures to prevent further fighting between our forces, he said, "In this matter we will cooperate."

Now that we had covered the coalition's main points, we had a brief discussion of how vehicles in the cease-fire zone would fly orange flags to signal peaceful intent. Then I asked, "Are there any other matters the general would like to discuss?"

"We have one point," he said. "You know the situation of our roads and bridges and communications." I nodded, thinking of the overwhelming damage our bombing had done. "We would like to fly helicopters to carry officials of our government in areas where roads and bridges are out. This has nothing to do with the front line. This is inside Iraq."

It appeared to me to be a legitimate request. And given that the Iraqis had agreed to all our requests, I didn't feel it was unreasonable to grant one of theirs: "As long as it is not over the part we are in, that is absolutely no problem. So we will let the helicopters fly. That is a very important point, and I want to make sure it's recorded, that military helicopters can fly over Iraq. Not fighters, not bombers."

Then Ahmad said something that should have given me pause. "So you mean even helicopters that are armed can fly in Iraqi skies but not the fighters? Because the helicopters are the same, they transfer somebody—"

"Yeah. I will instruct the Air Force not to shoot at any helicopters flying over the territory of Iraq where our troops are not located."

In the following weeks, we discovered what the son of a bitch had really had in mind: using helicopter gunships to suppress rebellions in Basra and other cities. By that time it was up to the White House to decide how much the United States wanted to intervene in the internal politics of Iraq. But to judge from intelligence reports we received at Central Command, grounding the Iraqi helicopter gunships would have had little impact. The tanks and artillery of the twenty-four Iraqi divisions that never entered the Kuwaiti war zone were having a far more devastating effect on the insurgents.

After that, there was only one moment at which Ahmad showed any emotion. He presented an accounting of coalition prisoners of war held by Iraq. "We have forty-one in all," he said. I made notes as he read them off:

17 Americans
2 Italians
12 British
1 Kuwaiti
9 Saudis

This left a number of people unaccounted for, and I quickly brought out our list of MIAs, but he stopped me. "And we would like to have the numbers of the POWs on our side as well."

"As of last night, sixty thousand," I replied. "Or sixty thousand plus, because it is difficult to count them completely." His face went completely pale: he had had no concept of the magnitude of their defeat.

When the meeting adjourned, we had to wait a few minutes while Colonel Bell verified that a full set of audiotapes had been recorded for each side. We gave the Iraqis their set and escorted them outside. The convoy was waiting. I walked Ahmad to the first humvee and Khalid walked Mahmud to the second. The press was all around taking pictures, but I wasn't paying much attention. I was focused on getting them out of there. We'd accomplished what we'd set out to do, and the sooner the delegation was safely on the road and out of our hands, the better.

When Ahmad reached the humvee he turned, stood at attention, and saluted. I returned the salute. He stuck out his hand. I shook it and wished him a safe journey. He looked at me and replied, "As an Arab, I hold no hate in my heart." Then he climbed in and the convoy rolled off in another cloud of dust, again escorted by M1A1 tanks, Bradleys, and Apaches.

Khalid and I held a short news conference and then went back into the meeting area where we exchanged congratulations with the coalition generals. Major General Mario Arpino of Italy was overjoyed to have learned that both his missing pilots were alive. General Jaber, who had greeted me before the meeting with a bear hug, was delighted to find out that the one missing Kuwaiti pilot was safe. Peter de la Billière showed mixed emotions: happiness to hear of the twelve British prisoners and grief that more of his missing countrymen weren't on the list. We were all relieved that the meeting had gone so well, but none of us would feel fully satisfied until all our prisoners had returned safely and all our missing had been accounted for. I called Powell and gave him a complete rundown, complimented Pagonis and Carter on the superb preparations, and then went out to thank the troops, shaking hands, signing autographs, and posing with soldiers for snapshots. After all, they were the people who had gotten us here.

Finally Franks and I climbed aboard his Blackhawk.

"Your men did a good job setting this up," I told him.

He thanked me and beamed.

As we flew back over the devastated landscape, Franks talked about the vast ammunition dumps his troops had found in southern Iraq. He pointed out that it could take weeks for his units to carry out the order I'd given that all enemy ammunition be destroyed.

"We have to blow up the ammo or haul it out," I insisted. "If we leave it behind, they'll use it again." I wanted him to understand that the job wasn't finished yet. I also pointed out that the Kuwait City airport was his responsibility and could become an exchange point for prisoners of war. He nodded in agreement.

When we reached Kuwait City, I immediately got on my plane and took off for Riyadh. I knew my headquarters was about to turn into an administrative meat grinder. We had to start moving forces and equipment home—a happy but gigantic and complicated task. We had to bring Kuwait City back to life, which meant repairing and turning on the water supply, electrical power grid, and telephones, helping the police maintain order, searching for booby traps and clearing the beaches of mines, reopening the harbor, and a thousand other tasks. And until the UN approved a cease-fire agreement that would permit us to end our occupation, we had to serve as the government of southern Iraq—maintaining order, providing basic services, and caring for the thousands of refugees fleeing from upheavals in the north. Finally, we had to help the Red Cross get what would turn out to be eighty thousand Iraqi prisoners out of Saudi Arabia as quickly as possible.

But all of that could wait until the plane landed. For the first time, I had a sense, not of triumph, not of glory, but of relief. I looked down at the Kuwaiti sky still darkened with the stain of war, and at the unspoiled Saudi sky ahead, and told myself again and again, "It really is over."

---

16 MAR 91 G+20/D+58

0830 Discussions with the congressional delegation led by Congressman Ford. One issue was women in the military— how did they do? The CINC said "Great!"

1100 The CINC departed the Ministry of Defense for a visit to Lieutenant General Khalid's hydroponic desert farm where he spent the day.

17 MAR 91 G+21/D+59

1725 Phoncon with the chairman. The CINC reviewed his most recent congressional delegation presentation, noting that the senators who voted against the war took up half the time explaining to the CINC the reasons for their votes.

I waited a month and a half before asking permission to come home. By then the government of Kuwait had been fully restored and the cleanup was well under way, though experts estimated it would be many months before all the oil-field fires were put out. We'd gotten back our prisoners, returned thousands of Iraqis, and helped the Saudis establish a huge camp to care for Iraqi civilian refugees. And we'd managed to send more than half our troops home. When I called Powell to say I thought the time had come to shift Central Command headquarters back to the United States, he asked dozens of questions to make sure we were leaving enough commanders behind to handle any problems that came up. Finally he said, "I'll clear it with the President."

I knew there would be victory celebrations when I arrived. Our troops had received heroes' welcomes in the States, and our Arab allies had already overwhelmed me with ceremonies and awards. But the day I stepped on my airplane to come home, all I could think about was my family. Even though I recognized that every other man and woman in Desert Storm had also been separated from their loved ones, for me it had been one of the toughest things to bear. I'd felt robbed of precious time with my children I had never wanted to lose: my daughter Jessica was just reaching the age where she was an adult, leaving home for college; my son was on the brink of growing from a little boy into a man. The war had started for me the day I'd had to walk out the back door and tell Cindy I didn't know if I'd be home for Christmas. It wouldn't end until I had them back again.

A big crowd was waiting on the apron at MacDill Air Force Base as we touched down and taxied in. As I emerged from the plane, I looked for an American flag and saluted. A few weeks before, our POWs had done that upon their arrival in Riyadh, and I was repeating the gesture for them. Then, as I started down the steps, I saw my family. They were all there, Brenda, Cindy, Jessica, Christian, Sally, and Bear, waiting at the front of the crowd a short distance away. I held out my arms and they rushed to meet me at the bottom of the steps. It was like a wonderful wrestling match. My kids were hugging me, Brenda was hugging me, Sally was hugging me, Bear was jumping all over us, and somehow there were reporters and photographers all mixed in.

There were thousands of people on the runway—old couples waving American flags, teenagers wearing "God Bless America" and "If you're not a patriot, you're a Scud" T-shirts, little kids in desert fatigues. I saw flashes of yellow everywhere because so many people had on yellow ribbons. As my staff and I worked our way to the podium, people shook our hands, patted us on the back, and held out their babies while a thousand flashbulbs went off. One guy, a Vietnam vet wearing jungle fatigues, a Fu Manchu mustache, and hair halfway down his back, threw his arms around my neck, crying. "Thank you, thank you! You finally made it right." I climbed up on the podium, saluted as the 24th Mechanized Infantry Division band played the national anthem, stood quietly beside Brenda as the Kuwaiti ambassador thanked us for freeing his country, and finally made a few remarks.

At last we went home. In our living room everything seemed to be happening at once: Cindy and Jessica and Christian were all talking and showing me the letters and things people had sent, Bear was barking, Brenda was asking me what I wanted to eat, and everybody was clamoring for me to open the Christmas presents they'd saved. The phone rang and it was Ruth, who promised we'd see each other soon. Sally kept jumping up every half hour to check the TV—she'd been glued to it throughout the war and hadn't broken the habit. What the news reports showed was *us*—hugging each other at the air base. "Come on, Sally," I laughed, "the war's over. You can turn that thing off." She shrugged and broke into a big smile. It was as hard for her to believe as it was for me.

The months ahead were punctuated with celebrations—the Tampa municipal homecoming, the Washington victory parade, the ticker-tape parade up Broadway in New York, and other events—but I still had work to do as head of Central Command. When the Iraqis failed to comply with the UN resolution regarding nuclear inspection, or threatened to interfere with the delivery of relief to the Kurds, I had to make plans to launch military operations if we needed to. I oversaw the preparation of long official reports on the war and was summoned to testify before four congressional committees.

Before I'd left Riyadh, Mike Stone, the secretary of the Army, had visited and asked what I planned to do next. "I have my heart set on you as chief of staff of the Army," he'd said. I'd told him I'd long ago made up my mind to retire when the crisis ended, and had pointed out that whoever succeeded Vuono would be called upon to downsize the Army. "I'd rather retire with a great victory than suffer a thousand defeats at the hands of Congress," I'd told him. The job went to General Gordon Sullivan, whom I'd known for many years and who had exactly the right combination of toughness and fairness.

As my successor, to my delight, Cheney and Powell picked Joe Hoar, my first chief of staff at Central Command. I busied myself for weeks with the planning of the change-of-command ceremony, which took on some of the proportions of a state occasion because of the dozens of princes and other foreign dignitaries who had asked to attend.

I made a final trip to Egypt, Saudi Arabia, and Kuwait to tie up loose ends. On the way home I stopped in England, where the warmth of the welcome I received from the government left me embarrassed—there was no way I could ever thank them enough for the support they'd given us in the gulf. While we were in Riyadh, Peter de la Billière had joked that I'd seen the kingdoms of the Middle East, but I knew nothing about his, and so after the official part of my visit he took me on a tour of some of the beautiful ruined castles of Herefordshire.

I also stopped in France, where Michel Roquejeoffre met me as I arrived at Aubagne, the home of the French Foreign Legion. In an elaborate ceremony General Maurice Schmitt presented me with the Order of the

Legion of Honor and General Raymond Le Corre, the Foreign Legion commander, made me an honorary lance corporal, the equivalent of a private first class.

After a ceremonial lunch, we took helicopters out to a château in the hills of Provence that the Foreign Legion had bought after the war in Indochina. It was the legionnaires' retirement home. Many, having joined under rules that allowed a man to enlist under an assumed name without divulging any information about his past, had no family or country to go home to and could never be reassimilated into society. They supported themselves at the château, which had its own vineyard, foundry, ceramics and woodworking shops, and bookbindery. As we walked into each shop, the men working there, seventy- and eighty-year-olds, snapped to attention. They still took fierce pride in being soldiers.

Outside my hosts had set up long wooden tables under camouflage netting. As the sun set and breezes off the mountains cooled the stifling heat, the legionnaires came out—white-haired old Germans, Austrians, Swiss, Bulgarians, Poles, and Frenchmen, many with full white beards and some without teeth. They'd put on civilian jackets over their old shirts and trousers, and had their medals pinned to their chests. Under the netting we drank champagne—in keeping with European military tradition, the legionnaires opened the bottles by chopping the necks with a saber. We then sat down for a French country dinner of pâté, sausages, fruit, vegetables, and bread that reminded me of the meals I'd eaten as a schoolboy in Switzerland—complemented, of course, by immense quantities of wine. Finally, when the meal ended, they began singing their old marching songs—slow, beautiful, almost dirgelike melodies all about families and girlfriends and countries left behind. As the men's voices rose, and the young legionnaires joined in, I found myself overcome.

Then it hit me: three weeks and I was out! I'd never thought of myself as one hundred percent a military man—I was confident I could make my way as a civilian—but suddenly I realized that from the time I'd left Princeton to join Pop in Tehran forty-five years before, I'd lived the military life. I knew I was going to miss the camaraderie of those who had suffered great adversity. It was a bond that linked all old soldiers, not just those from our army but from the Foreign Legion, the German Panzer Corps, the Red Army, and I supposed even the Vietcong. Looking at those old war-horses, I knew I was going to miss the troops.

On Friday, August 30, I put on my battle fatigues and reported to the personnel office at Central Command. A young female soldier handed me my discharge form and said, "Sir, this is your DD-214. We recommend you put this form into your safe deposit box because this is the only real proof that you have that you were ever in the service." I signed the papers, received my retiree ID card, and, after posing for a snapshot with all the young troops in the office, walked out to the car. Craig "Max" Maxum, the sergeant major who'd been in charge of my bodyguards since the beginning of Desert Storm and was still constantly at my side, asked, "Is that all?"

"Max, that's it."

"Sir, it's not right. Thirty-five years in the military and you just sign a piece of paper and it's over? Sir, it's not right. We ought to *do* something."

"We've had enough parades." But Max was disturbed.

The following night some friends gave Brenda and me a dinner party. We got home shortly before midnight. I'd just parked the car in the garage when Max said, "Only seventeen seconds more, sir."

At first I didn't understand. "What do you mean?" I asked. He looked at me funny and I realized he was talking about my retirement. "Shut up, Max. I don't want to talk about it." I laughed.

"Sir, it just doesn't seem right. No rockets in the air, no big parade, no flyovers."

By then it was midnight. My Army career was over.

AFTERTHOUGHTS

Since my retirement from the Army a year ago, I have traveled extensively throughout the United States and Europe. Everywhere I go I am asked the same questions regarding the conduct and the outcome of the Gulf War. As the postwar euphoria receded, the analyses began. Some people started questioning, and some criticizing, both what we accomplished in the gulf and how the war was fought. Here are my answers to the five questions I am most often asked.

The first question, of course, is, *Why didn't we go all the way to Baghdad and "finish the job"?*

It should be clearly understood that the option of going all the way to Baghdad was never considered. Despite all of the so-called experts who, with twenty-twenty hindsight, are now criticizing that "decision," at the time the war ended there was not a single head of state, diplomat, Middle East expert, or military leader who, as far as I am aware, advocated continuing the war and seizing Baghdad. The United Nations resolutions that provided the legal basis for our military operations in the gulf were clear in their intent: kick the Iraqi military force out of Kuwait. We had authority to take whatever actions were necessary to accomplish that mission, including attacks into Iraq; but we had no authority to invade Iraq for the purpose of capturing the entire country or its capital.

If we look back to the Vietnam War we should recognize that one of the reasons we lost world support for our actions was that we had no internationally recognized legitimacy for our intervention in Vietnam. In the gulf the case was exactly the opposite; we had no less than nine United Nations resolutions authorizing our actions, and we had the support of virtually the entire world. But that support was for us to kick Iraq out of Kuwait, not to capture Baghdad.

If we look at the battle maps of the ground war, we can see that no Arab forces ever entered Iraq. Only British, French, and American troops fought on Iraqi territory. In this book I have discussed in some detail the sensitivity of our allies concerning one Arab nation's attacking another. I am convinced that had a decision been made to invade all of Iraq and capture Baghdad, the coalition that we worked so hard to preserve would have fractured. I am equally convinced that the only forces that would have participated in those military actions would have been British and American. Even the French would have withdrawn from the coalition.

Had the United States and the United Kingdom gone on alone to capture Baghdad, under the provisions of the Geneva and Hague conventions we would have been considered occupying powers and therefore would have been responsible for *all* the costs of maintaining or restoring government, education, and other services for the people of Iraq. From the brief time we did spend occupying Iraqi territory after the war, I am certain that had we taken all of Iraq, we would have been like the dinosaur in the tar pit—we would still be there, and we, not the United Nations, would be bearing the costs of that occupation. This is a burden I am sure the beleaguered American taxpayer would not have been happy to take on.

Finally, we should not forget how Saddam tried to characterize the entire war. He was quick to proclaim that this was *not* a war against Iraq's aggression in Kuwait, but rather the western colonialist nations embarking as lackeys of the Israelis on the destruction of the only Arab nation willing to destroy the state of Israel. Had the United States and the United Kingdom alone attacked Iraq and occupied Baghdad, every citizen of the Arab world today would be convinced that what Saddam said was true. Instead, they know that the armed forces of western *and* Arab nations fought side by side against Iraq's aggression and that when Kuwait was liberated the western nations withdrew their military forces and went home. For once we were strategically smart enough to win the war *and* the peace.

The next question I inevitably get is a follow-up one: *Since Saddam is still alive and in control in Iraq, wasn't the whole war fought for nothing?*

I will confess that emotionally I, like so many others, would have liked to see Saddam Hussein brought to some form of justice. He may still be. But to best address the question, we must consider what would have happened if Saddam had been allowed to succeed with his aggression—if the Gulf War hadn't been fought.

First, he would now control all the oil from Kuwait and perhaps from the entire Arabian Peninsula. Let's not forget that prior to the war, Saddam's threats were against *both* Kuwait and the United Arab Emirates. The only way to get to the United Arab Emirates from Kuwait is through Saudi Arabian oil-producing territory. But even if we assume that he would have limited his aggression to Kuwait, he would have sent a powerful signal to the rest of the gulf nations which they could not have ignored. They would have been intimidated in every future decision. Saddam would have achieved his stated aim of dramatically raising the price of oil on the world market, with the resultant stress on an already shaky world economy. Worse yet, if he followed the patterns of the past, his greatly increased oil revenues would have gone to the strengthening of his already strong (relative to other Middle Eastern nations) military forces and the expansion of his developing nuclear and biological and existing chemical arsenals. It is not hard to imagine what this could have meant to the future of Israel and the cause of world peace.

Instead, a defanged Saddam has been forced to retreat behind his own borders. His nuclear, biological, and chemical military capabilities have been destroyed and will stay that way if we can figure out how to prevent him from getting them in the future the same way he got them in the past— from unscrupulous firms, both western and eastern, more interested in the corporate bottom line than in world peace. Saddam's military forces suffered a crushing defeat and are no longer a threat to any other nation. Perhaps of greatest importance, because he did the unthinkable, attacked a brother Arab and subsequently lost face in a humiliating military rout, Saddam's irrational, militant voice is no longer relevant in Arab politics. Largely as a result of this and the coalition's gulf victory, the Middle East peace process is moving forward; Palestinians, other Arabs, and Israelis are sitting down at the negotiating table, and our hostages have been freed. Do I think it was worth it? You bet I do.

Finally, despite what we may see in *Rambo* films, catching and bringing to justice someone like Saddam is not a simple task. In Panama, a small country where we had thousands of American eyes in place even before military operations began, we still couldn't find a guy named Noriega for quite some time. I'm not sure that even with a full-scale invasion we would have ever found Saddam in the large armed camp that is Iraq.

What about all of the incidents of friendly fire we have heard about since the end of the war?

I detest the term "friendly fire." Once a bullet leaves a muzzle or a rocket leaves an airplane, it is not friendly to anyone. Unfortunately, fratricide has been around since the beginning of war. The very chaotic nature of the battlefield, where quick decisions make the difference between life and death, has resulted in numerous incidents of troops being killed by their own fires in every war that this nation has ever fought. Even at the National Training Center, where "kills" are simulated by lasers and computers, many incidents of fratricide are observed. This does not make them acceptable. Not even one such avoidable death should ever be considered acceptable. And in a war where so few lives were lost on our side, the tragedy is magnified when a family loses a son or daughter in such a way.

In the Gulf War our problem was that our technological ability to engage targets exceeded our ability to identify targets clearly. For years we had been working on the ability to attack enemy targets at great ranges since, in order to succeed against massed Soviet tank forces, we would need to destroy as many of them as possible before they could engage our forces. We found that the desert environment enhanced this ability to acquire and engage targets at great distances.

Early on, we became aware of the danger posed to our own forces by this enhanced capability and challenged the development community to come up with some way to discriminate definitely between friend and foe. Unfortunately, no technological solution was found that wouldn't have increased the danger to our forces of being destroyed by the enemy. Simply stated, anything that would have made our forces more recognizable to us would also have made them more recognizable to the enemy. We then had to rely on other procedures for identification, which we emphasized and reemphasized at every level. The most common of these of course was to look at "position on the battlefield." If you know that no friendly forces are in front of you, then anything you see must be the enemy.

Regrettably, in the confusion of battle innocent mistakes were made and lives were lost. We must find a better and safer way to do our jobs. In every after-action report submitted by my former headquarters and those of my component commanders, this problem has been highlighted as one that demands immediate attention and action. All the services are dedicated to finding a technological solution to this long-standing dilemma.

Another question I am often asked is, *How did our high-tech equipment really work?*

My answer is always the same: "Beyond our wildest expectations." In the early days of our deployment we did run into unanticipated problems as a result of the harsh desert environment. We found that the fine, dustlike sand of Saudi Arabia caused the air filters to clog on some of our armored vehicles. This problem was quickly solved when American technology came up with new filters. We found that sand eroded our helicopter blades, so the experts came up with tape for the blades that reduced the erosion. Just like other extreme environments, such as the Arctic and the jungle, the desert environment posed special challenges that we had to adjust to, but good old American ingenuity always came through. We learned to adapt, and our equipment continued to operate despite all the predictions to the contrary. After four days of battle, our maintenance levels were higher than those found in most units during peacetime.

Certain systems have been singled out for criticism by individuals serving their own purposes. One of these is the Patriot missile. The critics have only succeeded in illuminating their lack of knowledge about what the Patriot was designed to do. The Patriot was designed to defend a *point* target—such as an airfield, supply depot, or headquarters—against incoming enemy aircraft or missiles. I don't know of a single case where the Patriot wasn't one-hundred-percent successful in defending the facility it was deployed to protect. The fact that it also often performed splendidly as an *area* defense weapon was pure gravy and provided a degree of protection for whole cities that we had never expected to have. Similar criticism has been leveled at Air Force precision munitions, stating that they didn't always hit their target the first time; sometimes it took two or even three to destroy a target. Maybe so, but were any of those critics in Vietnam? I would have given my left arm if our Air Force could have had half the capability in Vietnam that it demonstrated in the gulf. Sure our high-tech munitions didn't work perfectly one hundred percent of the time, but that is not unusual considering their complexities and the fact that many were developed at an accelerated pace because of the war. But they were so vastly superior to anything we had before, and to anything our enemies have now, that the American people can feel very proud of the *American* technology that produced them.

Finally, I am often asked to comment on *the nature of future conflicts and the size of our armed forces*.

I feel that retired general officers should never miss an opportunity to remain silent concerning matters for which they are no longer responsible. Having said that, I believe a few general (no pun intended) comments are in order. I am quite confident that in the foreseeable future armed conflict will not take the form of huge land armies facing each other across extended battle lines, as they did in World War I and World War II or, for that matter, as they would have if NATO had faced the Warsaw Pact on the field of battle. Conflict in the future will be similar to that which we have seen in the recent past. Both of the military operations in which we were involved in the Middle East were a result of regional conflicts that grew to proportions that began to impact the rest of the world. The "tanker war" was a result of the Iran-Iraq war, and, of course, the Gulf War came about as a result of a dispute between Iraq and other oil-producing nations. As I have stated earlier, when I took command of Central Command there were thirteen such conflicts occurring in my area of responsibility alone. Since that time many have abated, but others far more troublesome have emerged to take their place. One need only look at the tragic events taking place in what we used to call Yugoslavia or the ethnic, religious, and nationalistic clashes in the former Soviet Union to realize that such dangerous regional conflicts will be with us for years to come. Any one of them could lead us to war.

What then does this tell us about the future size of our armed forces? First, it does tell us that reductions are possible. But it does not tell us that reductions by arbitrary amounts set *solely* on the basis of political or fiscal considerations are the answer. It frightens me when I hear someone propose a hundred-billion-dollar cut in our armed forces without any rationale other than that the money can be used elsewhere. The purpose of our armed forces is to protect our national interests and defend our country. Before we allow deep cuts in our forces we should be sure that we have made a thorough analysis of what our national interests will be for the next twenty years and where and how we might be required to commit our forces. Only then can we honestly assess what size our armed forces should be. Then the cuts can be made. I am told that just such an analysis is currently under way in the Department of Defense.

Finally, we must ensure that our forces remain flexible enough to handle unforeseen contingencies. The future is not always easy to predict and our record regarding where we will fight future wars is not the best. If someone had asked me on the day I graduated from West Point, in June 1956, where I would fight for my country during my years of service, I'm not sure what I would have said. But I'm damn sure I would *not* have said, "Vietnam, Grenada, and Iraq."

The day I left Riyadh to return to the United States, General Khalid made a statement in a speech that every American should think about. He said, "If the world is only going to have one superpower, thank God it is the United States of America." When I think about the nations in the past fifty years that could have emerged as the world's only superpower—Tojo's Japan, Hitler's Germany, Stalin's Russia, Mao's China—and the darkness that would have descended on this world if they had, I appreciate the wisdom of Khalid's words. Because we have emerged as the only remaining superpower, we have an awesome responsibility both to ourselves as a nation and to the rest of the world. I don't know what that responsibility will mean to the future of our great country, but I shall always remain confident of the American people's ability to rise to *any* challenge.

ACKNOWLEDGMENTS

The first person I want to thank is Peter Petre, my coauthor. He is a superb writer. More important to me, he took my accounts and captured on paper not only the events but the emotions of the events. During the many months we worked together he challenged me and probed aggressively to make sure that we got to the truth. In the writing of this book we were a team.

Marvin Josephson is the man who enlisted me in the book business when I retired from the Army. I couldn't have picked a better mentor. He guided me step by step through the Byzantine process of launching a book and faithfully offered critiques of our work that were right on target, even when we didn't want to hear them.

My personal staff laid the foundation for the book. During and after the gulf crisis, Colonel B.B. Bell, Major Roger Murtie, and Chief Petty Officer Rick Rieger volunteered many off-duty hours to collect information and help compile my private journal. Lynn Williams, my executive assistant, did our photo research even as she deftly managed drafts, copies, faxes, mailings, phone calls, factual queries, travel arrangements, and countless trips to my house. Beth Lefft and Anne-Marie Giacobone of Marvin Josephson's office and Mary Buckley of mine also handled hundreds of faxes, phone calls, and mailings connected with the work.

Kathy Robbins backed up Peter Petre every step of the way, offering incisive comments on successive drafts. She deserves a medal. We also received fine support from Elizabeth Mackey and Steven Bromage of The Robbins Office. Marshall Loeb, managing editor of *Fortune* magazine, allowed my coauthor to join me on short notice and was most understanding about extending Peter's leave of absence so that we could complete our work.

I am indebted to Jack Hoeft and Linda Grey of Bantam Books for their confidence that I had a book in me and their faith that we could deliver. To help make sure that would happen, Linda Grey shrewdly relieved us of many of the housekeeping chores authors ordinarily get stuck with when they have all the time in the world to write their book. Our editor, Beverly Lewis, had to withstand my wrath on more than one occasion—and did so with real grace. She doubled as our project manager; with her remarkable ability to juggle complicated tasks, she'd have fit right in at Central Command. Our copy editor, Len Neufeld, did a great job keeping us straight.

Jean Kidd has to be the smartest, fastest transcriber in the world. Whereas many others type what they *think* they hear, Jean captured what I actually said, despite my use of military terminology and acronyms, not to mention foreign names. And she did it all at lightning speed. Natasha Perkel was a wizard at putting together maps that were both understandable and complete. Even when I sent her back to the drawing board for the twentieth time on the same map, she displayed inexhaustible patience and was a joy to work with.

Vicky Sufian and Sari Wilson did the bulk of our research, dealing expertly with a manuscript full of names, dates, places, historical references, military accounts, and military terminology. They were ably assisted by Anne Tardos, Jackson Mac Low, and Chris Gray. Among the sources on whom they depended were Janet Bacon, Peter Bechtold, Walter Bradford, Anna Branner, Richard Bulliet, John Carland, Jeffrey Clarke, Karl Cocke, Vincent Demma, Ingeborg Godenschweger, Martha Guenther, Geraldine Harcarik, William Hartley, Richard Hobson, Susan Keogh-Fisher, James Knight, Colonel Shirin Labip, Gladys Mazer, Captain Steven Michael, Jean Nichols, Lieutenant General Gus Pagonis, Carolyn Piper, James Speraw Jr., Major Rick Thomas, Joyce Weisner, and Captain Darlene Wilson. The Project for Public Spaces and The Writers Room provided not only work space but a congenial atmosphere for the writing of much of the manuscript.

Peter's wife, Ann Banks, was the manuscript's first reader and provided valuable editorial advice. Their daughter, Kate, tolerated her dad's long absences with understanding beyond her years. Our thanks to Colonel Richard Banks and his wife, Isabel, for supplying Peter with insights about military life as well as transportation during Peter's Tampa tour of duty.

Both my sisters provided Peter with insights into our family and my boyhood that I never could have supplied. Ruth Ann Schwarzkopf Barenbaum contributed stories and photos that helped fill crucial gaps in the narrative, and sent a steady stream of encouraging letters. Sally Schwarzkopf supplied original correspondence from my father's years in Iran and proved an invaluable source of information concerning our childhood and years abroad. I am grateful for their love and understanding.

When I retired, Brenda, Cindy, Jessica, and Christian thought they were finally going to have a full-time husband and father. Instead I disappeared for days, nights, and weekends into the study where Peter and I worked, while the house became cluttered with boxes, records, photographs, and tapes. I hope that what we've written will make them proud. Without their love, patience, and support, I could never have done the work.

Bibliographic Note

Besides Grant's memoirs, a number of books proved useful in our writing:

Stephen E. Ambrose, *Duty, Honor, Country: A History of West Point* (Baltimore, 1966).

C. D. B. Bryan, *Friendly Fire* (New York, 1976).

Leo J. Coakley, *Jersey Troopers: A Fifty Year History of the New Jersey State Police* (New Brunswick, N.J., 1971).

Stanley Karnow, *Vietnam: A History* (New York, 1983).

David Lamb, *The Arabs: Journeys Beyond the Mirage* (New York, 1987).

T. H. Vail Motter, *The Persian Corridor and Aid to Russia* (in the series *The United States Army in World War II*; Washington, D.C., 1952).

Col. John A. Warden III, *The Air Campaign: Planning for Combat* (Washington, D.C., 1988).

Among the journalists who covered Desert Storm, a number wrote articles that we found valuable in establishing a context for events in this book: Dean Fischer, Joe Galloway, Youssef Ibrahim, David Lamb, and Molly Moore.

INDEX

Note: "HNS" signifies "H. Norman Schwarzkopf." Page numbers in *italic* refer to maps. Small roman numerals (e.g., xi) refer to the preface. Photographs and captions are not included in this index.

Under chronological subheadings (e.g., "in 1988–91" and "7/90 to 9/90"), sub-subheadings are listed chronologically (i.e., in page order) rather than alphabetically. Subheadings like "7/90 to 9/90" refer to the period of the Iraq-Kuwait crisis and Gulf War.

Army military units are listed under "Army," where numbered units (e.g., "1st Infantry Division" and "V Corps") precede all other subheadings. Other countries' military units are listed under the name of the country.

In Arab names, the element "al-" is inverted (e.g., Mizyad al-Sanii is listed as "Sanii, Mizyad al-"). Members of Arab nobility are generally listed by first name (e.g., "Khalid Bin Sultan al-Saud").

A

AAFES (Army and Air Force Exchange Service), 260, 261
Abadan, Iran, *357*
Abdulaziz al-Saud (king), 277, 329, 354
Abdulaziz al-Shaikh, 424, 425, 426
Abdullah Bin Abdulaziz al-Saud (prince), 279, 304, 477
Abdul Rahman, Ahmad, 275
Abdul Rahman Bin Abdulaziz al-Saud (prince), 275, 277, 304
Abqaiq, Saudi Arabia, *349*
Abrams, Creighton, 148, 169, 188, 344, 358
Abu Dhabi, United Arab Emirates, *347*
Abu Nidal, 317
Abu Shanaf, Safy, 275, 389, 446–447
Abu Taleb, Youssef Sabri, 389, 476
Ad Dammam, Saudi Arabia, 348
Afghanistan, 220, 275, 280, 286
Africa, 275

Ahmad, Sultan Hashim, 479, 481, 483, 484–485, 488–490
Airborne (U.S. Army), *see numbered airborne units under* Army
Air Campaign, The: Planning for Combat (book), 318
Air Force (U.S.), 68, 118, 220, 222, 269, 280, 294, 302–303, 330, *see also references to air campaign under* Iraq-Kuwait crisis and Gulf War
and Central Command, 272–274
funding for, 69, 73
in Iraq-Kuwait crisis and Gulf War, *see also* Horner, Chuck; *references to air campaign under* Iraq-Kuwait crises and Gulf War
and Al Khafji, defense of, 424
in beginning of air campaign, 414–421
in buildup for Desert Storm, 376, 408
and Bush's Thanksgiving visit, 377–378